Understanding
The Family

Understanding The Family

STRESS AND CHANGE
IN AMERICAN FAMILY LIFE

Edited by

CATHLEEN GETTY, R.N., M.S.
Associate Professor
School of Nursing
State University of New York at Buffalo
Buffalo, New York

and

WINNIFRED HUMPHREYS, M.S.W.
Associate Clinical Professor
School of Nursing
State University of New York at Buffalo
Buffalo, New York
Former Director of Field Education
School of Social Work
University of Connecticut
West Hartford, Connecticut

Appleton-Century-Crofts / New York

81 82 83 84 85 / 10 9 8 7 6 5 4 3 2 1

Prentice-Hall International, Inc., London
Prentice-Hall of Australia, Pty. Ltd., Sydney
Prentice-Hall of India Private Limited, New Delhi
Prentice-Hall of Japan, Inc., Tokyo
Prentice-Hall of Southeast Asia (Pte.) Ltd., Singapore
Whitehall Books Ltd., Wellington, New Zealand

Library of Congress Cataloging in Publication Data
Main entry under title:

Understanding the family.

   Bibliography: p.
   Includes index.
   1. Family—United States—Case studies.   2. Problem
families—United States—Case studies.   3. Social change.
I. Getty, Cathleen, 1937-   II. Humphreys, Winnifred,
1927-   [DNLM: 1. Family.   2. Life change events.
3. Stress, Psychological.   HQ 536 U55]
HQ536.U52   306.8'0973   81-10874
ISBN 0-8385-9266-X   AACR2
ISBN 0-8385-9265-1 (PBK)

Text design: Dana Kasarsky
Cover design: Jean M. Sabato

PRINTED IN THE UNITED STATES OF AMERICA

Contributors

Sister Joan Therèse Anderson R.S.M., R.N., M.S.
Formerly Counselor
Diocesan Counseling Center
Diocese of Buffalo
Buffalo, New York

Rigmor Asmundsson, D.S.W.
Assistant Professor
Human Development and Family Relations
University of Connecticut
Storrs, Connecticut

Evelyn L. Barbee, R.N., Ph.D. (Anthropology)
Assistant Professor
Department of Psychosocial Nursing
University of Washington
Seattle, Washington

Theresa T. Chen-Louie, D.N.Sc.
Vice Chairman and Associate Professor
Department of Nursing
San Francisco State University
San Francisco, California

Carolyn Woods Daughtry, M.S.W.
Formerly First Deputy Commissioner
Department of Social Services
Erie County, New York
Currently Dean of Students
Virginia Union University
Richmond, Virginia

Margaret Duggan, R.N., M.S.
Instructor and Interim Chairperson
Advanced Nursing Department
Niagara University
Niagara Falls, New York

Joy Feldman, R.N., M.A.
Assistant Professor
Undergraduate Nurse Education
State University of New York at Buffalo
Buffalo, New York

Michael P. Farrell, Ph.D. (Sociology)
Associate Professor
Department of Sociology
Center for the Study of Human Groups
State University of New York at Buffalo
Amherst, New York

Betty S. Furuta, R.N., M.S.
Assistant Clinical Professor and Coordinator for Academic Services
Department of Mental Health and Community Nursing
School of Nursing
University of California, San Francisco
San Francisco, California

Lee Ann Hoff, M.S.N., M.A.
Assistant Professor
School of Nursing
Boston University
Boston, Massachusetts

Gillian Ingall, M.A., M.S.
Genetics Associate and Coordinator
Birth Defects and Genetic Counseling Clinic
Henry Ford Hospital
Detroit, Michigan

Hope L. Isaacs, M.A., Ph.D. (Anthropology)
Assistant Professor
Department of Graduate Nurse Education
School of Nursing
State University of New York at Buffalo
Buffalo, New York

Sharon S. Kern, M.S.W., A.C.S.W.
Director of Social Services
Niagara County Chapter, New York State Association for Retarded Children, Inc.
Niagara Falls, New York
Instructor/Faculty Liaison to Field Supervisors

State University College
Department of Community Social
  Services
Buffalo, New York

Suzanne Czamara Lema, R.N., M.S.
Formerly Assistant Professor
Division of Nursing
D'Youville College
Buffalo, New York

Aileen Lucero, Ph.D. (Sociology)
Postdoctoral Fellow
NIMH Program in Social Problem
  Solving
Department of Sociology
Washington State University
Pullman, Washington

Irene R. Mahar, R.N., M.P.H.
Associate Professor
School of Nursing
State University of New York at
  Buffalo
Buffalo, New York

Anthony N. Maluccio, D.S.W.
  (Social Welfare)
Professor
School of Social Work
The University of Connecticut
West Hartford, Connecticut

Ann McCreery, R.N., M.S.
Instructor
Department of Psychosocial Nursing
University of Washington
Seattle, Washington

Nomsa Vanda Meindl, R.N., M.S.
Community Mental Health Nurse
Psychiatric Institute
New York, New York

Marjory Nelson, Ph.D. (Sociology)
Sociologist, Writer and Activist
San Francisco, California

Marilynn Petit, R.N., M.S.
Psychotherapist and Instructor
School of Nursing
University of Rochester
Rochester, New York

Joan Evans Rawson, R.N., M.S.
Veterans Administration Medical
  Center
Palo Alto, California

George Fred Rivera, Jr., Ph.D.
  (Sociology)
Associate Professor
Department of Sociology
University of Colorado
Boulder, Colorado

Harriet Rosenberg, M.A.
Research Associate
Department of Psychiatry
Dartmouth Medical School
Hanover, New Hampshire

Stanley D. Rosenberg, Ph.D.
Professor of Psychiatry
Dartmouth Medical School
Hanover, New Hampshire

Polly Taylor, M.S.W.
Retired from Private Practice
Editor and Publisher of
  BROOMSTICK, a Periodical By,
  For and About Women Over 40
San Francisco, California

Wilma G. Watts, R.N., M.S.N.
Faculty Assistant for Student Affairs
  and Clinical Assistant Professor
School of Nursing
State University of New York at
  Buffalo
Buffalo, New York

Contents

Preface

Most human services professionals see the family as representing a central focus for their concern. Their work is rendered infinitely complex by virtue of the fact that the family, along with our other social institutions, is subject to the relentless onslaught of stresses deriving from rapid social and technological change. Distressed families increasingly find that they must begin to rely on outsiders, whereas previously they had been comparatively self-sufficient, less isolated from extended family ties, and buttressed by natural social networks. Professionals are therefore faced with the necessity of continually expanding the range and variety of their services. Because they are called upon to achieve a broader perspective on contemporary family functioning as well as to come to terms with the practice implications of these changes, it is vital that a relevant body of literature continue to evolve. This book represents a partial response to these imperatives.

From its inception we have seen the volume as a collection of interrelated, topical presentations, united through a common focus—the family and its functioning. We approach the family from an ecological systems perspective which centers on the complex interrelatedness of man and his environments. It is intended that each chapter of the book be considered within this context. Some of the chapters are offered as "think pieces," while by contrast, others are emphatically clinical in nature. We see these two emphases as complementing each other and contributing to an action base for practitioners.

Because of the scope of the material, we have sought contributors with expertise in a variety of theoretical and practice areas. A broad conception of family service provision is inherent in our orientation, with modalities as diverse as family therapy and genetic counseling being represented. At the same time, we make no claim to providing an exhaustive treatment of the subject matter. It is our expectation that human services students and professionals—especially those in nursing and social work—will find the content useful both in broadening their perspectives on the family, and in spurring further investigation of this primary social unit.

Introduction:
A Life-Model Perspective on the Family

Anthony N. Maluccio

It is generally recognized that families are dynamic social units with complex internal organization, constantly changing and engaging in ongoing interaction with their environments. Therefore, the most productive efforts to conceptualize families and their functioning will be those that attempt to account for the complexity of these phenomena. It is the view of the editors of this book that the life model, which incorporates both developmental and ecosystems concepts, represents a comprehensive approach that has special promise for guiding practice. In the following chapter, Maluccio examines this model, providing a lucid discussion of its theoretical bases and exploring its broad utility for work with families. Although subsequent chapters emphasize diverse dimensions in family life, all may be viewed productively from within this perspective.

In recent years there has been growing discussion of a new approach to practice, the *life model*, whose essence is that the worker's intervention into a client's situation is patterned after life itself. The approach provides concepts and principles based on life processes and designed to strengthen coping patterns by changing the transactions between people and their environments (Gitterman & Germain, 1976).

The model originated within the social-work profession, but it suggests a number of implications for the enrichment of practice in other applied disciplines as well. It provides an alternative to the disease or medical model that is predominant in the helping professions. It highlights the practitioner's responsibility to identify, mobilize, and ally himself or herself with the client's progressive forces, adaptive patterns, and resources. It focuses on the interface between the person and the environment, on the practitioner's role in facilitating the person's natural life processes, and on matching the client's needs with environmental supports.

This chapter presents an overview on the life model as a promising approach to work with families within an ecological-systems perspective. Selected practice examples are used to illustrate application of the model to treatment of family problems by practitioners in the human-service professions.

CONCEPTUAL FRAMEWORK

The life model in a sense is quite old. As early as the first part of this century, social-work pioneers such as Mary Richmond noted the importance of paying attention to the client's life situation and the need to change the interaction between the family and its social environment (Richmond, 1917). Lindeman (1940), a social philosopher, described social planning as an attempt to establish a dynamic balance between people and their relevant environments. Angyal (1941), a psychiatrist, proposed a holistic approach to the study of personality: He emphasized the concept of "the organism as a whole" and the "effect of life upon the living."

There is no doubt that the ideas of the life model have been germinating for some time. The difference at present is that there are important efforts underway to develop it conceptually and practically in a systematic fashion by taking advantage of emerging knowledge from a variety of disciplines. In particular, the life model derives its philosophical and theoretical underpinnings from General Systems Theory, ecology, biology, and ego psychology.

General Systems Theory, Ecology, and Biology

From General Systems Theory comes the notion of the human organism as constituting one part in an interconnected, interdependent, and complementary set of parts. As with any other living organism, the human being is constantly influenced by—and in turn exerts influence upon—other systems of varying levels, such as family, school, community, work, or culture.

In ecology, human beings are seen as engaged in dynamic transactions with their environment, and specifically in a continuing struggle to maintain a "moving equilibrium" while being constantly faced with a complex and changing array of environmental challenges. Similarly, in biology there is emphasis on the interplay between the person and the environment. As explained by Dubos (1968), this interplay represents a process of mutual adaptation in which each human being responds in a personal and creative manner.

General Systems Theory, ecology, and biology are vast fields including numerous concepts and diverse elements. The interrelated ideas from these disciplines most pertinent to the life model may be summarized as follows:

1. Living organisms and their environment form a reciprocal system characterized by their interdependence and influence on each other. Everything in the universe is related to everything else through an elaborate network of interconnections.
2. Living systems (including human beings and family units) are characterized by their self-maintaining quality, that is, the tendency toward achieving a "moving equilibrium" or "dynamic homeostasis."
3. The combination of living organisms and the physical features of their environment forms an *ecosystem*, that is, an ecologic complex such as a family, a city, a school, or a hospital. An ecosystem is in constant change, although it is usually in balance in the short run.
4. While they are governed by the same biologic laws as other species, human beings have managed to modify their environment sufficiently so as to be able to survive under a variety of conditions.
5. As people respond to environmental challenges, there is a dynamic interplay between them and their environment. This interplay frequently leads to conflicts and tensions, but it also provides opportunities for human growth and improvement in the environment.

The Family as a Living System

On the basis of concepts and propositions such as those described in the preceding section, in the life model the family is viewed as an open and living system that is engaged in a continuous and dynamic process of elaboration and differentiation. The family is an organic unit characterized not only by a complex set of internal organization and interaction but also by intricate interchanges with other people, groups, institutions, and external forces. Change in one member or subsystem of the family will affect its other parts as well as its interaction with external systems.

As with individuals, the family has a distinctive life cycle and is faced with time-specific developmental stages and natural crises, such as the birth of a child or loss of a member (Rodgers, 1973). The family is required to adapt itself to different tasks in each developmental phase and to the changing needs and qualities of its members.

In the process of change and continuity, the family is confronted with challenges and pressures from internal and external sources. An example of internal challenges is the middle-age crisis in men and women. Research is increasingly showing that, as one of its members experiences this crisis, significant changes occur in the family's structure and functioning. Similarly, external pressures influence family expectations, roles, and interaction.

As noted by Gitterman and Germain (1976, p. 602), industrialized society has created complex adaptive tasks both for individuals and for families: "The family's capacity for fulfilling its integrative functions has been taxed by its members' divergent opportunities, needs, responsibilities, and interests." Because of differences in their ages and developmental phases, individual family members may have conflicting or discordant needs. As an example, it may be difficult for a family to meet simultaneously the adolescent's strivings for emancipation and the middle-aged parent's need to feel wanted and worthwhile.

In response to multiple and complex demands, families frequently find themselves in a turbulent condition rather than in the state of harmony or equilibrium depicted in the popular media and at times even in the professional literature. Stress and crisis are normal features of a family's functioning throughout its evolution.

In short, ecology, biology, and General Systems Theory point to the importance of viewing the family within its overall ecologic context by analyzing the interrelationships among three different sets of factors: (1) the internal structure and processes within the family unit; (2) the unique qualities and functioning of each family member; and (3) other impinging environmental systems.

Ego Psychology

Ego psychology also offers various concepts that contribute to a conceptual framework for the life model. In particular, the concepts of *adaptation*, *autonomy*, and *competence* are useful in understanding the functioning of individuals within the family. This understanding is essential in work with families, since each family member and the family as a whole influence each other through a reciprocal process of interaction.

Adaptation. Adaptation refers to the process through which each human being strives to achieve a satisfying and acceptable compromise in dealing with the environment. As conceptualized by Hartmann (1958, pp. 22–37), adaptation involves a reciprocal relationship between organism and environment: The person's biologically endowed potentialities emerge and develop in response to the reality situation encountered throughout the life cycle. Hartmann defines three forms of adaptation: (1) *autoplastic*, i.e., change within one's self; (2) *alloplastic*, i.e., change in the environment; and (3) *seeking a new environment* that is more advantageous for the individual. The organism not only adapts to the environment but can also change it to meet his needs.

Adaptation may be described as the bridge between person and environment. It is a dynamic, creative process that demands continuous effort and a variety of strategies on the part of the human organism. It does not imply passive submission or mere adjustment of the person to the environment. On the contrary, the formulations of ego psychologists and others underscore the notion of the human organism as an active rather than merely reactive participant in interaction with the environment. Thus Dubos (1965, p. xviii) stresses: "Experience shows that human beings are not passive components in the adaptive systems. Their responses commonly manifest themselves as acts of personal creation. Each individual person tries to achieve some self-selected end even while he is responding to stimuli and adapting to them."

Autonomy. The concept of adaptation is closely related to that of autonomy, i.e., the person's capacity for self-government with relative freedom from instinctual and environmental forces. Autonomy may be viewed as an inner feeling of safety and well-being, and the higher the degree of one's autonomy, the greater the number of available adaptive responses. The development and maintenance of ego autonomy require inputs or stimulus-nutriments from within as well as from outside the organism.

A key function of nutriments from the external world is to provide opportunities to use and develop ego skills. In other words, to develop necessary skills, such as making decisions or dealing with anxiety-provoking matters, a person must have adequate opportunities to practice them in real-life situations. Environmental inputs should support and nourish the individual's efforts to cope and to grow. When they do not, the human being's autonomy is undermined.

Competence. Competence refers to the network of skills, knowledge, and talents that enable the person to interact with the environment. White (1963) has modified the orthodox drive theory of human motivation by postulating the existence of "effectance," that is, a set of "independent ego energies" or biologically given motivation toward dealing with the environment. He defines competence as one's achieved capacity to interact effectively with one's environment. In his view, the ego is strengthened through the cumulative experience of producing desired effects upon one's surroundings.

M. Brewster Smith (1968), a social psychologist, has proposed an integrative conception of competence. In his formulation, competence involves intrinsic as well as extrinsic motivation, social skills as well as personal abilities, and effective performance for *self* as well as for *society* in one's social roles. Other psychologists have also stressed that competence is an important force in human behavior. As noted by Allport (1961, p. 214):

> It would be wrong to say that "a need for competence" is the simple and sovereign motive of life. It does, however, come as close as any need (closer

than the sexual) to summing up the whole biological story of development. We survive through competence, we grow through competence, we become "self-actualizing" through competence.

SIGNIFICANCE FOR PRACTICE

From these interrelated ideas on the ecologic perspective and the life model flow several propositions with special significance for practitioners working with families:

1. Human behavior represents attempts at achieving satisfying levels and kinds of adaptation, autonomy, and competence.
2. Life experiences play a key role in the process of adaptation and the individual's quest for autonomy, competence and self-fulfillment.
3. The outcome of each human being's efforts to cope successfully with life is dependent upon the availability and purposive use of varied environmental resources and social supports.
4. As a basic social system affecting every individual, the family plays a critical role in the development and functioning of human beings.
5. A major function of other social systems or institutions should be to facilitate the family's adaptive tasks, by enhancing the mutual fit between the family and its impinging environment.

On the basis of these propositions, the entire helping process in work with families is redefined. The focus of help is on identifying, supporting, and mobilizing the natural adaptive processes of the family and its members. The "unit of attention" is the family within its ecologic context. The focus is on transactions between the family and the environment and on interactional patterns and communication processes within the family itself.

The environment encompasses not only natural or physical features (e.g., housing) but also sociocultural elements (e.g., social networks) and the individual's internalized needs and responses. This view is derived from the assumption that the exigencies resulting from people's efforts to cope with the natural and social world emerge, in human action, as psychologic, interpersonal, and sociocultural patterns or problems. In any given family situation, the environment does not consist of the total universe but of the part that significantly *environs* or impinges on the family or any of its members.

The life-model perspective influences the entire helping process, from the initial phase of "studying" the family situation to the phase of intervention into the family system.

Study Phase

In the initial phase, the emphasis is on gathering relevant data within the context of the family's life space and its transactions with environing systems. There is careful exploration of significant life events that impinge on each person, within as well as outside the family. Particular attention is devoted more to systemic elements or patterned relationships (such as the quality of interaction within the parent-child subsystems) than to single or discrete variables (such as a parent's intrapsychic conflicts).

Intensive study of historical events is not of paramount importance. Greater significance is attached to the here-and-now situation of the clients and to relatedness rather than fragmentation. Naturalistic methods of observation are stressed more than clinical methods, so as to gather information leading to a broad understanding of the clients in their overall ecologic context, as well as to in-depth knowledge of their particular needs, qualities, and patterns of functioning. For example, the practitioner can obtain a sampling of family interaction through home visits at strategic points in the life of the family, such as mealtimes.

Assessment Phase

In the assessment phase, as the principal arena for change shifts from the past to the present, there is a broad analysis of the relevant forces in the family's transactional field. The practitioner needs to understand the dysfunctional transactions between the family and its environment. He or she also needs to understand the unique coping styles and adaptive patterns of the family unit as well as its individual members. This includes examination of where the family is in its developmental cycle and how it is performing the tasks associated with that particular stage. There is also analysis of particular patterns of individual or family functioning in terms of their meaning for system maintenance. A parent's depression, for example, may represent an attempt to control an adolescent's strivings toward emancipation and to insure the family's survival.

Family functioning is explored and assessed in light of pertinent sociocultural, economic, and other environmental variables. Thus, in families that have emigrated from rural areas to urban centers, it is seen that the resulting loss of support from the kinship system can precipitate a crisis for the family unit. Family functioning is also examined in relation to the developmental tasks or crises with which its members are confronted at any given moment. For example, crises such as those of adolescence or menopause influence the family's "dynamic equilibrium" and may result in role changes, attitudinal shifts, and realignments.

In the assessment of the family's ecology, there is in particular a deliberate effort to locate resources and supports as well as points of stress or obstacles to growth and adaptation. The family structure is probed intensely to identify sources of strength, areas of potential changes, and ways of releasing latent capacities for growth.

Many of the current approaches to family therapy overemphasize dysfunctioning and pathology; as earlier the individual was seen as the "sick" patient, currently the family is viewed as "sick." By comparison, little attention has been devoted to the family's potentialities and adaptive mechanisms:

> Even the recent search for "strengths" in the family has at times been heavy-handed. Humor has often been taken as a clue to hidden pathology rather than as a basis for integration and solidarity, while ritual has been viewed as a form of obsession rather than a pleasurable activity associated with sentiments of continuity. (Leichter, 1974, p. 216.)

In the life model, on the other hand, there is a shift from preoccupation with pathology to appreciation of the rich variety of human responses to environmental challenges and externally imposed conditions. Families in trouble are viewed as open systems struggling to cope with life challenges due to the dysfunctional patterns in their transactions with the environment.

Human difficulties are conceptualized as "problems of living." The major categories include *developmental crises*, such as the impact of a child's birth; *situational crises*, such as the pressures and tensions in a family that is coping with the parents' divorce or the retirement of one of its members; and *discrepancies between the family's needs and environmental resources*, such as the situation of a family with working parents who are unable to provide for their young children's needs due to lack of day-care services.

Throughout the helping process, the family's definition of the problem is sought and highlighted. This is crucial, since the clients have a right to determine the target problems. In addition, the clients' perception of the problem strongly influences the process and outcome of any interventive efforts. For example, little progress is likely to occur in treatment so long as a family sees a child's academic underachievement as the responsibility of the school while the practitioner defines it as a symptom of family disturbance.

Frequently, however, family members have different needs or define the problem in divergent or conflicting terms. The practitioner's task then is to help the family members deal with their differences and to achieve some commonality. Gitterman and Germain (1976, p. 605) observe:

> In families and groups, the worker also helps members to separate out their individual developmental goals and tasks from the expectations exerted by

the collectivity and by environmental forces. At the same time, the worker encourages family and group members to be responsive to one another as they seek areas of common developmental expectations and tasks.

Intervention Phase

In intervention, the focus is on restructuring the environment and setting in motion natural adaptive processes in the family and its members. The key objective is not to "treat" or "cure" but to aid family members in promoting growth-producing environmental conditions and in mobilizing their own resources and adaptive patterns. Through planned changes in its ecologic context, the family is enabled to fulfill its functions more effectively. Its members then are more likely to have experiences that are more positive and conducive to their individual fulfillment as well as to mutual need-meeting.

Along with use of the environment, in the interventive phase there is emphasis on life experiences, family tasks and activities, and other opportunities for enhancing personal autonomy and competence. While clinical activities such as insight-oriented procedures may in some instances be valuable and appropriate, there is extensive use of less traditional methods that are responsive to the family's unique styles, sociocultural traditions, and values. Psychic healing, for example, can be an effective tool in work with members of certain minority groups.

Help is provided as much as possible outside the office and in the family's natural life situation—not only in the family setting but also in other contexts, such as school, hospital, work, or play, i.e., the "crossroads of life." Some social agencies, for example, are joining with labor unions and/or industries to offer counseling around personal or family problems in the context of the world of work.

The practitioner plays flexible roles that at one point or another may include those of therapist, educator, advocate, social broker, strategist, guide, and supporter. Whatever the specific role may be at any moment, the practitioner becomes an important part of the family system and therefore influences family functioning in ways that may be positive or negative. The practitioner therefore needs to examine carefully his or her actual or potential influence on the family.

PRACTICE APPLICATIONS

As presented thus far, the life model focuses on the dynamic transactions between people and their environments. The model challenges practitioners in the human services to move from concentration on pathology and weakness to emphasis on human strengths and the potentially healing powers of human relationships. It embodies a shift from an "id" focus on conflicts and instincts to an "ego" focus on tasks and autonomous functioning.* It highlights life experiences and environmental instruments as integral components of interpersonal helping.

The life-model perspective on the family in turn suggests a variety of principles that can guide intervention with families. Some of the most important ones will be discussed in further detail in this section in order to illustrate their application in practice. They are (1) using the environment, (2) using life experiences, and (3) using tasks.

Using the Environment

The environment is used as a primary means of helping, as a dynamic force for facilitating the family's efforts to fulfill its functions and for promoting each member's drive toward competence. A critical role of the practitioner therefore is to aid the family in seeking, modifying, or creating significant environmental opportunities. This often involves restructuring of the environment, which can be accomplished through one or more of the following interrelated approaches.

1. Changing the family's internal environment to make it more responsive to individual and collective needs. This can involve changing such aspects as the family's organization (e.g., dealing with the scapegoating of a family member); enhancing the competence of individual members (e.g., finding new roles for a newly retired family member); or introducing new resources into the family (e.g., a home health aide, a homemaker, or a volunteer). As vividly demonstrated by Minuchin (1974), the practitioner makes use of the family matrix in the "process of healing" by modifying family organization and transforming dysfunctional patterns of interaction.

2. Enriching the family's external environment. This can be done, for example, by involving key persons or forces such as the kinship system as instruments of help or by providing environmental nutriments such as recreational, cultural, or educational opportunities. In their formulation of network therapy, for instance, Speck and Attneave (1973) help families by bringing together their friends, relatives, and neighbors, thus releasing the dormant, therapeutic powers of a family's social networks.

---

*See, for example, Germain, C. B., An ecological perspective in casework practice, *Social Casework*, 1973, 54, 323–330.

3. Facilitating the family's exchanges with its environment. The thrust of this approach is to promote mutually satisfying feedback processes between the family and other systems in its environment. Toward this end, obstacles in the family's transactions with key systems are removed; for example, the practitioner may provide information and/or advocacy to parents who are trying to deal with a school or welfare system. Significant forces in the environment are identified and mobilized in support of the family. Alliances between the family and important members of its social networks are stimulated; for example, the family may join with others in its community to promote recreational opportunities for children and youth.

Various examples of "using the environment" may be drawn from practice. In the first one that follows, a family that was overwhelmed by situational stress is helped to locate and use badly needed resources. Professional intervention leads to a more nutritive environment for family members and helps them to move toward more active coping with life challenges.

Mrs. Lewis, a recently divorced 35-year-old woman, was finding it hard to cope with the demands of her three school-age children. Each of the children was encountering school difficulties and rejection from peers. The mother was providing minimal care and supervision for the children, who were frequently left outside on their own late at night.

When a neighbor complained to the police, a social worker from a protective service agency visited the family on several occasions and observed how they related to each other. The worker recognized the children's fear of making demands on their mother as well as the mother's desperate efforts to meet their needs while on public welfare. Their small apartment, for example, was in a dilapidated building in a section of town awaiting redevelopment.

During several family meetings, the social worker supported Mrs. Lewis' role as a parent and helped the children to express their needs and feelings openly rather than by staying away from home and thus further undermining the mother's self-esteem. In addition, playing the role of advocate with the Housing Authority, the worker helped Mrs. Lewis to find more adequate resources.

The family eventually moved to a better dwelling, following a long struggle to find a rent they could afford within the real limitations imposed by the welfare allotment. Mrs. Lewis went to work part-time. She began to relate to her own future in terms of going back to school and being determined to escape from the dehumanizing conditions of welfare dependency. As her own future broadened, so did this mother's ability to help her children to grow.

In the following case, a family is helped through environmental modification involving renewal of the family's ties with certain members of its kinship system.

The Brown family was trying to adapt to the recent discharging of the father from a psychiatric hospital where he had been confined for nearly a month because of a psychotic episode. Since she was afraid to leave him alone, Mrs. Brown had not been going to work, even though she knew that she might thus lose her job. The two children, both in junior high school, had been missing school regularly, because of their inability to sleep or their waking up with severe stomach aches. Mr. Brown was beginning to withdraw again into his own world as he sensed his wife's and children's growing anxiety and panic. He was also upset about having been laid off from his job during his hospitalizaton.

The psychiatric nurse who had been visiting the family since Mr. Brown's discharge tried unsuccessfully to reassure the family members that he was all right and could be left alone during the day. She then asked the family whether there was any relative or friend who could keep Mr. Brown company during part of the day. At first, neither Mr. nor Mrs. Brown could think of anyone. Eventually, they began talking about two aunts living nearby who had previously been close to the family but had been staying away ever since they had witnessed Mr. Brown's "strange" behavior at the time of his psychotic episode.

With the Browns' permission, the nurse called on each of the aunts. After explaining about Mr. Brown's recovery, the nurse found that each aunt was still quite interested in Mr. Brown but was reluctant to visit for fear of embarrassing him and his wife. Eventually, it was arranged for each aunt to visit Mr. Brown daily. As both the aunts and the family enjoyed these visits, Mrs. Brown was able to leave her husband and go to work. As their anxiety was also alleviated, the two children were able to resume regular school attendance.

In the next case, the internal environment of a family is restructured through changes in the communication patterns of its members.

Roy Albert was a 17-year-old brought to a psychiatric clinic by his parents following a suicide attempt. Both Mr. and Mrs. Albert as well as Roy expressed interest in counseling, and a psychologist was assigned to work with them.

Several family sessions were held which included Roy's younger siblings, 15-year-old Mary and 12-year-old David. It was soon apparent that a "family secret" was interfering with the family's functioning. The secret concerned the parents' growing marital dissatisfaction and recent decision to seek a divorce.

Although the Alberts had not shared their difficulties with their children, the children had been sensing those difficulties for some time. Mary and David had been responding with various behavioral problems at home and in school, while Roy had become increasingly depressed. Roy's suicide threat and Mary's and David's acting-out behavior appeared to represent their desperate efforts to avert the parents' divorce.

As the psychologist helped the parents and children communicate their feelings and fears more openly, they were able to give each other some support and to accept their individual needs. As the children were reassured of the parents' caring for them, they no longer had a strong need to hold on to them by acting out, even though the parents proceeded with their plans to obtain a divorce.

Using Life Experiences

Especially as the environment is enriched through restructuring, life experiences such as activities or relationships can be used as effective aids in treatment. In his discussion of the role of extratherapeutic experiences in psychoanalysis, Alexander (1946, p. 40) stresses that success in significant activities encourages new trials and enhances the person's sense of well-being. He notes that the performance of activities can be a powerful therapeutic factor: "Successful attempts at productive work, love, self-assertion, or competition will change the vicious cycle to a benign one; as they are repeated, they become habitual and thus eventually bring about . . . change in the personality."

As I have discussed in greater detail elsewhere (Maluccio, 1979), effective engagement in natural life experiences can help family members improve their coping skills and interact more effectively with each other. In turn, this can facilitate the family's adaptive tasks and integrative functions. As shown in the following example, life situations can be manipulated so as to render family structure and functioning more "therapeutic" or growth productive for each member.

The Jones family was rapidly drawing apart following the parents' divorce. Mrs. Jones had custody of her three teenagers. She was preoccupied not only with her own feelings and needs but also with the children's increasing behavioral and learning problems. When her oldest son dropped out of high school, Mrs. Jones talked with a guidance counselor and shared her desperation about herself and the children. With her permission, the counselor arranged a joint session with Mrs. Jones and the son and daughter who were still in school. In this session, the counselor recognized this family's struggle to cope with the impact of the divorce by avoiding each other. At the same time, he sensed their tender feelings for one another and their wish for closer relationships.

The family responded positively to the counselor's suggestion that, for the next two weeks, they arrange to participate in a variety of activities together, including dinner at least every other night, visiting the maternal grandmother in a convalescent home, and attending a basketball game. All family members agreed to participate in each of these activities and to discuss their experiences with the counselor in a follow-up session.

In the subsequent session, the children reported that, as they and their mother came together, they were able to share with her their confusion over the divorce, anger toward both parents, and fears of further losses. Mrs. Jones, on the other hand, indicated that she was able to let her children know about her growing dissatisfactions and disappointments in the marriage and her self-doubts since the divorce. The son who had dropped out of school still refused to return but appreciated his mother's concern for him and his future. All family members expressed their satisfaction in being able to come together. The children also began to talk about maintaining their relationship with the father by including him in selected family activities.

Action is particularly crucial as a means of providing opportunities for need satisfaction, task fulfillment, crisis resolution, and learning of social skills. As emphasized by White (1963, p. 150) in his formulation of the concept of *effectance*, the ego is strengthened through the person's successful action in dealing with the environment and his or her resulting feelings of efficacy. "Doing" can lead to greater self-respect and satisfaction and to an enhanced sense of competence and autonomy. With adults as with children, "action constitutes an essential instrument for learning, for development of one's reality testing, and for self-actualization.*

As suggested by the following example, typical case situations provide opportunities for engagement in purposive, goal-directed activities that can be a major means of stimulating a family's adaptive processes and progressive forces:

A disorganized, multiproblem family with several young children was living in a depriving environment. Through the combined efforts of a nurse, a social worker, and school personnel, the family was helped to engage more successfully in its struggle toward survival through participation in a variety of meaningful activities and experiences. These included structured family sessions in which two therapists taught the parents to cope more effectively with disciplining their children; enrollment of the children in a day-care center where the mother was also given various responsibilities as a volunteer

---

*For further discussion of the rationale for the use of action, see Maluccio, A. N., Action as a tool in casework practice, *Social Casework*, 1974, 55, 32–33.

aide; and involvement of both parents with a group of neighbors who were trying to obtain increased police protection to control the flow of drugs into their neighborhood.

As the preceding illustrations suggest, life itself can be viewed as the arena for change. The potentially therapeutic value of life experiences and processes can be exploited to provide more effective help to families (Maluccio, 1979), and to enhance the competence of family members (Maluccio, 1981).

Using Tasks

The concept of action is interwoven with that of task, which, as used here, refers to explicit definition of what is to be done by family and practitioners in any specific situation so as to meet the family members' needs or enable them to deal successfully with environmental challenges. As a task is clearly spelled out and agreed upon by the worker and family members, its implementation can proceed more smoothly.

Client and worker roles and tasks need to be redefined so as to maximize opportunities for the family and its members to interact effectively with their environment. Problems, needs, and conflicts are translated into adaptive tasks providing the clients with opportunities for growth and maturity and facilitating the family unit's integrative and developmental functions.

A variety of examples come to mind. A couple experiencing marital discord becomes engaged in the task of identifying factors leading to their persistent arguments. A family with an alcoholic father concentrates on the task of identifying, in conjunction with the therapist, the conditions leading to his drinking and the changes that may be required to make family interaction mutually satisfying and supportive. A father who is overwhelmed by his wife's sudden death is brought together with his parents to consider alternative ways of caring for his two young children so as to avoid placement in a foster home. A young couple who are moving apart following the birth of their second child are encouraged to share their individual needs with each other and to consider ways of meeting them both within and outside their relationship.

In each of these examples, the focus is on formulating tasks that are geared as closely as possible to family members' needs, qualities, and aspirations. Selected tasks can be assigned as "homework" to be carried out between sessions by the family and/or individual members.

The concept of task can lead to greater emphasis on the family's participation in the helping process. The focus in interventive activities is on the family and the joint or individual tasks of its members. The practitioner plays an important role, however, especially by planning for the provision or development of those conditions that facilitate the family's optimal coping with its tasks. In the case of the young couple mentioned above, for example, the counselor would need to help the clients to bring out and work through their feelings toward each other before they would be able to carry out their other tasks.

The casting of client and practitioner roles in terms of differential tasks could result in clearer definition of responsibilities, greater specificity of functions, and more precision in interventive strategies. This could lead to less discrepancy and confusion in the expectations of family members and therapist and more effective mobilization of their energies.

The client-worker contract can be used as a dynamic tool for engaging family members in assessing their situation, selecting appropriate tasks, and implementing interventive plans.* Client-worker interaction becomes more productive as all parties go through the process of formulating the contract and reaching agreement on specific goals, tasks, and approaches. Mutual expectations and obligations can thus be minimized and dissonance can be avoided. Participation in the deliberative process leading to the contract can be useful as a means of restructuring family organization and improving communication patterns. At the same time, the contracting process can serve to stimulate each family member's cognitive growth and mastery, broaden his knowledge of different alternatives and their consequences, and mobilize his decision-making function.

CONCLUSION

Through further development and application of a life model of practice, practitioners in the human service professions can provide more effective services to the families that come to their attention. A major reason for this is the model's emphasis on interventive plans and helping approaches based on full appreciation and use both of environmental supports and of the functioning, natural processes, progressive forces, and adaptive mechanisms in the family and its members.

At the same time, the model directs attention to the importance of changing the internal organization and functioning of each family and its relations with other systems, so as to provide mutually satisfying and growth-producing transactions. In addition, the model relies heavily on use of actual and potential resources existing within each family and its social networks.

---

*See, for example, Maluccio, A. N. & Marlow, W. D., The case for the contract, *Social Work*, 1974, 19, 28–36.

This perspective on practice also serves to conceptualize "help" in such a way as to include not only "treatment" but also the use of a variety of resources, services, and practice modalities. Ultimately, this approach could best be implemented through the strategic locations of practitioners at the "crossroads of life," at critical points in the developmental cycles of individuals and families.* The approach also underscores the urgency of a multidisciplinary orientation to systemic change in which various professions play complementary roles and no single profession has regal status.

REFERENCES

Alexander, F. Extratherapeutic experiences. In Franz, A., & French, T. M., (eds.), *Psychoanalytic Therapy*. New York: Ronald Press, 1946.

Allport, G. W. *Pattern and Growth in Personality*. New York: Holt, Rinehart and Winston, 1961.

Angyal, A. *Foundations for a Science of Personality*. Cambridge, Mass.: Harvard University Press, 1941.

Dubos, R. *So Human an Animal*. New York: Scribner's, 1968.

Dubos, R. *Man Adapting*. New Haven, Conn.: Yale University Press, 1965.

Germain, C. B. An ecological perspective in casework practice. *Social Casework*, 1973, 54, 323–330.

Gitterman, A., & Germain, C. B. Social work practice: A life model. *Social Service Review*, 1976, 50, 601–610.

Hartmann, H. *Ego Psychology and the Problems of Adaptation*. New York: International Universities Press, 1958.

Leichter, H. J. Some perspectives on the family as educator. *Teachers College Record*, 1974, 76, 175–217.

Lindeman, E. C. Ecology: An instrument for the integration of science and philosophy. *Ecological Monographs*, 1940, 10, 367–372.

Maluccio, A. N. Action as a tool in casework practice. *Social Casework*, 1974, 55, 30–35.

Maluccio, A. N. Promoting competence through life experiences. In Germain, C. (ed.), *Social Work Practice: People and Environments*. New York: Columbia University Press, 1979, 282–302.

Maluccio, A. N. (ed.), *Promoting Competence in Clients—A New-Old Approach to Social Work Practice*. New York: The Free Press, 1981.

Maluccio, A. N., & Marlow, W. D. The case for the contract. *Social Work*, 1974, 19, 28–36.

Meyer, C. H. *Social Work Practice* (2nd ed.). New York: The Free Press, 1976.

Minuchin, S. *Families and Family Therapy*. Cambridge, Mass.: Harvard University Press, 1974.

Richmond, M. E. *Social Diagnosis*. New York: Russell Sage Foundation, 1917.

---

*For elaboration of this point, see Meyer, C. H., *Social Work Practice* (2nd ed.), New York: The Free Press, 1976, 189–199.

Rodgers, R. H. *Family Interaction and Transaction—The Developmental Approach.* Englewood Cliffs, N.J.: Prentice-Hall, 1973.

Smith, M. B. Competence and socialization. In Clausen, J. A. (ed.), *Socialization and Society.* Boston: Little, Brown, 1968, 270–320.

Speck, R. V., & Attneave, C. L. *Family Networks.* New York: Pantheon, 1973.

White, R. W. *Ego and Reality in Psychoanalytic Theory.* New York: International Universities Press, 1963.

section

I

FAMILY ROLE RELATIONSHIPS

A society provides its citizens with a set of definitions regarding appropriate patterning for familial roles. These definitions evolve over time, so that the norms regulating parental and conjugal roles slowly crystallize. The prescriptions serve as guides for families who are engaged in carrying out their vital function of socializing future citizens. On the other hand, they may be challenged as social change gives rise to new expectations. The chapters in Section I address this process from a variety of perspectives, focussing on the American family's management of the stresses inherent in role transition during this turbulent era in our history.

1

The Meaning of Cultural Variations in Child-Rearing Practices

Hope L. Isaacs

What do the families of Egyptian farmers, Rajput landowners, North American Iroquois, and New Zealand Maori have in common with the families of urban Americans? In essence, this is the question addressed by Isaacs in the chapter that follows. In it she provides a series of brief ethnographies drawn from widely divergent cultures, using them to illustrate a paradigm in which the family is represented as the crucial vehicle in the acculturation of the young. From this perspective, child-rearing practices can be more fully understood as part of a complex, ongoing process of cultural transmission through which children are prepared to take on the roles, tasks, and identities of their parents' generation. Her model is useful in clarifying the way in which the family functions in the service of the larger social system, while at the same time retaining the prerogative of placing its own unique stamp on its progeny. She does identify a cluster of personality traits, observable in the children of the majority of contemporary American families, suggesting a common imperative in socialization practices. However, she points out that it is erroneous to reduce "the American family" to a single stereotypic form.

Over the past century anthropologic perspectives on the family have followed an evolutionary trajectory that is intrinsically significant and informative. The earliest anthropologists, who tended, as Harris has demonstrated, to confuse evolution with progress (1968, p. 36), argued that *das Mutterrecht* held sway in the dawn of mankind and that the matriarchy was the prevailing structure of both the family and society (Bachofen, 1939). The appeal of this notion is attested to by the sheer frequency of its resurrection after repeated burial under refuting evidence. Indeed a recent revival (Morgan, 1962) has provoked a refutation from Bamberger (1974, pp. 263–280).

For the most part, however, the culture-bound postulations of the nineteenth century as to the origins of the family fell before an onslaught of enthnographic data indicating that a broad spectrum of sharply different family structures existed concurrently around the world. The accumulation of these data was initiated by Lewis Henry Morgan and first published in a massive work, *Systems of Consanguinity and Affinity of the Human Family* (1870).

Morgan's research introduced an era of scholarship that elucidated kinship structures in all parts of the globe and at all levels of culture evolution, from simple hunting and gathering bands to complex industrial states. These studies led, inevitably perhaps, to new epistemologies concerning the family. The family was examined, for example, in the perspective of a territorial or residence unit (Goodenough, 1956), an economic unit (Engels, 1884), a functional unit (Murdock, 1949; Parsons, 1955), and so on. Each of these approaches, in turn, led not only to explanations of the variations in family structure among human societies, but also to a new understanding of the dynamics of culture and of the global variations in culture.

It is the aim of this chapter to explore another approach to understanding family structures and their relationship to culture by examining the family in the perspective of its function as the principal child-rearing unit of society. It is my position that this function is bi-valent; that is, in the process of socializing its children a family simultaneously transmits the culture of its society to future generations.

The richness of cultural detail and the completeness of the network of social and cultural relationships transmitted from one generation to the next via child-rearing practices cannot be overemphasized. As Margaret Mead has pointed out, "Everything that has been patiently accumulated on the subject of child-rearing in different cultures has demonstrated the most minute correspondence between the overall patterns of a culture and the patterns of child-rearing in that culture" (1963, p. 184). It is inferred, therefore, that a reciprocal bonding dynamic may be operative in the child-rearing process. The following "mini ethnographies"* are intended to serve as a sample for testing this proposition and as a springboard for further discussion.

EGYPT

In the farming village of Silwa on the banks of the Nile River a sparse subsistence is carved out of land that is enriched and irrigated entirely by the river. Each family owns a small plot that has been handed down from

---

*A full-scale ethnography is an anthropologic description of a society, encompassing all of the major aspects of its culture.

father to son for as long as anyone can remember. Survival depends upon every member of the family working on the land under the absolute authority of the father. Older parents who are too old to work in the fields are treated with respect and supported by their children out of money earned from the family's plot of land.

The mode of working the land and selling its products places all authority in and prestige with the male head of the household. The religion, Islam, reinforces this alignment of power with its emphasis on sacred male ancestry. From birth on, boys are regarded as an asset. Girls, on the other hand, are trained to scurry along the house walls and leave the center of the village paths for boys and men.

In pregnancy the Silwan woman must continually be on guard against the evil eye, which can deform the fetus. The newborn baby is swaddled in its parents' old clothes, and for the next 40 days the mother and child are kept apart from society. It is believed that angels entertain the baby during this period and that during infancy the baby acquires its personality through its mother's milk. A professional "good man" is hired to transmit moral virtue to the baby. He does this by giving the baby a sweet to eat on which he himself has sucked. Extended nursing is frowned upon, especially for a boy, since it induces compassion and "darkens the mind." Weaning, therefore, begins early. Toilet training begins at four months. Otherwise, however, children are treated with much compassion, fondness, and permissiveness up to the age of four years. Even sleeping hours are unregulated and Silwan children learn to sleep "anywhere and through anything" (Honigmann, 1967, p. 218).

At the age of four the patterns of gratification are deliberately and sharply reversed. Children are deliberately ushered into rivalrous situations with siblings and other village children and encouraged to fend for themselves. At five or six, boys undergo public circumcision and girls undergo clitoridectomy in private. The purpose of the latter operation is to reduce sexual excitement and therefore diminish the temptation to premarital or extramarital sex.

Social pressures to conform are thus imposed early and severely in rural Egypt. Hamed Ammar, an Egyptian anthropologist who studied the village of Silwa, theorizes that the severity of socialization leads to the placing of covert value on revenge, retaliation, and trickery. Religious training attempts to deal with these, and the Koran threatens severe corporal punishment for misbehavior, which the teachers "are not slow in administering." The result, Ammar suggests, is that young people become timid, apprehensive, and withdrawn; such qualities complement and maintain the power roles of the elders.

Although Ammar suggests that the elders holding these power roles may rely on maximizing restraints during adolescence "in order to secure the individual's energetic participation in adult life," he later indicates that such active participation is restricted to males, and that women "remain excessively repressed and dependent" throughout their lives (1954, pp. 183–201). Indeed, he points out, the linking of severity in childhood socialization to unequivocal sexual dichotomization explains the strong in-male and in-female group solidarity characteristics of adult rural Egyptian society.

On closer inspection, however, this apparent crystallization of roles and options in adult life is threatened with disruption by the very same cultural framework that gave rise to it in the first place, for any behavioral deviation from prescribed norms on the part of a female who has passed puberty brings "shame"* upon her male relatives and thereby diminishes their status and power in the community. Ultimately, then, the strength and security of adult Egyptian males depends upon the response of the females to the weakness and insecurity that the males impose upon them. The result is a precarious social equation that gives expression to the retaliative personality traits instilled in childhood.

INDIA

In northern India the village of Khalapur is a representative community of about 5000 persons. According to Honigmann (1967, p. 237) there are a half-million villages in India of around this size. Although several other castes were represented in the village. Leigh Mintura and John Hitchcock, the anthropologists who studied it, concentrated on the culture of one caste, the Rajput landowners. In India the caste system is rigid, and life-ways are sharply differentiated from one caste to another.

The religion of the Rajput caste is Hindu, and, once again, all authority is vested in the males. Males and females live out most of their lives in physical separation, even after marriage. Men and adolescent boys live in "men's houses"; women and girls in the women's compound. A bride who comes as a stranger to Khalapur goes at once to live with the wives of her husband's brothers. The women's compound also houses unmarried daughters, preadolescent boys, and the wives and children of married sons of the older women. At least three generations of females thus live together in the compound. The bride who joins the compound group at marriage leaves it only at death.

Since a Hindu man jeopardizes his own salvation if he does not beget a son, and since marrying off daughters is very expensive, a couple is under great pressure to produce sons, and elaborate ceremonies mark the birth of

---

*The reader is referred to Peristiany's work (1966) on the honor and shame syndrome in circum-Mediterranean societies.

a boy. Infant mortality is extremely high and is often attributed to the evil eye. The baby is therefore surrounded with protective charms. One, which is hung around the neck of male infants, protects them against impotence.

Rajput mothers sleep with their infants at night and nurse them whenever they seem to desire it. Weaning takes place at about one year although solid food is started much earlier. Although toilet training is carried on casually and with minimal stress, the daily bath is administered with considerable roughness. This apparent contradiction is discernible in other aspects of child rearing. Thus, although children are expected to learn by observation and there is little training toward responsibility and self-reliance, they are required to exercise self-control and to cooperate with others. While the system requires passivity and obedience to the male adults, children learn to vent their anger and frustration upon each other and upon their mothers.

Rajput mothers, in turn, vent much of their hostility on their sons. Tenderness is directed toward their daughters whom they expect to lose while still very young. Rajput mothers sleep with their daughters until they are eight or nine years old and express deep love for them. They tend to be hostile and punitive toward their sons and this may be what is projected in the terrifying bloodstained Hindu goddess Kali. Honigmann (1967, p. 245) postulates that the childhood experiences of Rajput men incline them in adulthood toward a generalized mistrust of people, a deep regard for renunciation of the world, and a longing to return to infantile dependency.

POLYNESIA

In the northern island of New Zealand, at one end of a fertile valley running between rugged mountains, a community of Maoris maintains its traditional culture in the midst of the English culture that now holds sway. The Maori bear a physical resemblance to the Polynesian peoples of the central Pacific, and, in fact, they trace their ancestral lineages back to the time of the great migration of Polynesians out of that area. Despite the comprehensive Europeanization of New Zealand, the Maori today vigorously maintain their ancient language, family names, social organization, and historic traditions. In other words, like so many of the subpopulations within our own borders, their cultural identity has survived the impact of contemporary western civilization.

Maori parents set a high value on large families. Home is defined as a place of many children. Despite such verbal avowals of love and welcome for many children, however, weaning takes place at four months, and toilet training soon after. Childhood, in terms of tolerance, indulgence, and gratification, ends between 14 and 18 months, and, except for attention from older siblings, the child is left thereafter to fend for itself. On the other hand, punishment for aggressive behavior is severe, and one gets the impression that young Maori children survive mainly through the care and concern of their older siblings. The result is that by the age of four, Maori children have learned to share, to respect another's property, and to repress aggression. The sudden cutoff of close parental attention at so early an age not only produces independence in very young children, but also a sense of caution and of wariness of others, verging on distrust.

In the middle childhood years, Maori children seem to be happy only when with their own age group. They interact with their parents without emotion, as if unrelated to them. The psychologist who studied this age group, Margaret Earle (1958, p. 107), described their adjustment as "miserable."

Interestingly, however, adolescence among the Maori appears to be a time of homecoming. Parents relate satisfactorily to their older children and reward them for doing their household chores. Competition with peers becomes more hostile, but since a nonassertive outward mien has been established in earlier years, hostility and aggression are habitually internalized. Since curiosity and experimentation were discouraged in childhood, teenage Maoris do not make good students in the New Zealand schools. The limitations imposed on their intellectual growth tend to reduce their functioning to a level far below their ability. An outwardly docile personality hides inner tension, self-doubt, and unfulfilled desires. Depression, hypochondria, and paranoia characterize the later teen years.

It is germane here to note the similarities in traits of culture, child-rearing practices, and personality development reported much earlier by Margaret Mead in her famous study of another Polynesian people, the Samoans of the Island of Ta'u, *Coming of Age in Samoa* (1928). Both Earle for the Maori and Mead for the Samoans call attention to two critical child-rearing practices, the early exclusion from adult interest and the use of child caretakers. Both psychologist and anthropologist note the relationship of these practices to the overall culture, and their impact on personality formation. Both attest to the great degree of conformity among young adults in these cultures, the lack of imaginative or creative activities, and the lack of individualism and initiative.

THE IROQUOIS

We referred earlier to a methodologic approach that employs the concept of the family as a territorial unit for its analytical tool. The traditional family structure of the Iroquoian tribes of northeastern United States and Canada exemplifies this concept. Indeed, the anthropologic literature refers to the

Iroquois Confederacy of the seventeenth and eighteenth centuries as "the classic example of a kinship state" (Fenton, 1951, p. 39).*

The cohesive interpersonal relationships engendered by this type of polity have been enhanced in the case of the Iroquois by the two dominant principles organizing their kinship structure. First, the classificatory principle as defined by Morgan (1962, p. 85) ordained that the relationship of mother's sister was equated with that of mother, and that the children of sisters were sisters and brothers. This merging of collateral lines of a family had the effect, as Morgan foresaw (1962, p. 86), of preventing the dilution of family ties through successive generations.

Second, the matrilineality principle ordained that the connection that counts in traditional Iroquois communities is the maternal connection. Except where drastic political revision has taken place, an individual's right to own land, to live on the Reservation, to have a voice in governance and religious affairs, to be legally entitled to a share of governmental treaty obligations, to inherit Reservation property, and so on all depend upon his place by birthright in his maternal lineage.

Under this system, then, Iroquois children are born into large extended families, and close ties with many relatives are the norm. Although collateral relatives seldom live in the same household today, it is still common to find at least three generations living together and collateral relatives living within easy reach of each other. Iroquois children therefore grow up with a strong sense of membership in a family group and a sharp awareness of the group's norms and values. The imprint of group membership, indeed, seems to take precedence over that of individual identity, and individual expectations tend to conform to goals the group can comfortably sustain. One effect of this thrust toward conformity is to limit individual ambition and striving beyond levels of attainment for all members of the group.

Despite these tendencies toward equalization of opportunity and achievement, there is one powerful division in Iroquois society that is impressed upon the children early in their upbringing, namely the clear-cut separation of male and female roles and relationships.† This division is not one of status, in the sense of the superior versus the inferior, but rather one of the assignment of tasks. Thus, in traditional Iroquois culture girls were trained to assist their mothers in household tasks and the care of younger siblings; to work in the fields with the cooperative women's group on a multifamily plot of land; to participate with older women in weaving, sewing, basket making,

---

*By definition, a kinship state is a territory inhabited by people who are related to each other by ties of kinship (Murdock, 1949, p. 79).

†The association of gender with the distribution of power and authority in Iroquois culture has been delineated in Isaacs (1977, pp. 167–184).

quilting, embroidery, beading, the shaping of bark utensils, etc. (Randle, 1951, pp. 170–171). The majority of these child-rearing activities and the social groupings to support them persist at the present time. Iroquois girls in the past and at present moved smoothly from infancy to maturity with few discontinuities, and even marriage did not and does not necessitate a major change in residence or social relationships. Indeed the woman's crucial and often dominant relationship is her position of daughter-sister-mother in the maternal family. This perhaps explains the minimal disruption of family relationships when children are born to unwed mothers. All children, in fact, are equally legitimate in terms of their affiliation in the maternal family, and there is always a close female relative available to help in their care and upbringing.

Iroquois males, however, have had to cope with severe discontinuities both in their upbringing and in their traditional roles. The child-rearing practices of the past involved a sharp interruption of the young boy's intimate association with the females of the household. Boys were not trained to perform household tasks; instead, they were sent out on hunting expeditions with the men or sent to help clear the fields for cultivation. They were assigned tasks requiring physical strength and endurance, and the qualities of the warrior, such as bravery and stoicism, were impressed upon them from an early age.

Anthony Wallace has argued that the pronounced dependency needs he witnessed among (Tuscarora) Iroquois adult males are the result of insufficient gratification of their oral needs in early childhood (1949, pp. 69–72). Wallace attributes the continuing dependence of some of these males on various forms of state and federal support to unfulfilled dependency cravings in early childhood.

The central problem for Iroquois males of today, however, is the break with the valued male activities of the past, which were associated with success as a hunter and warrior. There is no place today for these behaviors, and since young boys are still prevented from participating in house and family-related chores, they are left with little to occupy their free time and with ambitions that often are "vague and impossible of execution" (Randle, 1951, p. 178); the pattern persists into adulthood and helps to explain problems like alcoholism.

The Iroquois woman of today, then, is often secure, confident and self-reliant. Although her identification with her role as a woman in her own society stands her in good stead in her interactions with other societies, it does not stimulate her to encourage her sons to ambitious undertakings (Randle, 1951, p. 180). In sum, then, the child-rearing practices prevailing among the Iroquois appear to be developing two distinctly different personality types: the independent and confident female and the dependent and insecure male.

FIGURE 1-1. The family as the child-rearing unit of a society.

DISCUSSION

In the introduction to this chapter it was suggested that the child-rearing function of the family is bi-valent, that at the same time and in the same ways in which a family socializes its children it also preserves and perpetuates its culture. A paradigm illustrating this concept is shown in Figure 1-1.

However, in the four "mini-ethnographies," two salient features that serve to modify that concept become manifest. First, it appears that the major impact of the child-rearing practices of each of these societies is upon personality formation. Second, the regrouping of the adults in each generation into a constellation of roles, tasks, and identities characteristic of the parent group seems to be inevitable in the light of that personality patterning. Personality, then, is a necessary and pivotal factor in the reciprocal bonding that takes place between the family and its culture.

In Egyptian culture the central feature of paternal authoritarianism is preserved by inculcating a personality configuration in young males that combines fearfulness with vengefulness. In young females the same feature is preserved by socialization practices that stress conformity, passivity, and self-depreciation.

In India, among the Rajput, where the central cultural feature is the search for other-worldliness, deep hostility toward the opposite sex develops as the core of a cluster of negative and punitive personality traits among the women. These traits, as we have seen, are engendered by the cultural practice of sundering young women first from their mothers and then from their daughters, thus cutting them off from the only love-filled relationships of their lives. While this custom provides the males with the equivalent of life-long indentured servants, thereby freeing them for their lives of contemplation, the women take out their bitter resentment upon their sons through their child-rearing practices. Rajput boys, as a result, grow up incapable of finding solace or support in interpersonal relationships, and in adulthood they tend to resort to mystical projective systems characterized by elaborately organized structures oriented to the certain attainment of spiritual solace and security.

In New Zealand, where the major values of the Maoris appear designed to maintain both the status quo within their own society and their traditional cultural patterning vis-à-vis the dominant European culture (and these may be related goals), the abrupt, turnabout shifts in nurturing that occur in infancy and again in early adolescence result in a personality pattern typified by distrust of others and reluctance toward individualism, initiative, and striving. Clearly, the impact upon a society of the predominance of this personality pattern is conservative, both in terms of socioeconomic progress and in terms of acculturative adaptation.

Finally, among the Iroquois we find that the child-rearing practices that differentiated male and female roles in the past so emphatically and were in large measure responsible for the success of the Iroquois Confederacy under aboriginal conditions are today maladaptive for many of the males. Thus, the present-day continuance of the exclusion of young boys from significant roles in family sustenance, no longer provides meaningful alternatives, instead tending to produce a frustrated adult male personality marked by dependency traits and yearnings for opportunities to display heroism, which only war, dangerous construction jobs, or phantasizing can provide.

Conversely, in terms of personality development, the traditional practices in socializing Iroquois girls appear to be as adaptive and positive as in the past. As we have seen in the case of Egyptian villagers and Rajput families in India, however, the differential socialization of boys from girls within a single culture ultimately has effects upon the whole society that are intertwined and inseparable. Thus, among the Iroquois, while the competence and security of the women has a stabilizing effect upon the society, their failure to channel the ambitions of their sons and husbands in realistic directions and into persevering efforts results in the perpetuation of a cultural adaptation to present conditions which is disadvantageous to the society as a whole.

In view of the impact of child-rearing practices upon personality formation illustrated in the foregoing reviews, therefore, it appears indicated that personality constitutes a central factor in the perpetuation of cultures. But personality formation, we have seen, is not the end-product of the child-rearing process; it is a way-station in an ongoing cultural process that is demonstrably engaged in its own preservation. Thus, as I have previously pointed out, the personality patterns engendered by the child-rearing practices of a society prepare the young people of that society for moving into the roles, tasks, and identities of their parents' generation and thereby for preserving and transmitting to *their* children the crucial aspects of the culture within which they themselves were socialized.

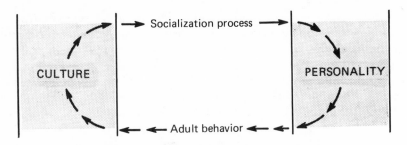

FIGURE 1-2. Culture and the socialization process.

My modification of the paradigm shown in Figure 1-1, accordingly, is designed to indicate recognition of the reciprocal bonding dynamic inherent in the socialization process. Since the foregoing analysis suggests that rather than diverging into two separate directions from its source, the socialization process is unidirectional but not terminal, I now conceive the process as shaping a characteristic typology of personality and *through* that process enabling, indeed *directing*, the maturing individual to take a preestablished place within a preestablished culture. Figure 1-2 illustrates this concept. It will be noted that the starting (and ending) point of this paradigm is the culture rather than the family. This indicates the major conclusion to be drawn from the foregoing cross-cultural ethnographic comparison: While the family may be the primary vehicle for carrying out socialization practices, it is the culture that decrees the content of those practices and the direction they take.

Finally, this paradigm may afford a new perspective on some of the current dilemmas we confront in observing the American family of the present.* It is evident from numerous studies (Kagan & Moss, 1962; Stolz, 1967; Baumrind, 1971; White & Watts, 1973) that the personality traits predominantly elicited and stimulated by socialization patterns among the majority of American families today are those that cluster around independence, individuality, and self-reliance. That these traits prepare their bearers for essentially isolated life styles is self-evident. It is also apparent that they are congruent with a technology that rests upon the continuous rapid transfer of goods and services. On the other hand, it may not be quite so manifest that these traits are related to the disintegration of close-knit family ties, of extended family households, and of mutual kin-based supports. The para-

---

*The notion of "the" American family is, of course, a fiction in the polygenetic, polycultural, and polyglot society of the United States. It is used here to refer to a preponderant patterning of familial relationships discernible as a numerically increasing phenomenon in the second half of the twentieth century.

digm developed above, however, in indicating an irreversible mechanism that welds personality to culture and culture to personality, strongly suggests that the narrowing of membership, the shrinking of obligation, and the geographic dispersal of ancestrally united, cohesive, and cooperative kin groups is in large part a function of the socialization process that presently prevails in the United States.

REFERENCES

Ammar, H. *Growing Up in an Egyptian Village*. London: Routledge and Kegan Paul, 1954.

Bachofen, J.J. *Antiquärische Briefe*. Berlin: W. Keiper, 1939.

Bamberger, J. The myth of matriarchy: Why men rule in primitive society. In Rosaldo, M.J., & Lamphere, L. (eds.), *Women, Culture and Society*. Stanford, Calif.: Stanford University Press, 1974.

Baumrind, D. Socialization and instrumental competence in young children. In Hartup, W.W. (ed.), *The Young Child: Reviews of Research* (Vol. 2). Washington, D.C.: National Association for the Education of Young Children, 1972, 202–224.

Earle, M.J. *Rakau Children from Six to Thirteen Years* (Victoria University of Wellington Publications in Psychology, No. 11). New Zealand: Victoria University of Wellington Press, 1958.

Engels, F. *Origin of the Family, Private Property and the State*. Moscow: Foreign Languages Publishing House, 1884.

Fenton, W.N. Locality as a basic factor in the development of Iroquois social structure (Symposium on Local Diversity in Iroquois Culture). *BAE Bulletin*, 49. Washington, D.C.: Smithsonian Institution, 1951, 39–54.

Goodenough, W.H. Residence rules. *Southwestern Journal of Anthropology*, 1956, 12, 22–37.

Harris, M. *The Rise of Anthropological Theory*. New York: Crowell, 1968.

Honigmann, J. *Personality in Culture*. New York: Harper & Row, 1967.

Isaacs, H.L. Orenda and the concept of power among the Tonawanda Seneca. In Fogelson, R.D., & Adams, R.N. (eds.), *The Anthropology of Power*. New York: Academic Press, 1977.

Kagan, J., & Moss, H.A. *Birth to Maturity, A Study in Psychological Development*. New York: Wiley, 1962.

Mead, M. *Coming of Age in Samoa*. New York: Morrow, 1971.

Mead, M. Socialization and enculturation. *Current Anthropology*, 1963, 4, 184–188.

Morgan, E. *The Descent of Women*. New York: Stein and Day, 1962.

Morgan, L.H. *Systems of Consanguinity and Affinity of the Human Family*. Washington, D.C.: Smithsonian Institution, 1870.

Morgan, L.H. *League of the Iroquois*. New York: Corinth, 1962.

Murdock, G.P. *Social Structure*. New York: Macmillan, 1949.

Parsons, T. The American family. In Parsons, T. & Bales, R.F. (eds.), *Family, Socialization, and Interaction Process*. Glencoe, Ill.: The Free Press, 1955, 3–33.

Peristiany, J.G. (ed.) *Honour and Shame: The Values of Mediterranean Society*. Chicago: University of Chicago Press, 1966.

Randle, M.C. Iroquois women, then and now (Symposium on Local Diversity in

Iroquois Culture). *BAE Bulletin*, 149. Washington, D.C.: Smithsonian Institution, 1951.

Stolz, L.M. *Influences on Parent Behavior*. Stanford, Calif.: Stanford University Press, 1967.

Wallace, Anthony, F.C., *The Tuscaroras: Sixth Nation of the Iroquois Confederacy*. Proceedings of the American Philosophical Society, 1949, 69–72.

White, B.L., & Watts, J.C. *Experience and Environment: Major Influences on the Development of the Young Child* (Vol. 1). Englewood Cliffs, N.J.: Prentice-Hall, 1973.

2

Identity Concerns in Early Motherhood

Stanley D. Rosenberg
Harriet Rosenberg

The birth of a child radically alters the relationship within the marital dyad, requiring the partners to take on new roles within a family system. Some studies conclude that this change assumes crisis proportions; others arrive at less extreme conclusions. In an effort to shed further light on this significant role transition in adult life, Stanley and Harriet Rosenberg studied a group of women with preschool-age children and asked them to describe selected aspects of their experience as mothers. They focused on factors thought to affect women's expectations of themselves in fulfilling the maternal role— for example, the mothers' recollections of their own experiences with their parents. Their findings lend some support to the view that motherhood is a hazardous event that precipitates a temporary identity disruption in most women. On the basis of the degree of crisis experienced by the women, the authors developed three prototypal profiles characterizing the social and psychologic import of the maternal experiences. This chapter should serve to challenge practitioners to examine their work with families in order to test the validity of these characterizations for their own practice.

The transition to parenthood is currently recognized as one of the most significant adult life changes, particularly for women. There is far less consensus about the affective and experiential qualities of the transition to the maternal role and its impact on female identity (Erikson, 1956). The issue is further complicated by rapidly shifting expectations and beliefs about women's roles and the nature of motherliness, changes that are partially associated with evolving patterns of participation in the labor force by mothers of young children. Such rapid change in the cultural milieu may be problematic not only for contemporary mothers, who are faced with complicated or ambiguous role expectations, but also for researchers and clinicians who are attempting to comprehend the experience. Despite a long history of theorizing and clinical observation in this area, particularly in the psychoanalytic literature, there exists no adequate contemporary phenomenology of the experience of early parenthood and its effects on a woman's psychologic adaptation.

In this chapter, we briefly review the development of thinking and empirical findings on early motherhood and report on our recent study of the experiences of parents with young first children. Our emphasis is on understanding the meaning mothers give to their parenthood, and how it impacts on their self-conception. Motherhood in our culture is a developmental watershed, a transformation requiring the woman to forge a new sense of herself. Her past, present, and future must take on a new coherence, one that includes motherhood as an aspect of her definition. The terms of this evolving identity, and the ways in which motherhood reinforces or undermines it, are intimately tied to the parent's affective responses to her new role, to the child, and to the stage of life.

The woman's self-conception, as it evolves in the parenting phase, is made manifest in many concrete spheres. Her experiences of marital, extended familial, community, and occupational relations tend to be reexamined in the context of becoming a parent, as does her perception of her history. The child may be seen either as reinforcing this larger conception of self or as undermining it. In the latter case, the mother experiences the child as the opponent in her struggle to control her own life space, to be the self she wishes to be. The depressive reaction so commonly observed in the mothers of young children is a reflection, at least in part, of the difficulties associated with this identity struggle. Drawing on the work of Ricoeur and Schafer we will attempt to put forth a framework for understanding this experience and its attendant conflicts.

OVERVIEW OF LITERATURE

Relevant findings on parenthood as a stage of life are found in several diverse research spheres. On the demographic or survey level we see evidence of widespread unhappiness among parents of young children (Campbell et al., 1976; McLaughlin, 1975). The mothers of preschool-age children, particularly, report a high level of depressive symptomatology (Radloff, 1975, p. 261); parents in this stage of life are high users of psychiatric outpatient services (Rosen et al., 1964).

In the sociologic literature there has been a two-decade–long debate over the question of whether the transition to parenthood represents a "crisis," and if it does, for whom. Stimulated by Lemasters' pioneering paper (1957), which suggested that the introduction of the child to the dyadic marriage situation precipitated sufficient stress to be considered a crisis, this series of studies has presented rather mixed conclusions. There are several investigators who find evidence of widespread crisis.* However, a somewhat greater number provide much more mixed data and find far less evidence of stress.†

LeMasters (1957), who did in-depth interviews with 46 couples, reports "extensive" or "severe" crises for 83 percent of his respondents in the period following the arrival of the first child. The extent of this crisis was not determined by the prepregnancy quality of the marriage, by the planned or unplanned nature of the pregnancy, by psychiatric disorder, or by personality adjustment. The crisis was linked more to the parents' naïveté about child rearing and their romanticizing the parental role.

On the opposite end of the spectrum are Hobbs (1968) and Russell (1974) who reported that 87 percent and 95 percent of their subjects, respectively, evidenced no more than "slight" crisis reactions in response to questionnaire items. Both agreed that mothers had significantly more difficulty with this transition than fathers. In a review article, Jacoby (1969) observed that the concept of crisis had been neither clearly explicated nor rendered comparable as used by these investigators. Since every major life transition requires a series of internal and interpersonal adjustments, he suggested that it might be more profitable to discuss the parameters of these changes, rather than arbitrarily to dichotomize them as crises and non-crises. Even if one is interested in making this distinction, a number of methodologic snares are encountered. There has not been comparability among the samples studied in terms either of social class or of the child's age. There is some evidence of a "baby honeymoon"; investigators looking at families with newborns (under one year) find less disruption than do those looking at somewhat older children (up to age five). It has been suggested that the checklist method tends to produce less evidence of crisis than does intensive interviewing. Social class may affect not only the reaction to parenthood but also the willingness to acknowledge any form of negative response. This line of research leaves us, then, with considerable ambiguity about the intensity, universality, and experiential nature of the crisis elements in the transition to parenthood.

---

*See, for example, LeMasters, E.E., Parenthood as Crisis, *Marriage and Family Living*, 1957, 19, 352–355; Dyer, E.D., Parenthood as Crisis: A Restudy, *Marriage and Family Living*, 1963, 25, 196–201; Wainwright, W.H., Fatherhood as a Precipitant of Mental Illness, *American Journal of Psychiatry*, 1966, 123, 40–44.

†Refer to Hobbs, D.F., Jr., Parenthood as Crisis: A Third Study, *Journal of Marriage and the Family*, 1965, 27, 367–372; Hobbs, D.F., Jr., Transition of Parenthood: A Replication and Extension, *Journal of Marriage and the Family*, 1968, 30, 413–417; Meyerowitz, J.H., & Feldman, H., Transition to Parenthood (Psychiatric Research Report No. 20), 1966, 78–84; Russell, C.S., Transition of Parenthood: Problems and Gratifications, *Journal of Marriage and the Family* 1974, 36, 294–302; Hobbs, D.F., Jr., & Cole, S.P., Transition to Parenthood: A Decade Replication, *Journal of Marriage and the Family*, 1976, 38, 723–731.

Rossi (1968) argued that the adjustment to the parental role is more difficult than the adjustments to marriage and career. She implicated the following factors in the stressful impact of parenthood: a lack of cultural options to reject parenthood or to terminate an undesired pregnancy; the shift from marriage to a first pregnancy as the major change in an adult woman's life course; the abruptness of the transition at the point of childbirth; and the lack of guidelines to successful parenthood in our society. While some dimensions of her argument remain cogent, others seem to have been rendered virtually obsolete by the changes of the past ten years (for example, availability of abortion and greater acceptance of childlessness).

Evolving patterns of labor-force participation are affecting both the practices and ideals of mothering. In 1948 only 13 percent of women with preschool-age children were employed outside the home. By 1976 the comparable figure was 37 percent (Kenniston, 1977). The great majority of women express the wish to combine a career with a marriage and motherhood (Roper Organization, 1974). Some of the conflicting elements in this set of choices are shown by the following data. Fifty-three percent point to motherhood as "the most difficult thing about being a woman today" (Harris, 1970, 1972). Ideals of female identity and motherhood are thus becoming more multifaceted and even internally contradictory.

The relation between employment and parental status is a complex one. Recent studies show that women commonly regard preschool children as a hindrance to personal freedom and find that "the loss of freedom the preschool child brings is itself a motivation for employment" (Hoffman and Nye, 1963, pp. 48–49). Indeed, post–parental-stage women show far less interest in employment than do women with young children. While findings are once again somewhat ambiguous, it appears that employed mothers of preschool-age children are more anxious and guilty than their unemployed counterparts.

The guilt experienced by these working mothers can be understood in the context of expectations that have traditionally surrounded motherhood in our culture. Popular notions of mother–child interaction have been highly congruent with psychoanalytic literature. Both have represented a high degree of exclusivity and intimacy as necessary and ideal. In putting forth such concepts as "instinctual mothering" and "infant bonding" on the one hand and "maternal deprivation" on the other, the psychoanalytic school has helped to reinforce traditional beliefs about the necessary conditions for mothering healthy, fulfilled children (Benedek, 1959; Winnicott, 1957; Fraiberg, 1959, 1977).

It is interesting to note that more recent studies, including Bowlby's own follow-ups, provide very little evidence of the long-term effects of maternal deprivation, and it is certainly not possible to demonstrate any relation between maternal employment and subsequent adjustment or growth of the child (Bowlby, 1952, p. 96; Yarrow, 1961; Schafer, 1976). In terms of the mother's development, a number of psychoanalytic writers have described the classical maternal role, which acts as both the mechanism and indicator for the achievement of mature femininity. This view finds early expression in Freud's description of the mother–son relationship. As Schafer (1976, p. 250) points out, Freud (1933, p. 133) seems to have made this a special type of relationship: "A mother is only brought unlimited satisfaction by her relation to a son; this is altogether the most perfect, the most free from ambivalence of all human relationships." Subsequent writers on motherhood have extended and given greater complexity to this view (Deutsch, 1945; Brody, 1967; Benedek, 1959; Winnicott, 1957). All continue to share the position that mothering is an instinctual role. Experiencing marked conflict in this role is an indicator of cultural interference with normal identity development, neurotic conflict, or more severe psychopathologic processes:

> The development of the ego, so intensely influenced by the cultural milieu of the individual, harbors the conflicts of motherliness. . . . In our culture the biologic and ego aspirations of women in the course of their psychophysiologic development toward motherhood incorporate also an active, extraverted, "masculine" ego ideal. This may conflict with the passive tendencies inherent in the propagation function. Consequently, many women cannot permit themselves the regression that lactation and the bodily care of an infant imply. The often anxious distance from the infant depletes their source of motherliness. Such women often respond with guilt and with a sense of frustration because of their inability to live up to their biologic function of mother with natural, intuitive ease (Anthony & Benedek, 1970, p. 151).

It is through performance of the parental role that one is supposedly able to rework childhood conflicts and find the possibility of full adult maturity and greater psychologic health (McBride, 1973; Fraiberg, 1959). At the same time, it is those who have suffered excessive maternal deprivation themselves (including all forms of disturbed mother–child bonds) who are least able to use this new opportunity and who will tend to experience extreme difficulty both in the task of reworking and in the parental role (Sampson et al., 1964).

While this view emerged primarily from clinical contact with symptomatic adults, longitudinal research has shown a far less deterministic relationship between childhood experience and parental role performance or conflicts. In a 1977 report, Fries traces the 28-year longitudinal development of Mary, one of 200 neonates studied from the time of the mother's pregnancy. Mary was born of a mother "resistive to the maternal role," a woman who was almost uniformly harsh and rejecting. The mother became psychotic and suicidal when Mary was 15. Almost every factor, save actual child abuse, was present, according to the case history, serving to undermine the chances for Mary's successful transition to motherhood. In actuality, her mother's death had a relieving effect, and Mary became more "active," "happy," and "poised." Follow-up, after the birth of a son and subsequent twins, showed her to be functioning well and "very content with her maternal role" (Fries, 1977, p. 32).

Many factors, such as genetic constitution or Fries' continued interest, might account for Mary's turnabout. It is nonetheless clear that there are many women who overcame glaring deficiencies in their own mothering while there are others who cannot adapt to the maternal role despite objectively adequate nurturing.

Psychoanalytic insights regarding the parental experience continue, however, to be valuable. Our phenomenologic investigation underlines the pervasive issues of reliving one's childhood through parenting, and the continued influence of one's own parental introjects. The introject may be a more or less accurate mental image of the parent as perceived by the child, but it is crucial to remember that the developing child's view of the world never corresponds directly to an adult view. Egocentric needs are dominant, coloring the child's reactions to the parents' behavior. The young child cannot adequately differentiate reality from dreams or fantasies; nor can the child understand the actions or explanations of the parents in adult terms. While these and other developmental features skew the child's initial impressions, the introject also changes and evolves as he or she grows older. Memories of the parents are lost; some are highlighted, exaggerated, transposed in time, and otherwise altered. Thus, while one's remembrances of one's childhood represent a dominant paradigm in the experience and enactment of being a parent, they can be more productively understood, not as "unconscious memories of actual past events [but] fantasies expressing unconscious infantile wishes" (Schimek, 1975, p. 845). These fantasies are not totally unanchored in actual events or stimuli, but as Ricoeur (1977, p. 841) comments: "Fantasies deriving from infantile scenes . . . in spite of their fragile basis in the real history . . . present a highly structured organization and are inscribed in scenarios which are both typical and limited in number."

What Ricoeur is alluding to, and what is also underlined by Schafer (1976, pp. 160–161, 251), is that these mental representations of one's parents are part of a larger self-conception. While the basic shape of the person's identity begins evolving early in life, it continues to change and develop through the specifics of his or her life experience. Parenthood represents a life event of almost unique significance for the women studied, one that produced an alteration or crystallization of their identities. Not only did these women become more aware of the parental introjects as they themselves became mothers, but the introjects could also become more complex and amenable to change. Both positive and negative images of the woman's own parents were awakened, often leading to reinterpretations of her own childhood. This reinterpretive process served to justify their particular reactions to motherhood, or to open up new possibilities for them in the maternal role.

METHODOLOGY

In 1976 the authors conducted a series of intensive, semistructured interviews with 15 sets of parents of preschool-age children. The respondents were randomly chosen residents of a specified area whose names appeared in the birth records of a regional New England medical center. At the time of contact, the firstborn children varied in age from one to four years. The parents were essentially working- and middle-class. A remuneration was offered for participation and there was a 100-percent acceptance rate. The taped interviews were conducted in two parts, the first being a home visit with the mother lasting from two to four hours. The second meeting was held in a university setting and involved joint interviewing of both parents. Although this provided information on the father's reaction to parenthood, we primarily used this interview to obtain another source of data on the woman's adaptation and the child's impact on the dyad. Secondarily, we sought to assess the impact of the father's responses and attitudes on the mother's feelings about and definition of her role. The interview schedules are given in Appendix A.

Our particular objectives in the interview were as follows:

1. To assess the emotional impact of the maternal experience.
2. To understand the woman's definition of the maternal role and her own experience of attempting to fulfill it.
3. To draw connections between the parents' recollections of their own upbringing and their approach to childrearing.
4. To understand better how the social environment of the marriage, extended family, and community affected the parenting role.
5. To examine role conflicts associated with changing norms of motherhood, particularly work and career conflicts.
6. To gain insight on how the transition to motherhood altered the woman's conception of her own identity.

We felt that intensive interviewing with a normal sample was required to gain a more accurate view of these phenomena. Currently available data from intensive contact tend to be from psychiatric populations, introducing obvious biases, while survey-type data involve the limitations discussed above. Moreover, data from as recently as five to eight years ago may well be rendered obsolete because of changing role expectations.

PHENOMENOLOGY OF THE PARENTING EXPERIENCE

There was a striking variation found in the affective responses and identity concerns related to parenthood, not only between individuals, but also across time for a given person. The chart in Appendix B conveys in condensed form the fluctuations in mood and meaning the parents reported. For descriptive purposes, we have designed three general types of responses to motherhood: (1) negative, (2) mixed, and (3) positive. These represent a continuum of responses from the most to the least affectively negative, and groups 1 and 2 can be described as undergoing crises in this life phase.

We note the relation of the mother's position on this continuum to those areas of life space most directly affected by her transition to parenthood (for example, marriage, her interaction with the child, work conflicts, and re-evoked images of her own childhood). The responses of mothers studied constituted a generally bell-shaped curve, highly positive or negative responses being less common than more ambivalent or mixed reactions. The mixed category was the most representative, describing eight of the fifteen families studied. Three were clearly positive and four were negative. Themes of control, vacillation, and confusion dominated many aspects of the experience for the mixed group. There was often a struggle for control in the marital dyad, deciding who would dictate the terms of parenthood. In addition, these mothers felt they were in a tug-of-war between fulfilling the child's needs and maintaining control over their own time and personal space. The mother had to work to find the limits of her obligations to the child and the degree to which the child should dominate the mother's ideation. For many, there was also a struggle to control the child's feelings, behavior and personality: Could the mother make the child become what she wanted the child to be? For most, there were elements of a confrontation with re-membrances of their own parents: The mothers wondered whether they would negate what their parents had done or whether they would fulfill their parental roles more effectively while following the guidelines established by their parents. We did observe, however, a generally depressive stance on the part of most of the mothers. This depressive affect was manifested primarily in a sense of confusion or suspension of time. They talked of feeling both that time was endless and yet that days were not long enough to accomplish all that needed to be done. Their parenting experiences seemed to engulf them. Life before the arrival of the child tended to seem unreal or like the life of another self.

In general, our findings support LeMasters' view that motherhood tends to engender at least a temporary identity disruption in most women, one that could reasonably be called a crisis. A few mothers, about a fifth of our interviewees, were not characterized by this sense of being overwhelmed. They reported that a sense of stability and coherence had been brought about through being a parent, and they acted as though such were the case. For them, motherhood acted as reinforcement to an evolving identity. Appendix B summarizes our interview findings. While space does not permit a full reporting of the interview data, the generalizations and conclusions that follow are based on the parents' responses to the appended interview schedule.

IDENTITY AND MOTHERHOOD

The accounts of entrance into the mothering role presented by our interviewees demonstrated several possible relationships between this transition and the woman's sense of identity. On the most obvious level, we can say that there were three types:

1. Those who found motherhood a negative experience, a disruption or impediment to their attempts to forge an acceptable identity. These women (n = 4) experienced motherhood as a profound crisis.
2. Women who found motherhood a mixed input, enhancing self-esteem and fulfilling certain identity imperatives at the cost of other equally significant aspects of their self-definitions. These latter concerns revolved around issues of career and external achievement. Disruption of their sense of adult autonomy and self-worth was of sufficient magnitude to represent a crisis (n = 8).
3. Women who found in motherhood an almost total identity, a life project that gave them a unique sense of purpose and a positive sense of self (n = 3).

Each woman obviously cast her particular identity strivings in personalized terms. At the same time, it was clear that the basic images of self they were trying to achieve were drawn from a limited set of cultural images or themes. The whole weight of shared stereotypes, common socialization experiences, and role expectations shaped and delimited the alternative identities sought. In this sense, we can say that the transition to motherhood evokes the utilization of several shared themes. The women used one or more of these themes as they attempted to understand, live through, and define themselves in their new roles. The themes were not only congruent with the specifics of the mothering experience but were also a basis for giving continuity to long-standing aspects of self-definition, memories, ambitions, values, and styles of interpersonal relatedness. They expressed underlying assumptions of the women's self-identity.

The first (or profound-crisis) group uniformly manifests an identity of deprivation. In this identity, the mother sees herself as an embattled figure.

These women typically felt victimized by a whole array of life events and people. They describe themselves as attempting to right these wrongs and to overcome adversity. The child is a crucial principal in this identity quest, the potential vehicle for the mother's triumph.

One of the ubiquitous components of this identity theme as it emerged in the cases studied was the image of maternal deprivation in the parent's own childhood. The mother talked about suffering a lack of maternal love and attention or, alternatively, of having been smothered and overcontrolled. Incorporating this theme into their self-conception, they felt trapped by their history and embattled by those introjects associated with it. The arrival of the child reactivated or heightened their feelings of deprivation and anger. The sense of emptiness, bitterness, and longing in these women was focused on the child as a means of self-fulfillment. The typical fantasy involved insuring fulfillment in one's own child as a means of finally feeling loved and wanted. However, in encountering the reality of having to provide this fulfillment, a number of internal obstacles often arose. For example, some women experienced intense feelings of emptiness in the face of the child's demand for love and nurturance, as if the continued malevolent presence of the introject was polluting the contemporary relationship. These feelings were associated with a pattern in which extreme solicitousness alternated with hostile withdrawal.

When this identity was the most extreme, we observed that the mother felt impelled toward emotional withdrawal from the child. As such withdrawal was threatening to the dependent child, it often resulted in an escalation of demands for assurance and, in addition, an expression of rage. The woman who, in fact, shared with the child many of these feelings of need and anger toward parental figures often found it impossible to give reassurance or confront the child's hostility. She then either tried to tune out the child's behavior by denying or distorting its meaning or by punitively forbidding expressiveness on the child's part.

These parents either experienced a sense of being dominated by these feelings or worked to transcend them. Some mothers, that is, began to reconstruct their image of self after the birth of the child. They found long-buried remembrances of positive maternal input and even reported the sense of seeing their own parents in an entirely different light. In all but the most extreme instances, the parental image seemed to be so ambiguous or multifaceted that the self had space for such reconstruction.

A far more diverse and complex set of identity strivings revolved around the quests for achievement and interpersonal approval as seen in the second group. While the two identity needs were not precisely the same, they shared important components in the sense that the mother was caught up in the pursuit of goals delineated either by the culture generally or by specific people in the environment. These women felt that a positive identity could only be achieved through winning approval and recognition for their accomplishments. This approval would demonstrate that they had become "new," better selves, somehow more than others had thought them to be. Once transformed into new selves, these women expected to conquer longstanding feelings of anxiety, self-doubt, and fears of inadequacy. The child was part of this image of fulfillment in the sense of being another aspect of self that would be seen and applauded by others: another demonstration of general capability and well-roundedness.

For these women, a career reversal or failure to achieve a degree or to win some important prize was experienced as a total cataclysm, as if the viability of their identity was dependent on these achievements. The sense of disaster associated with failure could be understood in terms of the conditional sense of identity of these mothers. They only felt worthwhile or substantial when "proving" their capacity to achieve some socially valued image. This equation between self and achievement led these new mothers to a sense of desperation. Some women in this group reported that a career hiatus made them feel as though their lives had come to a halt. Women for whom this theme was central often became tremendously disorganized and depressed when the birth of the child threatened career continuity.

The child could, nonetheless, be seen as a necessary element in achievement. These women still experienced a sense of being viewed as incomplete or insufficiently "womanly" if they did not become mothers. Our respondents almost universally reported familial pressure to produce grandchildren and a sense of being somehow excluded or questioned by peers and neighbors while they prolonged their childless state.

This general responsiveness to culturally defined goals is associated with certain dilemmas and paradoxes. There were at least two sets of contemporary, prepackaged role images these women experienced as prescriptions for their own identities. The first was a picture of an independent, competent career woman; the second was that of a charming, carefree young mother. While these images seemed like mere caricatures when overtly stated, women in the study still tended to measure themselves against or attempt to enact them. When attempting to fulfill both roles simultaneously, they encountered some fairly harsh realities. They reported an increasing feeling of the impossibility of success, as though they had to devote their energies exclusively to the achievement of one of the roles. Perhaps even more fundamentally, these women encountered discrepancies between their own experience in either role and what was represented to them as "good" or "normal."

Each image is, in itself, a fiction that may grossly distort the reality of one's actual performance in the role. Rather than feeling utterly competent, the mother–career women reported often feeling harassed and fraudulent in their attempts to appear in control. In place of serenity and warmth, the nonworking mothers told of experiencing anguish and rage. Some women were able to detach themselves from both images and attempted to come to grips with their own experience in relating to their child and to their status of motherhood. This shift usually involved a sense of relief—a giving up of the effort to be the "ideal" woman. It also had elements of surrender or the abandonment of the pursuit of perfection, reflected in their relinquishing their strong need for admiration and praise from others. In giving up this identity quest, these women were thrown back onto their own spontaneous feelings, the depth and variability of which were sometimes reported as alarming. The intense emotionality of motherhood, good or bad, was a very new experience for these typically controlled, cerebral women.

The thematic that characterized the most positive mothers (group 3) in the study involved an image of a near-perfect childhood, of a "paradise lost." The image here of motherhood is one of a return to the paradise, a re-creation of the happiness and security associated with the remembered past. In this return, the mother does not relive her childhood directly, but rather through her offspring. These women looked back upon their own upbringing with a sense of fulfillment. They expressed no uncertainty about their parents' love, goodness, or dedication to their well-being. Concomitant with this image was the wish to recreate this perfect family setting for their own child, to relive this idealized past.

In each case of adherence to this belief structure, the birth of the first child was the stimulus for activation of the identity of the stereotypical "perfect mother," a figure out of a Norman Rockwell painting. Some of these women attempted explorations of new living environments or life styles as young adults. However, moving into the maternal role invariably evoked a conservative response, experienced as a need to establish roots in an environment the same as, or highly similar to, the one remembered from childhood. Once this identity began to be lived out, it was seen as inevitable. Earlier life movements, although they might have been divergent, came to be interpreted as no more than preparations for or vacations from the mother's "real" life. The conservatism in this real life went beyond the issue of residence. It was also reflected in other dimensions, such as occupational choice, daily life routines, and the style of family interaction. This latter involved a sense of very close, "natural" family interaction, an almost organic unity between parents and child, and, if at all possible, including the extended family. There was a demand that family be the main focus of interest, emotional commitment, and pleasure.

While this identity might seem to foster the most idyllic adaptation to parenthood, it also involved certain delimitations of self and often an unwillingness to recognize the child as a person. It represented comfort and certainty but also engendered feelings of oppressiveness or servitude. These women's lives no longer seemed controlled by the self but were experienced as totally predetermined by the images of the past. This state led some women to a feeling of premature aging, as if youth, middle age, and old age were collapsed into a single experience.

At another level, we observed the vulnerability of this identity quest to circumstances in the external environment. Since it was believed that the traditional way was the only satisfactory one, the prospect of relocating for economic or career reasons produced real dread. The self-defined need to remain close to the extended family in some cases became a crippling limitation.

CONCLUSIONS

The mothers we observed continually worked to keep their personal identities viable, attempting to integrate new role demands and elements of experience into their particular ongoing definitions of themselves. Since these definitions represented ideals, the realities of motherhood could never fully be in accord with them. This discrepancy created a continual tension, pressing the mothers to revisions of their identities on the one hand, or to distortions of experience on the other. The attempt to maintain their self-definitions appears to be the first priority for the mothers. Indeed, the basic elements of these identities seemed to be experienced as crucial. While the components of maternal identities varied widely, certain factors came repeatedly into play in focusing the general experience of childhood and influencing the quality and degree of crisis associated with it.

The image of one's own upbringing, and particularly the kind of mothering experienced, was probably the most pervasive element in the mothers' development of a parental identity. This implies that the psychoanalytical approach, and particularly that of the object-representation school, is applicable to normal as well as to patient populations. Each of the three identity types we have discussed is based in large degree on a continuation of, or response to, perceived inputs from the family of origin. Some of the parents in the study struggled to become like their parents and thus relive their childhoods. Still others sought to fulfill perceived parental expectations and thus win love and approval. In each case, the parental image was experienced as a ubiquitous force. No type of encounter between mother and young child seemed to transpire without there being some sense of actual or potential repetition from the mother's own construction of her childhood.

In the case of the deprivation thematic, the choice was obviously tinged with bitterness and defiance. In contrast, the "paradise lost" thematic tied the woman's identity to a re-creation of these childhood images. The relation of the achievement thematics to the image of childhood was often more variable. When they were tied to an essentially benign image of upbringing, mothers involved with them almost unthinkingly reproduced large components of their own parents' perceived styles and values. More characteristically, achievement needs were expressed in the woman's continued effort to please her parents by becoming the person they seemed to expect.

The woman's sense of her identity was thus made problematic by the parenting experience in a number of ways. It was often the wish for self-transformation, a new or enhanced identity, that led the parents to desire children. As prospective parents, they expected that a new sense of self would be created in the process of bringing a child into the world. There was thus considerable pressure on the children to fulfill their mothers' often unarticulated expectations. Gaining a sense of control over their own lives instead of a sense of domination by other people was one of the major alterations these women hoped to bring about through motherhood. Images of motherhood and social adulthood were intertwined. It thus represented a very direct assault on their aspirations when the child became—as all children sometimes do—another source of demands. The child's attempts to control its parents in order to satisfy its needs were experienced as a challenge to these women's images of self as parent. Similarly, the child's looks, talent, and good behavior were expected to be used as visible evidence of the mother's basic competence, a way to secure acknowledgment and approval from others. The reality of the child's capacity to be dirty, to have flaws and weaknesses, or to misbehave could conversely undermine the mother's attempts to enhance her sense of identity.

In general, the basic terms of the mothers' identity quests largely defined and colored their reactions to parenthood, while the chance factors or externals surrounding this life stage served to modify and further define the experience. Either elements of reality coalesced with and reinforced the identity the mothers worked to construct in this life phase or they were discrepant, requiring modification or the collapsing of such self-concepts. Finances, health, career contingencies, and extended familial input all had such effects.

Changing and ambiguous social demands also seem to impinge directly on the mothering experience. The social environment thus continually interacted with the woman's psychologic needs and her sense of her own history in shaping her responses to becoming a mother. The cultural images of woman's role and motherhood represented the basic elements out of which identity strivings were formulated. These images as perceived by young women in our culture contain contradictory elements and impossible demands. Part of the depressive response and identity disruption noted in this population is due to the unrealistic nature both of the expectations young women have about motherhood and the expectations communicated by others about how the role should be performed. In the current study the most troublesome issue frequently was the setting of priorities among the women's needs for freedom, autonomy, career, or intellectual achievement, and the demands of motherhood. For women with needs for simultaneous reinforcement in several of these spheres—common certainly among middle-class women—early motherhood represented a deprivation of identity inputs. The sense of being trapped or deprived in the maternal role, moreover, engendered considerable guilt. Such doubts or negative feelings about motherhood are not part of the stereotyped image of the "good mother."

A factor that has probably not received adequate attention in the literature is that of the immediate interpersonal environment of the mother. The availability of support systems can often serve to temper the depressive response to the role change and temporally delimit the sense of crisis. The opportunity to share child-rearing tasks with spouses or other families, for example, could greatly relieve the sense of servitude and entrapment. In the experience of our subjects, communication with other women going through similar problems in adapting to the maternal role served to relieve the sense of isolation, guilt, and inadequacy so commonly experienced. In the face of ambiguous role expectations and competing identity needs, the attitudinal support of spouses, friends, and extended family helped to inhibit or facilitate such options as combining work and parenthood. A woman's identity strivings in this, as in other life stages, are affected both by social expectations on the one hand and by internal needs and imagery on the other. Her adaptation requires that there be a creative modification of these images, in closer accord with her own decisions about how to fulfill the maternal role.

REFERENCES

Anthony, E.S. & Benedek, T. (eds.). *Parenthood: Its Psychology and Psychopathology.* New York: Little, Brown, 1970.

Benedek, T. Parenthood as a developmental phase. *Journal of the American Psychoanalytic Association*, 1959, 7, 389–417.

Bowlby, J. *Maternal Care and Mental Health* (WHO Monograph Series, No. 2). Geneva: WHO, 1952, 96.

Campbell, A., Converse, P., & Rogers, W. *The Quality of American Life.* New York: Russell Sage Foundation, 1976.

Dyer, E.D. Parenthood as crisis: A restudy. *Marriage and Family Living*, 1963, 25, 196–201.

Erikson, E. The problem of ego identity. *Journal of the American Psychoanalytic Association*, 1956, 4, 58–121.

Fraiberg, S. *The Magic Years.* New York: Scribner's, 1959.

Fraiberg, S. *Every Child's Birthright.* New York: Basic Books, 1977.

Fries, M.E. Longitudinal study: Prenatal period to parenthood. *Journal of the American Psychoanalytic Association*, 1977, 25, 132.

Freud, S. *New Introductory Lectures on Psychoanalysis* (Standard Ed.), Vol. 22. London: Hogarth Press, 1933.

Harris, L., and Associates, Inc. The Virginia Slims American women's opinion poll, 1970, 1972, 10–11.

Hobbs, D.F., Jr. Parenthood as crisis: A third study. *Journal of Marriage and the Family*, 1965, 27, 367–372.

Hobbs, D.F., Jr. Transition to parenthood: A replication and extension. *Journal of Marriage and the Family*, 1968, 30, 413–417.

Hobbs, D.F., Jr., & Cole, S.P. Transition to parenthood: A decade replication. *Journal of Marriage and the Family*, 1976, 38, 723–731.

Hoffman, L.W., & Nye, F.I. (eds.). *Working Mothers: An Evaluative Review of Consequences for Wife, Husband and Child*. New York: Rand-McNally, 1963.

Kenniston, K. *All Our Children*. New York: Harcourt Brace Jovanovich, 1977.

LeMasters, E.E. Parenthood as crisis. *Marriage and Family Living*, 1957, 19, 352–355.

McBride, A.B. *The Growth and Development of Mothers*. New York: Harper & Row, 1973.

McLaughlin, M. Parents who wouldn't do it again. *McCalls*, November 1975, 37–38.

Radloff, L. Sex differences in depression: The effects of occupation and marital status. *Sex Roles*, 1975, 1, 261.

Ricoeur, P. The question of proof in Freud's psychoanalytic writings. *Journal of the American Psychoanalytic Association*, 1977, 25, 841.

Roper Organization, Inc. The Virginia Slims American women's opinion poll, Vol. 3, 1974.

Rosen, B.M., Bahn, A.K., & Kramer, M. Demographic and diagnostic characteristics of psychiatric clinic outpatients in the U.S., 1961. *The American Journal of Orthopsychiatry*, 1964, 34, 455–468.

Rossi, A.S. Transition to parenthood. *Journal of Marriage and the Family*, 1968, 30, 26–39.

Russell, C.S. Transition to parenthood: Problems and gratifications. *Journal of Marriage and the Family*, 1974, 36, 294–302.

Sampson, H., Messinger, S., & Towne, R. *Schizophrenic Women: Studies in Marital Crisis*. Englewood Cliffs, N.J.: Atherton Press and Prentice-Hall, 1964.

Schafer, R. *A New Language for Psychoanalysis*. New Haven: Yale University Press, 1976.

Schimek, J.G. The interpretations of the past: Childhood trauma, physical reality and historical truth. *Journal of the American Psychoanalytic Association*, 1975, 23, 845.

Wainwright, W.H. Fatherhood as a precipitant of mental illness. *American Journal of Psychiatry*, 1966, 123, 40–42.

Winnicott, D.W. *The Child and the Family*. London: Tavistock, 1957.

Yarrow, L.J. Maternal deprivation: Towards an empirical and conceptual reevaluation. *Psychological Bulletin*, 1961, 58, 459–490.

APPENDIX A

Interview Schedule

1. INTRODUCTION

Nowadays, there are many different ideas of what women should do and be. Since there is no longer any one predominant model for raising children, we are trying to get a clearer idea of some of the diverse styles of bringing up young children. Also, some ideas about what it feels like to be a mother. I'd like to start by asking you a few questions about your family history. How long have you been in this area? In the same house? Where did you live before? Do you work? What does your husband do? How long have you been married? How long were you married before the baby came? If you didn't work, what occupied your time before the baby came?

2. FAMILY ACTIVITY PATTERNS

Could you tell me what a typical day is like for you?

[Attempt to assess type of mother–child interaction; friendship patterns of mother; attitude toward household tasks; division of labor: cooking, cleaning; etc. See also supplemental questions for working mothers.]

Does your child have a play group, nursery school, etc.? What do you do with your free time? Do you visit friends? Does your child play well alone when you're occupied with chores, etc.? What kind of games? What kind of games or type of play do you do *with* your child? What is it like when your husband comes home from work? Can you tell me what you do on the weekends?

3. FAMILY OF ORIGIN

Before talking more about the changes in your life since the baby came, we'd like to find out a little more about what it was like for *you* as a child, what your family was like.

Where were you born and raised? Can you describe what kind of a person your mother/father is—for example, physical characteristics, personality, occupation? Do you think that you were like/unlike your child [at comparable stages of development]? In what ways? Are there similarities in personality?

Do your parents seem different to you now than when you were a child? Do you think you are raising your child differently from the way you were raised—for example, discipline, day care, babysitting? Do you remember who took care of you at the preschool age? Do you see your parents and/or in-laws much? What do you do with them? Do they babysit? How do your mother and father act with your child? Is this different from the way they acted toward *you* as a child?

4. MAJOR CHANGES SINCE CHILD'S BIRTH

I imagine that having a child has changed your style of living in some ways. We'd like to explore this. [If not already covered, ask about occupational changes and/or changes in daily activities.]

Have you changed friendship patterns? Do you have a mixture of friends or only married friends with children? Have there been changes in your social life? What do you do when you go out with your husband? How often do you go out? Do you think having a child has changed your marriage? In what ways? Do you argue? Do you argue about different things than before? Do you do more or fewer things together (for example, movies, sports)? Has there been a change in your physical relationship? What things have increased/decreased in importance for you since your child was born? For your husband (for example, social life, free time)? Has having a child changed how you feel about your husband? Do you feel closer to your husband? Has having a child changed how you feel about yourself? Do you have a more or less positive feeling about yourself? Do you feel that sometimes being a mother gets in the way of being yourself?

5. CHANGES AS THE CHILD GROWS

We'd like to ask you some more specific questions about your child.

Has he had any major health problems? Are both you and your husband generally in good health? About what age did your child walk? Talk? Any feeding/eating/sleeping problems? Did toilet training present difficulties? What kind of play does your child like best? Does he have playmates? Do you try to teach him anything (a,b,c's, drawing, etc.)? Can you describe a situation where you had to discipline him? Do you feel that you can communicate with your child (and he with you)? Does he express opinions, ideas, and how do you respond to this? Is he stubborn about certain things? Is there a battle of wills? For example, does he consistently resist you about certain things? Can you describe something he did that particularly amused you?

Do you feel his personality is changing as he grows? Do you have any impressions now of what he will be like as an adult? Do you feel that it is easier or harder for you to deal with your child now than a year ago? Are you eager for the future, for his growing up? What do you think has influenced the way you are raising your child—for example, books, magazines, parents, friends? Do you have any philosophy, any guidelines in mind for the way you want more children? Have you thought about any timetable for raising your family?

6. SUPPLEMENTAL QUESTIONS FOR WORKING MOTHERS

What are the main things that make work worthwhile for you?

[If there is a financial necessity for working, ask: If there were no financial pressure, would you still work?]

If your job folded, how do you think the transition to staying home would be for you? What are the pros and cons? Are your friends work related and/or do you know full-time housewives with young children? Do you talk to them about your child's developmental problems or progress? If not, do you have any other source for advice—for example, parents, doctor, books? Has anyone expressed any opinions to you about your trying to combine motherhood and work? Criticism or praise? Has your husband received any flak because of your stepping out of the traditional role? If your child developed problems which required a parent at home (for example, illness, emotional upset), would you be the one to step in, or would you continue to attempt to share the responsibility with your husband?

APPENDIX B

Identity Concerns in Early Motherhood

NEGATIVE	MIXED	POSITIVE
DEPRESSIVE MANIFESTATIONS		
Masked depression punctuated by overt and severe depressive affect Considerable use of denial Fear of being emptied by child	Overt depressive symptomatology Chronic tiredness, boredom, irritability, sense of being trapped	Absence of depressive symptoms
TIME EXPERIENCE		
Time with child is oppressive Feeling of being trapped in time Attempt to define time away from child as "real" life	Time confusion: unreality of preparenting phase of adulthood (belongs to another self) In present life phase child rearing seems, at points, omnipresent and endless Slowing down of time, boredom mixed with feeling that days are not long enough to accomplish what needs to be done	Collapse of time: mother experiences sense of her own past as "present"; day-to-day dealings with child often seem a reenactment of her childhood Earlier period of marriage seems "preparation" for parenthood
EFFECT ON MARRIAGE OF BIRTH OF FIRST CHILD		
If both parents have negative attitude: impact minimal If one parent negative, one positive or mixed: highly divisive and stressful Birth of child tends to reactivate feelings of emptiness, bitterness, longing; images of maternal deprivation in mother's own childhood	Stress on marriage, divisive if parents' orientations differ May create competition for maternal attention More stressful if experience is faced with naïveté and romanticised	Stimulus for beginning of reenactment of "perfect" childhood Bond or unifying symbol in marriage Transition nonstressful Extra work, fatigue, monetary burden, restructuring of interaction and communication patterns, need to "share" attention—all are dealt with as "expected" price of child rearing

continued

NEGATIVE	MIXED	POSITIVE
	GUILT THEMES	
Guilt over emotional inadequacy	Guilt evoked by wish for separateness from child and/or use of time for self	Lack of guilt vis-à-vis child-rearing issues
Guilt for inability to be different from their own maternal imago	Guilt over anger towards child	
	Guilt over limits of mother's competence, or limits of her capacity for warmth	
	CHILD CENTEREDNESS	
Highly circumscribed modes of contact with child	Fluctuations in degree of child centeredness	Integration of child into general social and leisure activities of mother
Consistent attempts by mother to be separate from or to flee from child	Contact with child compartmentalized; maintenance of exclusively adult activities	Decrease of non–child-oriented activities with birth of child
		Reluctance of mother to overcommit herself to work
		Mother seeks diffuse contact with child
	QUALITY OF INTERACTON WITH CHILD	
Demand for adult-like behavior from child	Attempts to mold in child qualities important to parent	Ability to accept and enjoy child's developmental level
Objectification of child	Limited tolerance for play with child	Mother acts as companion, teacher, entertainer
Stress on perception of defects in child	Concern for external standards of child and/or parent behavior and achievement	Little or no pressure for child to "grow up" quickly or to meet or surpass behavior of other children at comparable developmental levels
General irritability toward the child		
Solicitude alternating with emotional withdrawal		
	DISCIPLINE/CONTROL	
Harsh, punitive controls	Much conflict and guilt about use of discipline	Unconflicted about applying discipline
Sense of child as willful, perverse	Sense of being unable to control child	Often use remembered techniques from mother's own childhood
Encounters between mother and child often seen as power struggles	Experimentation and inconsistency in search of "correct" techniques of control	Good manners, controlled behavior seen as important

continued

NEGATIVE	MIXED	POSITIVE
	IMAGE OF CHILD	
Child seen as an object to be controlled so he does not intrude Child often seen as "evil," demon-like Child viewed as reflection of mother's "bad" self or reincarnation of persecutory figure (sibling or parental imago)	Ambivalence toward child: child sometimes seen as pleasurable, sometimes unbearable View of child's behavior, appearance, etc., polluted by ambivalent images of past—i.e., child is reflection of "good" or "bad" aspects of mother's own parents and siblings Child's behavior seen as proving ground, test of parent's self-worth Child seen as reflection or proof of mother's ability: much emphasis on child being smart, attractive, popular, successful	Child seen as reflection of good in self Child seen as confirmation of mother's ability to recreate own happy childhood Child a necessary object in parental drive to recreate own childhood Lack of concern with child's personal qualities or traits, but general view of child as cherished, precious Considerable investment in perceiving child as happy and healthy
	WORK ORIENTATION	
Work is essential focus in life, given priority over child rearing	Self-esteem linked ambivalently to professional achievement Conflict between priorities of work/motherhood	Belief in child rearing as central work in life Capacity to experience self-worth without external (occupational) employment Willingness to curtail outside work during this life stage
	COPING DEVICES	
Withdrawal—use of any available alternative caretakers Isolation from other parents to avoid potentially "upsetting" comparisons Isolation of child, e.g., confining to room for long periods Denial of child's demands	Seeking of diversions with and for child Quest for interpersonal supports Attempt to retain contact with adult competencies and activities Reliance on "socially acceptable" means of having child cared for (nursery school, play groups)	Glorification of experience Reliance on familial contact and support Insistence on parenthood as central value and achievement (makes difficulties in other life projects easier to handle)

continued

NEGATIVE	MIXED	POSITIVE
IMAGES OF MOTHER'S OWN CHILDHOOD		
Childhood seen as oppressive	Was object of parents' striving	Organic unity of nuclear family, nearly perfect childhood
Distance from or rejection by parents	Cleavage or conflict with one parent	Family's closeness and dedication
Negative self-image as child	Ambiguous sense of self-worth or acceptance as child	Remembrance of caring and opportunity for freedom
Intrafamilial conflict		
Maternal deprivation		

3

Parent–Child Relations at Middle Age

Michael P. Farrell
Stanley D. Rosenberg

While midlife has long been identified as a stage of development and growth, it has recently come under closer scrutiny. For many adults, entry into middle age coincides with the late adolescence and young adulthood of their children. Farrell and Rosenberg studied the family life of middle-aged men, focusing on how the parents managed the "launching" of the children out of the family and into their roles as independent young adults. The authors describe the dynamic forces influencing the parents' participation in this process and conclude that they reexperience their unresolved conflicts through the lives of their teenaged children, covertly encouraging them to take a preferred direction. Because parent and adolescent needs run counter to each other during this phase, Farrell and Rosenberg propose that some degree of turmoil is inevitable. However, they suggest that the process need not have only negative outcomes, since adolescents are frequently able to achieve satisfactory compromises between their own aims and the pressures of the parents, while the parents may find a constructive resolution of old conflicts. Such problems are, of course, not always managed without recourse to outside help. In such circumstances the authors' thesis provides practitioners with a framework for anticipating the hazards of this stressful stage of family development and for understanding the behavioral manifestations of this type of struggle.

Our children are often the measuring rods that drive home to us the fact that we are aging. Psychologically and physically we may not feel any older, but our children's yearly changes in height, interests, and maturity are objective indicators of the years going by. One of the most concrete indicators that one is reaching middle age is a teenage child around the house. When the family reaches the "launching stage" of development (confronting the problems of parental disengagement and adolescent individuation), we can be sure the parents are wrestling with the problems of middle age. In this chapter we examine the evolving relationships between middle-age parents and their child as the child moves through adolescence. We are particularly interested in the ways in which parents make use of children in working through ambivalence about themselves and accepting who they themselves have become.

PERSONALITY PROCESSES DURING
THE LAUNCHING PHASE

Parsons and Bales (1955, pp. 16–22) have argued that the modern family has become a more specialized unit than in the past, performing social-emotional functions for its members rather than being a unit of work or political life. It is a retreat from the pressures of everyday life, where one can shed the facades of external roles and release intense emotions that have been suppressed.

But it is not simply suppressed feelings from everyday life that get acted out in the home. The privacy of the home also creates a context where parents gain some important gratification through temporary regression in play and involvement with children. This "regression in the service of the ego" in this isolated setting contributes to the integration of the adult personality. Enmeshing oneself in the play and fantasy of the child can be an important means to discharging residual tensions from one's own childhood as well as a means to escape from adult pressures.

Benedek (1959) elaborates on this line of thinking by suggesting that parents rework resolutions to critical life issues throughout the life cycle by vicarious participation in the development of their children. For example, the parent of a two-year-old controls him by setting limits and expectations, but he also identifies with the rambunctious toddler's attempts to explore and master his world. By vicariously participating in the child's growing sense of autonomy, a parent may rework his own styles of relating to the world and develop a greater sense of self-confidence and autonomy himself. By reliving some of the issues of that stage of life, the parent can "try on" styles of relating to the world other than those originally adopted. This process can then lead to a therapeutic change, the letting go of maladaptive patterns of thinking and behaving and the taking on of more effective patterns. However, Benedek's analysis focuses on the early preschool stages of life. The extension of her theory to adolescence remains to be done.

Some of the more macroscopic overviews of family life when children reach adolescence indicate that parent–child relationships are most problematic at this point. Blood and Wolfe (1960) find that parents begin to report conflicts over children at this stage, while Rollins and Feldman (1970) report that parents are least satisfied with family life during this period. Reiss (1976) finds that parents become most conservative in their standards of sexual behavior at this point. After the children leave home, the parents become more liberal again. In our own study (Farrell & Rosenberg, *forthcoming*) we find that fathers become more rigid and authoritarian in their attitudes towards child rearing. Apparently this stage of family life is likely to be stressful and associated with conflict between parents and children.

At least one factor that contributes to the turmoil is parental identification with children and the attempt to enlist the adolescent child in their reworking of their own resolutions to adolescent life-cycle issues. At adolescence a life-and-death struggle is in progress, with the parent's and child's self systems at stake. Perhaps this turmoil is an inevitable climax to the warm family-centered home, where parents become intensely involved in the children's development. Reaching for individuation, independence, and a separate self, the adolescent must either disrupt the cocoon of warmth and nurturance or stay enmeshed in dependency. Trying to piece together a separate self that truly feels like his or her own, the child is likely to break out of the self-validating drama of the parents' life structure. If the child is to establish his or her own reality, the child must step out of theirs.

Of course many children never make the break and establish their own life structures. The adolescent's identification with a parent, and the parent's hold on the adolescent are then so strong that the child lives out a life that mirrors the parent. By recapitulating this parental life structure, the child validates the parent and avoids the problem of individuation.

GROUP PROCESSES DURING THE LAUNCHING PHASE

In most families the role relations and family culture have crystallized by the time the children reach adolescence. Procedures for decision making have been worked out, and the grooves are well worn. Through repeated interactions the couple and children have built a shared conception of their social world that is taken for granted by family members. Beliefs about the relations, the neighbors, school, and other community groups are as solid as the walls of the house and are just as much a part of the taken-for-granted reality (Berger & Kellner, 1964) as the family members orient themselves to the world. "Stay away from so and so," or "go to this person if you want that," are proscriptions that are carved in stone in the family culture. These assumptions and guidelines form boundaries around the thinking and behavior of family members. It would take a major anomaly to unfreeze this family paradigm and lead the family members, for example, to seek out a new doctor, grocer, political party, or religion.

However, the paradigm most likely was put together by the parents at an earlier point in their development. Since that time, changes in the culture and social structure have occurred. The family may have changed its position in that structure by moving up or down on the class hierarchy or simply by moving to a new neighborhood. Thus, for example, parents who are children of immigrants may find themselves now living in a world quite different from the ghetto they grew up in. They formed their images of husband–wife relations, politics, religion, and so on in response to characters and events in that setting. Now, as their child is reaching adolescence, they are in a very different social landscape—perhaps in a suburb, a small town, or a high-rise apartment.

Boundary Testing, Deviance, and Scapegoating

As the adolescent child wrestles with the problem of finding a place in that social landscape, he or she may act as boundary tester for the family culture. In adapting to the new environment, the adolescent takes on and brings home ideas and even dress patterns and hair styles that are not accepted in the family culture. Although the adolescent may feel like a separate person simply trying to find a place in the world, he or she is still a member of the family group. Trying on new identities, the adolescent is likely to become more or less deviant in relation to the family culture.

The parental response to the boundary testing is critical to their own development at this stage as well as to the adolescent's. As the child brings home new ideas about sex, religion, or art, the parents may respond defensively, or they may go through a healthy reevaluation of their own conceptions. If they are able to sort through the new patterns being fed into the family in an open fashion, they may enrich their culture and find wider opportunities for fulfillment for themselves and their younger children. At the very least, open consideration of alternative life styles may lead to a deeper appreciation of and commitment to their own values. If they respond defensively and actively try to suppress any signs of deviance, they not only squelch the adolescent's development of a sense of identity but also reduce their own chances for growth through new inputs into their culture.

Essentially, we are arguing that the boundary-testing adolescent can serve the same positive functions for the family that the deviant serves for other social groups (Erikson, 1966; Dentler & Erikson, 1959). Rather than being a sign of cultural decay or disorganization, a limited amount of deviance can serve very positive functions. The outrage over the behavior brings members of the family or group out of the ruts of everyday life and into communication with each other. The shared feelings of outrage and hostility bring the rest of the group closer together (Redl, 1942). Through communicating about the behavior and expressing shared values, the members replenish understanding of and commitment to old values. The confrontation with the "not us" makes the "us" more clear. Thus, a limited amount of deviance ultimately contributes to social organization.

The constructive effects of deviance can be even more profound under some conditions. By acting out shared but suppressed impulses in a family or group, the deviant may contribute toward the members working through anxiety-provoking ambivalence or conflict, For example, the deviant may act out the suppressed urge to be more independent of an oppressive leader or father. On one level the members may be outraged, while on another level they identify with the deviant. They respond to the behavior, reconsider the group's values and social structure, and by vicariously participating in the conflicts, they work through their ambivalence about the constraints in question. Perhaps the outcome will be to put more group members in touch with their ambivalence and ultimately lead to a change in social structure that reduces the ambivalence.

In the family the adolescent child sometimes serves such a function for family members. He or she acts out urges suppressed by parents. On one level the parents act to control the child; on another level they identify with and encourage the behavior. In some cases the situation may lead to classic double-bind communication (Bateson et al., 1965).* The parent says, "If you do it, I'll punish you." Then, at another level the parent also says, "If you don't do it, I'll punish you." Finally the parent says, "If you try to talk about this dilemma, I'll punish you. Now, go to it!"

In other cases this split in levels of communication may lead to the kinds of mystification and "efforts to drive the other person crazy," which Laing (1970) and Searles (1959) describe so well. The results can be disastrous for the adolescent.

Scapegoating.   These tensions over the integrity of the family boundaries are manifest in several prominent issues and dynamics that recurred in the families under study. The first of these dynamics is scapegoating, the use of one or more of the children to symbolize or divert conflicts from within or between the parents. The parent, that is, experiences an undesirable trait or unacceptable feeling of his or her own as if it were coming from the child. The child then becomes the target of parental hostility from which there is no escape. He or she is induced by the parents to behave so as to justify

---

*Although the term *double-bind* was originally developed in an effort to shed light on the family relationships of persons labeled as schizophrenic, it has been used elsewhere in the literature to describe disturbed parent–child communications in situations in which schizophrenia is not an issue. See, for example, the discussion of the double-bind with reference to delinquent behavior (Ferreira, 1960).

their anger. As a number of writers have discussed (for example, Vogel and Bell, 1960), this process of scapegoating can become a central facet of the family's culture. This is especially true when the child is used to stabilize relations between the parents, as when all the anger they might evoke in each other is instead focused on one of their offspring. The parents may then reinforce and validate each other's distorted view of the scapegoated child, since the child is serving needs common for them both. In this context, other siblings are easily induced to join in the aggression toward the victimized child. The family's stability as a system can come to depend on this definition of one child as "bad" or "different," and the concomitant illusion that all other family members are well and harmonious.

More commonly, the scapegoating process is less extreme and more fluid: Different children occupy the position at different points in their development. The process, moreover, is not entirely negative or destructive. In projecting onto and then battling with their children in a relatively controlled, loving context, the parents may rework neurotic positions and gain a sense of closeness with their offspring. The scapegoated child may gain a greater sense of autonomy in the difficult process of differentiating his or her own intentions and feelings from parents' attributions.

Idealization. A second dynamic may be characterized as the opposite of scapegoating: idealizing the adolescent child. In our cases the child was sometimes viewed as an agent of redemption by one or both parents. In this role, the adolescent became the agent charged with fulfilling dreams that had been shattered or left dormant in the parents. The child's successes could be defined as a vindication of the parent, providing compensation for a marred or incomplete identity. Again, identifying with the child may strengthen the parent. The parent who dropped out of school may vicariously return; one who abandoned interests in art or business may gain new inspiration.

In both the scapegoating and idealizing relationships the parents are relating to the child through projective identification. However, in the latter case the child is seen as possessing positive traits and crossing desirable boundaries. In both cases the parental identification with the child may generate positive change in the parent's sense of self. Old aspirations, fears, and urges are reawakened and may lead to attempts at altering the self. Of course, the resulting turmoil may also lead to defensive withdrawal. Our primary point is that such projective identification is more or less ubiquitous and that it represents a stimulus for parental self-examination and change.

Transformation of Role Relations. A third group-level process that occurs during the launching phase is the transformation of the parent–child role relationship. As the child moves toward independence, the parents must relinquish their authority. This process often does not unfold with ease. Parents are ambivalent about giving up their positions, and children are often ambivalent about giving up dependency. The ambivalence leads to vacillation and over-reaction on both sides. The child becomes counterdependent, attempting to prove that he or she does not need guidance or support by openly staging confrontations and deliberately doing what the parents forbid. The parents, in turn, may stage their own confrontations over money, attitudes, or behavior, attempting to prove they are still in control, "not just another pal." The ambivalence on both sides may continue into young adulthood, until the child is established in the adult world.

Taken together, all these processes would lead us to expect a great deal of conflict during this period. Disengagement is never easy. Disengagement coupled with these processes that lead to reconsideration of the self-concept can be particularly problematic.

Two Case Studies

In this section we present two family situations that illustrate some of these processes. The first involves John Nash, a middle-class engineer with eight children. In the Nash family we find that the mother's unresolved ambivalence about herself is central as the parents deal with the individuation of their adolescent children. The second situation involves Bob Wilson, a social worker in the midst of identity crisis. In this instance we find the son acting out impulses and goals that are blocked in Wilson. In both cases we find the children enmeshed in unresolved tension between the parents and within one or both parents.

We selected these cases from a subsample of 20 follow-up, whole-family interviews in our study of adult male development. The original sample consisted of 300 middle-aged men. The follow-up subjects were contacted by phone and offered $100.00 to allow us to visit them for dinner and interview them and their families at our offices. The objectives were twofold: first, to observe the family interacting in the home environment, and second, to obtain a historical picture of the development of the family.* Family members were interviewed both together and separately.

---

*Schram (1979, p. 11) suggests that in order to capture more fully the level of satisfaction experienced by middle-aged marital partners, it is important to utilize intensive whole-family interviews, which make it possible to gain access to the subjective dimensions of their experience. She maintains that research based solely on objective methodology is likely to produce a limited interpretation of the processes that occur in families as they pass from one stage to another.

THE NASH FAMILY

For the past 8 years the Nash family had lived in a large, old wood-and-shingle home in a neighborhood that looks like the Norman Rockwell vision of America. Mrs. Nash greeted the interviewers on the front porch. Her black hair was loosely bundled in a blue scarf and she wore a light cotton housedress that revealed an ample figure. At forty she was still a beautiful woman, and it was hard to believe she was the mother of eight children.

Mr. Nash greeted the interviewers in the hallway. He wore Bermuda shorts and a striped polo shirt with brown street shoes. He stood about 6'2" and had begun to develop a pot belly. He seemed alert but friendly, speaking softly out of the corner of his mouth.

Throughout the evening we discovered evidence of Mr. Nash's investment in his home and family. He commutes across town to work, but doesn't consider moving because the family is so entrenched in the neighborhood. He painted the house himself with a second-hand compressor he acquired at work. In the kitchen, the benches and tables were built by him from remnants salvaged from second-hand stores. Out in the yard was a used sailboat he was fiberglassing.

Besides these concrete signs of his presence, there were also other manifestations of his involvement in family and neighborhood activities. His detailed stories of his children's activities, his knowledge of neighborhood gossip, and his involvement in local church affairs made it clear that his interests extend beyond his career.

He presented himself in muted tones, as if he was shy about bragging over his abilities and accomplishments. He said he had a few tools and liked to "tinker a little." And then on the basement wall we found that he had a more complete set of tools than most hardware shops, and he has built professional-looking shelves, cabinets, and beds all around the house.

He worked as a mechanical engineer, designing equipment in a company that makes camping supplies. He said he was next in line for the top engineer position, and he was on his own a lot. More than this he didn't offer. Rather, he seemed more interested in talking about the home, family, and neighborhood.

The Nashes viewed their home as a sanctuary from the pressures of the outside world. Mrs. Nash said that in high school, "the world becomes a battlefield" for children. The children, especially Jan—the second oldest girl—could get "swept away" by forces out there and "get herself into real trouble." She would have hated to see Jan get "swallowed up by crazy culture out there." She said, "With all the sophisticated, phony talk, they are so lost." In contrast, the home was described as a relaxed and nurturant place, a place where mother served each person their own individual breakfast in the morning. It was a place where people could retreat from pressures to have to "impress somebody." Even some local priests came to the Nash house at times to relax because there they can "be themselves."

This picture of the nuclear family as a refuge from the outside had not always fit the reality, and even now daughter Jan was an abrasive, unassimilated part of this family nest. We will return to Jan later, but first let us look briefly at the history of the relationship between the parents.

Both of the Nashes were children of Irish immigrants and they felt this contributed to their happiness: "Each isn't pulling in different directions," said Mrs. Nash. They both grew up in the same neighborhood where Mr. Nash's father was an "uppity Irish policeman," according to Mrs. Nash. Mr. Nash had an irregular college career. He quit to join the navy for a period, then taught high school mathematics for one year. He went back to school, and after graduating began his career as a mechanical engineer for the camping-equipment firm.

They reported that their courtship was stormy. Their son, Peter, even knew the story about how they were fighting during this time. Mrs. Nash also told us that she had been the most rebellious of her own mother's four daughters. Repeatedly we were told that adolescence was a period of rebellion and discontent for Mrs. Nash. Eventually they married and bought a small home. Mrs. Nash said that during her first pregnancy she "thought the walls would come in." She hated the confinement. The first child was born in 1953; the second, in 1954; and so it went, with 14 pregnancies in all. She said they lost their closeness, with all the babies around. She worked for a while as a laboratory technician before marriage but was not happy in the position. She had hoped that by getting married she'd be happy. Then she hoped that having children would do it; then that it would happen when the children left. She says that she and her husband had been distant for 15 years although "I wanted him and he wanted me." To illustrate the distance between them, Mrs. Nash told about the summer vacations, when she stayed at the beach with the children while Mr. Nash stayed in the city to work.

As for power to make decisions, she told us she was after as much as she could get, and so was he. However, she had to make decisions for the children that could not wait until he got home from work. One got an impression of the couple being in a state of siege, with the wife combatting the problems of the children and the husband lost in problems of making a living. During the siege the mother formed closer ties with the children; Peter told us that the children first made requests of her when permission was needed from their father.

After 15 years of marriage, they began to make moves to change the pattern. They bought a larger house and gave up the summer beach cottage. They joined a club in town where swimming and boating were possible and they could all be together during the summer. A few years later they went to a weekend sensitivity retreat for married couples, sponsored by their church.

The experience crystallized a number of insights about themselves that helped them restructure their relationship. Mr. Nash faced up to his pattern of hiding feelings and was able to express misgivings about always being seen as strong. They became more open with each other and accepted themselves and each other more. The self-acceptance was apparent in many areas of their life. It came through in their nondefensive orientation to their religion and the size of their family. It was apparent in their matter-of-fact responses to the satirical, critical images of middle-class life portrayed in popular plays and movies. They did not condone these images, but accepted them as out there while they tried to create an inner world based on values of authenticity, affection, and family togetherness.

For Mr. Nash the self-acceptance was apparent in his ridicule of men his age and older who tried to be "young tigers" and married young girls. He saw them as trying to avoid growing old. He felt his own relationship with his wife was more comfortable and relaxed now that they did not have to impress each other. The only kinds of people that overtly troubled them were those (such as Mr. Nash's older sister) who were described as very superficial and showing no give-and-take in conversations. These "uppity people" who never let themselves out were a solid negative reference point for this family.

They described their family as being divided into two separate groups: the four older children who had clear and separate identities, and the four younger children, ranging in ages from 6 to 9, who seemed to be treated as a group. The three youngest girls were squeezed together on the same piano bench at the dinner table. At this point in the family development, the center stage seemed to be taken up by the adolescents going through the problems of the launching phase. A week before the interview they were busy with the wedding of Amy, the oldest daughter. The wedding ceremony was modeled after that of a friend. The couple constructed their own vows, and most of the guests were friends and cousins, even though this might have antagonized some of the Nashes' older friends. Mrs. Nash was surprised and felt guilty about how easy the first week had gone without Amy around. But every once in a while she had to remind herself when she got the urge to tell her to help with dinner or the children. She described Amy as competitive and restless, while her new husband was gentle and kind. The couple was living just a few blocks away, and Mrs. Nash laughed when she told us that Peter, the 16-year-old son, did not think the marriage would last because of the differences in temperament.

Mrs. Nash described her oldest son, Thomas, as gentle and "full of nature, full of love." But he was "confused about what he wants. He reminds me more of his father." Thomas went to a private school during his high-school years. Now he commuted to the University, where he wanted to get a degree in biology. During his first year there he did poorly, so his father stopped paying expenses. Tom went to work at a supermarket warehouse to earn money for college. Seeing the men who were his father's age who had worked there all their lives had increased his motivation to complete his education. He respected people who knew what they wanted, but he did not know what he wanted yet. Maybe he would start a real-estate business. He would buy cheap old houses, the way his father bought their home, then refurbish them and sell them. But he was not sure how long he would be content with that. He had no steady girl-friend, though he saw his friends starting to get married. He told us that marriage leads to more responsibilities and less freedom. When his father had been his age, he said, he had driven a truck delivering cement, but then pressures from the family had forced him to finish school. Mrs. Nash said Tom did not want to grow up to be superficial and status-oriented like many adults he sees.

Peter was the youngest of the older four children—the Nashes' first family. His mother described him as bright and perceptive, the family psychologist. He was currently in a private school as a freshman. He had not wanted to go to this school where he thought only sissies went, but now he had come to respect "mental toughness." John Kennedy was one of his heroes and he told us that the day Kennedy had been shot his own father had been away on a business trip. He said that at the time he and Kennedy's son, John, had been the same age. The episode had stayed with him, but now the idealization of Kennedy was fading. He wanted to go to an ivy-league college and major in some scientific area, which he saw as being like his father. He was described as an observer and analyzer of the family. He ferreted out information and fed it to his parents in after-dinner discussions.

It was Jan who was currently a focal point in the family's attempts to deal with the strains of launching. Mrs. Nash told us: "Jan has no head on her. She crosses us. I'm afraid for her. She reminds me of myself. She is like me, but she can't stand me saying that. 'Let me go!' she says. She wants to take care of herself too much. My mother used to say I was cursed. I was drawn to the antihero (Oh, I plead guilty!) during the ages of 13 to 19. I had many riles with John [Mr. Nash]. Jan hates to be told she's like me. But I'm damn glad I was like that. It's healthy. Jan sees me as old fashioned in the same way as I saw my mother."

The mother's identification with Jan was obvious. Jan seemed to represent those parts of the mother that had been brought under control during the courtship and early stages of marriage, the parts that had been continually unhappy in the early stages of family life. In fact, this identification of the mother and Jan seemed to present in the mind of son Peter also. He told us briefly that mother and father had always been fighting during their courtship, but never any more, never any yelling or screaming. They had not even had any clashes as mother was going through the change of life. Then, in the very next breath he went on to talk about the problems with Jan, as if there was a logical connection between the parental truce and Jan's problems. He told us that Jan evoked "furor" from her parents for doing some things that he and the other children did with impunity. It was not clear whether she brought attacks down on herself or was being singled out for special attention. In spite of the fact that everyone in the family liked to be close, Jan went out every night. "If she wants to go out, she goes. And then comes in late." Her parents feared the field where she hung out. Someone had been shot there last year. There were fights often, bikes got stolen, and some of the kids used drugs. Mrs. Nash said that all Jan's friends talked about was getting abortions or living with someone. When Jan came home late, Mr. Nash was "full of furor." He beat on her and slapped her and yelled. Jan responded with "too bad," or went on brushing her teeth nonchalantly. At times, father would retreat to the basement where he pounded out his frustrations with a hammer.

Recently, Mrs. Nash had been cleaning in Jan's room and had found an ounce of marijuana in a plastic bag. She said she had found it in a drawer, but her son reported she had found it while searching through Jan's purse. She had come downstairs in a rage, had stood in front of the dining room table and beat on it with both hands. "I swore and made a terrible scene. That's how I feel, I wasn't logical. I know I can't control it, but I wanted them to know my complete disapproval." Now she felt guilty about intruding on Jan's privacy. She would have loved to give the marijuana back and say she was leaving it to Jan to decide. Her husband said no, that would be showing approval, but Mrs. Nash would have liked her not to use it out of respect for her wishes.

In private, Peter told us he smoked pot too but was more careful about it. He also used to smoke cigarettes and his mother had said nothing even though she knew. He told us that when his parents got angry at Tom and Amy they did not yell the way they did with Jan. He saw mother as the intermediary between the children and the father. If he wanted to go to the beach, he asked his mother and she asked his father. More pertinent to the issue of Jan, he told us that his mother controlled the amount of attack Jan received from his father.

There was one final element to Jan's story. Jan wanted to be a nurse. She wanted to move downtown and live in a dormitory while going to one of the better nursing schools. Her father had vetoed this plan. Instead he had arranged for her to live at home and commute to a local school. In this way he said she would be safer and less likely to get into trouble. "It'll be better for her until she is more mature."

The overall picture that begins to emerge is that Jan has moved into the role of family scapegoat and helps to reduce tension in this family on a number of dimensions. By her boundary testing on the dimensions of rebelliousness, selfishness, independence, and impulsiveness, Jan makes the other brothers and sisters look good in comparison. She reduces the potential heat they might receive. She also appears to be a pawn in the husband–wife relationship, with the wife encouraging her to act out the rebellious, impulsive sides of herself. The husband's attacks on these sides of his wife are redirected toward Jan. She incorporates the parts of the mother that Mrs. Nash reports have now come under control in herself. She becomes the rebellious and ambitious young woman who wanted a career and hated the oppression of the pregnancies, the babies and familial life. Mrs. Nash sends messages that encourage her to act this out. Implicitly, she says, "Run! This is terrible! Fight it!" But at the same time she must reject these sides of her daughter, for if her daughter succeeds, then perhaps she was wrong to capitulate. If her daughter's responses are right, then the mother's whole life structure is negated. The husband, for whom she capitulated, is a willing accomplice in the suppression of the daughter.

On a more general plane we see the dynamics of middle-aged parents confronting adolescent children. As the adolescents makes bid for individuation, the parents enlist them in a drama of reworking their own adolescent tensions through projective identification. In the Nash case we see the father playing a less direct role in the individuation drama. As the daughter is making her bids for individuation, the mother is enmeshing her in a web of acting out her own unresolved ambivalences about her wife-mother role. The husband is enlisted to play the part of parental superego figure in the drama, though he may be reliving some of his own rage at his wife during the early stages of the relationship. By absorbing his anger, Jan contributes to the stability of the marital relationship.

THE WILSON FAMILY

The Wilsons' oldest son was born just before Mr. Wilson made the decision to go to graduate school with the "great and glorious dream" of getting a degree in philosophy and becoming a college professor. His inability to meet the requirements led him to shift toward a career in social work because "it was practical." It would provide him with a means to support a family. His early career as a bureaucrat in an employment agency was frustrating because of a limited income. He finally drifted into a job as a counseling social worker for adolescents in a children's hospital, where he hoped to help young people avoid the mistakes he had made.

When we met them, the Wilsons seemed confused and desperate. In talking about the compromise decisions he had had to make in life, Wilson often pointed to his head and said, "Dumb." Until this year the only piece left of his college-professor dream was his position as second in command of the children's hospital counseling program. However, he had lost that job, having been fired because he and his younger supervisor had "different philosophies" about the job. To make matters worse, Mr. Wilson had a recent heart attack, but in spite of these difficulties, he and his wife seemed to see as their most serious problem the rebelliousness of their son, Bob, Jr.

It was this son who seemed to emerge as the emotional center of the home after Bob's early setbacks. His precocious development and successes as a youngster compensated for many of the losses. "He was number one," Mrs. Wilson reported, and they structured their lives around his needs and built a dream of his one day becoming a politician.

In retrospect, this reliance on Bob, Jr., as the compensation for a lifetime of disappointments had become increasingly problematic in the past four years. At work, a younger man had come into the office and Bob had been asked to be his "guiding light." Before this he had been on his own; counseling families, running the evaluation program—"the chief cook and bottle washer." In the emerging team structure, Bob had found he had more and more differences with his co-workers: "I was the only one there who had on-the-job experience. I didn't want to overshadow this kid who had his first job as director. But his and my philosophies didn't get along." The conflicts had finally culminated with Bob's dismissal. Although he would be out of work in September, when we spoke to him in July, he still did not have a position for the fall. One of the factors holding Bob back from looking for a job was a sense of being trapped. Practically, he said, "I'm committed. I'm stuck in social work for the next 10 or 15 years." At the same time, he felt strongly that he "has had it with counseling." He had reached a point where he had stopped believing in the values and goals he tried to instill in his adolescent clients. He was tired of listening to "the same old pipe dreams of not working and living on nothing." He did have the hope of being an assistant director of a charitable organization, a secure job not subject to political whims and where he could try to work in a number of administrative domains, but he did not see much chance of obtaining such a position.

As the problems at work began to emerge, Bob also ran into some physical difficulties. He "pulled his back out" lifting a five-gallon can of paint, and this had led to chronic problems. But perhaps the most disturbing problem to emerge at this time was that young Bob began to rebel, to "change his personality." He had been a model child, an outstanding student, very religious, president of the local youth organization, even an active door-to-door campaigner in the previous elections. He had been good at anything requiring public speaking, and it seemed he was inclined toward politics. In this period their relationship was rewarding for both of them. Mr. Wilson "always tried to encourage him to be independent and creative" and Bob, Jr., described his father as "firm and effective," and reported that they had had "amazing intellectual discussions."

However, as Bob, Jr., had moved into his teenage years everything had begun to change. He had let his hair grow long, had begun talking back and "walking around moody all the time." He had developed the ambition of becoming an actor and playwright—a profession that his parents feared because of its "seamy side," its association with drugs and sex, and its economic uncertainties. Bobby said his parents would have rather had him be an insurance salesman, something concrete, and he felt they were trying to "squelch" him. He had developed an intense interest in existentialist philosophy, which he said his parents found threatening because they were very religious. His mother said the things he reads were "not nice anymore" while his father, favoring the classical philosophers, was not interested in his son's readings. The previous year, as a senior in high school, Bobby had produced and acted in a Sartre play. He has been accepted into a 6-year program in a dramatic-arts college and during the summer had spent time there working as an apprentice on some productions. He had thought he would hate the remote area, but had grown to love it. Although the prospect of going into drama was "scary," Bobby was certain he wanted to do it.

Bobby had been dating a girl that his mother considered a "loose woman." He responded by saying that his parents were old-fashioned and exceedingly strict about sex, describing his mother as a "wicked prude." In the home interview his mother expressed disdain for "this woman who drives over with her car to pick him up." However, Mr. Wilson quickly pointed out that when they were dating, she had often picked him up in her car. It was unclear to the interviewers whether Mrs. Wilson's anger was directed more toward her son or her husband. Sexual freedom or constraint represented one issue over which the Wilsons were split in regard to expectations for Bobby.

Bobby saw his mother as the instigator of attacks on him. At one point he told her she would have made the best director of drama there ever was. She did not know whether to feel complimented or insulted. His father was described as "cool" and "holding his feelings in." However, Mrs. Wilson seemed to be in a rage against Bobby; at times she seemed to view him as dead, as if a stranger were dwelling in her son's body. Bobby related the story of the family visits to a psychiatrist. His mother had urged it. At one point the psychiatrist had asked her, "Do you love your son?" She had said, "Yes." And he had asked, "Do you like his school?" She had said, "No." "His clothes?" "No." "His hair?" "No." "What do you like about him?" She could not say. After three visits they had stopped going because Mrs. Wilson had thought "the psychiatrist wasn't too bright."

The growing rift in the family had reached a culmination during the previous winter. Bobby had been president of the youth organization at his church. They met on Saturday afternoons in a church-owned house that happened to be next door to the police station. In addition to discussing business, the members also smoked marijuana at these meetings. One afternoon a police officer caught a whiff of what was happening and raided the place. Bobby had been booked and placed on parole. His father had been calm and controlled throughout the episode, but his mother had just "yelled and yelled," repeatedly asking herself and anyone who happened by, "Where did I go wrong?"

The next week Mr. Wilson had been sitting at home in the living room reading the paper when he felt classic heart-attack symptoms. He had known immediately what was happening, but before calling for help he had decided to lie down on the couch and just bear the pain for awhile, offering his suffering as a prayer in hope that it would lead to Bobby's giving up drugs.

In this case we see a range of parental styles of relating to the adolescent child. In the early stages the relationship is characterized by idealization, but as the son moves into the boundary-testing stage the parents' hopes that he will compensate for their setbacks are shattered. His attempts to relate to the culture outside the home are interpreted as a betrayal. However, a close look at the case reveals a complex array of the dynamics of the launching phase. Beneath the feelings of betrayal the father seems to support his son's pursuit of a difficult occupational goal, perhaps regretting his own abandonment of his dreams. The mother, on the other hand, shifts from using her son as a vehicle for redemption of her lost dreams of success to using him as a target for her pent up anger at her husband for his failure. Once again, the use of the child as scapegoat contributes to the stability of the marital relationship.

DISCUSSION

In both cases we see the children enmeshed in parental conflicts. In the Nash case, Tom, the older son, is recapitulating his father's slow start in life. His identification with his father is apparent in his self-support while going through college as well as in his dreams of rebuilding old houses, the way his father did their current home. His father's encouragement of the recapitulation is apparent in his refusing to pay college tuition after his son's poor first year in school. The move forced the son to go to work and pay his own tuition the way his father did. The move may also have set limits on his son's abilities to progress in college, thus making it even more likely that the son would recapitulate and validate his father's life structure. The younger son, Peter, also shows signs of identifying with his father in interpersonal behavior as well as in his orientation toward scientific work.

The straightforward identification of father and sons contrasts with the complex relationships with the daughters. We have little knowledge of the older, recently married daughter, except that she was seen as an extension of her mother, aiding in the care of the children and maintenance of the house. There are some hints that this daughter's husband resembles her gentle, taciturn father, while she herself resembles her more explosive mother. The family's valuing of closeness is manifest in her moving only one block away from home. Other than these hints, we have little knowledge of the extent of her enmeshment in parental conflicts.

However, the involvement of Jan is obvious and dramatic. The mother's "unhappy, rebellious" self is reincarnated. Through Jan the mother is reliving that whole, unresolved period in her life, but with the added perspective of age and parenthood she has the opportunity to learn from Jan's problems. Perhaps the vicarious participation in Jan's plight will enable her finally to accept the self she backed into: the traditional Irish wife and mother with strong ties to family and neighborhood. Perhaps she will see alternatives to the depressions brought on by this choice and the unfocused rebellions of her early adulthood. Perhaps she will see options beyond entrapment or rebellion that she can choose for herself or help Jan to see. At present the outcome is undecided, but if Jan's bids for professional nursing are not frustrated by the parents' problems, she may succeed in finding a middle ground.

It is important to note that the father's role in this drama is somewhat peripheral. He, too, acts as an extension of the mother. He acts out the controlling parts of her, encouraging the traditional home-centered orientation in Jan. His association with Mrs. Nash's own entrapment may facilitate this role, and his playing out this part frees Mrs. Nash to identify with the rebellious sides of Jan.

In the Wilson case the father is more actively involved in the son's enmeshment. We hear about his misguided compromises in life from high school through young adulthood. Now we hear of his disillusionment and alienation. He tells of his inability to believe in the dreams he offers to clients in his role of counselor, his own "grand and glorious" goal of being a college philosophy professor having been abandoned long ago. His wife speaks with disturbing admiration of the successful neighbors—self-made men who made the right moves in life. Together, the couple has invested their hopes for vindication in their son. He showed all signs of succeeding in that world where they had failed.

Unfortunately, the son heard the disillusionment message more loudly than the vindication message. Like his father, he takes to philosophy, but unlike him he values the disillusioned existentialists over the classical philosophers. Rather than settling for the secure, moderately ambitious lifestyle of his father, he chooses the insecurity of a career in drama. As the pressures toward a conventional life mount, he retreats into moody passive resistance and lets his hair grow long. Finally, he gets into trouble in the outside world over marijuana.

His bids for individuation, for disengagement from his parents' compensatory defenses, are interpreted as craziness. Their son has inexplicably gone astray and the mother, at least, has the urge to disown him. All that has been invested in him is being squandered. Their ticket out of the gray world of compromises, into the shining world of conventional success, has been destroyed.

What they do not see is the relatively healthy adaptation their son has made to the confusing, contradictory messages they have been sending him. On the one hand the world is a heartless place where one compromises away one's dreams. The father implicitly says, "If you act like me, you'll wind up in a meaningless life of alienation." On the other hand he urges the son to stay on the conventional path, because the alternative to meaningless alienation may be something even worse: "Damned if you do, and damned if you don't."

The son's compromise is to opt for a career that has the potential of conventional reward but allows him to express and even act out the alienation from the conventional. The father passively smiles on the choice. Perhaps at some level he understands the ingenious synthesis his son is attempting. He may be vicariously involved in this young man's adamant commitment to his dream in the face of obstacles. Conceivably, the father's reliving of this phase of his life, when he compromised his dreams away, will rekindle hopes of fulfillment and strengthen his own commitment to internal dreams.

The mother's sense of betrayal is more manifest. Her husband having failed her, she invested in the son and she worked hard to pound him into the conventional mold: "Dress nicely; date nice girls; go to church; go to college," and so on. During his childhood he was "number one," and she was the "best director he ever knew." Now, as he breaks free of his role in her life and she must deal with disengagement, she finds herself unable to let go. Rather than simply letting go and allowing her son to find himself, she must reject him. Perhaps he is receiving the pent-up anger over her husband's failures; the anger is directed at the father's namesake. What is more likely is that he is receiving the brunt of the anger from a woman whose planned escape from life's torments has been closed off.

Can she benefit from this episode? Possibly her son's involvement in the theater will help her regain contact with the self she was when she first met her husband, working on props and lighting in the college theater. Being freed from the investment in her son she may be able to reinvest in her self and her husband, and this may lead to building a life structure on a firmer foundation.

Parents show a range of responses to their children's bids for individuation. The responses vary from avoidance to encouraging recapitulation, from enmeshment in old conflicts to encouraging growth and development. Most of the 20 families we examined in depth were in the early stages of launching their children. In virtually none of our case studies did the parents show an easy, unconflicted reaction to the children's individuation. As the children acted as boundary testers, the parents played the parts of police and judges. Perhaps the families who agreed to be in the follow-up interviews did so because they were having problems. A more representative sample may find parents encouraging growth and learning new skills and values through their children's boundary testing. However, at this point we feel that the turmoil may be a more common response to this stage. The literature on interpersonal relations in other settings (for example, Mills, 1964) has shown that the termination of relationships is usually problematical, generating an upheaval of unresolved tensions and anxieties about loss. The family is no exception. If the children are a part of the defensive cocoon that encases the parents' life structures, then the disruption of that cocoon is going to be problematical. It may be that the more positive inputs into the parental culture do not appear until after this stage, when parent–child relations are reconstituted on a more adult-to-adult basis.

REFERENCES

Bateson, G., Jackson, D.D., Haley, J., & Weakland, J. Toward a theory of schizophrenia. *Behavioral Science*, 1956, 1, 251–264.

Benedek, T. Fatherhood and providing. In James, E., & Benedek, T. (eds.), *Parenthood, Its Psychology and Psychopathology*. Boston: Little, Brown, 1970.

Benedek, T. Parenthood as a developmental phase—a contribution to the libido theory. *Journal of the American Psychoanalytic Association*, 1959, 7, 389–417.

Berger, P., & Kellner, H. Marriage and the construction of reality. *Diagnosis*, 1964, 64, 1–25.

Blood, R.O., Jr., & Wolfe, D.M. *Husbands and Wives: The Dynamics of Married Living*. Glencoe, Ill.: The Free Press, 1960.

Dentler, R.A., & Erikson, K.T. The functions of deviance in groups. *Social Problems*, 1959, 7, 98–107.

Erikson, K.T. *Wayward Puritans*. New York: Wiley, 1966.

Farrell, M.P., & Rosenberg, S.D. *Men at Midlife*, forthcoming, Auburn Press.

Ferreira, A.J. The "double-bind" and delinquent behavior. *Archives of General Psychiatry*. 1960, 3, 51/359–59/367.

Laing, R.D., & Esterson, A. *Sanity, Madness and the Family: Families of Schizophrenics* (2nd ed.). London: Tavistock, 1970.

Mills, T.N. *Group Transformation*. Englewood Cliffs, N.J.: Prentice-Hall, 1964.

Parsons, T., & Bales, R.F. *Family, Socialization and Interaction Process*. Glencoe, Ill.: The Free Press, 1955.

Redl, F. Group emotion and leadership. *Psychiatry*, 1942, 5, 573–596.

Reiss, I.L. *Family Systems in America*. Hensdale, Ill.: The Dryden Press, 1976.

Rollins, B.C., & Feldman, H. Marital satisfaction over the family life cycle. *Journal of Marriage and the Family*, 1970, 32, 20–28.

Schram, R.W. Marital satisfaction over the family life cycle: A critique and proposal. *Journal of Marriage and the Family*, 1979, 41, 7–12.

Searles, H.F. The effort to drive the other person crazy—an element in the aetiology and psychotherapy of schizophrenia. *British Journal of Medical Psychology*, 1959, 32, 1–18.

Vogel, E.F., & Bell, N.W. The emotionally disturbed child as the family scapegoat. In Bell, N.W., & Vogel, E.K. (eds.), *The Family*. New York: The Free Press, 1960, 385–397.

4

Power Relationships in Marriage: The Fine Print in the Oral Tradition

Marjory Nelson
Polly Taylor

Most marital therapy is predicated upon a belief that a couple, if sufficiently motivated, can restructure their relationship in such a way as to meet their mutual needs. Nelson and Taylor, explicit about their radical feminist bias from the outset, assert that it is society *that shapes the institution of marriage and that individuals, therefore, are comparatively powerless to change the structure of the role relationships. Fundamental to their thesis is a definition of power as coercion. Some may charge that this characterization minimizes the interactive dimension of the process of interpersonal influence and does not fully acknowledge the importance of persuasion and other means of influence. However, despite the fact that radical rhetoric is frequently dismissed as overstatement, the views of these authors are included here to add a crucial dimension to the understanding of family functioning against the backdrop of a sexist society.*

Nelson and Taylor grant that both males and females are penalized by their diminished power in reference to defining their mutual roles. Nevertheless, it is their view that since men are accorded the dominant position in our society, women, vulnerable because of their inferior power, become ready victims in the unequal struggle. (This premise provides a cogent context within which to view Petit's chapter on battered women, later in this volume). The authors therefore see collective feminist action as the only viable solution to a dilemma in which change depends on the wresting of power from the powerful.

In recent years, there has been much discussion about improving the quality of married life. Various concepts have emerged, such as open marriage and individually designed marital contracts. The privatization of the individual and the family has convinced each couple and every counselor that, in spite of indisputable divorce statistics, marriage can be improved by loving, well-intentioned couples. Every couple sets out to make a marriage better than that of their parents and friends. They break patterns and try new ways, reassign housework and wage earning, live collectively, develop loving relationships outside the marriage, wanting to believe that somehow *they* will be different. If things go badly, they consult therapists to help them work out their personal problems, still never believing that the problem is not in *their* marriage but in the structure of marriage.

We believe that personal lives of individuals cannot be isolated from the political context in which they live, and the personal marriage contract cannot be unaffected by the power relationships established from outside. A non-sexist marriage, one not oppressive to women, cannot exist in a sexist society, no matter how hard the couple and the therapist try. Therapeutic intervention cannot make any significant change in the quality of individual lives and individual marital relationships except insofar as it is part of a movement for change in the larger society.

The women's movement has become very clear in its conviction that the personal is political; such has been the case in area after area that has come under its scrutiny. What this means is that individualistic approaches, such as "open marriages," cannot resolve social problems. It is our contention that there is a basic political structure to marriage imposed upon the individual couple. There is a real and preset power relationship that is operating over and against the individual lives. An income to pay for rat-free housing and healthy child care is available only through a mother's full-time attention; banks lend money for down-payments on suburban houses, not for time off to picket the utiltities.

A couple may work out one "contract," but their contract in marriage is not only with each other but is a contract to take certain roles in the state. The capitalistic state requires that the man be tied into the labor force by his responsibility for wife and children, and it requires that the wife take care of her husband so that he can work and that she produce and raise children who meet the state's needs.

The state has a vested interest in traditional marriage and nuclear families, and it has the power to protect that interest. Counseling must understand and relate to this power; that is, counseling must assume a revolutionary or change-directed function if it is to do more than add guilt as another bar in the woman's cage or ineffectually bandage her wounds.

We have explicit bias and purpose. We are feminists who approach the subject of power relationships in marriage from an understanding of the political structures within which marriage is imbedded. We want the reader to see individual marriages as part of a pattern of relationships making up our culture. We want to feed the feminist perspective in the disciplines of counseling. Feminism understands that women cannot be healthy (mentally or physically), happy, or adult unless real change takes place in society.

THE NATURE OF POWER IN OUR SOCIETY

Power can be defined as the ability to make someone act against his or her will. It eliminates choice or narrows it to the trivial. It is backed by physical force, economic control, negative or positive sanctions that are built into our traditions, customs, and laws. It provides the ability both to change things and to keep them the same. Power is not neutral; it works for those who possess it. It is protected by myths and ideologies that mask its workings and hidden assumptions. "Someone has to be boss" *means* that those who are controlled by the boss ought to shut up and do what they are told. "All men are created equal" invalidates the feeling of powerlessness that women and most men share. "This is a classless society" perpetuates the myth that it is laziness that keeps the poor impoverished. "Woman's place is in the home" makes her wage earning unimportant and exploitable and keeps her dependent.

These ideologies are perpetuated by the educational system, the media, the church, and social scientists. All these institutions are historically particular to this society, although they maintain the illusion of the existence of universal "truth." It is the nature of ideologies to deceive the oppressed about the nature of the oppression. Thus, the most basic ideologies are the ones that run, "Women are not oppressed," "The poor are lazy," and "Blacks have rhythm."

Women are socialized to be weak, passive, and dependent, but that is only a partial explanation of their oppression. It obscures the workings of power that continually beat women back when they do manage to assert themselves. For example, a woman may want to end her marriage, but if she has spent 20 years working only in the home and thus has few salable skills to support herself, she is a victim of economic power. It is not her own husband who is keeping her out of a job when she decides to leave him, but men are the ones who fill the choice jobs already and receive the vocational training. The oppression of women within the family has been fundamental to the expansion of capital. We live in a system that is both capitalistic and patriarchal. Under capitalism, the people who own the processes of production have power over those who sell their labor. Patriarchy means the power of the male parental figure. It is as old as recorded history, giving power to judges, kings, and priests. The father as the head of the family has controlled the labor, property, wages, and bodies of his wife and children. This power has been written into law and enforced by church and state.

In our society, patriarchy has been supported by the growth of capitalism. The structures of class are intertwined with those of the family, creating in our day that new phenomenon we call the nuclear family: an isolated unit of mother, father, and children, and no others, excluding other generations and relatives. The nuclear family is new. And so is one of its products, the alienated, isolated housewife.

When the home ceased to be the center of production, a fundamental change occurred in the organization of the family. It began to emerge as the core of what we call "private life." Private life has been extolled as offering individuality, expanded opportunity, and a personal control over destiny never before available. But that "privacy" is only a smokescreen that hides the essential functions of the family for the survival of capitalism.

It is through the family system that social classes reproduce and socialize new members. The individual home is a basic unit of consumption. It is also the dumping ground for surplus labor, which provides a rationale for keeping women on low wages. Women were the first factory workers in the nineteenth century. Women and children were seen as a pool that could be drawn on when labor was scarce and discarded when work was scarce. Women are still viewed in that way, even though they now make up 40 percent of the labor force. It is their relation to the home that continues to maintain that myth. The woman is expected to labor *in* the home; however, housework is not called labor because it is done for free. At home the wife services the husband so that he can return daily to his "real" work in the outside world. That is the critical relation. She may also do "real" work outside but she is paid less than he, and she gets little encouragement to identify with that work as anything that is important or serious.

The family is idealized as a sanctuary in a dog-eat-dog world, ministered to by mother angel who is expected to eradicate dirt and dispell woes. It seems incredible (but it is the case) that the compulsive obsession with dirt inside shiny new homes not only sells lots of consumer goods but keeps the wife constantly busy and obscures the real dirt in the world outside the home.

Just as the home is defined as private, the workplace is seen as belonging to the "boss" or the company. An iron curtain screens the quality of these "private" environments from each other. For example, it was certainly not general knowledge in 1970 that every year 14,000 workers were killed on the job and that more than 2.2 million additionally were either permanently injured or temporarily disabled as a result of work-related accidents (HEW, 1970).

The illusion of privacy around the home and workplace keeps women from getting together and sharing notes about what is really going on. They believe that they can live happily, if only they find the right partner, sex, or neighborhood. And in order to maintain this so-called privacy, the man ties himself into a job he hates and a lifelong debt in order to buy a house and lots of things to fill it, so that the woman will have enough to do to take care of it all. Even though she may also work outside the home, she is encouraged to maintain her primary identity as wife and mother. Thus, both husband and wife fulfill the roles expected of them within the structure of patriarchal capitalism without really seeing how essential these roles are for that structure.

A society's power structure is propagated through the education of children in their roles as children, teaching them the behavior that will be expected of them as men or as women. They are also instructed in the behavior appropriate to members of different social classes. Roles are complementary. The role of child requires the existence of the role of adult. The expected behavior of the wife and that of the husband fit like jigsaw pieces. The family built up by these roles fits into its slot in the class structure of the larger society. The interlocked stability of these roles is power in action. The forces of economics, social approval, and personal comfort (including "privacy") continually press for conformity and assure that a woman in marriage does not gain equality with her husband nor her husband with his boss. In other words, power is not established by decree but maintained by constant vigilance and exercise.

Power also is internalized in self-image. Young children perceive themselves as gaining power as they grow bigger. Females perceive a levelling off of their power as they become women, with males gaining ascendancy. Men perceive their power as superseded by that of other men (e.g., the boss, the rich). And this relative power is not subject to the choice of individuals. A man cannot choose to give his power to a woman; a couple cannot change the power relationship by reversing roles.

POWER MANIFESTED IN PERSONAL LIFE

Power, and the understanding of the locus and nature of power, is built into the system and taught more surely than most forms of information. It is not that school children (including college students) read in books about its existence; rather it is experienced in day-to-day-living from early childhood, with a pervasive system of positive reinforcements and negative penalties to consolidate the role behavior consonant with society's assignment of power. It is clearly and surely taught in spite of the extraordinary complexity of power relationships, the inherent contradictions in the system, and the incongruity between what is declared and what is actual.

Human children, like other animals, develop extreme sensitivity to emotional tones. Since they are totally dependent on the good will of adults, they would not survive without that sensitivity. The training begins there, so that the child is taught by the teacher's sniff that rudeness or asking questions on taboo subjects is unacceptable. The male child learns from the flicker of a grin on father's face that the aggressive behavior verbally condemned is really desirable. Millions of such moments bring about the socialized adult, trained to accept that others have power over him or her. However, part of what *he* learns is that although there are limits on *his* power, *he* is the one who has power over *her*. This power is constantly reinforced by a community of men that reminds him that his manhood depends upon the clear separation of the sexes and freedom from womanly traits.

Training in power relationships continues to take place in adulthood: some-times in formal ways, such as contracts and agreements about work and services; sometimes in the same "sniff is *no*, grin is *yes*" manner. The concept of learning a body of knowledge or establishing a contract gives the false impression that a power relationship is a static matter, like a cage or a wall. The contract concept also implies that these are things that are worked out between essentially equal parties. While the power functioning in a marriage may be concealed, it is neither dormant nor static. While it may be denied, it is still exercised, and while it may show only small effects, the larger effects are always in the background. For example, if a man comes home from work and his wife serves him a drink in the living room, she may only feel that she is being a good person and doing something nice for him because she wants to. But if we shake the image a bit to see what makes it tick, asking how this ritual developed whereby *she* serves *him*, we find that it is assumed in the timing and the goal (his relaxation) that because he goes to work all day he deserves service. That is an example of power in operation. If the action were logical, it would be found that since she has worked all day and all evening too, she deserves service, relaxation, and rest. The idea that she should serve him is a general principle, reflecting, illustrating, and reinforcing his power over her, not an *ad hoc* response to the actual situation each is in. Because she is responsible for his creature comforts, he has the power to demand that she serve him. If she does not, any court may declare her to have broken the contract of making a home for him.

There are the large political forms that determine the drink-serving scene, and there are also immediate muscles flexed in that moment. If he wants the drink and she doesn't want to serve it or wants him to take care of the children or wants to get on with dinner, she may well have logic on her side, but she has very little recourse against his power. He can choose to make it uncom-fortable for her in a variety of ways: from simple griping, to complaining to their friends, to beating her or leaving her penniless until she makes a long and usually futile struggle for funds through the courts. He puts her in the position of figuring that it isn't worth the fuss, so she continues to serve him in all the small ways that add up to a full-time job. THAT IS POWER!

There are additional factors that add to the wife's subordinate role, rein-force the pressures keeping her in that position and contribute to the sense of powerlessness that persists in women (including those who are not in a marriage). This is the mythology of sex difference, which is believed by the vast majority of members of the culture. Almost every wife believes that her husband is physically and psychically capable of flattening her with a single blow should she "go too far." She believes herself to be totally incapable of fighting back. This mythology is reinforced by those husbands who do beat up their wives, and by a tremendous amount of overt violence against women in the culture. As long as the woman believes these things, they are true, even if her husband has never raised a hand against her.

In addition, vast numbers of women believe that they are incapable of making the decisions and carrying out the plans necessary to supporting themselves and their children. They believe it and the men believe it, and that makes it true in spite of the fact that vast numbers of women have the role in fact of the single head of household. (Even though their number is increasing, the fact that many of these women are living in independent poverty does not help the situation.) In the belief system, women are fearful. They despair of changing their situations, and they convey whatever last shreds of power and dignity they have to the men in exchange for protection against their own perceived inadequacy.

To the objection that we have given a description of a Victorian "life with father" marriage that is no longer necessary or encouraged, we contend that the change is in the outward forms (true, no woman now calls her husband "Mr. Jones"), not in the reality. Moreover, the vaunted mutuality of accommodation built up in the course of a marriage continues to reflect at each step the power of the husband. Each partner learns what irritates the other and the relative size of the irritations; however the husband's irritation is taken seriously as the wife's failure to do right by him, while her irritation is laughed off as emotionalism or dependency. Even if he decides to humor her, it is he who makes the decision; she does not have the option to decide whether to please him. Such decision making is his right. It is her role to take care of his emotional as well as his physical needs. He is expected to provide financial support, but if he fails, this can also be defined as her fault, since he cannot be expected to succeed when his wife creates distracting, painful scenes at home.

Power peaks and plateaus in human development. We all know the classic progression of the infant: Born totally helpless, it learns to breathe alone, to cry and provoke feeding, and to stand up and assume control of body, bowels, and buttons for whatever purpose it chooses. When the child goes to school, lessons in being controlled from outside are stepped up and she or he sees the adults controlling children en masse. But she or he imagines that the key variable is age, not still another level of control from impersonal institutions. It is naively supposed that when she or he grows up, her or his turn will come. For the adolescent female, that illusion is shattered in the myriad prohibitions against asserting one's own self vis-á-vis potential (male) mates. She cannot be too bright, too well coordinated, too knowledgeable, or too sure of wanting to go to the movies instead of the ice-cream parlor. For the male, something equivalent happens on the job when he becomes a worker. But it happens to the female first. She is left behind the male in power in the same process that leaves the male behind the boss and the boss behind the owner and the black behind the white.

POWER OPERATIONS IN MARRIAGE

The marriage contract is a conglomeration of written and unwritten law, covert and overt interpretations, injunctions recalled from the years of life before marriage, and fantasies and myths from the individual's imaginative life. Each partner entering a marriage believes that she or he will benefit from the relationship. A few years later, in a very large percentage of cases, the marriage is on the rocks. We believe this happens because of the way in which power operates in the marriage, particularly in defining the woman's role.

What are the gains and losses for each partner in marrying? There are a number of social and emotional gains for the woman, which may be differently valued by different women. In general, she feels that she is now an "adult" and joins the "club" of that acceptance—no longer defined as her parents' child or a teenager who is fair game for everyone's correction. She is granted the self-esteem that comes with having proved herself capable and successful in the work of getting a man (the work that has been given so much importance in her life by the media, if not by her own family). She has someone to take care of her without the stigma of childishness. It is approved behavior to turn to her husband about all matters that are frightening to her or about which she is insecure. She has some assurance of financial protection if her husband acts responsibly. He can earn more than she, and his wages are not interrupted by pregnancy. She has a father for her children, both as a financial and day-to-day helper and in the sense that her having children is thereby socially approved. She has the reassurance and confidence derived from having someone else in the house—i.e., not feeling alone, even if the husband is not actually present at any given moment. She has a social companion and sexual partner. At the same time that her sexual needs are given a socially approved outlet, she is offered protection from being a sexual object to other men. She is no longer "up for grabs" and does not have to justify refusing advances. She is launched on a new "career" of nest-building, which legitimizes making a pleasant setting for herself to live in and encourages others to give her things she will enjoy.

The losses for the woman when she marries are high in the area of work and its rewards, while the gains are high in dependency and security. She is denied the sense of being successful and valued that comes from a paycheck and promotions. She loses the independence and self-direction that come from earning one's own wage and making the decisions about spending it. She loses the accumulated benefits from years of employment-pension plans, increased marketable skills and advancement, and seniority on the job. She loses the continuing and varying contacts with other people that would be available were she not in the home so much. As her life comes more and more to be defined in terms of other people (her husband and children), she loses the decision-making power in her own life. This means that she also loses the growth that comes from making choices and suffering their consequences. And she is trapped in the house for long hours of exhausting and nerve-wracking work.

The loss of self-esteem and self-direction is clearly apparent in the area of sex and the control of her own body. The woman upon marriage may gain some freedom from the constant pressure to look lovely to win a husband and may be less ensnared in the routines and rituals of decorating and bullying her body to fit a social image. She may even be less impinged upon by the men around her. But she cannot rest with that relief. In fact, whatever small protection marriage may give a woman from the advances of strangers and from the fears of being a sexual novice or having an unpredictable partner, she remains a sex object for the whole world of advertisers, and her physical attractiveness is still used as a gauge of her huband's success and her own. The threat, "You'll never get a man that way," may be nullified by marriage, but if the man in particular is not dealt with, pleased, or made to look good, new threats come to bear: displeasure, the withholding of money and small freedoms, abandonment.

Are the wife's losses in the marriage the husband's gains? One of the myths of the common culture, perpetuated by the myriad jokes about hen-pecked husbands, is that a man must be strong and assertive and put his wife in her place in order to maintain any control over his own life. This assumes that all the power and all the decisions about it are between the two spouses, that if the man seems powerless, it is because his wife has usurped his power. The husband's felt oppression does not disprove his wife's oppression in the relationship between them. Most men do not have any real power in the outside world, and for vast numbers of them, having power over the wives is poor compensation. Being able to compel sex from his wife (not called rape because of the marriage) and being able to beat her with virtual impunity is only a tension releaser. It does not solve the man's problem with powerlessness, but the wife still feels, very literally, the power he has over her.

Marriage often seems essential for a woman's social and economic survival, but it does not offer her very much (Bernard, 1973). What does it offer to the man? Studies show that a man is much better off married than single (Bernard, 1973, Chap. 2). He is healthier both physically and emotionally. He gets a better job with higher pay, and his social status rises. He is freed from many of the self-support chores and can therefore pursue his career, build up seniority, and develop his pension for the future. He can have children to bear his name and give purpose to his life without being vulnerable to loss of work-time and reliability because of their needs. His home is taken care of for him, and his physical needs for food, clean clothes, and available supplies are met. If he runs out of razor blades, he is entitled to squawk. He has a sexual partner on demand, a woman who is constantly admonished by counselors and the media to make him feel good. He has a home that is a retreat from the pressures of the outside world, protected by his wife's efforts.

And what does the husband trade off for these gains? His major loss is the freedom to make changes and run risks that jeopardize income. Nor can he spend money freely without first considering the additional needs of children, such as education and stable living. There are also some limitations on his choice and exercise of friendships and activities. He cannot be so open about his involvement with other women or his search for sexual variety, nor can he spend as much time as a bachelor can in activities his wife dislikes. (The concept of open marriage does resolve some of these losses, as suggested later in this chapter.)

The woman's cooperation in her caste relationship to her husband and other men is enforced basically from the structure of society. Her conformity is reinforced within the smaller social group of family and friends. They are threatened by her attempts to renounce the powerless role. And beyond these sanctions lie the myths and commandments that have taken root in each woman's mind. These subject her to guilt, anxiety, and fear when she steps outside her role.

It is important to understand that this role assigned to women and so well enforced is not only one of powerlessness in the face of power but also one that is highly demanding of time, energy, skills, and intelligence. It is also riddled with internal contradictions. A wife is not simply a slave who must jump to the command of the master, though that would be bad enough. She is also held responsible for a variety of matters: for guests' happiness; the children's use of drugs; her husband's ability to sustain an erection; his boss' picking him for promotion. The combination of responsibility and the lack of power to carry out the responsibilities is a classic crazy maker. These pressures and contradictions impel incredible numbers of women into neurotic and self-defeating behavior. Some are obsessed with small decisions and details. Some make desperate attempts at controlling their children. Some drink. Others turn to doctors who offer only tranquilizers and narcotics, not solutions.* The contradictions in the structure of women's lives make it *seem* as though women have difficulty making up their minds, making decisions.

---

*Women are legally drugged twice as much as men. For example, 70 per cent of all those receiving Valium are women (*New Women's Times*, 1980, p. 4).

Women need release from the contradictions, not more ways to adjust to them.

Since happiness depends on self-esteem, it is clearly impossible to be responsible for someone else's happiness. She then becomes a ready consumer of the products and ideas advertised as sure to make her husband happy (and thereby hangs a large part of the Gross National Product). She must be a good sex partner, so she buys seductive makeup and clothes. Because of these trappings, if she is raped, she is accused of asking for it; meanwhile husbands joke about their earnings being wasted on their wives' clothes. Learned journals discuss how the female of the species is described as devious and manipulative rather than honest and assertive.

A final turn to the rack upon which the woman is stretched is the fact that her options for self-esteem and self-support outside of marriage are severely limited. In most instances her self-esteem plummets if she cannot define herself as a good wife and mother: What, then, is she good for? And the woman who is not married is stung by the same nettle. On most jobs open to her, she must have the same credentials of sexual attractiveness and willingness to nurture. At the same time she is being told she is not really capable because she is a woman—and not really a woman because she is unmarried or childless.

Couples, becoming aware of the power differential between husband and wife and the inequity in roles, have tried to make fairer contracts and to reapportion or reverse roles. Books, articles, and groups have sprung up to give them guidance. The resulting changes fall short of eliminating wives' oppression because they disregard societal enforcement of the traditions.

The couple trying to increase the man's share of work at home finds he cannot earn a living wage without spending all day out of the house. His wife cannot compensate with wages because her pay-scale is lower. They are admonished from all sides about the quality of their child rearing and her supporting her husband. Everyone is ready to tell them how bad crash-pad living is for babies, how dangerous living in the city is for children, how essential it is to earn extra money and send the children to college. They will be reminded constantly of how well their peers are doing (John has bought a new house; Mark has a sailboat).

Talks with women who have entered into "open" marriages indicate that they gain little increase in sources of self-esteem. What is more likely to occur is that their husbands compensate for their own loss of power by taking advantage of the opportunity for sexual variety. The women are hurt by this, since it strikes at their socialized need to be sexually attractive and at their security in the relationship. But they are told that they must be "liberated" so they now feel not only hurt and angry but guilty that they should not be able to accept what they bargained for.

Financial troubles and social attack may make a couple so anxious that they retreat to traditional roles, but at best their reversals of role do not really change their relative power. The male homemaker knows how much less prestige and power he has than a wage earner, but he has more than a woman homemaker. Imagine him in the supermarket. The manager cashes his check politely: Men have better credit than women. Passers-by are sympathetic as his children raid the cookie shelves: The poor fellow's wife is probably ill, so he must bumble through "her" work. If he gets depressed, everyone agrees that it is the role that depresses him, he should indeed be doing more important work. But the woman is criticized because her "more important work" takes a job away from a man. She is berated for having "balls": being unnatural, a bad mother and worse wife.

Power between husband and wife is not a one-to-one contract they can negotiate as they please. Although it remains a man's choice whether he will exercise some forms of power over his wife, it is he who has the choice; she does not.

CHANGING WOMEN'S POWERLESSNESS IN MARRIAGE

Since we believe that the source of power in marriage lies in the larger institutional structure, it should be clear by now that we also believe that any real change in personal relationships is going to have to come from changes in those structures. It is the system that produces unresolvable conflicts, pain, and untold suffering, yet we go on trying to help individuals and ignore the system. We equate innocence with happiness, call women "girls" and dress them immaturely in puffed sleeves and short skirts; they want to do good but are unable to come to grips with power (they needn't "trouble their little heads" with that). Privacy and individualism justify this denial of reality and hide the conformity of their lives. They have been taught to fear change and the agents of change (wide-eyed radicals and women's libbers) and to believe that they live under the best of all possible systems.

In a society where women earn 59 cents for every dollar a man earns (U.S. Department of Labor, 1977), where rape and wife beating are the most rapidly increasing violent crimes, where women are (legally) drugged twice as often as men, where our waterways are becoming cesspools, where we choke on the air, and where our elderly, tied to chairs and drugged, are allowed to sit in their own filth, in this kind of world, we apparently do not want to see how much is wrong.

Why *are* women so afraid to give their support to a women's movement, to any serious movement for change? They are afraid because men and the system have power over them. People who want to change things can get hurt, because those who have power never relinquish it freely. Maybe the woman's husband will not beat her up if she starts going out to meetings at night, but maybe he will. And if he does, where does she go for support? If her husband "allows" her to become politically involved, the police may refuse her right to picket or change the route of a march. At every level power reasserts itself.

When we talk about change, we mean changing lives, changing institutions, changing heads. It is impossible to change your head and go on living in the same old way. Women who truly recognize their oppression become angry and are compelled to act or go mad.

To be an adult is to claim the right to be, to act, and to define. To be human means to be an adventurer, explorer, builder, shaper, and thinker. Women are not only afraid of success. They are afraid of the failures that go with venturing. They have accepted lonely pedestals, deluded into thinking that they have value as the guardians of moral virtue, making them rigid and keeping them passive.

Women need to become aware of their relatedness to each other as women. The essence of patriarchal domination is the isolation of women from women: Each is taught and constantly reminded that the only way she can find herself as a human being is through her relation with some man. With such training there is no way to talk about equality in marriage.

A social movement begins when enough people recognize that whatever they are experiencing as personal distress has a collective, societal base. The movement grows as issues are defined, new symbols, rituals, and celebrations developed, and organizations formed. Social movements may cut across the traditional fabric of society: Therein lies their power, in the coalitions that form, threatening the established power structure. A significant turning point in the suffrage movement occurred when women began to recognize that they could use the vote collectively, as a power bloc. A similar turning point occurred when the civil rights movement began to talk about Black Power.

It is to the advantage of those who gain from established power to keep the oppressed in isolation, passive, and unaware of their potential as collective power. Ridicule is an effective weapon, and that is why women's gatherings are defined as hen parties and coffee klatches. As an individual a woman has no power. Women derive strength from collective action and organization. They need the women's movement. They need to know, to tell each other, the good news that as individuals they can fail and succeed and be *bad*. They need to show each other that together they can be powerful.

Release from oppression requires that women become public figures. Gaining control of public space is essential to change. Public space is the opposite of the kind of "private" space, the "nuclear family" we have been discussing.* Equality and democracy are useless abstractions until they are tested to see who has access to public institutions and public space.

When the blacks struggled for power, they struggled for space. The freedom walkers walked in the streets and sat in the public restaurants. Workers enforce their demands for better wages and working conditions by their *absence* on the job and their highly visible *presence* on a picket line outside. When women wanted the vote, they organized parades in the streets, stood on soapboxes to make speeches, and picketed the White House. They knew (or some of them did) that by itself the vote would not be very effective until women began to overcome their isolation. The radicals who organized the movement caused a scandal, and many of them were arrested; after all, a "lady" did not go out without a chaperone. Women in the streets were considered "street-walkers," prostitutes (Nelson, 1976). Even today, women are told, "Don't be conspicuous," "Don't make a spectacle of yourself," "Speak softly." A woman raped on a city street is asked why she was there alone. Women are virtually under house arrest when the sun goes down.

To be fully equal women must demand the right to take up space, to be visible, to be known. It is relatively easy to say to oneself that women are oppressed or that things are really bad, and it is not too difficult to say those things to a sympathetic therapist or close friend. But how does one make a public issue of it? How does one move across that huge gap that separates the public from the private, that keeps women powerless and isolated within the family structure or on the job, and that also keeps men slogging along, paying the bills on a house that ends up becoming a prison?

What is the direction of real change? Is all of this just a pipedream that has nothing to do with what is possible in our lives? If not, who are the agents of change, and what forces can bring it about?

Under capitalism, each individual is pitted against every other in the competitive, profit-motivated economy. However, with the advent of advanced technology, education rather than tradition is the criterion for job qualification. More and more women are able to enter the labor force. As a result, they have fewer children and become economically independent. One of the most striking changes that has occurred in the past few years is the increase in the number of families headed by women.

These trends do not necessarily mean more power for women; they only provide the framework in which political change is also possible. Our society maintains all sorts of myths about change agents. We believe, for instance,

---

*This is equally true on the job. To be *public* on the job means to organize there, too. Since this chapter is on marriage, that aspect is not developed here. However, we want to emphasize the importance of women taking leading roles in organizing at the workplace.

that government intervention will subdue oppression because we do not understand that government is tied to the oppressive capitalist system. When women struggled for suffrage it was *not* the vote that liberated them; it was the movement itself, the movement that drew women into public places. When they ceased to struggle, when their organizations became *non*political, they began to fade from view; women born in the 1930s and 1940s scarcely knew of their predecessors' existence. Change in law and affirmative action have clout only when the oppressed are organized to see that the law gets enforced.

Neither can therapy rescue women caught in the oppression of traditional roles. Therapy, too, is a part and instrument of the system: It is based on psychologic study that has not used the learning of politics and the political movements. Psychology has been trapped in a circle: It defines women according to their behavior and then calls their behavior inevitable because of their basic "femininity." It does not see beyond the circle to the social causes for women's "feminine" behavior.

Therapy and the other counseling disciplines must cease colluding in maintaining women's stereotypes. They must stop punishing women for assertion (called "hostility" or "aggression") and for ambition (called "neglecting the children for a job"). It must stop rewarding women for their dependency by reassurance, intercession, advice, and comforting. Counselors must understand that women can assert themselves more than they do, and they must help women do so. But they must also recognize that women are powerless in their relationship to their husbands, as elsewhere, that women cannot simply walk out of that relationship with impunity. Therapy can help women make the initial step toward self-esteem and self-help. It can only hold them back if it does not step aside and allow women to organize to help themselves.

It is not for us to tell other women what they need. Part of the process of liberation is for the oppressed to do that for themselves. That is the beginning, as women get together to identify just what is going on in their lives. The agents of change are the oppressed themselves, not their leaders, and certainly not the professionals who treat them.

How can women organize? The answer is always that women can organize where they already are, at work and in the community. But now they are beginning to understand that their organizations must no longer be ladies' auxiliaries to movements that benefit only men. They must organize specifically for women. It is crucial for women to understand the negative forces against female solidarity. Women's talk is labelled "gossip." Women's meetings are called "hen parties." Remember all those jokes about women's clubs. The joking hides attempts to keep women isolated and suspicious of each other. The women's club movement was basic to getting women the vote, in addition to a host of urban services that all citizens now take for granted:

libraries, public health, pure foods and drugs, and garbage collection, among others. Women need to know their history, and they can be proud of it.

Women need to build political parties in their communities that will pressure for women's needs (homes for battered women, anti-rape squads, apartment houses with cooperative child care, community kitchens): services that break down the isolated family unit while giving more support and aid to the individuals within it. Women need decent low-cost health care and control over their own reproductive systems. They need jobs that pay adequately.

In the past, women were persuaded that their primary job could not be working outside the home. Therefore, they did not join unions or press for benefits—consequently, wages and benefits for women were kept down and women's jobs were kept ghettoized. Who else but a "wife" could afford to take those jobs? Thus, the distinctions between work and home (both of which were defined as private) were maintained. But now, as more and more head-of-family women are working, they are beginning to demand that unions recognize their particular needs as women workers and that they get the same wages and benefits as men. Working mothers need changes that touch both the home and the work place.

The earliest stages of a movement, and often the most difficult, come in little neighborhood groups, in sessions in the washroom, and in tentative efforts to share ideas and give support. When Betty Friedan wrote *The Feminine Mystique* (1963), she blew the whistle on the plight of suburban housewives. Thousands of women responded to the liberating news that they were not unique in their craziness but were the object of massive social forces that denigrate women. The women's movement had its manifesto and women had a new way to define what was happening in their lives. Since then, a growing body of research has catalogued the breadth and depth of women's oppression, and incidentally brought to light information about women's movements in the past.

Today, women are organizing in countless different ways, struggling for greater representation in public institutions as well as for the creation of independent, woman-defined space. Meanwhile, all women make personal adjustments to the problems of daily life. Women must not kid themselves, however, that these "solutions" are a substitute for political change; first, they must begin to deal with the question of power in their private lives. For example, if six women live together and four of them go out to work while two are unemployed, those who bring in the money can begin to exert power over those who do not: It is easy for the wage-earners not to do their share of the housework, to expect those who spend more time in the house to be responsible for the climate of the home. To the extent that women only look for better "personal" solutions, they will not solve the problem of power.

SUMMARY AND CONCLUSIONS

Marriage is a socially designed relationship within which the man has power over the woman. Power is institutional and operates in the socialization of women and in the ongoing, continual oppression of women. Marriage as a private contract affecting only private life is an illusion that masks the need for societal change. Individuals may make relatively successful or disastrous adjustments within this structure, but no one escapes. An individual couple, acting by itself, can neither change the basic institution nor reverse its members' roles. The sanctions and reinforcements are too pervasive, too firmly entrenched. Even the most cursory study of the lives of women makes the need for change apparent. The source of change is less readily visible. Hopes are placed in government programs, progress in professional understanding, and resolution within the family unit.

If women doggedly work their way out of this smokescreen, they find that real change will come only if they organize to take power to solve the problems of their own lives.

We have written this chapter in an attempt to lead the reader through this smokescreen of myths and illusions. This belief system keeps all of us from seeing what is really coming down and distracts women from effective action on their own behalf. We see the solution coming from the women's movement because the women's movement means that women are learning to politicize their personal, private lives. Politics is another word for power.

REFERENCES

Bernard, J. *The Future of Marriage.* New York: Bantam, 1973, Chap. 1–3.

Friedan, B. *The Feminine Mystique.* New York: Norton, 1963.

Nelson, M. *Ladies in the Streets: A Sociological Analysis of The National Woman's Party, 1910–1930.* Dissertation, State University of New York at Buffalo, Buffalo, New York, 1976.

New Women's Times, April 1980, 6, 4. Victims of valium usually women.

U.S. Department of Health, Education and Welfare. *Environmental Health Problems.* Washington, D.C.: Government Printing Office, 1970.

U.S. Department of Labor, Bureau of Labor Statistics. *U.S. Working Women: A Databook.* Washington, D.C.: Government Printing Office, 1977.

ADDITIONAL READINGS

Ashley, J. About power in nursing. *Nursing Outlook,* October 1973, 21, 637–641.

Brownmiller, S. *Against Our Will: Men, Women and Rape.* New York: Simon & Schuster, 1975.

David, D. S., & Brannon, R. The male sex role: Our culture's blueprint of manhood, and what it's done for us totally. *The Forty-Nine Percent Majority: The Male Sex Role*. Menlo Park, Calif.: Addison-Wesley, 1976, 1–45.

Ericksen, J. A., Gancey, W. L., & Ericksen, E. P. The division of family roles. *Journal of Marriage and the Family*, 1979, 41, 301–313.

Gornick, V., & Moran, B. (eds.). *Women in Sexist Society: Studies in Power and Powerlessness*. New York: Basic Books, 1971.

Kjervik, D. K., & Martinson, I. M. (eds.). *Women in Stress—A Nursing Perspective*. New York: Appleton, 1979.

Reeves, N. *Womankind—Beyond the Stereotypes*. Chicago: Aldine, 1971.

Roberts, J. L. (ed.). *Beyond Intellectual Sexism—A New Women, a New Reality*. New York: McKay, 1976.

Rollins, B. C., & Bahr, S. J. A theory of power relationships in marriage. *Journal of Marriage and the Family*, 1976, 38, 619–627.

5

Women at Work:
Stresses Within the Family

Rigmor Asmundsson

Whatever the attitude adopted regarding the role of women in the workplace, they are there, and in unprecedented numbers. However, their increasing engagement in work in the public arena has not been accompanied by a concomitant redefinition of their role within the family. As it is now, the addition of the work role generates problems in that the traditional functions of women have not been redistributed within or outside the family. This lack of redistribution taxes to the utmost the resources of both working women and their families. In this chapter, Asmundsson discusses the stresses that result from the disparities in role definition within the society. The attendant difficulties tend to be seen as problems that each family must solve on its own, as opposed to their being defined as the responsibilities of society-at-large. Asmundsson's perspective adds an important dimension to the consideration of these families, providing a useful contrast to the traditional view that has inhibited the emergence of forms of social provision that might enable the family to develop more creative solutions.

Interwoven in Asmundsson's assessment are suggestions as to how society might take an active role in supplying resources that would serve as ongoing supports for working parents. Basic to her analysis is her belief that both sexes must be socialized toward greater flexibility in role definition. It is intriguing to note that Asmundsson shares Isaacs' view that independence and self-reliance may be outcomes of current socialization practices. However, she reaches a somewhat different conclusion in that she views the outcomes of training for independence as highly functional in an environment that requires that families and individuals take on new role relationships for which there are only inadequate models.

One out of every two women of employment age is now in the labor market (United States Bureau of the Census, 1979:400). They got there gradually: A continuous, although unsteady, movement of women into wage labor has been traced back to 1890 (Department of Labor, 1969, p. 10). Yet that movement went largely unheralded until the 1960s when unprecedented economic growth and the women's movement focused public attention on women as wage earners. Spotlighted were inequities in salary and job opportunities for women. Federal legislation to correct discriminatory practices followed (Department of Labor, 1973). Such legislation served to acknowledge that a change in work roles was taking place, but it could not update attitudes about work roles that lagged behind existing employment practices. For, while some women pursued egalitarian work roles, the existing values, norms, socialization processes, and support systems for families continued largely to represent and foster separate and unequal work roles. Although it is not unusual for attitudes to be shaped by behavior, the resultant change may cause confusion and stress. Thus, a portion of the stress felt in working women's families may be related to the complexity of the changes that occur when traditional values give way to egalitarian values. In addition, such a change process requires the creation of supports for changing work roles of the sexes. These increasing strains in working women's families will be explored in the following pages, after traditional and egalitarian roles are defined.

TRADITIONAL VERSUS EGALITARIAN WORK ROLES

Industrialization, which moved the work site from home to factory, led to clearly defined task assignments for men and women. In the 1950s Talcott Parsons conceptualized these as the "instrumental-adaptive" role for men and the "expressive-integrative" role for women (Parsons, 1954, pp. 305–307). Males were to be socialized to lead active, policy-making lives in the larger community; they were to be the breadwinners. Meanwhile women managed the home; they were to be socialized for more passive, nurturing, family-oriented roles. They were responsible for transmitting society's norms to each generation, whereas men were responsible for observing and influencing those norms. Child-caring and homemaking tasks for women were essentially similar from household to household, although affected to some extent by class and residence factors. Men's tasks varied according to the type of work they did. Perhaps because of this variety, the status of the family was derived from the man's occupation. Thus, the employment of men was pivotal to the functioning and rank of the family. Parsons and Bales (1955, p. 339) described the dichotomy of roles:

> It seems quite safe to say that the adult female role has not ceased to be anchored primarily in the internal affairs of the family, as wife, mother,

and manager of the household, while the role of the adult male is primarily anchored in the occupational world, in his job and through it by his status giving and income-earning functions in the family. The distribution in the labor force clearly confirms this general view of the balance of sex roles. Thus, on the higher level typical female occupations such as those of teacher, social worker, nurse, private secretary, entertainer all have a prominent expressive component and often are "supportive" to masculine roles. Within the occupational organization they are analagous to the wife–mother role.

In the traditional view women were socialized to work only in the home setting and not for wages. If they did enter the workplace, they were expected to take jobs of the "expressive-integrative" type. Parsons presents a view that prevailed during the first half of the twentieth century, even though more and more women were seeking paid work. Employed women were found primarily in the fields he mentions (Department of Labor, 1976, p. 7). However, job selection was not simply a matter of personal preference; women were limited in job choice by sex discrimination. The latter is what the legislation of the 1960s and 1970s has sought to alter. The pervasiveness of the traditional division of work roles will become more apparent as its effects are described in relation to women's present-day reasons for working, their attempts to combine home and work roles, and the interdependency of family members.

Not everyone agreed that what Parsons described was necessary for societal survival. Myrdal and Klein were among the first to raise questions that became popular once public attention was paid to women's infiltration of the marketplace. These authors pointed to the social isolation and loss of purpose experienced by women who remained at home. Myrdal and Klein believed that men, as wage earners, suffered from physical overexertion and isolation from family life. As they so dramatically put it:

> Something must be wrong in a social organization in which men die a premature death from coronary thrombosis, as a result of overwork and worry, while their wives and widows organize themselves to protest against their own lack of opportunities to work (Myrdal and Klein, 1956, pp. 145–148).

Two decades have not weakened the cogency of their comment. The unequal distribution of roles came to be examined by economists and sociologists as well as by spokespersons of the women's liberation movement.*

An alternative, egalitarian role theory was postulated by Alice Rossi. She saw full-time motherhood as insufficiently absorbing for women, and also felt it was deleterious to children's development. Children, she thought,

---

*See for example, Huber (1973); Lloyd (1975); Sullerot (1973).

needed their father's influence. Rossi (1964, p. 608) disagreed with Parsons that marriage was too fragile an institution to sustain competition at comparative skills levels and proposed:

> . . . a socially androgynous conception of the roles of men and women, in which they are equal and similar in such spheres as intellectual, artistic, political and occupational interests and participation, complementary only in those spheres dictated by physiological differences between the sexes. This assumes the traditional conceptions of masculine and feminine are inappropriate to the world we live in. An androgynous conception of sex role means each sex will cultivate some of the characteristics usually associated with the other in traditional sex role definition. . . . [It] means that achievement need, workmanship, and constructive aggression should be cultivated in girls and approved in women.

Under such a model no distinctions would be made between men's and women's spheres of work. Role boundaries would be blurred by crossovers and sharing. Choice of options would be increased. The security provided by clear-cut and limited perspectives would be weakened. Uncertainty as a source of stress for the family would probably be heightened, particularly if uncertainty was seen only in a negative light and societal support for innovation was minimal. Essentially the choice lay between a rigid traditional view and a diffuse egalitarian view.

Signs point toward a societal decision in favor of the egalitarian intention. Women are entering positions formerly identified as masculine: telephone lineperson, truck driver, lawyer, business manager. Fewer become secretaries, nurses, teachers, dieticians, and social workers. Equal-employment opportunities are mandated, as are equal vocational-training options in public schools. Textbooks and television, prime socialization forces, portray a variety of work roles for both sexes. Yet a disquieting note is sounded by the discrepancy between men's and women's salaries and by the preponderance of female over male participation in part-time positions, those that pay least and are devoid of fringe benefits. It is likely that discriminatory attitudes about work role will generate stress for women, their men, their families, and their communities as long as traditional attitudes retard the emergence of egalitarian benefits.

The attitudinal lag may reflect more than a natural resistance to change. Perhaps it also stems from reluctance to assign equal values to homemaking–child care and wage labor. Status within the family under the traditional dichotomy was assigned, after all, according to paid employment rather than according to quality and quantity of home and child care. To be "just a housewife" connoted neither special qualifications nor high aspirations. If homemaking were to be considered a high-skill task and to have a substantial market (dollar) value attached, it might compete with wage employment for participation by both sexes. In addition, women who had denigrated their home tasks might then develop more pride about their competence and be more confident should they wish to undertake other paid employment.

A further explanation for the delay in recognition of women's labor participation and their need for societal support is offered by homosocial theory. Lipman-Blumen (1976, p. 16) defines homosocial as "the seeking, enjoyment, and/or preference for the company of the same sex." A pattern of sex-segregated play that began in childhood is carried into the labor marketplace. Men, having higher status, exclude women from workplace decisions and perpetuate the "old boy" patterns. Until the advent of the feminist movement, women were generally content to take their status from men. However, as women's consciousness was raised and their earned income increased, they secured greater decision-making powers. This power, which represented a challenge to the exclusiveness and higher status of men, might have been a further factor contributing to a delay in reassessing and equalizing the values of home and workplace routines, because to do so threatened a long-standing affinity for association with members of the same sex, and men would therefore reluctantly have to abandon their higher status roles.

WORKING WOMEN'S FAMILIES

The majority of working women are mothers in nuclear families. In 1975 more than half of the married women with children of school age were in the marketplace; two-fifths of those with children under six were working (Department of Labor, 1976, pp. 2–3). The stresses on women who are married and living with husbands are different from those in one-parent families.

Single-parent families headed by women constituted nearly one-fifth of working women in 1975. They were even more likely to be working than were women in intact families. More than half of those with preschool children and two-thirds of those with school-age children were employed at that time (Department of Labor, 1976, p. 4). These parents without partners lacked the option of traditional role division unless they lived in communes or extended families. Neither did they have another adult with whom to share the income-producing and home-managing tasks. As the rate of divorce increases, as unmarried pregnant women more commonly elect to keep their children, and as more unmarried persons of both sexes adopt children, the single parents will carry greater weight in society.

Family stress related to women at work will differ, then, with the type of family structure. Single parent families may be expected to experience the most stress since neither traditional nor egalitarian support systems are available to them. Ideally, communal families would provide the most balanced work–home distribution of roles, but sparse data are available to support such a supposition.

Since the nuclear family is still the predominant American family form, the following discussion of stress related to working women will focus primarily on the family that consists of working mother, working father, and children living together as a separate unit.

PARAMETERS OF FAMILY STRESS
RELATED TO WORKING WOMEN

Many personal factors, in conjunction with each other and with family and societal transactions, determine whether the balance within a family falls toward stress or pleasure when the woman works. Does the woman want to work? Does she need to work? Do her partner and/or children support her working? Is her health good? Is the family physically well?

Conditions of the workplace also affect the home situation. How far is it to travel? Is the work monotonous or challenging? Is the woman paid well? Can she advance at that job? Are there side benefits, such as recreation and interest clubs for the worker and her family?

Arrangements for child care probably represent the most crucial factor influencing the level of stress in the family. Who meets the emotional and physical needs of the children while the mother is absent? What provision is made for different age-level needs? Have the children been taught appropriate self-reliance? How are interactions managed with other systems in the child's life, such as peers, school, physicians, sports, and religion?

Household care can be complicated by employment. Who finds time and energy to shop, cook, and clean? How are repairs and new purchases arranged? Who takes care of the banking?

Perhaps the most neglected area affecting pleasure–stress is that of meeting adult needs within the family. How is adult affection, dependence, and sex given and received? What special interests are pursued? How are friendships maintained? What is the relationship between privacy and interpersonal involvement?

The flexibility of arrangements also becomes crucial to the family balance. What happens if a member is ill? Must each person be within the home at prescribed hours? How are vacations, travel, and absence handled?

Until the 1970s there was little sharing of information about complications of work for working women and their families. Failure to acknowledge the growing trend toward female employment heightened a sense of uniqueness for working women and their families, further isolating them within the traditional norm rather than encouraging egalitarian planning.

REASONS WOMEN WORK: INTRINSIC AND EXTRINSIC FACTORS

In an egalitarian society both sexes would be able to choose among home and work roles, as well as both combined. In the traditional society exceptions to the prescribed labor roles were acceptable for extrinsic reasons stemming from reduced family income. Women did not work unless their husbands earned inadequately or were ill or unless the women were separated, divorced, widowed, or single. Currently, the woman's greater ability to choose participation in the labor force may be a factor either in reducing or in increasing stress within the family. For those families still maintaining strong traditional vestiges, the stress may be greater because secure role formulations become blurred. Such stress is apt to be intrafamilially determined. Egalitarian families would be more likely to experience stress related to inadequate or nonexistent extrafamilial support for dual work roles.

The woman who works because she wants to do so for her own satisfaction, rather than because circumstances necessitate her employment, is likely to view herself as a career worker and to plan for a sequence of jobs. Her sense of purpose and permanence in the labor market may be expected to lead to greater conviction in planning for the family. Reasonable family stability permits her to pursue her career. The greater the satisfaction she receives from progressing at work, the more pleasurable her working is likely to seem to the family. However, the cycle can also reverse itself so that dissatisfaction with either home or work progress becomes stressful to the second system. Ambivalence or guilt about working will heighten family tension.

Failure to progress at work as planned can have deleterious effects not only on the woman, but also on a family that has accommodated to her work plans. Special problems arise for women who enter fields that were traditionally occupied by males. She is not likely to receive support on the job for the "pioneer" role, so family support becomes particularly important, especially since the woman may experience severe individual stress. A 16-year-old girl in her junior year at a vocational school with a predominantly male student body was one of two remaining females of the first group of young women admitted. She became hysterical and needed emergency psychiatric care. Despite her family's backing, she had, after two years of taunting by male fellow students, become unable in her sixth semester to complete her work academically. She was seen as responding to an accumulation of tension, increased by failure of peer and community support. Her dilemma highlights another factor: Socialization for career choice begins in childhood.* Thus, the balance of pleasure and negative aspects of stress related to a woman's working will affect her children's choice of work role.

In contrast to the woman who works for personal, intrinsic reasons, the woman who is forced to seek employment for extrinsic reasons, such as financial need, is more likely to feel ambivalence about working and to convey to her family her resentment about employment. Her potential departure from the labor market when the family's economic situation improves introduces a transitory note to planning for the family. The temporary nature of her working may inhibit her advancement at work, ironically interfering with her income-producing ability in the long run. If the woman works because her husband earns inadequately, the potential for competition, shame, and resentment between the couple is ever present. Children of such a couple may view the parents' work as a reflection of inadequacy in the family. On the other hand, the woman who works to "get the extras" may insure more optimism within her family, and her temporary employment may be translated as the completion of a family task. Some women "stumble" into work for lack of something better to do. The friend of a traditional housewife, mother of seven children, asked her to fill in on a job as receptionist. After three weeks of objecting to work and feeling nervous, encouraged by her husband and children to continue, she suddenly discovered she enjoyed her job, was administratively talented, and wanted to continue working. Her family had been so busy supporting the mother throughout her initial stress that they had failed to notice the way they all pitched in to cover household duties.

A single working mother may have intrinsic reasons for working, but she usually works because her income is needed. Alimony, child support, and pensions are seldom adequate to support a family. Welfare payments as currently administered are inadequate and demeaning. In fact, low-income families sometimes remain together against their better judgment because they cannot afford the two households necessitated by separation and divorce. Stress related to the single parent at work may actually be stress related to that parent's attempt to perform all the roles usually shared by two people. One divorced mother found very little time to be with her children since she worked full-time as a laboratory technician and over-time four nights a week.

---

*Ginzberg (1966, pp. 47–57) describes occupational choice as a six- to ten-year process that begins in childhood and is basically irreversible.

Mealtimes were at the discretion of the children, aged 8 to 14; the mother knew little of how or where the children spent their after-school hours. The family lived in a neighborhood where traditional values prevailed; the children were labeled as "different" because their mother was not home, and community support was not available. This was a mother who needed every cent she could earn just to maintain the family. Under other circumstances she might have elected to be employed anyway, but now she was too pressured to even consider her reasons for work or to plan toward future change. Her children were neglected; one was experiencing school failure, and another was becoming obese.

The reasons women work relate to the kind of stress experienced by their families, and vice versa. Ideally, a choice may be made, with the recognition that some disadvantages exist regardless of the basis for the choice.

OVERLOAD: HOME AND WORK ROLES

The traditional, Parsonian division of roles provided an advantage in that women had less to do while they were "just housewives." Once in the labor market most women, conditioned by generations of traditional child-rearing and household responsibilities, simply added the home tasks to the paid tasks. Now they were doing two jobs instead of one. In similar fashion, since males were socialized to leave the home chores to women, the likelihood was increased that the male family members would not notice what was needed at home. Even where men were willing and able to share responsibility for the home, they were often not attuned to what was needed. As long as home chores were seen as unimportant "women's work," it was not too likely that there would be a spontaneous sharing of duties.

The need to carry both home and wage work roles creates stress for many women and their families. There is need for great organization and efficiency and for good health and energy, because time is limited. Few family tasks can be eliminated; stringent priority assignments must be made. Ironically, at the point where it would most benefit the family, women may find they have no time to teach the home tasks to the other family members. Simple misunderstandings may grow because no time is found to clarify and straighten out the issues. A secretary, who was invited to attend an evening meeting, explained that she could not come because she still had three hours of housework to do when she got home each night. She explained that she "just had boys" and her husband "didn't go for that stuff." In her case, she not only had no time to teach, but she adhered to the old division of roles at home even after she had entered the marketplace.

The working woman may find herself struggling with issues of competence. Despite jokes about "supermom," many women and their families believe women should perform wage and home roles equally well. A working women's failure to maintain exemplary care of children and home may be a source of complaints, anger, and frustration for family members. The woman's resentment of her overload may be buttressed with guilt that she has let her family down, that she is not providing a "proper home atmosphere."

Choices have to be made between human and household needs. Few would disagree that relaxed family time should have high priority, but in practice, cooking, cleaning, and doing laundry may come first. These are concrete, measurable services and therefore may be easier to provide than the abstract, psychologic services to the family. The media, particularly television advertising, have directed attention to housework performance. In order to sell consumer goods, advertisers encourage families to compare and compete in household performance.

Delegation of the more impersonal household tasks could offer relief to families of working women. One solution might be to equip apartment buildings with central kitchens and laundries from which hired staff could dispense prepared meals and finished laundry to the occupants.* Neighborhood groups have occasionally reported the success of eating clubs through which large quantities of food are prepared by alternating families and are shared communally or distributed to members' homes. The proliferation of packaged frozen foods and fast-food eating places, despite the generally low quality of food offered, has met some of the needs of the families of working women. A sharp increase in restaurant eating in the past few years appears to be a partial response to increased income and lessened free time in families of employed women (*New York Times*, 1977b, p. 1). Increased evening and weekend hours of operation for stores and banks have provided further accommodation. Perhaps these isolated changes are harbingers of societal adaptation to a more egalitarian distribution of home roles and work roles.

Because of a new approach to work schedules, in some instances employees are permitted to choose work hours convenient to themselves and their families. "Flexitime" permits the worker to distribute working hours on an individual basis. Some industries have moved to shorter work weeks with longer daily working hours. Occasionally, two persons share one job. Part-time work is increasing. However, when these alternative patterns of work hours do not provide fringe benefits, the advantages to family functioning may be cancelled by concern for coverage in illness, loss of job, or retirement.

---

*Rossi (1964) recommends a change in suburban housing–urban employment patterns such that workplace and home be located closer together, reducing travel time and making it easier to obtain services needed at home.

FAMILY NEEDS:
INTERDEPENDENCE AND SELF-RELIANCE

The traditional division of roles clearly assigned nurturing and the meeting of dependency needs to the female; the self-reliant role was assigned to the male. A self-reliant woman and a demonstrative man were considered anomalies. Some of these attitudes still prevail, but there is greater recognition that both sexes have needs and capacities for autonomy and for dependency. Agreement may not yet be sufficiently widespread to be incorporated in socialization patterns for children; nor is there appreciation that adults themselves may have a strong need for nurturing, and children a need for their self-reliance to be recognized prior to adolescent years.

The woman who works may become a less nurturing person to her family. Whether this promotes growth or stress within the family will depend upon age-related needs of each family member and how sustaining members can be to each other. Nurturing can be provided by fathers and siblings, with gratification to provider as well as to receiver. It may be, as suggested by Binstrock (1973, p. 54), that mothers in the past kept their children tied to them longer than necessary in order to confirm their own need for a purposeful function in the family. If children are to be socialized to allow for greater adult options than previously available, self-reliance may become a particularly desirable character trait for both sexes. Striking a balance between dependency and self-reliance for various age levels is a difficult task for a family, and perhaps a certain amount of stress is inevitable as attempts are made to reach flexible balances. A particular risk in a working couple's marriage is that adult needs for nurturance are overlooked, either through denial of their existence or through the belief that they are incompatible with self-determination.

It was formerly believed that the personality development of a child was likely to be damaged if the mother were not available in the home. Hoffman and Nye (1974, pp. 163–166) have reviewed research of the past two decades and found that the employment of the mother is not usually associated with problems in children. In an earlier study they reported that children whose mothers worked part-time had fewer difficulties than children whose mothers remained in the home or whose mothers worked full-time (Nye and Hoffman, 1963, p. 80). It seems likely that the sex- or blood-tie of the caretaker may not be as essential to the child's ego development as the consistent, attuned warmth, affection, and ability to set limits. The attitude of parents, kin, and community toward the surrogate parent may influence the way in which the child construes this experience.

Finding a substitute caretaker is often a problem and source of family upheaval. Nursemaids and babysitters are generally held in low esteem. It is hard to find a substitute with the same value system and priorities as the natural parents. Parental worry and guilt about leaving children may confound the sharing of responsibility with the surrogate. Parents and children are prone to anger and regret at missing key experiences with each other, and children may need assurance of their importance to the parents.

Preferred character traits are to an extent culturally determined. As more women enter the labor market, perhaps the expectations of children may alter in regard to assertiveness, affection, and self-reliance. There still remains the risk that children may develop a brittleness to their personalities if pushed to mature too rapidly.

The child's need for parenting changes with age. Entrance to school brings new stresses for the family of the working mother. After-school supervision is hard to arrange, particularly for children reaching an age of exploration and active peer play. Working parents may find it difficult to arrange school conferences, play and club transportation, homework supervision, and dental and medical appointments. Children, tired after a day in school, need to find a friendly, nurturing listener at home. If the children are being socialized in school for primarily traditional role patterns, they may be confused and resentful of working parents. The parents may be trying to encourage independence in the child while the school asks for compliance.

Society has not yet provided child-care facilities as needed by working parents. Historically, day-care centers have increased in wartime and closed in peacetime. A few industries have experimented with nurseries at the workplace, but these have not caught on, perhaps because of the need for providing transportation for young children and because of the leverage such an arrangement gives the employer over the parent's production. Only 5 percent of children of working mothers are cared for in day-care facilities (Department of Labor, 1973, p. 2). The majority spend their time with relatives and neighbors or are cared for by older siblings, but there remains a need for trained parental substitutes. Ideally, these would be located in the child's own neighborhood. Schools could be used after class hours for recreational and group care activities. The Scandinavian system of park mothers might be organized in urban centers. Children would then be brought as needed to playgrounds where qualified caretakers would care for and instruct them. Comprehensive planning for children of working mothers cannot be expected to materialize as long as the view holds that women ought to remain at home as caretakers.

School vacations present particular problems for families of working mothers, as do times of illness in children. Few employer–employee arrangements provide for such contingencies. Intact families with egalitarian employment attitudes might be able to distribute time spent at home between the parents, at least on a short-term basis. An innovative approach would be to develop a core of homemaker–visiting-nurse services, funded either publicly or privately by fee.

Parental needs for solitude, companionship, and excitement are not easily obtained in the family of the working woman. Conscious effort and deliberate planning become necessary; even so, a certain amount of strain is probably inevitable as various solutions are tried. Parents may benefit from adapting some of the child's play attitudes, and children from recognizing that adult life is not all hard work and seriousness. Working parents may find it difficult to sustain relationships with their own peers because of their preoccupation with home and work lives. It may be more important to the parents, particularly if they work different hours, that adult satisfactions be drawn from the marital bond. Once both partners are in the labor market, performing instrumental roles, both are almost obliged to sustain and nurture each other as well as the children. Socialization of both sexes toward such role expectations would reduce strain generated by the attempts of egalitarian partners to follow traditional prescriptions for role division.

SUMMARY

Potential for the evolution of egalitarian work roles increases as more and more women move into the labor market. Since systems reverberate with and alter each other, changes in homemaking and child-care practices would be expected to accompany swelling ranks of women entering employment, but such is not the case. Traditional norms and support systems still prevail. The discrepancy between egalitarian expectations and traditional behavior is seen as a major cause of family stress related to women at work.

The balance of pleasure and stress within a family reflects the woman's reasons for working, the amount of overload she experiences by trying to fulfill home and work roles, and, perhaps most significantly, the distribution of dependence and self-reliance of family members. The woman who works for primarily intrinsic reasons seems likely to contribute less to family stress than the one who works for extrinsic reasons. The family in which homemaking and child-care tasks can be shared in a reasonably equal distribution should experience less pressure than one in which the working woman attempts to fill both home and work roles. Family tension may be reduced through encouraging the development of characteristics like self-reliance in children and interdependence in adults. In addition, there is real need for peer and community support and planning to meet concrete needs of the working woman's family.

Rossi has commented (1965, p. 103) that when "changes are in process, they are defined as social problems, seldom as social opportunities." Perhaps it would be appropriate to view stress related to working women as opportunity for beneficial change within the family unit.

REFERENCES

Binstrock, J. Motherhood: An occupation facing decline. *The Futurist*, 1973.

Ginzberg, E. *The Development of Human Resources*. New York: McGraw-Hill, 1966.

Hoffman, L.W., & Nye, F.I. *Working Mothers*. San Francisco, Calif.: Jossey-Bass, 1974.

Huber, J. (ed.). *Changing Women in a Changing Society*. Chicago, Ill.: The University of Chicago Press, 1973.

Lipman-Blumen, J. Toward a homosocial theory of sex roles: An explanation of the sex segregation of social institutions. In Blaxall, M., & Reagan, B. (eds.), *Women and the Marketplace*. Chicago: University of Chicago Press, 1976.

Lloyd, C.B. (ed.). *Sex, Discrimination and the Division of Labor*. New York: Columbia University Press, 1975.

Myrdal, A., & Klein, V. *Women's Two Roles: Home and Work*. London: Routledge and Kegan Paul, 1956.

New York Times, Rising popularity of eating out puts a pinch on supermarkets. April 10, 1977(b).

Nye, F.I., & Hoffman, W.L. *The Employed Mother in America*. Chicago: Rand-McNally, 1963.

Parsons, T. *Essays in Sociological Theory*. Glencoe, Ill.: The Free Press, 1954.

Parsons, T., & Bales, R. *Family, Socialization, and Interaction Process*. Glencoe, Ill.: The Free Press, 1955.

Rossi, A. Equality between sexes: An immodest proposal. *Daedalus*, 1964, 93, 607–652.

Rossi, A. Equality between the sexes. In Lifton, R.J. (ed.), *The Woman in America*. Boston: Beacon Press, 1965, 98–143.

Sullerot, E. *Woman, Society and Change*. New York: McGraw-Hill, 1973.

United States Bureau of the Census, *Statistical Abstract of the United States: 1979* (100th ed.). Washington, D.C.

U.S. Department of Labor. *Brief Highlights of Major Federal Laws and Orders on Sex Discrimination*. Washington, D.C.: Government Printing Office, 1973.

U.S. Department of Labor. Day care facts. Washington, D.C.: Government Printing Office, 1973.

U.S. Department of Labor. *Handbook on Women Workers*. Washington, D.C.: Government Printing Office, 1969.

U.S. Department of Labor. *Women Workers Today*. Washington, D.C.: Government Printing Office, 1976.

SUPPLEMENTAL READINGS

Baxandall, R., Gordon, L., & Reverby, S. *America's Working Women: A Documentary History—1600 to the Present*. New York: Vintage, 1976.

Blaxall, M., & Reagan, B. *Women and the Workplace*. Chicago: University of Chicago Press, 1976.

Dreitzel, H.P. *Family, Marriage, and the Struggle of the Sexes.* New York: Macmillan, 1972.

Fogarty, M., Rapoport, R., & Rapoport, R.N. *Sex, Career and Family.* Beverly Hills, Calif.: Sae, 1971.

Kreps, J. *Sex in the Marketplace: American Women at Work.* Baltimore, Md.: The Johns Hopkins Press, 1971.

Kundsin, R.B. (ed.). *Women and Success: The Anatomy of Achievement.* New York: William Morrow, 1974.

Lifton, R.J. (ed.). *The Woman in America.* Boston: Beacon Press, 1965.

Matthews, E., Reingold, S.N., Berry, J., Weary, B., & Tyler, L.E. *Counseling Girls and Women over the Life Span.* Washington, D.C.: American Personnel and Guidance Association, 1972.

Oakley, A. *Woman's Work, the Housewife, Past and Present.* New York: Vintage, 1974.

Richardson, E. *Work in America: Report of a Special Task Force to the Secretary of Health, Education and Welfare.* Cambridge, Mass.: MIT Press, 1975.

Seifer, N. *Absent from the Majority: Working Class Women in America.* New York: National Project on Ethnic America, The American Jewish Committee, 1973.

Smuts, R.W. *Women and Work in America.* New York: Schocken, 1971.

6

Sex Roles:
Dilemmas for Women and Men

Winnifred Humphreys
Suzanne Czamara Lema

The two preceding chapters have addressed several dimensions of current problems in marital and family role definition. Humphreys and Lema, acknowledging the profound effects of the role incongruities, focus on the parallel and at the same time reciprocal nature of the role strain experienced by both men and women. They maintain that continually attempting redefinition of roles based on persisting stereotypes is futile and suggest that professionals, eschewing the concept of sex role–appropriate behavior, move instead to assist couples and families in developing interactional patterns commensurate with their mutual needs and proclivities.

The burgeoning of the women's movement, a phenomenon of the past two decades, was accompanied by an upsurge of interest in examining and comprehending the constraints and burdens inherent in the role of women in our society. Society's expectations and constrictions had placed great burdens on women and injustices were in need of redress. Characteristically, the rhetoric of the movement depicted "outsiders" as laudable or contemptible depending on their stance on women's issues. The zeitgeist was such that social science researchers and mental health professionals who were interested in the study of sex roles focused heavily for a time on women's issues. It was almost inevitable that during this period comparatively little attention was paid to the impact of societal role expectations on *men*, as well as the implications of women's role changes vis-à-vis their male counterparts.

However, the 1970s brought increasing evidence of role strain for men and growing interest in investigating its nature as well as its diverse sources.* At

---

*See, for example, Bednarik (1970); Kaye (1974); Pleck (1976); Harrison (1978).

the same time, a significant literature has begun to emerge that moves beyond the traditional perspectives on sex roles.* It attempts to examine the phenomena traditionally subsumed under the rubric of sex role in ways that do not anchor particular aspects of social role performance to either sex. Such a shift in thinking is fraught with crucial implications for professionals since it calls for a substantial reshaping of our conception of interpersonal relations, much of which has been tied to a view of sex (and, by extension, social) roles, as being biologically determined.† However, before considering the implications of a departure from the familiar characterization of sex roles, we will briefly examine factors central to the current functioning of both men and women in America.

STATING THE CASE FOR WOMEN

Traditionally, our society has socialized women to be dependent, passive, fragile, nonaggressive, sensitive, nurturant, subjective, intuitive, and unable to take risks. During the past 60 years, however, the role has evolved. Since 1920 women have received the right to vote, to enter any career in the man's world, and to expect equal opportunities and pay. This transition has created new stresses for women because it provided them with the chance to choose careers that might have been closed to them in the past: careers other than or in addition to that of wife and mother. However, the demands society has placed on women have not changed as rapidly as have the opportunities for personal achievement. As recently as the 1950s, writers were describing the modern woman as having the choice either of pursuing a career *or* of marrying, while her male counterpart was permitted to combine a career with marriage and a family (Rose, 1951). At that time most of the female labor force was made up of widows, "never marrieds," or divorcees. By contrast, in the past two decades, growing numbers of married women have been embarking on careers not only to supplement their family incomes in the face of spiraling inflation but also to satisfy their own needs and to utilize their intellectual capacities in stimulating occupations outside of the home.

Combining the roles of wife, mother, and person with a career (or "work," since not all working women view themselves as having careers) has afforded

---

*See, for example, Bern (1974); Rebecca, Hefner, & Oleshansky (1976); Kaplan & Bean (1976).
†A striking example of the persistence of this biologic determinism, in this case in relation to women, is represented in *Our Bodies, Ourselves*, the otherwise laudable publication of the Boston Women's Collective (1976). Although considered avant-garde at the time of its first edition in 1971 and aimed toward the freeing of women to *accept* their bodies, its very title imposes constraints on their identity and implies biologic determination of their social role.

women the opportunity of widening their boundaries. On the other hand, it has been accompanied by considerable controversy concerning a woman's right to take away time from her husband and children—i.e., time that might have been devoted to performing those homemaking tasks once considered the only legitimate and meaningful responsibilities included in the social role of women. In view of the foregoing, it is ironic to note that women in the current inflation-ridden period are expected to be simultaneously proficient on both fronts. There is continuing evidence that domestic and occupational expectations are intertwined in very complex ways for females, whereas the two arenas are comparatively unconnected for males who continue to view their career goals as not being contingent on their marital and/or family situations (Aneshensel & Rosen, 1980, p. 129).

The dilemma extends to women of all ages. What, for example, is the price in role strain paid by adolescent girls who hear contradictory messages from family and teachers? They are commonly urged to train for a vocation but at the same time not to be emotionally committed to the training; to prepare for a future acquiescent marital role, even while becoming actively involved in the educational process, and competing with young men (Epstein 1971, p. 64). Furthermore, young girls are commonly not socialized to tolerate the stress and mental anguish inevitable in the struggle to reach difficult-to-achieve career goals; they tend to reach adulthood without having been encouraged to deal with the anxiety of commitment as males have been since childhood (Symonds, 1971, p. 33; Stake & Levitz 1979 p. 157).

Most women continue to prefer the traditional coupling relationships, but increasing numbers have become discontent with their subordinate status. The time-honored vow to "honor and obey" does little to enhance the quality of a marriage in which the female partner accedes at the expense of stifling her own social and psychologic needs. The language used to describe the status of each marital partner vis-à-vis the other emphasizes the inequality of the partnership: The woman is referred to as "the little woman" or "the wife." The very phrase "man and wife" accords the male his identity as a man while the female is represented as deriving her identity reciprocally (O'Neill & O'Neill, 1972, pp. 195–196).

For the American woman, then, the world of education, paid employment, business, and professional careers has steadily opened up, but to take advantage of the beckoning opportunity she must be prepared to contravene early socialization that has influenced her to consider marriage and motherhood as her primary life goals. At the same time, she must compete in a labor market that grudgingly acknowledges her competence, and she must work constantly to "prove" that she is indeed the peerless wife and mother to which every husband and child is entitled. Merely to characterize her struggle as "role strain" is to underestimate her dilemma.

MEN AND THEIR EXPERIENCES

Traditionally, men in American society have been socialized from earliest youth to be strong, confident, and independent; to exhibit a capacity for daring and aggression; to display physical prowess and suppress tenderness, avoiding any behavior or traits that might be construed as effeminate. They have been expected to pursue success and status in the work world while demonstrating competence as breadwinners (Brannon, 1976; Pleck, 1976). Considerable pressure is exerted on men, then, to be action- and achievement-oriented. Dominance (power) characterizes their handling of interpersonal relations. However, they should be wise and "level-headed" in their inter-actions with others, as well as in their management of themselves. (One can already discern grounds for incipient role strain!) As the foregoing implies, primary life goals for the traditional man tend to focus around "bringing home the bacon"; the gaining of a secure status in the work world, however killing (literally) the pressures of the marketplace; the acquiring of material possessions along with attractive and acquiescent daughters and ambitious, aggressive, yet respectful sons, reared by a compliant wife who is a competent housekeeper, agreeable bed-mate, and nurturant mother.* The man, ex-pected to be the somewhat detached, yet benevolent and strong, proprietor of such an establishment, would appear to be in an enviable position. But how is he to reconcile the contradictory demands of his role? He is at once required to scrabble for a living, be a man among men ("just one of the boys"), as he aggressively, even violently, competes for his share of the trophies of the occupational and athletic arenas while at the same time as-suming the benign but aloof position of *pater familias* with all of the impli-cations of authority and the prerogatives to demand respect and compliance.

With the evolution of contemporary culture and, at least in part, in relation to the changing demands of women, another constellation of role expectations has emerged to constitute what Pleck (1976, p. 156) refers to as the "modern male role." Closely paralleling the characteristics of a middle-class lifestyle, this set of role expectations incorporates the positive sanctioning of intellec-tual accomplishment as opposed to the physical achievement valued in the traditional male role. Interpersonal skills are also more highly esteemed; along with sexual expertise, heterosexual tenderness and emotional intimacy are encouraged, although, contrary to the traditional male role, same-sex rela-tionships tend to be weak except in work situations, where a high level of competence in managing "on-the-job" relationships is expected (Pleck, 1976, p. 157).

Particularly for the man who has early been socialized to the requirements

---

*Apropos the division of labor in this vital aspect of American family life, see Polatnick (1975).

of the traditional role with its emphasis on physical prowess, athletic ability, and the viewing of women as valuable largely for their nurturant and sexual functions, the discontinuity embodied in the transition to the modern male role is fraught with strain and trauma. Moreover, at a time when his female counterparts have been discovering and enjoying the boon of the increased support and esteem of same-sex peers, he is pressured by society to look only to women for the satisfaction of his emotional needs, thereby losing the potential for vital sustenance and enrichment available from other men. Ironically, he is at the same time expected to look to his work (and therefore usually to associations with other males) as a central source of self-esteem.

Perhaps the most disturbing indication of the degree to which role strain impacts on men's lives is to be found in this century's health statistics. While improved nutrition and health services account for an increase of more than 20 years in the life expectancy of both males and females since 1900, with women consistently living longer, the difference in expected longevity between men and women has climbed from 2 years in 1900 to 7.8 years in 1977 (HEW, 1977). While biogenetic factors have for decades been held largely responsible for the discrepancy, those who view the situation from a psychosocial perspective are accumulating evidence of the substantial implication of sex-role–related factors in accounting for the difference.*

TOWARD A CHANGE IN PERSPECTIVE

The power dimension, which forms an important aspect of social interaction, is an especially crucial element in marital relationships by virtue of the fact that society has accorded, and, in large measure continues to accord, superior power to the male partner. The cry of "power to the powerless" currently emanating from oppressed groups (women among them) carries with it the suggestion that a reallocation of power will, in itself, ameliorate the problems of the disenfranchised. However, in American families, mere occupancy of the male's power position has hardly served to secure for him an existence free of role strain. Professionals have noted that even in those situations in which couples have engaged in serious efforts at sex-role accommodation, the necessity for a continuing struggle against conservative external forces has made the task extremely difficult.

Since it is clear that both men and women in America are suffering almost intolerable role strain, it would appear that professional attempts to understand and offer help to distressed couples based on current sex-role definitions—even when those efforts include moves toward role accommodation—will fall short of the mark. Such deeply embedded stereotypes are unlikely

---

*For a useful discussion of the cumulating data in this regard, see Harrison (1978).

to yield sufficiently for families to make the necessary shifts in allocation of roles. It is in this regard that the work of social scientists exploring the concept of sex-role transcendence may have particular cogency for professionals.

However "enlightened" we are, along with our clients we have been deeply conditioned to become uneasy when confronted by traits and behavior that deviate in any marked way from those that accord with the sex-role expectations of our culture. It is therefore almost inevitable that we will have difficulty both in accurately assessing and in productively intervening with couples and families. For this reason the reader is asked to consider the intriguing and important implications of moving beyond the structures of sex-role definitions as a means of shaking free his or her thinking from these conventions that subtly but strongly influence our view of the social functioning of clients.

With reference to the foregoing, Rebecca et al. (1976) propose a three-stage model of sex-role development. In the first two stages, developing human beings are represented as taking on, through a very complex learning process, the attributes seen as appropriate to their sex. According to the model, a third stage provides individuals with new opportunities for experience and learning. By now, they have a well-developed role repertoire and a fairly sophisticated knowledge of the behavior, feelings, and personality traits expected of both sex roles. They are in an advantageous position to test out any of them, not on the basis of their sex-role appropriateness, but rather in terms of how they suit particular situations or "fit" with the individual's own integrity as a person (Rebecca et al., 1976, p. 204). That is, individuals have multiple choices open to them. Unbound by the strictures of stereotyped role expectations, they may choose to test out new ways of reacting or behaving. They may accommodate in some way to the role(s) of others. On the other hand, they are also freed to assess each situation on its own merits, perhaps reaching the conclusion that the requirements do not accord with their own self-image and that therefore the situation or role is in need of change.

Extended to couples and families, this model has considerable potential for adding flexibility to the professional's repertoire. Although it is not the purpose of this chapter to detail practice solutions, it seems important to consider the following beginning applications of the model.

If our thinking can transcend sex-role stereotypes, families can be more clearly assessed in terms of their functioning in the situations in which they find themselves. There is a reduced likelihood of confusing the issue of functionality by judgments emanating from biases about the degree to which each member's personality and behavior is sex-role appropriate. In addition, there are crucial implications for the socialization of children who, though heavily exposed to the prevalent cultural expectations, may, through a different family life experience, be helped to achieve a more creative lifestyle, one less dominated by the role strain that characterizes the lives of their parents' generation.

REFERENCES

Aneshensel, C.S., & Risen, B.C. Domestic roles and sex differences in occupational expectations. *Journal of Marriage and the Family*, 1980, 42, 121–131.

Bednarik, K. *The Male in Crisis*. New York: Knopf, 1970.

Bern, S.L. The measurement of psychological androgyny. *Journal of Clinical and Consulting Psychology*, 1974, 42, 155–162.

Boston Women's Health Book Collective. *Our Bodies Ourselves*. New York: Simon and Schuster, 1976.

Brannon, R. The male sex role: Our culture's blueprint of manhood and what it's done for us lately. In David, D., & Brannon, R. (eds.), *The Forty-nine Percent Majority*. Reading, Mass.: Addison-Wesley, 1976.

Epstein, C.F. *Woman's Place*. Berkeley: University of California Press, 1971.

Harrison, J.B. Warning: The male sex role may be dangerous to your health. *Journal of Social Issues*, 1978, 34, 136–150.

Kaplan, A.G., & Bean, J.P. (eds.). *Beyond Sex-Role Stereotypes: Readings toward a Psychology of Androgyny*. Boston: Little, Brown, 1976.

Kaye, H. *Male Survival*. New York: Grosset and Dunlop, 1974.

O'Neill, G., & O'Neill, N. *Open Marriage*. New York: Avon, 1972.

Pleck, J.H. The male sex role: Definitions, problems and sources of change. *Journal of Social Issues*, 1976, 32, 155–164.

Polatnick, M. Why men don't rear children: A power analysis. In Petras, J. (ed.), *Sex Male, Gender Masculine*. Port Washington, N.Y.: Alfred, 1975.

Rebecca, M., Hefner, R., & Oleshansky, B. A model of sex-role transcendence. *Journal of Social Issues*, 1976, 32, 197–206.

Rose, A.M. Adequacy of women's expectations for adult roles. *Social Forces*, 1951, 30, 69–77.

Stake, J.E., & Levitz, E. Career goals of college women and men and perceived achievement-related encouragement. *Psychology of Women*, 1979, 4, 151–159.

Symonds, A. The psychology of the female liberation movement. *Medical Aspects of Human Sexuality*, 1971, 5, 24–33.

U.S. Department of Health, Education and Welfare, Public Health Service. Life tables. In *Vital Statistics of the United States*. Hyattsville, Md.: National Center for Health Statistics, Vol. 2, Sect. 5, 1977.

7

Blended Families: One Plus One Equals More Than Two

Rigmor Asmundsson

With the increase in the incidence of divorce and the corresponding rise in the rate of remarriage, the merging of already formed families is becoming commonplace. The resultant complex family form makes unusual demands on its members. The newly married, childless couple must come to terms with its mutual interrelationship; the blended family additionally must come to grips with the continuing dilemmas posed by past ties to family members. Some relationships must be given up and others require redefinition. In either case, grieving will be an unavoidable part of relinquishing the old and taking on the new. Asmundsson addresses herself to understanding and elucidating these crucial processes. While she acknowledges the strains inherent in blending, she is also optimistic about the ability of families to meet the challenge. Professionals will find her analysis useful in formulating strategies for working with families attempting to manage these tasks. However, there is abundant evidence that many are seeking the help of professionals who are called upon to meet this challenge. Asmundsson's analysis will prove valuable to the development of an understanding of the special circumstances of such families and will supply a base for the formulation of strategies for working with them in their attempts to forge a new family identity.

When Peter Dayton was 10, his father was killed in a car accident. At 12, his mother remarried. In addition to getting a new father, Peter gained six more siblings, including, for the first time, sisters. In fact, one of his new sisters was Peter's own age. That sister became a thorn in his side. She took a bath every day, idolized rock stars Peter had never heard of, and devoted herself to reforming Peter from his grubbiness and poor manners. Peter, who had been the oldest of three brothers, became third youngest of nine children. Whereas Peter's first extended family had been small, consisting only of the nuclear family, two grandfathers, and one married uncle with children, his new family was huge. There were additional grandparents, uncles and aunts, and many, many cousins. Most of the added relatives lived in the immediate neighborhood of Peter's new home. There was a great deal of visiting back and forth; Sundays were saved for the family. For the first time in his life, Peter found there was always someone available with whom to fish or play ball. No longer did he hear, "Go play with your brothers."

Moving to the new house had been sad for Peter. He missed his old friends and school. The special science program he had entered did not have an equivalent in his new school. His new classmates were tougher than his old pals, but he had survived their initial hazing. He still had not made a close friend. One puzzling new involvement was with church. Having been raised as an indifferent Catholic in a mixed marriage, Peter did not have the personal connection to church that his new family showed. Sometimes he felt a little ignorant about church.

Peter felt pretty good about his new family. He seemed like his old happy self, except for complaints about his sister's intrusiveness. His mother, now Mrs. Rossi, noted that Peter stayed closer to home than in the past but saw that as a natural consequence of the slow rebuilding of friendships. However, Peter confessed to a friend from his old town that he "didn't want to miss anything." He knew how quickly things could happen because he had seen his mother become a grandmother the day she had married his new father!

Peter had become part of a blended family, one in which two established, partial families joined to form one family. Referred to also as "reconstituted families," blended families are an old phenomenon, currently undergoing an accelerated growth of numbers as the divorce rate increases. Many of us met our first blended family in Cinderella's household. Nowadays most of us have more personal experience with blended families, either as participants or as observers within the neighborhood or among friends.

It will become increasingly difficult not to have personal contact with blended families since the divorce rate continues to escalate and divorced partners tend to remarry. In 1977 there were half as many divorces as new marriages.* Bohannan (1970, p. 138) reported that 26 percent of all marriages in 1970 were the second or third marriages of one or both partners. Surely that percentage has also risen over the past few years. Far from being an isolated phenomenon, blended families reflect one important aspect of changing family life.

Peter's family experience illustrates an example of some of the pressures attendant upon reconstituting a family. In his new immediate family 11 people are undergoing the transition from a single-parent to a blended family.

---

*In 1974 there were 10.5 marriages and 4.6 divorces per 1000 population; in 1977 those figures were 10.1 marriages and 5.0 divorces (National Center for Health Statistics, 1977).

The extent of adaptation necessary to merge the families becomes immediately apparent. Those embarking on a blended-family venture frequently find themselves floundering, in part because norms have not yet been established for the blended family. Additionally, starting with Cinderella, the blended family has had a "bad press." "Step-parent" and "step-child" have pejorative shading. Perhaps because divorce carried a stigma until recently, it has been assumed that blended families would have trouble reconstituting themselves. Researchers such as Duberman (1975, pp. 27–30) have commented that widowed parents are more accepted by society than are divorced parents and that there is greater ease in reconstituting widowed families. Her research on 88 blended families and the author's own interviewing experience with them has indicated that parents in a reconstituted family do not deny complications and strains in unifying the family, but most have also spoken of the excitement and pleasure that comes in the process.

Guidelines for the nuclear family do not apply realistically to second families since the blended family is distinguished by certain attributes not found in the first family. In the first place, the blended family starts with two past histories of "being a family." Some of the members have functioned together previously in a family unit. Not only do the parents have an earlier experience of family, but the children also enter with past history in family experience. Second, the members of a blended family have suffered a past loss, either through divorce or death. Members know that a parent can withdraw or disappear. A third distinguishing feature of the blended family is that it is an "instant" family. Members are not added gradually (although later more members may be born to the family); they are "there" from the start. They may be many in number, frequently with double sets of grandparents, uncles and aunts, cousins and friends. The instant increase in size often leads, in turn, to practical complications of space, timing, and location. Some members will have to change plans, expectations, and use of space for the reconstituting to succeed.

PAST HISTORY

The groundwork for one's self-esteem, sense of competence, and the expectations of family and society are laid in the primal family. Experiences there have a cumulative consistency. They are not readily discarded or altered. Children tend to believe that what they observe in their own family is typical of other families. The newlywed, even after a long courtship, can expect to suffer some shock at seeing how differently the beloved person views life. Adjusting one's self-image and value system to that of the marital partner is a natural phase in any marriage.

The blending of a marital pair for the second time implies that some childhood observations have already been modified. The second time around may be either harder or easier. Familiarity with the necessity and the process of change may facilitate adaptation. However, if much change is necessary, or if the changing process in the first marriage was particularly painful, the blended partners may feel so apprehensive or frustrated as not to want to give up the past. Thus, a husband who originally came from a "tight-lipped" family had married and been divorced from a garrulous wife. Hoping for more communication, he had sought a different marital pattern from that of his primal family but he had been unprepared for a wife who insisted upon "sharing" everything. When he remarried he found himself very confused about how much to discuss with his second wife and her children. The new marriage represented less of a communication threat, but the memory of his painful experience in the previous marriage added to his hesitancy to pursue what he knew he wanted.

Unique to the blended family is the fact that the children, as well as the parents, have past family histories. Ways of relating to mother and to father have been established with strength of ties, expectations, and disappointments already known. Ordinal position has been established among siblings, with the expected advantages and disadvantages of each position already experienced. Certain memories have been treasured already. Role assignments (the "smart one," "scapegoat," "softee," "loner," etc.) have been made and acted upon. The security that comes with successful adaptation is likely to be weakened as children struggle to maintain behavior and values learned in the past. Even such relatively small changes as seating arrangement at the table may become traumatic because they conflict with past experience. Thus, Jane, a 4-year-old, who had always sat next to her mother before the second marriage, did not want her mother at the head of the table, even when her new father explained that that was how it was "always done." It had not been done that way in her earlier family!

Comparisons are inevitably made between two family patterns as the families engage in the blending process. Even when not verbalized, the expectation of comparison is there. Sexual adaptation is particularly vulnerable to the question, "Which was better?" Patterns of housekeeping, handling money, and, almost universally, disciplining children, draw comparisons. When the comparisons place the new partner in a favorable position, the task of reconstituting may be lightened. Occasionally, the positive comparison may represent an overidealization that can lead to disillusionment later. Adolescents, facing their own developing independence and sexuality, may take unkindly to remarriage except as it provides them more distance from the parent. The adolescent whose life task is to refine his or her self-definition is already faced with many choices. It may be easier for the adolescent to base these choices on experiences from the past than to watch the evolving patterns in the new marriage for boundary signals. There is a certain time-limited urgency to resolving adolescent issues that perhaps cannot wait for blending to take place.

Loyalty to past relationships may interfere with relationships in the blended family. Duberman (1975, p. 48) comments that "even in the case of widowhood the child is likely to maintain a relationship with the deceased biological parent. . . . " In Peter's case, it is a tribute to the honesty and forcefulness with which his mother faced and discussed the death of her 35-year-old first husband, that Peter was able to relate so readily to Mr. Rossi. Peter brought fond memories to the paternal relationship; he expected the same kind of loving attention his natural father had provided. A child of divorce who sees the missing natural parent may find it harder to accept the new parent because of a sense of disloyalty or of sorrow for the natural parent. One 7-year-old, upon being told of his divorced father's impending remarriage, replied, "I've got a mother and I don't need another one!" Not until he was well through adolescence did he describe the confusion he had always felt about having two mothers.

Loyalty to the natural parent within the home unit may also interfere with acceptance of the new parent. During the period of earlier loss of the natural parent the child may have drawn so close to the remaining parent that it becomes difficult to share that parent with the new spouse. The new parent may be seen as an intruder in the support system that parent and child had earlier offered each other.

LOSS

Whether through death or through divorce, loss of a significant adult has been experienced by the children and at least one parent in the blended family. They know one can be left, dismissed, abandoned; parents can disappear or leave a family. Loss through death may be more dramatic and clear-cut because of its finality. Once the mourning has been accomplished, family members are free to involve themselves with others. Yet the ghost of the departed person is likely to impede the firming of new family ties. Loss of a living parent may be total or partial. The parent with visiting rights simply is not around for routine comforting and the combative tasks of daily life. Children's needs cannot be scheduled to occur when the parent is available. The loss is thus one of natural and appropriate timing as well as of person.

Some process of mourning seems to be required in relinquishing the ties of daily living to the divorced as well as the deceased partner and parent. Sadness, introversion, and anger at being left are to be expected. Occasionally, a parent remarries before he or she has had time to pass through these stages, and the mourning continues into the second marriage. For example,

Sue Wallace remarried before experiencing the full extent of the fury she felt toward her divorced first husband; it came out as continual complaints about Tom Wallace. She was ready to dissolve her second marriage after six months. Her children, ready at first to accept their new father, withdrew when they saw their mother's displeasure. They could not risk losing another parent. Since Sue had not been able to complete the withdrawal of attachment to her first husband, there was no way in which her recent marriage could function. It was necessary that she first see her husbands as separate and different.

Children in a blended family may also continue to mourn the lost parent, making it impossible for them to engage with the new parent. After many years of drug rehabilitation, Bill, a young man of 19, was finally able to say to his father of five years, "I love you," and to ask for acceptance as a son, the role he had pursued repeatedly and unsuccessfully with his natural father. As long as he had been looking for an attachment to his natural father, Bill had been unable to relate to anyone in his new family except his familiar mother whom he was now sharing with four siblings after 14 years of being an only child.

Mourning for past relationships may be a long, drawn-out experience, especially when complicated by external factors. Joe Jenkins, a divorced father, married Marcia, a divorced mother of two teenage children. Joe's three children of his first marriage lived in a distant state with their mother and her new husband. Marcia was furious at her new husband's inability to involve himself with her children. These two precocious, provocative children were constantly defying both parents. Peace occurred for the Jenkins only when the children visited their father and his new wife on alternate weekends, but the kids usually came back complaining of boredom and disrupted the Jenkins' calm. In some ways, Marcia seemed to conspire with the children to exclude her husband. The children complained of their mother's vigilance over them and sent overtures to their new father to interfere. The more family members reached out to him, the more silent Joe became. Finally it emerged that he was still in mourning for his lost children who had been adopted by their new father and had severed communication with Joe. Unwittingly, he had been protecting himself from another loss by walling himself off from his new children with whom he urgently wanted and needed to be attached. Recognizing vulnerability to loss led to more overt efforts toward family cohesion. It took a long time and much testing before all were reassured that there was little likelihood of family dissolution.

Because of a wariness about family disruption, disagreements in the blended family may be exaggerated in importance. What starts out as simple bickering about household tasks may come to be seen as a prelude to divorce. In the case of loss through death, the resulting apprehension about illness may be such that each sickness is seen as potentially fatal. Thus, one child, whose natural father died of a heart attack as a young man, had unobtrusively but regularly checked her mother's breathing in the morning. This was never noticed until the mother remarried and the new father objected to the child's presence in the bedroom. At that point the behavior was more habit than meaningful. (One can speculate that watching might have been given new impetus by overheard sounds of intercourse, which young children tend to translate as aggressive sounds.)

Children in a blended marriage may push the parents to the limit in order to test the strength of the marital bond. Uncertainty of outcome can then be replaced by evidence pointing toward continuation or severance of relationships. Sometimes parents are so attuned to their children's sense of loss that they feel guilty and bend over backwards to protect them from any pain. The effect in a blended family is to stifle natural reactions, particularly those calling for aggressiveness or discomfort. A family that cannot express its irritations is in just as much trouble as one in which affections are not shown.

INSTANT FAMILY

Unlike the nuclear family, which starts with two and slowly grows, the blended family comes into existence as a ready-made unit of parents and children. It takes a single, short ceremony to put together a three-generational blended family. Peter's mother became a grandmother at her wedding. Peter's father became the father of nine. Peter became one of the younger children instead of the oldest in the family. Two new sets of grandparents were added, for Mr. Rossi's parents and the parents of his deceased wife were actively involved with the family. As a wife in a blended family commented face-tiously, "It takes a cast of thousands!" Ironically, the increase in number of relatives must be managed in even less time than that available to the smaller nuclear family. While wariness might be appropriate for the first year of a reconstituted family's life, no such luxury is possible. Too many details of living hinge on setting up family alliances. Blended family members are in a sink-or-swim position.

"His" and "her" children are commonly found in instant families. It is natural that, immediately following the loss of the original parent, the remaining family members draw closer together to close the boundaries of the family. Their past history as a family unites them. Yet the task of the blended family is to change the old boundaries and merge the members into one unit that is not readily divisible. The concept of "our" children calls, first of all, for a jelling of the marital bond and, second, for a willingness to deemphasize the earlier parent–child tie so that a new parent may share the pleasures and responsibilities. That this is hard to do can be deduced from the results of both Duberman's (1975, pp. 105, 112) and Messinger's (1976, pp. 186, 197) studies of blended families in which problems regarding children were found to occur more frequently than other difficulties. As Messinger (1976, p. 196) points out, this contrasts with the nuclear family in which "partners' immaturity" and sex are described as the leading problem areas.

It might be interesting to study whether families with greater tolerances for ambiguity—i.e., those who tolerate the uncertainties of family ties—delay the instant melding and follow more closely the gradual, evolving relations of the nuclear family. Does the family that tries to hold out against the instancy factor fare better or worse than the one that accepts the pressure to blend quickly? Surely, the age of the children will be important. Adolescents, trying to work their way to independence, may have an easier time if they cling to the fantasy of the family as it was and resist joining the new family too quickly. Younger children, with their stronger nurturing needs, may find safety in the instancy of new relations. This seemed to be the case for 12-year-old Peter.

Some instant families jell too slowly or too unevenly. One couple who believed themselves to be satisfied with each other found themselves constantly defending the 7-year-old children whom each had brought to the marriage. The boy from the husband's first marriage was seen by the wife as too raucous, mean, and irresponsible, and her son was seen by the husband as a busy-body and a sissy. The boys had no chance to become friends because the parents were so busy protecting each one of them separately. To the outside world and to their extended family, they represented the picture of a cohesive family unit, but to themselves they were living in past worlds. Discipline was irregular because the parents could not agree on their children's virtues and errors. A different set of rules seemed to apply to each child. Unfortunately, discipline issues are seldom dealt with in courtships; a couple may be totally unprepared to moderate differing values systems when faced, early in a marriage, with decisions regarding punishment and reward, which are in need of immediate implementation.

Changes in family structure may be dramatic and overwhelming. One grandmother, Mrs. Levine, felt she had lost her grandchildren when her son and his wife swapped partners with another couple. Her former daughter-in-law took the children to another part of town. Her son often brought her grandchildren's former playmates to the house as new grandchildren. She seldom saw the children she had grown to think of as her grandchildren and found it difficult to respond to her son's new children as if they were also grandchildren. Mrs. Levine prided herself on her tolerance and understanding of the partner change, but she had not glimpsed its far-reaching implications until she found herself an instant grandmother.

Physical boundaries are also instantly defined. One child, who had had her own room, suddenly gained two roommates when her new siblings moved in. Jane's spacious bedroom became so crowded that one had to enter sideways once the new beds and dressers were added. Toy space and closet space were lost. She was outnumbered in her own quarters. Personal possessions of two partial families joining may not only crowd: They may jar the senses. Consider Peter's reaction to his record-loving sister. His house was suddenly a noisy place. Food habits may abruptly need to be abandoned. Pets may be added or relinquished. It is no wonder that many blended parents find themselves moving to new locations within a year. Two families have been squeezed into the space of one: Part of the family serves as host family; the other has guest status.

The acquisition of an expanded family prompts realignments in dyadic and triangular relationships. For example, a divorced mother and her only child find their relationship weakened by the inclusion of a new man in the family. He finds his loving partner must be shared with a child. Children, like Peter and his brothers, who had been rivals, unite to find strength against their new siblings. One child sees the new sibling joyously as a companion, and the parent feels unwanted. Parents, happily in love, "neglect" their children. These are the types of adjustment that occur in any expanding family, but, in contrast to the instant family, there is a period of preparation when children are added through pregnancy. In addition, the parents have ordinarily had time to know each other intimately before they deal with children.

Instant family leads to instant cash outlay. Even where the actual amount of money spent is not greater for the blended family than it was for the two partial family units, attitudes toward the earning and use of money may be different. Apportioning and timing the use of income must take into account a larger number of people's needs. This was vividly illustrated in a situation in which a widowed woman and her two children joined the household of a divorced man and his three children. The couple were attracted to each other and believed that "two families could live as cheaply as one." The woman brought her welfare and social security payments to the home, and the man worked two separate jobs. Friction soon arose over the woman's complaints that she was used as a household drudge and the man's complaint that he could never use his hard-earned money for occasional self-indulgences. When they both found their positions to be untenable, the woman left with her two children. Two weeks later she returned to take the man's children with her because they had been so upset at losing their new found mother. For a brief period, before the couple aired their differences more successfully and decided to reunite, the woman had ended up with twice as many children to share her limited income. It had not been quite so easy and so practical after all to make an instant family.

FUTURE DIRECTIONS

In summarizing their review of the literature on remarriage after divorce, one set of authors commented: "Remarriage is a growing phenomenon for which its members are likely to be poorly prepared, due to inadequate institutionalization of this form of the nuclear family and to a divorce process which tends to place obstacles in the way of remarriage family organization" (Walker et al., 1977, p. 276). They point out that little attention and research have been directed to blended families and recommend the use of longitudinal studies as potentially the most useful way to understand them and their institutional needs (Walker et al., 1977, p. 285). It is my impression that it takes at least two years for a blended family to reconstitute itself. Significantly, almost all of the family experiences used herein as illustrations come from families experiencing their early years together.

Information on blended families is still at the impressionistic stage. Some work was done in the 1950s, but changes in social and sexual roles and in economic family structure have to a large extent invalidated those earlier findings.* In fact, while there is a renewed interest in blended families currently, the literature is still sparse.

One of the few attempts to establish guidelines for reconstituting families drew its sample from newspaper advertisements. Seventy remarried Canadian couples indicated that "they felt poorly prepared for the many problems they had encountered and in retrospect would have been grateful for consultation" (Messinger, 1976, p. 198). This led the authors to outline an educational program in preparation for remarriage, including discussions on the following:

1. Feelings related to first marriage and divorce.
2. Remarriage adjustment between the various persons involved.
3. Division of labor in the present marital household.
4. Perception of role relations.
5. Responsibilities of new partner.
6. Exchange of views between present couple on childrearing.
7. Feelings about financial arrangements.
8. Perceptions of what constitutes a "happy family life."
9. Feelings about continued relations between ex-spouse and kin.
10. Feelings about partner's children living with ex-spouse.
11. Recognition of difficulties related to time factor for privacy and instancy of relating (Messinger, 1976:198).

---

*The outstanding study of that period, Jessie Bernard's *Remarriage*, was reissued in 1971. Although Bernard's sample was large it was composed of relatives of college students and the results therefore could not be presumed to be valid for the population at large. (Duberman's sample is also self-selected). Cf. Bernard, 1956.

They also recommend legislative changes to relieve stress during separation, divorce, and remarriage.

Norms for the blended family are not yet established. Duberman compared characteristics of the traditional nuclear family and the reconstituted family to those of the ideal family. Of the 24 traits compared, the nuclear family was found to be partially similar in 17 characteristics, and the reconstituted family similar in 20 of the 24 characteristics. She felt there were "implications that in time the reconstituted family will become even more like the ideal type" (Duberman, 1975, pp. 130–131). Her assumption was in large part based on the self-consciousness of the blended families she studied and their strong wish to constitute themselves as viable, satisfying family units.

While the blended family may be distinguished as one in which all family members have a past history as family members, have experienced loss, and have faced the task of constituting a family in a collapsed time space, the actual experiences in blending a family are to an extent only exaggerations of some of the adaptational tasks of the nuclear family. A study of blended families may therefore offer insights into the nuclear family as well as into defining norms for the blended family. Sibling rivalry, generational differences, boundaries between parental and child units, and ties to the primal family are issues with which all families must involve themselves.

PRACTICE CONSIDERATIONS

In work with the blended family, it is necessary to go beyond the considerations basic to any therapeutic work with families. Their dilemma calls for particular attention to the effect on each member of past family memories, reactions to earlier loss of significant partner or parent, and the manner in which the need for instant adaptation has been handled. It is important that the family appreciate some of the positives of the earlier relationships. The past cannot be disregarded, and for some family members it may need to be validated as meaningful. The family therapist may take cues from the "bridging" efforts manifested by various family members when interventive strategies are developed to assist the family experiencing pain in blending.

In the meantime, oblivious of the concerns of family researchers and therapists, widowed and divorced parents remarry and blend the family units with combinations of joy, confusion, and pain.

REFERENCES

Bernard, J. *Remarriage*. New York: Dryden, 1956; reissued 1971.
Bohannan, P. Divorce chains, households of remarriage and multiple divorces. In Bohannan, P. (ed.), *Divorce and After*. Garden City, N.Y.: Doubleday, 1970.

Duberman, L. *The Reconstituted Family: A Study of Remarried Couples and Their Children.* Chicago: Nelson-Hall, 1975.

Messinger, L. Remarriage between divorced people with children from previous marriages: A proposal for preparation for remarriage. *Journal of Marriage and Family Counseling*, 1976, 2, 193–200.

National Center for Health Statistics. *Vital Statistics of the United States.* Washington, D.C.: U.S. Government Printing Office, 1977.

Walker, K.N., Rogers, J., & Messinger, L. Remarriage after divorce: A review. *Social Casework*, 1977, 58, 276–285.

section
II

PERSPECTIVES ON ETHNICITY AND THE FAMILY

For many years the literature pertaining to American families has been focused heavily on the white middle class. This inevitably gave rise to a limited portrayal of what was seen as "normal" family form and functioning. Those families that deviated from the stereotype came to be seen as defective in some way, as not meeting the standard. This stereotype has not only failed to take into consideration the life-styles of the families of ethnic minorities, it has actually proved inadequate in depicting altered contemporary middle-class family forms. In recent years this standard has been subjected to increasing scrutiny, and the literature has reflected a growing interest in investigating and describing varying social class and ethnic patterns. In keeping with this orientation, several chapters in Section II consider these issues, and others focus on selected ethnic minorities in order to sensitize the reader to the inherent richness and diversity of family life in this pluralistic society.

8

Families of Ethnic People of Color: Issues in Social Organization and Pluralism

Evelyn L. Barbee

Barbee is concerned about the family research of social scientists. She maintains that they have been blinded by fixed notions regarding an ideal family structure in the form of the white middle-class nuclear family. Because there is considerable variety in family forms among ethnic groups, large portions of these populations diverge from this ideal and have been found wanting. Social-science findings have been uncritically accepted and applied by practitioners who inevitably, then, found the stereotyped family structure, behavior, and pathology they anticipated. They have been prone to act therefore in ways that may serve both to undermine the integrity of families with whom they work and in fact to negate their own best efforts to be helpful. Barbee maintains that the multiple forms common among ethnic people of color have not only had a crucial adaptive purpose in their survival in a perpetual one-down position vis-à-vis the white majority, but are a sign of creativity and strength.

The major task of the social sciences is to examine various kinds of human experiences and then attempt to draw conclusions about them. The ultimate goal of these studies is to make generalizations or predictions with regard to how, why, and when human beings engage in specific types of behavior. As a social scientist, the approach of the sociocultural anthropologist involves the examination of social relations among individuals and groups in an effort to explain how social relations are related to and influenced by cultural beliefs. The idea of social relations implies the presence of both social units and social institutions. Studies of the family, a social unit that mediates among its members and the community, can provide social scientists with an opportunity to examine the relationship between a micro social unit (the family) and a macro social institution (the society). This paper examines the families of ethnic people of color* using the concepts of pluralism and social organization in order to explore some of the adaptations these families have used to survive in this plural society. Further discussion is devoted to two major concepts that have been used to explain the forms of family organization of ethnic people of color.

The society of the United States is composed of people from diverse ethnic and racial backgrounds. However, as Hall (1969, p. 183) points out: *"we have consistently failed to accept the reality of different cultures within our national boundaries."* This failure has resulted in a lack of understanding about ethnic groups in general and about ethnic groups of color in particular.

Gordon (1964, p. 27) defines an ethnic group as any "which is defined or set off by race, religion, or national origin, or some combination of these categories." According to the 1970 census, there are approximately 34 million ethnic people of color in the United States. This group includes approximately 23 million Afro-Americans, 9 million Spanish-surnamed people, 760,000 Native Americans, 586,000 Japanese Americans, 400,000 Chinese Americans, and 300,000 Filipinos (Department of Commerce, 1970a, pp. 593–595). The presence of these large numbers of ethnic people of color requires that any effort to understand family organization in the society as a whole take into account the diversity among cultural groups.

PLURALISM

As Bennedict (1962, p. 1235) notes, pluralism is a classificatory concept rather than an analytical one. For the purposes of this chapter, social pluralism and cultural pluralism need to be distinguished. Cultural pluralism refers to the presence of two or more cultural groups in a single society. Awareness of this concept sensitizes the observer to the existence of different ethnic cultures that have their own traditions, values, and life-styles.

Aspects of social and cultural pluralism in the United States include (1) the coexistence of several distinct ethnic and racial groups sharing a common economic system (making these groups interdependent), (2) interaction among the groups characterized by cleavages along ethnic and racial lines and differential incorporation of the various groups into the common political society, and (3) the groups' having a set of discrete institutional structures in other spheres of social life, notably the family and religion. The institutional structure with which we are concerned is that of the family.

---

*The phrase *ethnic people of color* is used in an effort to achieve more accuracy in identifying those groups that have been subjected to the most intense discrimination. This group includes all groups whose skin pigmentation contains "color": Asians, Afro-Americans, Native Americans, and Spanish-speaking people (Western Interstate Conference for Higher Education in Nursing, 1976).

SOCIAL ORGANIZATION

Although family form and structure differ widely in this country, only one form, the nuclear family, tends to be viewed as dominant. A nuclear family generally consists of wife, husband, and their offspring, living in relative isolation from the rest of their kin. Emphasis on the nuclear family has virtually ignored the fact that the "family" is not a monolithic unit about which one can make definitive statements. A much more viable approach would look at the family as a form of social organization with its own cultural and social dynamics. As Firth (1951, pp. 34–40) points out, the concept of social organization allows one to examine how the forms of basic social relations are capable of variation. It also makes possible an examination of continuity and variance as they are expressed in social relations and helps to explain the variance.

The advantage of viewing the family as a form of social organization is that it allows one to look at the settings (for example, political, social, economic) and the results of choice and decision as they affect activity and social relations. Any examination of the families of ethnic people of color should take into account the processes in operation between the family as a form of social organization and the plural society. Such an examination would more clearly reveal the adaptive responses of the micro social institution (the family) and the macro social institution (society).

FUNCTIONS OF THE FAMILY

The social system of a society is a complex of interrelated parts, and the family as one of these parts is functionally related to the other parts of the social system. As a group, the family is intermediate between the individual and the community. As such, the family reflects some of the functions of the larger community. Among the general functions of nuclear families are replacement of members, primary socialization, and the maintenance of motivation for participation in the society. Specific family functions include basic personality formation as well as conferral of status and management of tension for the individual (Bell & Vogal, 1968, pp. 7–34). The underlying assumption in this thesis is that the above functions can only be or are best met in the husband–wife–present family. Although many writers have stressed the socializing function of the family, little attention has been paid to the ways ethnic children of color are socialized by their families to deal with the plural society.* Moreover, little notice has been taken of the social

---

*Ladner (1972) is one of the few authors to look at the socialization of ethnic children of color to the plural society.

organization of these families and of how it may change in response to economic social changes. For example, in parts of Southern Africa, as a result of the migration of male labor, women have been making many decisions that were previously made by their husbands.

Many studies of ethnic people of color (Moynihan et al., 1965; Davis & Dollard, 1964; Drake & Cayton, 1962) have focused on what has been perceived as family disintegration: They have identified desertion, "illegitimacy," and "female dominance" as destructive characteristics typical of these families. A notable exception is Billingsley (1974, p. 19) who writes:

> Our mission is not simply to exist and certainly not simply to conform to what other families look like or do, but to produce competent individuals able to conquer some major aspects of our inner and outer environments in order to survive, perpetuate the race and make some contributions to the larger society.

In their effort to survive, these families have adapted their social organization in response to the social and economic changes in the plural society. As a result of these adaptations, many families have been labeled "disorganized," "broken," or "matriarchal" by social scientists because they deviate from the Anglo-American cultural ideal of the nuclear family.

ASSIMILATION

Assimilation is based upon the concept of acculturation. The process of acculturation usually occurs in a situation of superordinate-subordinate relationships between societies and groups. In the process, the weaker group is often obligated to acquire cultural elements from the dominant group. The wholesale borrowing of cultural traits usually comes about as a result of external pressure on the weaker group. In assimilation, the wholesale borrowing occurs to such an extent that the weaker group takes on the characteristics of the dominant one.

In writing about ethnic people of color, Kitano (1974, p. 275) proposes that their experiences and relationships with the dominant white majority fall into three different patterns: forced immigration (African slaves); voluntary immigration (the Asian groups, Puerto Ricans, and more recently Mexicans and Cubans); and groups overwhelmed and conquered (Native Americans, Chicanos, and Indochinese). He further suggests that, other things being equal, the voluntary immigrant makes an easier adjustment to American culture than do those whose contacts were of a different order. Unfortunately, he does not elaborate on what he means by "other things being equal." Voluntary immigrants have a difference in motivation toward "becoming American" and therefore have the most adaptable orientation (Kitano, 1974). Presumably, this motivation is based upon the fact that they willingly came to this country, whereas the forced immigrants and those who were overwhelmed and conquered have a more difficult time "becoming American."

Part of the adjustment to American culture required of all ethnic groups has been the expectation that they replace their cultural institutions with Western cultural forms. For many decades the nuclear family has been the preferred structural form in urban America. Deviance from this norm by the families of ethnic people of color has been "explained" by using the concepts of the "melting pot" and the "culture of poverty." Essentially, the melting-pot notion is based upon Anglo-American conformity, since it requires assimilation to Anglo-American cultural norms and institutions. The melting-pot concept virtually ignores the contribution of ethnic people of color to the society.

Although the process of acculturation and eventual assimilation has been required of all ethnic groups in this country, the means used to "facilitate" the assimilation of ethnic people of color have been particularly blatant. For example, Africans were enslaved, the Japanese were interned during World War II, and Native Americans have been subjected to pernicious legislation. The underlying intention of these acts has been to destroy the cultural beliefs and norms of these groups in order to replace them with those of the dominant majority. If a group is having difficulty assimilating to the culture of Anglo-America, then the culture of that group must be so strong and so pervasive that it interferes with assimilation. This is a major premise underlying the culture-of-poverty concept.

CULTURE OF POVERTY

The culture-of-poverty concept was originally proposed by the anthropologist Oscar Lewis. Like the notion of the melting pot, the concept of a culture of poverty influenced legislation that was ostensibly based upon helping the families of some ethnic people of color. The two groups usually discussed in this regard are Afro-Americans and large numbers of those whom the Census Bureau terms the "Spanish surnamed."

The concept of a culture of poverty is an attempt to understand poverty and its associated traits as a culture or subculture. According to Lewis (1970, p. 68), poverty has its own structure and rationale and, as a way of life, is passed down from generation to generation along family lines. In addition to identifying the societal conditions in which the culture of poverty flourishes, he delineates what he claims to be the major traits of the culture of poverty at the family level:

. . . absence of childhood as a specially prolonged and protected stage in the life cycle; early initiation into sex; free unions or consensual marriages; a relatively high incidence of abandonment of wives and children; a trend toward female or mother-centered families; and a much greater knowledge of maternal relatives; a strong predisposition to authoritarianism; lack of privacy; verbal emphasis on family rivalry, and competition for limited goods and maternal affection; a high incidence of maternal deprivation; a high incidence of orality; weak ego structure; confusion of sexual identification; lack of impulse control; strong present time orientation; relatively little ability to defer gratification and plan for the future; sense of resignation and fatalism; widespread belief in male superiority; and a high tolerance to psychological pathology of all sorts (Lewis, 1968, pp. 10–11).

Lewis initially proposed that improved economic opportunities would not be sufficient to alter the subculture of poverty because it has self-perpetuating mechanisms. He later modified his position by acknowledging the importance of the basic structure of the larger society in perpetuating poverty (Lewis, 1968, p. 180). However, the idea of a self-perpetuating culture of poverty appealed to many powerful people who used it to justify a series of discriminatory policies (Valentine, 1968, p. 75). As Hylan Lewis (1971, p. 363) points out, the idea of a culture of poverty matters to persons in applied fields and policy-making positions who are shopping for ideas and are primarily interested in the usefulness of the idea in shaping and implementing their programs.

Oscar Lewis' (1968) emphasis on the self-perpetuating mechanisms of the culture of poverty practically obscured the role of the dominant white society in the perpetuation of poverty. As a result, the poor became responsible for their own poverty (Valentine, 1968, p. 15). The *Moynihan Report*, with its emphasis on "the tangle of pathology," best exemplifies this position in its focus on self-perpetuating patterns of poverty in the family. For Moynihan (1965) the family became the independent variable that "caused" problems such as crime and delinquency. He went so far as to claim that "at the heart of the deterioration of the fabric of Negro society is the deterioration of the Negro family" (Moynihan, 1965, p. 5).

A theoretical framework that includes the concepts of pluralism and social organization provides us with a basis for better organization of information about the families of ethnic people of color. The next section of this chapter is devoted to an examination of the family forms of Native Americans and Afro-Americans in an attempt to illustrate how the social organization of their families has been modified as a result of social and economic changes in the plural society of the United States. Many of these adaptations in the social organization of the family have been basic to the surivival of these groups.

NATIVE AMERICANS

An important fact about attempting to force acculturation and eventual assimilation is that people cannot be swiftly remodeled to adapt to cultural patterns that are not in harmony with their ideals and aspirations. As a result of federal legislation that was ostensibly enacted in order to hasten the process of the assimilation of Native Americans, both the culture and the survival of Native Americans were placed in peril. For example, the General Allotment Act of 1887 (the Dawes Act) allowed the distribution of reservation land into individual allotments. Each family head was eligible for 80 acres of agricultural land or 160 acres of grazing land (Sorkin, 1978, p. 2). The underlying intent of this Act was to pressure the Native Americans into becoming individual farmers and thereby hasten their assimilation into white society. Since these farms were too small to generate an adequate income and because few Indians were interested in agriculture, most of the allotments were sold at low prices (Sorkin, 1978). As a result, by 1933 two-thirds of the Native American land base (91 million acres) passed into non-Native American hands.

Deloria (1969, p. 185) notes that culture is the expression of the essence of a people. This essence is composed of such things as language, knowledge, laws, and religious beliefs and generally refers to the customary ways of thinking and behaving that are characteristic of a particular people. How the essence of a Native American family is expressed in this pluralistic society depends upon the demographic, economic, and social setting in which one finds the family. In the United States there are members of more than 350 different tribes of Native Americans residing either in rural reservation communities or in urban areas.

In discussing contemporary plains reservation communities, Wax (1971, p. 75) points out that a reservation is not a unified nation composed of Native Americans speaking a common language and sharing many traits. The inhabitants of these rural settings see themselves first and foremost as members of bands of kith and kin. *Kith* can generally be defined as acquaintances, friends, and neighbors living within the same locality who form a more or less cohesive group. *Kin* refers to affinal (by marriage) and consanguineal (by blood) relatives. Although their family organization has been described as extended, the networks of kith and kin more accurately refer to the groups that have been essential to the survival of Native Americans since, within the networks of kith and kin are found the processes of sharing, voluntary cooperation, equality, and solidarity (Wax, 1971, p. 76). Because the central problem of most reservation communities is economic, the real unit of survival is neither the nuclear nor the extended family, but a complex of families that are most often situated quite close to each other (Wax, 1971, p. 80).

The importance of kin and kith for the Native American closely parallels what Hsu (1971, pp. 69–70) refers to as "social baggage." In writing about the Chinese, Hsu points out that the preexisting network of family and kinship has priority over other human ties, and the individual is not as free to move away from it as his or her counterpart in other cultures. When a person does move away from these ties, he or she finds it difficult to form new associations without reference to the old ones. Thus, a Chinese person may be seen as facing the world with a large amount of social baggage. The Native American has a similar network of preexisting human ties with which she or he can relate. The ethnocentric reference point of the nuclear family has made it extremely difficult for reformers to understand Native American kith and kin organizations. Therefore, one of the main targets for reformers has been to break up the patterns of obligations and sharing that form the basis for Native American kith and kin groups (Wax, 1971, p. 76). The significance of this strategy can best be appreciated if one recognizes that in the Native American world, to be without relatives is to be really poor (Backup, 1979, p. 22).

Within Native American families, individual freedom and independence are two highly valued attributes. Wax and Thomas (1961, p. 311). refer to the Native American's belief in the right of self-determination as the "ethic of non-interference." All behavior, from gentle meddling to outright meddling is defined by Native Americans as outside the realm of proper action (Wax and Thomas, 1961, p. 310). In effect this means that interference in the behavior or actions of one person by another is neither allowed nor tolerated (Backup, 1979, p. 22). The ethic of noninterference holds even when an individual is engaging in behavior that may be destructive to self or others (Wax & Thomas, 1961, p. 309). As Good Tracks (1973, p. 30) notes, the extent to which a Native American adheres to this ethic depends upon the degree of acculturation and assimilation of the individual.

Backup (1979, p. 22), in discussing the importance of kith and kin to Native Americans, points out that the two most important groups in the family are grandparents and children. According to tradition, the very old and the very young "are safe within the universe and carefully watched by the Great Spirit." Native Americans view children as assets to the family. In the rural reservation communities, the primary socializing agent of the Native American child is her or his peer group (Wax, 1971, p. 84). Although the concept of parenting may be extended throughout the adults in the kith and kin network, many times children in the rural reservation communities are reared by their grandparents because their parents have migrated to urban areas (Wax, 1971, p. 71). In their socialization, Native American children are encouraged to be independent (there are no rigid schedules for eating and sleeping) and patient and to behave in an unassuming manner (Backup, 1979, p. 22). Furthermore, they are taught that the family and tribe are of foremost importance. Grandmothers are very important, and the aged in general are looked to for wisdom and counsel. The aged occupy the important position of relating traditions, beliefs, and customs through the role of storyteller (Backup, 1979, p. 22).

Although the popular image of the Native American is that of a rural Western reservation dweller, at least three-quarters of this population lives in urban areas and in the eastern portion of the country (Deloria, 1969, p. 251). Like previous migrants to the city, Native Americans tend to cluster together residentially and to elaborate distinctive institutions that are neither traditional nor urban middle-class. The question of survival in the urban areas has led to the formation of institutions such as Indian Centers. These centers provide a place where Native Americans can meet peer-group members. In addition, traditional activities, such as basket weaving and powwows, take place in the Indian Centers. Institutions like these enable Native Americans, as a community, to create a meaningful existence in the urban environment.

Although the nuclear family form can be found among some rural Native Americans, generally this form is more common among those who reside in urban areas. A recent study of Native Americans suggests that families at home in both the Native American and white world have a greater ability to survive and adapt to the city than those who are not. Using a bicultural model, these researchers point out that the urban Native American who learns both white and Native American ways is "best able to maintain a strong sense of self-esteem and thus make a satisfactory adjustment to the city" (Native American Research Group, 1975, p. 56). These researchers also found that urban Native Americans attempt to complement traditional peer group friendship patterns by frequenting centers, parks, and common meeting places for Native Americans.

A major issue that is being addressed by urban Native Americans today is that of identity. The migration of people from diverse tribes to the urban areas has promoted the rise of pan-Indianism. Concomitant with pan-Indianism has been the evolution of a tri-level sense of self: that of being a tribal person, a Native American, and an individual human being (Native American Research Group, 1975, p. 56). This issue of identity has been the impetus for a variety of courses designed to teach the Native American the skills to survive in white society while maintaining her or his own identity.

Not all Native Americans in urban areas use uniquely Native American institutions in their attempts to cope with urban life. Some have adopted the nuclear-family form. For others, the urban environment presents insurmountable obstacles to family life, and portions of the family may have to return to the rural reservation. A third group is likely to have preserved strong attachments to their kith and kin in the reservation communities. As a result, they may journey to the reservation frequently and may send their children there during vacations from school (Wax, 1971, p. 71).

The family form of Native Americans, with its emphasis on a wide network of kin and kith, has enabled many tribes to survive despite efforts to destroy them in the name of acculturation and eventual assimilation. In a pluralistic society, the concern should not only be with full cultural sharing but also with cultural diversity. In a situation of cultural diversity, the success of both individual and family in acting in accordance with expectations depends not only on the beliefs, values, and skills adopted for self, but also on an awareness of those with whom the individual interacts (Hannerz, 1971, p. 184). For the Native American, this cultural diversity can best be seen in the variability of family forms.

AFRO-AMERICANS

There has been a selective focus on the negative aspects of Afro-American family life because scholars do not seem to be interested in the Afro-American family as an institution in its own right (Billingsley, 1968, p. 197). In addition there seems to be little recognition that the study of these families can shed light upon American society in general. The essence of the general charge against the Afro-American family has been that the family is at least partially responsible for the economic, social, and personal problems faced by Afro-Americans in this society (Heiss, 1975, pp. 5–6). Since Billingsley brought attention to this selective focus on Afro-American family life, several works (Ladner, 1972; Staples, 1971; Hill, 1972) have been published in order to counteract the previous bias in the studies of these families.

Controversy remains as to whether Afro-Americans have their own unique culture and hence a distinctive family organization; some hold that the norms and values that Afro-Americans hold are simply a reflection of social class factors. For example, Glazer and Moynihan (1965, p. 33) state: "It is not possible for Negroes to view themselves as other ethnic groups viewed themselves because . . . the Negro is only an American and nothing else. He has no values and culture to guard and protect."* On the other hand, Herskovitz (1958) argues that many "Africanisms" survived slavery and are to be found in the present life-styles of Afro-Americans, including family structure, religion, music, dance, and the arts. A more balanced viewpoint is presented by Billingsley (1968, pp. 8–10) who, while noting that social class is a powerful dimension that helps to determine the condition of life for Afro-American families, also points out that the concept of ethnic subsociety helps to explain many of the commonalities of Afro-Americans in general.

---

*In the second edition of *Beyond the Melting Pot*, Glazer edits this passage to read "He bears no foreign values and cultures that he feels the need to guard from the surrounding environment" (1970, p. 53).

The debate as to whether an Afro-American subculture exists has only relative importance. The position taken in this chapter is that Afro-American families should be viewed as forms of social organization with their own cultural dynamics. The social organization of these families adapts to economic and social changes in the American plural society. This position allows one to better understand the differences in Afro-American family form.

For the most part, the literature about Afro-American families has concentrated on the female-headed household. As a result, there has been an erroneous impression that the majority of Afro-American families are female-headed. In reality, publications like the *Moynihan Report* only deal with one-quarter of Afro-American families. Furthermore, these families have been characterized as "broken" and "unstable." For most social scientists, the term *stability* implies a situation where both husband and wife are present (Scanzoni, 1971, p. 3). The term *broken* usually refers to father absence in a family; *attenuated* would be a better term simply because it means that someone important to the family constellation is missing (Billingsley, 1968, p. 19). Thus, *attenuated* would refer to situations in which either of the biologic parents or parental surrogates is missing from the family.

In discussing the female headed attenuated family (Hill, 1972, p. 21) suggests that the self-reliance of Afro-American women as primary breadwinners exemplifies their adaptability in family roles. Unfortunately, this position comes perilously close to the stereotype of the Afro-American woman as a matriarch. As Ladner (1972, pp. 41–42) states:

> In recent years the Black woman has almost become a romantic, legendary figure in this society because the vast conceptions of her as a person are largely dictated by these stereotypes. The idea that she is almost super-human, capable of assuming all major responsibilities for sustaining herself and her family through harsh economic and social conditions has been projected in much of the popular as well as academic research.

Furthermore, the representation of single-parent families as "broken" and "unstable" tends to deal with these families as though they are "nonfamilies" (Herzog, 1966, p. 9). These negative views of the female-headed family lend support to the position that somebody should do something to make sure that all Afro-American children are put into families headed by males.

Few works point out the adaptability of Afro-American men in family roles. Billingsley (1968, p. 25) comments:

> It is not at all uncommon for Negro men to engage in expressive functions with respect to the maintenance of family solidarity and to help with child rearing and household tasks. Researchers have found Negro men to be more helpful around the house than a sample of white men, *but they have chosen to give this fact a negative reading.* [Emphasis added.]

One can seriously question these negative interpretations. Perhaps these social scientists make these evaluations because they do not view the fulfillment of expressive functions in the family as a culturally legitimate role for males. To suggest that a family is inevitably stable and organized when the male is present is equally questionable.

Dichotomizing male- and female-headed families ignores the number of variations that exist among Afro-American families. Three basic forms of Afro-American family organization have been identified: nuclear, extended, and augmented (Billingsley, 1968, pp. 16–21). These are further subclassified into 12 basic forms that depend upon the presence or absence of either household head and other household members, including children, other relatives, and nonrelatives. Essentially, these adaptations can be viewed as responses to social and economic changes in the pluralistic society. Two forms of particular interest are the extended and the augmented.

Billingsley (1968, p. 20) describes four classes of relatives who may reside together in extended Afro-American families: (a) grandchildren, nieces, nephews, cousins, and young siblings under 18; (b) peers of the parents, for example, siblings, cousins, and other adult relatives; (c) elders of the parents, for example, aunts and uncles; (d) parents of the family heads. The length of time that a relative may live with the family is variable and is often dependent on the reason that the individual came there. The authority structure of the family may shift considerably, depending on the status of the relative who moves in.

Martin and Martin (1978, p. 6) are two of the few social scientists to explore the social organization of the extended family. These authors suggest that the extended family has four defining characteristics: (a) It is comprised of four generations of relatives; (b) it is headed by a dominant family figure to whom the other members look for leadership in holding the family together; (c) it is interdependent in that relatives depend upon each other for emotional, social, and material support; (d) the dominant family figure always resides in the extended family's base household (this base is usually the center of extended-family activities).

From their study of Afro-American extended families, Martin and Martin (1978, p. 8) suggest that what may appear to be a nuclear family may in actuality be a subextension of an extended family base. Therefore, a family with a missing parent is not necessarily a "broken home" but may, in fact, be a vital part of a viable extended family (Martin & Martin, 1978, p. 9).

Although there has been little written about the extended-family form, even less reference has been made to augmented families. Essentially, augmented families are those that have unrelated individuals living with them as roomers, boarders, lodgers, or other relatively long-term guests. In 1970 there were 361,219 Afro-American families who had nonrelatives living with them (Department of Commerce, 1970b, p. 154). Often these unrelated persons exert major influence on the social organization of the family.

How the social organization of a family adapts to the social and economic changes in the plural society is closely related to the dynamics of the cultural group. For example, several authors (Stack, 1974; Hill, 1972; Billingsley, 1968) illustrate the kinship networks of Afro-Americans and how these are used, particularly in terms of crisis. The importance of kinship to Afro-Americans is exemplified by the number of fictive kin terms in an Afro-American community. Thus, one can find reference to a wide range of "play" relatives, for example, "play mother," "play sister," "play brother," etc. Each of these terms refers to a status and identifies the relationship between the speaker and the person being addressed. The classification of a friend as a kinsperson is accompanied by respect and responsibility (Stack, 1974).

These forms of Afro-American families can be seen as adaptations to changes in the plural society. It has been these adaptations to social organization that have allowed the Afro-Americans to survive as a group. In the face of oppression and sharply restricted economic and social support, the Afro-American family has proved to be a very resilient institution. As Martin and Martin (1978, p. 100) point out, the extended family is a powerful mechanism for meeting basic needs and providing its individual members with a sense of solidarity. As the dominant white majority in this plural society continues to deny opportunities for Afro-Americans to become full participants in its economy, the extended family remains a meaningful unit in sustaining its members.

IMPLICATIONS FOR HEALTH AND SOCIAL-CARE PRACTITIONERS

There are multiple implications for health and social-care practitioners working with families of ethnic people of color. Social scientists' goals of generalization and prediction have produced a myriad of problems in that, in essence, these goals have been propagated in the literature as though they were absolute truths. In reality, these same generalizations and predictions have been based upon inadequate data (as in the case of many studies on Afro-American families) and knowledge (as in the case of studies of Native Americans). Health and social-care practitioners have compounded these problems by reading this literature and then attempting to apply faulty findings to the families of ethnic people of color.

The first conclusion that can be drawn from the discussion in this chapter is that there is no one family form that is applicable to all Native Americans and all Afro-Americans. Quite obviously, if one is to find out the type of organization in a given family, it is necessary to ask questions as to who are to be seen as the significant members. Second, although the nuclear family may be viewed as the ideal form for the social and health-care practitioner, it may not be ideal for the clients. Cultural sensitivity combined with an intellectual awareness of the impact of the plural society on ethnic people of color will give the practitioner an understanding of the different types of family organization found among these peoples. Third, in regard to Native American families, *if* they endorse the ethic of noninterference, there are questions as to how far a practitioner can expect to intervene. Knowledge of the ethic of noninterference can alert the worker as to what to expect in relationships with Native American families. As Good Tracks (1973, p. 33) notes, practitioners must not intervene in family problems unless they are requested to do so. With regard to working with Native Americans in general, Good Tracks suggests that the one virtue that the worker must possess is patience.

Unfortunately, since most of the literature focuses upon pathology in Afro-American families and reinforces stereotypes of the Native American, social and health-care practitioners have tended to look for (and therefore find) the pathologic and stereotypic instead of the positive characteristics of these groups. All family forms have their strengths and their limitations. Since the presumed weaknesses of Afro-American and Native American family organization have been widely publicized, perhaps it is now time for those who have helped to perpetuate these emphases to begin to work with and publicize their strengths.

SUMMARY

In this chapter the concepts of pluralism and the family as a social organization have been used to explore some of the adaptions that ethnic people of color have used to survive in this society. A classificatory concept like pluralism calls attention to the fact that a society can be characterized by cultural diversity and social cleavage. In the United States, this social cleavage is based in part upon ethnic and racial lines.

Within our plural society, ethnic and racial groups are differentially incorporated into the mainstream of society. Because of this, the task for many ethnic people of color has been survival. In order to enhance their chances for survival, the basic institution, the family, has adapted to the economic and social changes.

The concepts of acculturation, assimilation, and culture of poverty do not account for the effects that the plural society has had upon the families of ethnic people of color, nor do they deal with the adaptations that the social organization of the family undergoes in response to social and economic changes in the society. The types of adaptations made by these families are highly dependent on the cultural dynamics of the particular group under discussion.

Some groups have been more willing to assimilate to Western culture than others. But, at the same time, others are questioning whether the nuclear family can meet many of the common human needs for both emotional and financial security. For example, Spencer (1965, p. 506) writes: "Indians believe that they can function with competence in modern society as *Indians*." Ironically, Afro-Americans have begun forming nuclear families in significant numbers while, at the same time, nuclear-family life is deteriorating in the white community (Martin & Martin, 1978, p. 100). To paraphrase Billingsley (1974, p. 19), regardless of preferred family form, the mission of ethnic people of color in this country is not simply to exist and certainly not to conform to what other families look like or do, but to produce competent individuals.

REFERENCES

Backup, R. Implementing quality care for the American Indian patient. *Washington State Journal of Nursing* (Special Suppl.), 1979, 20–24.
Bell, N., & Vogel, E. A *Modern Introduction to the Family* (rev. ed.). New York: The Free Press, 1968.
Bennedict, B. Stratification in plural societies. *American Anthropologist*, 1962, 64, 1235–1246.
Billingsley, A. *Black Families in White America.* Englewood Cliffs, N.J.: Prentice-Hall, 1968.
Billingsley, A. *Black Families and the Struggle for Survival.* New York: Friendship, 1974.
Davis, A., & Dollard, J. *Children of Bondage.* New York: Peter Smith, 1964.
Deloria, V. *Custer Died for Your Sins.* New York: Avon, 1969.
Drake, St. C., & Cayton, H.R. *Black Metropolis.* New York: Harper & Row, 1962.
Firth, R. *Elements of Social Organization.* London: Watts, 1951.
Glazer, N., & Moynihan, D.P. *Beyond the Melting Pot.* Cambridge, Mass.: MIT Press, 1965.
Good Tracks, J.G. Native American non-interference. *Social Work*, 1973, 18, 30–34.
Gordon, M. *Assimilation in American Life.* New York: Oxford University Press, 1964.
Hall, E.T. *The Hidden Dimension.* Garden City, N.Y.: Anchor, 1969.
Hannerz, U. The study of Afro-American cultural dynamics. *South Western Journal of Anthropology*, 1971, 27, 181–201.
Heiss, J. *The Case of the Black Family: A Sociological Inquiry.* New York: Columbia University Press, 1975.
Herskovitz, M. *The Myth of the Negro Past.* Boston: Beacon Press, 1958.
Herzog, E. Is there a breakdown of the Negro family? *Social Work*, 1966, 11, 3–10.
Hill, R.B. *The Strengths of Black Families.* New York: Emerson Hall, 1972.
Hsu, F.L.K. *The Challenge of the American Dream: The Chinese in the United States.* Belmont: Wadsworth, 1971.
Kitano, H.H.L. *Race Relations.* Englewood Cliffs, N.J.: Prentice-Hall, 1974.
Ladner, J.A. *Tomorrow's Tomorrow: The Black Woman.* Garden City, N.Y.: Anchor, 1972.
Lewis, H. Culture of poverty? What does it matter? In E. Leacock (ed.), *The Culture of Poverty: A Critique.* New York: Simon & Schuster, 1971, 345–363.
Lewis, O. Book review of Valentine's 1969 Culture and Poverty: Critique and counter proposals. *Current Anthropology*, 1969, 10, 189–192.

Lewis, O. *Anthropological Essays*. New York: Random House, 1970.

Martin, E.P., & Martin, J.M. *The Extended Black Family*. Chicago: University of Chicago Press, 1978.

Moynihan, D.P., Ballon, P., & Broderick, E. *The Negro Family: The Case for National Action*. Washington, D.C.: Office of Policy Planning and Research, U.S. Department of Labor, 1965.

Native American Research Group. *Native American Families in the City: Final Report, American Indian Socialization to Urban Life*. San Francisco: Institute for Scientific Analysis, 1975.

Scanozi, J.H. *The Black Family in Modern Society*. Boston: Allyn and Bacon, 1971.

Sorkin, A. *The Urban Indian*. Lexington, Mass.: Heath, 1978.

Spencer, R.F., Sennings, S.D., et al. *The Native Americans*. New York: Harper & Row, 1965.

Stack, C.B. *All Our Kin: Strategies for Survival in a Black Community*. New York: Harper & Row, 1974.

Staples, R. (ed.). *The Black Family: Essays and Studies*. Belmont, Calif.: Wadsworth, 1971.

U.S. Department of Commerce. *Census of the Population: Characteristics of the Population* (Vol. 1, Part 1). Washington, D.C.: Government Printing Office, 1970 (a).

U.S. Department of Commerce. *Census of Population Subject Reports: Persons by Family Characteristics*. Washington, D.C.: Government Printing Office, 1970 (b).

Valentine, C. *Culture and Poverty: Critique and Counter Proposals*. Chicago: University of Chicago Press, 1969.

Wax, M. *Indian Americans: Unity and Diversity*. Englewood Cliffs, N.J.: Prentice-Hall, 1971.

Wax, R.H., & Thomas R.K. American Indians and white people. *Phylon*, 1961, 22, 305–317.

Western Interstate Council for Higher Education in Nursing. Position paper: The phrase ethnic people of color. 1976.

9

The Black Family: Poverty and Health Care

Wilma Watts

Family functioning is a complex phenomenon that can be understood from a variety of vantage points. The individual capacities of each member, the interaction of the family as a group, or the cultural context within which families interact may assume differential importance to students of the family, depending on their orientation. In this chapter, Watts addresses the last of these as she examines the impact of poverty on the health status of black families in the United States. She identifies several critical health problems, seeing them as directly related to the economic and social deprivation experienced by a major proportion of the black population. She challenges the practice of "blaming the victim," a means of holding the sufferer responsible for his misfortune, and proposes instead that poverty, low social status, and institutional racism have caused the dilemmas confronting this minority group. Solutions to these problems require changes in health-care planning and policies and can be brought about only through the joint efforts of professionals and black consumers. Although this theme is not new to the family literature, it bears reexamination in light of the fact that the problems addressed yield slowly to change in a society in which the victims occupy a largely disenfranchised status.

In 200 years, the health status of blacks relative to that of whites has gone virtually unchanged. The health of black Americans continues to lag far behind that of their white counterparts. To gain a better understanding of this phenomenon, it would seem worthwhile to examine the organization and behavioral patterns of the black family, and to determine whether family structure affects the family's capabilities for meeting its health-care needs. Features of the contemporary health-care system that hinder black families in caring for health on their own, as well as jointly with health professionals, can also be identified.

The experiences of black Americans in this country differ from those of dominant groups and other minority groups. Blacks are unique because of their history of enslavement.* Slavery was responsible for establishing a caste system that relegated blacks to an inferior status. Since the Civil War, black people have been constantly striving for equal rights. There has been an overwhelming migration from Southern rural areas to Northern industrial cities. This migration has occurred in an attempt by blacks to better their social and economic conditions. In Northern cities the majority of blacks have found themselves forced to live in ghettos and faced with long periods of unemployment. They still must contend with discrimination, insult, segregation, the threat of violence, and poverty.

From the breakup of the black family during slavery to the urbanization of black people in the 1970s, black family life has been in a constant process of change. An analysis of the family structure of blacks gives evidence of the adaptations made to the social and economic conditions encountered (Gutman, 1976).

THE BLACK FAMILY IN THE 1970s: DEMOGRAPHIC CHARACTERISTICS

As of March 1975 there were approximately 23.8 million black people in the United States, constituting 11 percent of the total population. A majority of black families (61 percent) had a husband and wife present; 35 percent had a woman as the head. Three-quarters of the black population lived in metropolitan areas and three-fifths in central cities within these areas (Bureau of the Census, 1976, p. 37). The average black family earned less money than the average white family although the average black family was larger. The average size of all black families in 1975 was 3.90 persons while that of all white families was 3.32 (Bureau of the Census, 1977, p. 83). The median income for black families was $7800 in 1974, compared to a median income of $13,400 for white families. Twenty-three percent of the black families had incomes under $4000 (Bureau of the Census, 1975, p. 24). These low income levels were the result of low paying jobs and unemployment. Representation in the professions and in some skill areas was proportionately small, and unemployment continued to be a major problem for black Americans. Fifteen percent of blacks 16 years old and older in the civilian labor force in March 1975 were unemployed (Bureau of the Census, 1976, p. 37).

Black families have been less likely than white families to own their own

---

*For more extensive information on this subject see for example Bennett (1969); Gutman (1976).

homes. In 1973, 43 percent of all black families owned their homes, as compared to 67 percent of white families (Bureau of the Census, 1975, p. 134). As might be expected, because of the low income levels, black households were less likely to have most major appliances. Refrigerators, kitchen ranges, and television sets were the three most common appliances in black households in the fall of 1973. One-half of them (51 percent) contained washing machines, as compared to nearly three-quarters (71 percent) of white households. Few blacks (16 percent) had clothes dryers, while one-half of white families (52 percent) had these appliances. Finally, only slightly more than one-half of black households (57 percent) owned an automobile, while more than four-fifths of white households (84 percent) did (Bureau of the Census, 1975, p. 139).

CONTROVERSIAL ISSUES REGARDING THE BLACK FAMILY

The study of black family structure has been characterized by distortions and misunderstandings. Most discussions of black families in the literature tend to focus on problems, thus creating the false impression that deviant behavior is characteristic. It is widely believed, for example, that the black community is characterized by a high percentage of female-headed families. Approximately one-third of all black families are headed by females; such families represent a minority. In the vast majority of black families, as in white families, the egalitarian or patriarchal patterns of family life are found (Middleton & Putney, 1960). The matriarchal pattern, with dominance vested in the female, is found mainly in the poorest black families. As soon as blacks achieve middle-class status, their family patterns become similar to those of economically comparable white families. Differences in patterns of family life between blacks and whites are largely a result of economic factors.

Regardless of the fact that a matriarchal pattern is found in a minority of black families, social scientists have focused on the "pathology" of families headed by women. Although two-parent families are preferred to one-parent families in American society, there is no justification for assuming that all two-parent families function "positively" or that all one-parent families function "negatively."

In March 1965 the Office of Policy Planning and Research of the Department of Labor issued a controversial report entitled *The Negro Family: The Case for National Action*, compiled by Daniel P. Moynihan, then Assistant Secretary of Labor. In this report, Moynihan stated: "At the heart of the deterioration of the fabric of Negro society is the deterioration of the Negro family. It is the fundamental source of weakness of the Negro community at the present time" (Department of Labor, 1965, p. 5). One of the allegations to support the charge held that almost one-fourth of all Negro families were headed by females. Other allegations were as follows: (1) "Nearly a quarter of urban Negro marriages are dissolved," (2) "Nearly one-quarter of Negro births are now illegitimate," and (3) "The breakdown of the Negro family has led to a startling increase in welfare dependency." The differences in interpretation of the figures documented led to a variety of opinions regarding this report. In looking at the rise in divorce and illegitimacy rates for blacks and whites, a case could be made for stating that "all" American families were deteriorating (Ryan, 1965). It was Moynihan's assumption, however, that the roots of black social and economic problems are embedded in the family structure of black people. He alleged that "weakness" of the black family was a "cause" of inequality; in other words, the black individual was trained to be poor by his culture and family life. The implication is, then, that efforts to end poverty and discrimination would be futile. This document is a classic illustration of the ideology of "blaming the victim."

Blaming the victim, according to William Ryan, involves identifying a social problem, studying those affected, and determining how they are different from the dominant group. The differences, then, are defined as the cause of the social problem itself. Finally, government intervention occurs through the invention of a "humanitarian action program to correct the differences" (Ryan, 1971, p. 8). Factors such as institutional racism tend to be ignored when the black family is focused upon as the cause of racial inequality. Institutional racism has been defined as:

> . . . the operating policies, priorities, and functions of an on-going system of normative patterns which serve to subjugate, oppress, and force dependence of individuals or groups by: (1) establishing and sanctioning unequal goals; and (2) sanctioning inequality in status as well as in access to goods and services (Ladner, 1972:265).

The dynamics of institutional racism have been responsible for both the strengths and weaknesses of the black family. The weaknesses of alleged deviant behavioral patterns have been blamed on blacks themselves, rather than on the overt and covert expressions of institutional racism that produced these behavioral adaptations.

The matriarchal pattern of family life found in poor black families results from poverty and not from "culture." There is no available evidence that family structure is inherited. Certainly, under slavery the mother-child unit tended to be the functional family, but each generation of black families has been subjected to economic and social stresses, and a variety of behavioral patterns has emerged as a flexible adaptation to these stresses. Differences in family patterns can more logically be related to conditions of poverty and unemployment. For instance, it has been found that the lower the income level, the higher the proportion of men living apart from their wives (Farley, 1970, p. 179). Periods of rising unemployment have correlated to time periods when the number of broken families was rising (Moynihan, 1970, p. 307).

Other significant factors contributing to the number of fatherless families include premature deaths of black males and illegitimate births. Nonwhite males between the ages of 15 and 44 have twice as great a chance of dying as white males have in that age group. (Bureau of the Census, 1975, p. 124). In this age range most of those who die leave children behind. This is hardly a cultural tendency but rather the result of poor physical and social health. Death rates are largely attributable to inadequate health care, although death rates attributable to homicide increased between 1970 and 1973.*

Some reasons for the high rates of illegitimacy among blacks include less use of birth-control methods (including abortion), differences in reporting, and the unemployed status of the father (Herzog, 1970, p. 336). Again, we see evidence of institutional racism in that the "problem" is the result of discrimination and poverty. Illegitimacy has been used as one of several indications of black-family breakdown. However, fatherless families can be an adaptation to poverty and may exhibit strengths of their own. Studies have shown that the extent of support or rejection by family members and relatives is a crucial factor in the effective functioning of the parent. Hill (1972, p. 24) reports a study indicating that support from the extended family was more likely to be found among blacks than among whites in families with illegitimate children. Thus it cannot be assumed that families headed by black women will function in a pathologic manner.

HEALTH STATUS OF THE BLACK FAMILY †

The health picture for black Americans is not a good one. The trouble begins during pregnancy. Prenatal care is received in the first three months of pregnancy by only 52 percent of pregnant black women, as compared with 75 percent of pregnant white women (HEW, 1975, p. 158). This situation contributes to the fact that mortality rates are two-thirds higher for black infants than for white ones. Rates are higher when the mother is poor or poorly educated, when the birth is illegitimate, or when the mother is under 20 or over 35 years old (HEW, 1975, p. 158). White children are more likely

---

*The death rate by homicide in white males remained constant during that period (Bureau of the Census, 1975, p. 125).

†Data on the black population in the United States are often combined with those of other "nonwhite" minorities. Since blacks constitute about 90 percent of this group, "nonwhite" and "black" are frequently used interchangeably. The figures quoted here will be deduced from the nonwhite categories.

than black children to be protected against such diseases as polio, diphtheria, typhoid, whooping cough, and measles (HEW, 1975, pp. 274–281). The average number of visits to a dentist is higher for white children than for black children (HEW, 1975, p. 422).

In the age group 17 to 44, twice as many persons in all American families with incomes under $5000 have some limitation in physical mobility because of poor health (HEW, 1975, p. 496). In many families a low income level is the direct result of illness. In the next age group, 45 to 64, the rate of persons with limitations of mobility due to chronic illness or injury is almost twice as high among blacks as among the white population (HEW, 1975, p. 496). The chronic illnesses referred to include arthritis and rheumatism, heart conditions, and impairment of lower extremities.

FACTORS CONTRIBUTING TO POOR HEALTH

In the literature the health-care functions of families have been neglected. As with many functions formerly performed by families, over recent decades health-care functions have been absorbed by specialized agencies. All families in the United States are highly dependent on the health-care system for services. Family failures in health care are largely due to defects in the organization and services of the health-care system itself.

All Americans face obstacles to health care; the poor find it especially difficult. Black Americans are particularly disadvantaged since they consti-tute a disproportionately large segment of the poor. In analyzing why the black family suffers from poor health, the pitfall of blaming the victim must be avoided. It is easy to say that poor health is "their own fault" because of certain "cultural" attitudes toward health that hinder the effectiveness of health services. The facts are very plain. The poor are less healthy because they cannot afford to buy health. In 1973 black persons were less likely than white persons to have visited a physician. The number of visits to a physician was associated with the income level of black families. Black persons with lower family incomes were less likely to have made such a visit and were more likely to have received care in an out-patient clinic or emergency room rather than in the physician's office (Bureau of the Census, 1975, p. 127).

The principal means by which most Americans assure themselves access to health services is through health-insurance coverage. For black persons such coverage varies substantially by income level. In 1972 about three out of five blacks had hospital-insurance coverage, as compared to four out of five whites. Only 31 percent of blacks with an income under $5000 had hospital insurance, while 85 percent of blacks with incomes of $10,000 and over had coverage (Bureau of the Census, 1975, p. 127).

The differences between the experiences of the poor person who is sick and the middle-class person who is sick have been documented. First, it is more difficult for a poor person to get admitted to a hospital. The poor person generally has no private physician to smooth the way. In addition, the poor person is not a good financial risk as he or she may not be covered by insurance and usually has no assets. Second, when the poor person does get admitted, the care received is inferior. Treatment is by medical students, interns, and residents who often function with little supervision. Care is usually obtained in a city or county hospital where staffing problems exist, and the poor person is usually placed in a ward situation with little privacy.

The black poor are often exploited by being uninformed subjects of medical research. In this country it has been established that every individual has the right to informed consent before being used as a research subject. Gray (1975, p. 139), in his investigation of the use of human beings as experimental subjects, found that the more dissimilar the subjects were from the physicians they saw, the more likely they were to be unaware of the research. He found that all clinic patients were more likely to be unaware of the research at the time their participation began than were private patients. Black clinic patients were more likely to be unaware than white clinic patients, and none of the physicians involved was black. These findings indicate that the greater the social distance between the physician and the prospective subject, the greater the problem of communication. It must be emphasized that the responsibility for the effective communication of material necessary to informed consent rests with the investigator, not with the subject.

Other factors in the health-care system that contribute to poor health care are related to the small number of blacks in the health professions. Only 2.2 percent of all doctors and 2.3 percent of all dentists are black; blacks constitute 7.5 percent of all registered nurses (HEW, 1975, p. 111). Due to the paucity of black medical doctors, less than one-fourth of black patients are able to receive medical care from black physicians. This situation is a result of individual and institutional racism in the system of education in the United States. Institutional racism is evident in the way medicine is learned and practiced. Blacks are poorly represented in the student bodies and on the faculties of professional schools. White students' contacts with blacks most frequently occur in the clinical situation. They get their training by practicing on the hospital ward or with clinic patients who are generally black. Later, their medical practice is largely comprised of white, paying clientele.

Employment and promotional procedures in hospitals tend to result in underrepresentation of blacks at higher administrative levels and overrepresentation of blacks at lower levels. Twenty-five percent of all nurse aides, orderlies, and attendants in hospitals are black (HEW, 1975, p. 112). Blacks, then, have little representation and control in the health-care field. Because they do not participate in decision making, allocation of resources is rarely in the direction of meeting the needs of black people as they themselves perceive them. Absence of the black perspective results in an insensitivity to the black experience.

WHAT CAN BE DONE?

To improve the health status of blacks, changes are needed both within the family and within the health-care system. It would seem that all families have the principal responsibility for initiating and coordinating services provided them by health professionals. Black families, however, generally have very limited linkage to the organizations and resources of the broader community; thus they are poorly equipped to develop their capabilities for meeting their personal health-care needs. Many patients do not go to white doctors or to traditional health-care agencies, fearing that they will not be treated with dignity and courtesy. They rely on patent medicines and home remedies. Early symptoms of disease are not recognized as clients have had very limited education in the detection of illness. Black families can, however, begin to accept more responsibility for their own health. For example, the fact that diet is directly and indirectly related to most major illnesses, including heart disease and hypertension, cannot continue to be disregarded. Efforts can be made to change eating habits within the confines of the family food budget. Family members can become more assertive in demanding explanations for whatever is done for or to them by any health worker. Efforts can be directed toward gaining more control over their own destinies and toward diminishing reliance on health professionals as well as on the health-care system as it exists.

In order to be effective, blacks must unite to attack problems of discrimination in health-care delivery and to increase their representation in the health field. Black professionals in the various health disciplines have an obligation to take the lead in the struggle to improve the health status of all blacks.

The health-care system must recognize its failure to meet the needs of this segment of the population. New patterns for the delivery of health care are needed, emphasizing prevention and early detection rather than crisis intervention. Neighborhood health centers and family-care teams are examples of efforts to distribute services more effectively. Neighborhood health centers are out-of-hospital institutions for medical care of the poor established under the Office of Economic Opportunity. Medical as well as social-welfare services are readily accessible, provided by a team of doctors, nurses, social workers, and health educators. A program of preventive medicine and health promotion using local health aides is included (Singley & Plaut, 1974, p. 13); clients participate in ways other than as patients, thus acquiring the necessary experience to initiate social and political change. Family medical care by way of the team approach is explored by Silver (1974) who describes the experiences of Family Health Maintenance Demonstration as initiated by the Montefiore Medical Group in New York City. Mount Sinai Hospital Medical Center in Chicago has also developed a number of neighborhood out-patient facilities in an effort to distribute services more effectively to clients (*Hospitals*, 1977, pp. 53–54).

Mechanisms for contacting individuals in greatest need and for encouraging them to use available health facilities should continue to be developed. All health programs should be derived from the needs of the target populations and based on their perceptions of need.

Applicants from a broader social spectrum must be encouraged to enter the health professions. More physicians are needed, but until the number can be sufficiently raised, allied health professionals can be better utilized. Nurse practitioners are the most likely immediate solution. Nurses are now being prepared to function in expanded roles. As primary-care practitioners, nurses become the client's first contact with the health-care system. The nurse uses assessment skills in determining how and by whom the patient's problems can best be resolved. The nurse serves as a point of entry, as well as a continuing contact for the client within the health-care system (Aiken, 1977, p. 1829). Third-party reimbursement for the services of this group, either from the government or private third parties, would offer more options to the consumer as well as incentives to the caregivers.

Health professionals have a major responsibility for the communication of health information on the client's level. Incorrect and insufficient health information influences behavior by limiting people in their use of sound health-care practices. Health workers must also attempt to demonstrate the value of health programs aimed at the prevention and early detection of diseases such as hypertension, diabetes, and sickle cell anemia. Finally, clients need information and support regarding what they should be demanding in the way of health services. In this way, the family is helped to develop its power to influence the health care system and to deal with it effectively.

SUMMARY

Health institutions in the United States have not done their job of promoting health for all in an equal manner, to the detriment of black Americans. Far too little attention has been given to the delivery of health care to the black population. The device of blaming the victim can no longer be employed to explain the poor health status of the black poor. It is the environment in which the black person lives that makes him sick. Low income, unemployment, poor housing, inadequate food, poor education, and discrimination contribute to his ill health and to his inability to obtain adequate care.

REFERENCES

Aiken, L.H. Primary care: The challenge for nursing. *American Journal of Nursing*, 1977, 77, 1828–1832.

Bennett, L. *Before the Mayflower: A History of the Negro in America*. Chicago: Johnson, 1969.

Farley, R. Trends in marital status among Negroes. In Willie, C.V. (ed.), *The Family Life of Black People*. Columbus, Ohio: Merrill, 1970, 172–183.

Gray, B.H. *Human Subjects in Medical Experimentation: A Sociological Study of the Conduct and Regulation of Clinical Research*. New York: Wiley, 1975.

Gutman, H.J. *The Black Family in Slavery and Freedom, 1750–1925*. New York: Pantheon, 1976.

Herzog, E. Is there a breakdown of the Negro family? In Willie, C.V. (ed.), *The Family Life of Black People*. Columbus, Ohio: Merrill, 1970, 331–341.

Hill, R.B. *The Strengths of Black Families*. New York: Emerson Hall, 1972.

Hospital-affiliated neighborhood health center designed for efficiency in care and energy use. *Hospitals*. 1977, 53–54.

Ladner, J.A. *Tomorrow's Tomorrow: The Black Woman*. Garden City, New York: Anchor, 1972.

Middleton, R., & Putney, S. Dominance in decisions in the family: Race and class differences. *American Journal of Sociology*, 1960, 65, 605–609.

Moynihan, D.P. The ordeal of the Negro family. In Willie, C.V. (ed.), *The Family Life of Black People*. Columbus, Ohio: Merrill, 1970, 299–309.

Ryan, W. Savage discovery: The Moynihan Report. *The Nation*, November 22, 1965. (Reprinted in Rainwater, L., & Yancy, W.L., *The Moynihan Report and the Politics of Controversy*. Cambridge, Mass.: The MIT Press, 1967, 462–463.

Ryan, W. *Blaming the Victim*. New York: Random House, 1971.

Silver, G.A. *Family Medical Care: A Design for Health Maintenance*. Cambridge, Mass.: Ballinger, 1974.

Singley, W.G., & Plaut, T.F. (eds.). *Training Community Health Workers*. New York: Dr. Martin Luther King, Jr. Health Center, 1974.

U.S. Bureau of the Census. *The Social and Economic Status of the Black Population in the United States, 1974*. Washington, D.C.: Government Printing Office, 1975.

U.S. Bureau of the Census. Population profile of the United States: 1975. *Current Population Reports*. Series P-20, No. 292. Washington, D.C.: Government printing Office, 1976.

U.S. Bureau of the Census., Characteristics of the population below the poverty level: 1975. *Current Population Reports*, Series P-60, No. 106. Washington, D.C.: Government Printing Office, 1977.

U.S. Department of Health, Education and Welfare, Public Health Service, Health Resources Administration. *Health United States 1975*. Rockville, Md.: National Center for Health Statistics, 1975.

U.S. Department of Labor. *The Negro Family: The Case for National Action*. Washington, D.C.: Government Printing Office, 1965. (Reprinted in Rainwater, L., & Yancy, W.L., *The Moynihan Report and the Politics of Controversy*. Cambridge, Mass.: The MIT Press, 1967.)

10

Life-Styles of Black Families Headed by Women

Nomsa Vanda Meindl
Cathleen Getty

Statistics provide descriptive information about populations. However, they deal in generalities and tend to add to the distance between reader and subject. They tell us, for example, that a large and growing proportion of single-parent families is made up of black female-headed households, but they cannot tell us about the people who constitute these populations and how they cope with the vicissitudes of their lives. This chapter embodies vivid portrayals of three such families, struggling to maintain themselves as viable units in the face of scant material resources and a threatening environment. Meindl and Getty present an assessment of the degree to which this family form permits maintenance of itself as an integral unit, providing for the fulfillment of the physical and emotional needs of members.

In recent years, the attention of social scientists has been turned to a type of family form that is steadily becoming more prevalent in the United States. Families headed by women have always existed, but their rapid growth in recent years due to the increasing number of divorced, separated, and never-married women has made them a subject for concern and study. They now account for 10.6 percent of all households (Bureau of the Census, 1979a, p. 3), their number having increased by 55 percent during the 1960s, and by 78 percent from 1970 to 1978 (Bureau of the Census, 1979b, p. 1). Further, statistics project continuing increases through the next decade. Such figures are disconcerting to those who view these changes as a threat to the "normal" structure of the American family.

Although research findings are extremely contradictory and inconclusive, it is most often assumed that these families are pathologic and deviant "simply

because the women and children are without a man" (Bould, 1977, p. 340).*
Black female-headed families are the subject of even greater controversy due
to their disproportionate numbers† and their being labeled by Moynihan
(1965, pp. 5, 30) as "the center of the tangle of pathology."

Allen (1978, p. 121) believes that the major discrepancies in the research
on black families have resulted from the ideologic and value differences of
the researchers. He and others emphasize the need for additional research,
but believe such work will be most productive if it is based on frameworks
and perspectives appropriate to the study of black families in this society
(Allen, 1978; Nobles, 1978; Peters, 1978). These authors underline the grave
limitations inherent in the "cultural deviant" perspective that compares black
families and society to mainstream white families and society, the latter being
assumed to represent the norm. Peters advocates a "cultural variant" perspective within which behaviors are not viewed as maladaptive or pathologic
simply because they differ from those sanctioned/valued within the mainstream culture. Instead, such behaviors may be interpreted as functional,
that is, having survival value within the Afro-American culture. She summarizes this position as follows:

> . . . black families are an important sub-culture of American society, dif-
> ferent in many ways from white families, but possessing a value system,
> patterns of behavior and institutions which can be described, understood
> and appreciated for their own strengths and characteristics. The black family
> has a history, and future, as well as a present, that are viable, worthwhile,
> understandable, and which serve the peculiar survival needs of a group
> which continues to suffer discrimination, prejudice and subtle institutional
> racism (Peters, 1978, p. 655).

It is important, however, to heed Allen's (1978, p. 126) note of caution,
warning against misuse of the "variant" perspective.‡ Such misapplication
can occur when social-science researchers and professionals ignore "factual
deficiencies," claiming instead a functional purpose for any aspect of black
family life.

It is clear that although black families have been the subject of fairly intense
scrutiny of late, further studies are needed: studies that more closely examine

---

*For an excellent critique of the research in this area, cf. Ross & Sawhill (1975).
†Blacks constitute one-ninth of the total U.S. population, and while the majority of black
families are headed by married couples, almost one-third of mother-only families in this country
are maintained by black women (Bureau of the Census, 1979b, p. 1; 1979c, p. 2). These families
may also represent a threat to mainstream white society because a large percentage of the
mothers are never-married women: 34 percent, as compared to 8 percent of the single-parent
white women (Bureau of the Census, 1979b, p. 1).
‡For a comparison of ideologic perspectives (cultural equivalent, cultural deviant, and cultural
variant), see Allen (1978).

the nature and quality of family life. In this regard, Bermann (1973, p. viii) has noted the heavy reliance on collecting family data by means of experimental, office interview, or survey methods, to the neglect of naturalistic observation. The neglected mode would provide more intimate detail on interacting families and on their management of stressful events.

The purpose of this chapter, therefore, is to describe observed patterns of family behavior in three lower-class, black female-headed families in an attempt to assess the effect of single parenthood on the functioning of the family unit.

THE STUDY

Three families who met the following criteria were selected for observation: urban; lower class; black; female headed, with two or more children; having no resident adult male for at least five years; and not labeled pathologic by community health agencies. The families were recommended for the study by social service, nursing, health and educational professionals with whom they had direct contact. All three families lived in the Model Neighborhood Area (MNA) of a large city in western New York State, a target area for federally funded poverty programs.

Conceptual Framework

A modification of Parad and Caplan's (1965) theoretical design for studying families was used as a means of classifying family behavior, while Ackerman's (1958) definition of the basic functions of the family provided the criteria for assessment. Pearsall's (1965) participant-observation procedures were used to gather and record the data.

Nathan Ackerman (1958, pp. 16–19) has conceptualized the family as a biosocial unit whose members are bonded together by a combination of biologic, psychologic, social, and economic factors. He, as have others, viewed the two basic purposes of the family as being the ensuring of man's physical survival and the building of essential humanness, the qualities essential for humanness being developed only within the matrix of the family "togetherness" experience. Ackerman (1958, p. 19) further specified the social purposes of the modern family as:

1. The provision of food, shelter, and other material necessities to sustain life and provide protection from external danger, a function best fulfilled under conditions of social unity and cooperation;
2. The provision of social togetherness, which is the matrix for the affectional bond of family relationships;

3. The opportunity to evolve a personal identity, tied to family identity, this bond of identity providing the psychic integrity and strength for meeting new experiences;

4. The patterning of sexual roles, which prepares the way for sexual maturation and fulfillment;

5. The training toward integration into social roles and acceptance of social responsibility;

6. The cultivation of learning and the support for individual creativity and initiative.

The utility of his conceptualization of the family and its functions is that it applies to all family units, regardless of race, social class or constellation.

Parad and Caplan (1965) studied family functioning during crises by using the interrelated concepts of family life-style, intermediate problem-solving mechanisms, and need-response pattern to guide data collection and analysis. The concept of family life-style was deemed to be particularly cogent for the purposes of the present study in that it refers to the "reasonably stable patterning of family organization" (Parad & Caplan, 1965, p. 57), that is, the fairly characteristic way in which a family manages its day-to-day existence. These everyday operations may be characterized by three interdependent elements: value system, communication network, and role patterning.

Value system may be understood as the organization of the family members' ideas, attitudes, and beliefs about the world, their place in it, and their relation to others. These shared person-nature, time, activity, and relational orientations help bind the members together in a common culture and provide them with a means of defining, understanding, and responding to the world around them (Parad & Caplan, 1965, p. 58; Speigel, 1971, pp. 162, 190–193). The term *communication network* is used to conceptualize both the provision of and participation in the process by which family members exchange information with one another (internal communication) and with the outside world (external communication). It is obvious that the family's value system will influence not only what gets transmitted, but how the transmission of messages is accomplished (Parad & Caplan, 1965, p. 58).

Role patterning refers to the provision within a family for the definition of what is to be done, who is to do it, and who is to make such decisions. Sanctions are an important component of the role system, spelling out means of dealing with poor task performance (Parad & Caplan, 1965, p. 58).

Observation Procedures

An initial interview was held with each prospective family to determine their willingness to participate and to advise them of study procedures. The first three families who volunteered and met all criteria constituted the study sample. The families were then observed in their homes for one hour, twice weekly, over the period of a month. Observation periods were usually scheduled after the dinner hour, when all members were likely to be present. Family members were observed individually and in groups, often at mealtimes or while engaged in household or child-care tasks. Approximately three-quarters of the time, all members were present during the sessions. Friends and relatives at times would drop in, but this was not discouraged since it was part of the natural life-style of these families. Data were systematically collected and assessed according to the procedures outlined by Pearsall (1965).

FAMILY PROFILES

THE SMITH FAMILY

Family Composition and History

The Smith family was recommended for this study by a registered nurse who treated Mrs. Smith at a medical clinic. The five members of the Smith family consisted of Mrs. Anna Smith and her four children, Peter, John, Jimmy, and Mary. Their home was sparsely furnished, but well kept. Neatness and cleanliness were evident at first glance. The house was in need of repairs because of its age (more than 50 years old) and inadequate upkeep by the landlords. The family had recently been to City Court demanding that service be provided as specified in the provisions of the lease.

Anna Smith was born in Alabama, the fifth of ten children. Her parents were poor farmers who maintained a disciplined household based on a foundation of strong religious convictions. At the age of 15, after dropping out of high school, she married her high school sweet-heart. The marriage lasted 8 years, during which time her four children were born. In 1960, shortly after the husband deserted the family, Anna left the children (aged 1 to 5) with their grandparents and went north, where she found employment as a housekeeper. She claimed that lack of finances was responsible for the breakup of the marriage, and she had felt at that time that if she could have contributed to family financial resources, her husband might have returned. He was, however, never heard from again.

After a year and a half, Anna had saved enough money to bring her children to live with her. She had an older sister in the area, and between the two of them, they managed to take care of the children. For the next two years, Anna was able to support the family with social-welfare assistance. Shortly thereafter her sister moved to the South, and Anna lost her job because she had to remain at home with the children.* From that point, the family became totally dependent upon social welfare for financial support. Chronic hypertension prevented Anna from seeking employment once the children had reached the age where constant supervision was no longer needed.

Peter, the oldest son, was 17 years old, and a high school graduate. He was tall, slightly built, articulate, and friendly. He was very interested in continuing his education but felt a strong responsibility to help his family with financial matters. He was planning to support himself by joining a federally funded youth work program when he became 18.

John, a 16-year-old high school junior, was tall and, because of past health problems, extremely thin. He had had cholera when he was 8 years old and had a history of rheumatic heart disease. These physical problems had limited his activities and caused him to miss one year of high school. Anna claimed that John had always been a "sick boy, who required a lot of attention." Even though his medical history had hindered his overall school participation, John was a good student. His hobbies included watching sports events, music, and woodworking.

Jimmy, a sophomore, was 15 years old, of average height, and like his two brothers, slightly built. His school work was adequate at best, and he had problems at school (fighting and truancy). His mother was concerned with the possibility that he might drop out of school and move out of the house. Jimmy was both physically and verbally aggressive, as was clearly observed in his attempts to dominate the family conversations. Recently he had become involved with a street gang, and it was reported to his mother, by friends, that he had also been experimenting with drugs (marijuana and amphetamines).

Mary, the only girl, was an attractive, quiet, 14-year-old high school freshman. She was very slender and looked younger than her stated age. A close attachment to her mother had developed, possibly as the result of her being the youngest and the only female child. This was illustrated by the mother's references to her as "my baby," a description Mary readily accepted and encouraged with her childish behavior. She referred to her mother as "Mommy" and used the baby role to gain favors from Anna.

---

*The loss of this relative appears to be one of the critical events in the life of the Smith family in that it precipitated the withdrawal of Mrs. Smith from community life and the provider role, causing the family to become totally dependent upon external sources for financial support. In this regard, Bould (1977) found that the *source* as well as the amount of income has important ramifications for single women and their families in that it impacts on the women's sense of "personal fate control": "poor women and women who must depend on AFDC (Aid to Families with Dependent Children), child support and other stigmatizing or unstable sources of income, feel less able to plan for their lives."

Family Life-Style

VALUE SYSTEM   The value system of the Smith family was characterized by an emphasis on education and religion within their ideas and attitudes. The religious training and background of Mrs. Smith's childhood continued to play an important part in family affairs. The children had a deep-rooted attachment to the Baptist church, attending not only service on Sunday but Sunday school and weekday church activities as well. The general feeling concerning religion and the family was best expressed by Mrs. Smith: "My children have grown up with the presence of God in mind." The children echoed John's belief that peer group and environmental influences that sought to weaken their religious connections were "the work of the devil." The children felt that many of their friends were "hooked on drugs" because "they put their faith in man and money instead of God." Mrs. Smith was concerned with what she described as "the moral decay of the country; the devil is working overtime." She was a determined woman who protected herself from the evils of the world by maintaining strong religious convictions. Many religious artifacts decorated the house. Religion seemed to be a force that gave meaning and depth to their existence and helped serve as a guide for setting life goals.

Education was viewed by Mrs. Smith as, "the salvation for the children from the suffering of the black world." The primary reason the children were brought to the North was to provide them with a higher standard of education. Both Anna and her children were concerned about the social problems of the ghetto schools and the resulting impediments to academic achievement. Anna stated, "I try to guide my children in my home, but when the schools let you down, it becomes so much more difficult." Mary expressed the sentiment that "school is as bad as the streets; it's not a matter of learning, it's just a matter of surviving."

Jimmy had been especially affected by the social problems that were a part of the school and neighborhood. He had recently joined a street gang that was primarily composed of both classmates and dropouts from his high school. His attitude toward school was generally reflected in his truancy record. Jimmy stated, "I dislike people [teachers] who don't give a damn about us [students], and are only thinking of their paychecks." He continued, "How can you expect them [teachers] to understand what it's like to live here? The only time they see the neighborhood is when they look out of their car windows—so why should I care?"

The remaining children echoed Jimmy's thoughts, but they differed in their approach to and management of the problem. Because they believed that education was a way out of the ghetto, they were willing to participate in the educational system with the hope of eventually attending college and consequently escaping their environment. At the same time, they were quite concerned about their ability to compete in a college environment. Peter, who had already graduated from high school, appeared to sum up the feeling of the other children, "I want to go [to college] and I can get in, but I don't know if I can do the work; my [educational] background is poor." The entire family, including Jimmy, agreed that education was important if one hoped to find a place in the mainstream of American life.

Fair play and freedom to express oneself were important elements of the family code. All the members were vocal and felt free to express their attitudes and ideas. Their opinions of the social system were often critical. The family was very aware of the "second-class citizenship" that blacks have been allotted and burdened with in American history. Mrs. Smith believed her children had the right to express their feelings on social issues: "They live with and have to deal with prejudice; better they talk about it in their home, rather than fight about it in the street."

The time orientation of the Smith family was in the present, except for their beliefs about education, which were achievement-motivated and future-oriented. Because of her trying life experiences, Mrs. Smith was determined that her family should have the basic necessities of food, shelter, and clothing. She maintained that if they did, the future would "take care of itself."

There was a strong feeling among family members that humor was important for the maintenance of family equilibrium. Joking and teasing constituted a great part of the family interaction. It also seemed to be used as a way of releasing tension by making light of social situations that seriously affected family life but over which they had no control. Much of the joking involved the Watergate proceedings, which prompted statements such as, "I guess it's . . . better to be white than right," and, "If the president was black there wouldn't be a trial, there would be a hanging."

The family members expressed the belief time and time again that their race was a handicap in social mobility. Schools, housing, jobs, and social acceptance were seen as the most notable areas of oppression. Feelings of second-class citizenship had developed. This was best described by John's statement: "It's the white man's world; we just rent a piece of it."

ROLE PATTERNING   Mrs. Smith was clearly the source of authority in the home, allocating tasks and responsibilities to her children. As example of task assignment was Peter's designation as family spokesman in issues dealing with the community. Mrs. Smith explained Peter's role as follows: "In the ghetto, force is a sign of power. Peter is the eldest and should be ready to deal with the problems of the neighborhood either by talking or fighting if necessary." Peter accepted this role and had mobilized his two younger brothers into a fighting force in order to be ready for action if, and when, necessary. He knew the problems that confronted his family, and as the eldest son, felt responsible for their safety. He accepted this role with pride and enthusiasm.

Living within the confines of the ghetto, the Smith family was naturally aware of, and concerned with, the threats to their safety. Their home was a virtual fortress with locks and window bars, and special emphasis was placed on being suspicious of strangers. The police were also looked upon with suspicion. Jimmy stated, "They are here to protect white folks from us." There was general understanding by all the family members that if trouble occurred, they would have only each other to depend on for help.

All the children were assigned day-to-day tasks in order to maintain the smooth functioning of the family household. The most important function of the task assignments was to develop a sense of responsibility in the children. Peter, in describing the importance of family acceptance of as-signed roles, stated, "If we're going to make it, we have to work as a group. You know, the old united we stand, divided we fall thing." The recognition by family members of the need for unity and cooperation was manifested in their willingness to work together for the benefit of all.

Mrs. Smith assigned many tasks on the basis of the age and sex of the family members. Mary was held responsible for many of the household chores. Because there was only one female child, it was necessary at times to enlist the help of the boys in these tasks. At that point, Mrs. Smith would explain the need for extra help and ask for volunteers. Most of the time one of the boys would step forward, but if this did not happen, Mrs. Smith would assign the household tasks on a rotation basis. If there was any resistance by the children, Mrs. Smith would quickly reprimand them. She not only delegated tasks, but also took responsibility for all matters of discipline: "Spare the rod, and you spoil the child," she explained.

All the brothers had the shared responsibility of "keeping an eye" on their sister. This was apparently not because they distrusted Mary, but rather because there was a high incidence of assaults and rape in the neighborhood. The boys seemed to overreact to this responsibility, almost hoping that someone would try to accost their sister so they could demonstrate their courage. The violent character of the neighborhood was reflected in the personalities of the children. Masculinity was equated with courage in fight-ing. Mrs. Smith expressed her concern: "I try to tell my children, only fight when you have no other choice, but here [in the ghetto] fighting is a way of life. People get killed. I pray that it's not one of us next."

In their mother's absence, the children showed flexibility concerning their roles. They were expected to apply peer pressure to any member who was not carrying out his or her assigned tasks. It was not "squealing" to report the negligent individual to the mother. This family norm insured that the children would put the family unit before individual needs and feelings. Interdependency within the family system was reflected in the support this mother gave to her children and the gratification she received from the role-performance of her children.

COMMUNICATION NETWORK   The internal communication network of the Smith family provided for relatively free and open communication between and among members. All family members were talkative and transmitted information freely. When there was an exchange of good news, the family used a good deal of body language to express themselves. Hand slapping, dancing, and singing, with exclamations "Hey, brother, that's real cool man! Ain't no one is gonna believe this!" illustrated their feelings of excitement. Body language and gestures were important indications in relating to the family members that information either pleased or displeased them. There appeared to be no family taboos on the expression of feelings and no restrictions based on the age or sex of members. All were encouraged to express themselves in relation to their feelings. Mary commented, "It's better to talk about things—especially your troubles. We all try to figure it out; Ma wants it that way."

Each member of the family was regarded as a possible source of important information that might be of relevance to the family as a whole. The exchange of ideas and the giving of information was crucial to the social life as well as to the survival of the family. Peter commented, "It's necessary to know what's going on out there in the street. Knowing what places or people are bad news is where it's all at." John illustrated the importance of communicating and how it helped the family to avoid trouble: "There was a street gang that came to our neighborhood and beat up a few guys real bad. My sister heard about their plans from her friend and told us not to go on the street that night." Much of family activity was governed by information exchanged among family members. Shopping and recreation are just two of the areas directly influenced by what a family member reported on a particular day.

Communication with both the black and the white communities was approached with suspicion. The black community was viewed as a threat by the family members. Peter expressed concern for the safety of the family: "Black folks need more respect for each other; they just go around ripping each other off. These people are dangerous, but so am I. If they don't bother me, I won't bother them." His sentiments were echoed by the other children. On the other hand, the white community was viewed as a ruthless oppressor that constantly exploited and dehumanized blacks. There was a family feeling that because of race, they, as individuals had been oppressed by the dominant white society. Jimmy stated, "Most white folks would just as soon see us dead. That would cut down on welfare. They put us on welfare in the first place, thinking they're doing us some big favor."

Communication with schools was poor. When Jimmy had school-related problems, school authorities failed to inform Mrs. Smith. She found out about his problems from the other children. The family had few friends, so that form of interaction was quite limited. Mrs. Smith stated, "Don't let your business get in the street; people will only make it sound worse than it is." The police were viewed as the oppressors rather than the defenders of the people: "Don't waste your time calling the police for help; you better be able to take care of it yourself," stated John.

External communications with the outside world were mainly channeled through the children. Mrs. Smith summarized the situation: "Outside of making sure of our welfare payments, there is just not much more for me to do. The children let me know what is going on in the neighborhood and on the streets." Except for church-related activities, she seemed to have purposely restricted her interaction with the community. She was, however, clearly the head of the family and made the final decision on most matters of importance. External communication was one dimension of family life in which they, especially Mrs. Smith, may have missed and needed an older male member. She once stated, "I sometimes wish we had a man in the house. It would make things easier for me. The children need guidance and Peter is just too young to be saddled with any major responsibilities. A man's place is in the world."

THE BROWN FAMILY

Family Composition and History

The Brown family was referred for this study by a social worker employed in an agency where one of the daughters had taken her baby for postnatal care. This six member family consisted of Mrs. Anita Brown, head of the household, her son, daughters, and grandchildren—Bob, the oldest, Sylvia and her 7-month-old baby girl, and Suzie and her 2-month-old daughter.

Their apartment, well-kept, clean, and cheerful, was located in a two-story wooden house that was badly in need of repair. Despite the poor condition of both the house and neighborhood in general, that the family went to great lengths to maintain a respectable residence was evidenced by fresh paint and makeshift home repairs.

Mrs. Brown was a very active 35-year-old woman who looked younger than her stated age. The eldest of a family of five girls, she had continued to maintain a close relationship with her sisters and parents, all of whom resided in the same city. After dropping out of high school, she was married at 16 to a neighborhood sweetheart whom she had known for a number of years. Shortly thereafter her first child was born. All three of her children were fathered by the same man, who was, according to Mrs. Brown, a good husband until financial pressures caused them to separate and eventually divorce. They divorced when the children were 8, 7, and 6 years of age. The family had received welfare assistance since that time. Mrs. Brown claimed that after her husband left, he continued to help support the family for a couple of years, then dropped out of sight completely. When the children reached their teens, she joined various job-training programs sponsored by the Department of Social Service and occasionally had been able to find employment to help supplement the welfare payments. At the time of this study, she was employed as a part-time secretary at a local hospital.

Bob, the only boy in the family, was a 17-year-old high school dropout. He was tall, of average build, and rather quiet and reserved. Since leaving high school, he had been involved in a federally sponsored job-training program that helped supplement family income. Bob claimed he was more interested in working than in returning to school, so he was quite satisfied with the program. His main interest was music. He played with a local group on weekends and expressed a desire to become a professional musician.

Sylvia, a petite 16-year-old, was also a high school dropout. Seven months earlier, she had given birth to a baby girl, Nanette. Sylvia's boyfriend, the father of the child, lived in the neighborhood. They had tried living together, but a combination of domestic difficulties and financial problems caused Sylvia to return with her child to her family. She claimed her only interest was to raise her child and help her mother in the running of the household. Mrs. Brown, who had condoned the living arrangement between Sylvia and her boyfriend, welcomed her daughter back into the family when the arrangement failed. Sylvia and her child received financial support from the Department of Social Services, but she had not become involved in any type of job-training program.

Suzie, 15 years old, was of average height and build and looked older than her stated age. Because of pregnancy she had dropped out of school during her junior year. As her sister before her, she had chosen to keep her baby and live with the Brown family. Suzie and her child, Tina, also received welfare assistance. At the time of this study, Suzie's boyfriend was in the Marines and had regularly been sending money to her (the payments were not reported to the Department of Social Services because she feared monthly assistance would be discontinued). There was an understanding between them that they would marry in the near future. Considered a good student by the other family members, Suzie was attempting to finish high school at night, and she hoped to be able to enroll in a two-year college nursing program.

Family Life-Style

VALUE SYSTEM   The Brown family placed emphasis on family unit, racial pride, and religion. Of these, unity was seen as crucial for maintenance of the family. There was a conscious effort by all the members to help one another in times of need. Mrs. Brown summarized the feelings of the entire family when she stated, "I've brought my children up to always respect their home, and in order to preserve that home, we all have to work together."

When both of the girls had babies out of wedlock, they were neither ostracized nor censured by Mrs. Brown or their brother. Bob stated, "There is nothing wrong with what my sisters did. If they get together with their man that's fine; if they don't, they don't. They still have a home." Mrs. Brown added, "This is the way colored folks have always lived; we're used to it. Most of the homes around here have no man at all. In most cases it's better that way." Recalling her own experience, she indicated that after her husband left and the family went on welfare, their financial position actually improved: "Most white folks don't understand that they created a welfare state for colored folks. The colored man is still a slave for the most part. Most of us can't help ourselves enough to survive. We need help, and to get help it's better to be without a man," continued Mrs. Brown. "I have no hatred toward the country or whites in particular," she emphasized, "but, the truth is the truth and that's the way things are." Both of the girls agreed with their mother, and felt that the newborn babies were good for the Brown family and for the black community as well. "We need all the black people we can get in this country," stated Sylvia. "I'm proud of my child and I know my family is too," Suzie added. "You didn't see us run to have an abortion like these white girls do."

Racial pride was strongly emphasized in the ideas and attitudes of the Brown family. Pictures and slogans of black leaders were clearly displayed throughout the apartment. Despite their lack of formal education, all the members were keenly aware of both the past and present problems of the black community. "You don't have to be in school to understand that blacks are having a tough time. All you have to do is look around and talk to people," stated Bob.

Religion was yet another important element in the value system of the family. As a result of her own highly religious background, Mrs. Brown strove to foster religiousness in her family. The children had a religious orientation but did not share their mother's views and expectations about personal and religious fulfillment. Sylvia summarized the feelings of the children when she stated, "I want something in this life, for me, my family, and my baby." Mrs. Brown countered, "This life is just a passing thing. I can withstand just about anything if I know there is something for me in the hereafter."

Education was not highly valued by the family. Suzie was the only member who was achievement oriented; she hoped to eventually attend college. Planning for the future was not much in evidence, and the time orientation of the Brown family was to the present. The general feeling was, "Let's get what we need now; the future will take care of itself."*

Good-natured joking and teasing was a predominant characteristic of family interaction. This appeared to help relieve some of the daily tension stemming

---

*Since such data are often viewed from a "cultural deviant" perspective, that is, compared with middle-class values that stress achievement and success as well as planning for the future, the reader is referred to Speigel's (1971) discussion of differing value orientations toward time and modes of activity.

from the financial and social problems indigenous to ghetto living. Music and singing were other observed family recreation activities.

Affectional ties between the mother and the children were very strong. Mrs. Brown emphasized that the children "always have had, and will continue to have, the best I can get for them." She continued, "We have gone through some tough times, but here we are and here we will stay. There is a lot of love in this family, always has been." The children responded to this feeling and openly exhibited affection for their mother. "She has kept us together, and we really appreciate that," said Sylvia. Mrs. Brown is quite proud of the fact that the family has survived: "They have always had the necessities of life. I've seen to that."

ROLE-PATTERNING   Mrs. Brown was clearly the source of authority in the family. She was expected to take on all matters of discipline, guidance, and task assignment. The children readily accepted her leadership, offering only passive resistance when assigned unpleasant or unwanted duties. "Our mother wouldn't ask us to do anything she didn't think was for our own good," stated Bob. "She has sacrificed and suffered for a lot of years to help us, and we appreciate and respect her for that." Mrs. Brown readily took on and enjoyed this role: "I've raised each one of these children, and things have always worked out for the best. As long as they are in my house, they will do things my way."

Mrs. Brown was both mother and father to her children: "I never wanted to burden my boy [Bob] with any of the responsibilities that the man of the household would have. He'll have a lifetime of responsibilities when he gets older; no sense in giving him all these headaches just because there is no man here." Mrs. Brown maintained that her role had been difficult because "sometimes I was so busy doing the man's job that I neglected the mother's responsibilities." She thought that both her girls had not received enough attention and consequently did not have a positive female figure with which to identify.* There was little doubt that she felt responsible for the girls' leaving school. Both Sylvia and Suzie disagreed with their mother's evaluation of the situation. "Our mother did everything in her power to guide us. I just got involved and had a baby," said Suzie. Sylvia added, "Everyone loves the babies. Mother just feels that we are going to miss out on a lot of things because of our age."

---

*Mrs. Brown's dilemma is shared by many women inasmuch as society has conflicting expectations of all female heads of families; the problems encountered in trying to meet these expectations are more acute for lower-class women. They are expected to be self-supporting (not welfare "burdens"), and yet, at the same time, must fulfill their responsibility to home and children. They can work if their children are well cared for, but society does not feel obligated to help arrange for that care. As heads of families, they must function as both mother and father, but they are expected to remain "feminine" to prevent their children from receiving distorted conceptions of male and female roles. [Cf. Glasser and Navarre] (1970.)

Bob seemed to be developing an increasing sense of family responsibility: "I know that when I was younger, things were not expected of me, but now that I'm getting older I have more responsibilities." In many ways he thought that he should be regarded as the man of the house. He stated, "Living in this type of neighborhood is bad news. There has to be a man in the house or people will walk right in and rip us off." This attitude troubled his mother. She worried that he was becoming too involved with both the violent nature of the neighborhood and the need to prove his masculinity. "I wish he would leave well enough alone and stick to his music. I've seen many young men hurt and even dead because they grew up too fast," she said tearfully.

Task assignment was mainly based on the age and sex of the children. The girls were responsible for all the household work, such as cleaning, washing, and cooking. Bob was assigned all the outdoor and repair tasks. "With my part-time job, I don't have the time to do all the things I once did around the house. The children understand and are able to attend to household duties while I'm working," stated Mrs. Brown. Everyone experienced a sense of gratification from their accomplishments, and would boast about their completed tasks.

Mrs. Brown's most prominent task, and the one where she took complete control, was the care of the two infants, Nanette and Tina. Sylvia and Suzie were involved, but only in a secondary capacity. Reminiscent of an apprenticeship program, Mrs. Brown would give instructions to her daughters; they would then apply the newly learned techniques under the mother's watchful eye. Mrs. Brown was adamant when discussing the welfare of her granddaughters: "I am not at all concerned if people think I'm too much in control of my daughters' babies; I'm concerned about the welfare of these babies, and that's the way it's going to be." Both daughters were in agreement regarding the need for the advice and experience of their mother. "Mom makes sure that the babies are well cared for, but she also makes sure that we learn by watching and assisting," stated Suzie.

COMMUNICATION NETWORK   There was a free interchange of ideas and opinions within the family. Everyone spoke openly on matters ranging from family maintenance concerns to neighborhood gossip. There was a democratic spirit that allowed all members to converse on any topic. There was one restriction: Because of Mrs. Brown's religious convictions, "foul" language was not condoned.

Body language was often used as a means of communication between the children. Suzie had a habit of crossing her arms and legs and tilting back her head when she was annoyed with either her brother or sister. She said, "When I get mad, it's better for me to keep my mouth shut, but I want them to know that I'm angry." This is an example of the discretion used by the children; they chose to express their feelings through the use of body language rather than use language that might have offended their mother.

Body language and other nonverbal means were also used to express feelings in other contexts. When the family or an individual member was experiencing a period of happiness, invariably soul music would be played, and it was accompanied by dancing and singing. The music played in the household seemed to reflect the moods of the occupants: A pleasant situation heralded rock or soul music, an unpleasant one gave rise to the blues, and religious moods brought on gospel music.

Mrs. Brown was a very open and forthright woman who believed the best way to "get your point across is to tell people what you think." She continued, "If my children want me to know something I want them to tell me in straight talk." She encouraged her children to express themselves without fear of reprisal. Both of the girls had not hesitated to ask their mother for advice when they were pregnant. Sylvia commented, "Mother was just great. She understood and encouraged me to try and make a go of it with Frank [the baby's father]. She asked me if I wanted to tell the others [Bob and Suzie] and when I said 'yes,' she arranged a family meeting. Everything was explained with love and understanding." Suzie stated, "Mother was the first person I went to when I was pregnant. She made me feel that my baby would be wanted."

The external communications between the family and the community were primarily Mrs. Brown's responsibility. This was in keeping with the authority role she maintained within the family system. Mrs. Brown was the spokeswoman for the family with the Department of Social Services: "I want to be sure all of the necessary information is received by the right people. Welfare is what keeps us alive, so I have to be very careful." She handled the situation even when it was the girls and their babies who were the object of welfare inquiries.

There was little communication between the family and school personnel. Even though Mrs. Brown had been upset when the girls had left school, she neither encouraged them to return nor made any attempt to contact school authorities concerning possible readmission. However, Suzie, who wanted to continue her education, independently contacted the school guidance counselor and was assured of readmittance. (The cause of this lack of communication is not clear. Perhaps it resulted from Mrs. Brown's viewing education as unimportant or irrelevant to ghetto life; perhaps it stemmed from beliefs that "family business" should not be revealed to public authorities for fear of recrimination and/or negative sanctions.)

Because their immediate neighborhood was viewed with suspicion, outside contacts were limited to a few time-tested friends. Neighborhood information garnered by the children was discussed with emphasis on its relevance to the family. For example, a rash of recent house burglaries prompted a discussion concerning the merits of acquiring a dog versus investing in additional security locks. It was decided that since a dog might be a danger to the infants, the locks would be more practical.

Relatives were communicated with every day since Mrs. Brown's parents and sisters all lived in the immediate area. They were frequent, and welcome, visitors to the house. Mrs. Brown, as the eldest, had been instrumental in the upbringing of her sisters. In the light of this, they continued to regard her as an authority figure and often sought her guidance.

Communication with the outside world did not seem greatly affected by the absence of an adult male representative; for the most part, Mrs. Brown was adequate and adept in her role as family spokeswoman. Since the reasons for the lack of communication with the school authorities are not clear, and its probable consequences not readily discernible, one can only speculate as to whether the presence of an adult male was needed and whether this would have influenced communications in that arena.

THE REED FAMILY

Family Composition and History

The Reed family was recommended for this study by a teacher from the high school attended by the eldest children. Mrs. Lenora Reed and her eight children resided in an old two-story wooden house that was badly in need of repairs. The interior was sparsely furnished with second-hand furnishings. Attempts to brighten and personalize the rooms were evidenced by the various athletic trophies, family pictures, and religious artifacts scattered throughout. The family's sleeping arrangements were cramped, the children sleeping two and three to a room and Mrs. Reed sharing a room with the youngest boy.

Mrs. Reed was 34 years old, the youngest girl in a family of nine. Her family still resided in Georgia, and Mrs. Reed expressed a desire to eventually return to her native state. Her mother had died when Mrs. Reed was 3; the oldest daughter became a substitute mother for the other children. Her father supported the family until his death some 10 years later. The responsibility for the care of the children was then divided among the relatives. Lenora was sent to live in another part of the state with a maternal aunt. She claimed her early years were difficult because of the separation from her brothers and sisters.

Lenora left high school in her second year to work and help supplement the family income. At the age of 16, she married Frank Reed, a field hand on the farm where she was employed. According to her, this was an act of desperation, an escape from the difficult farm work and the stern discipline of her aunt. She had four children in the first five years of the marriage. Hoping for better economic opportunities, the Reed family moved to a northeastern industrial city. Although Mr. Reed obtained a job in a local factory, his income was not sufficient to support his large family. He began to drink excessively, and a year after the move, deserted his family. The children were very young and Mrs. Reed was forced to turn to welfare, which continued to be the family's means of support. A year after her husband deserted the family, Mrs. Reed met James Young, a Canadian, who subsequently fathered her four other children. Mr. Young did not live in this country and did not contribute to the support of his children. Mrs. Reed claimed that marriage was decided against since it would result in the loss of the welfare benefits that were, in her view, her only dependable and stable source of income. For the past few years, Mr. Young had visited the family infrequently, usually three times a year during the Easter and Christmas holidays. Mrs. Reed believed that he had become angry and felt rejected when she would not marry him.

Earl, the eldest son, was an 18-year-old college sophomore. He was very tall, athletic, and ambitious. Hoping for an athletic scholarship, he spent many hours on the neighborhood basketball courts. Education took a high priority in his life.

Flora, the eldest daughter, was a 17-year-old college freshman. She had hopes of one day studying nursing. Her activities were primarily church-related—Sunday school, church choir, etc.

Cindy was an extremely attractive 15-year-old high school sophomore. She had been involved with the law because of a number of juvenile offenses. Running away from home and chronic truancy were just two of her problems.

Edward was an obese 14-year-old high school freshman. He was popular with his peers, and although he was a good student, he had recently gotten into trouble in the neighborhood and school. His mother worried over the possibility that he was becoming involved with a gang.

Brenda was 10 years old and the first child fathered by Mrs. Reed's boyfriend. A quiet and reserved girl, she isolated herself much of the time from the rest of the family.* The slightly built girl was an excellent student who had won a number of grammar school awards.

Kathy, a fragile-looking 9-year-old, was in the fourth grade at the local public school. Unlike her sister, Brenda, she was an extroverted child who spent most of her free time outdoors playing with the neighborhood children.

Vicky, the youngest girl, was in the first grade. She was a pleasant, friendly child who was constantly at either Mrs. Reed's or Flora's side.

---

*The reader is referred to Asmundsson's perceptive analysis of the problems of blended families, which may lend an added perspective within which the interactions of the Reed Family may be examined. See Chapter 7 of this volume.

Billy was a chubby 4-year-old, who had the pleasure of being the baby of the family. He was almost constantly being cuddled or fussed over by one family member or another.

Family Life-Style

VALUE SYSTEM   The value system of the Reed family was a mixture of ideas, attitudes and beliefs that emphasized the here-and-now, living only for the known present. It did not appear that the family lacked vision or hope for a better future, but the stark realities of poverty and deprivation made the basic necessities of life the primary focus of attention. Mrs. Reed had lived with poverty all her life as a child in the rural South and as the head of a family of nine. She had hopes for a better life for her children, but could not help viewing the future in terms of her own past experiences: "My main concern is that the children are fed and healthy. We can't look to tomorrow until we take care of today." The family was bound together in their attempts to survive. Mrs. Reed provided this explanation for her refusal of Mr. Young's marriage proposal: "Our welfare payments would have been cut, and I'm not going to take food off the table to put on a good appearance." Although very aware of the harsh realities of lower-class life, she did as much as she could to improve the family situation: "I've got eight of God's children and the only person on this earth that really cares about them is me."

The children were also conscious of the poverty of their environment. Earl commented, "I'm thinking college, but I may have to go to work to help improve things at home." There was little doubt that Mrs. Reed placed a premium on the worth and value of her children. They appeared to feel loved and appreciated, and willing to do what they could for the other family members. This type of attitude had bound the family members together. "We do our best with what we got, and if we stick together, things will improve," said Edward.

Other than the concern with the basic necessities, the emphasis on education was the most important aspect of family life. Both Earl and Flora discussed the benefits of finishing college. Mrs. Reed thought of education as the "key to their future, if there is a future." Two of the children had excellent school records and were a source of great pride in the family. Flora, who planned a nursing career, and Brenda, who, at the age of 10, envisioned herself as a teacher, had both received numerous certificates of academic achievement that were prominently displayed in the house.

Humor was important to the family. Joking, teasing, and "goofing and jiving" were part of the everyday behavior of the family. In a joking manner, Cindy stated, "You know us black folks, always laughing, singing, dancing." "Yeah, singing the blues and dancing the funeral march," added Edward. This was not atypical; most of the "humor" concerned the oppressive manner in which society treated the black community. This seemed to be their way of masking true feelings or relieving hostility.

Personal safety was another subject of great concern to the family. The condition of the neighborhood lent credibility to their fears. Mrs. Reed was especially concerned with the violent nature of their surroundings: "I'm very worried about Cindy and Edward. They have been in trouble recently, and I can't do much about it. You open your front door and there's nothing but trouble waiting in the street for the kids." Edward explained that the reason he joined a gang was for his safety and to help his family: "If I'm in the gang, they won't beat up on me or my brothers and sisters."

Their house was never left unoccupied. "If you want your belongings, you better make sure someone is at home," commented Flora. Mrs. Reed felt very bitter about the lack of law enforcement in the neighborhood: "The things that go on here are more than criminal; they're sadistic. If this was a white neighborhood, it would be a different story."

The family believed society to be oppressive toward them because of their race, and there was much general hostility and anger directed toward whites. The children shared mutual feelings of despair and bitterness. They believed there was a double standard of justice in America—one for the whites, the other for the blacks—and questioned the American value system, denouncing middle-class values as being selfish and racist.

ROLE PATTERNING   The source of authority in the family was Mrs. Reed. She had established a chain-of-command system, giving the responsibility of ensuring that assigned tasks were carried out to the two eldest, Flora and Earl. She was in firm control of the children, and used physical punishment when necessary. "I find that one spanking is worth a thousand words," she jokingly related. The children were well schooled as to their mother's expectations of them. Each child had specific duties, and carried them out with few complaints. Tasks were distributed according to age and sex or were adopted by other members in order to meet specific individual and family needs. The traditionally female tasks of cooking, cleaning, baby-sitting, etc. were assigned to the four oldest girls. The two oldest boys took care of the painting, house repairs, heavy moving and lifting, etc. There was a high degree of willingness to work together to complete a group task. Mrs. Reed stated, "We all live here, eat here, and work here. These kids know that I need help, and they all do their best." Peer pressure was freely applied to keep all members in line. However, Mrs. Reed did not allow the children to strike each other: "If there's any hitting to be done, I'll do it."

Earl had assigned himself the responsibility of ensuring the safety of the family. He would investigate strange noises in and around the house and would also challenge outsiders who "hassle my brothers and sisters in the street." He was assisted by Edward in the defense of the family against abuse or violence.

In addition to her assigned tasks, Flora had taken on the role of surrogate mother to the two youngest children. She often tended to their needs before leaving for school, at bedtime, and so on: "My mother needs extra help. I think the best way of helping is to take care of Vicky and Billy; they take so much time and energy."

Their required participation in maintaining the household helped to develop a sense of responsibility in the children. "Responsibility is a part of growing up. The quicker we learn this, the better off we'll be," stated Brenda. Everyone seemed to appreciate the need for cooperation.

The children made use, to some degree, of fictive roles. Perhaps as an escape from the harsh realities of ghetto life, they sometimes envisioned themselves as other people, in other places, living in a different style.

The emotional needs of her children were well provided for by Mrs. Reed. "I always want my kids to be able to come to me when they have things on their minds," she stated. The children were quick to turn to their mother in times of stress. Even though Cindy and Edward had problems with the police, they still were able to discuss their problems with their mother. "They are both good kids," stated Mrs. Reed, "it's just this neighborhood, everywhere they turn there is trouble, trouble, trouble."

COMMUNICATION NETWORK   The internal communication network provided for open expression, pleasant as well as unpleasant subjects being discussed and evaluated by the family as a group. All members were talkative, especially when focusing on favored topics. Mrs. Reed commented, "Nothing is so bad that we can't talk about it."

Communication within the family was strongly influenced by its value system. An example of this was the manner in which the subject of the two fathers was handled. Mrs. Reed confronted the subject directly and honestly and tried to prevent any rivalry or jealousy from springing up between the children. She explained the reasons for the failure of her marriage and her decision not to remarry. The children were allowed to ask questions and give their opinions on the subject: "I want them to know about their fathers, and if they have any questions to get it off their chests."

Body language was an extensively used tool of communication. This was especially true of happy or pleasant news, when the family exhibited many of the "soul expressions or movements" to convey their feelings.

The family, recognizing that its survival was dependent on keeping channels open in order to receive needed resources, regarded communication with the outside community as being of utmost importance. However, such communications were undertaken cautiously, as they trusted neither the motivation nor the actions of social-service agencies. For example, communications regarding the welfare situation were of high priority with Mrs. Reed; they had to be undertaken even though she saw the agency as obstructive and noncaring. "We have had so many problems with welfare it makes me sick," she said. "They don't care if we starve."

Since the immediate community was viewed with suspicion, Mrs. Reed did not engage in many community activities. The children spent a great deal of time in the neighborhood but were always aware of its dangers. Everyone was responsible for relaying information from the immediate neighborhood to the family; this was primarily to ensure the safety of the family. As Earl commented, "It's a matter of survival—this is a hard place to live in and an easy place to get hurt." Decisions concerning the family's activities were dependent on the information obtained in the streets. Their entire external communication system was used primarily to investigate and evaluate the community in terms of its impact on the family.

THREE FAMILIES: ASSESSMENT OF FUNCTIONING

As previously indicated, Ackerman (1958) identified six functions or purposes served by the modern family. An assessment of the three families has been made in terms of these functions. They have been treated and discussed as one unit, since it was not the purpose of the study to make comparisons of their functional levels. Therefore, references are made to a particular family only as needed for illustration or clarification.

Function 1

. . . the provision of food, shelter, and other material necessities to sustain life and provide protection from external danger, a function best fulfilled under conditions of social unity and cooperation . . . (Ackerman, 1958, p. 19)

The determination of these women to meet the responsibilities of parenthood is typified by their functioning in this arena. In all three families, the maintenance of the family unit through the provision of the basic necessities was given highest priority. All the women had known poverty and deprivation, both as children and as adults. They were determined that their children would be affected as little as possible by the conditions of poverty.

Their previous experiences had made these women extremely conscious of the necessity for maintaining communication with social-service agencies. Welfare assistance, in particular, was the area of greatest concern for them. They were quick to express their demands that the necessities be provided for their families. All three women hoped for a better future for their children, but as Mrs. Smith expressed it, "There can be no tomorrow, if we don't live through today." This statement would seem to sum up the feelings of all three women.

Function 2

. . . the provision of social togetherness which is the matrix for the affectional bond of family relationships . . . (Ackerman, 1958, p. 19)

The families exhibited strong bonds of unity and togetherness. This was understandable since survival was a key issue for them. Their neighborhood was viewed as dangerous, therefore the families needed to develop close ties as a protection against their environment. The concept of person–nature orientation, in which the human being controls the surroundings and triumphs over environmental obstacles, had little relevance for them. Nothing was taken for granted in their environment of poverty and violence. These harsh realities unified the family members; consequently, strong affectional bonds were developed.

Many of the subjects adopted informal roles, and carried out self-appointed responsibilities. For example, the oldest boy in each of the three families assumed the responsibility of guarding his family's safety. This was done voluntarily, in response to the violent nature of their neighborhood, and it indicates the strong feelings of responsibility and closeness felt by family members toward one another.

Function 3

. . . the opportunity to evolve a personal identity, tied to family identity, this bond of identity providing the psychic integrity and strength for meeting new experience . . . (Ackerman, 1958, p. 19)

Each family member appeared to have a clear sense of personal identity. All were very conscious of race and took pride in their heritage; this was especially true of the older children who exhibited a high degree of black pride. The two daughters in the Brown family, who had babies of their own, discussed and believed in the merits of black women having large numbers of children. The family was seen as the vehicle for survival: The "more members in our family, the better," Mrs. Brown asserted.

Each of the three women believed in the worth and value of their children and effectively communicated this belief to them. The children consequently had developed strong identities. They were especially adept at handling new experiences; this skill was necessary because of the unpredictable nature of their neighborhood. It was the children's responsibility to relay information from the community to the family, where it was assessed in terms of its usefulness or relevance to the family members. This was an additional indication of the interdependence of the family members. The relational orientation of their value system emphasized the collateral aspects of family life (Speigel, 1971, pp. 167–168). In this regard, the families tended to be large in number, with members closely tied to one another. The welfare and/or goals of the family had primacy for all individuals, and members worked together for the greater good.

Function 4

. . . the patterning of sexual roles which prepares the way for sexual maturation and fulfillment . . . (Ackerman, 1958, p. 19)

The women functioned as role models for their children, providing especially clear prescriptions for the way a woman ought to function as a mother. The three mothers were devoted and self-sacrificing, and their influence on their daughters was particularly evident. For example, Mrs. Brown instructed her two daughters in the care of their infants, and by following her example they were able to fulfill their responsibilities adequately as mothers.* While expectations and behaviors related to how a woman should be as a wife were obviously less apparent, all the women appeared to sanction their children's relationships with the opposite sex.

The children's experience with adult males within a family (or extended family) context was extremely limited. Except for Mr. Young's infrequent and brief visits, there were no adult males in residence to whom the girls, as well as the boys, could look in order to learn first-hand how a man should participate as a husband and father. The mothers, however, appeared to give clear messages to the children regarding sex-appropriate behavior, for example, through the assignment of tasks. On the other hand, sons were often called upon to help where needed; they thereby gained experience in non–sex-linked role behaviors.

While the sons did not appear to have any special problems in their sex-role identification, the absence of an adult male figure did appear to have certain disadvantages in that the teenage boys prematurely took on several major responsibilities that otherwise would have been allocated to a father. The primary task assigned to them, and one they themselves tended to assume, was that of protector. The ghetto environment combined with the absence of a father seemed responsible for the overemphasis on masculinity by the older male children. Especially in the ghetto, an adult male residing in the home is a definite deterrent to crime. The women, who in most other

---

*Again, this needs to be considered in light of the families' emphasis on the maternal aspect of a woman's role and on the importance of ensuring the continuity of black families in this society.

instances managed to compensate for the absence of a male figure, were not able to ensure the safety of the family effectively.

The other task taken on by the sons was that of community liaison. The women tended to limit their participation outside of the home (except for their intense interest and investment in dealings with the Department of Social Services). This seemed to put pressure on the oldest boys to assume this additional role, which is one usually not taken on by teenagers.

All the women had to assume the dual role of mother and father. In general, the social system was blamed for the absence of the men. In all three families the lack of finances was given as the reason for the marital problems. The women were bitter toward the society that, while placing so much emphasis on monetary gains, kept them fettered, controlling them and the lives of their children through the bureaucratic dispensation of welfare payments. In one instance, one mother refused a proposal of marriage because she believed that marrying would jeopardize her welfare status. Rather than take a second chance with a marriage that might result in financial difficulties, she decided to remain a welfare recipient, thereby ensuring a steady (if low) income.

Function 5

> . . . the training toward integration into social roles and acceptance of social responsibility . . . (Ackerman, 1958, p. 19)

The families generally viewed the dominant, white culture as oppressive and prejudiced. Consequently, there was little value placed on the acceptance of traditional social responsibilities and roles. There was a general stance of resistance to authority. A lack of faith in the social system was evident, and police and health agencies, in particular, were seen as doing disservice to the black community. Welfare, although it provided for their basic necessities, was also viewed with suspicion and resentment. It was felt that the social system was responsible for the poverty and despair that plagued the black community and that society looked with indifference on the plight of blacks, the "second-class citizens." As a result, there was a great deal of resentment and bitterness evident in all the families. "We worked for nothing, for 300 years," commented Mrs. Lenora Reed, "everything we get, we deserve." This statement best summarizes the feelings of the majority of the members of the three families.

Attempts were made to adjust to social expectations only in the areas of education and religion. Education was generally viewed as a means of escaping from the ghetto, and all family members, except for the Browns, recognized its importance. Although their time orientation emphasized the here-and-now in most situations, an exception was made for education, with its future-looking implications and achievement orientation. Religion was another area in which the subjects integrated and accepted the traditional middle-class values. They believed strongly in church doctrine. Much of the social activity of the Smith and Brown families revolved around the church.

Function 6

. . . the cultivation of learning and the support for individual creativity and initiative (Ackerman, 1958, p. 19).

The value system of two of the three families, the Smiths and the Reeds, emphasized the need for education. In both cases, one motivating factor for the family's move from the South had been the opportunities provided by the New York state educational system. Mrs. Smith described her children's schooling as "a salvation for the children from the suffering of the black world." Mrs. Reed believed that a high-quality education would provide the "key" to her children's future. These beliefs were not held by Mrs. Brown, although one of her daughters intended to finish high school and enter the field of nursing.

The children were generally aware of the need for a good education in order to "make it" in the world outside the ghetto. In many instances, the older children were planning on attending college, and academic achievement was held in high regard despite members' bitterness about not receiving a high-quality education from the local ghetto schools. They believed that the educators did not take sufficient interest in the students, and they felt that in many cases the students were "pushed through" without the proper preparation for college.

There was a continuous process of learning within all three families. The mothers gave guidance and direction to their children in various ways. Much of this guidance was expressed either through religious references ("keep the faith," "The Lord is thy shepherd," etc.), in practical application (Mrs. Brown instructing her daughters on the care of the infants), or by generally giving useful information to help the children in their daily existence (crime information, neighborhood activities, shopping tips).

SUMMARY

In summary, it appears that these black families parented by women provided the climate in which healthy psychologic, physical, and social growth was possible. The women, although heavily burdened and leading rather restricted lives, appeared to feel gratified at the degree to which they have been successful in providing their children with the necessities of life. The children appeared to have gained a clear sense of individual, family, and racial identity and to have learned a variety of coping skills crucial to survival in the ghetto and adaptable to life in the wider community. Despite the stereotypes that characterize so much of the commentary on such families, this small sample provides evidence that these single-parent families can meet many of the needs of their members, even though limited by an unyielding environment.

In general, the limitations of this family form appear primarily related to the socioeconomic environment, rather than to their being single-parented and headed by females.

REFERENCES

Ackerman, N. *The Psychodynamics of Family Life.* New York: Basic, 1958.

Allen, W. The search for applicable theories of black family life. *Journal of Marriage and the Family*, 1978, 40, 117–129.

Bermann, E. *Scapegoat—The Impact of Death-Fear on an American Family.* Ann Arbor: University of Michigan Press, 1973.

Bould, S. Female-headed families: Personal fate control and the provider role. *Journal of Marriage and the Family*, 1977, 39, 339–349.

Glasser, P.H., & Navarre, E. The problem of families in the AFDC Program. In Sneeden, L. (ed.), *Poverty: A Psychosocial Analysis.* Berkeley: McCutchan, 1970.

Moynihan, D.P. *The Negro Family: A Case for National Action.* Washington, D.C.: U.S. Department of Labor, 1965.

Nobles, W.W. Toward an empirical and theoretical framework for defining black families. *Journal of Marriage and the Family*, 1978, 40, 679–694.

Parad, H.J., & Caplan, G. A framework for studying families in crisis. In Parad, H.J. (ed.), *Crisis Intervention: Selected Readings.* New York: Family Service Association of America, 1965, 53–72.

Pearsall, M. Participant observation as role and method in behavioral research. *Nursing Research* 1965, 14, 37–42.

Peters, M. Notes from the editor. *Journal of Marriage and the Family* (Special Issue on Black Families), 1978, 40, 655–658.

Ross, H.L., & Sawhill, I.V. What happens to children. *Time of Transition—The Growth of Families Headed by Women.* Washington, D.C.: The Urban Institute, 1975.

Spiegel, J. *Transactions—The Interplay between Individual, Family and Society.* New York: Science House, 1971.

U.S. Bureau of the Census. Projections of the number of households and families: 1979–1995. *Current Population Reports—Population Estimates and Projections*, Series P-25, No. 805, 1979(a).

U.S. Bureau of the Census. Divorce, child custody, and child support. *Current Population Reports—Special Studies*, Series P-23, No. 84, 1979(b).

U.S. Bureau of the Census. Households and families by type: March 1979. *Current Population Reports—Population Characteristics*, Series P-20, No. 345, 1979(c).

ADDITIONAL READINGS

Allen, W.R. Black Family Research in the United States. *Journal of Comparative Family Studies*. 1978, 9, 167–189.

Brandwein, R., Brown, C.A., Fox, E.M. Women and children last: The social situation of divorced mothers and their families. *Journal of Marriage and the Family*, 1974, 36, 498–514.

Gurin, P., & Epps, E. *Black Consciousness, Identity and Achievement*. New York: Wiley, 1975.

Hill, R.B. *The Strength of Black Families*. New York: Emerson Hall, 1972.

Mathis, A. Contrasting approaches to the study of black families. *Journal of Marriage and the Family* (Special Issue on Black Families), 40, 1978, 667–676.

Meyers, L.W. Black women and self-esteem. In Millman, M. & Kanter, R.M. (eds.), *Another Voice*, New York: Anchor, 1975.

Moen, P. Developing family indicators—family hardship, a case in point. *Journal of Family Issues*, 1980, 15–30.

Peters, M.F. Nine black families: A study of household management and childrearing in black families with working mothers. Dissertations Abstracts International, Ann Arbor, Michigan (xerox, university microfilms), 1976, 37(07), 46–48A.

Willie, C.V. *A New Look at Black Families*. Bayside, N.Y.: General Hall, 1976.

11

The Chicano Family: Myth and Reality

George Fred Rivera, Jr.
Aileen Lucero

Americans are becoming increasingly aware of the prejudice and biases that influence their everyday social interaction. The communications media are rife with subject matter that demonstrates this changing consciousness. However, these belief systems have been in fact so deeply implanted in the social consciousness that the extent to which they have shaped the research on ethnic families has not been fully recognized. *

Rivera and Lucero, reporting on a survey they conducted in one Colorado barrio, call into question myths they believe have colored prior research on Chicanos. On the basis of their data, they attempt to dispel the negative picture of the Chicano family that emphasizes cultural differences. They advocate a view that, while acknowledging differences, takes into consideration the degree to which the Chicano family, subject to common societal influences, is similar to the Anglo-American family. Although their position may benefit from the support of further research, the work of these authors challenges professionals to examine distortions in their perceptions of this growing segment of the American population.

Ever since the policy of Manifest Destiny extended Anglo domination into the northern territories of Mexico (what is now known as the southwestern United States), American ideology has seized upon cultural differences as a determining factor contributing to the subordinate status of Chicanos in American society. Though cultural differences between Chicanos and Anglos do exist to some extent, they have often been highly exaggerated or misin-

---

*See Chapter 8 in this volume for a discussion of this subject.

terpreted to the detriment of Chicanos.* Such emphasis on differences has functioned to victimize Chicanos because they have become causal explanations for behavior ranging from lack of educational achievement of Chicano youth to the unacculturated status of Chicanos. This perspective, focusing on cultural differences, continues to pervade much of the social-science literature and has contributed to a myth-filled portrait of Chicanos.

A social institution that has commanded much attention as the prototype of cultural differences has been the Chicano family. Many researchers have found the Chicano family to be almost the exact opposite from the Anglo-American family in value orientations and authority structure. In fact, their observations lead one to conclude that the Chicano family is more similar to the Mexican family of Mexico than it is to the Anglo-American family. The Chicano family has been described as being different from the Anglo-American family in sex-role definitions, but generally the family remains the most misunderstood institution in Chicano culture.

The studies that exist on the Chicano family have, for the most part, been based on qualitative research. Social scientists have often used participant observation as a methodologic approach to the study of the Chicano community, including in their studies a description of the Chicano family.† Another popular approach to the study of these families has been the use of case studies.‡ Though these ethnographic accounts represented much of the early research, they have serious limitations. Since these studies were conducted in rural settings, they are limited in their application to urban Chicano families. In addition, concentration on a few cases of selected observations over limited time periods made it difficult to generalize to an entire Chicano population. Thus, there is a need for empirical research to verify the conclusions reached in these early descriptive studies.

Though quantitative research on the Chicano family is needed, there has not been much empirical inquiry into this area. Many of the studies that exist in the literature are actually analyses of the Mexican family of Mexico.§ Intermarriage rates have received some attention, and it appears that Chicanos are experiencing an increase in the rate of exogamous marriage.‖ Ramirez (1967) has conducted an interesting study of sex roles and the family in Chicano culture, but he restricted his study to an analysis of Chicano college students.

---

*For an excellent discussion of the relationship between racism and cultural differences, see Memmi (1969, Chap. 14).
†Two examples of Chicano community studies that have included sections on the Chicano family are Madsen (1964) and Rubel (1966).
‡An excellent example of the case-study approach is Humphrey, (1944).
§See Diaz-Guerrero (1955); Fernandez-Marina, Maldonado-Sierra, & Trent (1958); Ramirez & Parres (1957).
‖See Panunzio (1942); Mittelbach & Moore (1968).

Recently, there has been some attention given to Chicano family types based on residential status and ability to speak English.* However, these studies lack the systematic analysis of Chicano and Chicana attitudes toward sex roles and the family in Chicano culture that is required for an examination of the purported differences. It was the purpose of this study to compare the attitudes of male and female barrio (community) residents in the following areas: (1) family attitudes toward education; (2) authority in the family; (3) machismo and its characteristics; (4) the role of the woman and children, and (5) perspectives on the Women's Liberation Movement.

METHOD AND SAMPLE

The research project was conducted in an urban area of Colorado in 1976. A barrio with a high concentration of Chicanos was chosen as the survey site. There were approximately 360 households located in the area; of these we selected a random sample of 120, approximately one-third of the barrio population. A self-administered questionnaire was left at each household, with instructions that only the "man or woman of the house" should participate in the study. In cases where respondents had problems filling out the questionnaires, we assisted them with clarifications or translations.

The sample of barrio residents included 52 males (43 percent) and 68 females (57 percent). The average age of respondents was 39 years, and their ages ranged from 17 to 79. Sixty-eight percent of the respondents were married; 22 percent were either divorced, separated, or widowed; only 10 percent of the respondents were single. Eighty-nine percent of the barrio residents had lived in Colorado more than 20 years, and 78 percent specified that they had lived in this particular barrio for more than 20 years. The majority of residents in our study were Catholic (87 percent) in religious orientation and Democrats (78 percent) in political affiliation. Most of the respondents preferred to call themselves *Mexican* or *Mexican-American* (41 percent) or *Hispano, Spanish-speaking,* or *Spanish-American* (36 percent). Only 19 percent preferred the term *Chicano.*

The 1970 Census reported that the median years of school completed by Spanish-surnamed males and females 25 years old and older in Colorado was 10.0 years and 9.8 years, respectively.† The Census statistics also revealed

---

*For an analysis of family types based on residential status, see Grebler, Moore, & Guzman (1970); for an analysis of family types based on language differences, see Tharp, Meadow, Lennhoff, & Satterfield (1968).

†The Census also reported that the median years of school completed by white males and females 25 years old and older in Colorado was 12.4 years. See Bureau of the Census (1973, p. 146).

that the median income for Spanish-surnamed families in Colorado was $7138 per year. The median income of white families in Colorado was $9635. In comparison, the median years of education attainment for our barrio sample was 10.4 years, and the median income was $7321 per year.*

FAMILY ATTITUDES TOWARD EDUCATION

Since the family is considered the first major agent of socialization, the literature has tended to focus on the Chicano family as an institution that transfers negative values on to its children. There has been some attempt at blaming the Chicano family for the lack of educational achievement on the part of its children. A case in point is Heller (1966) who contends that

> . . . few Mexican-American homes stress higher education or intellectual effort. Lack of parental encouragement to pursue a formal education may be directly tied to the parents' belief that higher education is useless for their children and would not result in achievement but rather lead to frustration and humiliation.

Although Heller does not provide empirical data to support her position on lack of parental encouragement, she finds it sufficient to report that Chicano children are failing to succeed in the school system. Our data suggest that her position on the value of education in Chicano families is not well taken. (Tables 11.1 and 11.2.) Barrio residents are almost unanimous (95 percent) in their view that education is a very important value in their lives. The difference between Chicanos (96 percent) and Chicanas (94 percent) appears slight in their consideration of education as a very important value in their lives. The data indicate that a majority of residents (60 percent) desire a college degree for their children. Slightly more men (65 percent) than women (57 percent) would also like (or would have liked) for their children to have (or have had) a college degree. Less than one-fourth of the sample (23 percent) indicated that they desired anything less than a college education for their children.

Since Heller implies that Chicano families do not provide parental encouragment to stay in school, we asked barrio residents about their reactions to the following statement: "It is better to stay in school and wait for financial rewards than to drop out and take a job." The results are given in Table 11.3. Almost three-fourths of the barrio residents believed it was better to

---

*Only seven barrio residents refused to report their incomes. The incomes of the remaining 113 who did provide information on this question were distributed as follows: below $4000 (26 percent); $4000–6999 (23 percent); $7000–9999 (12 percent); $10000–14999 (22 percent); and $15000 and over (17 percent).

TABLE 11.1
Importance of Education

DEGREE OF IMPORTANCE	CHICANOS (%)	CHICANAS (%)	TOTAL (%)
Very important	96	94	95
Fairly important or not important	4	6	5

stay in school and wait for financial rewards. Slightly more men (75 percent) than women (70 percent) also agreed with the statement. Although only a small percentage of the sample disagreed, interestingly, more women (18 percent) than men (14 percent) disagreed with the statement. However, the difference is too small to venture into explanations based on sex roles.

Our data do not support the position that education is not highly valued. Not only is education highly valued, but it is also greatly desired that Chicano children achieve a college education. In addition, barrio residents feel strongly about the merits of staying in school and not dropping out. Moreover, there do not appear to be any sex differences in these attitudes. Thus, we would conclude that the position taken by Heller on educational attitudes in the Chicano family is highly deceiving and in error. Chicanos do not appear to be that different from other Americans who desire the best for themselves and their children. Any other view is more myth than reality.

AUTHORITY IN THE FAMILY

There is general agreement in the literature that the Chicano family is highly patriarchal. Murillo (1971, p. 21) maintains that the husband and father is the autocratic head of the household and represents authority in the family. Heller (1966, p. 34) observes that "the husband is regarded as the authoritarian patriarchal figure who is both the head and master of the family." In addition, Simmons' research (1974, p. 60) reports that the Chicano family

TABLE 11.2
Educational Aspirations for Children

LEVEL OF EDUCATIONAL ASPIRATIONS	CHICANOS (%)*	CHICANAS (%)	TOTAL (%)
Less than college	26	21	23
Some college	10	22	17
A college degree	65	57	60

*Total does not add up to 100 percent because of rounding.

TABLE 11.3
Attitudes toward Staying in School

ATTITUDINAL PERSPECTIVE	CHICANOS (%)*	CHICANAS (%)	TOTAL (%)
Agree	75	70	72
Disagree	14	18	16
Do not know	12	12	12

*Total does not add up to 100 percent because of rounding.

is characterized by the dominance of the father. Tharp and associates (1968, p. 405) note that masculine dominance is central to the Chicano family, and Rubel (1966, p. 60) asserts that the husband and father is expected to dominate. Moore (1970, p. 105) and Madsen (1964, p. 48) maintain that male authority extends beyond the father to other males who are ranked by age. The results in Tables 11.4 and 11.5 indicate what barrio residents themselves think about the patriarchy that everyone agrees is part of their lives.

When barrio residents were asked who should have authority in the family, more than three-fourths (77 percent) indicated that both the man/husband and woman/wife should have equal authority. A much higher percentage of women (88 percent) than men (62 percent) believed in egalitarianism in familial authority. Almost three times as many men (35 percent) as women (12 percent) still upheld a patriarchal ideal. It is also interesting to note that no women and only 4 percent of the men favored a matriarchy.

Barrio residents were asked the following question: "When a major decision is made in your family, who makes it?" Almost three-fourths of the sample (71 percent) indicated that both the man/husband and woman/wife together make major decisions in their family. This egalitarian trend in decision making holds for both men and women. That there are still rudiments of the patriarchal ideal in the Chicano family is evident in the fact that more men (29 percent) than women (14 percent) indicated that the man/husband should be the major decision maker.

There is also some evidence in the literature to indicate that Chicano males have complete control of the family income. Humphrey (1944, p. 622) ob-

TABLE 11.4
Authority in the Family

AUTHORITY	CHICANOS (%)*	CHICANAS (%)	TOTAL (%)*
Man/husband	35	12	22
Woman/wife	4	0	2
Both	62	88	77

*Total does not add up to 100 percent because of rounding.

TABLE 11.5
Major Decision Maker in the Family

DECISION MAKER	CHICANOS (%)	CHICANAS (%)	TOTAL (%)
Man/husband	29	14	20
Woman/wife	0	15	9
Both	71	71	71

served that the father/husband functioned as the food provider for the family. Jones (1948, p. 451) has also noted:

Family authority is usually vested in the principal wage earner or the person in control of the family finances. This is typically the father or the eldest male wage-earner, who is consequently considered to be the head of the family.

However, Grebler and associates (1970, p. 361) maintain that it is primarily older respondents who are more notably traditional in their attitude on who should control the family income. Our findings on attitudes about the husband's having complete control of the family income are shown in Table 11.6. Almost two-thirds of the barrio residents disagreed with the statement that the husband should have complete control of the family income. Fifty-eight percent of the men disagreed, as did almost three-fourths (71 percent) of the women. A much higher percentage of men (40 percent) than women (24 percent) agreed with the statement.

There are many researchers who indicate that the Chicano family is highly patriarchal. They qualify their positions by stating that the Chicano family is undergoing changes resulting from acculturation;* nonetheless, their position is that the patriarchy is the prevailing form of authority in these

TABLE 11.6
Attitudes toward the Husband's Controlling the Family Income

ATTITUDINAL PERSPECTIVE	CHICANOS (%)	CHICANAS (%)*	TOTAL (%)
Agree	40	24	31
Disagree	58	71	65
Do not know	2	6	4

*Total does not add up to 100 percent because of rounding.

*All the researchers who write about it note the effects of acculturation on the Chicano family. Though they specify that there is a shift from the patriarchal ideal to a norm of equality, they maintain that the Chicano family is still primarily a patriarchy.

families. Only Grebler and associates (1970, p. 362) have data to indicate that "the ideas of younger, better paid, and less ghetto bound Mexican-Americans about the father's role are no longer quite so tenaciously patriarchal as some of the literature suggests." Our data strongly indicate that there is an egalitarian trend in the authority structure of the Chicano family. Although we note that Chicanos tend to support this trend less than Chicanas, we found that a majority of the men still expressed a preference for egalitarian modes. With the exception of Grebler and associates, our findings indicate that much of what has been written on authority in the Chicano family is more myth than reality in Chicano culture.

MACHISMO AND ITS CHARACTERISTICS

In the *American Heritage Dictionary*, machismo is defined as "an exaggerated sense of masculinity" (Davies, 1975). Moore (1970, p. 104) maintains that machismo is of great importance to the Chicano family and Chicanos in particular. Heller (1966, pp. 35–36), contending that the image of the ideal male in the Chicano culture is one of sexual prowess and adventurousness, concludes: "The norm is that the husband being a male, cannot be expected to remain faithful to his wife. . . ." Madsen (1964, p. 49) upholds this position, stating:

> Marital conflict results from the male desire to prove his machismo outside the home. The young husband must show his male acquaintances that he has more sexual energy than his wife can accommodate. To prove his prowess, he often continues the sexual hunt of his premarital days.

Moreover, Hayden (1966, p. 20) asserts that Chicanos desire large families because large families are evidence of an adequate machismo.

Those descriptions of machismo in Chicano culture perpetuate a view of the Chicano as an oversexed male who is forever proving his masculinity to himself and his friends. The importance of machismo to Chicanos and moral perspectives regarding extramarital affairs are shown in Tables 11.7 and 11.8.

TABLE 11.7
Importance of Machismo

ATTITUDINAL PERSPECTIVE	CHICANOS (%)	CHICANAS (%)	TOTAL (%)*
Agree	58	46	51
Disagree	26	32	29
Do not know	16	22	20

TABLE 11.8
Morality of Extramarital Sexual Relations

MORAL PERSPECTIVE	CHICANOS (%)*	CHICANAS (%)	TOTAL (%)
Morally wrong	71	74	72
Not a moral issue	30	26	28

*Total does not add up to 100 percent because of rounding.

Slightly more than half the sample (51 percent) agreed that machismo was an important quality for Chicano men to have. More men (58 percent) than women (46 percent) agreed that machismo was important. Slightly more women than men did not think machismo an important quality, and slightly more women than men did not know whether it was an important quality for Chicano men to have. A slight majority agreed that machismo was important, but that does not necessarily mean that extramarital sexual relations are part of the definition (Table 11.7).

Almost three-fourths (72 percent) of the barrio residents perceived extramarital sexual relations to be morally wrong; both men (71 percent) and women (74 percent) overwhelmingly considered this to be so. As expected, more men than women considered extramarital sexual relations not a moral issue, but the difference between them is slight indeed. It appears that extramarital sexual relations are not condoned by either men or women.

If machismo does not mean highly valuing extramarital sexual relations, what does it mean? What are some of the characteristics that make up a "macho" in Chicano culture? We suggest three areas as important determinants of the contemporary meaning of machismo (Tables 11.9, 11.10, and 11.11). Respondents were given a list of qualities that men can have and were asked to indicate the importance of each of these qualities. A majority of the barrio residents (59 percent) indicated that it was very important for a man to keep his feelings under control. Slightly more men (63 percent) than women (55 percent) indicated that this quality was very important for men. The fact that there has been less range for men to express their emotions is a conclusion generally reached by researchers of sex-role behavior. Men have

TABLE 11.9
Importance of a Man's Keeping His Feelings under Control

DEGREE OF IMPORTANCE	CHICANOS (%)	CHICANAS (%)	TOTAL (%)
Very important	63	55	59
Somewhat important or not important	37	45	41

TABLE 11.10
Importance of a Man's Putting Family before Anything Else

DEGREE OF IMPORTANCE	CHICANOS (%)	CHICANAS (%)	TOTAL (%)
Very important	90	89	89
Somewhat important or not important	10	11	11

been socialized to believe that it is not masculine to show one's emotions. Chicanos are no exception. Thus, it is our finding that part of the definition of machismo includes controlling one's feelings.

Tables 11.10 and 11.11 indicate some contemporary components of machismo. There was high general agreement by Chicanos (90 percent) and Chicanas (89 percent) that putting the family before anything else was a very important quality for men to have. In addition, both men (85 percent) and women (90 percent) agreed that being a good provider was a very important quality in a man. These qualities would appear to have become important definitional aspects of the meaning of machismo. What is respected by family, friends, and peers are qualities contributing to good family relations, and those that contribute to marital discord are not valued.

We strongly contend that the image of machismo as projected by social scientists has given a highly distorted, exaggerated image of Chicano behavior. The social scientists seized on deviant behavior and suggested that it was the cultural norm. Their studies, which have no basis in empirical fact, focused on exotic behavior (extramarital sexual relations) and made the serious error of describing this behavior as an integral part of machismo in Chicano culture. Since these studies were primarily descriptive accounts, Montiel (1970, p. 62) maintains that "Terms like machismo are abstract, value-laden concepts that lack the empirical referents necessary for construction of sound explanations." We agree that the meaning of *machismo* remains to be defined, but we hold that it is still important to Chicano culture. In addition, we maintain that the meaning of *machismo* is very different from what the lit-

TABLE 11.11
Importance of a Man's Being a Good Provider

DEGREE OF IMPORTANCE	CHICANOS (%)	CHICANAS (%)	TOTAL (%)
Very important	85	90	88
Somewhat important or not important	15	10	12

erature suggests. It is in the descriptions of it that more myth than reality abounds in studies of the Chicano family.

THE ROLE OF THE WOMAN AND CHILDREN

Tharp and associates (1968, p. 405) observed that spouses in Chicano culture tend to live in separate segregated worlds; in addition, Rubel (1966, pp. 67–68) suggested that the segregation of women has created an image of the Chicana as an "unworldly" person. Burma (1961, p. 11) holds a similar position, noting that young Chicanas are taught that their place is in the home. Hayden (1966, p. 20) contends that "the mother assumes the traditional subservient and severely proscribed role of homemaker." Simmons (1974, p. 60) concurs that the wife is primarily concerned with household duties. Without exception, they describe the home as the "place" of Chicanas. Our data suggest otherwise (Table 11.12). A majority of barrio residents (57 percent) disagreed with the statement that a woman's place is in the home. A higher percentage of women (62 percent) than men (51 percent) disagreed with the statement, while slightly more men (33 percent) than women (29 percent) agreed with the statement. It appears that men were not in accord with the restrictions placed on a woman, but more women realized the limitations placed on them by being restricted to the home.

If Chicanas are defined as homemakers who take care of children, is having children the most important thing that can be done by a married woman? The responses to this question are shown in Table 11.13. More than two-thirds of the barrio residents agreed with the statement that having children is the most important thing that can be done by a married woman. Seventy-two percent of the men considered it very important, compared to 65 percent of the women. Thus, children still appear to be an important aspect of Chicano family life, and having children is still considered an important function for married women.

Social scientists who contend that a woman's place is in the home in Chicano culture are in serious error concerning the attitudes of the Chicano

TABLE 11.12
A Woman's Place Is in the Home

ATTITUDINAL PERSPECTIVE	CHICANOS (%)	CHICANAS (%)	TOTAL (%)*
Agree	33	29	30
Disagree	51	62	57
Do not know	16	9	12

*Total is less than 100% because of rounding.

TABLE 11.13
Having Children Is the Most Important Thing That Can Be Done by a
Married Woman

DEGREE OF IMPORTANCE	CHICANOS (%)	CHICANAS (%)	TOTAL (%)
Very important	72	65	68
Fairly important or not important	28	35	32

community. Chicanos and Chicanas alike are moving beyond such role restrictions and appear to be part of an egalitarian trend growing in the barrio.
Although Chicanos do not believe in restricting Chicanas to the home, they
still believe that having children is very important. The two attitudes are
not incompatible. Egalitarian families can believe in freeing the woman from
the household and also consider having children as important. Researchers
who claim that Chicano culture views the woman's place as being in the
home confuse the high value accorded to having children with "the place"
of the woman. Again, we find that much myth exists regarding the role of
the woman in Chicano culture.

PERSPECTIVES ON THE WOMEN'S
LIBERATION MOVEMENT

The involvement of Chicanas in the Women's Liberation Movement has
always raised serious problems for the Chicano Movement. Should Chicanas
identify themselves with a movement based on sex or with one based on
ethnic differences? It has been suggested that Chicanas should view themselves as part of the Chicano Movement because racial and ethnic identity
transcend other problems, including the special problems confronted by
women in American society. Moreover, it has been argued that the Women's
Liberation Movement is primarily a movement of middle-class women, and
as such it does not relate to the problems of minorities. However, the issue
of Chicana involvement in aspects of the Women's Liberation Movement is
far from resolved. Nieto (1974, p. 42) writes that the Chicana should

> . . . participate in the mainstream of the women's rights movement. She
> is needed here to provide the Chicana perspective as well as to provide
> support for the activities designed to help all women. Moreover, her unique
> role as a liaison person is crucial.

In contrast, Vasquez (1971, p. 204) writes that "when a family is involved
in a human rights movement, as is the Mexican-American family, there is

TABLE 11.14
Attitudes toward Chicanas' Being Involved in the Women's Liberation
Movement

ATTITUDINAL PERSPECTIVE	CHICANOS (%)*	CHICANAS (%)	TOTAL (%)
Agree	33	44	39
Disagree	35	27	31
Do not know	31	29	30

*Total is less than 100% because of rounding.

little room for a women's liberation movement alone." Thus, the appropriateness of the Women's Liberation Movement continues to be a debated question within Chicano Movement circles.

In our study we concerned ourselves with attitudes toward Chicanas being involved in the Women's Liberation Movement (Table 11.14). Barrio residents seem to be split on their attitudes toward this issue, although a higher percentage (39 percent) tended to agree than disagree. Forty-four percent of Chicanas, as compared to 33 percent of Chicanos, agreed that Chicanas should be involved in the Women's Liberation Movement. Chicanos appear to be a little more conservative on the issue. Chicanas are highly in favor of such involvement because they probably perceive the advantages of identification as women much more clearly than Chicanos are willing to concede. It is also interesting that almost one-third of the sample does not know whether Chicanas should be involved in the Women's Liberation Movement. Apparently, the debate on the issue has caused confusion, or the views of respected Chicanos has caused cognitive dissonance. Our data generally support the fact that different views still exist on the issue of Women's Liberation and that viewpoints have not yet crystallized into a definitive position.

CONCLUSIONS

Whenever cultural disparities are emphasized, there exists the possibility that myths will be created, based on the so-called differences. Since Chicanos are the nation's second largest minority and constitute an ethnic group that has kept most of its culture and language intact, all aspects of Chicano culture have been subject to analysis emphasizing cultural differences. As a consequence, a mythical portrait of Chicanos has been created that is far removed from the social reality of Chicano culture.

The Chicano family has received much attention as an institution that is substantially different from the Anglo-American family in values and sex-role perceptions. However, we found that there exist many myths regarding the Chicano family in the prevailing literature.* These include the myths of (1) the Chicano family's devaluation of education, (2) the patriarchy in Chicano culture, (3) the definition of machismo, and (4) the role of the woman in Chicano culture. We did not discover a mistaken view in the literature on barrio attitudes toward the Women's Liberation Movement; there were differing viewpoints. We found the Chicano community to be fairly divided on the issue. Though Chicanos tended to be more conservative than Chicanas on most issues concerning the family, a majority of Chicanos and Chicanas in our community study held the following beliefs: They strongly believed in the value of education and supported egalitarianism in family authority; they valued machismo as important but viewed extramarital sexual relations as morally wrong; they believed that a woman's place was not exclusively in the home.

Though there are Chicanos and Chicanas who exhibit traditional attitudes approximating those found in the family structure of the Mexican family, they constitute a minority within the barrio. Apparently, acculturation and urbanization have had an impact on the Chicano family, but it may not only be the Chicano family that has changed. Since differences have been emphasized to the detriment of Chicanos, the Chicano family has been described negatively. Perhaps the only thing that may have changed is the viewpoint of researchers who are beginning to present the Chicano family in a manner devoid of exotic descriptions. It appears that social scientists who focused on negative interpretations of the Chicano family were in error in either their observations or in their interpretations of what they saw.

There are probably some very real differences between the Chicano family and the Anglo-American family. Although there has been some acculturation of Chicanos, the influence of Chicano culture persists even in the most acculturated individuals. However, what is different in the Chicano family probably cannot be discovered until what is considered "different and negative" is put to rest. Until then, it will probably be more important to emphasize what is "similar and positive" in the Chicano family so that relations between Anglos and Chicanos will not be grounded in false assumptions.

ACKNOWLEDGMENTS

The authors would like to thank Richard Acosta, Vivian Pompa, and Edward Salazar for their invaluable aid in collecting the data for this study. We especially wish to thank Edward Salazar for directing the field work portion of this study.

---

*For a discussion of the "masculinity cult" as a myth in the literature on the Chicano family, see Montiel (1970). The myth of political inactivity on the part of the Chicano family is strongly refuted by Zinn (1975).

REFERENCES

Burma, J.H. *Spanish-Speaking Groups in the United States*. Durham, N.C.: Duke University Press, 1961.

Davies, Z. (ed.). *The American Heritage Dictionary*. New York: Dell, 1975.

Diaz-Guerrero, R. Neurosis and the Mexican family structure. *American Journal of Psychiatry*, 1955, 112, 411–417.

Fernandez-Marina, R., Maldonado-Sierra, E.D., & Trent, R.D. Three basic themes in Mexican and Puerto Rican family values. *Journal of Social Psychology*, 1958, 48, 167–181.

Grebler, L., Moore, J.W., & Guzman, R. *The Mexican-American People*. New York: The Free Press, 1970.

Hayden, R.G. Spanish-Americans of the southwest: Life style patterns and their implications. *Welfare in Review*, 1966, 4, 14–25.

Heller, C.S. *Mexican American Youth: Forgotten Youth at the Crossroads*. New York: Random House, 1966.

Humphrey, N.D. The changing structure of the Detroit Mexican family: An index of acculturation. *American Sociological Review*, 1944, 9, 622–626.

Jones, R.C. Ethnic family patterns: The Mexican family in the United States. *American Journal of Sociology*, 1948, 53, 450–452.

Madsen, W. *Mexican Americans of South Texas*. New York: Holt, Rinehart and Winston, 1964.

Memmi, A. *Dominated Man*. Boston: Beacon Press, 1969.

Mittelbach, F.G., & Moore, J.W. Ethnic endogamy—the case of Mexican Americans. *American Journal of Sociology*, 1968, 74, 50–62.

Montiel, M. The social science myth of the Mexican American family. *El Grito*, 1970, 56–63.

Moore, J.W. *Mexican Americans*. Englewood Cliffs, N. J.: Prentice-Hall, 1970.

Murillo, N. The Mexican American family. In Wagner, N.N., Haug, M.J., & Hernandez, C.A. (eds.), *Chicanos: Social and Psychological Perspectives*. St. Louis: Mosby, 1971, 15–25.

Nieto, C. The Chicana and the Women's Rights Movement. *Civil Rights Digest*, 1974, 6, 36–42.

Panunzio, C. Intermarriage in Los Angeles, 1924–33. *American Journal of Sociology*, 1942, 47, 690–701.

Ramirez III, M. Identification with Mexican family values and authoritarianism in Mexican Americans. *The Journal of Social Psychiatry*, 1967, 73, 3–11.

Ramirez, S., & Parres, R. Some dynamic patterns in the organization of the Mexican family. *International Journal of Social Psychiatry*, 1957, 3, 18–21.

Rubel, A.J. *Across the Tracks: Mexican Americans in a Texas City*. Austin: University of Texas Press, 1966.

Simmons, O.G. *Anglo Americans and Mexican Americans in South Texas*. New York: Arno Press, 1974.

Tharp, R.G., Meadow, A., Lennhoff, S.G., & Satterfield, D. Changes in marriage roles accompanying the acculturation of the Mexican-American wife. *Journal of Marriage and the Family*, 1968, 30, 404–412.

U.S. Bureau of the Census. *Census of Population: 1970, Characteristics of the Population*, Colorado, Vol. 1, Part 7. Washington, D.C.: Government Printing Office, 1973.

Vasquez, E., The Mexican-American Woman. In Babcox, D., & Belkin, M. (eds.), *Liberation Now: Writings From the Women's Liberation Movement*. New York: Dell, 1971, 200–204.

Zinn, M.B. Political familism: Toward sex role equality in Chicano families. *Aztlan*, 1975, 6, 13–26.

12

Ethnic Identities of Japanese-American Families: Implications for Counseling

Betty S. Furuta

The clinical literature has been deficient in its treatment of issues concerning Asian-American families. This chapter represents a needed addition to the small but growing body of available information.

Mental health professionals have for some time been cognizant of the limited numbers of Japanese-Americans who have sought their services, although they have not been clear as to why this has been so. Furuta believes that this behavior is an outcome of this ethnic group's rooting in the traditional orientation of ancestral Japan. However, it would be erroneous to assume that this orientation can be found intact at all levels of acculturation in contemporary Japanese-American society. Instead, one degree or other of Anglo cultural influence has intermingled with the traditional over time to produce a complex mix of ethnic identities. Furuta elucidates an ethnic identity model that provides counselors with a way of classifying, and thereby understanding, the products of this complicated acculturative process. In addition, she spells out a set of counseling guidelines that articulate with the ethnic identity types, allowing the counselor to implement this understanding of the needs of Japanese-Americans, distinguishing one subgroup's orientation and needs from those of another. Rich clinical material illustrates potential counseling strategies.

With the greater availability of mental health care through community clinics, the health professions have been faced with the need to treat an ever-broadening spectrum of ethnic clientele. Outcomes have been less than salutary. Mental health professionals have been considering what it is that constitutes effective treatment for a culturally diverse clientele. One of the problems appears to be related to the fact that psychotherapy ordinarily requires persons whose cultural values mesh well with those of the therapist, who can feel comfortable or at least can tolerate an ambiguous therapeutic relationship, who believe in change and the future, and who value their "I." A transcultural therapeutic situation is likened to a game where one side plays by the rules and the other side does not, probably because the latter have not learned the rules in the first place (Mazur, 1973). For those few Asian-Americans who might appear for counseling, the dropout rate after the initial interview is disproportionately high: 52 percent, compared to 28.9 percent for non-Asians (Sue & McKinney, 1975).

Japanese-Americans have been conspicuously absent from mental health facilities. Even when compared with other ethnic minorities, all of whom underutilize services, Japanese-Americans appear to be among the lowest of all users (Hatanaka, Watanabe, & Ono, 1975; Miranda & Kitano, 1976; Sue & Sue, 1973). Indeed, among the helping professions, the popular conception regarding mental illness among Japanese-Americans is exemplified by the question, "Is there any?" Kitano (1969) questioned 16 Japanese-American professionals on their recollections and impressions of mental illness in the Japanese community in which they worked. All agreed that if mental illness were defined as use of mental health services or hospitalization, the Japanese-Americans were a mentally healthy people. They differed, however, on whether there was need for treatment, with 60 percent stating that all generations needed services, and 40 percent maintaining that mental health was good.*

A different picture emerges when one looks at Japanese community agencies. As the number of ethnic personnel employed at health and social service centers increases, the number of clients of Japanese ancestry who either seek help or become identified as requiring mental health care also increases. The greatest need appears among the older generation, especially single men who are aging without the traditional family and cultural supports, and among the "war brides," i.e., Japanese nationals who married U.S. military personnel (Kitano, 1976, p. 152; Wake, 1975; Whitenack, 1978). Recent experiences have demonstrated that when Asian-American personnel are deployed as teams or units rather than singly dispersed throughout a mental health service, utilization and effectiveness rates are markedly enhanced. Both community-based and government-funded projects corroborate increased usage with the utilization of team approaches (President's Commission on Mental Health, 1978, p. 793).

The symptoms and conflicts that prompt the seeking of mental health care

---

*The 1970 United States Census reports that of 1.3 million Asians, 588,300 were Japanese. Of the 134,000 Japanese families, 114,600 households were composed of husband, wife, and children 18 years of age and younger. Of the 203 million residents in the United States, Japanese represented 3.5 percent. By far the largest contingent of Japanese reside in Hawaii and the western United States, especially California. New York, Chicago, and Boston also have sizable Japanese populations. (Bureau of the Census, 1973).

may well depend upon an individual's identification by generation. Having some familiarity with the ethnic terminology helps one to learn about the Japanese and their culture. There is a convenient mode for designating each generation. The *issei*, first generation, is an immigrant from Japan. Members of this generation, most of whom arrived between 1885 and 1924, are now between 70 and 95 years old. The American-born *nisei*, second generation, is a child of at least one *issei;* most of the *nisei* are now between 45 and 70 years old. The *sansei*, third generation, is a grandchild of an *issei; sansei* range from late teens to about 45 years old. The *yonsei*, fourth generation, is a great-grandchild of an issei; this group consists chiefly of infants and school-age children. The term *kibei*, literally "returned to America," refers to *nisei* who were sent to Japan to be educated and then returned to the United States, a common practice prior to World War II. While persons may be informally reassigned to another grouping, the conception of generation remains intact as a working reality. For example, an offspring of *nisei* parents who was born while they were in Japan might jokingly call himself an *"issei."* An older *sansei* who is strongly characterized by traditional values might be seen as *"nisei."* The *nisei* who is very Americanized might be regarded a *"sansei,"* and so on (Lyman, 1970, p. 83; Kiefer, 1974, p. 96).

> The Japanese are the only immigrant group in America who specify by a linguistic term and characterize with a unique personality each generation of descendants from the original immigrant group. In contrast, for example, to the United States Census and the Chinese, the Japanese do not merely distinguish native-born from foreign-born but rather count geo-generationally forward or backward with each new generational grouping. Moreover, from the standpoint of any single living generational group, the others are imputed to have peculiar and distinctive personalities and attendant behavior patterns which are evaluated in positive or negative terms. Each generation removed from Japan is assumed to have its own characterological qualities, qualities which are derived at the outset from its spatio-temporal position. . . . Thus, each generation is living out a unique, temporally governed lifetime which shall not be seen again after it is gone (Lyman, 1970, p. 83).

A MODEL OF ETHNIC IDENTITY

Ethnic identity stands out as a critical concept in any productive study of the mental health of Japanese-Americans. Therefore, this chapter will review traditional and cultural values together with their influences on the Japanese-American family. An ethnic identity model that emphasizes acculturation will be used as the theoretical framework (Clark, Kaufman, & Pierce, 1976). Some clinical implications for mental health practitioners will then be presented with guidelines for structuring the counseling milieu for Japanese-American clientele.

Japanese-Americans reflect to a greater or lesser degree both traditional Japanese and American cultural values. What needs to be remembered is that the Japanese-American family is neither exclusively Japanese nor exclusively American but a hybrid product of both cultural contexts. There is an underlying assumption that people who live in regular contact with more than one distinctly different culture will be confused in thought and action unless some clarity develops with regard to the conflict in beliefs and habits in their environment. The following model places the acculturative process in perspective.

The ethnic identity model addresses the issues of both ethnic identity and acculturation by studying the relationships of the two dimensions in the same individual. Acculturation becomes one measure of ethnic identity, an even more complex construct. Ethnic identity is then examined on three dimensions: acculturative balance scale, traditional orientation, and Anglo face. These dimensions were conceptualized from a research design using picture identification, questionnaires, and interviews with a Japanese-American and a Hispanic-American urban population (Clark, Kaufman, & Pierce, 1976; Pierce, Clark, & Kaufman, 1978; Pierce, Clark, & Kiefer, 1972).

Acculturative Balance Scale (ABS). This ethnic identity dimension is determined by an individual's correct answers to a picture-identification test that measures knowledge of traditional versus contemporary American popular culture. The test essentially shows a person's simple familiarity with everyday Japanese life, as compared with everyday American life. Substantial differences between generations in residence in the United States were revealed, making this scale a useful indicator of acculturation. As might be anticipated, the younger generation showed greater cognitive acculturation than the immigrants (Clark, Kaufman, & Pierce, 1976). These results are shown in Figure 12.1.

Traditional Orientation (TO). This dimension is derived from a series of questions about social relationships and level of participation within one's ethnic group—for example, speaking Japanese, celebrating traditional holidays, holding membership in ethnic organizations, attending ethnic church, eating Japanese food, the proportion of total friends who are Japanese, and so forth. TO indicates the degree to which an individual behaves as though he or she were a member of the traditional society (Clark, Kaufman, & Pierce, 1976).

Anglo Face (AF). This dimension is drawn from a series of questions about social relationships and level of participation with the majority or American

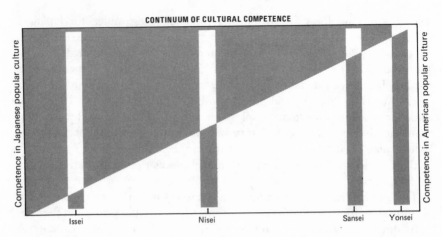

FIGURE 12.1. Japanese-American cultural competence by generation.

culture—for example, celebrating American holidays, attending Anglo movies, proportion of total friends who are nonethnic, eating American foods, and so forth. AF indicates the degree to which an individual behaves as though he or she were a member of the American or Anglo society (Clark, Kaufman, & Pierce, 1976).

ETHNIC IDENTITY TYPOLOGIES

The above dimensions, ABS, TO, and AF revealed six patterns called *ethnic identity types*. These statistically tested patterns showed that the critical factors in formulating the profiles were age, generation of residence in the United States, and personal choice, but not ethnicity, gender, adaptation rating, or education. These typologies are viewed as six bicultural life-styles that are generalizable beyond a single ethnic group (Clark, Kaufman, & Pierce, 1976).

Types 1 and 2. Types 1 and 2 are almost entirely immigrant first generation. The major difference between the two generational types is TO, that is, the personal choice either to move away from or to stay within the ethnic community. Type-1 individuals showed predominant traditional life-styles, while Type-2 individuals move within a broader social circle and feel themselves to be American.

Types 3 and 4. Types 3 and 4 are almost entirely middle-aged second generation. The difference between the two generational types is AF. Type-

3 individuals are slightly more traditional as compared to those of Type 4, but at the same time they are higher in AF. Type 3 emphasis in AF is shown by heavy involvement in American activities and social relationships with nonethnic friends, residing in Anglo neighborhoods, and the like. Type-4 persons, on the mean for ABS and TO, also show more "ethnic face" than their age peers or even than the issei generation. They emphasize their traditional culture in their self-presentation. Clearly, persons who approach biculturality can modulate the strength of their ethnic identity through face behavior (Clark, Kaufman, & Pierce, 1976).

Types 5 and 6. Types 5 and 6 are almost entirely young third generation who are highly Anglicized on the ABS and in TO. The striking difference between the two generational types lies in AF. Type-5 individuals reveal a strong blossoming of "ethnic face" but with a lack of knowledge about Japanese culture and an inability to speak or read Japanese. They are striving to reconnect with the traditional culture and are often active in Asian-studies programs, Asian consciousness-raising activities, Japanese celebrations and festivals, and the like. Type-6 persons show that they are Americanized. Their interests and behavior are no different from those of majority adolescents, and they show little concern with Japanese culture (Clark, Kaufman, & Pierce, 1976). At the group or generational level the total knowledge about the traditional popular culture appears to be on the wane with each successive generation (Connor, 1974, p. 161; Kiefer, 1974, p. 112).

THE TRADITIONAL JAPANESE CULTURE

Although ethnic identity of Japanese-Americans proceeds inexorably toward anglicization, traditional culture (including beliefs and habits) continues to influence families and the life-styles of their members. Assuredly, individuals of Types 1 through 5 of the ethnic-identity model are being affected by traditional Japanese values, however pronounced or attenuated. Values guide the choices people make. What distinguishes one cultural group from another is not simply the rules themselves but how they are assembled—that is, determining the priorities, how they are structured, and how they are employed. The way values are assembled, like the pieces of a puzzle, creates the rich cultural variety.

The plethora of culturally relevant data calls for the establishment of some criteria for separating the wheat from the chaff. Therefore, in constructing this model, I have chosen to include only those traditional values or practices that (1) provide insight into Japanese-American behavior, especially in families, and (2) introduce a perspective or principle that would help develop some guidelines for mental health counseling of Japanese-Americans. The following cultural patternings were selected.

Household System

The *issei* immigrants, most of whom arrived between 1885 and 1924, brought with them the culture of the Tokugawa (1680–1867) and Meiji (1868–1911) eras. Philosophical precepts of Confucianism, Buddhism, and Taoism pervaded the society. Probably the most important transplanted institution was what can be termed the household system called *Ie* (pronounced *ee-yeh*), which served as the primary unit for all social action. The household held strict precedence over the individual. Members maintained their role and comportment under the authoritarian direction of the head of the household and suppressed any personal yearnings that were unbecoming to their position. This is not to say that relationships precluded feelings of affection, but role, duty, and responsibility always took priority (Beardsley, Hall, & Ward, 1959, p. 216; Fukutake, 1967, p. 49; Kitano, 1976, p. 43).

The *Ie* was perceived as a corporate, living organism that included a past, present, and future. The family continuum encompassed not only the present generation but also ancestors and those members yet unborn. The *Ie* served a legal function, too, for births, marriages, deaths, adoptions, and residence in the foreign country were all recorded in the name of the household system and not in the name of the individual (Nakane, 1972). Some splitting off of nuclear families was allowed, but these were still subject to the governance of the *Ie*. Permitting some independent family existence accounts for the delimited Japanese extended family network that is nowhere comparable to the fully developed Chinese clan system (Lyman, 1970, p. 90).

Shame as Social Control. The omnipresent household system imposed social control by *haji* (shame), those feelings of painful embarrassment or a sense of mortification and humiliation so profound that the individual wishes simply to disappear. Members of a household system, who were raised from infancy to perceive themselves as representatives of the family, knew they were subject to public scrutiny. Because of role models and the collective orientation monitored constantly by selective rewards and punishments, members were quite aware of what constituted proper conduct (Kitano, 1976, p. 44; Maykovich, 1972, p. 30; Stierlin, 1974).

A corollary to the sanction of shame was the ethic of achievement as well as work. The idealized posture for a family member would be to discharge his role and responsibilities in such a way as to bring praise and approbation to the household. Families inculcated the belief that however humble one's origins, courage, hard work, and perseverance could take one anywhere. Educational achievement, a strong traditional value, was particularly respected (Maykovich, 1972, pp. 34–36; Okano & Spilka, 1971).

Making an Interdependent Personality. Of course, the *Ie*, a corporate entity, provided a natural arena for fostering the development of an interdependent rather than individuated personality. Children were typically raised with large doses of affection, physical contact, and indulgent support, coupled with concerted attempts to meet as many of their needs as humanly possible ("outrageous spoiling" from an Anglo viewpoint). Strong maternal-child attachment was valued; it, in turn, prepared the way for an easy maturational transferring of the child's trust toward other people. Children often slept with their parents until age 12 before being moved into another room with siblings. Nursing frequently continued through early school age. The net result of these practices mutually reinforced strong emotional attachment and interdependent investment among each member (Caudill, 1976, p. 164; Caudill & Doi, 1963, p. 412; Kiefer, 1974, p. 177).

The traditional interpersonal dynamic of *amaeru* or *amae* (pronounced *ah-mah-yeh-roo*), first learned in the *Ie* between parent and child, has been cited as a cornerstone in the traditional Japanese personality. *Amaeru*, an intransitive verb that resists easy translation, essentially means to depend upon or to avail oneself of another person's benevolence, to receive indulgent support from other people (Doi, 1962, p. 132–139; Doi, 1973). With experience, one discerned the social intricacies of *amaeru* interaction, which was mostly nonverbally apprehended. One needed to learn to modulate with whom and under what circumstances one could *amaeru*. Thwarting of the core dependency led to the behavioral consequences of *kodawaru*, anxiety about the personal relationship and its discovery, which in turn led to *sumanai*, feelings of guilt and obligation with failure to comport oneself as one ought to have done (Doi, 1962, pp. 132–139; Lyman, 1970, p. 89). Minor illnesses provided a convenient condition for *amaeru*. Sickness legitimized getting nurturance and having dependency needs met. One also could communicate love and affection in action, since traditional Japanese were unlikely to verbalize feelings such as "I want to be taken care of," "I want some attention," or even "I love you" (Caudill, 1976, p. 164).

The Household System in America. The household system, transplanted to the United States, grew to encompass not only family and kin but also the larger Japanese-American community. Intense cooperation within the ethnic group enabled its members to succeed at most common enterprises (Kiefer, 1974, p. 13). Appeals to the common ethnic identity were regularly heard: to be good and to do good so that behaviors reflected well on all Japanese-

Americans. Earning an academic degree, and higher education generally, remained highly valued and prestigious. Conversely, collective controls coupled with insistence upon proper comportment, particularly toward authority, kept crime and delinquency rates very low. One did not dare step out of line, for parents would be certain to hear about it and that would bring shame on the family. Unhappily, with Anglicization, juvenile delinquency rates are noticeably increasing (Kitano, 1976, pp. 140–156).

The sanction of shame remains the major suppressant of deviant behavior, including mental illness. Mental illness has no role within the culture and becomes both embarrassing and shameful. It is little wonder that people of Japanese ancestry are unseen at mental health clinics and hardly visible in mental hospitals (Kimmich, 1960; Kitano, 1976, pp. 150–158).

The popular notion is that the *sansei* generation is completely Anglicized. Studies report, however, that the *sansei* evidently retain enough of the traditional caretaking style so that differences from nonethnic infants are noticeable in infant behavior by age 3 to 4 months. Compared to their Anglo counterparts, *sansei* mothers exhibited more general indulgence, more breast and bottle feeding, more carrying, more lulling, and more playing with baby (Connor, 1974).

Japanese-Americans are largely unaware of the influence of *amaeru* on their personality structure, for the term is used only in reference to a spoiled child's behavior. In fact, conflicts within many *nisei* appear related to core dependency needs for love and affection, and to their feelings of guilt for the wish and shame for its expression (Lyman, 1970, p. 89; Babcock, 1962). Meredith (1965) hypothesized that the patterns revealed in studies of intraversion (turning inward) of *sansei* males and the anxiety of *sansei* females represent nonpathologic cultural parallels of the *amaeru* dynamic. Males apparently seem more disturbed over personal relationships *(kodawaru)* and seek an early resolution of frustrated *amae* by turning inward; females evidently express more anxiety and guilt *(sumanai)* due to conflicts between harboring feelings of family obligation and wanting Anglo freedom of individual choice.

Hierarchical (Complementary) Society

Another major influence on traditional culture was the *samurai* (warrior) ethic, essentially a lord-vassal relationship that stressed authoritarian principles and moral precepts and became the model for behavior. The *samurai* character, stereotypically depicted in movies as a solitary warrior enduring incredible adversity and calamity with inner control and stoicism, held some truth in fact. There developed social patterns of etiquette, that is, rigid formalism, humility and deference, modesty before superiors, and self-control. The vertical lord-vassal relationship, basically a complementary relationship, was emulated in parent-child, husband-wife, older sibling-younger sibling, elder-youth: virtually all familial and social relationships. Within the family, the father was the final authority; the parent-child relationship, not the spousal, took precedence (Frager, 1969; Lyman, 1970; Maykovich, 1972, pp. 30–32; Nitobe, 1912, p. 160).

The society was traditionally chauvinistically male oriented. By both role and upbringing, women were socialized to defer to men. The patriarchal, patrilineal emphasis, and all it denoted, placed woman in the subordinate position. Her role was primarily nurturant: raising children, maintaining the house, and keeping relationships proper and harmonious. The mother lived without status until she was widowed and her eldest son became head of the household. She then assumed the role of matriarch with all the privileges accorded the position (Maykovich, 1972, pp. 30–31; Shon, 1977).

Hierarchical Society in America.　Western egalitarianism unquestionably has been altering the traditional hierarchical relationships among Japanese-Americans. Nevertheless, vertical structuring still appears to characterize *nisei* and *sansei* families, ethnic Types 3 through 5, and even some Type-6 *sansei* families. In public presentation, men are accorded status and respect in the role as head of the household system and women tend to defer to them. (In actuality, inside the home, women are commonly in command.) The role of the oldest son, the major cultural transmitter and authority in the household, tends to remain operative. *Nisei* parents complain that their *sansei* children and *yonsei* grandchildren lack the proper deference toward authority, but observable attempts are made to raise offspring to respect their elders and superiors.

Males and females continually wrestle with the issue of autonomy conflicts between family role and obligations, on the one hand, and individuation and personal choice on the other. Increasingly, women are earning college degrees, being employed outside the home, trying to move out of the household prior to marriage, and generally liberating themselves from many traditional role constraints. Men are unavoidably affected by the changes in women's behavior in addition to the stress of trying to strike a workable compromise with the strong traditional male role-set (Kiefer, 1974, pp. 188–229; Asian American Mental Health Services, 1979).

Another vestige of the traditional hierarchical society is the Japanese-American tendency to be sensitive to status distinctions between conversational partners. The awareness of the status of a person, with appropriate modulation of behavior, is a conscious dimension not only in situational contacts but also in ongoing relationships. This concern for propriety in the presence of one's superior will manifest itself during therapist-client interactions as well. Silences, lack of verbal questioning or contradiction are often misinterpreted as implying assent when in actuality the client might simply be showing deference toward the therapist (Johnson, Marsella, & Johnson, 1974).

Reciprocal Obligation

The interpersonal dynamics of reciprocal obligation originated with Buddhism, where the diety conferred *on* (ascribed obligations, blessings) upon individuals who, in turn, were obliged to repay them by service and honor. Buddhism specified that a parent was one of the select few personages to whom repayment was due. Theoretically, the parental gift of life itself and of subsequent nurturance can never be repaid fully during one's lifetime. Therefore, one of life's greatest obligations was to care for one's parents. This meant caring for aged parents and honoring them even after their death (Kitano, 1976, p. 123; Maykovich, 1972, p. 29).

Another order of reciprocities was called *giri* (contractual, moral obligations). *Giri* might more accurately be referred to as quasi-contractual, for these transactions were tacit understandings only within the ethnic group. It was understood that all favors and gifts, goods or services, would be repaid by the recipient. There existed a scrupulous balancing of favors and obligations. If at all possible, the preferred position was to avoid indebtedness (Kitano, 1976, p. 123; Shon, 1977). Reciprocal obligations did not preclude the existence of genuine feelings of affection and helpfulness that the parties might hold for one another. (This dynamic is illustrative of Japanese emphasis on form or style regardless of the content.)

Reciprocal Obligations in America. Japanese-Americans are probably guided by reciprocal obligations more than they themselves are aware. Some examples might be informative. If friends and neighbors help with painting the house, it is tacitly understood that one will offer to help them paint their house or, barring that specific activity, assist with something comparable. One repays a gift with a gift; for example, the bowl that contained fresh fruit is returned with some homebaked cookies, perhaps. One must be mindful to select an appropriate repayment, for a return that is too generous could create still another round of reciprocal obligations.

When proffered help in time of need, the recipient incurs a debt of gratitude that is returned "with interest." For example, a person might decline a better, more lucrative job because a debt has been incurred to the employer who hired him when he was unemployed and needy. Despite payment of a fee for service, a family might feel especially grateful or obligated toward the therapist as they sense a resolution of their problems. If the therapist thwarts their attempts to discharge that obligation, the family might try to linger in counseling.

JAPANESE-AMERICAN NORMS

Norms refer to shared meaning within a culture and provide the context for communication. Norms enable individuals to determine the acceptable modes of behavior for both themselves and others (Kitano, 1976, p. 122). The following are some common normative behaviors utilized by Japanese-Americans; some of them all of the time, all of them some of the time but not by all of them all of the time.

ENRYO SYNDROME

Enryo (pronounced *end-yoh*) encompasses a cluster of self-effacing behavior connoting polite refusal and modesty. Of all the normative forms of behavior, Japanese-Americans employ *enryo* the most frequently. The norm originated with the Confucian ethic of proper comportment toward one's superiors. Contemporary usage of *enryo* includes such diverse circumstances as ambiguity of social interaction, feelings of embarrassment, not wishing to appear assertive, uncertainty about the status of a conversational partner, and masking of personal anxiety. Some concrete examples include hesitancy to speak up at meetings, particularly with nonethnic persons present; hesitancy to ask questions; selecting a less desired object when given a free choice; refusal of social invitations, especially the first time; declining a second serving of food although one might wish more; not asking for a promotion when one deserves it—the list is endless (Kitano, 1976, pp. 124–125). Caudill (1970) and Johnson and associates (1974), among other scholars, have corroborated the Japanese-American investment in self-effacement, modesty, and apology that has been frequently misunderstood outside the culture.

Hige (pronounced *he-geh*), a part of the *enryo* syndrome, is a prohibition against praise of oneself or one's family, especially in public. It is simply considered poor taste. The preferred self-presentation is modesty and humility. From the Anglo context, this norm would constitute a double message. For example, a parent might be very proud of a child's scholastic achievement but would disparage the accomplishment in the presence of persons outside the immediate family. One wonders about the possible negative outcomes for the child, since the social understandings are usually nonexistent in the American idiom (Kitano, 1976, p. 125).

Hazukashi (pronounced *ha-zoo-kah-she*), also a part of the *enryo* syndrome, is being shy and reticent. This norm is associated with the sanction of shame, that is, in the reflected appraisals of others. Thoughts like "People will laugh at me," "I don't want to make a fool of myself," or "People will think I'm showing off" are all examples of *hazukashi*. For those who understand the cultural usage of *enryo*, there is a neat balancing that occurs where another's accomplishments can be ascertained in a variety of subtle, indirect ways and can be modestly communicated. The norms for high individual and group achievement coexist with *enryo* (Caudill & DeVos, 1956; Okano & Spilka, 1971).

Other normative behaviors include *gaman (gah-mān)* and *shikataganai (she-kah-tah-gah-nye)*. *Gaman* can be translated as meaning the determination to persist or persevere. In times of frustration, pain, or adversity, one has the will to endure. *Shikataganai* holds a fatalistic connotation that one must endure the inevitable, accept what cannot be changed. Collectively, the normative behaviors are constraining on individuals and families. Inner control and outer emotional equanimity are the preferred modes of self-presentation. Japanese-American perception of a situation as unchangeable and as, therefore, merely to be endured, may be misperceived by outsiders as a lack of assertiveness or initiative. The submissive, collective compliance of 110,000 Japanese-Americans who were evacuated into concentration camps during World War II, has been attributed to the influences of these norms. In the main, they have been functional. However, there is no question that these repressive patterns exact their price.

The prohibition against self-expressiveness, including violence and aggression, combined with the absence of traditional cultural outlets for sensual enjoyment (baths, massage, hot springs, and the like) has led investigators to question how normal anger and frustrations are discharged. Not surprisingly, relatively high incidences of hypochondriasis and psychosomatic illnesses, gastrointestinal and hypertensive in particular, have been noted among Japanese-Americans (Babcock & Caudill, 1958, pp. 436–437; Kiefer, 1974, pp. 217–219; Kitano, 1969, pp. 196–199; Lyman, 1970, pp. 94–95). One wonders to what extent the physical symptoms mask an underlying depression or depressive reaction. Symptomatology, however, needs to be analyzed from the cultural context. Traditional Japanese medicine is closely associated with the normal, everyday, ongoing health maintenance of keeping one's "body in balance." The sensitivity to climatic change and emotional disturbance that adversely affect health is reflected in the capacity of the Japanese language to define precisely the nuances of bodily imbalance (Caudill, 1976, p. 161).

To provide mental health care for persons of Japanese ancestry, a therapist must take cognizance of acculturative balancing that includes the interplay of traditional cultural values based upon a compelling family orientation and

Anglicization that highly values individuation and autonomy. The household system, the hierarchical society, the reciprocal obligations, and the normative forms of behavior constitute dimensions of such a magnitude that counseling must be guided by them.

COUNSELING IMPLICATIONS AND GUIDELINES

The major difficulty in formulating counseling guidelines for Japanese-American clients lies in the paucity of empirical or documented clinical case studies. Undoubtedly, as use of mental health services increases (and it will), more substantial clinical insights will become available. For the present, we must be content to work from information drawn from a limited data base. In this chapter, the following implications for counseling guidelines have been derived from interviews with Japanese-Americans conducted by the author and from information provided by other ethnic mental health professionals, together with understanding gleaned from the literature.* The discussion will relate to ethnic identity Types 1 through 5, those family members who are influenced by traditional values to a greater or lesser extent.

Mental health practitioners have long known the crucial therapeutic significance of the client's initial overture for help, whether that contact is by telephone or in person. The therapist needs to be mindful particularly of the personal and social obstacles that the prospective Japanese-American client or family has hurdled even to make a contact. This is a fragile period in the counseling process. The following guidelines include strategies useful to the counselor who wishes to adopt, from the outset, practices that have the potential for enabling the family to remain in counseling beyond the first interview.

Support the Father's Role

However the family has defined the problem, they have already perceived the situation as a failure on their part; this is especially so for the father. As head of the household, the father will feel that he has failed in his overseer role, in his duty to ensure that members of his family are living properly, productively, and peacefully. He obviously will be vulnerable to any messages that imply his inadequacy in guidance or his contribution to the symptoms of the identified patient.

---

*The participating mental health professionals included two psychiatric nurse specialists, three psychiatrists (one Korean-American), two psychiatric social workers, one clinical psychologist, and two pastoral counselors: all Japanese-Americans from the greater San Francisco Bay Area. Information was obtained during 1978–79.

Because traditionally oriented fathers tend to be reticent, self-controlled, and economical with words (all these are culturally congruent traits that are interpreted as resistance by conventional psychotherapeutic norms), the therapist will be prone to turn to the mother for leverage. (Japanese-American females generally are more informative and talkative than are males [Johnson, Marsella, & Johnson, 1974].) The maneuver constitutes a therapeutic error. This subversion of the father's role and the failure to accord him appropriate deference will at best retard and at worst jeopardize treatment. Although the client or family members will almost never verbalize their discomfort during the interview, for that is disrespectful to the authority figure the therapist represents, they simply will not return for their second interview.

The preferable mode is to communicate first with the father and to acknowledge explicitly that he is the head of the family. Should the father not be present at the interview, it behooves the therapist to follow the protocol of consulting him by telephone, if necessary, to determine what he believes the problem to be, requesting his participation in formulating a beginning plan, and soliciting his support. One can then proceed with engaging the other family members in the treatment process. While there are no guarantees that this strategy will always work, one is increasing the probability that the family will remain in treatment.

Avoid Exacerbating Feelings of Shame

The problem must be particularly compelling or of such lengthy duration that the family members are at the end of their endurance, for they are breaching the sanction of shame and risking public exposure. Typically, a family member has desperately tried to seek private counsel through a trusted friend or relative or, perhaps, a respected member of the Japanese-American community. The therapist would enhance rapport with the family and patient if he were to acknowledge the strengths that enabled them to seek help and to mention that "they did the right thing." Supporting even tentative communications that reveal a desire to look at the problem, share a reaction, or try something different will help toward mitigating feelings of shame and developing greater comfort. In brief, even in response to a member's hostile remarks, it is important to provide support by commenting on positive intention.

To belabor the obvious, honoring the family's need for confidentiality becomes of paramount importance. The therapist's explicit statement that confidentiality will be maintained will be reassuring to the family. The issue undoubtedly would be on their minds, but they are unlikely to make an assertive inquiry. Japanese-Americans will go to great lengths to conceal what they perceive to be embarrassing or shameful situations. They will travel to another town, locate a non-Japanese therapist or, most problematic but still probable, avoid seeking counseling altogether rather than risk exposure. The more prominent and respected the family in the ethnic community, the greater the risk entailed.

Place Mental Health Problems in Perspective

Therapists might begin to help Japanese-Americans see that psychologic problems are human problems, that the cultural taboo against psychiatric care might be obsolete. "What happened is not so bad" or "We have helped families with worse problems than you have" or "There are other *nisei* families in the same situation" are statements representative of the type of support needed by these persons whose circumstances have left them feeling shamed and inadequate. It is essential to be honest about the treatment that might be required and also to provide large doses of "matter-of-factness" whenever possible. A *nisei* sociologist once advised the author, "Japanese are so skillful at conforming, that if you could somehow make psychiatric care (ethnically) normative, it would solve a lot of troubles." The idea is undoubtedly true, but the complexity of changing a value is also a reality.

For the above reasons, when Japanese-Americans do appear at the therapist's doorstep, the problems are often very severe and well entrenched (Kitano, 1970; Moteki, 1978). Primary prevention is unusual and probably nonexistent. Any message, implied or otherwise, that suggests, "Why didn't you bring him earlier?" will only serve to exacerbate the feelings of shame and guilt and probably contribute still another statistic to the Asian-American dropout rate.

Provide Hope and Direction

Conscious and explicit provision of hope that the situation can be different is a crucial early therapeutic task. Japanese-Americans would find it intolerable to remain in a state of ambiguity where answers to "What went wrong?" and "What can be done about it?" remain unclear. It is vital to help the family members get to the point of recognizing that their quest for a solution to their problem has some chance of succeeding. Any of the following issues imply hope for change:

- What behaviors are bothersome, and what do the family members want instead?

- What are strengths in the family network? Who are potentially supportive people?
- How might the identified patient (or any family member) signal when stress is too great?
- What is an average day like, and how might it be improved?

The point is that the therapist becomes more effective by being directive rather than nondirective with Japanese-Americans who are accustomed to prescribed roles, doing one's duty, and fulfilling responsibilities.

Be Scrupulous Regarding Tact, Courtesy, and Clarity

The conventional psychotherapeutic norm of encouraging expressiveness and candor is contraindicated with Japanese-Americans. As has already been noted, these people have a high investment in propriety, deference, self-effacement, avoiding shame, and not shaming others. Forthright, confronting messages are experienced as rude, coarse, and offensive and might hasten the client's departure. Negative reaction to verbal aggression and candor is apparently typical across Asian cultures (Shon, 1977).

When a simpler, more direct communication might indicate emotional involvement or be provocative, Japanese-Americans will employ euphemism, circumlocution, tangentiality, and tonal control. The listener must apprehend the important issue that is buried beneath the verbiage. The linguistic indirection serves to maintain emotional equanimity and self-control, that is, to mute one's own feelings and to prevent the disruption of another's composure. Japanese-Americans also tend not to volunteer any more information than they have to regarding feelings, opinions, and activities, especially before employers, colleagues, and guests. Because the face is vulnerable to unwitting emotional disclosure, avoidance of looking into another's face and averting one's gaze with conversational partners are commonplace; to do otherwise is considered rude. The characterologic ideal is the ability to mask one's true emotional state (Johnson, Marsella, & Johnson, 1974; Lyman, 1970, pp. 85–94; Yamagiwa, 1965, pp. 186–223).

At least initially, the therapist might be fortified with patience and permit indirection, circumlocution, euphemism, and speaking in the third person. A gradual move to directness may be effective. The therapist does need to serve as a role model who is a tactful yet an appropriately clear communicator. I am convinced that even with ethnic groups that place high value upon self-effacement, propriety, and indirection, the direct "I–thou" dialogue needs to be learned for behavioral change to occur.

Select the Proper Therapist

The introduction to the mental health facility is typically characterized by the transferring of the client from one person to another; this procedure should be avoided, if possible. Having to encounter a receptionist, followed by an intake worker, and then a therapist, who may or may not prescribe psychometry with still another practitioner tends to foster feelings of unworthiness, of being excess baggage (Miranda & Kitano, 1976). The client must be treated as an important person; introductions to a chief of service might be included, if that is convenient, for such an act carries prestige in the traditional culture.

The assignment of a therapist who would mesh well with a Japanese-American client becomes a bit more complicated. If one assesses that the individual adheres strongly to traditional culture, one would ideally assign a *nisei* clinician. Lacking such a person, the client might respond to an Asian who was conversant with traditional norms and who possessed sufficient insight into his or her own bicultural conflicts and acculturative processes. For *issei* and military "war brides," even though they might speak English, a bilingual therapist would help enormously.

Should no ethnic therapist be available, as a minimum requirement the practitioner must make available a consultant familiar with the culture. *Nisei* therapists, themselves, have divulged that because of the relatively rigidly defined modes of behavior, it becomes troublesome to differentiate clearly where role-set ends and psychiatric symptomatology begins. Reactions to anxiety and conflict with controlled affect, withdrawal, and ritualistic behavior are readily diagnosed as problematic among Anglos, but they are not necessarily problematic with Japanese-Americans (Kitano, 1970).

While not of overriding priority, chronologic age and ethnic identity type of the therapist might be considered in making an assignment. A traditionally oriented person of an older generation could conceivably find it both confusing and demeaning to expose his or her problems and miseries to someone the age of his or her child or grandchild.

Some *nisei*, *sansei*, and most especially *yonsei* request Caucasian therapists. Nonethnic practitioners have reported that several *sansei* females were adamant that they wanted only an Anglo therapist. The general issues with which each of them was struggling involved her relationship with a tradition-bound father who did not understand his offspring's liberal ways, her relationship with a mother who preferred that her daughter date Japanese boys rather than nonethnic boyfriends, and her own attempt to live away from home before marrying, a move interpreted by her parents as evidence of their failure in childrearing. Ethnic identity type, coupled with the client's preference, could serve as a valid basis for selecting a therapist.

Establish Goals Mutually

To reiterate a fundamental traditional value, the family (household system) takes precedence over the individual. Families are identified through time and are central to the self concept of Japanese-Americans. To establish goals, the therapist balances those traditional goals of interdependence and social acceptance that are juxtaposed with Anglo goals of individuation and self-reliance. The questions become, how does the identified patient and family perceive the situation, and what are their expectations of counseling? If the therapist is both nonethnic and unfamiliar with Japanese popular culture, the value systems of client and therapist probably will be disparate. Attempting to impose the therapist's values upon the family will effect no change at all or, as noted previously, will discourage the family from returning. Pragmatics dictate that goals be mutually formulated by the family and therapist. This will permit more exact meshing of the therapist's and the family's differing orientations and expectations (Mazur, 1973).

Broad goals commonly associated with counseling include the following (Glick & Hessler, 1974, pp. 60–64): first, facilitate communication of thought and feeling both of the individual and the family as a whole. Beyond the words, Japanese-American families need help in identifying and decoding the myriad nonverbal messages, both culturally prescribed and familially derived, that are apprehended and misinterpreted among themselves. Second, attempt to shift disturbed, inflexible roles and coalitions. Assess how the members' interdependence and complementary roles are functioning. Using tact and appropriate timing, help members to examine any false respect, counterfeit nurturing, interpersonal deceit, pathologic parenting, or other negative processes that are impeding the family's growth. Third, serve as a role model and educator. Because of the deference and respect accorded authority, the therapist holds a persuasive position for effecting change by role modeling. Members do need to communicate thoughts and feelings with clarity and with cultural sensitivity.

Utilize Family Therapy If Possible

Family therapy beckons as the treatment of choice for at least two reasons. First, it focuses on immediate, transactional family information that both family and therapist can experience together. It is a doing rather than a thinking orientation that lends itself to Japanese-American communicative style. Interdependence of roles and family networks for maintaining pacts, secrets, evasions and myths are more likely to be accessible. Second, the family as a cultural microcosm provides data for the therapist. Families can be helped to distinguish between those forms of behavior that are relevant within the household system and those that need to be modified in the outside world (Mazur, 1973; Speck & Rueveni, 1971, pp. 312–332).

Intergenerational family therapy is a modality that would appear to be well-suited to Japanese-American families. The bonds of relationship are perceived as ethically mandated rather than as simply emotional and cognitive in nature. Family members do keep in their heads a kind of ledger of credits and debits for and against other members as individuals and for families as a whole. The therapist's goal is to assist in rebalancing family loyalties and relationship debts or, to put it in other words, in effecting a rebalancing of justice. While a certain degree of imbalance may be constructive, unchangeable imbalance may become as pathogenic as a rigidly balanced system (Boszormenyi-Nagy & Spark, 1973, pp. 53–64).

At least initially, individual therapy would appear more useful than group therapy, for the feelings of shame and difficulty in self-disclosure before others may be a deterrent to participation. However, if one wants the client to learn by example, observing member interaction may be helpful.

COUNSELING EXAMPLES

The following case examples of an individual, a marital couple, and a family will illustrate application of the ethnic identity guide for counseling.

EIKO YAMADA

Mrs. Eiko Yamada, a 42-year-old *nisei* social worker, ethnic identity Type 4, sought counseling because of persistent feelings of guilt and shame regarding an assertive action she took against an uncle 2 months previously. In her family of origin, she was the second of four children; the others were Toshio, the older brother, Sumiko, a younger sister, and Ken, the youngest brother, who was severely handicapped by congenital cerebral palsy. All the siblings except Ken were married and raising children. Shortly after their father's funeral a year before (their mother had been deceased already), a maternal uncle laid claim to some property in the father's estate. Neither parent had ever spoken about an outstanding debt, nor were written contracts, title ownership, or informal notes substantiating the claim ever located.

Because the uncle, who was independently wealthy, was known to proffer monetary gifts to some members of his family periodically, the siblings conceded that he probably did pay for at least a portion of the property since an old bank statement revealed a certain cash flow. However, the uncle insisted on the property and would not accept financial reimbursement.

How were the children of deceased parents to settle a verbal claim against their father's estate, lodged by an older-generational relative? After hours of agonizing discussion, and on advice of legal counsel, the siblings sold the disputed property.

Four more months elapsed. Then Eiko carefully drafted a letter to the uncle stating at the outset that she was writing only for herself and not for her siblings. She had had periodic social contacts with him in the past and wanted to normalize the relationship. She shared the painful process that the siblings underwent in attempting to resolve the dispute fairly and honorably. At one point she inquired, "But how does one balance the account on the kinds of giving that family members do for one another?" For example, her mother, the uncle's sister, had paid for a portion of the family home purchased over a generation ago to which she had never laid claim and in which the uncle held title. In addition, in years past, the uncle himself had received assistance from his sister when she agreed to assume full physical care of an elderly, senile parent for 5 years so that he could devote time to his career. Eiko joined her brother and sister in establishing a trust fund from the inheritance for Ken; the money was not for themselves or their children. She appealed for the uncle's understanding and expressed a desire to see him again. The uncle never answered the letter. Instead, he telephoned Toshio and irately declared that he refused to see or hear from Eiko again, that he felt attacked, and that he was robbed by the children of his sister. Toshio, who knew nothing about the correspondence, asked sister Sumiko to inquire of Eiko just what had been written and why she chose to act when she did. While the estrangement with the uncle remained, Eiko and Toshio readily resolved their differences.

Discussion

Family conflicts that emerge from differing acculturative balancing, coupled with intergenerational reciprocity, are illustrated in this case presentation.

Self-Esteem Is Determined by Fulfilling Family Roles and Obligations. In writing the letter, Eiko was behaving normatively by Anglo standards but inappropriately by traditional standards. Toshio, the eldest son, who assumed the role of head of the household upon his father's death, was responsible for handling any communication with the uncle. Propriety of form is followed no matter what the content. Eiko knew that Toshio, more traditional than she, managed interpersonal conflicts by not handling them. Therefore, it was Eiko's view, "If I still feel unsettled about my relationship with Uncle, then I ought to take care of my own 'unfinished business' "; this is an Anglo orientation toward self-assertiveness. The uncle, obviously tradition-bound, felt violated not only by the lack of deference but also by the breach of protocol that entailed the eldest son's contacting him. The end result was that the self-esteem of everybody suffered. Eiko felt guilt for a positive intention that backfired, shame for bringing embarrassment and pain to her siblings and for possibly worsening the estrangement with the uncle.

Another family obligation was the care of Ken, the handicapped brother. A vigorously operant traditional norm is "taking care of one's own." Not to do so is shameful. Without questioning, the siblings continued the care where the parents had left off.

Communication Is Restrained, Indirect, and Controlled. It is important to note the interplay of both traditional and Anglo values in Eiko's communication with the uncle. The communication was at one and the same time restrained and controlled (a letter was used rather than a telephone call or a personal visit) and direct and assertive (she shared the explicit reasons for her decision not to accede to the uncle's claim).

The uncle as well as Toshio used a third party for communicating conflictual, emotion-laden issues; this typical traditional practice permits the parties involved to "save face." The uncle responded to Eiko indirectly through Toshio; Toshio contacted Eiko through Sumiko. Both instances exemplify indirect communication.

Goals of Counseling Mutually Defined between Therapist and Client. In seeking counseling, Eiko hoped to get help in alleviating her feelings of guilt and shame as well as in resolving the problem of estrangement from her uncle. To be of assistance, the therapist knew that Eiko needed both to explore her own acculturative processes and those of the family and to come to terms with the process of balancing intergenerational obligations and debts. Eiko examined each family member, in turn, and determined their approximate acculturative balance of traditional and Anglo orientations. It was revealing to her to discover different ethnic identity types within a single generation. Personal choice, an added determinant in any situation, further complicates the assessment of ethnic identity. This process of reframing the family conflict from a cultural context was enlightening for both Eiko and the therapist.

Any family dynamic would involve intergenerational reciprocity, an attempt to rebalance familial loyalties and debts in a ledger that was begun in generations past. The siblings, in their bookkeeping, arrived at one set of figures while the uncle balanced the books differently. On an interpersonal level, Eiko came to realize her role as an intergenerational emissary for her mother when she confronted the uncle, something the mother was unable to do. This insight enabled Eiko to cite other instances where she "settled accounts" for her mother.

As for resolving the estrangement with the uncle, Eiko discovered that doing the "right" thing meant doing nothing, although, at some future time through an intermediary, a reconciliation might be effected, perhaps. Counseling was terminated by mutual agreement after four sessions.

MR. AND MRS. SATO

Mrs. Anne Sato, a 37-year-old *nisei*, ethnic identity Type 4, had become increasingly depressed over an impasse between herself and her husband, George, age 39, ethnic identity Type 3, regarding the care of George's invalid mother. George and Anne were totally responsible for the care of George's invalid mother. Personal resistance and social prominence of the family in the Japanese community precluded her seeking mental health counseling. She chose to confide in a *nisei* friend, Mary, a psychiatric social worker.

Anne, a former schoolteacher, was devoting herself to raising three sons, ages 3, 9, and 12, and caring for her invalid mother-in-law, who resided with them. George was the only son and oldest child in a family of four children; Anne resented her husband's shouldering the total burden for the care of his mother. The financial expense did not deprive the children of basic necessities, but it did greatly curtail any extra amenities. George's sisters assisted with parent sitting occasionally, but they did not share significantly in their mother's care, and their husbands did not support their doing so. When Anne asked George why he did not insist that his sisters help, just on general principle, he replied, "Can't you understand that I'm the Sato? It's my job and I've just got to do it. I can't ask them."

Mary readily perceived that for a full exploration of the dilemma, George's presence was necessary. Although skeptical that George would consent to attend, Anne saw that they owed it to themselves at least to clarify the assumptions and priorities in their lives. Anne was to tell George that she had spoken to the social worker and was to call Mary when she had done so. Mary, in turn, would then contact George and attempt to make an appointment for marital counseling. With many reservations, George agreed to attend, provided the meeting was indeed held at Mary's home, as had been indicated already.

At the marital counseling session, Anne, who was normally cheerful and energetic, was depressed; she felt guilty for causing trouble, for she liked and admired her mother-in-law. George appeared basically calm and collected but was obviously concerned about his wife's turmoil. He volunteered that he felt caught in an untenable situation, for he felt obliged to assume full responsibility for his mother's care. There was never any question in his mind that it should be otherwise. Anne concurred that George should care for his mother but could not understand why all the offspring should not bear their fair share of the burden. She noted, "If our kids weren't so young, I'd feel differently. But we're shortchanging them of our time, energy, and money now." Eventually by thorough discussion of the conflict, George and Anne reached an understanding with one another and a compromise was reached.

Discussion

This case presentation illustrates the marital conflicts that arose from a husband and wife's differing cultural orientations regarding a mutual problem.

Presentation of Self Is Derived from the Familial Context. In addition to his role in the nuclear family, George identified himself as the "only Sato," that is, the only male generational carrier of the family name; he was the son of Hajime Sato, grandson of Takatoshi Sato, and so forth. Traditional self-identity is based upon the *Ie* household system, the lineage and relationships among family members living and dead.

Self-Esteem Is Determined by Fulfilling Family Roles and Obligations and Enduring Adversity. As the only son and head of the household, George felt his decision regarding the care of his mother was the correct one. Because she and George were parents raising three young children, Anne believed that a more egalitarian distribution of the burden was indicated. This created the tug-of-war, a power struggle.

With a good airing of the issue, Anne saw the additional burden she was placing on George by insisting that he change a role function he perceived as one he *could not* change. George appreciated the sheer physical load that Anne was assuming in helping him fulfill his role. He felt it reasonable to ask his sisters to help for a few hours weekly, in rotation if necessary, to relieve Anne. He would also make more time for Anne, to be used the way she wished, alone or with the children. It was important to Anne that George respect himself by fulfilling what he saw as his duty. She deferred to him and accepted the responsibility for continuing care of the mother-in-law.

The Goal Was Focusing on Interdependence, Not on Individuation. A critical factor in this marital conflict was in not insisting that George separate from his mother, that he "get untied from his mother's apron strings." This direct contradiction between an Anglo and a traditional value poses conflict for many Japanese-American couples, for an eldest son who is truly tradition-bound would feel compelled to put his mother before his wife (Kiefer, 1974, pp. 214–216).

The Preferred Therapeutic Modality Was Family (Marital) Counseling. The social worker defined the problem as a marital one involving issues of interdependence and individuation. In order to resolve the conflict, the participation of both husband and wife was necessary. The strategy used to get George to the family sessions was a deliberate one. First, Anne was to be honest about having confided in Mary, a psychiatric professional, to prevent any secrets between spouses. Second, after Anne had informed George, Mary was to contact him for an appointment. She would initiate the contact rather than making Anne responsible for getting her husband to accept counseling and waiting for George to call. Third, this procedure allowed George to maintain "face." That is, not he, but his wife was in need of help. Mary's communication to George was a direct request made to the head of the household and included an assessment by a professional that the matter was of sufficient concern to require his attention. Explicit assurance of confidentiality and privacy of meeting site also made it easier for George to attend.

Counseling Was Kept Focused and Brief. The problem was focused; the marital conflict explored; a solution using consensus was found; and the sessions were terminated after three meetings. One might legitimately argue that a number of other interpersonal dimensions needed exploration, including the spouses' expectations of one another and how they expressed feelings like affection, anger, or disagreement. However, keeping the sessions supportive and oriented to problem solving suited the communicative style of George and Anne. There was a high probability that the couple would return to counseling in the future if the need arose.

Ethnic Preference in a Therapist. Anne disclosed that she sought a *nisei* professional for she wanted someone who was familiar with Japanese popular culture because George had traditional inclinations. While this would not preclude a nonethnic therapist's counseling George and Anne, the problem was quickly defined and resolved because of the therapist's familiarity with the cultural dynamics.

THE SUZUKI FAMILY

John Suzuki, a 15-year-old *sansei*, ethnic identity Type 6, a B+ student and only child, was caught selling marijuana to some classmates on school grounds. The principal summoned the parents for a conference attended by John and the school security officer. The parents were told of John's infraction and that he would be reported to the juvenile probation officer.

Mrs. Yamato, a *nisei* school nurse specialist at the high school, was available.

Immediately following the conference the family turned to her. She found an impromptu crisis session developing. Tension and massive feelings of guilt and shame permeated the room. Mrs. Suzuki wept openly. Her first words were, "How could you do this to us? We can never face people again." The father, a proud, controlled man who had reddened eyes and tensed jaw, agreed with his wife. "You've brought shame on us," he said, berating his son and then wondering aloud what they had done wrong in raising John. Standing away from his parents, John, too, cried and expressed remorse. When asked why he had sold marijuana, he stated that he was looking for acceptance: "I wanted them to like me. I don't have any brothers or sisters, and I just like to make friends."

Mrs. Yamato supported the family as they painfully released feelings. People did not have to know, she said, for juvenile cases did not get published by name. She understood the family's need for privacy. In the parents' presence, she spoke to John saying that although she did not condone his behavior, she understood the pain he was experiencing. She would contact the probation officer and help the family in whatever way she could. Prior to concluding the session, she said it was important that the parents continue with their respective employment and that John attend his classes. They were free to reach her at school and, in any event, she would contact them in a week.

Five days later, Mrs. Suzuki called Mrs. Yamato asking to speak to her. The school nurse agreed to a home visit. She discovered that although the parents did go to work and John attended classes, the family had noticeably withdrawn from virtually all social contact. They did not attend their clubs; Father declined a golf date; Mother missed the church's women's auxiliary meeting; and John withdrew from both his parents, spending his free time either alone at the park or in his bedroom. Mr. Suzuki had his hypertension medication increased because of dizziness; Mrs. Suzuki said she had headaches and thought she needed to have her glasses rechecked. All of them suffered from insomnia and lack of appetite.

Mrs. Yamato recognized that her main task was to get the family to accept counseling. John and his mother were receptive, for both of them knew the situation had become untenable. Father, however, refused, for he felt that talking would accomplish nothing; the damage was done. Mrs. Yamato honored his refusal for the moment and did not insist that he attend (she sensed that nothing would be gained except more resistance). She was supportive regarding their feelings of shame and mentioned that there were other *nisei* families in a similar plight, a revelation the family found reassuring. Mrs. Yamato did direct John to spend some time with his best friend regularly.

Ten days later, Mrs. Yamato met John at school. He now felt hostile toward his parents. All he heard from them were "shame messages and guilt-trips." "They don't care about me," he muttered, "just about what other people will think." His grades had slipped to Cs; he was still essentially withdrawn

TABLE 12.1

Ethnic identity guide for counseling Japanese-Americans

Client Dimensions	Traditional Orientation (Japanese)	Acculturative Balance	Anglo Orientation (American)
Self-presentation	Interdependent, other-oriented Self-controlled Self-effacing Identifies self within familial context		Independent, self-oriented Self-expressive Self-assertive Identifies self as an individual
Self-esteem determined by	Fulfilling family roles and obligations Bringing honor to family, "doing good" Enduring under adversity		Fulfilling own needs for mastery, self-actualization, "doing own thing" Taking responsibility for own behavior
Shame and/or guilt caused by	Bringing embarrassment, dishonor to family or group Failing to fulfill family role and obligations		Violating one's conscience Failure to meet one's standards and expectations
Conflict and anxiety dealt with by	Internalizing, somatizing, withdrawal, depression, autism, or rarely, acting-out		Various behaviors including acting-out
Communication	Restrained, emotionally controlled, indirect, more nonverbal than verbal		Spontaneous, direct, verbal
Therapist ethnicity preference	Japanese-American or nonethnic who is acculturated to Japanese-American values and mores		Anglo or may have no preference

Counseling Considerations		
Goals	Interdependence, functioning within family (household) system Mutually defined by client and therapist Rebalancing of intergenerational obligations	Individuation, autonomous functioning Defined by therapist or client and therapist Alleviation of symptoms or actualization of individual potential
Preferred therapeutic modality	Preference for family, then individual therapy	Family, group and/or individual therapy as appropriate
Therapist role	Active participant-observation Directive intervention	Nondirective or directive intervention as appropriate
Requirements of therapist	Understanding of Japanese popular culture (have consultant if necessary) Education and training in family and individual therapies Bilingualism (if client is issei, older nisei, or kibei)	Understanding of Anglo popular culture Education and training in therapies appropriate to clients; family, group, individual
Therapy site	Clients' home; community facility (nonpsychiatric)	Counseling or mental health facility
Duration and frequency	Preferably brief, 1 to 6 months Weekly	Variable according to therapist and client assessment of need

from his peers. Mrs. Yamato contacted the juvenile probation officer to share information about the particular vulnerability of this Asian-American family whose culture is so strongly family-centered and shame-oriented. The officer was sympathetic and noted that this was John's first offense.

Now Mrs. Yamato made a direct appeal to the father, as head of the household, to enter counseling for the sake of his son. He, too, could see that John was suffering. The boy's grades had slipped, and he no longer socialized; he had closed himself off. He learned that the probability of John's receiving probation became greater if the family showed a serious attempt to get help. The family, including the father, entered counseling 6 weeks after the son's apprehension. John was, in fact, given only probation.

The Caucasian therapist who treated the Suzuki family consulted Mrs. Yamato to corroborate her information regarding Japanese-American cultural values and practices. The interviews were characterized by a gradual, painstaking process of helping the family members share thoughts and feelings with one another. Mr. Suzuki eventually learned that John's action was basically a plea for attention, especially for his father's attention. John discovered his father's enormous pride and affection for him, although he had never felt it. Mother found how she habitually deferred to her husband, how she mediated between husband and son, what that role served, and how she might relinquish that intermediary position. Father and son grew noticeably closer, spending time in each other's company and attending outings together. The family attended weekly sessions for 4 months and terminated by mutual agreement.

Discussion

Mrs. Yamato's intervention with the Suzuki family is illustrative of how a Japanese-American family may be helped to participate in counseling through the professional's sensitivity to popular culture and to the acculturative process.

Shame and Guilt Are the Result of Bringing Embarrassment and Dishonor to the Family. The parents' reaction to the son's "delinquency" was immediate shame and a sense of failure. The school nurse specialist, Mrs. Yamato, supported the family members in their expression of feeling. After Japanese-Americans have lost control of emotions, they frequently feel ashamed about having expressed their feelings in front of other people. By responding in a matter-of-fact way and informing them that other *nisei* families had similar troubles, the nurse helped to attenuate that shame reaction. She became directive and task-oriented, a communicative mode familiar to the Suzukis. She told the parents to continue to work and John to attend school. She took on the more technical tasks of community contacts and facilitated ongoing communication by offering to contact the family in a week. Conflict and anxiety were expressed by withdrawal, somatizing, and internalizing. The Suzukis were unaware of the psychogenic component in their bodily ailments and in the subsequent exacerbation of these somatic symptoms. They also responded to stress with marked withdrawal. While treating the symptoms was important, getting the family into counseling to deal with the interpersonal trauma was of primary importance.

Self-Esteem Is Enhanced by Fulfilling Role Obligations. So long as father interpreted the situation as one of family suffering, then he could *gaman*, endure the adversity. However, once he realized that he needed to enter counseling for the good of his son (caring for one's children is a normative traditional value) he was convinced that his attendance was mandatory. Initially, Mrs. Yamato simply dropped the suggestion of counseling and let the idea incubate, knowing full well that Mr. Suzuki would resist. After she had more concrete data on the probationary process and John's handling of his offense, she became more directive in her appeal to his duty as head of the household and caretaker of his son.

Interestingly, one of the strategies adopted in order to help this family to heal and grow was to move the parents toward the Anglo orientation and the son toward the traditional orientation. With John, an ethnic identity Type 6 *sansei*, it was essential that the parents deal with Anglicization. Father also learned how to express affection behaviorally by spending time with his son, an Anglo practice. Mother removed herself as the sole caretaker and the mediator between father and son, a traditional aspect of the mothering role. John realized that he had some traditional responsibilities as the only son and he began to appreciate the patrilineal linkage of the Suzuki family.

The foregoing treatment considerations are summarized in Table 12.1.

SUMMARY

Currently, Japanese-Americans are among the lowest users of mental health services in this country. However, as acculturation inexorably proceeds and the cultural stigma on mental illness abates, they are likely to increase their usage. This development will almost inevitably require that therapists of differing ethnic backgrounds provide mental health care for persons of Japanese ancestry. The therapist must be aware of the acculturative balancing that involves the interaction of traditional values and those of contemporary Anglo society. Knowledge of key elements in the traditional orientation, such as the household system, the hierarchical social structure, the repertoire of reciprocal obligations, and other normative behavior is essential for effective counseling of Japanese-American clients.

REFERENCES

Asian American Mental Health Services of Oakland California. Symposium on Perspectives on Japanese-American Mental Health, Berkeley Buddhist Church, March 1979.

Babcock, C. Reflections on dependency phenomena as seen in nisei in the United States. In Smith, R. & Beardsly, R. (eds.). *Japanese Culture: Its Development and Characteristics.* Chicago: Aldine, 1962.

Babcock, C., & Caudill, W. Personal and cultural factors in treating a nisei man. In Seward, G. (ed.), *Clinical Studies in Culture Conflict.* New York: Ronald Press, 1958.

Beardsley, R., Hall, J., & Ward, R. *Village Japan.* Chicago: University of Chicago Press, 1959.

Boszormenyi-Nagy, I., Spark, G.M. *Invisible Loyalties; Reciprocity and Integrational Family Therapy.* Hagerstown, Maryland: Harper and Row, 1973.

Caudill, W. The study of Japanese personality and behavior. In Norbeck, E., & Parman, S. (eds.), *The Study of Japan in the Behavioral Sciences.* Houston: Rice University Press, 1970.

Caudill, W. Cultural and interpersonal context of everyday health and illness in Japan and America. In Leslie, C. (ed.), *Asian Medical Systems: A Comparative Study.* Berkeley: University of California Press, 1976.

Caudill, W., & DeVos, G. Achievement, culture and personality: The case of the Japanese-American. *American Anthropologist,* 1956, 58, 1102–1126.

Caudill, W., & Doi, T. Interrelations of psychiatry, culture and emotions in Japan. In Goldstone, I. (ed.), *Man's Image in Medicine and Anthropology.* New York: International Universities Press, 1963.

Clark, M., Kaufman, S., & Pierce, R. Explorations of acculturation: Toward a model of ethnic identity. *Human Organization,* 1976, 35, 231–238.

Connor, J. Acculturation and family continuities in three generations of Japanese-Americans. *Journal of Marriage and the Family,* 1974, 36(1), 159–165.

Doi, T., Amae: A key concept for understanding Japanese personality structure. In Smith, R., & Beardsley, R. (eds.), *Japanese Culture: Its Development and Characteristics.* Chicago: Aldine, 1962.

Doi, T. *The Anatomy of Dependence.* Tokyo: Kodansha, 1973.

Frager, R. The psychology of the samurai. *Psychology Today,* 1969, 2, 48–53.

Fukutake, T. *Japanese Rural Society.* Tokyo: Oxford University Press, 1967.

Glick, I., & Hessler, D. *Marital and Family Therapy.* New York: Grune & Stratton, 1974.

Hatanaka, N., Watanabe, B., & Ono, S. The utilization of mental health services by Asian-Americans in the Los Angeles area. In Ishikawa, W., & Archer, N. (eds.), *Proceedings of Service Delivery in Pan-Asian Communities.* San Diego: Pacific Asian Coalition Training Center, 1975.

Johnson, F., Marsella, A., & Johnson, C. Social and psychological aspects of verbal behavior in Japanese-Americans. *American Journal of Psychiatry,* 1974, 5, 580–583.

Kiefer, C. *Changing Cultures, Changing Lives: An Ethnographic Study of Three Generations of Japanese-Americans.* San Francisco: Jossey-Bass, 1974.

Kimmich, R. Brief communication: Ethnic aspects of schizophrenia in Hawaii. *Psychiatry,* 1960, 23, 97–102.

Kitano, H. Japanese-American mental illness. In Plog, S., & Edgerton, R. (eds.), *Changing Perspectives in Mental Illness.* New York: Holt, Rinehart and Winston, 1969.

Kitano, H. Mental illness in four cultures. *Journal of Social Psychology*, 1970, 80, 121–134.

Kitano, H. *Japanese-Americans: The Evolution of a Subculture* (2nd ed.). Englewood Cliffs, N.J.: Prentice-Hall, 1976.

Lyman, S. Generation and character: The case of the Japanese-Americans. In Lyman, S. (ed.), *The Asian in the West*. Nevada: University of Nevada Press, 1970.

Maykovich, M. *Japanese-American Identity Dilemma*. Tokyo: Waseda University Press, 1972.

Mazur, V. Family therapy: An approach to the culturally different. *International Journal of Social Psychiatry*, 1973, 19, 114–120.

Meredith, G. Observations on the acculturation of sansei Japanese-Americans in Hawaii. *Psychologia*, 1965, 8, 41–49.

Miranda, M., & Kitano, H. Barriers to mental services: A Japanese-American and Mexican-American dilemma. In Hernandez, C., Haug, M., & Wagner, N. (eds.), *Chicanos: Social and Psychological Perspectives*. St. Louis: Mosby, 1976.

Moteki, R. Nikkei shame hides mental illness. [As reported by B. Resenberger in] *Pacific Citizen*, July 18, 1978, pp. 1, 4.

Nakane, C. *Human Relations in Japan*. Tokyo: Ministry of Foreign Affairs, 1972.

Nitobe, I.O. *The Japanese Nation; Its Land, Its People and Its Life; With Special Consideration to Its Relations With the United States*, New York: G.P. Putnam, 1912.

Okano, Y., & Spilka, B. Ethnic identity, alienation and achievement orientation in Japanese-American families. *Journal of Cross-Cultural Psychology*, 1971, 2, 273–282.

Pierce, R., Clark, M., & Kaufman, S. Generation and ethnic identity: A typological analysis. *International Journal of Aging and Human Development*, 1978, 9, 19–29.

Pierce, R., Clark, M., & Kiefer, C. A "bootstrap" scaling technique. *Human Organization*, 1972, 31, 403–410.

President's Commission on Mental Health. *Report of the Special Population Subpanel on Mental Health of Asian/Pacific-Americans*, February 15, 1978.

Shon, S. The Asian family. In *Three Perspectives of Asian-American Mental Health: The Individual, The Family and the Community*. Symposium presented at Canada College, San Mateo, Calif., October 1977.

Speck, R., & Rueveni, U. Network therapy. In Haley, J. (ed.), *Changing Families*. New York: Grune & Stratton, 1971.

Stierlin, H. Shame and guilt in family relations: Theoretical and clinical aspects. *Archives of General Psychiatry*, 1974, 30, 381–389.

Sue, S., & McKinney, H. Asian-Americans in the community mental health care system. *American Journal of Orthopsychiatry*, 1975, 45, 111–118.

Sue, S., & Sue, D.W. Understanding Asian-Americans: The Neglected Minority. *Personnel and Guidance Journal*, 1973, 51, 386–396.

U.S. Bureau of the Census. *Census of the Population: 1970 Subject Reports*. Final Report PC (2)-10: Japanese, Chinese and Filipinos in the United States. Washington, D.C.: Government Printing Office, 1973.

Wake, M. *Counseling the Japanese Family in the United States* (Monograph). Berkeley: Asian Center for Theology and Strategies, 1975.

Whitenack, J. Personal communication. Asian-American Community Mental Health Services, Oakland, Calif., March 10, 1978.

Yamagiwa, J. Language as an expression of Japanese culture. In Hall, J., & Beardsley, R. (eds.), *Twelve Doors to Japan*. New York: McGraw-Hill, 1965.

13

Bilingual Families:
A Chinese-American Example

Theresa T. Chen-Louie

Like Furuta, Chen-Louie examines the experiences of Asian-American families whose traditional beliefs and values have had to undergo the vicissitudes of acculturation over time. While the traditional precepts have undergirded the functioning of Chinese-Americans, changes in each succeeding generation have contributed to value discrepancies and intergenerational strains. Chen-Louie pays particular attention to the custom of saving face, a prototype of the behaviors most highly valued in traditional Chinese culture, but esteemed in varying degrees by generations less steeped in the old ways. She sees the bilingual, Chinese-American family as epitomizing the intergenerational strain and distance, in that each faction uses a preferred language both as a tool to advance a particular cultural view and to manipulate the other. She stresses that the complexities and subtleties of this type of interaction must be understood by all persons called upon to help in the resolution of the familial conflict. A vivid, verbatim case example adds depth and clarity to the author's presentation.

For the past decade, Chinese-American clients in the vicinity of San Francisco have traveled a great distance to obtain bilingual counseling services in the city. A survey of Asian American Community Mental Health Services (1974) documented an underutilization of government clinic services while Asian clients inundated an Asian-American mental health agency in Alameda County. The need for individual or family counseling is pressing not only for new immigrant families, high school and college dropouts, and youth gangs, but also for young adults struggling with identity problems or discrimination, native-born families experiencing life crises, or elderly immigrants coping with social isolation and poverty. However, the needs of the new immigrants are most urgent as they have the fewest available resources.

In the meantime, regardless of the group they belong to or of the seriousness of their problems, they all share in common cultural conflicts, effects of institutional racism, and frustrations in their attempts to gain economic, social, or political status. These conflicts and struggles are in and of themselves sources of mental anguish and emotional upheaval.

The underutilization of Anglo psychiatric services is a comment on the inadequacies and ineffectiveness of white psychiatry for ethnic people of color.* Linguistic barriers obviously contribute to the ineffectiveness of English-speaking therapists with Chinese-speaking clients. A lack of appreciation of the cultural and racial experiences of Chinese-Americans leaves these same therapists unattuned to the sensibilities of English-speaking Chinese-American clients.† On the other hand, bilingual Chinese-American therapists may be plagued by the same Anglo-dominated psychotherapeutic methods and white middle-class values. They can therefore be just as insensitive to their clients' needs and can add to their problems. Bilingual therapists have begun to confront this problem and have attempted to sort out what it is in the Anglo-oriented methodologies that is not congruent with the Chinese-American experience. The process of identifying and sorting is slow and ambiguous. In this paper I spell out some of my own experiences and reflections on this subject. I hope that this will stimulate greater refinement and integration of these ideas.

THE LITTLE LOGIC‡

The basic problem encountered in transcultural therapy is ethnocentrism in both theoretical and methodologic formulations as well as in the therapists' subtle racist values and attitudes. As therapists, we learn these assumptions in a taken-for-granted manner. Even in process-oriented therapy, ethnocentric values may still be unintentionally imposed. I would like to begin with an examination of issues in racism in the theoretical arena. Since it is important to approach clients' experiences phenomenologically, it is valuable to be familiar with some patterns in cultural groups. Their experiences must be viewed in the historical, social, and political context of intergroup and interracial relationships. The Chinese-American experience will be described in that context. I will draw on Erving Goffman's (1955) analysis of com-

---

*Nurses in the Western Interstate Commission for Higher Education have adopted the term *ethnic people of color* in preference to the term *minority*, which connotes inferiority.

†This issue was fully addressed in the proposal on mental health presented to the California Department of Health in 1975 as drafted by the Bay Area Concerned Chinese Americans for Mental Health.

‡Sociologist Barney Glaser, in his seminars, has referred to the central theme of a composition or book as the "little logic."

munication and social interaction to elucidate Chinese custom and value conflicts. After illustrating how face-saving concepts may be applied to clinical situations, I will offer some observations that may be useful in transcultural therapy.

ISSUES OF RACISM IN SOCIOLOGIC THEORIES

Billingsley (1968, pp. 3–4) aptly observes that black families have been mistreated by social scientists and the mass media. In like manner, other ethnic families of color are also misrepresented. Theoretical frameworks on ethnic people of color are limited by biases toward Anglo conformity. Whether the phenomena be viewed under the guise of "the melting pot" or "cultural pluralism," the assumption made about ethnic people of color is that they are to become American through amalgamation and/or through fusion of their cultural contributions. Central to this notion of assimilation or acculturation is an ethnocentric coercion toward Anglo conformity (Mindel & Habenstein, 1976, p. vii). Juxtaposed to this Anglo conformity is the American myth of individual opportunity. The democratic ideology of individualism and equality promises that ethnic immigrants can be upwardly mobile and eventually successful. In their striving, diversity is left behind. Immigrants will be given equal access to individual opportunity, depending on the date of their arrival. Differential success will rest on their different innate racial abilities and talents (Dickeman, 1973). These ethnocentric premises are pervasive in our educational and value systems as well as in everyday practices. It is not uncommon to find negative stereotypes about ethnic people of color in literature—e.g., Negroes' inferior intellect, sociopathology of the Negro matriarchy, or social disorganization of Chinatowns.

The sociology of the family emphasizes the functioning of the white middle-class American family while examining ethnic families with emphasis on their problems. Frequently, the writers are not members of the ethnic groups under investigation. Even if the writers are ethnic people of color, it is likely that they have unwittingly taken on the pervasive institutional racism common in academia. It is only in the past decade that these writers have begun to question the Anglo-dominated sociologic assumptions and to write from the perspective of their own experiences.* The problems, pathologies, or disintegration of the groups in question are now being put into the perspective of racism through an examination of the historical, economic, and political development of the ethnic experiences. In like manner, Asian-American writers, social scientists, and therapists are looking at what actually is Asian-

---

*Kagiwada (1973), Staples (1971), and Billingsley (1968) have referred to the inappropriateness of using certain established sociologic theories to explain particular racial or ethnic groups.

American experience rather than accepting the stigmatization of their language as "sophomoric" or "pidgin" English, their gangs as illustrative of "social disintegration," their clients as "passive aggressive."* What is Asian-American experience in and of itself? What theoretical postulations can we make beside those of conflict and marginality? What are the effects of cultural dissonance? What about the discounting process in racial oppression?

THE SOCIOHISTORICAL CONTEXT OF CHINESE-AMERICAN EXPERIENCE

Chinese-American bilingual families exist in a social context that is rooted in the historical interaction of Chinese and Americans. The lack of integration necessary for them to become truly Chinese-Americans has been and remains a problem. Chinese-American citizens are still overtly or subtly disenfranchised and treated as foreign.

The Chinese who immigrated to this country some 150 years ago were largely male peasants from southern China. To escape poverty, political repression, and natural catastrophe many came as indentured laborers. They intended to remain temporarily and eventually rejoin or establish their families in China. However, there were no easy fortunes to be found in California. Exploited and oppressed, while enduring extreme hardships, they provided the manpower for the frontier economy. In the meantime, while their civil rights were violated, discriminating taxes were levied upon them to enrich the state treasury. No Chinese could testify in courts even to defend themselves. When the gold mines were exhausted and the railroads built, and the Chinese immigrants began to contribute to the building of California's agricultural economy, anti-Chinese sentiments were on the rise. Exclusionary immigration laws restricted Chinese who visited their homeland from returning to America or from bringing their spouses along.†

Unlike the exploited and oppressed European immigrants who came with their families to establish households in America, Chinese families, because of discriminatory immigration, widespread anti-Chinese violence, and restriction of occupation and services, were prevented from forming and being transplanted in this country in the late nineteenth and early twentieth centuries (Lyman, 1970, pp. 3–8). With pressures from the host society, the Chinese congregated in urban enclaves. With the lack of women and family

---

*Asian-American experience and Chinese-American experience are used interchangeably. Chinese-Americans share many oppressive experiences with Japanese-Americans, Korean-Americans, etc. For references on Asian-American language, consult Chin et al. (1975), and Wand, (1974).

†For additional details regarding the early experiences of Chinese immigrants, see Chun-Hoon (1975), Kung (1962), Siu (1952), Wu (1972), and Sung (1971).

lives, Chinese men turned to the ghettos' established mercantile power elite for work and recreation (Lyman, 1974).

In the past two decades, although second- and third-generation Chinese-Americans have moved out of the ghettos as occupational, educational, and residential opportunities opened up, many families have remained trapped in these small communities. Chinatown provides services and opportunities as well as cultural support for both the residents and recent immigrants. For example, there are no career opportunities in the host society for immigrant professionals who do not speak fluent English. Chinese immigrants of both professional and unskilled backgrounds must seek jobs that are available in Chinese commercial operations, e.g., in restaurants, laundries and groceries or sewing factories. They vie for the limited opportunites to be laundrymen, busboys, kitchen helpers, dishwashers, janitors, stockboys, or seamstresses (Sing, 1970). In the meantime, the entrenched Chinatown mercantile power elite remain staunch against pressure to increase wages or admit external union control (Lan, 1971). They argue that their profit edge may erode if they change the traditional long-hour–low-wage tactics that make their competition viable with similar American enterprises.

Chinatowns are characterized by poverty, overcrowding, oppressed labor conditions, and high unemployment. Those who live and work in the community have little direct contact with white society. When they lack English language skills, they are trapped in Chinatown with little chance to improve their English. Children from these families are socialized into the American culture through the educational system and mass media. Whether they are native-born or from China, their parents continue to be essentially monolingual. Many children speak Chinese in their homes (HEW, 1970). When they grow up, they may choose to speak only English. Their lives are engrossed in work and education. Trapped in this existence for survival, they are not aware of or are indifferent to the social, political, and economic interchange between their community and white society. Unfortunately, this ghetto mentality still operates in Chinatown (Wang, 1970).

BILINGUAL CHINESE-AMERICAN FAMILIES

Value Discrepancies

The preference for speaking one or the other language in bilingual families is indicative of the varying cultural experiences of the members. Chinese-speaking parents, reared in the mother culture with little exposure to the American culture, continue to retain expectations deriving from the Chinese family culture. Children who are secure in neither the Chinese nor the American culture have not yet found a place in the American culture for their unique Chinese-American contribution. They come to dislike what they have while searching for those elements of the Chinese-American culture that will be valued by the host society.

Parents' Experiences and Expectations. The parents' expectations derived from Chinese family rules center around keeping the family order and unity through harmony, deference, and conformity to parental authority. In deference to the elders, communications flow one way: from parent to child. Dissension is discouraged. Emotions are best kept under control; external manifestations of emotionality indicate a lack of cultivation and civility. Older children are expected to assume disciplinary and economic responsibilities.

The parents' American experiences are tied up with the necessity for long, hard work to make a living. They view the capacity for hard work as necessary for their survival and upward mobility. In China, education was highly revered. The parents' American experiences serve to heighten the urgency for education. It becomes the only viable hope and vehicle for their offspring to break out from the laborious cycle of hard work. They hope that their achievements will be expressed through their children (Jen, 1971, pp. 24–26). In order to inculcate responsibility in their children, they believe in constant admonition and close supervision.

Mainland Chinese-American parents, in general, share values similar to those found among the Chinese-Americans in Hawaii. They are pleased when their children do well in school, are responsible for chores and their personal care, respond to discipline, refrain from fighting, and exhibit friendliness to the young. Parents are angry at disobedience. They do not like messiness or aggressive behavior (Young, 1972).

Children's Experiences. The children's experiences revolve around education and, at times, around work as well. After attendance in regular public schools, they are sent to Chinese schools to learn their language and culture.

In public schools, they do not learn about Asian-Americans viewed in an Asian-American perspective. They learn about themselves as white Americans portray their race. Occasionally, successful Chinese-Americans are held up as examples of those who have made it. However, by citing these shining examples, there is an inevitable playing down of the conflict and struggle of those who are still caught in institutional racism (Chun-Hoon, 1975). Chinese-American students therefore cannot even find their own cultural heroes to identify with. Teachers, in the meantime, finding the students to be studious and quiet, reinforce those qualities since they do not present disciplinary problems; they do not realize that studious and quiet students may have problems with language and self-expression or may be plagued with timidity regarding any show of aggressiveness. Thus, Chinese-Americans are repeatedly confirmed by society as quiet achievers, "math geniuses," and law-abiding citizens. Given no Asian role model to identify with, Chinese-Americans are left with white values for self-confirmation. The psychologic colonialization of the quiet, studious, Chinese-American is thus perpetuated (Tong, 1971). Few of these quiet, law-abiding citizens who have high grades in colleges now hold managerial positions, however, this is the price the Chinese-American pays to be in this society.

In Chinese schools, students are supposed to learn about the values and language of their parents' culture. However, they can see that their parents have not reached any desirable status with their "fine" culture and endless hard work. Rarely do the students find affiliation in learning Chinese. These schools become another social institution where students gather to share the illusion of learning language. It is a place where they complete the process of being disciplined, obedient, and of "bowing to the teachers."

Ironically, Chinese-Americans socialized in this lengthy educational process can neither accept "Chineseness" or "Americanness." In the resulting dilemma, those who dare challenge the unfairness of their experiences find themselves turning to spurts of self-hatred, anger, or depression (Chun-Hoon, 1975; Tong, 1971).

Within the family system, parents cultivate the values of the work ethic and educational achievement, compliance, and nonaggressiveness (Fong, Gee, & Wong, 1973). All these injunctions have molded them into developing qualities that they do not like about themselves: lack of aggressiveness and language expressiveness (Watanabe, 1972). This, together with their skin color and racial characteristics, serves to prevent them from penetrating places most Americans can aspire to and reach. The children comply; however, they are angry that they are unable to overtly demonstrate their rebellion.

Saving Face in Bilingual Families

The values extolled by Chinese-American parents—such as deference, compliance toward authority, emotional control, and politeness—are closely related to the custom of saving face among Chinese. To maintain harmony and the respect of others in social relationships, the individual is to act in such a formalized way as to always preserve his own face and prevent the loss of face in others. Chinese-American children, whether they are asserting their adolescent identity or being socialized toward individualism and expressiveness, find the face-saving custom hypocritical and burdensome; however, although the children may not like the custom, they have been brought up with it. To further the process of saving face, communication is usually nonconfrontational.

Face-Work Analysis. Our concept of self is derived through a series of interactive processes. Each interactant's self is developed and confirmed through the interpretation of the symbolic representations and gestures of the other. The definition of self emerges as one interactant communicates his or her perception while the other validates or discounts the former's interpretation. The latter in turn receives feedback from the former and can also validate or disconfirm the interpretations. Through these continuous feedback loops each interactant receives from the other his or her reflected self-appraisal. In each event of a face-to-face encounter, interactants express their views through verbal and nonverbal acts, evaluate self and other to arrive at a joint definition of the situation. Goffman's (1955) face-work analysis deciphers the interactive rituals in these encounters in which each party attempts to present a favorable self appraisal. His explanation elucidates the communication processes in Chinese face-saving situations as well.

The analysis of interactive processes is based on the theoretical framework of symbolic interactionism.* In this analysis of interaction, points of reference are derived from the actors themselves. There is not a predetermined norm from which biased interpretations are made. The hazard of value imposition can thus be reduced. For instance, it is important for the therapist to understand that saving face is inherent in Chinese interaction, both in family and therapeutic situations. If the therapist is in touch with the Chinese client's point of reference, the cultural roots of face-saving behavior may become visible. Instead of imposing the value of "open communication" or promptly labeling clients as resistant, the therapist might then see that proffering a favorable image may still be used as a coping mechanism for some Chinese in a discriminatory environment.

People attempt to guide and control the impressions others form about them. They employ various strategies to sustain the good impressions. In social rituals, people expect considerate behavior from self and others to sustain each other's face. Face embodies the positive image, interpretations, or social attributes that one claims for oneself or perceives others to have accorded one. Human nature is such that in social encounters most people attempt to avoid making fools of themselves, and should they unfeelingly contribute to another's losing face, they would be considered heartless (Brown, 1971). Goffman refers to all face-saving processes as "face-work."

In an encounter where one's taken-for-granted self-image is sustained, one will probably have few or no different feelings about oneself from those one ordinarily has. If an encounter establishes an image that is better than one's own self-image, one is likely to feel good. One can use tactics to "give face" to others and thereby "gain face" or "get face" from them. If one's ordinary expectation of self is not confirmed, one feels bad or hurt. One is said to be

---

*According to Manis and Meltzer (1972, pp. ix–xiii), there are many theoretical contributors to symbolic interactionism. Some of their emphases are the "processual character of human behavior" and the need for "sympathetic introspection"; the reconceptualizing of self in structural terms; and the active, self-aware nature of human conduct. In the study of human behavior, these social psychologists take the "actor's point of view."

"in the wrong face," "out of face," "in shamed face," or to have "lost face." In order to save face, the individual must have perceptiveness and a willingness to exercise social skill to preserve face.

There are two ways to save face: by defending one's own face and by protecting the face of others. To save face, one prevents loss of face by withdrawal from experiences that will cause loss of face. One also gives face to enhance one's own face. To restore lost face, one counteracts by retaliation or reassertion after being humiliated. Saving face is an anticipatory or ongoing process. Face restoration is an after-the-fact remedying process.

Face-saving Tactics.   Defensive tactics to save face include avoidance of direct confrontation by use of an intermediary, avoidance contact, or gracious withdrawal. Nonconfrontation can also be achieved by deliberate ambiguity, unstated facts, or delaying time by hedging. Once caught in a potential face-losing situation, one may shift by changing the topic or by noting that the subject is not "really serious." To save one's own face various protective maneuvers can be used. One might first extend face to others. One might exhibit politeness, make certain that ceremonial dues are extended, avoid direct confrontation through ambiguity, and make use of circumlocution or even deception.

Face-restoration Tactics.   There are defensive and protective strategies to restore face once it has been threatened. Defensive corrective tactics include maintaining composure and not giving away the inward threat one feels. When caught in a wrong-face situation, one might acknowledge that the incident has happened without one's knowledge and disclaim responsibility. Furthermore, there are protective maneuvers used to restore face. Both parties can make light of the situation; that is, one offers and the other agrees that the difference is indeed not very serious. The wrong-face person may also belittle her- or himself, expecting the other to be generous. When forgiven, she or he responds with sighs of gratitude. The interactants can mutually assume the stance that no loss of face has really taken place. Both play at being blind so that face can be regained.

Saving Face among Chinese-Americans.   Saving face is not unique to the Chinese culture. While face-saving rituals are part of conventional diplomacy, Asian-Americans are particularly noted for their use of innuendo and politeness (Lyman, 1970). The Chinese are adept in the use of nonconfrontative communication in face-work. The Chinese perceives the Westerner's custom of frank honesty and confrontation as abrupt and uncivilized; on the other hand, Westerners complain that Chinese don't say what they mean.

People who are accustomed to employing politeness and innuendo do not perceive face-work to be vague or ambiguous. Circumlocution is employed so that in the indirect communication the message sender can render the report ambiguously to maximize the options from which the receiver may define the command or relationship.* The receiver can either accept or reject the sender's message without outwardly offending the sender's feelings. This style of communication purports to create an atmosphere of harmony. Negative reactions to the injunction of the messages are also suppressed. Perceptive people do, however, pick up negative sentiments through analogic communications. They will mediate in such a way as to change the original message to ensure the receiver's acceptance. The ability to communicate according to the clues from metacommunication is indeed an accomplished social skill. Not all Chinese are deft face savers. Those who favor direct communication are branded as being too straightforward or tactless.

There are various communication tactics in Chinese face-work. Defensive tactics include the use of a go-between to avoid embarrassment, deliberate noncommitting statements, hedging, the use of innuendo, talking superficially, leaving important detail until later, or leaving others to make inferences. Protective maneuvers to save face include politeness, claiming respect for elders, calling on the generosity of others, and making light of situations. To restore face, the tactics are controling facial expression, denying any threat of face, discounting intended harm, and mutually disclaiming the seriousness of the situation.

Saving face in Chinese-American families can be problematic. Communication from parent to child is unidirectional with clear do's and don't's. Parents expect children to perform so as not to lose the family's face. They expect children to be considerate and take care of them when they grow old. They have sacrificed for the children, and the offspring are to reciprocate by being well-disciplined, neat, compliant, and academic achievers. They are expected to obtain high status and secure jobs, to marry and procreate. Family, and particularly parents, will lose face if children behave in a contrary fashion.

In the parent-child relationship, parents are not expected to give face to children; children must behave respectfully so parents can gain face. In bilingual families, children who are more exposed to the American culture really feel the value discrepancies. On the one hand, they are always pressured to save face; on the other hand, in the face-to-face encounter with parents, they are not given opportunities to enhance their self-concepts unless they fulfill the face-saving expectation. Children who have learned the value of self-expression, honesty and direct communication in American schools do not find a place for free self-expression at home. It is not surprising that as adults, many continue to experience constraints in linguistic expression.

---

*For further discussion of these elements, refer to Watzlawick, Beavin, and Jackson (1967, pp. 51–52, 60–71).

THERAPY WITH BILINGUAL FAMILIES

In this section, a case study will be used to illustrate some characteristics of a dysfunctional bilingual family, the face-saving ploy in therapy situations, and the specific contribution of bilingual therapists.

THE CHUNG FAMILY

The Chung family of four consisted of a native-born father who married a non–English-speaking wife in China through a matchmaker. Both were in their forties. Their adolescent children included a son who avoided involvement with the family through isolation, occasional angry intimidation, and the exclusive use of English. The daughter, the face watcher of the family, was compliant. She spoke both Chinese and English and wanted to take care of both parents. The mother was the identified patient. She described herself as having no brains, neither memory nor education. She had tremors and fainting spells that had been diagnosed once as epilepsy. She was further incapacitated by arthritis. She appeared to manage her situation by begging to be exempt from household responsibilities and by allowing herself to be patiently tutored so that she would not get exasperated and nervous. When she felt threatened, she "could not hear." The family members acted on the premise that mother was "dumb" and easily excitable and that her illness was irreversible. The father changed his occupation from laundryman to grocery owner to postal clerk as his wife progressively relinquished her role and function. He took on all the responsibilities that the others refused to take. He was frustrated. In therapy, all family members expected to be "taught" new ways to cure the mother's sickness.

In the Chung family, teaching and learning were referred to by all four members, particularly the mother. She assumed the mother/authority role. She professed to be teaching while she was actually commanding, and exacted compliance from her children which indicated that they had learned their lessons. She saw teaching as the parental responsibility and prerogative. Children were to study and not watch television, to keep their rooms neat, and to be polite and responsible for their chores. She related how her own mother did not love her, exhorting her to behave, not to show irritation or anger when she met her prospective suitor. She did not at that time think she was irritable, but "obeyed" her mother's teaching anyway. Others in the family held up the ideal of teaching as well. The husband referred to having to teach his wife patiently. The daughter taught the mother how to go to the grocery to purchase milk.

In a face-saving context, to ask another to be a teacher is to give face. To be able to teach is to gain face. To learn well in the family is to save the family's face. Inherent in the teaching process is the expectation of an unquestioning and receptive attitude on the part of the "learner." The conflict arises when parental demands, couched in the name of "teaching," are perceived by the children as unreasonable or trivial. When the mother's constant blocking in learning taxed the patience of the husband and the daughter, it went beyond their endurance to give face or restore face. This however violated the norm, since despite underlying tensions, family members were not supposed to express dissatisfaction.

Characteristics of Dysfunctional Bilingual Families

The inherent value discrepancies within bilingual Chinese-American families have been cited earlier in this chapter. When family members have little time together except to work and study, their opportunities to negotiate the value discrepancies decrease. Furthermore, they may only feel the conflict and may not have identified its relationship to the value discrepancies that have resulted from their Chinese-American experience. In a dysfunctional family, communication further deteriorates as a result of the frustrating experiences deriving from family conflict. Each member operates on his or her individual premise.

The insistence on using one language in a bilingual family effectively sustains the family dysfunction. The communication gap will decrease to the extent that members acquire proficiency in both languages. In the Chung case, it would help if the mother learned English, and the son Chinese. It was difficult to assess to what degree they comprehended each other's language. However, the ploy of preferring to communicate monolingually served to perpetuate their dysfunctional pattern. The linguistic barrier also gave them an excuse not to teach or learn well.

Let us examine the premises of the monolingual ploy. Insistence on the use of two distinct, unrelated languages perpetuates the value discrepancies. Both the message sender and the receiver have access to the analogic communication. They can opt to disregard the digital communication.* However, because communication consists of multilevel messages, digital communication adds a further dimension to the level at which the receiver can choose to respond. On the other hand, the rule in the interaction in the families under discussion is mutually to pretend that face is being saved through indirect communication. Their options for response are maximized. For instance, in the context in which a parent (A) speaks some English but chooses to speak Chinese, and a child (B) understands some Chinese, but chooses to speak English, B has these options:

---

*According to Watzlawick et al. (1967), analogic communication encompasses the whole nonverbal repertoire as well as the interactional context (p. 62); digital communication is verbal (p. 61).

1. Understand A's verbal message and acknowledge it in English. (A's message is received, understood and acknowledged, but the acknowledgment is unlikely to be comprehended by A.)
2. Deny understanding of the Chinese message. (Here B negates the verbal message. B is in the one-up position of defining their relationship on his or her own terms. This strategy would be particularly useful to B in that he or she can evade the issue, especially if B does not wish to comply. At the same time, both A's and B's faces are preserved.)

On the other hand, if A sends a Chinese message with an accompanying incongruent nonverbal message to B, B's options, based on his or her ability to understand Chinese, are as follows:

1. Perceive the Chinese verbal message alone and acknowledge it verbally in English. (This avoids dealing with an important aspect of the message.)
2. Perceive the nonverbal message and respond with another nonverbal message. (The communication now remains on the nonverbal level. Therefore B can always deny whatever meaning is attributed to the nonverbal behavior. B can discount intended harm or disclaim the seriousness of his or her intent.)
3. Receive both verbal and nonverbal messages and negate them by denying understanding. (B can thus gain the satisfaction of challenging the incongruence as if he or she had not done so. B gets a stab at this usually avoided area in face-work without being penalized. Since B does not acknowledge either message, he or she can thereby claim control by not controlling.)
4. Respond to the nonverbal message in English. (If B's face is threatened, he or she can call attention to A's lack of English comprehension, thus averting further loss of face.)
5. Receive the message on the verbal and nonverbal level and comment on the lack of congruity.
6. Understand the message on the verbal and nonverbal level and acknowledge in Chinese. (This unequivocating response has the potential for fostering mutuality and deescalation of the one-upmanship in the interaction.)

The use of the monolingual ploy can effectively block communication. It also allows one to withdraw from taking responsibility. One can opt to be irrelevant. One can thus work into a complementary relationship by maneuvering oneself into a one-up position.

Let me illustrate with an example drawn from the work with the Chung family*:

Mother to Son: (C)	I have fainting sickness—you like it?
Son: (E)	I don't know.
Mother: (C)	You like it? (E) You don't know! (C) Talk now. I have sickness. I teach you. You don't listen. Make me more nervous and I can't get well. You want Mother to get well or not?
[Son keeps silent.]	
Therapist: (E)	What's going on?
Father: (E)	Mother asked about her illness. He [the son] wouldn't say anything.
Mother to Son: (C)	Don't waste time. Talk! Don't laugh! Don't look at me sideways. [It is impolite to do so.] Now I am mad at you. [Soft voice:] I am not mad at you. [Hard voice:] I am *teaching* you.
Daughter to Therapist: (E)	He's ignoring her.
Therapist to Daughter: (E)	Tell your brother.
Daughter to Son: (E)	You are ignoring her.
Mother to Son: (E)	What you say? (C) How did I just teach you? Scold you? Talk!
Mother to Therapist: (C)	Look, he doesn't like me. I ask him. In his heart, he doesn't like me.
Mother to Son: (C)	You don't talk, you waste time. I can't get better, Son. I wish you would talk slowly and clearly.
[Son remains silent.]	
Therapist to Son: (E)	How do you feel?
Son: (E)	I don't feel nothing.
Therapist to Son: (E)	Tell Mom.
Son: (E)	I can't speak Chinese.
Therapist to Son: (E)	Tell her in whatever way you want.
Son: (E)	I can't.

The example demonstrates that the verbal language itself bore little significance in the messages. The tone of voice and the posture conveyed the mother's anger, helplessness, and demands. The son responded with anger and silence. He chose not to respond verbally. When he did respond, he negated his mother's and everyone else's messages. He could thereby continue to avoid being drawn into the family interaction.

In conventional social encounters, people attempt to save face mutually.

---

*(C) stands for Chinese. (E) stands for English.

That is to preserve self-esteem, however superficially. In a dysfunctional bilingual family, saving face is also used, but in general, members do not usually communicate to enhance each other's self-esteem. Their experiences have been frustrating. They discount each other through blaming and denial.

Therapeutic Situations

There are some cultural attitudes that may act to deter functional communication in therapy. Most people attempt to preserve a façade by controlling emotional expression, and this is particularly the case for the Chinese. Open expression of anger is unacceptable, although the conventional language is replete with verbal hostilities and abusiveness. Efforts to bring out sentiments and emotions in therapy can be met with great resistance. To show anger is also to lose face. When anger is exposed, it may be met with a "so-what" attitude to minimize the wrong face. Members of the Chung family were asked on various occasions to express their private pain. Even though this would cause the participants to lose their face, as a result of repeated focus on the individual family members, some members finally expressed inner feelings that had been hitherto guarded in the face-saving processes:

> Father (with moistened eyes): I am helpless. No one else helps. They don't really trust me.
>
> Mother (voice and limbs tremulous): I can't do anything I should as a wife and mother. I have only my stupidity to be angry at.
>
> Daughter (uneasy): I am in between. I don't know what to do.

To show that one is not happy or that one's family is not harmonious is to lose the family's face. Various face-saving rituals help to screen out true feelings and build up resistance to acknowledging their existence. In dysfunctional bilingual families, even though each blames the others, all go to great lengths to save the face of the family, especially in initial therapy sessions. To attempt to rescue in order to save face can be costly to the member who helps. In the end, no one feels the caring that might have motivated the rescue. There is only the sense of being burdened with unexpressed feelings.

> Father (to Mother): You are sick. You can't help it. I don't mind taking care of you.
>
> Mother (to Father): I can't perform as a normal wife should. You teach me. You are patient and kind.

Son (in answer to Father's complaint of mistrust):	Sure I trust you!
Daughter (to Mother):	We will baby-sit you. We will take you out and walk you to the day-care center. I like going out anyway!

Everyone in this instance was considerate and was enhancing the other's self-esteem. However, they were also cheating themselves out of expression of their authentic feelings.

In family therapy, all members are expected to participate. This is not the norm in bilingual families. Children are expected to listen and learn from adults. Therapist, assigned the adult and expert role by the family, are expected to speak and be listened to. For instance, a common feeling experienced by the father was expressed in these words: "It's the same old thing at home. She [his wife] asks me to teach her. She never listens to me completely. She has to check it out with someone else. We want to get someone outside the family, maybe a professional person, you know, to get some new ideas. Maybe she will listen to an outsider, but certainly not to me!" Here the father was giving face to the therapist and was asking the latter to give face in return by complying with his wish.

In Chinese communication, most responses to messages center on the digital communication. However, using the analogic communication as well, the receiver is to make inferences regarding what the sender means. This custom is contrary to the goal of communication in therapy where clear and direct verbal and nonverbal communication is of prime importance. Frequently this may mean that emotions underlying digital communication will have to be made explicit. Bilingual therapists are in a position to make some unique contributions here. They can effectively mediate the dysfunction perpetuated by the monolingual ploy. By constantly using one or the other language, like a traffic cop, the therapist can open the communication and cut through blocking. For instance, in commenting on underlying emotions, the therapist can employ both languages to facilitate their expression in metaphors but not in gestures. On the other hand, if the therapist speaks only one language, he or she may perpetuate some of the dysfunction inherent in the monolingual ploy.

In my therapeutic work with bilingual families, when there has been a communication overload, I have employed both written and spoken language to slow down, sort out, and clarify messages. For instance, I have written down messages for members' examination and response. This was useful, for example, in the preceding illustration, when the mother professed that she could not hear. In using both languages in the written and spoken form, an empathetic context is created for the interaction in both the Chinese and English sectors. No one is left out.

TOWARDS TRANSCULTURAL THERAPY

Understanding the culture is not just knowing the unique values held by the Chinese. It means understanding the experiences of Chinese-Americans: the interplay, the conflict of value discrepancies as well as the oppressive experiences of institutional racism.

A bilingual therapist is better able to avoid the subtle racism that might characterize treatment by a nonbilingual therapist with no transcultural experience. Clients may be frustrated when therapists unwittingly reinforce traditional Chinese values (i.e., those subscribed to by the parents), thereby alienating the children of the family. Similarly, if they fall into the trap of appearing to identify with the Americanized value system of the children, they may lose the parents. With an understanding of the probable parent-child discrepancies, the therapist is more likely to recognize and therefore bring out the caring inherent in the communication of family members.

The author does not maintain that only bilingual therapists can help dysfunctional bilingual families. In order to gain sensitivity to the unique culture of Chinese-Americans, the therapist needs to have a firm understanding of the social history of these people, and to know that the older and younger generations have had very different experiences. Instead of emphasizing the parents' "maladaptation" with reference to their social status, their accent, or their tenacious clinging to Chinese values, the therapist must stress the strength of their sheer determination to survive and their aspirations toward upgrading their families' circumstances. Instead of emphasizing its adolescent rebellion, the younger generation's progress toward identity and racial pride must be encouraged. One must also come to grips with the taken-for-granted nature of racism. In fact, both clients and therapists may be holding an Anglo perspective without being aware of it. Since certain family dysfunctions are indirectly the results of racism, it is important, in the best interests of clients, that these areas be sensitively and honestly examined.

REFERENCES

Asian American Community Mental Health Services. *Survey on Asian American Utilization of Mental Health Services in Alameda County, Calif.*, 1974.

Bay Area Concerned Chinese Americans for Mental Health. *Proposal on Mental Health.* Presented to the California Department of Health, San Francisco, Calif., 1975.

Billingsley, A. *Black Families in White America.* Englewood Cliffs, N.J.: Prentice-Hall, 1968.

Brown, B. Saving face. *Psychology Today*, 1971, 4, 55ff.

Chin, F., et al. *Aiiieeeee! An Anthology of Asian-American Writers.* New York: Anchor Press, 1975.

Chun-Hoon, L. Teaching the Asian-American experiences: Alternative to the neglect and racism in textbooks. *Amerasia*, 1975, 3, 40–58.

Dickeman, M. Teaching cultural pluralism. In Banks, J.A. (ed.), *Teaching Ethnic Studies*. Washington, D.C.: National Council for Social Studies, 1973, 4–25.

Fong, L, Gee, J., & Wong, H. *The Assimilation of Chinese Americans—A Study of Chinese Undergraduate Nursing Students in The University of California at San Francisco*. Unpublished senior paper, June 1973.

Goffman, E. On face-work: An analysis of ritual elements in social interaction. *Psychiatry*, 1955, 18, 213–231.

Huang, L.J. The Chinese American family. In Mindel, C.H., & Habenstein, R.W. (eds)., *Ethnic Families in America*. New York: Elsevier, 1976, 124–147.

Jen, L. *Oppression and Survival, Asian Women*. Berkeley: University of California at Berkeley Press, 1971.

Kagiwada, G. Confessions of a misguided sociologist. *Amerasia*, 1973, 2, 157–164.

Kung, S.W. *Chinese in American Life: Some Aspects of Their History, Status, Problems and Contributions*. Seattle: University of Washington Press, 1962.

Lan, D. The Chinatown sweatshops: Oppression and an alternative. *Amerasia*, 1971, 1, 40–57.

Lyman, S. *Chinese Americans*. New York: Random House, 1974.

Lyman, S. *The Asian in the West*. (Social Science and Humanities Publications, No. 4). Reno: University of Nevada, 1970.

Manis, J.G., & Meltzer, B.N. (eds). *Symbolic Interaction*. Boston: Allyn and Bacon, 1972.

Mindel, C.H., & Habenstein, R.W. *Ethnic Families in America*. New York: Elsevier, 1976.

Sing, L. Chinese in San Francisco 1970. Testimony of Employment Problems of the Community as presented before the California Fair Employment Practice Commission, December 1970.

Siu, P. The sojourner. *American Journal of Sociology*, 1952, 58, 34–44.

Staples, R. (ed). *The Black Family: Essays and Studies*. Belmont, Calif.: Wadsworth, 1971.

Sung, B. L. The story of the Chinese in America, New York: Collier, 1971.

Tong, B.R. The ghetto of the mind: Notes on the historical psychology of Chinese Americans. *Amerasia*, 1971, 1, 1–31.

U.S. Department of Health, Education and Welfare. A study of selected socioeconomic characteristics of ethnic minorities based on the 1970 census. Publ. No. 05, Vol. 2, Asian Americans. Washington, D.C.: Government Printing Office, 1970.

Wand, D.H.S. *Asian-American Heritage*. New York: Washington Square Press, 1974.

Wang, L.C. Chinatown in transition. In Ting, (ed.), *The Cauldron*. San Francisco, Calif.: Glide Urban Center, 1970, 91–105.

Watanabe, C. Culture and communication: Self expression and the Asian American experience. *Asian American Review*, Ethnic Studies Department, University of California at Berkeley, Spring 1972, pp. 10–20.

Watzlawick, P., Beavin, J., & Jackson, D. *Pragmatics of Human Communication*. New York: Norton, 1967.

Wu, C. (ed.). *Chink*. New York: Meridian, 1972.

Young, N. Socialization patterns among the Chinese of Hawaii. *Amerasia*, 1972, 1, 31–51.

section
III

TRAUMATIC DISRUPTIONS IN FAMILY LIFE

The family, as the primary social unit, is subjected to intense internal and external stressors in contemporary American society. The stress of unusual circumstances often places intolerable demands on resources already heavily invested in managing the strains of everyday life—this at a time when the nuclear family is increasingly removed from primary social networks. The increase in stressors, accompanied by diminished resources for managing them, leaves the family more vulnerable and less capable of coping with disruption. This section scrutinizes some of the disruptive circumstances germane to a study of families in contemporary America. Descriptive and interventive considerations provide the reader with a base for critical examination of the selected problematic situations.

14

Violence in the Family

Margaret Duggan

The communications media bombard us daily with evidence of the violent currents in our society. American families are confronted with the necessity of functioning within this context. In addition, statistics suggest that family members are more frequently resorting to violence in response to the frustrations and demands of daily living. Duggan examines these phenomena, paying particular attention to the complex issues inherent in any attempt at defining violence. Such definitional considerations are vital in that they serve to guide research and interventive efforts. The author presents a conceptual model that characterizes violence as occurring along a continuum that ranges from acts of omission, as in neglect, to acts of commission, the extreme being murder. These apparently disparate forms are portrayed as having some similarities in that all have both physical and psychologic effects on the victim. Duggan's work provides a frame within which the two succeeding chapters on spouse and child abuse may be viewed.

It is well recognized that violent crimes in America have reached epidemic proportions. The media confirm again and again the risk one takes walking city streets. We are shocked to learn that elderly tenants in certain areas of New York City remain locked inside their apartments for days and weeks on end, fearful of venturing outdoors even for so essential an item as food. For years disreputable businessmen were known to burn their businesses to collect insurance money; now there are arsonists in urban ghettos who, deliberately, in retaliation for real or imagined grievances, set fire to buildings that house sleeping tenants. What has happened to American values? A recent news article suggests that even a top government law-enforcement agency may be impressed by violent tactics:

> Making the FBI's Most Wanted Criminals List these days is a little like winning admission to a top-notch graduate school. There are few openings and only those with outstanding qualifications get accepted. . . . We're after the best fugitives. . . . We select the ones who are most violence prone . . . (*Buffalo Evening News*, 1979a).

All of this, however shocking, seems relatively remote for most of us. Since the names and places are out of our immediate sphere of contact, after the initial reaction we usually manage to remain relatively complacent. Yet an even more disturbing fact has recently surfaced to rock the American dream boat. The fact is that for many Americans at all economic levels, home is no longer the haven that Norman Rockwell portrayed (if indeed it ever did exist). A recent survey used conflict-tactics scales to measure the use of reasoning, verbal aggression, and violence in a nationally representative sample of more than 2000 families (Straus et al., 1980). The results suggest that violence among family members is common enough to be considered a routine part of family life. A yearly figure depicting the level of family violence in America is mind-boggling. At least 6 million men, women and children are physically attacked each year by a family member (Straus et al., 1980). Nearly one out of four murder victims in America is killed by a member of his own family (Gelles, 1979, p. 11). These data are especially disturbing if considered from the point of view that the family is the basic unit of American society; in other words, that is, as the family goes, so goes the nation.

Violence in the family is hardly a new phenomenon. For example, since the Code of Hammurabi, 4000 years ago, laws have existed condemning infanticide (Radbill, 1974). In the prerevolutionary days of China, and well into the twentieth century, both infanticide and the selling of children (especially females) were carried out. In our own country, the commonly used phrase, "rule of thumb," came from an 1867 North Carolina court case in which a man was acquitted of beating his wife on the grounds that the switch used was "smaller than his thumb" (Martin, 1976).

What *is* new is the beginning social awareness of the pervasiveness of family violence. The American myth of the happy, conflict-free family is crumbling. The notion that violence in the family is rare and carried out solely by mentally deranged persons simply won't sell anymore.

The first real breakthrough in bringing the problem to light occurred in the United States in 1871 with the founding of the Society for the Prevention of Cruelty to Children. The courts had refused to take legal action against the parents of a young girl who was being maltreated, since the right of parents to chastise their child was held "sacred." Church workers finally appealed to the Society for the Prevention of Cruelty to Animals on the grounds that the girl was a member of the animal kingdom, so her case would be eligible for inclusion under the laws against animal cruelty. The formation of the Society for the Prevention of Cruelty to Children occurred as a direct result of this case (Fontana, 1964). Kempe's coining of the phrase "battered child syndrome" in 1961 shocked American society into taking a second look at the supposedly "rare" problem of child abuse (Helfer & Kempe, 1974). Kempe actually proposed the term at the 1961 symposium of the American Academy of Pediatrics in an attempt to focus attention on the seriousness of the problem. Still, the public largely viewed matters like child abuse as something only the "sick" person could do. In fact, this view was supported by theoreticians who postulated that parents who abused children were psychopathic (Steele & Pollack, 1974). The fact of the matter is that violence between family members cuts across all socioeconomic levels, all racial lines, all ethnic groups. It is really difficult to pick out child abusers or wife beaters, for example, from any other group of Americans on the street. As the English phrase "gram-slamming" suggests, victims come from all age groups as well as in all sizes, shapes, and colors. However, awareness of the problem is of little avail unless we identify contributing causal factors in order to plan effective intervention.

Violence is a global term. Depending on one's definition and perspective, one's focus may vary considerably. For instance, physicians might concentrate on the extent of physical injury, such as circumoral bruising, fractures in various stages of healing, malnutrition, and the like. Social workers might tend to look at the milieu in which the violence occurred. Psychologists in their orientation to the problem might concentrate on the psychologic components, such as the personality characteristics of both victim and perpetrator.

If we examine synonyms for the term *violence*, the problem of definition becomes more apparent. A violent incident might be described variously as physical assault, abuse, battering, brutality, or aggression. Yet even these terms fall short of the mark. Do we consider threat, force or coercion to be violence? If so, do we include only the *means* by which threat, force, or coercion are carried out? Goode (1971) has distinguished between violence and force in terms of legitimacy; that is, violence is seen as the illegitimate use of physical force, whereas force itself is viewed as a legitimate act. This suggests that social approval, or the lack of it, plays a role in defining violence. Again, do we differentiate between physical and psychologic coercion? Is one form violent and the other nonviolent?

Another related term, the word *conflict*, can be used to describe a clashing of interests that is a normal everyday occurrence in life. Yet the term *conflict* can also be used to describe aggression and even warfare. The Korean Conflict of the 1950s was never labeled a "war," yet that was small comfort to the troops of both sides who lay wounded and dying on the battlefield.

Can neglect be considered an act of violence? Initially, one might argue that neglect is not violence. This is especially true if one confines one's definition to the immediacy of the act itself, disregarding long-term results. On the other hand, violence can be defined in terms of omission or commission. In this regard, child abuse is often separated into categories, with neglect and abuse-neglect at the omission end of the scale and abuse on the commission end. In keeping with this view, Young (1964, p. 9) defines the failure to feed a child satisfactorily as severe neglect based on the assumption that "to eat is the most necessary and elemental of all human needs." The devastating effects of this form of abuse are depicted in the following exchange between a caseworker and a severely neglected 8-year-old child. The caseworker asked the girl what she wanted to be when she was grown up; the child replied simply, "I don't want to be" (Young, 1964, p. 25). For some, death may seem preferable to some forms of existence.

Does our definition of violence vary according to intent? The word *neglect* connotes a lack of action while the term *deprivation* suggests deliberate action. On the basis of the concept of intentionality inherent in this differentiation, the starvation of millions of people in concentration camps during World War II was not only a heinous act, it was also violent action.

A definition of *violence* is incomplete without the inclusion of a consideration of psychologic abuse. Psychic blows leave no immediately visible scars, yet the victim's very sense of self can be eroded by repeated verbal attacks. The terms *abuse* and *violence* are often used interchangeably. Does this apply in the case of psychologic abuse? Just how muddy the waters can be is illustrated in the problem of incest. Incest has rarely been discussed in polite society. Many people confuse the terms *rape* and *incest*. Rape has become recognized in recent years for what it is: an aggressive, hostile act rather than primarily a sexual one. However, incest can be much more complex, in many cases beginning subtly, for example, with fondling by a loved parent and then progressing to sexual intercourse that often continues over a span of years. While threats or bribes may be used against the young child, violence in the sense of physical aggression is absent in many cases. The child is often only 4 to 5 years old at the onset, and may perhaps be only dimly aware that something is wrong without comprehending totally what is taking place. Is the betrayal of innocence to be considered violence, that is, psychologic violence/abuse? While incest is labeled a crime in every state in our country, there remain important ambiguities regarding whether such a betrayal of trust and subtle distortion of a child's gender and sexual identity are to be considered violence if battering or force is absent.

Muddy indeed are the waters! Definitions of terms are essential in order to formulate and test out theories. Multidisciplinary concurrence is needed on the notion of just what constitutes violence in the family. It is not easy to research a problem whose dimensions are so difficult to categorize and operationalize. In an effort to develop a comprehensive view, it may be helpful to place violence, of all the types mentioned earlier, on a continuum according to the act itself and the resulting severity of the act (Fig. 14.1). As the diagram indicates, death can occur from one end of the spectrum to the other and all categories of abuse have both physical and psychologic components. Obviously, the risk factor, in terms of severity, increases with the more severe forms of violence.

Straus et al. (1980) conducted the first national study on family violence. Conflict tactics scales were used to measure the families' responses to conflict. There was a total of 19 items in the scale. The first ten, used to designate comparatively nonviolent behavior, ranged from efforts at reasoning to acts of verbal aggression. Of the remaining nine categories, eight were constructed to measure frequency of actual use of physical force to settle family differences. (The nineteenth item allowed for interviewers to probe for additional data.) The eight items descriptive of use of physical force were as follows:

1. Threw object at other
2. Pushed, grabbed or shoved other
3. Slapped or spanked other
4. Kicked, bit, hit with fist
5. Hit, or tried to hit, with object
6. Beat up other
7. Threatened with knife or gun
8. Used knife or gun

Therefore, the act itself was considered and rated according to severity. Violence was separated by these researchers into two types: "normal" violence and "abusive" violence (Straus et al., 1980). The distinction was based on the degree or severity of the physical act as well as on the intent. Normal violence encompassed acts ranging from a slap to murder. The term *normal* suggested everyday occurrences not necessarily recognized as having a high potential for injury. Abusive violence incorporated physical acts with a "high potential for injuring the person being hit," for example, punching, kicking, stabbing, or shooting. Abusive violence was characterized as severe violence on the conflict tactics scales and included only the last five items listed above.

VICTIMIZATION

In any definition of *violence*, the effect on the victim and his or her responses, and the victim's internal and external resources are crucial considerations. The wide-ranging potential effects are illustrated in Figure 14.1. For example, verbal abuse may affect one individual more deeply than another, and responses to assault may differ. One woman described her reaction to her husband's verbal attacks in the following manner:

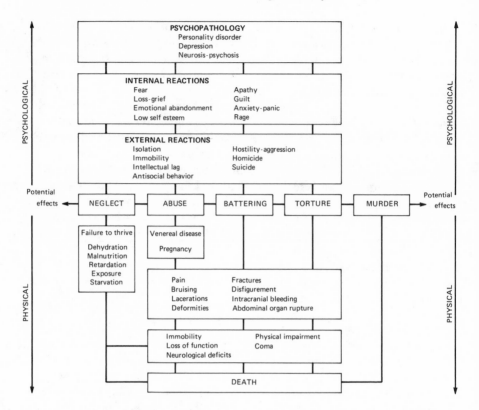

FIGURE 14-1. The continuum of violence. The diagram depicts the potential effects despite the variability in intent.

> He would leave me with such a low opinion of myself I couldn't function for days. Sometimes I would even cower in front of him, get down on my knees and apologize for having provoked him, but yet not knowing how I had (*Buffalo Courier Express*, 1977).

Another victim might respond in kind, for example, by retaliating with a verbal assault on her husband. Despite the type of violence employed, there are certain similarities in reactions as well as individual differences. Initially, the victim (whether wife, child, or other) may feel confused in that one who supposedly cares is inflicting pain. While anticipated disapproval by a significant other is well recognized as a threat to the security of the self, victims of battering are subject to threats to biologic integrity as well. There may be massive denial of the experience itself, or of the affect associated with the event due to the severe anxiety experienced. It is also common for the victim to express guilt for having provoked the attack: "It's my fault; if only I had been a better wife (husband, child), it wouldn't have happened." Fear of future attacks produces feelings of apprehension, tension, and difficulties in concentration. The victim may rationalize, saying, "It can't happen again," or "He (or she) didn't mean it." Anger resulting from the attack may be displaced onto "safe" objects in the environment. The battered wife may direct anger toward the children. An abused child may act out against siblings, playmates, or pets. If alternative modes of living and substitute support systems are not readily available (or perceived as available), the victim can become increasingly depressed, feeling impotent in a situation that looms as hopeless and unresolvable.

The family unit may respond to violence within its perimeter by tightening its boundaries, forming coalitions, or dispersing. If boundaries are tightened, the family group tends to isolate itself from neighbors and community. This response usually occurs out of shame and fear: "People won't understand"; "They'll take my children away"; "How will I survive, where will I go?"

Coalitions may develop among family members in an attempt to maintain homeostasis. Children may stay away from Mommy when she is in a "bad mood." The development of both gender and role identity may influence coalition formation in the children. Female children may side with the mother if she is the target of abuse, while male children may side with the father and identify with his behavior. The victim may become the scapegoat for the rest of the family. Many cases have been reported in which one child is treated in a completely different manner from the other children in the family. The scapegoat is usually seen as special, different, or disappointing in some way (Friedrich & Boriskin, 1976).

Dispersal is a flight response to the problem on the part of some of the members. For example, teenage runaways frequently cite parental abuse as a factor in their decision to leave home. Younger children may opt for strong peer-group identification or join gangs in an attempt to replace the family as primary group. The gang provides its own set of norms, values, rules, and beliefs. This pseudofamily group can offer a troubled youngster some sense of the security lacking at home.

The most serious result of violence in the family is the "spiritual" disintegration that occurs in the system. The family is the real (but often unidentified) victim; one member simply carries the more visible signs of its dysfunction.

IMPACT OF CULTURE

What impact does the larger culture have on the development of family norms and values? Every society develops concepts of what is acceptable, normal, or natural, and these concepts are closely related to its notion of good and evil (Benedict, 1934). Culture constantly shapes our thoughts and behavior, in many cases outside of our awareness. Cultural influences may be manifested subtly, resulting in behavior that is often labeled as "just human nature." Cultural beliefs and values are learned through imprinting that begins immediately after the infant is born. Gradually, she or he learns what it is to be female or male, how grown-ups handle anger and frustration, how they gratify their needs, and how they view the world around them. People from different cultural backgrounds make unconscious assumptions about personal space, interpersonal relations, and the function of time (Hall & Hall, 1976).

The influence of culture on human behavior has been illustrated by comparing two Native American groups, the Eskimos and Ojibwa. These societies have markedly different cultural approaches to child rearing. The Eskimos believe that the child is the repository of the soul of a recently departed family member, thereby commanding singular respect. As a result, the child is treated in a kind and permissive manner. The Ojibwa, by contrast, believe a child is "empty" when born and needs severe, early discipline in order to remove the opportunity for the entry of evil spirits. The outcomes of these differing modes of parenting are noteworthy. Adult Eskimos develop strong cooperative and communal values; they are described as spontaneous, open, empathetic, and carefree (Parker, 1977). In contrast, Ojibwa behavior is marked by both stoicism and inhibition; their general attitude has been described as sullen, reticent, aloof and restricted (Parker, 1977). The impact of cultural beliefs on behavior is clearly deep and far reaching. It seems logical, therefore, to infer that individual norms regarding violence are similarly derived.*

America's culture is one of violence. One way to measure what we value is to examine what we are willing to pay for. For example, among recent film successes there are several that are graphically violent. Producers package salable commodities: What the public says it wants and what it pays for at the box office may be two entirely different matters, and box office receipts are the determining factor. As a nation, we support violence in contact sports. Just imagine for a moment, a television blackout during a Super Bowl game. This would be viewed as a "national disaster" in homes across the entire country.

Public approval of violence can also be demonstrated by the growing support for the death penalty. Disturbing as the fact may be, as a nation we place a certain value on violence. At the same time, we continue to proclaim to ourselves and to the world the myth of a nonviolent America and a conflict-

---

*For an in-depth discussion of the interdependence of child rearing and the transmission of culture, see Chapter 1 in this volume.

free, happy American family. The family, as a unique unit of American society, not only incorporates these values from the larger culture, but also perpetuates them in future generations.

THE FAMILY IN TRANSITION

Changes in the larger culture over time have been reflected in the American family. For much of the first half of the twentieth century the extended family group held a firm place in American society. While individual liberty may have been sacrificed, security and continuity were fairly well provided. Parents, children, grandparents, maiden aunts, and unmarried uncles were often part of the same household, sharing in family decisions and responsibilities. Family unity was usually a more important consideration than personal needs or attitudes. Sex and age roles were clearly defined and limited, as were, of course, educational and job opportunities. Tradition and family customs were an important part of family life. Ethnic groups had a tendency to cluster in specific neighborhoods. There was awe of the powers in Washington, and estrangement from them. With the coming of the Depression, people lost faith in government, banks, and jobs that failed to offer them security. Security became the byword and primary goal of many families in the late 1930s.

World War II brought many important, far-reaching influences to bear on American family life. Defense plants needed workers, and with most of the able-bodied male population in service, women were called upon as patriots to perform many jobs formerly held by men. Thus, Rosie the Riveter appeared on the American scene in slacks and goggles, a welding torch in her hand, and her hair pulled back in a snood. Before this time a wife and mother working outside the home was frowned on by society in general and was often viewed as reflecting adversely on her husband's ability as a provider.

The post-World War II baby boom caused an upsurge in the provision of needed services, such as schools and new housing. The move to suburbia began in earnest and old-style ethnic neighborhoods were left behind. Many women continued to work, through personal desire, need for extra income, or in many cases for both reasons. The new, smaller houses influenced the transition from the extended to the nuclear family. Estrangement from and awe of government changed to cynicism with the introduction of television into American homes in the 1950s. Government came under scrutiny nightly in living rooms across the nation. Officials who had been just names before, now became visible, vulnerable human beings. The aura of mystery disappeared and, in many cases, disillusionment set in.

The 1960s brought about confrontation between individuals and authority at all levels. On college campuses the drug scene, riots, and rock music produced sit-ins, lie-ins, and dropouts. "Relevance" replaced tradition and middle-class values. The gap between the generations widened and became more clearly defined. Emphasis on the individual encouraged a new narcissism in American society that was reflected in the breakdown of the traditional American family unit. "Doing your own thing" led to exploration of previously unthinkable goals and roles. Many established churches were questioned as to their social policies and relevance to social needs. God and Country came under fire simultaneously. The Protestant work ethic, threaded throughout the tapestry of American culture, faltered in the turmoil of the 1960s, but it rebounded strongly. College students in the 1970s became noticeably more career-oriented and competitive.

Many American males met the Women's Liberation Movement in the 1960s as if the gauntlet had been thrown down. Role blurring, confusion, and threats to the traditional male-oriented marketplace abounded in the 1960s. Women became increasingly unwilling to accept second-rate jobs or pay. In the communications media, males were beginning to exhibit emotions, helping to set the stage for their moving into nurturing roles. Child-custody cases were being fought and won by fathers.

Families in the 1970s were highly mobile and took on varying forms and lifestyles. During the past 20 years, single-parent families have increased more rapidly than have traditional two-parent families (*Buffalo Evening News*, 1979b). Most of these single-parent families have a woman as head of household. The rapid rise in divorce rates is an important contributing factor. Blended families, consisting of partners with children from previous marriages are also on the increase. Marriage is no longer "till death do us part" but rather till the relationship is no longer "meaningful." Other "meaningful" relationships include those of unmarried couples, with or without formal or informal prenuptial legal agreements, and groupings of the same sex, with or without children.

The composition of the family has changed drastically along with its values and traditions. Mom and apple pie have given way to MacDonald's and Supermom. Women, facing increased responsibility in the marketplace (in many cases without an easing of home duties), have also become more vulnerable to stress-related disease.

Looking back on the 1970s it appears that the idealistic social commitment and soul searching of the 1960s were replaced with a more calculating approach (i.e., "What's in it for me?"). There remains skepticism toward organizations and institutions, as well as belief in the potential of the individual. Health fads, spas, jogging, and nutrition cults enjoy wide popularity because of the constant effort to stave off the aging process. America is youth- and productivity-oriented. The Protestant work ethic has survived these decades of change far better than has the traditional concept of the American family.

FAMILY: A MINI-SOCIETY

In the movie *Wizard of Oz*, Dorothy clicks the heels of her magic ruby slippers, repeating, "There's no place like home; there's no place like home. . . ." What is there about the family that makes it different from other units in our society? People may establish membership in many different groups during the course of a lifetime. Certainly, there are pressures and stresses in any task-oriented group, and in many social groups as well. It is common knowledge that power struggles go on every day in large corporations. Aggressiveness and drive are the name of the game in the climb to the top of the corporate heap. Yet, we rarely read about "free-for-alls" in the board rooms. If violence in the family has become common enough to be considered routine, as mentioned earlier (Straus, 1976), then what makes the family as a group so different?

There are several factors that are unique to the family (Straus, 1976). For instance, the way in which it is organized distinguishes it from other groups. Families are composed of members of different sex- and age-groupings, and these differences are conducive to both gender and generational conflict. What the children value is frequently at odds with what the parents value. A husband may see the family income-tax refund as a chance to buy a power saw, while his wife has entertained visions of a new dishwasher. The wide range of activities and interests shared by family members provides more areas for possible disagreement. There is also a more intense involvement of the members as compared with the intensity of involvement in groups whose membership is elective. For instance, if Johnny gets into trouble with the law, the parent usually feels a personal sense of responsibility coupled with the right and duty to influence the child's behavior. The neighbors expect this; the police expect it; the entire community expects it. The message is, "He's your child; you'd better straighten him out." Implied, of course, is the understanding that the parent, as responsible party, will resort to whatever means are necessary. The methods or degree of influence are never really spelled out. Results count.

America is action-oriented. The community at large continually sends out signals reinforcing the old notion that "a man's home is his castle." The police refrain from intervening in domestic squabbles, not only because of the danger to themselves, but also because of their reluctance to interfere in "private family matters." This attitude has been deeply ingrained in American culture and stems historically from the old frontier notion of the family as an island in the savage wilderness. Long before any sense of organized law and order of community developed, the family stood alone and solved its problems. Along these lines, when a group of Pennsylvania State University students were tested to determine their reactions to fights between men and women, according to how they perceived the relationship, 65 percent of the students tried to help when they believed that strangers were fighting each other, but only 19 percent did so when they thought the parties were married (*Psychology Today*, 1977). The frontier notion persists.

Since membership is not an elective matter, escape is not always feasible; this limitation is another source of intrafamilial conflict. Where is a 5-year-old child going to go? For that matter, a wife with no special skills, money, or training has a similar problem, especially if she has dependent children. Free day-care centers are still about as rare as dinosaur saddles.

Members must cope with the stresses inherent in an intrafamilial living situation, day after day, over a span of years. The usual course of events includes a series of maturational and situational changes that can be crisis producing for one or all members. This series includes births, marriages, deaths, job losses or changes, accidents (both major and minor), and illnesses. What other group in our culture faces as wide a range of stresses as does the family?

This social unit is expected to clothe, house, nurture, and educate its children, regardless of the resources at its disposal or of the extreme economic factors over which it has little or no control. Society expects the family to produce well-educated, healthy, law-abiding citizens. Many families face these enormous expectations with severe instrumental deficiencies. Basic intellectual endowment may be limited; finances for survival (let alone education) are often lacking; and the only nearby recreation area for many poor urban families is a garbage-strewn alleyway or a playground that is run by the street gang that happens to be in power at the moment.

The family is recognized as primary educator of the young. If the family is a battleground, the children learn battle tactics. To a child, love can be inextricably linked with violence in that those to whom she or he is closest also punish. If a child sees parents managing stressful situations by striking out, then a specific script for such actions has been provided (Bandura, 1973). Often the child learns violence only too well and later her- or himself becomes an abusive parent or spouse. It has been found that parents most likely to injure a small child are those who themselves were severely punished as children (Kempe & Helfer, 1972).

America has reached a stage of illusion regarding sexual equality. Whenever the media pay particular attention to a subject, people begin to feel that the accompanying issues have been resolved, or that they are at least in the process of resolution. Census documents, insurance forms, and many legal papers still reserve the first line for the "head of the household," with a second line for "wife." Significant salary differences between men and women persist despite the write-ups about the salary gains of the few women who have become corporate executives.

For the family, this period of transition toward a more egalitarian relationship between the sexes is a source of much overt and even greater covert friction. There have been no role models for men and women in transition.

Roles have to be redefined, reinvented. Men moving away from traditional tasks and sharing in household chores are moving into areas previously defined as "women's work." Even if the man initially supported his wife's move into the job market, for example, resentment over the additional burden placed on him, or any threats to his masculinity, can produce anger and a sense of losing control. Hostility, if indeed he feels he must mask it, often erupts over trivial matters, such as deciding which partner is more tired at the end of the day or who is to take out the garbage, or he may use emotional withdrawal as a subtle, and even deadlier, form of sabotage. Violence, in one form or another, can then become a final, desperate expression, a kind of last resort. Rollo May (1972) has described violence as an expression of powerlessness—of impotence.

The interplay of cultural and emotional factors provides fertile ground for battle. These factors include notions of the sanctity of family privacy, of the husband as head of the household, and of economic inequality of the sexes, as well as the frustrations inherent in role transitions related to gender identity. Of importance, too, are society's expectations of the family and the general societal trend toward narcissistic gratification. In families with immature parents whose understanding of both the parenting role and the normal process of development in children is impaired, or parents to whom violence has become an acceptable response to life's problems, internal resources are severely limited. While contemporary families have gained mobility, they have suffered the loss of crucial external support systems. Not only are they deprived of a network of relatives, but also of that special sense of historically belonging in one place over generations. In 1938, Thornton Wilder described this notion in his play, *Our Town*. Goodbye, Grover's Corners!

The crucial social unit, the family, is assembled primarily by sheer dumb luck, in most cases with little or no preparation. It harbors our most intense emotions and is expected to solve our deepest social problems.

IMPLICATIONS FOR THE FUTURE

Considering the impact of the larger social system on the family in terms of learning violence and approving of violence as a social norm, one is forced to conclude that levels of intrafamily violence are not likely to decrease until significant change occurs in the larger system. Cultural norms and values are slow to change, and the traditional state of the family, involving role modifications, will continue to generate additional stress. We cannot expect rapid enactment of legislation or the adoption of new, nonviolent parenting methods overnight. The problem exists, and it is likely to continue in the foreseeable future. What are the implications, then, for service providers?

Case Finding

The abusing family's point of entry into social and health service systems can be a crucial factor in determining the success or failure of treatment. If, for example, focus is placed entirely on the identified victim, without the acknowledgment and identification of the family's underlying problems, maladaptive patterns are likely to continue. It is a "finger in the dike" approach at best. Professionals in emergency rooms, community health agencies, schools, social service agencies, and the like are in especially strategic positions for identifying cases of abuse and neglect. A diagnosis of abuse is often difficult for the professional to make unless the symptoms are so obvious that there is no room for doubt. Many have to deal with their own feelings, including that of denial that family members do abuse one another. If the clients are well-dressed and come from middle or upper socioeconomic levels, the professional, identifying with them, may be reluctant to make "accusations." The gathering of data and initial assessment do not have to include accusations. A nonjudgmental focus on the presenting problems can help the worker appear less like a district attorney and more like a caring professional. Certain aspects of the history may suggest the need for further assessment. The professional should be alerted to the possibility of abuse (1) if the description of the incident causing injury to a child does not correspond with the child's developmental ability, (2) if there has been an unreasonable delay in seeking treatment, (3) if the description changes considerably with additional questioning, or (4) if the description conflicts with the child's version of the injury.

Along with the history, the worker can rely on his or her skills of observation. Does the child appear withdrawn, neglected, exceptionally fearful, or act in ways inappropriate to his or her role by attempting to comfort the parent? Does the parent avoid contact with the child or react inappropriately to the severity of the injury? All of these factors taken into consideration can help in making an accurate problem assessment.

Physical findings from accidental injury are often difficult to differentiate from abusive injury. Some questionable findings would include malnutrition, additional injuries in various stages of healing, cigarette burns, belt-buckle marks, oddly shaped bruises, rope burns, bruising on or near the genitals, venereal disease, or ruptured abdominal organs.

There are problems with all age groups in the identification of abuse. While small, helpless creatures readily call forth a protective response in professionals, adolescent victims evoke little sympathy in many cases because of their arrogant and hostile attitudes. These "unlovelies" are usually identified as victims only after complaints of abuse are lodged against them by their parents. Professionals should consider every runaway as suspect for a history of abuse or neglect unless data obtained point to other causes. In addition, it is important for the interviewer to remember that a surly attitude may spring from a lifetime of abuse during crucial stages of development. Because of past difficulties in developing a sense of trust, the adolescent is convinced that no one really cares. Hostility and testing behavior are often directed toward any authority figure, including the professional. Awareness of these factors, and a patient, caring approach are vital if the worker's efforts are to be therapeutic in managing these transference phenomena.

Case finding is also made more difficult because many victims deny that a problem exists. Shame, guilt, dependency, and fear of retaliation are major factors promoting the victim's tendency to cover up the abuse. This is especially true of the elderly victim and the battered wife. Workers must be alert constantly to the sense of futility in these victims. Since they feel helpless, alternatives should be presented in a manner that clearly indicates their attainability. Lowered self-esteem and accompanying depression leave little energy for facing major challenges. However, if change is to occur, the client needs help in sensing that the situation is not without hope.

An additional concern in case finding is the potential danger of employing a crisis-intervention approach indiscriminately. Battering may clearly appear as a crisis to the professional, but to many victims battering is perceived not as a crisis but as a way of life. One cannot overlook the victim's perception of the situation.

After an initial assessment, it is important that the worker collaborate with other health and social-service professionals to plan appropriate referrals for further evaluation. Once the problem has been identified as one of abuse, the tone of empathetic problem solving should be maintained. This is an exceedingly difficult time for the entire family, since feelings of shame, guilt, and fear frequently accompany the abuse label.

Treatment Approaches

The approach to treatment will vary according to the types and severity of the problems, the client system's willingness to accept treatment, and the resources available. Past experience with professionals will also influence the client's attitudes toward treatment.

When appropriate, efforts should be made to restore and support the family unit. However, a word of caution is necessary. In setting priorities, the safety of the victim is the first consideration. It has been found, for example, that a battered wife who returns to her husband is likely to be battered again, often more severely than before (Martin, 1976; Straus, 1977). Professionals are doing little for the victim by insisting that the couple "kiss and make up." In battering cases, the woman must be prepared to leave and cancel the marriage contract, if necessary. If the abuser is willing to take part in counseling sessions, he can demonstrate his intent while living apart from the victim. All too often, a battered wife, who was encouraged to return home by her spouse's promise to "reform" and seek counseling, reappears at a refuge days later, having undergone additional beatings.

In cases of father-daughter incest, the rate of recidivism is low if the offender receives psychotherapy (Gebhard et al., 1965; Foreman, 1979). However, this does not necessarily suggest that every offender should be rehabilitated in his own milieu. Underlying maladaptive family patterns that permit incest to take place must be dealt with, along with the devastating psychologic damage to the victim. In addition, options for treatment are often influenced by the legal system. In cases of incest in New York State, for example, sexual intercourse in consanguineous relationships is a felony, yet the Domestic Relations Law in New York State labels the act a misdemeanor. The application of these charges and laws is up to the prosecutor. "Treatment," then, might involve a jail sentence or a release on parole. A stipulation might be made by the judge that the offender receive psychiatric treatment at a state facility; this often means release to an outpatient clinic in a short time without the offender's having received anything that could reasonably be viewed as rehabilitative psychotherapy. If the offender is released on a misdemeanor charge as a first offender, he is free to return home and resume the incestuous relationship. Moreover, in cases where the safety of the victim dictates a separation, it is all too often the victim who is uprooted rather than the perpetrator.

Treatment options, which may be used separately or in combination, include individual psychotherapy, group therapy, marital counseling, and family therapy. Clients who respond poorly to professionals frequently respond better to peer groups such as Alcoholics Anonymous, Parents Anonymous, and women's support groups. These clients also respond well to lay service providers such as parent aide volunteers who act as role models, babysitters, and transporters (in effect, extended family) within the client's home. Residential treatment centers are geared to provide a variety of services to the entire family including individual psychotherapy, as well as parenting and financial counseling. Unfortunately, such centers are few and far between at this point.

Recommendations for professionals in strategic settings would necessarily include awareness of responsibility regarding reporting cases of abuse, examination of personal values toward victims and perpetrators of intrafamily violence, and knowledge of the specific resources available in their community. Most areas have child-protective services, and many have access to a crisis hot line. If there are no shelters for battered women in the immediate area, agencies such as the Salvation Army will often provide emergency housing. The National Center on Child Abuse and Neglect in Washington, D.C., provides information on programs available in each state, and local chapters of the National Organization for Women offer information on refuges for battered women.

Prevention

The phrase "and they lived happily ever after" should be stricken from our vocabulary. Infants are born every day who are not "bundles of joy." Some are not cuddly, many are colicky, and a few may remind one of that awful Aunt Edna or Uncle Herman. The normal process of giving birth does not guarantee nurturing behavior. Yet the myth of motherly love is so strong in our culture that a mother would be loathe to admit to feelings of rejection toward her newborn. Educational systems should include classes on marriage and parenting in every curriculum. The notion should be stressed that it is okay to have hostile and rejecting feelings but that it is important that they be managed in constructive ways. Professionals can play a supportive role in parent-child bonding relationships, in prenatal classes involving both parents and in the period immediately following delivery. In these early stages it is important to encourage the parents to touch and hold the child so that the parents learn how to provide the child with needed stimulation and security. This in turn fosters their attachment to the infant and gives them an opportunity to gain feelings of gratification and success from their parenting. Infants considered especially at risk for possible problems in the bonding relationship are the premature, sick newborns, and those with birth defects. Further supportive measures may include referral to a community health nurse for in-home follow-up visits.

A second myth that needs exploding is the one that the spared rod means a spoiled child. No one should be hit. Why is it okay to slap a child but not an adult? If a spanking on the "well-padded bottom" of a child is okay, as the vast majority of American parents believe (Stark & McEvoy, 1970; Erlanger, 1974), then does not a spanking on the more abundantly padded bottom of an adult make even better sense? Adults are now punished for their offenses by loss of a liberty or payment of a fine, whereas in the distant past they were publicly whipped. The spanking of the child is usually done by an angry, exasperated parent. Would she or he use the same method to the same degree an hour after the incident, or was it carried out primarily to relieve angry feelings? Children who are spanked, while perhaps learning not to do whatever caused the spanking, are also learning that it is all right to hit children (Gil, 1970; Kempe & Helfer, 1972; Steele & Pollack, 1974). Alternative modes of discipline can teach valuable lessons to a child. Loss of playtime, a brief period of isolation from other family members, or involvement in cleaning up a child-created "disaster" teach the child responsibility for his or her own behavior at least as effectively as does a spanking.

Victims, whether assaulted by a stranger or by a family member, deserve, but do not often receive, equal redress under existing laws. The judicial system is oriented to the preservation of the family: this is evidenced in the treatment of wife beating as a "domestic disturbance" rather than as an assault. Women are frequently discouraged from filing charges and encounter delays when they attempt to do so. Ours remains primarily a male-oriented legal system that is patriarchal in nature, supporting the traditional myth that the husband is the head of the house. Successful prosecution depends on wife beating's being defined in the legal system as assault and subject to criminal charges in every state. This is one method of eroding a cultural norm that permits and legitimizes wife beating.

Finally, the myth of the "happy family" needs to be exploded. Conflict in the family is inevitable because of the very nature of the family. Label the family what it is: a conflict-prone social microcosm. Recognition of the inevitability of conflict can open the way to learning productive methods of conflict resolution.

REFERENCES

Bandura, A. *Aggression: A Social Learning Analysis.* Englewood Cliffs, N.J.: Prentice-Hall, 1973.

Benedict, R. Anthropology and the abnormal. *Journal of Genetic Psychology*, 1934, 10, 59–82.

Buffalo Courier Express. Brutality not just physical, psychological blows hurt too. November 20, 1977, p. E-5.

Buffalo Evening News. You've got to be good to make the FBI top ten. June 30, 1979(a), p. A-2.

Buffalo Evening News. Single-parent outpacing two-parent unit. July 2, 1979(b), Sect. 1, p. 16.

Erlanger, H. Social class and corporal punishment in childrearing: A reassessment. *American Sociological Review*, 1974, 39, 68–85.

Fontana, V.J. *The Maltreated Child.* Springfield, Ill.: Thomas, 1964.

Foreman S. *Betrayal of Innocence: Incest and its Devastation.* New York: Penguin, 1979.

Friedrich, W., & Boriskin, J. The role of the child in abuse; a review of the literature. *American Journal of Orthopsychiatry*, 1976, 46, 580–591.

Gebhard, P., Gagnon, J., Pomeroy, W., Christenson, C. *Sex Offenders: An Analysis of Types*, New York: Harper and Row, 1965.

Gelles, R. *Family Violence.* Beverly Hills: Sage, 1979.

Gil, D. *Violence against Children: Physical Child Abuse in the United States.* Cambridge, Mass.: Harvard University Press, 1970.

Goode, W. Force and violence in the family. *Journal of Marriage and the Family*, 1971, 33, 624–636.

Hall, E., & Hall, E. How cultures collide. *Psychology Today*, July 1976, 91, 66–71.

Helfer, R., & Kempe, C. (eds.). *The Battered Child*, 2nd ed. Chicago: University of Chicago Press, 1974.

Kempe, C., & Helfer, R. (eds.). *Helping the Battered Child and His Family.* Philadelphia: Lippincott, 1972.

Martin, D. *Battered Wives*. New York: Pocket Books, 1976.

May, R. *Power and Innocence*. New York: Norton, 1972.

Parker, S. Eskimo psychopathology in the context of Eskimo personality and culture. In Landry, D. (ed.), *Culture, Disease, and Healing*. New York: Macmillan, 1977, 349–358.

Psychology Today. Newsline. The bystanders' creed: Don't meddle in family fights. February 1977, 10(9), p. 29.

Radbill, S.T. A history of child abuse and infanticide. In Steinmetz, S. & Straus, M. (eds.), *Violence in the Family*. New York: Harper & Row, 1974, p. 173.

Stark, R., & McEvoy, J. Middle class violence. *Psychology Today*, November 1970, 4, 52–65.

Steele, B. & Pollack, C. A psychiatric study of parents who abuse infants and small children. In Helfer, R., & Kempe, C. (eds.), *The Battered Child*, 2nd ed. Chicago: University of Chicago Press, 1974, 89–134.

Straus, M.A. A sociological perspective on the prevention and treatment of wife-beating. In Roy, M. (ed.), *Battered Women*. New York: Van Nostrand, 1977, 195–237.

Straus, M.A. Sexual inequality, cultural norms and wife beating. *Victimology*, Spring 1976, 1, 54–76.

Straus, M.A., Gelles, R.J., Steinmetz, S. *Behind Closed Doors: Violence in the American Family*. Garden City, N.Y.: Doubleday, 1980.

Young, L., *Wednesday's Children; A Study of Child Neglect and Abuse*, 2nd ed. New York: McGraw Hill, 1964.

15

Battered Women:
A (Nearly) Hidden Social Problem

Marilyn Petit

Although women have long been beaten, the beating has often been viewed as part and parcel of the expected exchange between man and woman and has therefore not been defined as seriously problematic. However, as evidence has accumulated, learning of the severity and frequency with which this form of abuse occurs has forced a different definition of the phenomenon. The statistics, alarming though they may be, only hint at the toll that battering takes of families that find themselves enmeshed in this tragic form of interaction. In this chapter, Petit spells out the nature of the problem, particularly addressing the needs of the battered woman within the context of the family. She critically examines traditional forms of service and finds them wanting. Her recommendations for alternative approaches to the problems of both the women and their families merit serious consideration, as do her suggestions regarding further research efforts.

The following is from a letter from a battered wife to a woman's crisis shelter:

> I have been married for ten years and my husband has kicked me and beaten me with a broom handle. . . . Six years ago I was 140 pounds, today 102. I would be more than thankful if you could help. Please be discreet in any attempt to contact me, as if he found out that I wrote you, he would kill me (*Newsweek*, 1973, p. 39).

A 1976 study by the Kansas City, Missouri police department revealed that 90 percent of the city's family homicides had been preceded by at least one "domestic-disturbance" call (Gingold, 1976). In 1969 a study determined that approximately one-third of homicides and even more assaults took place within a family context. According to some investigators, family-disturbance calls represented the single most frequent source of injury and death to police officers (Barocas, 1973).

Legal experts believe that wife or woman abuse is one of the most underreported crimes in the country, even more so than rape, which the FBI estimates is ten times more frequent than statistics indicate. A conservative estimate puts the number of battered wives nationwide at well over a million (Durbin, 1974). A 1976 nationwide study conducted by researchers Straus, Steinmetz and Gelles revealed that of more than 2000 couples representative of all American couples, 28 percent had been involved in physical violence at some time during their marriage. Additionally, for the 12-month period preceding the interview survey, 3.8 percent of the respondents reported one or more instances of wife beating. Applying this incidence rate to the approximately 47 million couples in the United States, approximately 1.8 million wives may be beaten by their husbands in any one year (Straus, 1977–78). If we consider that only couples living together were sampled, that "excessive" violence is a major cause of divorce, and that divorced persons were only asked about their current marriage, it is probably accurate to assume that the data are considerably underrepresentative. The researchers suggest, in fact, that the true incidence rate is probably closer to 50 or 60 percent of all couples than to the 28 percent of those who were willing to describe violent acts in a mass-interview survey. This truly represents a health and social problem of national dimension.

In this chapter, some of the social and cultural considerations surrounding the problem of wife abuse* will be examined. In addition, the needs of the victims and the views of the service providers will be identified in considering the development of effective services. Two final sections will highlight trends in service to battered women and suggest implications for therapeutic intervention by professional health and social-welfare providers.

SOCIAL AND CULTURAL CONSIDERATIONS

Violence is an ever-present phenomenon that, according to some sources, may even be increasingly characteristic of our society (Steinmetz & Straus, 1974; Martin, 1976). Numerous investigators are currently studying the extent to which the average citizen is exposed to violence through the media and the possible influence of such exposure. For example, George Gerbner, dean of the Annenberg School of Communications at the University of Pennsylvania, has been investigating television violence and its possible effect on

---

*For the purposes of this chapter, the term *wife* is used to refer to any woman, whether a legal wife, a common-law wife, or a cohabitee spouse, who lives with a man. The terms *battered wife* or *battered woman* refer to any woman who is beaten by her mate.

individuals for the past decade. A 1977 court case in Miami, Florida, raised the issue of whether the youthful perpetrator of a violent act had himself been a "victim" of exposure to television violence and was therefore not fully responsible for his act. Again, in July 1978, after 4 years of legal maneuvering, a mother in California finally went to trial claiming her daughter's "gang rape" in 1974 was the result of a television movie that was aired 4 nights before the act. Traditionally, the major institutions of our society have sanctioned the use of violence as a means of social control: the church in its punishment of heretics and in its condoning of "mortification of the flesh"; the state in its corporal punishment of criminals. According to Steinmetz and Straus (1974), however, only the police and the family today have a "clear legal mandate" to use violence as a method of social control.

Despite cultural norms that depict and demand a view of the family as a refuge of nonviolent, loving, and integrative relationships between individuals, statistics point to the fact that today's nuclear family is instead perhaps the most violent of all living arrangements (Whitehurst, 1974; Campbell, 1974). These emphatic antiviolence norms may actually account for the fact that intrafamily violence typically occurs as a climax to suppressed conflict. That is, we are so set on a loving and peaceable image of family life that conflict between members cannot be safely and positively acknowledged. Paradoxically, despite a general myth of family harmony, data from the National Commission on the Causes and Prevention of violence revealed that 25 percent of the men in the survey and 16 percent of the women would approve of slapping a wife under certain circumstances (Fojtik, 1976, p. 34). In addition, a number of investigators have documented what they feel is implied social approval of police, mental-health, and social-service agencies toward familial violence (Micklow & Eisenberg, 1975). There is a belief by prosecutors and police that if women are being beaten they should leave or seek a divorce instead of going through the judicial process: "A lot of beaten women continue to 'take it' because society tells them to take it. Their families tell them to take it. Their religion reminds them it is for better or for worse, and other institutions offer no alternatives" (*The Eccentric*, 1975). "Some of those cry babies call us three or four times a week," a Michigan police department officer was quoted as saying. "As soon as everyone sobers up and talks it out, everything is back to normal until the next little scuffle" (Ypsilanti Press, 1976, p. 3A).

WIFE ABUSE AS A MAJOR SOCIAL PROBLEM

It is only within the past two or three years that the problem of wife battering within marriage, or woman abuse in general, has gained recognition as a significant social problem in the United States. The magnitude of the problem and the extent of the disruption of families because of the threat or exercise of physical violence from within is also beginning to be confronted by some American citizens. So long (almost) hidden from view by victim, violence perpetrator, and a large majority of "others" who hesitated to get involved in the "private concerns of somebody's marriage," the problem of wife abuse is finally gaining exposure and eliciting concern on a national level.

A growing awareness of the enormity of the problem of violence to women has been facilitated by the resurgence of the women's movement. As women have become more conscious of the social conditions associated with their own and other women's lives, the problems of the battered woman have come more clearly into view. The needs and concerns of battered women were addressed by English women in the years between the late 1960s and the early 1970s, and it was through the pioneering efforts of one of these women, Erin Pizzey, that a number of legal and social reforms designed to aid battered women were established in Great Britain. Besides working for improved legal and social measures, Pizzey established Cheswick Women's Aid, the first of many women's shelters to be opened in England (Pizzey, 1975). Its establishment in 1971 was the starting point for the current international trend to create shelters specifically for battered women. Today, these refuges exist all over England and in Ireland, Scotland, Holland, Germany, India, Australia, Canada, and most recently the United States (Martin, 1976, p. 198).

Benefiting from knowledge of the experience of English women in their efforts to highlight the problem and to bring about social reform, American citizens have, in addition, begun to be exposed to a growing body of research and literature concerned with the problem of violence in the family (Scott, 1974; Steinmetz & Straus, 1973; Steinmetz & Straus, 1974; Gayford, 1975a; Gayford, 1975b; Gelles, 1972; Gelles, 1975; Dewsbury, 1975). The results of these recent investigations as well as the contributions of many feminist authors (Martin, 1976; Warrior, 1977; Leghorn, 1976) have contributed to an increased awareness of the reality of violence in our own lives and have served to reinforce the efforts of newly formed groups of Americans to provide services to protect women and family members from violent abuse. Secondary to, and it would seem in response to, citizens' raised consciousness and voices, some community social-service agents and agencies have now begun to look into this previously nonvisible social problem.

THE COMMUNITY AND ITS VIEW OF THE PROBLEM

It is the intent of this chapter to present an overview of the variety of positions, viewpoints, and services (proposed and actual) that groups within a number of urban communities presently offer to victims of wife battering;

however, before moving to explore the views of the providers of service and the needs of the victim, it may prove useful to provide first a definition of *community* and then briefly to examine the phenomenon of stigma and its effect on service provision.

In speaking of the "competent community," Cottrell (1976, p. 208) points out that the discovery that individuals and their neighbors can take effective collective action to cope with their common problems, that "they can become meaningful and effective actors in the life of the community" is, in itself, a step toward the development of mental and emotional health of the members of that community. The conditions of a modern mass technologic society tend increasingly to depersonalize and dehumanize much of life, and it is indeed a significant process when a community is able to provide an arena for effective participation by the individual in the vital processes of his or her society.

Chatterjee and Koleski (1970, p. 82) describe a number of ways of looking at the "community." One definition presents community as "the aggregate of all the institutional means available to some given groups in interaction toward the accomplishment of an aggregate of all the institutional ends": a community of persons concerned with, and interacting around, a common interest area. This conception of community provides us with a framework that will underlie our examination of each group's interaction with other groups in relation to the delivery of services to the consumer.

THE PROBLEM OF STIGMA

A common phenomenon noted when working in social problem areas is the attachment of stigma to the victim or victims of the problem. To avoid being stigmatized an individual may hide from recognition and refuse to be designated as "one of them" by the larger community. Individuals may, and in fact apparently do, resist detection even by others of "their own." In one community investigated by the author, several counselors interviewed noted the "great resistance" their battered clients maintained toward inclusion in a group for therapy purposes. Efforts in each case were subsequently discontinued and no group was successfully instituted in the four community mental health agencies surveyed. There are a number of problems associated with the phenomenon of the "hidden victim." Services may be greatly hampered and/or tangential and inappropriate since service planners frequently must rely on means other than consumer input and direction in defining needs. In addition, in terms of eliciting community response the authority or authenticity of a "person who has been there" may evoke emotional impetus toward a solution that an appalled professional may never duplicate.

Bumbalo and Young (1973, p. 1589) note that those who have experienced a problem may in fact have available a store of knowledge not easily tapped by those who have not themselves been personally involved. Groups who have "come out" to declare themselves and form self-help collectives may move more directly toward confronting society with the problems as they know them and toward more appropriately defining their needs. The increased visibility of "gay" groups of the past 10 years, for example, shows movement in these directions. Society has, to some extent, adjusted to their demands for recognition and definition of the problems.

In a community surveyed by the author, women who had been or were still being battered remained primarily isolated and anonymous; though some were active in a volunteer task force initiated by the local chapter of the National Organization for Women, most victims did not identify themselves as participants in a battering syndrome. This seems to be a characteristic inherent in many task groups working on the problem of battered women. There is a common bond emerging from the problems of being a woman in a modern patriarchal society, though many battered women within the groups do not openly declare the basis for the bonding. Because of this phenomenon there are few "consumer" voices collectively raised in protest, few women personally attesting to the seriousness of assault within their families. Upon occasion the news media highlight a prototypical battered woman and her story, but in many communities these incidents continue to be viewed as singular, perhaps occurring to only a few luckless women.

VIEW OF THE PROVIDER

How the particular organization or help provider defines the problem of the battered woman appears crucial to the development of service. Perusal of literature on the subject reveals an inordinate concern with the psychology and "pathology" of the female—the victim of the crime. The author uncovered only two or three articles concerning themselves with the violence and explosiveness of the husband/attacker. Typically, journals of medicine, psychiatry, and psychology seemed fascinated by the pathology of a woman who would remain in a battering environment. Surely, she must require, perhaps thrive on, sadomasochistic relationships; she probably precipitated the man's behavior or "carried the conditions of her early family situation into marriage, setting up a duplication of earlier battering experiences" (Hanks & Rosenbaum, 1977, p. 291). Even when it was found that battered women did not, in fact, "fit" well into a homogeneous profile, a variety of categories were proposed in an effort to be helpful to clinicians in need of spotting and understanding the dynamics of the battered woman. The battered woman's mother might thus be categorized as subtly controlling, submissive, or disturbed. Her father might be labelled figurehead, dictator, or a multiple-type!

Even in Britain, psychiatrists and other physicians were regularly invested either in identifying the characteristics of the (deviant) battered woman or in playing down the abnormality of explosive behavior. Scott and his associates (1974, p. 433), a committee composed of eight men from the Royal College of Psychiatrists, note that "wife battering is best regarded as a failure of adaptation, . . . a failure to acquire the necessary social lessons." They add that some degree of physical assault is very likely to occur at times of special stress, and that this should surprise no one. Much (even grievous) assaulting of wives is culturally determined, they hold, and neither partner would welcome interference. In addition, they believe that true battering necessarily implies "thoroughness and repetitiveness, in contrast to the milder or isolated blow which could scarcely constitute a marital problem."

In another investigative effort, three psychiatrists from the Court Clinic in Framingham, Massachusetts, were charged with the responsibility of finding out more about wife-beaters, and to this end 37 men who had assaulted their wives were referred to them during the years from 1957 to 1962. They discovered early on that the husbands resisted the interviews, tending to deny that any problems warranting outside help existed in their marriages, while the wives were eager to "tell their story." Consequently, the doctors decided to take the course of least resistance. "The Wifebeater's Wife" was subsequently published in *Archives of General Psychiatry* (Snell, Rosenwald, & Ames, 1964): another contribution to the literature of blaming the victim.

Another study (Field & Field, 1973) concluded that official acceptance of violence between "consenting" adults leads to a belief among police, courts, and citizenry in general that such violence should remain a private affair. As a result, according to sociologist Richard J. Gelles of The University of Rhode Island, most agencies and legal organizations are unprepared and unable to provide useful assistance to women who have been beaten by their husbands (Bell, 1977).

The literature reveals that the identity of the care providers, their definition of the problem, and their views of the participants are central in defining the nature of services provided. A shift in focus from a psychiatric, psychologic, or medical world view to one reflecting sociologic and cultural perspectives begins to suggest more promising avenues for understanding the problem and for planning intervention. In 1971 *The Journal of Marriage and the Family* published an entire issue focused on the problem of violence in the family. Though not specifically dealing with the problem of wife abuse, the articles concerned themselves with the problems of force and violence, conflict and power and the occurrence of homicide within the family. As earlier noted, the ensuing few years witnessed further acknowledgment of the reality of sociologic, economic, legal, and physical problems faced by the battered woman. She began to be seen not as a person trapped by her own pathologic psychic processes, but rather as an individual with a host of social problems that converged to keep her in her violent familial environment.

NEEDS OF THE VICTIM

It is difficult to know how battered women define their problems and their needs. Since they are, on the whole, a relatively anonymous group, decisions on the nature of needed services are often based on mere inference. Study of those projects begun in other countries (notably England, Scotland, Wales, and Canada), as well as research beginning to be pursued in our own country, is vital in order to assess the needs of such women more accurately. The literature reveals, for instance, that women *will* leave their homes at times of crisis if there is a suitable, safe alternative living space provided for them in the community. As of June 1977 there were 28 women's shelters in Great Britain with dozens more being planned (Bell, 1977). There were approximately a dozen women's emergency shelters fully operating and a number of others in the planning stages throughout this country in early 1976 (Martin, 1976). Though the public may debate the pros and cons of the appropriateness of providing shelters, consumers have in fact shown that they are readily acceptable as a temporary measure in many cases.

While the problem of identification and consumer input continues to hamper development of services for the battered woman, we are beginning to reach her and in so doing to gain some understanding of the multifaceted nature of the problem she faces. The situation of Mary L. may serve as an example:

> Mary L.'s husband asks her to forgive him again. He asks her to drop the charges she made against him in court after the last beating. He says it will cost a thousand dollars to pay the lawyers if she goes through with it, and that he might go to jail. How will she manage then?
>
> Mary has a blood clot on her head now. X-rays of her head show scars from old skull fractures. The doctors told her one more hit on the head from him and she's dead. She's afraid of that, and remembers other beatings. . . . The last one when he came home drunk early in the morning asking for his supper. When he found it wasn't waiting for him he exploded and "started in on my head like he always does when he's drunk," choking her with a pillow or socking her on both sides of her face. Her husband says, "You must like it—you let me do it."
>
> Mary's family refused to get involved. Her mother says, "You are married, you should stick. Maybe you are doing something to make him hit you. It's probably your fault." She thinks a woman should stick with a man no matter what he does.

Mary is afraid to stay at home, yet afraid to leave. "Where will I go with my child? How will I support us? With unemployment so high, how will I get a job so we have money to live on? I don't know what to do." (*Buffalo Courier-Express*, 1977.)

How does the community begin to meet the needs faced by Mary L. and thousands of others like her? Where can she turn for help? Mary L. was lucky in one sense. She happened to consult a doctor who recognized the seriousness of her marital problems as well as the seriousness of her injuries and impressed her with the danger of her situation. One wonders, though, how likely it is that Mary will be able to extricate herself from this destructive relationship. If she were left to deal with the realities of economic dependence and emotional isolation alone, without a supportive network of community resources, how likely is it that she would continue to resist her husband's demands that she drop charges and "forgive and forget?"

As was demonstrated in the experiences of Mary L., the battered wife is likely to have a variety of needs. She may require police protection and legal advice, medical and/or emergency treatment, and shelter or funds with which to escape from the violent environment. She may have no job or means of support for herself and children, and she may need counseling to help her learn to view herself as a worthy being. The battered woman may require the efforts of many social services to emerge from her situation. However, lack of knowledge about the working of the service system in combination with exhaustion and fear of being alone with these problems may leave her feeling immobilized. In addition, lack of collaboration between service providers leaves each agent to perform his service in his own peculiar way. Differing philosophy and viewpoints may make a tremendous difference in the way in which the battered woman's problems are defined and dealt with.

Though social, medical, economic and legal systems may all be involved at some point in providing services to a battered woman, in many communities no specific program recognizing her special needs and experiences has been developed.

DEFICIENCIES IN SERVICES

Though most formal agencies and social-service professionals recognize the plight of the battered woman as a complex of many problems, there are influencing biases and views that determine the nature of service provision. One organization approached by the author indicated that it was traditionally and primarily concerned with maintenance and support of the family. Provision of "a healthy family life" for the raising of children was its primary goal. Until very recently this organization offered no official recognition of the problem of wife abuse within the home, though it is likely that the problem was frequently uncovered in work with family members. Until recently, psychotherapeutic counseling was offered to family members, or the wife might be encouraged to "take a vacation" from the situation (visit mother?) "until tempers cooled." The strategy was to utilize existing resources and existing support groups in meeting the crisis. Family of origin, friends, and relatives might be sought out to "put up" mother and children until the family could be restored or until alternative plans were arranged for the woman. Unfortunately, very frequently, adequate support groups such as these are absent.

Many social-service agencies in the United States and abroad have been criticized for continuing to minimize the significance of the violence inflicted against women and for taking a casual attitude toward the woman's physical and emotional well-being. An excerpt from Elizabeth Kobus' article, "Stay Away from My Body," (1975, p. 4) illustrates how the attitudes of traditional social-service agents may undermine the needs of the battered woman: "When I said that I was so afraid of my husband because he had tried to strangle me the night before, the therapist answered: 'But ma'am, do you ever think how terrible it is for your husband that you're so afraid of him?' "

Most frequently the crisis nature of the problem receives little attention. The woman in crisis might be referred to the local Salvation Army or a convent for a safe night's sleep and told to return for counseling at a later date. (If she's lucky and has a charge plate, she might be able to secure a safe refuge away from home longer than the two to three nights allowed at any of the few other charitable organizations.)

There may be two further reasons for the failure of social-service agents either to perceive or to act swiftly in regard to the problems of battered women. First, they have usually been trained to believe in the importance of the family as the instrument for the socialization of children and therefore to work always for its maintenance. Second, family breakdown means more expense to the State, and these professionals also have a role as guardians of the State's resources (Wilson, 1975, p. 296).

Many current services available to the battered woman continue to be traditional in perspective and nonspecific to her particular life situation: individual counseling, referrals for financial help, legal service, and so on. It is because of perceived major gaps in health-service provision to women in general (and to the battered woman in particular) that groups of individuals throughout the United States have begun working together. The formation of task- and problem-oriented health groups has given rise to a variety of creative approaches to services for the battered woman and will be the focus of the following section.

TRENDS IN SERVICES TO BATTERED WOMEN

Though conventional approaches to service continue to be the only ones available to battered women in most communities at the present time, the number of innovative and more specific approaches to the problem is rapidly increasing in many areas of the country. Many of these approaches were initiated by self-help collectives, often associated with members of the National Organization for Women. In some communities formal social service agencies are also now trying to address the problem of the battered woman and to offer more specific, less fragmented services.

Voluntary Shelter Homes

In a number of communities, networks of temporary emergency shelter homes have been formed comprised of families willing to take in another family in an emergency. Typically, the abused woman and her children would stay at the volunteer home for a few days to a few weeks to provide time to allow for legal, financial, and family assessments to begin.

Some problems associated with an approach based on volunteer shelter homes should be considered. It is often unrealistic to expect that one family can be relied on to provide the emotional and financial resources needed by another family in crisis. Few families have sufficient resources to provide a refuge for more than a short period of time, and the task may quickly become burdensome and unmanageable. In addition, the battered woman may be reluctant to place herself in the position of being a burden on these immediate caregivers, and thus she may return home or hesitate to leave in the first place rather than face the guilt and shame involved in meeting her needs in this way.

Another problem has been observed: Family members who take in the battered woman and her children are frequently already deeply involved in the disturbed relationships of the situation. Research indicates that most battered women have previously attempted to use familial sources unsuccessfully before turning to outside help (Martin, 1976). Often there is no time to make the needed assessment during the crisis. Moreover, an irate husband frequently follows or finds his runaway wife, and there is inherent danger both to the woman and to those who take her in. It may be impossible to maintain adequate security of the private home (Gayford, 1975a, p. 196).

An approach that utilizes private voluntary homes promotes continued isolation of the woman and her problem. There is no group orientation built in, thus there is little probability for raising consciousness or gaining strengths through meeting and living with others sharing similar problems. The problem remains a personal one rather than one that is collective and shared.

A final consideration concerns the extreme nature of the problem. The usual features of total exhaustion, perhaps severe physical and emotional collapse, lack of any means of financial support, and the burden of children who require continuing care suggest the need, at least temporarily, for a total nurturing, accepting, and supportive environment that can help rebuild broken spirits as well as broken bones.

Crisis Shelters

Another trend in services to battered women has been the establishment of crisis shelters. The idea of shelters for women in abusive living conditions is centuries old, yet the shelters of the past had significant differences from those rapidly being established in many parts of the world today.

In the past, most sanctuaries for women were affiliated with religious bodies, charitable organizations, or community governmental groups. Convents, hospitals, and poor-houses might offer a refuge for a woman in crisis. Rather than serving the long-term well-being of the women who used these shelters, however, they functioned to serve the family unit, the community, and the status quo. The philosophy and goals of traditional shelters upheld the idea that when the interests of men, the family, or community were in conflict with women's needs, the needs of the women were secondary or were to remain unmet. Because of the often deplorable conditions and/or rigidly imposed restrictions that existed in the early sanctuaries for women, many were reluctant to enter, and for them the streets or brothels became the escape from family or community. In reality, most shelters for women were not shelters at all but served as such because there were no better alternatives (Warrior, 1977, p. 1).

Today, a feminist orientation is considered to be crucial as the framework for maintaining focus on the interests of the women who use shelters. The philosophy behind most refuges is that the battered woman's greatest need in times of crisis is for shelter in a supportive, self-help environment that facilitates self-respect and self-reliance (Ridington, 1977–78, pp. 563–575). For the individuals working and living in many feminist shelters there is an assumption that it will be women who resolve their own problems and that men cannot be relied upon to be sensitive or particularly amenable to action for women's relief. The problems of being a woman in a male-dominated society are addressed and it is acknowledged that women exist in subordinate, dependent life positions, economically and emotionally tied to a male provider. Frequently not able to stand against the myriad pressures that serve to "keep her in her place," the battered woman is considered in need of a network of others who will support her in her attempts to resolve her problems. The self-help ideology—women helping women—is most visible here.

In the United States the problems of battered women were first addressed by the National Organization for Women. In 1975 this organization identified marital violence as a major issue and established a National Task Force on Battered Women and Household Violence. This task force works to coordinate efforts of groups and individuals throughout the country who are working on the problem and seeks to put them in touch with each other.

At the present time there are sheltered crisis centers operating in Michigan, Minnesota, Arizona, California, Oregon, Washington, Pennsylvania, Florida, Idaho, New York, and Massachusetts. Shelters in other cities throughout the country are in various stages of development. Problems associated with overcrowding, lack of funds to pay for operating expenses, and community ambivalence or outright hostility toward the opening of a neighborhood women's shelter are common phenomena. Often, with the desire to offer immediate help to victims, these problems are not addressed in advance; they are managed in one way or another as they appear. For the first 5 months of operation, one shelter (Transition House, Cambridge, Mass.) received no formal funding. The two women who began the project supported the operation with their own AFDC checks, food stamps, and donations of clothing, food, and money.

The harsh realities that many early shelters faced have led other groups of interested women to take steps toward developing comprehensive funding proposals before opening their doors. Here the belief seems to be that living conditions should be better (not only safer, but more humane) than those from which the women were forced to flee. Conditions of severe overcrowding and inadequate food and basic supplies are not at all conducive to making decisions involving important and perhaps permanent life changes. Reliance on part-time, voluntary, and unpaid staff is viewed as problematic for the maintenance of a stable, on-going program. There is likely to be strong professional and specialist input in the planning, organizing, and actual operation of these shelters. The organizational structure may be one that relies on a traditional board of directors composed of influential and professional members of the community. Major decision making tends to take place within this body. In addition, there is an emphasis on utilizing existing social services available within the community to supplement the specific service the shelter provides.

Major criticisms have been raised about groups that choose to work within the system in this manner. The process of planning, organizing, and obtaining funding is often slow, and the feeling of some more radical workers is that priority ought to be given to providing immediate services (meager as they might be), with organizational needs being met later. Many women workers in this area also acknowledge frustration and mistrust with regard to working within the system and believe that some professionals and bureaucrats have an interest in exploiting the issue of the battered woman to their own advantage. Where were all these human services before the women's movement and before funding was a possibility? An additional critical question that concerns many feminists centers around a possible shift in basic service orientation and decision-making powers: a move away from self-help toward service provision that differentiates between the care provider and the recipient of care.

Comparative assessment of the differing ways in which shelters are currently structured and managed and evaluation of the resultant benefit to the consumer are much needed. Though there may well be room for a variety of tactical approaches to service it does seem judicious to take time to evaluate these efforts knowledgeably.

Counseling Approaches

Both professional and peer-group counseling are additional services available in a number of communities. However, there is a good deal of controversy as to the appropriateness of each in responding to the problems of the battered woman. The view of many feminists is that the woman and her interpersonal situation should not be viewed or treated as a medical or psychologic problem. Traditional counseling methods that tend to focus on the individual psychologic dynamics of the client or other medical approaches that aim to help the woman cope with her situation (e.g., a prescription of Valium) are inappropriate and ineffective, they say.* Though uncovering psychologic dynamics may be beneficial to some individuals at a later time, and the relieving of anxiety and depression might be a necessary component of service, the feminist proponents of a peer-group approach believe that what is needed to effect long-term change for the battered woman are viable real-life alternatives and resocialization as a woman. These needs are best met, they feel, within self-help or peer-group environments.

Peer-Group Counseling   Most women's crisis shelters have on-going consciousness-raising or support groups that offer the opportunity for women to share their experiences and to gain support through experiencing what some refer to as "active" or "creative" listening with one another. Active listening may be defined as listening in a caring, nonjudgmental way, that is, hearing the message behind the speaker's words and letting her know that

---

*Gayford (1975a, pp. 288–289) reports that battered wives frequently visit their general practitioners, and out of 100 women studied, 71 percent were prescribed antidepressants or tranquilizers.

she is really heard, so that she can eventually clarify for herself what her fears and feelings are, what her situation is, and then proceed to sort out options. A skill used by many professional counselors, active listening is an approach widely used and ideologically consistent with a self-help support-group focus. As one shelter resident put it, "It's the House specialty." The battered woman frequently feels isolated and experiences fear and shame about her life situation, and being listened to in this way may be the first healing experience.

"Feminism as therapy" is the orientation most emphasized in women's peer-group counseling approaches. Through it the group seeks to strengthen the development of a female identity as a positive force. Professional counselors (either volunteer or staff) may be included in feminist consciousness-raising or support groups, and most often they relate to the group in two ways: as peer members, able to share and relate personal experience and feelings, and as individuals who are able to use learned skills to facilitate the growth of members of the group. The emphasis on developing active listening skills among members rather than advice-giving approaches, for instance, may be one way in which the professional may help to facilitate the group process in support groups.

Marriage and Family Counseling　Professional agency approaches to counseling the battered woman sometimes take the form of marital or family therapy. Marriage therapy may focus on helping the couple develop more effective communication patterns. The physical expression of violence in the marriage is viewed as an individual's response to extreme frustration and stress in his life, and the violent outburst is considered the only way the individual knows to manage the feelings. Therapy efforts may thus be directed toward helping both the husband and wife to learn new ways of expressing their needs and new ways of releasing and/or managing stress.

A family therapy approach emphasizes the effect of all members of the family system upon each other as well as upon the total functioning of the family unit. This mode of therapy encourages total family involvement and includes input from the children as well as from other significant members of the extended family in efforts designed to reverse dysfunctional family patterns.

Though these approaches are based on sound theoretical tenets, problems have been cited in practical experience. Many therapists note that a large number of husbands of battered wives lack motivation to engage in marriage or family counseling (Nichols, 1976; Snell, Rosenwald, & Ames, 1964). Often, the wife is too meek or too frightened to insist on the husband's continuing counseling. A few courts of law, have attempted to combat this problem by ordering the abusive husband to "get treatment" in lieu of other judgments. Court-ordered therapy, however, has a record of very limited success.

Marital and family therapy approaches are attacked by critics who believe that these strategies for dealing with the problems put the interests of the marriage or the family (and thus the husband) above those of the woman. Radicalization of the female is necessary to effect equal balance of power within the family, they say. In addition, these critics reject the assumption that the battering husband desires relief from his psychic pain. The man who can get his way through force is not likely to voluntarily give that up because power itself is considered to be pleasurable (Leghorn, 1976).

Despite problems associated with a marriage or a family therapy approach to the problem of wife abuse, for the family in which both partners express a desire to stay together and a genuine motivation for changing behavior, these counseling approaches are considered to be appropriate and effective, with the capability of providing real help to troubled families.

Additional Services

In addition to developing effective emergency shelter systems and utilizing new counseling approaches, there is a wide range of other activities and services which are currently being carried out in behalf of battered women.

The Establishment of a "Hot Line." A priority in many communities, this telephone crisis line serves to put the battered woman in touch with trained volunteer counselors prepared to offer crisis counseling services as well as legal, medical, and housing referrals. In some communities a 24-hour capability has been effected, and in others a referral system has been developed in which local police precincts and hospital emergency rooms provide known and suspected victims of spouse abuse with the hot-line number.

Crisis-Intervention Training for Police Officers. Domestic calls have long been known to be among the more unpopular calls to which the police respond. Statistically, there is a high risk of personal injury to all parties involved, and police officers frequently express feelings of frustration and pessimism about the probable outcomes of their intervention. Education in the use of crisis theory has been provided by a number of groups on a consultative basis to local police precincts. Illumination of practical strategies designed to deescalate violent and intense emotions are possible within this framework.

In conjunction with this service there is special emphasis placed on educating the police about the problems of the battered woman. Efforts to raise the consciousness of the law-enforcement community have met with some success. The comments of Commander James Bannon of the Detroit Police Department, demonstrate the changing attitudes of police officers:

> It is my view that police and later prosecutors and courts contribute to domestic violence by their laissez faire attitudes toward what they view as essentially a personal problem. Further, that this view is held because police are socialized to regard females in general as subordinate. The superordinacy of the male coupled with his socially mandated self-reliance on violence to resolve personal problems without outside assistance, assures us that wives will continue to be battered in record numbers (Bannon, 1975, p. 4).

Legislative Lobbying. Growing numbers of women have become active in drafting and lobbying for legislation that would benefit battered women. Some of the issues of concern include acquiring state funds for shelters, drafting legislation that would define battered women as priority cases in eligibility for emergency public housing, securing legislation aimed at changing the right of disclosure that often permits husbands to retrieve wives under the guise of the husband's right to know the whereabouts of his children, and supporting legislation seeking to enforce a police officer's responsibility to inform the battered woman of her legal rights and to suggest resources for help (Leghorn, 1976).

Research. Some groups have begun research on current legal, social-service, and law-enforcement practices and have monitored local systems of treatment of spouse-abuse cases in the courts. Data gathered in this way have proved of vital importance in educating the public to the problems of battered women and in serving to define areas for further work.

Advocacy. A number of groups offer the services of client advocates who will accompany women through legal, courtroom, and social-service procedures. These individuals are trained, committed volunteers who are knowledgeble about the rights of the individual and are able to provide needed support and advice to the battered woman while she is attempting to navigate through the social and legal systems. The advocate knows ahead of time what kinds of questions the battered woman will have to be able to answer and what kinds of identification will be needed for court or welfare procedures. This kind of practical and supportive assistance often proves of great help to the woman in crisis. Frequently, battered women cite the advocacy role as a "lifesaving" service.

Other activities and services undertaken by groups and individuals in a number of communities have been designed to help the victim of wife abuse by increasing public awareness of the problem, as well as to include planning for long-term comprehensive service.

"Fact Sheets." Informational brochures about battered women are being developed and distributed to a variety of human service agencies as well as to other local community groups interested in community welfare.

Grant Writing. An especially important activity for groups aiming to set up a refuge has been the acquisition of skills and resource persons for writing comprehensive funding proposals.

Presentations. Speeches and workshops to educate members of the community about the problem of spouse abuse are being conducted in many communities.

New approaches to meeting the needs of the battered woman continue to develop and testify to the imaginative and resourceful nature of individuals and groups working on wife abuse. One New York group, for example, decided to sponsor seminars for local judges to sensitize them to the legal situations and specific needs of battered women. This same group followed through by writing a legal manual for domestic relations attorneys to encourage them to handle more cases of marital violence. It may be that similar strategies could beneficially be used to increase the awareness of practitioners of medicine, nursing, religion, psychotherapy, and other human-service fields.

IMPLICATIONS FOR PROFESSIONAL HEALTH AND SOCIAL-WELFARE WORKERS

Today's statistics, as well as the evidence coming from newly established crisis shelters, testify to the seriousness and prevalence of wife beating. The local newspaper is likely to contain a number of items informing us of violence committed today against women. More than likely the violence will have occurred at home; more than likely the incidents will have occurred between husband and wife. Women's own life experiences tell them that violence toward women is indeed commonplace. From grade school through old age women fear physical attack, assault, molestation, and rape at the hands of a stronger male. It is not a new problem, though it is a newly acknowledged problem. Wife or woman assault—including its most extreme form, wife battering—has been with us for a long time. Despite this, it has remained a hidden problem even to health and social-welfare professionals. There are many factors that have contributed to keeping the problem undercover to this extent. Adequate exposition of these factors would constitute a major and important piece of research, but it is possible, I think, to point out a few factors that have special implications for professional health and social-welfare workers.

Problems with Identification

Identification of the battered woman is a continuing problem that exists in part because definitions vary on what constitutes a "battered woman." How many blows (or slaps or stitches) does it take? Some states go so far as to have a "stitch law:" the husband is held accountable legally only when the stitch count exceeds a set number; less than that and the situation is viewed as an unfortunate family squabble. How frequently does an assault have to take place? What is the interval between assaults that converts a mere family fracas into wife battering? Once a month? Every other Friday night? Four times a year? Nightly? As health professionals, we must come to terms with these questions in a personal way, for our own philosophical beliefs and values play an enormous part in determining our actions. How we define the battered woman in large part determines how we will work with her, or if, indeed, we will even *see* her as "battered."

There are many who believe assault is to be expected within the close confines of a family environment, that human nature is such that we are naive to expect harmonious (that is, assault-free) resolution of differences. Others believe that the woman should have the right to be protected from even the *first* blow; the woman on the street is protected by law from assault, yet the woman at home is treated with a different set of values by law and by health professionals. We expect her to absorb a certain number of blows perhaps.

A few health researchers have attempted to delineate a working definition of the battered woman for the purposes of their investigations. In one such study (Dewsbury, 1975, p. 290) the woman qualifies as battered if she has been subjected to "repeated deliberate physical assault including at least one experience of moderate injury (battery)." According to another study (Scott, 1974, p. 434), her injuries must be serious and repeated. These characteristics are then graded: "Serious" may range from 1 (not requiring medical attention) to 4 (death); "repeated" may range from 1 (regular or habitual) to 4 (terminal).

Legal definitions of the battered woman vary from one state to the next. One definition recognizes the woman as battered if she has received "deliberate, severe and repeated demonstrable physical injury from her husband," while minimal injury is considered to be severe bruising (lasting long enough, it is hoped, for her to "demonstrate" to the judge), and mental and emotional cruelty are not taken into account at all (Gayford, 1975a, p. 194).

The current interest in the battered woman may in the future expand to include consideration of those who are emotionally and mentally abused, as well as those who are, in fact, denied individual control and self-assertion in their own lives by fearful remembrance of that "once-or-twice-a-year blow."

Another problem that has hampered identification of battered women is the disguise the problem often takes or that we, as professionals, perpetuate. If we believe that the battered woman is not presenting herself for service, it may be that her problems have been translated into a relationship or communication problem. Similarly, the violent act itself may not be seen as wife assault at all, and work may instead focus on her husband's drinking problem, his frustrations with his job, his under- (or over-) employment, and so on.

There is much to be said for focusing directly on the problem at times, attending to the presenting problem and the crisis aspects of battering as well as to the interactional ones. Perhaps this kind of focus will not improve the dysfunctional family system, at least initially, but it may be the beginning of assisting one member of the system—the one under attack—to begin to recognize the significance of her experience and to begin to know that there are others who believe it is intolerable.

Role Adaptation for Professionals

Clinicians working with battered women frequently speak of the frustrations involved in trying to promote change in the lives of these women since husband and wife seem glued together in their destructive relationship. Too often both individuals are resistant to traditional approaches to service, and these usual approaches help neither the family as a whole nor the woman as an individual. Perhaps we might better look at the possibilities of the peer-group self-help approach, one that uses the professional health and social-welfare worker as a facilitator rather than as an individual with primary responsibility for bringing about change.* The professional in this role may begin by coordinating efforts designed to resolve the massive social, economic, and medical needs of the battered woman, yet plan and structure for the major intervention to come about through resocialization and peer support: a group solution to the problem rather than a private one.

The consultative or facilitative role for the professional working with self-help groups is not inactive or nondemanding. This role frequently necessitates a willingness publicly and actively to confront and explore many issues of direct concern to the battered woman. The worker may, for instance, initiate efforts directed at organizing needed new services for women: long-term safe housing accommodations or improved community crisis-intervention policies, for instance. The professional working as a consultant to in-

---

*For an illustration of professional functioning in this manner, see Rounsaville, Lifton, & Bieber (1979).

dividual self-help groups needs interpersonal skills that permit the sharing of appropriate knowledge and skills, as well as personal commitment that allows involvement in this group as a sensitive and perceptive member.

Providing services within a self-help framework requires the ability to be comfortable working in new and frequently unconventional surroundings. The traditional 50-minute office counseling session is, for example, not appropriate for most of the work taking place in women's crisis shelters. In addition, working within a self-help group framework necessitates the relinquishing of control that has traditionally been allocated to the professional. Instead, this framework calls for a basic confidence in the ability of the individual and peer group to come to healthy and satisfactory personal decisions through the experience of the group process.

Reconciliation of Personal Values and Professional Ethics

One of the major considerations facing feminists who work as professionals providing services to battered women is the reconciliation of personal values with professional ethics. As professionals they learn that it is crucial that the client's values be respected whether or not they are consistent with feminist beliefs. In addition they are taught to respect the right of the client to self-determination and personal decision making; they are there to help the client explore his or her world, and although they may work to bring options and alternatives more clearly into view, they avoid giving advice. Unless a life-threatening situation exists, they are prepared to accept the decision their client makes. Essentially, they avoid "laying their own trip" (their own values and beliefs) on the client. Though they indirectly reflect many of their values in practice (belief in and respect for self-determination for example), they hesitate to espouse and promote a particular point of view directly.

A feminist orientation has few concerns regarding direct assertion of its philosophical bases. The philosophy *is* the "therapy." Raised consciousness and resocialization are considered essential for the woman who has been in a battering situation. The approach is direct, task- and decision-oriented, and though supportive measures and listening skills are used, the bases in feminist philosophy are freely verbalized.

Some individuals believe reconciliation of these points of view is impossible. The issue thus becomes polarized into feminist versus professional points of view. It is the author's contention that the service provider who has an awareness of the contributions of both viewpoints and an ability to select critically from both views, has much to offer in assisting the battered woman. We do not need to shy away from our personal values. In fact, it is both impossible and dishonest to do so. The sharing of a personal philosophy can be a lifeline to hold on to or grow with, and it is an integral part of all self-help modalities. For many women it will be welcome. On the other hand, indiscriminate proselytizing to a woman in crisis is irresponsible and damaging. A sensitive approach that acknowledges where the individual woman is "coming from" and that remains accepting and flexible may well integrate both feminist and professional orientations.

RECOMMENDATIONS FOR FUTURE RESEARCH

Though interest in the problems of battered women is emerging in many parts of the country, currently there is a critical lack of available research to guide service efforts. Establishing crisis shelters and crisis intervention for battered women, though essential, usually is viewed as a mere "band-aid" solution. Pursuing the image, in addition to stopping the bleeding and providing the possibility for healing to begin, we need to increase research efforts that will enable us to plan appropriate and comprehensive long-term solutions.

There are many unanswered questions that merit investigation. A number of these research questions have been addressed earlier in this chapter. A final few are offered for consideration here.

First, there is a need to uncover the meanings of aggression in a variety of socioeconomic, cultural, and minority groups. Frequently, we hear of violence toward females being accepted as a fact of life or even as evidence that "he cares about me." We need far more familiarity with the special meanings of aggression, the many forms it takes and the special problems that ethnicity creates for minority women.*

Second, intensive research investigations of current and proposed intervention strategies are needed to determine "what works" to bring about change in the life situation of the battered woman. Evaluation of the variety of approaches to counseling the battered woman may be one place to start, for example. The number of approaches needing scientific investigation of effectiveness include traditional one-to-one psychotherapy, women's consciousness-raising support groups, assertiveness-training strategies, group treatment of family or marital couples involved in abusive interaction, "feminism as therapy" models of psychotherapy, resocialization/education for men as well as women, direct advocacy and intervention for the battered woman, and group treatment of men who are known to be abusive.

There is a pressing need for creative adaptations of the marital or family-

---

*It is particularly important that we improve knowledge about useful intervention strategies for these groups. It is essential that we include professional and nonprofessional minority women in planning efforts and in service provision in behalf of battered women in order to broaden the awareness and understanding of all workers in this area.

treatment modality for abusive families. Research efforts need to be initiated to determine the effectiveness of these endeavors. Two creative approaches come to mind. The first is suggested by Sanford Sherman, executive director of the Jewish Family Service of New York: The husband and wife are put together in the same room, and the therapist prompts them into the beginning stages of a fight so that she or he can point out to them how they interact with one another. There is an effort to teach the man nonviolent ways of behaving when he is enraged, to show him that he can translate the anger into words and take it out on objects rather than people. In contrast, Murray Straus, sociologist at the University of New Hampshire, has observed that verbal violence often leads to physical violence. Instead, he suggests that there must be a recognition that it is as wrong to insult, yell, and scream at another person as it is to hit that person. In its place he proposes reeducation of individuals to ways of arguing without hurting others. Marriage "rules" are developed between the partners. They are encouraged to face the issues and have confrontations but not by hurting one another verbally or physically.

Third, investigation of the impact of newly established crisis shelters and follow-up on battered women after they have received services is an area needing study. What happens to the woman after she leaves a shelter? Is the service of any real help, or does she just go back into a similar situation? How has her life been affected by the peer-group experience within a shelter? How do we measure "success?" What do we consider improvement in her life situation?

Another area in need of study is the organizational structures and staffing patterns of the shelters being developed. Again, what are the benefits to the consumer? Is a totally voluntary self-help group the most effective vehicle for facilitating change, or are professional staff members with particular skills needed? If so, what skills, and how would these skills be used? What about groups who have integrated both professional and self-help volunteer members? Are there significant benefits for the battered woman that can be documented among varying group approaches?

Finally, epidemiologic studies are currently hampered by the lack of a generally accepted legal or medical definition of what constitutes spouse abuse or battering. There is a need for exploration of present definitions and to arrive at more common definitions. If we define *abuse* as more than *battering*, that is, as mental and emotional cruelty as well as occasional episodic physical attack, are we prepared to defend a woman's right to be protected against these as well? Epidemiologic efforts to identify the battered spouse must include attention to the male partner as well; certainly our cultural norms are such that "husband abuse" (if in fact it does exist) might well be hidden even more deeply than wife abuse.

CONCLUSION

Although this chapter has focused primarily on women, it is important to recognize the need for the development of adequate outreach systems designed to reach the abusive and violent man. No treatment will be complete without improving treatment methods for the violence-prone husband. Men's consciousness-raising groups may be one place to begin to address problems inherent in cultural stereotypes and role prescriptions that cripple men as well as women. Discussion of violence and aggression as a socially expected and accepted yet ultimately damaging means of conflict resolution might begin here. It is time for professional men working in the health and social-welfare field to take active roles in developing services for abusive husbands. Failure to speak out against the dehumanizing stereotypes our culture imposes on both sexes suggests cooperation with a system that not only condones private abuse of its female members but continues collective abuse through maintenance of social, political, and economic policies that damage women.

REFERENCES

Bannon, J. Law enforcement problems with intra-family violence. Paper presented to the American Bar Association Convention, August 12, 1975.

Barocas, H.A. Urban policemen: Crisis mediators or crisis creators? *American Journal of Orthopsychiatry*, 1973, 43, 632–639.

Bell, J.N. Rescuing the battered wife. *Human Behavior*, June 1977, 6(6), 16–23.

Buffalo Courier-Express. A year of married horror: battered wife asks what's going to happen. October 30, 1977, 1 (Section E).

Bumbalo, J., & Young, D. The self-help group. *American Journal of Nursing*, September 1973, 73(9), 1588–1591.

Campbell, J.S. The family and violence. In Steinmetz, S.K., & Straus M.A. (eds.), *Violence in the Family*. New York: Harper & Row, 1974.

Chatterjee, P., & Koleski, R. The concept of community and community organization: A review. *Social Work*, 1970, 15, 82–92.

Cottrell, L.S., Jr. The competent community. In Kaplan, B., Wilson, R., & Leighton, A. (eds.), *Further Explorations in Social Psychiatry*. New York: Basic, 1976.

Dewsbury, A. Research on battered wives. *Royal Society of Health Journal*, 1975, 95–96, 29–40.

Durbin, K. Wife beating. *Ladies Home Journal*, June 1974, 62–64.

The Eccentric (Birmingham, Mich.), June 12, 1975.

Fojtik, K. *Wife Beating: How To Develop a Wife Assault Task Force and Project.* Ann Arbor: National Organization for Women, Domestic Violence and Assault Fund, 1976.

Field, M., & Field, H. Marital violence and the criminal process. *Social Service Review*, 1973, 47, 221–240.

Gayford, J.J. Wife battering: A preliminary survey of 100 cases. *British Medical Journal*, January 25, 1975(a), 1, 194–197.

Gayford, J.J. Research on battered wives. *Social Health Journal*, 1975(b), 95–96, 288–289.

Gelles, R.J. Violence and pregnancy: A note on the extent of the problem and needed services. *The Family Coordinator*, 1975, 24, 81–86.

Gelles, R.J. *The Violent Home: A Study of Physical Aggression Between Husbands and Wives*. Beverly Hills, Calif.: Sage, 1972.

Gingold, J. One of these days—pow—right in the kisser. *Ms.*, August 1976, pp. 51*ff.*

Hanks, S.E., & Rosenbaum, C.P. Battered women: A study of women who live with violent alcohol-abusing men. *American Journal of Orthopsychiatry*, 1977, 47, 291–306.

Kobus, E. Stay away from my body (trans. Janice Weiss). Appeared in *Urij Nederland*, July 19, 1975.

Leghorn, L. Social responses to battered wives. A speech given at the Wisconsin Conference on Battered Women, Milwaukee, October 2, 1976.

Martin, D. *Battered Wives*. San Francisco: Glide, 1976.

Micklow, P., & Eisenberg, S. Wife beating serious issue. *Ypsilanti* (Michigan) *Press*, April 9, 1975, p. 4A.

Newsweek, July 9, 1973, p. 39.

Nichols, B.B. The abused wife problem. *Social Casework*, January 1976, 7, 27–32.

Pizzey, E. Cheswick Women's Aid—a refuge from violence. *Social Health Journal*, 1975, 95–96, 297–308.

Ridington, J. The transitional process: A feminist environment as reconstitutive milieu. *Victimology: An International Journal*, 1977–78, 2, 563–575.

Rounsaville, B., Lifton, N., & Bieber, M. The natural history of a psychotherapy group for battered women. *Psychiatry*, 1979, 42, 63–78.

Scott, P.D. Battered wives. *British Journal of Psychiatry*, 1974, 125, 433–441.

Snell, J., Rosenwald, R., & Ames, R. The wifebeater's wife. *Archives of General Psychiatry*, 1964, 11, 107–112.

Steinmetz, S.K., & Straus, M.A. The family as a cradle of violence. *Society*, 1973, 10, 50–58.

Steinmetz, S.K., & Straus, M.A. (eds.). *Violence in the Family*. New York: Harper & Row, 1974.

Straus, M.A. Wife beating: How common and why? *Victimology: An International Journal*, 1977–78, 2, 443–458.

Warrior, B. *Working on Wife Abuse* (5th Supplemental edition). Cambridge, Mass.: Woman's Center, 1977.

Wilson, E. A social worker's viewpoint. *Royal Society of Health Journal*, 1975, 95–96, 294–297.

Whitehurst, R.N. Alternative family structures and violence-reduction. In Steinmetz, S.K., & Straus, M.A. (eds.), *Violence in the Family*. New York: Harper & Row, 1974.

Ypsilanti (Michigan) *Press*, July 11, 1976.

ADDITIONAL READINGS

Ball, P., & Wyman, E. Battered wives and powerlessness: What can counselors do? *Victimology: An International Journal*, 1977–78, 2, 545–552.

Davidson, T. *Conjugal Crime*. New York: Hawthorne, 1978.

Dobash, R., & Dobash, R.E. Wives: The appropriate victims of marital violence. *Victimology: An International Journal*, 1977–78, 2, 426–442.

Fleming, J.B. *Stopping Wife Abuse.* Garden City, N.Y.: Anchor, 1979.

Langley, R., & Levy, R. *Wife-Beating: The Silent Crisis.* New York: Dutton, 1977.

Roy, M. *Battered Women: A Psychosocial Study of Domestic Violence.* New York: Van Nostrand Reinhold, 1977.

Shainess, N. Vulnerability to violence: Masochism as process. *American Journal of Psychiatry,* 1979, 33, 174–189.

Straus, M.A., Steinmetz, S.K., Gelles, R.J. Violence in the family: assessment of knowledge and needs. Presentation to the American Association for the Advancement of Science, Boston: 1976.

Symonds, A. Violence against women—the myth of masochism. *American Journal of Psychiatry,* 1979, 33, 161–173.

Walker, L.E. Battered women and learned helplessness. *Victimology: An International Journal,* 1977–78, 2, 525–534.

Walker, L.E. *The Battered Woman.* New York: Harper & Row, 1979.

Walker, L.E. Who are the battered women? *Frontiers: The Women's Study Journal,* April 1977, 2(1), 52–57.

16

An Ecologic Perspective of Child Abuse

Carolyn Daughtry

It is estimated that at least 1 million children are now abused annually in the United States, and that of these, more than 2000 die. The magnitude of the problem is such that it can no longer be overlooked by a public reluctant to infringe on the parental domain. Although professionals have long been concerned about the welfare of children at risk for abuse and neglect, the increase in legal requirements for reporting evidence of child abuse has confronted them with the necessity of becoming more involved in active intervention. Various explanations have been offered in efforts at understanding the motivations of the abuser and the consequences for the abused. Perhaps because our most immediate means of comprehending a social phenomenon is to try to understand the individuals involved, workers have typically relied on a psychologic approach to the problem. While Daughtry acknowledges the merit of this and other explanatory models, she views them as having major limitations. It is her contention that an ecologic-systems perspective has the greatest potential for conceptualizing this multi-faceted phenomenon and for laying a base for the development of interventive strategies. Some professionals may have difficulty initially in taking on this approach because it calls for intervention at political as well as the more familiar individual or family levels. However, Daughtry provides convincing evidence of its promise in the remedying of this distressing social problem.

A sensational media account of the details and horror of the abusive death of a small child continues to have the power to stir a community to action. People are deeply troubled by individual cases of mutilation and brutality inflicted on children. Sympathy for the child victim is only exceeded by the outrage directed at the offending parent or at the failures of the social-control agents paid by the public to see that these problems do not occur.

Patterns of public opinion have played a major part in affecting the attention that violence receives in the broad arena of public policy, whether it applies to "cop killers" or "child abusers." The first child-protective agency in the United States was established in 1874 in response to a massive public furor aroused by the unspeakably brutal treatment of a little girl in New York City. Subsequent legislative developments have occurred in response to such shocking incidents.

Not all cases of child abuse are as dramatic as those that capture the attention of the public, nor are the incidents of brutal, sadistic destructiveness inflicted on the children in their homes as isolated or infrequent as we might like to imagine. Maltreatment of children can be traced through centuries of recorded history. Infanticide has served as a means of population control in impoverished societies. Disfigurement and mutilation have been inflicted on children in order to invoke the pity of adults and to enhance a child's capacity to beg coins more abundantly to benefit the family. Under some ancient laws, fathers were not restricted in their right to inflict cruel punishment and even death on their children under certain circumstances (Sherman, 1976; Bakan, 1971).

While violence against children by their own parents is as old as mankind, the paradox is that such patterns can persist today in a caring, informed, and affluent society. It is perplexing that the deeply valued family system can be the source of physical injury, death, torture, disfigurement, or permanent impairment of defenseless, dependent children. It is also hard to understand how a nation that emphasizes quality-of-life issues and invests massive resources to promote the education of its youth can be so halting in its initiatives to develop a national policy on family life including a broad-scale attack on conditions conducive to child abuse and other forms of intrafamilial violence.

Three pervasive and interlocking attitudinal views seem to operate to maintain society's highly ambivalent posture regarding its responsibility in relation to the violence that occurs within the context of the family. First is a deeply embedded *private-ownership view* of the family as a private system and the children as the possessions of their biologic parents. Parents are accorded by law the authority and responsibility for the direct, intimate, and continuous care of their children—including the right to discipline them in their own style. A strong belief persists that parents act in the best interests of their children when they punish them. When parental discipline results in injury, it is explained as punishment that went a little too far. The tenacity of this view is reflected universally in state statutes that require that investigations of alleged child abuse distinguish between those situations in which parental punishment simply went too far and resulted in accidental injury and those nonaccidental acts intended to hurt the child.

Second, we find it almost impossible to believe that people like ourselves could participate in such unthinkable, violent behavior against a small child. The *mad/bad parent view* holds that child-abusing parents are mentally defective, deranged, or socialized to the values of the lowest class of society. This view of abusive parents as being significantly different from the mainstream of parents is reinforced by the causal explanations that emphasize parental psychopathology.

These views help shape our programmatic approaches to resolution of the problem and our allocation of resources to combat child abuse. By 1967, every state had enacted legislation on child-abuse reporting and developed protective-service operations for the child supported by public funds. In 1974, 100 years after the first protective agency had been established, the National Child Abuse Prevention and Treatment Act was signed into law. Subsequently, the National Center on Child Abuse and Neglect was established to promote study and research into the causes, treatment, and prevention of the problem. However, resources have not been allocated to develop the needed support services and treatment resources to the same extent that they have been allotted to the social-control aspects of programming. The heavy investment in investigative and monitoring programs leads the public to believe the problem is being addressed adequately.

This emerging *adequate social control view* diverts attention from the development of social policies that would help build cohesive families and address the larger social and economic conditions that affect them. The overemphasis on control of child abuse by paid protective-service agents and law-enforcement agencies relieves the conscience of the community and promotes a false sense of service adequacy. When children die after their abused status has been reported to the public agencies, scapegoating of these organizations follows.

Douglas Besharov, director of the National Center, cogently stated: "Child abuse laws provide only the legal and institutional framework for action. A law lives in the way it is used. Child abuse and child maltreatment are family and community problems. If we are to prevent and treat them, we must have a community commitment to fostering the emotional and behavioral hygiene of the individual, the family and the community" (Besharov, 1975, p. 2).

Informed observers are in agreement that the occurrences of abuse are increasing at an alarming pace. The National Center projects that 1 million or more children a year are the victims of familial maltreatment. Of this number, it is estimated that close to 300,000 are physically abused; 100,000 are sexually abused; and more than 2000 die each year in abuse-related situations (HEW, *Model Act*, 1977, p. 1). Other projections based on estimates, surveys, studies, or interpretations of other source data have set the prevalence of abuse as high as 2 million children per year and the fatalities at over 100,000 (Bronfenbrenner, 1975, p. 7). Some scholars consider child abuse to be the leading cause of death among young children. Deficiencies in data allow great discrepancies in establishing the size of the problem. It is recognized that a reliable and accurate incidence rate cannot be established until there is an adequate and operational definition of *abuse* that is used uniformly in systematic reporting systems across the nation. Every state has written into its statutes a legal definition of *child abuse* that delineates the range of cases and the particular circumstances to be addressed by the protective programs. These definitions vary from state to state. What may be considered abuse in one state may not come within the purview of the law in another. This not only limits generalizing about abuse with any degree of certainty, it also leads to ambiguity and inconsistency in the interpretation and application of standards within a single state statute. A legal definition is, in the final analysis, what the local courts adjudicate it to be (Polansky, 1975, p. 26). The formality of the judicial process obscures the fact that decisions about child abuse are largely dependent on judgments and values.

From a comparative analysis of state statutes on child abuse, Kamerman and Kahn (1976, p. 146) identify three basic characteristics that exist in all the legal definitions:

1. The behavior violates a norm or standard of parental conduct.
2. The infliction is deliberate, a nonaccidental injury.
3. The abuse is severe enough to warrant intervention, whether medical, social, legal, or a combination of these.

In the absence of promulgated operational standards to guide decision making, each of these characteristics requires the exercise of discretionary judgments. Cultural and class factors have considerable impact on the form, content, and style of child rearing, and the absence of social consensus militates against establishing either one point of view or a single standard that is universally accepted. Years ago, Caplan (1959) observed a pattern among lower-class black families of assigning to the grandmother the primary responsibility for the nurturing care of the infant. He interpreted this pattern as a form of role reversal that could adversely affect child development and adult-role performance. Within the culture and class there was no confusion of roles for any of the actors. For the family this represented a culturally sanctioned support system for child rearing relevant to the family's realities, while being at variance with the more pervasive nuclear pattern in our society. Hill (1972) interprets similar patterns as strengths of black families reflecting strong kinship bonds and adaptability of family roles. The assessment of a pattern or standard of child rearing as functional or dysfunctional is largely a matter of perception, values, and point of view.

The difficulties are mind-boggling in developing an empirically derived set of standards reflective of differences in community norms and cultural, social-class, ethnic, and religious orientations. The current requirement to apply a parental conduct standard in adjudicating child abuse not only allows for variation across jurisdictions but contributes to strong differences of opinion and conflict across agencies and among professionals. Some react negatively to the judicial fact-finding process of determining whether the home is safe for the child. Child-protection workers feel helpless and angry when the courts do not substantiate their concerns with adjudication. Physicians, at times, find themselves in strong disagreement with judges and lawyers over the interpretation of medical evidence. In a widely publicized, sensational case involving the death of a 3-year-old boy, the medical report included in its multiple findings an opinion that the child had been sodomized. Sodomizing of a small child offends any standard of parental conduct and likewise establishes the deliberateness of abusive behavior, whereas accidental injury is no one's fault. When pressed by the caretaker's attorney as to whether the rectal injury could have occurred from a fall on a toy or other object, the physician could not refute this remote possibility.

The establishment of intent is equally difficult and often unproductive in relation to the objectives of protection of the child and engagement of the parents in a therapeutic plan for remediation. A 5-year-old child was seen at the emergency clinic with a deep gash below the eye requiring suturing. The mother explained that the child resisted her instructions and hid under the bed. In her attempts to get him out, she poked under the bed with the handle of the broom and accidentally poked him in the face. The nurse on duty reported the incident to the child-protection hot line. Subsequent investigation of the situation resulted in the determination that the injury was accidental and child abuse was ruled out. The mother did not see the need for accepting help with her problems of managing the child or developing more appropriate forms of discipline. There was considerable difference of opinion about the parental judgment in poking at a small child with a broom handle, about the amount of force behind the thrust that would imply anger, and about the substantial risk to vision had the poke been a bit higher. Nevertheless, without a determination of abuse or maltreatment and an order from the court, the parent can refuse to become engaged in a service intervention. Such a child may be left in a deteriorating parent-child situation that may lead to more serious injury.

The issue of severity of injury also militates against early intervention and preventive services. In the case above, if the child had sustained permanent injury to his eye or lost some degree of visual acuity, the court could well have ordered involvement in a therapeutic or parent-training program. Staff with considerable experience in protective work feel particularly defeated when they perceive indicators of substantial risk to be present but are helpless to intervene until pernicious damage has occurred. Operating statistics of protective agencies reflect a high rate of subsequent reports of serious physical impairment or even death of previously investigated children who, because of the legal ambiguities, were not adjudicated abused, and thus the right to intervene was not granted.

The institutional framework for the protection of children is established in law. The spirit of the law enunciates a guiding philosophy on the intent of protective measures with regard to families and children and specifies those conditions under which society can intervene in family life against the wishes of the parents: "The Courts can mandate the rehabilitation of the parents but it cannot rehabilitate them. Ultimately the prevention and treatment of child abuse depends less on laws and more on the existence of sufficient and suitable helping services for children and families" (HEW, *Model Act*, 1977, p. 36).

The definitional problems contribute to difficulties in developing an effective system of service delivery to abusive families. Professionals have expressed concern about the legislative tendency to transfer clinical judgments away from mental health professionals and to place them increasingly in the hands of judges. Professionals of all disciplines have tended to disengage from child-abusing parents and to view the courts and public child-protection services as the responsible service agents. Threats to professional autonomy and to judgment- and value-orientation have been identified as factors that contribute to professional disengagement from public agencies with their bureaucratic relationships and decision-making hierarchies (Gilbert & Specht, 1974). The discrepancies in viewpoints and purposes that are being emphasized in the increasingly legalized domain of child abuse tend to militate against heavy professional involvement in the problem. In a recent study conducted by the American Humane Association (1978) it was found that private social agencies accounted for less than 1 percent of initial reports of abuse, and private physicians for less than 2 percent. These figures exist despite mandatory reporting for professionals, which includes negative sanctions for willful failure to report an incident of abuse. Many experts in the field view the accusatory climate of blame, the constraints on the therapeutic relationship, apprehension that reports may further endanger the child, and the resistance to legal proceedings as factors that influence the lack of cooperation among professionals.

Conceptual definitions and practice-based definitions are critical to the development of practice theory and practice modalities that will be effective in improving the quality of parenting, the family environment, and enhancing the development of vulnerable children. The clinical picture of the "battered-child syndrome" provided a base for the specific identification and labeling of the most severe form of abuse in small children. This conclusion was substantiated by verifiable medical evidence including multiple fractures in the long bones, fractures of the skull, soft-tissue injuries and bruises, and subdural hematoma. Often the fractures were in various stages of healing, suggesting a pattern of injury over time. This medical evidence not only served to provide a medically diagnosable condition of abuse that may have been unsuspected otherwise, but also began to dispel the myth that we were dealing with a single-accidental injury that resulted from punishment simply going too far (Kempe et al., 1962).

The identification of a battered-child syndrome stimulated interest, research, and active involvement of pediatricians, psychiatrists, and other related medical and public-health professionals in problems of child abuse. This focus on the health consequences of the battering behavior for the child began to legitimize the problem as one falling within the purview of the medical profession. Subsequent medical study and research on abused children has documented that such children suffer varying degrees of neurologic damage and sustain permanent physical and mental impairment. Morse, Sahler, and Friedman (1970) reported in a follow-up survey of children hospitalized from abuse during a 3-year period, that 71 percent were outside the normal range of intellectual, emotional, social, and motor development, and 43 percent of this number were mentally retarded. Other medical studies present similar findings and relationships (Elmer & Gregg, 1967; Martin, 1972).

While the battered-child syndrome is usually the easiest form of abuse to prove in court, it is only a subset of the larger problem of abuse of children. In addition to understanding the health consequences of battering, we are beginning to understand and document the social consequences of intrafamily violence and child abuse. There is increasing documentation of the psychologic and sociologic crippling of abusive child-rearing patterns, the intergenerational cycles of abnormal parenting, an increasing incidence of reported histories of childhood abuse by perpetrators of violent crimes, and the deficits of interpersonal skills in adulthood that contribute to maladjustment and other social problems.* Despite this growing appreciation, practice definitions continue to retain the concept of intentionality. That is, child abuse is usually defined in terms of two concepts: (1) nonaccidental injury perpetrated by a parent or guardian and (2) severity, which includes the notion of a continuing pattern over time (Zalba, 1967; Young, 1974; Gil, 1970; Justice & Justice, 1976).

Newberger (1973) departs from the field as he does not restrict his definition to deliberate injury. He suggests that situations in a child's home (family) that jeopardize survival with or without observable injury constitute abuse. This definition, while less operational and verifiable, suggests a preventive perspective to guide policy development and programming. A similar approach is reflected in the "maltreatment syndrome" conceptualized by Fontana (1973), which includes children with multiple minor physical evidence of nutritional deprivation, neglect, and emotional and physical abuse. It is

---

*See Alfaro (1978); Silver (1969).

Fontana's assertion that the presence of these conditions eventually leads to serious physical trauma in children. Some investigators propose a continuum of types of abuse that range from "failure to thrive" in infants through severe physical trauma. Many feel that neglect and abuse should be reflected in a single-problem definition. Others feel abuse and neglect have different etiologies and should be defined separately to promote more effective control and treatment strategies.

Preoccupation with achieving definitional clarity is warranted as it establishes directions for policy formulation, program development, and the specification of interventive modalities and strategies. To some extent, our understanding of the causes of the problem is as illusory as our ability to define it operationally.

EXPLANATORY MODELS OF CHILD ABUSE

The popular misconception of child abuse as a single-problem condition is not supported by current knowledge and understanding. To date, theorists have approached this problem from different perspectives, identifying varying causative factors. These explanations have not resulted in a comprehensive theory package that satisfactorily accounts for all the observations that have been made about the manifestations or causes of child abuse. The major theories and assumptions may be summarized in terms of four model types. Each model contains a central core of determinants considered basic to its position on causation.

The Clinical/Psychologic Model

The clinical/psychologic model is probably the most widely known and accepted explanation of why parents abuse their children. This model places the locus of the problem in the psychologic makeup of the parents. Their personality structure, character traits, or psychologically induced dynamics, in confrontation with the demands of the child, precipitate an internally directed rage reaction that results in abuse of the child. While the developers of this explanatory approach recognize other sources of stress as contributory, they hold the position that parents without the requisite psychologic profile are not capable of committing abusive attacks on their children.

The abusive-dynamic construct developed by Kempe and others (Kempe & Helfer, 1972; Pollock & Steele, 1972) appears to be the most dominant of the clinical/psychologic theories in the literature. While other theorists have used one or more of the individual dynamic factors in their generalization, the strength of this model is based on the presence and interaction of the dynamics with each other. Kempe utilizes seven "dynamics" in his formulation: mothering imprint, isolation, self-esteem, role reversal, spouse support, perception of the child, and crisis. These dynamics affect the parents' attitudes and behavior toward children. Selective explication of the dynamics follows.

"Mothering imprint" refers to the deeply embedded capacity to nurture that is learned in one's earliest childhood experience of being loved and cared for in a nurturing way. Parents who were not cared for on the basis of their own needs as children and who were deprived of consistent nurturant mothering as infants tend to become parents who are incapable of providing the necessary nurturant care to their own children. Such parents are unable to perceive the true needs of the dependent child because their own dependency needs are so overwhelming that they blur the perceptive capacity. Cherished childhood memories are not a part of the experience of these parents, and they are incapable of intuiting the infant's needs or responding empathically. The crying and the helplessness of the infant or small child does not evoke tender concern or sympathy but instead stirs up old hurts and uncontrollable feelings that must be released. Pollock and Steele (1972, p. 11) further elucidate this dynamic phenomenon:

> One of the most common precipitants of abuse is the persistent crying of an infant, despite parental efforts to comfort or care for the child's needs. . . . [Such] behavior is interpreted as criticism. . . . [The] parents feel attacked and may release abusive punishment.

Psychoanalytic theory emphasizes the crucial importance of the emotional union of mother and infant during the oral stage of psychosocial development as the foundation for trust and relationship capacity. The infant experiences the world first through the symbiotic union with the mother. Attachment behavior and issues of bonding are concepts receiving considerable attention today as critical ingredients in healthy development and as underlying factors in disordered development when they do not occur in the proper time frame. In their work with abusive parent couples, Rita and Blair Justice (1976) observe the amount of "emotional and physical stucktogetherness" the parents exhibit. These couples are seen as fused together in a symbiotic relationship constantly seeking love and approval from each other. It is their view that when a spouse is losing the battle to be cared for, the abuse follows to eliminate the competition the child represents.

These clinical interpretations of the concept of symbiosis in the abusive pattern appear to blend the dynamics of mothering imprint and role reversal as used by Kempe.

"Role reversal" occurs when the parent turns to the small child for emotional nurturance and for gratification of the parent's dependency needs.

Parents attribute adult powers to the child, and failure of the child to live up to the parental expectations results in abuse. The child's display of assertiveness or resistance is viewed as a deliberate attempt to exert power over the parent and to deprive the parent of what is desired and needed. The report of the investigation of an alleged abuse case by a child protection worker demonstrates the dynamic of role reversal.*

9/8—Report of Abuse

A paternal aunt, Mrs. B., reported that Lucy, age 4, was seriously mistreated by her mother, Mrs. J. (her sister-in law), and that yesterday the child had been pushed down the steps: "I took Lucy to the Children's Hospital and told them the child fell down the steps, but today I can't live with my conscience and let that child return to that situation. That woman thinks that child is grown! My poor brother is in jail for desertion and child support. He just couldn't cope with that wife of his. She drains everybody."

Mrs. B. went on to relate that Lucy's mother expects her to be perfect; to help supervise and keep the baby occupied. If Lucy complains, she gets beaten within an inch of her life: "My brother's family lives in the upper flat over us. Last night the child was screaming and we could hear the blows through the ceiling. I called on the phone and told her if it didn't stop, I was coming up there. When I pretended I was coming up the stairs, the door opened and she [Mrs. J.] shoved the child down the stairs saying, 'The both of you go to hell and see if I care. You deserve each other.' " The child fell six or seven steps before her aunt could grab her.

9/8—Verification of Injury

Called hospital and found Lucy had been admitted with a broken collarbone. It had been noted that the aunt seemed quite concerned and comforting to the child. It appeared to be an accident, and they had expected to discharge her today. However, x-rays show several healed bone injuries, suggestive of abuse. They had phoned the mother and asked her to come in, but she has not visited.

9/9—Home Visit

Mrs. J. was somewhat nervous as she talked with me. We sat in the kitchen as she prepared lunch. The kitchen was neat and clean and the boys were fully dressed. Fred, age 3, was holding onto his mother's skirt as she moved around, pulling him along without paying any attention to him. Tommy, 8 months, was in his highchair, quietly sucking his thumb. Mrs. J. blamed

---

*Some of the case material in this chapter was developed by the author when she was a faculty member and Project Director of the Child Abuse and Neglect Training Program at the State University College at Buffalo.

my visit on her in-laws. "I know they asked you to come. They've always interfered in my life. Why can't they leave me alone?" She continued, "It's their fault my husband is gone and that Lucy hurt herself. . . . They were always partial to Lucy, fawning over her and making her feel she was so special that she didn't owe her own mother anything. I'm the one who almost died when she was born, and do you think she cares about that? No, she likes their sweet talk and all that baby cuddly baloney. No one thinks about what I go through; it's just Lucy, Lucy! Now here you are about Lucy! Well for your information, Lucy hurt herself trying to run down there to them instead of staying close to me where she belongs. Serves her right! What am I supposed to do now . . . show her sympathy? No one ever showed me any." At this point Mrs. J. began to sob quietly, Fred wrapped his arms around her legs and began to hum a little tune and Tommy began to rock himself in the chair.*

While the role of these dynamics remains unsupported by research findings, the overall clinical profile is strongly supported by the observations of practitioners working with abusive families.

Other psychologic explanations have been advanced in the literature. Kaufman (1962) has used diagnostic categories of character disorder to explain abusive behavior and to outline treatment programs. Others propose a description of personality or character traits as explanations of abusive behavior. These explanations take the form of identifying traits that are typical of the abusing parent (such as emotional immaturity, inability to cope with stress, poor impulse control, and chronic hostility) and precipitate rage reactions in them when they are frustrated or under stress (DeFrancis, 1963; Galdston, 1968; Pollock & Steele, 1972).

Several investigators have developed typologies for the classification and treatment of child abuse. Zalba (1967) developed a six-class typology: (1) psychotic parent; (2) pervasively angry and abusive parent; (3) depressive/passive-aggressive parent; (4) compulsive, disciplinarian parent; (5) marital-family system problem; (6) person-environment system. The locus of the problem in each of the first four classes is the personality system of the abuser with the basic determinant being personality structure. Abuse that occurs in the first three classes is considered uncontrollable, and treatment would require separation of the child from the parents. In the fourth classification, that of the compulsive parent, the problem is also centered in the basic personality or character structure of the abuser; however, the abuse is considered controllable since the parent can respond to a firm limit-setting relationship with an external agent and benefit from social-environmental pressure to conform. In the fifth instance, the problem resides primarily in the

---

*For an in-depth discussion of role reversal and the other dynamics of abuse, see Daughtry, et al. (1975).

marital or family-interactional system, and conflicts from this domain are displaced onto the child through abuse. In the sixth, the locus of the problem is in the person-environment system, and status loss or achievement tensions are displaced in abuse to the child. In each of these latter classes, the abuse of the child is controllable so that treatment methods less radical than the separation of children and parents are generally successful. Zalba's typology has similarities to other classification systems conceptualized in the literature (Delsordo, 1963; Merrill, 1962) in its description of the personality characteristics of the abusing parents. This formulation, however, with its integration of causal variables, assessment of severity and controllability, and differential treatment strategies, is more amenable to practice research. All of these typologies share the shortcoming of not having been empirically validated through systematically constructed practice research. They, like most of the work that supports the development of the psychologic theories of child abuse, have been patterned from clinical practice. The cases from which the generalizations have been formulated are of families in which clinically significant abuse has been identified. There is no substantiation that the cluster of personality traits, or the dynamic characteristics of parents described, are unique to the outcome of child abuse, and this weakens substantially their value as predictive or explanatory constructs. Do other parents with these psychologic profiles manage the stress of child rearing without resorting to abusive behavior? Are there significant numbers of abusive parents who do not display these profiles? Without more carefully constructed studies that include a broader population of parents, we cannot conclude cause and effect relationships.

Sociologic/Environmental Model

The clinical/psychologic explanations of child abuse emphasize the private troubles of abnormal or psychologically impaired parents who are unable to handle the stressful tasks of child rearing without resorting to abuse. On the other hand, sociologic/environmental explanations of child abuse emphasize the public troubles of our social environment that affect family life negatively and promote violence. Intolerable life circumstances either diminish parental self-controls to a degree that elicits and maintains abusive behavior or stimulate and reinforce, through social or cultural sanctions, those values and behavior patterns that are conducive to the expression of violence. The most consistent themes that support these views are as follows:

1. Histories of extreme deprivation and exposure to multiple stress. The unrelenting press of poverty, poor health, unemployment, dilapidated and overcrowded housing, limited tangible amenities and

resources, and persistent failures in adaptation that set the stage for violent child rearing.

2. Social isolation and the absence of supports to alleviate the normal stress of child rearing.
3. Class-related family life-styles that are aggressive, authoritarian, and overdetermined in the use of physical punishment in both the guidance and management tasks of child rearing.
4. Subtle but widespread societal and cultural sanction of violence and the use of physical force as acceptable control/conflict-resolution strategies, encouraging the use of violence in family life activities and child rearing.

A resource-deficiency explanation of poverty has been advanced by some theorists as both an outcome of poverty and a variable that contributes to its development and maintenance. Some investigators have adopted a similar explanation of child abuse as an outcome of the aggressive child-rearing strategies of lower-class families and the conditions impinging on these families as developing and maintaining such aggressive patterns. This explanation is reinforced by the fact that poor families are more heavily represented in identified populations of abusing families. Studies of the characteristics of these families reflect sociologic or environmental indicators usually associated with lower social class. The work of David Gil (1970; 1975) links child abuse to the socioeconomic pressures on poor families that weaken parental mechanisms of self-control and permit life frustrations to be expressed through attacks on their children. This view is also consistent with reported observations of behavioral changes that occurred in persons subjected to the pervasive brutality and extreme environmental stress of concentration or prisoner-of-war camps. Persons formerly viewed as well adjusted, when subjected to prolonged and extreme environmental stress, as prisoners, exhibited disordered behavior and resorted to primitive forms of bodily attacks on persons with whom they had previously held meaningful relationships (Bettleheim, 1943). The unrelenting and all-encompassing nature of the stress, the threat to both physical survival and psychologic integrity, and the absence of hope for change seem to be factors that corrode the coping capacities of humans and permit the release of primitive and base instincts.

It is a reality that poor families are more likely to be subjected to multiple stresses in their life circumstances than are those of other socioeconomic classes. Their economic status is marginal and most often unpredictable. They are more often unemployed or, when employed, receive substandard pay, have low-level job security or predictability, and derive little or no job satisfaction from their work. Income security is often bolstered by public means income support programs with the family eligibility determined by a means test. The degrading quality of the interactions and the dehumanizing transactions with public bureaucracies mandated to help, are often ego assaultive and lead to the internalization of negative attitudes about the applicant's adequacy. Dilapidated, energy-inefficient, and vermin-infested housing facilities are common. Overcrowding militates against privacy or the opportunity for even transitory relief. The absence of basic labor-saving equipment, such as washing machines, contributes to harsh daily realities that make child rearing difficult. Basic items taken for granted by most of us are absent, such as hot running water, storage space, electricity, a bed of one's own, or refrigeration. The day-to-day drudgery and the costs of survival escalate together. Barely to survive, some families have to turn to a remote and impersonal suprastructure in which the potentially available help may result in further suffering, punishment, and rejection reminiscent of the abused child's experience.

> A child-protection worker responded to a reported threat made by Mrs. S. to her welfare worker that she was going to kill her children if she did not get her check. The home visit revealed living circumstances of the most inhuman and degrading sort. The kitchen was filthy. Empty bean cans and scraps of bread were the only visible signs of food. The refrigerator was not working because the electricity was off. Three dirty mattresses with no sheets comprised the total equipment other than a gas range in the house. Dirty clothes were piled in boxes in the two bedrooms. The commode was malfunctioning, and feces floated around in the almost overrunning bowl. Mrs. S. was depressed and subdued, and the four small children were dirty, frightened, and clinging together. They had been beaten for begging food from one of the neighbors. The mother had refused to allow the neighbor in and had rejected the offer of a bowl of stew. The children had revealed the family's business and had caused her trouble. The neighbor reported her for neglect.
>
> Mrs. S. expressed total inability to cope with the situation any longer. Her welfare check had been suspended for two cycles for failure to comply with certain regulations related to paternity action. The problems with "the welfare" had caused fights with her boyfriend in which she sustained a black eye and a broken tooth. She had secured a peace warrant to prevent his coming to the house, but she still did not feel secure; he was furious that he might be implicated with "the welfare." Her mother helped out from time to time but she was receiving social security and lived some distance away. The only answer to her predicament as she saw it was to give her children to the welfare agency.

Situations like this lend credibility to the environmental-stress explanation. Such obscene and degrading circumstances not only render the management of family functions and child-rearing tasks impossible, but in the absence of promised respite could lead to unthinkable violence. Yet many poor families survive in the context of similar oppressive circumstances without resorting to abusing their children.

Many researchers endorse the notion that social stress, particularly poverty, contributes to neglect, but they are less inclined to establish such a relationship to abuse (Polansky, Hally, & Polansky, 1975). Universal support is lacking for the view that abuse and neglect are a part of the same problem continuum. Giovannoni and Billingsley (1970) studied a sample of low-income women and grouped them according to their child-care behaviors into the categories, adequate, potentially neglectful, and neglectful. The current life circumstances of those judged neglectful had many similarities, but their social histories and familial backgrounds failed to distinguish the neglectful mothers from the other two categories. The authors concluded that neglect is more typically a product of currently experienced stress than of the mothers' personality traits or earlier life experiences. Similar findings in a recent national study indicate "that the family factors involved in child abuse are different than in child neglect. In neglect, the relative importance of environmental stress factors is greater than the personal characteristics or inability to cope factors present in cases of abuse" (American Humane Association, 1978, p. 16). Child abusers are said to come from all socioeconomic levels of society, and the overrepresentation of lower-income families is believed to relate to biases of reporting systems, frequent use of public services, lack of access to private practitioners and physicians, and societal tendencies to abrogate their rights. Failures to differentiate abuse and neglect incidents in some reporting leaves the findings of surveys like Gil's lacking in the sharpness needed to establish necessary relationships between social class and abuse.

Social isolation has been identified as a contributory variable in abuse within all the models of causal explanation. Kent (1978) compared 500 children and families referred for direct abuse to a group of 185 families referred for other stated reasons, such as alcoholism, mental illness, or inadequate parenting. While both groups were defined as economically poor, the abusive families were found more often to be new to the neighborhoods, to have few friends, to be without phones or transportation, and to have had more complications during pregnancy or at birth.

According to the clinical/psychologic model, social isolation results from the parents' inability to develop and maintain relationships and to ask for, receive, and use help. The pattern is not class-related but psychologically determined. It develops and is maintained as a result of the parents' pervasively low self-esteem, fear of rejection, mistrust of others and their massive defense against unmet dependency needs. From the standpoint of the social-learning/socialization model, forms of behavior that support social isolation are learned. In a study conducted by Young (1974), 95 percent of families with a history of severe abuse and 83 percent of families with a history of moderate abuse demonstrated social isolation in their relationship patterns. These families had almost no continuing relationships with others outside the immediate family. More significant from a socialization viewpoint was the finding that such families actively prevent their children from developing relationships or friendships with others. Family members were socialized to maintain distance, keep the family secrets, and to steer clear of relationships and social experiences that would encourage interpersonal engagement.

Within the sociologic/environmental view, social isolation is an environmental condition, much like poor housing or unemployment, that contributes to the social stress of poor families. Social isolation is the absence of resources necessary to support parents in their child-rearing tasks. Not only do families *feel* deprived and isolated, they *are* deprived and isolated. The lack of telephones, transportation, and nominal cash for fees to participate in organized group activities restricts involvement. Limited education correlates with limited skills and limited information about the existence of resources useful in resolving problems and performing life tasks. These families are not indifferent to the appeal of mainstream values expressed so vividly in the media. The issue is not one of repudiation of achievement, independent functioning, and self-reliance. Rather, the environment is less likely to provide them with the opportunities to participate and to learn from the social and interpersonal competences of the institutional activities of community life. They are more likely to experience rejecting societal attitudes through frequent and negative exposure to bureaucratic systems such as public welfare, hospital clinics, police, schools, courts, attendance officers, and the like. Isolate behavior is understandable if one perceives that opening one's family life to public view results, not in help, but in additional suffering, punishment, or forced separation and destruction of the family unit. Isolate behavior is also understandable if encounters with community agents provide families with a "mirror reflection" of themselves as failing, inadequate, and devalued units of society.

There is a prevailing consensus that social isolation reduces access to the relationship supports and tangible resources that would ease the stress of child rearing and promote the coping abilities of parents. Adaptation and mastery of life tasks within the current social structure require a high degree of interdependence among people and societal organizations. Coping skills are bolstered or fragmented by the continuity or discontinuity the person experiences in the context of prevailing societal attitudes and in his access to and use of interpersonal and societal resources. The resource theory of violence (Steinmetz & Straus, 1975) takes the view that one subjected to extreme stress attempts to cope by using familiar problem-solving patterns and all the internal and external resources available to one. When such coping efforts fail, one turns to violence as a tertiary resource to alleviate an intolerable life situation.

Gil (1970) proposed that the level of child abuse is reflective of our society's sanctioning of physical abuse as an appropriate form of conflict resolution. This general climate, predominant at a societal level, provides the context for the use of such measures in child rearing and in the resolution of intra-familial conflicts. Professional football and hockey, both saturated with brutal physical encounters, are big business in this country. Film and television superstars are often heroes in their roles of enforcers and intimidators. There is fascination with the violence presented in our homes as entertainment in television movies. The media are extremely powerful in exalting the macho image of the outlaw or "Dirty Harry" type of character. A 5-year content analysis of television programs conducted by Gerbner (1970) revealed that 75 percent of the viewings contained violence. Educators and parents are beginning to concern themselves seriously with the effects of such television programming on the developing child. In 1979 an attorney defending a teen-aged boy accused of a brutal murder presented a highly detailed brief of the relationships between violent television programs and the boy's behavior. There is a growing concern that the levels of violence in society are being mirrored in family-interaction patterns.

Gelles (1973) believes that environmental stress is as inadequate an expla-nation of the causality of violence as are theories of personality aberration. He proposes a more dynamic blending of the two views in a sociopsychologic perspective. His formulation proposes that the causal force of child abuse emerges from the interaction of the following multidimensional stress factors: the social position of the parents, their socialization experience with abusive role models, their personality and character traits, their class and community values, situational events, and broad prevailing norms of violence. Stress in this model may be situational, as in marital friction; structural, as produced by conditions of unemployment or social isolation; or child-specific, growing out of the interactional demands of a special, deformed, or hyperactive child. Like the sociologic/environmental model, Gelles' paradigm takes into con-sideration the psychologic context as well as a multidimensional stress per-spective.

Socialization/Social Learning Model

A widely accepted causal explanation is that child abuse is transmitted from one generation to the next through the process of socialization. Cultural perpetuation of child-rearing patterns and procedures from one generation to another has been richly documented in the history of human life. Child-rearing styles are defined by the culture, and the learning necessary for the taking on of customs, traditions, attitudes, and beliefs occurs within the socialization process. Socialization refers to all the processes, conditions, and interactions involved in transforming the child into a socially oriented person equipped for harmonious living with others. This training is carried out by caretakers in an environment that promotes close, frequent, and intimate contact and allows for the shaping of behavior through identification, modeling, and the selective use of rewards and punishments. This process is the means by which children learn to take their adult roles in the culture and learn the technology of parenting, in their turn socializing the succeeding generation.*

Throughout the literature on child abuse one finds reference to the fact that abusive parents themselves have histories as abused children. These early abusive experiences are proposed by many theorists as the critical factor in shaping the parental capacity for abuse (Galdston, 1968; Pollock & Steele, 1972; Bakan, 1971; Wasserman, 1967; Helfer, 1976). While most of these investigators subscribe to the "early-learning" hypothesis, there are variations among them.

Pollock and Steele (1972) stress the interpersonal qualities of the parents as the significant variable leading to the development of a similar interpersonal gestalt in the child, rendering him or her incapable of effective parenting at a later date. The child is socialized by parents incapable of nurturing, empathic responses. They cannot minister to the child's affective needs, and punishment is meted out without the expression of warm, caring support and direction. The child learns that those to whom one turns for support are punishing and rejecting. The punishment is often untempered and brutal because there is no capacity to empathize with the child's pain and suffering. The child in the context of this emotional climate fails to incorporate the capacity for nuture and empathy, while adopting the parental model of punitive child rearing.

A somewhat different view emphasizes the use of the child as a hostility sponge to absorb the noxious feelings and anger of the parent, so as to terminate the unbearable tension of his deeply embedded rage (Wasserman, 1967). Rage, as differentiated from anger, is not an emotional reaction to current stimuli but a suppressed infantile terror and anger. The threat, submerged in the fear, is of annihilation and destruction. The danger of loss of control is always present. At a later point, in the role of parent, he or she is in the power position and can act out against the child the destruction he or she longed to inflict on his or her own parents (Holmes, et al., 1975). This interpretation suggests that the battering of the child not only serves to reduce the parent's tension but also to feed the need to feel superior and powerful. The goal of the socialization process has been displaced from meeting the developmental needs of the child to meeting the needs of the parent. "The perpetuation of the species has been sacrified for the maintenance of the

---

*See Chapter 1 in this volume for further discussion of these concepts.

parent's psychological homeostasis" (Galdston, 1968, p. 2). Individuals, thus socialized, may come to hold a deeply embedded belief that the parent-child configuration exists for the primary purpose of serving the parent's needs. The behavior is, therefore, doubly determined because it serves both a release and pleasure purpose. There is a sense of justification and prerogative in the parent's claim to this role, which renders the family boundaries closed to cues and expectations of change from the external environment.

Helfer (1976) has conceptualized a cycle of intergenerational imprinting, which he labels the "World of Abnormal Rearing (W.A.R.)." His explanatory model pushes toward meshing more discrete clinical concepts into an organized theory of abnormal child rearing that describes the acquisition of the behavior and the forces that maintain it into the next generation. His first assumption seems to be that abusive parenting is learned in the process of being parented in a certain way. The second assumption is that there are identifiable elements and processes by which this parenting pattern is transmitted. The elements he identifies include unrealistic expectations of the child (compliance and role reversal), lack of trust (isolation and poor self-image), selection of friends and mates, and conception, pregnancy, and the resultant child.

From the beginning of the child's entry into this world, such parents hold unrealistic expectations. Their requirements are not congruent with the child's maturational or developmental capacity to respond. Performance demands are usually unrealistic, and the child's failure elicits punishment, verbal belittlement, and rejection. The constant failure, the fear associated with trying, and the continuing sense of diminishing competencies, deprive the child of the normal experiences of graded practice and the mastery of age-appropriate skills. The child not only fails to develop a repertoire of instrumental competencies, he or she learns to evaluate him- or herself as inferior:

> Mary, age 4, was expected to keep her room clean. At bedtime, the covers on her bed were on the floor, and she sought help from the parents who had settled down to read the paper at the end of a long day. She said, in a whining manner, that her covers were off. After a round of escalating orders to get to bed, the child was hurled to the floor and pushed out of the room by the father's foot: "You dirty, lazy wench, if you took care of your room like any decent person you wouldn't have this problem. Get your ass out of here and go to bed. I don't care if you sleep on the floor."

Such parents also exact speedy compliance to their wishes and demands and become enraged at any protestations or expressions of anger on the part of the child. Compliance demands are rigidly enforced through punishment:

John, age 9, the oldest of four children, was looking forward to the football game on television after supper. He rushed through the meal, not eating too well. However, when dessert was served, John quickly ate his cupcake and asked for another. His mother explained that there were only enough for each person to get one. John began to pout and complain, "Why can't we ever have lots of cupcakes like Tim's folks? This is such a stingy house." Father became enraged and, lifting John out of his chair by the back of his collar, he demanded: "You greedy bastard, what makes you think you deserve two cupcakes? I'm the man of the house and I only have one. What makes you so special? If you open your big mouth again, I'll rub your face in that plate. I'm warning you, don't make me lose my temper. Get these dishes done and earn your keep, then get out of my sight. Maybe that'll teach you that other people have needs besides you."

The child learns to submit to the power of the parent, to submerge self-expression and displeasure. He or she is deprived of opportunities to develop skills in the control and expressive domains. His or her control mechanisms are primitive, and while he or she capitulates to external power, it is at a cost to regulatory and emotional development.

Roles are often reversed in this child-rearing system. The parent looks to the child for emotional support, nurture, and satisfaction of the parent's dependency needs. While some children are described as quite successful in developing a pattern of reciprocation aimed at pleasing and gratifying the parent, this is not a normal childhood expectation. Such children pay a heavy price in terms of their emotional and interpersonal development. They do not know how to be children. They have, in Helfer's terms, "missed the childhood experience" (1976, p. 36).

The child moves on in the developmental cycle without a solid foundation. The skills of basic trust have not been developed; the child feels inferior and worthless and is incapable of the emotional give and take that will further interpersonal growth and meaningful engagement with others. The child elicits rejection from others and is emotionally isolated. He or she has not been integrated into the family in a healthy way and has not developed a separate self. The family members seem joined together tenuously but tenaciously, and this relationship quality colors their selection and attachment to friends and eventual mates. Similar relationship qualities have been described and labeled as symbiotic (Justice & Justice 1976) or undifferentiated-fused (Bowen, 1971). W.A.R. children will, as teenagers or young adults, seek to reestablish another symbiotic union, conceive a child and become enmeshed in the recycling of the abnormal world of child abuse. Helfer and Justice maintain that such parents are essentially alike, no matter which one actively abuses the child. The merger is of two insufficiently differentiated persons seeking to meet their primitive needs to be cared for. The child is

awaited with high expectations that he will bring the fulfillment and gratification that has eluded them thus far.

There is wide acceptance among investigators and practitioners in the field
of child welfare that childhood experiences of abuse predispose the individual
to demonstrate this kind of behavior in rearing his or her own child. The
socialization model comes closer than others to a workable formulation of
the reason the expression of violence is directed toward the child. Nevertheless, this explanatory model has weaknesses similar to the others. The
concepts used in this model were developed from clinical insights and practice
that involved a skewed sample. Further, there has been no empirical validation of the theory. Helfer seems to have made a contribution to a beginning
base for generating research efforts. Perhaps the persuasiveness of his abnormal model of child rearing will stimulate efforts to develop a testable
model of adequate child rearing. The absence of consensus on what constitutes such a prototype not only limits the feasibility of empirically testing
a model of abnormal child rearing, it limits the objective and uniform adjudication of child-protective orders.

A final weakness of Helfer's formulation is the absence of consideration
of other influences on the family and W.A.R. children. The larger societal
perspective, although not encompassed in Helfer's work, is richly documented in the sociologic/environmental explanation. The impact of television,
the school experience, and the influence of latency-age peers and playmates
as socializing agents need further exploration. Comparative cultural studies
document the role of a wide range of societal units, customs, and sanctions
in socialization outcomes (Mead, 1970).

Ecologic/Systems Model

There have been dramatic and widespread increases in the incidence and
prevalence of child abuse, other forms of violence, and destructive behavioral
responses within and across socioeconomic classes and families of all types
within our society. These broad-scale changes have led to some disaffection
with the existing causal explanations as being too narrow in perspective and
interpretation. While each model offers some cogent and persuasive insights,
each falls short of accounting for all the clinical and empirical observations
made to date. The concept of multicausality of human problems has broad
support in the literature and many investigators, rejecting the psychologic-
versus-environmental view, have searched for multidimensional explanations
to achieve a more dynamic and unifying theory.

Bronfenbrenner (1974), a renowned authority in the field of the family,
believes child abuse can occur as a function of the degree to which the human
ecology enhances or undermines parenting. In this view, one does not look

for the etiology of the problem in the psychologic makeup of the parents, their past life experiences, or in the structural characteristics of the family. Each or all of these variables may be important, but when pursued in isolation they tend to produce models that fall short in accounting for abusiveness.

Ecologic inquiry seeks to recognize and examine the relationships among variables rather than their defined characteristics. Failures in adaptation are conceptualized as problems in living (even such faulty adaptations as abusive parenting), requiring an emphasis on the conditions and resources necessary to bring about more effective coping and adaptiveness. The focus is not on the characteristics of the person or on those of the problem condition but rather on the interaction of all the elements in the situation that impede social functioning and produce deviant outcomes (Pincus & Minahan, 1973, p. 11).

Ecology is the science concerned with the adaptive fit of organisms and their environments and with the means by which they achieve a dynamic equilibrium and mutuality (Germain, 1973, p. 326). Human ecology concerns itself with relationships between human beings and their interpersonal, physical, and organizational environments and the degree to which these modify or enhance the performance of life tasks. It is concerned with maintaining life-support systems that have potential for sustaining and improving our existence.

Child abuse as a social problem cannot be considered in isolation from other grave difficulties that plague families today. Problems of family violence are the result of an interlocking array of cause-and-effect connections related to disruptions in the relationships of the ecosystems of which they are a part. Although the family is the major and most intimate unit involved in directing the social development of its members, it is embedded in a network of other social systems that support, neutralize, or counteract that direction. Parental child-rearing performance is deeply affected by the entire living experience, not simply by the parents' early history. Problems of child rearing are problems in living, and the focus of help must be on the ability of the parent-child system to perform its life tasks in mutual interdependence with its environment.

An examination of some of the empirically documented ecologic issues and propositions may be useful at this point (Ehrlich, Ehrlich, & Holdren, 1973, p. 4). They are as follows:

1. The extent of human dependence on the natural environment and the fundamental character of our disruption of it.
2. The exponential properties of growth both of the human population and of its impact on the environment.
3. The importance of time lags and irreversibility in the man-environment system.

4. The interlocking nature of present problems of environmental deterioration, resource consumption, and of social organization.

Human beings, like all other living systems, are dependent on their environment for survival. Ecologists inform us that all living systems are open, that is, involved in a reciprocal exchange of energy between one system and another. All living systems take something from the environment, use it for survival and growth, and return to the environment some substance that has been modified to the further benefit of this life-sustaining process (Meyer, 1976). Living systems that are not engaged in such vital exchange processes within their ecosystems are headed toward disintegration or destruction.

"The human population, its consumption of resources, and its adverse impact on the environment are all growing exponentially, in other words, at compound interest" (Ehrlich et al., 1973, p. 8). In such a growth process, each addition contributes new additions, and a problem viewed over time as negligible in size and as the private trouble of a subset of the population suddenly and dramatically emerges as a major social problem. "It is probably no accident that certain environmental problems have seemed to materialize so suddenly in the last two decades; more likely, the abruptness with which these problems have appeared is the usual manifestation of an exponential growth process approaching a threshold" (Ehrlich, et al., 1973, p. 10). The social problem of child abuse in its observed escalation is growing exponentially. If the momentum of this growth continues uninterrupted, violence in the family may be the norm rather than the exception, with dire consequences for our society.

Ecologic changes take place over a much longer time-span than the yearly or monthly changes that are apparent in our accelerated life context. Delays between the initiation of environmental insults and the emergence of negative consequences blur our understanding of cause-and-effect relationships and render corrective action ineffective or impossible. The Love Canal incident in western New York is an example of this concept. Massive amounts of chemicals disposed of in landfills bubbled to the surface, and their toxic effects became identified with serious health conditions of residents living on developments laid over these dumps. The disposal practices of the chemical plant, the responsibility of government for allowing it, and the culpability of the residential builders for using this land space for homes and schools were all at issue, but much of the damage that had accrued was irreversible. Problems of violence in families need to be examined in such a perspective. Modifications to our social scene, which connote progress at one point in time, often produce unanticipated consequences that impact negatively on human development and family life.

"Environmental degradation is not the sum of independent causes, it is the multiplicative product of inter-connected ones" (Ehrlich, et al., 1973, p.

12). The delays in recognizing the symptoms of environmental degradation make it impossible to disentangle the causes and tackle them separately. As a matter of fact, the effort to isolate a simplistic causal relationship may be as unproductive as it is difficult. The rapid conversion of the world's resources into waste by rich countries has contributed to serious economic, environmental, and political problems. It is difficult for the lay public to conceive of the relationships between our affluent life-styles, our personal and industrial consumption of natural resources, and current global problems. Yet the human plight of the American hostages in Iran gave most of us an initial grasp of this concept and brought home the extent to which one cannot establish simple cause-and-effect relationships. Rather, a "web-of-responsibility" concept seems more appropriate. So it is with complex social problems like child abuse.

Meyer (1976) has given particular attention to the role of societal institutions and the critical role that formal, bureaucratized organizations have played in the ecology of our society: "Our world has become so complex that despite the continuing American dream that people can do everything for themselves, it is no longer possible for a single American family or any economic class to be independent of some socially organized, government-supported system of social utilities and social services" (Meyer, 1976, p. 45). She perceives a systemic relationship between people and the social institutions with which they intersect at the various stages of life. Social policies and institutions require modification in order to respond to the needs confronted by families at various stages in family life. It is possible to perceive services and practitioners located within those institutions, which are the normal intersecting points in the life space of parents. The challenge is to identify points at which normal life crises will occur, as well as where pathologic crises might erupt, and to locate sites of support in the family's ecosystems (for example, prenatal clinics or nursery schools). "The view that the internal dynamics of family life as reflected in the quality of child care and the internal functioning of society's institutions are symbiotic is not fully accepted" (Axinn & Levin, 1979, p. 542). Nevertheless, because of the dramatic increase of violence in families, as well as of other significant family changes, we are led to seek new ways of understanding, explaining, and responding to the issues at hand.

Meyer proposes structuring a developmental model of service delivery consonant with life development and at the same time related to the organized services that are the hallmark of the technologic, urban society. She matches in a transactional field (1) individual developmental age-specific tasks and needs, (2) expectable transitional crises and typical problems, and (3) available institutions providing social services.* This model takes the view that support

---

*For further elaboration of this approach, see the developmental chart in Meyer (1976).

systems are essential to the performance of life tasks for all people and all families. The developmental model focuses on life tasks, not pathology, and is not directly related to explanation of child abuse or specialized programs designed for that population. It is, however, useful in understanding and planning services for abusive parents who are experiencing problems in their child-rearing tasks. Meyer (1976, pp. 182–183) illustrates this approach as follows:

> Assuming that feelings of emotional deprivation, often traced to the oral period, can affect people at vulnerable times of their lives, the clinically oriented practitioner might psychologically "feed" the person through an intensively supportive psychotherapeutic relationship, perhaps aided by chemotherapy. A social worker using an ecosystems perspective would help the person seek out in his life space some source of gratification, no matter how small, to begin with. With the support of the worker, the client could slowly begin to master even infinitesimal life tasks, building a sense of competence through the activity itself. Simultaneously, the worker would attend to environmental supports—would seek someone in the social network, some improvement in the physical quality of life, some environmental response that would reinforce the client's own sense of his worth.

This practice approach is consistent with the ecologic position that support systems must be provided for parents in order to prevent child abuse. This model has a preventive orientation. Its methods engage the client's active involvement in real-life encounters and offer a range of supports in order to provide relief from the pressures of the parenting role as well as educational development opportunities for the parent. "Where the human ecology provides adequate support, child abuse is minimized; where support is inadequate and stress great, the factors cited by Gil are manifested in child abuse" (Garbarino, 1976, p. 178).

Meyer's work, with its developmental focus, contains a universal approach to human beings in the context of the transactions of living. To the extent that abusing families are to be maintained as families, we need to engage their participation in programs of community services that are responsive to their special needs as well as to their developmental life crises: "A renewed sense of respect for the human growth of all individuals within the context of the family (ecosystem) would do more to lower violence and aggression against the young than any number of social agencies which can become involved only after the process of family breakdown has progressed almost past the point of irremediable damage" (Besharov, 1975, p. 3). Meyer's conceptualization of service design and organization in an ecosystem model involves significant shifts in fundamental ways of thinking and behaving. She has begun evaluation of the constant changes in the broader environment and the effects of these changes on the types and quality of transactions that need to occur between service organizations and the people who use them. History and traditional attitudes about individual responsibility continue to affect the structure of service provision in this country, and these outmoded attitudes and approaches undermine parenting. Our public policy development is more often aligned with economic values and the interests of business than with the needs of humans performing their life tasks: "Several European countries have explicit family policies in which the well-being of families with young children is a criterion by which all policy development is assessed" (Kahn & Kamerman, 1977, p. 86). Our values, beliefs and public policies are as nostalgic as our image of family life, centering around the ideal of the nuclear family with an employed male head and a housewife mother caring for the children, despite the fact that at least 46 percent of all women now are in the labor force (Kahn & Kamerman, 1977).

Working mothers no longer come only from the ranks of the poor, and self-actualization needs as well as survival needs are motivating forces. The number of children whose mothers work is increasing at a phenomenal rate. Approximately 6.5 million children younger than 6 and 18 million children between 6 and 14 years of age have working mothers (Authier, 1979, p. 502). Yet publicly supported day-care services are still not available to families of all income levels as a means of improving the quality of care.*

In a recent study of American families (Yankelovich, et al., 1977), a "new breed" of parents was identified; it tended to be more affluent, better educated, more self-oriented, more "now"-oriented, and its members tended to be firm believers in equal rights of children and parents. This new breed, according to the authors, represents 43 percent of all fathers and mothers of children under 13 years of age. These parents, compared to the 57 percent of "traditionalists," have been affected by changing viewpoints in our society, and a clear majority of both groups felt parents should have lives of their own even if less time were available for their children.† While one may not infer cause-and-effect relationships from these observed changes in family behavior and attitudes, an ecologic explanation is strongly supported. The contributing factors are many and have occurred through varied human activities directed at modification of the environment over a period of years. The rapid changes being observed in family structure, ideology, and life-styles may be the result of man's environmental modifications and of the growth process reaching a threshold. Whether these changes will enhance

---

*For further discussion of the organization of child-abuse and child-welfare services in the United States and in an international comparison, see Kamerman and Kahn (1976, Chap. 3); Kahn and Kamerman (1977). In the latter the concept of universalism of social services is considered from the point of view of strengthening rather than undermining family life and parenting.

†See the special issue on family policy, *Social Work*, 1979, 24, for a variety of viewpoints on changes in family ecology and public policy concerns.

family adaptiveness in today's world or lead to increases in family violence is not clear. What does seem clear is that they will result in further modification of the environment and, in an open systems mode, further affect the total family ecosystem. Viewing these changes in the family as faulty solutions to social stress or as the result of personality characteristics of a new breed is to miss the point.

We are not talking about a few deviant families or even of families locked in poverty. We are observing a distinct trend toward new family forms and patterns that require new and different responses from the environment, i.e., new and different patterns of relationship and transactions within the ecology of which they are a part. In the face of such rapidly changing family conditions, the professions and public policy makers need to rethink and reshape the supportive features of the ecology to enhance family functioning. The emerging ecologic models represent such a theoretical thrust.

Pincus and Minahan (1973) have probably constructed the most complete model for practice that is consonant with the ecologic perspective. The model uses a general systems approach in the organization of its elements and, as such, allows for the integration of a number of theoretical orientations within the overall framework.

In this model, problems are viewed as attributes of the interaction of the elements in the social situation that are frustrating or blocking the performance of life tasks. The interdependence of people and resource systems is acknowledged. The kinds of resource systems with which people have relationships in their ecosystems are organized into three categories: (1) natural resource systems, consisting of family, friends, neighbors, co-workers and the like; (2) formal resource systems, such as membership organizations, formal associations, labor unions, welfare rights groups, tenants' unions, etc.; and (3) societal resource systems, which include schools, hospitals, day-care centers, employment places, social-service agencies, housing authorities, social security programs, and the like. Further, the model entails looking at three related aspects of social situations to make assessments and to plan goals and action strategies: (1) the life tasks that people confront and the resources and conditions that would facilitate their coping with these tasks; (2) the interactions between people and their resource systems as well as the interactions within and among resource systems (natural, formal, or societal);* and (3) the relationships between the private troubles of people and the public issues that bear on them.

A reexamination of the case of the S. family presented earlier in this chapter will illustrate how this framework may be used to conceptualize

---

*Cohn (1979) in her national evaluation of treatment services in programs for child abuse, found that lay or parent-aide counseling and/or Parents Anonymous were the most successful interventive approaches observed. These services are alternative forms of natural resource systems.

problems, formulate objectives, and enlarge the arena from which help may be drawn. The presenting situation is the same. The reader may recall that the worker found, on arrival, an anxious and upset family group. The children were hungry, dirty, and bruised from the punishment meted out by the mother. The home was filthy, the electricity was shut off, and the plumbing clogged up. The family system was completely overwhelmed in its inability to satisfy its most fundamental needs. The withdrawal of resources by the welfare system had weakened the mother's ability to perform her parenting tasks. Not only had the exercise of a restrictive policy severed the lifeline between this family and the source of its funds for food, shelter, clothing, and medical care, thereby presenting a major threat to survival, but the withdrawal of the relationship had also heightened feelings of abandonment and loss. The interlocking crises severed or strained all the meaningful relationships and support systems in this family's ecosystem. The mother, caught in the crosswinds, lashed out at her hungry children. Her adaptive functions overtaxed, she had no one to turn to. She not only felt powerless, she was indeed powerless and consumed by fear and anger. Her call for help was sent in the form of a threat of violence.

> [Our] helping institutions have begun to carry out a coercive function beneath a genuinely charitable intent. Our national welfare system has become notorious for legislation whose covert policy seems designed to break up or weaken poor families and place their members into self-perpetuating cycles of helplessness (Pincus & Minahan, 1973, p. 313).

From the perspective of the Pincus and Minahan model, the S. family's problems are viewed as arising from, and being maintained in, the interacting elements that are blocking this family's effective transactions with its crucial support systems. Using this model, the helping focus would be on the reestablishment of vital relationships between this family and its resource systems (societal and natural). The transactions with the welfare system would have to be disentangled. The protection worker would act as an advocate to secure an immediate response to meet basic needs for food and shelter and then participate in the negotiations on the issues that have disrupted the support line. The emotional, practical, and personal help of the grandmother would need to be elicited by reengaging her in a mutual support mode as opposed to requiring her to drain her already scarce financial resources. Information and linkage to other societal resource systems for housing and social-support services would also be required. No family, however intact its members' psychologic domain may be, can manage significant life tasks without minimum essentials. This family had retreated into behavior approximating a closed system, cut off from supportive and energizing exchanges with the environment. From a systems perspective, the case demonstrates how one disruptive event can set in motion a series of other events that, in interaction, can lead to violence or disintegration. The core caring qualities of the parent-child unit may be revitalized through a similar supportive process. Mrs. S. needed opportunities to engage in goal planning for herself and her family with support that would allow her to gain a sense of parental competence, as well as a measure of control over her personal life choices. Focusing on the mother's personality traits, her control mechanisms, and the deviance from child-care norms in the context of the present situation would serve no helpful function. Such an approach would only stimulate the regression forces already at play and lead to the family's being segmented and separated*:

> On the contrary, this approach [ecosystems] is predicated on the belief that individual problems in social functioning are to varying degrees both cause and effect. It rejects the notion that individuals are afflicted with social pathologies, holding rather that the same social environment that generates conformity, makes payment by the deviance that emerges (Pincus & Minahan, 1973, p. 299).

For a start, there must be support from the environment in the form of concrete resources and encouragement of new life skills at a rather basic level. The resolution of one aspect of the life problem could have a positive synergistic effect that reenergizes coping capacities and begins to restore a balance of necessary relationships.

The ecologic model has as its concern the maintenance of life-support systems to enhance the adaptive qualities of individuals and families and to promote their coping capacities, growth and development as they perform their life tasks and pursue their personal aspirations. The model provides insights that permit a focus on people and milieux simultaneously. Family life in our highly technologic system is characterized by an extreme degree of interdependence of individuals, groups, organizations, and social institutions. National policy, the organization of societal-resource systems, and the reinforcement of natural support systems are requisite to effective parenting. Child abuse, in this context, is viewed as a disruption of this mutuality and an absence or distortion in the essential support systems of the family ecology.

Ehrlich et al., (1973) commented on humanity's overreliance on technology to solve environmental problems and observed that the technologies required

---

*The actual case from which this material was abstracted has been abbreviated and disguised for confidentiality and space purposes. In the actual situation, the children were removed, neglect adjudicated, and the children remanded to the public agency for foster care. The mother subsequently became enraged in a struggle to get her children back, removed one without permission, and was charged with kidnapping and required to go for psychiatric care.

to deal with the disruption may themselves bring further damage or shift the impact to new problem sources. The same observations may be made about some of the social institutions and organizations designed to deal with family problems: services that segment families, then place children and leave them in limbo; that adjudicate but offer no lifelines to permit correction of the "offense"; and on and on.

It is a paradox not only that the family institution that represents the touchstone of emotional nurturance can become destructive of its own dependent members, but also that our public policy, our social institutions and organizations, and our social sanctions and artifacts can contribute to the emergence of destructive violence in the family context. The ecologic systems perspective has the potential for examining these interrelationships simultaneously, and for directing our attention to altering public policy, social institutions, and professional practice so that they may be more supportive of human development in our national life space.

SUMMARY

Table 16.1 summarizes the salient features of each of the major theories developed to date to explain child abuse. We do not, as yet, have a comprehensive theory that has stood the test of empirical verification. However, the historical and conceptual stage is set for more effective use of what is known in serving abusing families and in attending to the tasks of preventing the escalation of violence.

The emerging ecologic-systems model appears to provide the framework through which we may use what has already been learned. The dynamics of abuse from the psychologic model present us with descriptive concepts for behaviors, often observed in abusive families, which may be pursued through research efforts. Helfer, in the socialization model, has isolated interacting variables presumed to impact on transactions within the socialization process, and Justice and Justice have examined the "cultural scripting" that occurs in the communication patterns and interaction of abusive parents and serves to maintain the destructive symbiotic relationship. Such interactions and transactions affect exchanges with the family ecosystem, and further study of those interactions that reinforce abuse would appear to be fruitful. The theorists of the environmental model have identified salient environmental forces that stress the family and overwhelm its social functioning. These guides are useful in the examination of the human ecology. The clinical/psychologic, the sociologic/environmental and the socialization/ social learning models, if viewed separately, fail to explain child abuse satisfactorily. However, all contribute valuable insights.

TABLE 16.1
Theoretical Models of Child Abuse

	CLINICAL/ PSYCHOLOGIC MODEL	SOCIOLOGIC/ ENVIRONMENTAL MODEL	SOCIALIZATION/ SOCIAL LEARNING MODEL	ECOLOGIC/ SYSTEMS MODEL
View of problem	Psychologically induced dynamics and personality traits that precipitate abuse	Socially induced stress, frustration, and aggression that precipitate abuse	Learned deviant child-rearing behavior that incorporates abuse	Dysfunctional interactional patterns among family members and with their resource systems that have abusive outcomes
Explanatory variables	Internally induced stress Individual deficiency	Situationally induced stress Resource deficiency	Learned, disordered behavior Role-model deficiency	Support-system deficiency Network deficiency
Unit of attention	Personality structure, character traits, or dynamics of abuse	Environmental stress factors and societal sanctions of violence	Habits of learning cultural sanctions, child-rearing patterns	Interactional patterns, support system, network Ecosystem transactions
Unit of change	Parents	Parent/environment	Parent/child	Family ecosystem
Knowledge base	Dynamic psychiatry systems of psychotherapy Psychoanalytic theory	Frustration-aggression theory Environmental stress theories	Learning theory Socialization theory	Systems theory Ecosystem theory

The ecologic-systems model may provide the framework by which the strengths of all these theories may be used in bringing improvement to the job at hand. To paraphrase Ehrlich et al. (1973, p. 221), it is time to stop quibbling about which factor in the human predicament is most important. They are all important. Failure to come to grips with factors that sustain human life-support systems (namely, the family) will surely sabotage the future. Child abuse may well be significantly reduced as we emphasize the alignment of the transactional processes of organizations, delivery systems, and public policies supportive of a human ecology that sustains family life and positive parent-child relations.

REFERENCES

Alfaro, J. *Report on the Relationship between Child Abuse and Neglect and Later Socially Deviant Behavior*. New York: Issued by the New York State Assembly Select Committee on Child Abuse, March, 1978.

American Humane Association. *National Analysis of Official Child Neglect and Abuse Reporting*. Englewood, Colo.: The Association, 1978.

Authier, K. Defining the care in child care. *Social Work*, 1979, 24, 500–505.

Axinn, J., & Levin, H. The family life cycle and economic security. *Social Work*, 1979, 24, 540–546.

Bakan, D. *Slaughter of the Innocents: A study of the battered child phenomenon*. San Francisco: Jossey-Bass, 1971.

Besharov, D.J. Building a community response to child abuse and maltreatment. *Children Today*, DHEW Publication No. (OHD) 76-30084 (1-6) September–October, 1975, Vol. 4.

Bettleheim, B. Individual and mass behavior in extreme situations. *Journal of Abnormal and Social Psychology*, 1943, 38, 417–452.

Bowen, M. Family therapy and family group therapy. In Kaplan H. and Sadock B. (eds.), *Comprehensive Group Psychiatry*. Baltimore: William & Wilkins, 1971.

Bronfenbrenner, U. The origins of alienation. *Scientific American*, 1974, 231, 53–61.

Bronfenbrenner, U. The disturbing changes in the American family. *Search*, Vol. 2, No. 1. Albany: State University of New York, fall 1975, 4–10.

Caplan, G. *Concepts of Mental Health Consultation*, Publ. No. 373. Washington, D.C.: U. S. Department of Health, Education and Welfare, Children's Bureau, 1959.

Cohn, A.H. Effective treatment of child abuse and neglect. *Social Work*, 1979, 24, 513–519.

Daughtry, C., Tapp, J., Wegenast, D., & Wijnberg, M. *A Self Instruction Booklet for Assessment of Child Abuse Potential*. Buffalo: State University College at Buffalo, 1975.

DeFrancis, V. *Child Abuse: Preview of a Nationwide Survey*. Denver: The American Humane Association, 1963.

Delsordo, J.D. Protective casework for abused children. *Children*, 1963, 10, 213–218.

Ehrlich, P., Ehrlich, A., & Holdren, J. *Human Ecology: Problems and Solutions*. San Francisco: Freeman, 1973.

Elmer, E., & Gregg, G.S. Developmental characteristics of abused children. *Pediatrics*, 1967, 40, 596–602.

Fontana, V. *Somewhere a Child is Crying: Maltreatment—Causes and Prevention*. New York: Macmillan, 1973.

Galdston, R. Dysfunctions of parenting: The battered child, the neglected child, the exploited child. In Howells, J. (ed.), *Modern Perspectives of International Child Psychiatry.* Edinburgh: Oliver and Boyd; New York: Brunner/Mazel, 1968. Reprinted in Ambrose, B. (ed.) *Child Abuse and Neglect,* Social Services Reader I. Albany: State University of New York, 1976, 45–54.

Garbarino, J. A preliminary study of some ecological correlates of child abuse: The impact of socioeconomic stress on mothers. *Child Development,* 1976, 47, 178–185.

Gelles, R. Child abuse as psychopathology: A sociological critique and reformulation. *American Journal of Orthopsychiatry,* 1973, 43, 611–621.

Gerbner, G. *Violence in Television Drama: A Study of Trends and Symbolic Functions.* Philadelphia: University of Pennsylvania, Annenberg School of Communications, 1970.

Germain, C. An ecological perspective in casework practice. *Social Casework,* 1973, 54, 323–330.

Gil, D. Unraveling child abuse. *American Journal of Orthopsychiatry,* 1975, 45, 352–355.

Gil, D. *Violence against Children.* Cambridge, Mass.: Harvard University Press, 1970.

Gilbert, N., & Specht, H. *Dimensions of Social Welfare Policy.* Englewood Cliffs, N.J.: Prentice-Hall, 1974.

Giovannoni, J., & Billingsley, A. Child neglect among the poor: A study of parental adequacy in families of three ethnic groups. *Child Welfare,* 1970, 49, 196–204.

Helfer, R.E. *The Diagnostic Process and Treatment Programs,* DHEW Publ. No. (OHD) 76-30069. Washington, D.C.: U.S. Department of Health, Education and Welfare, 1976.

Hill, R.B. *The Strengths of Black Families.* New York: Emerson Hall, 1972.

Holmes, S., Barnhart, C., & Cantoni, L. Working with the parent in child abuse cases. *Social Casework,* 1975, 56, 3–12.

Justice, B., & Justice, R. *The Abusing Family.* New York: Human Sciences Press, 1976.

Kahn, A., & Kamerman, S. *Social Services in International Perspective,* (SRS) 76-05704. Washington, D.C.: U.S. Department of Health, Education and Welfare, 1977.

Kamerman, S., & Kahn, A. *Social Services in the United States.* Philadelphia: Temple University Press, 1976.

Kaufman, I. Psychiatric implications of physical abuse of children. *Protecting the Battered Child.* Denver: American Humane Association, 1962.

Kempe, C.H., Silverman, F. & Steele, B. The Battered child syndrome. *Journal of the American Medical Association,* 1962, 181, 17–24.

Kempe, C.H., & Helfer, R. *Helping the Battered Child and His Family.* Philadelphia: Lippincott, 1972.

Kent, J. T. As reported in the *1978 Annual Review of Child Abuse and Neglect Research,* DHEW Publ. No. (OHDS) 79-30168. Washington, D.C.: U.S. Department of Health, Education and Welfare, September, 1978.

Martin, H.P. The child and his development. In Kempe, C.H., & Helfer, R. (eds.), *Helping the Battered Child and His Family.* Philadelphia: Lippincott, 1972.

Mead, M. *Culture and Commitment.* New York: Natural History Press, 1970.

Merrill, E.J. Physical abuse of children: An agency study. In DeFrancis, V. (ed.), *Protecting the Battered Child.* Denver, Englewood, Colo.: American Humane Association, 1962, 1–16.

Meyer, C. *Social Work Practice: The Changing Landscape.* New York: The Free Press, 1976.

Morse, C.W., Sahler, O.Z., & Friedman, S.B. A three year follow-up study of child abuse and neglect. *American Journal of Diseases of Children,* 1970, 120, 439–446.

Newberger, E. The myth of the battered child syndrome. *Current Medical Dialogue,* 1973, 40, 327–334.

Pincus, A., & Minahan, A. *Social Work Practice: Model and Method.* Itasca, Ill.: Peacock, 1973.

Polansky, N., Hally, C., & Polansky, N. *Profile of Neglect.* Washington, D.C.: U.S. Department of Health, Education and Welfare, Social and Rehabilitation Service, Community Services Administration, 1975.

Sherman, E. Historical and characterological aspects of child abuse and neglect. *Social Services Reader I.* Albany: State University of New York at Albany, 1976.

Silver, L. Does violence breed violence? Study of the child abuse syndrome. *American Journal of Psychiatry,* 1969, 126, 404–407.

Steele, B. & Pollock, C., A therapeutic approach to the parents. In Kempe, C.H. & Helfer, R.E. (eds.), *Helping the Battered Child and His Family.* Philadelphia: Lippincott, 1972, 3–21.

Steinmetz, S.K., & Straus, M.A. *Violence in the Family.* New York: Dodd and Mead, 1975.

U.S. Department of Health, Education and Welfare, Office of Human Development Services. *Model Child Protection Act with Commentary.* Washington, D.C.: Government Printing Office, 1977.

Wasserman, S. The abused parent of the abused child. *Children,* 1967, 14, 175–179.

Yankelovich, Skelly, and White. *The General Mills American Family Report 1976–77: Raising Children in a Changing Society.* Minneapolis: Yankelovich, Skelly and White, 1977, 27–32. Reprinted in *Human Ecology Forum,* 1977, 8, 10–11.

Young, L. *Wednesday's Children: A study of Child Neglect and Abuse.* New York: McGraw-Hill, 1974.

Zalba, S. The abused child: II. A typology for classification and treatment. *Social Work,* 1967, 12, 70–79.

17

Divorce and the Children

Joy Feldman

Parental divorce represents one of the most common family crises in contemporary America. While for divorcing adults the dissolution of the marriage may be seen as having certain positive aspects, for the children in the family, vulnerable in their developmental immaturity, it is likely to be perceived as portending calamity. Feldman emphasizes that during this period of disorganization, parents, entangled in their mutual difficulties, may have little energy available for recognizing and dealing with the distress of their bewildered and fearful children. Professionals, too, may tend to become caught up in dealing with the parents' upset without fully recognizing the impact of the experience on the children. Feldman addresses the complexities of the cognitive and emotional responses of children at varying developmental levels and provides recommendations for timely family intervention.

Over the past 25 years there has been on ongoing rise in the national divorce rate. Between 1968 and 1971 the national marriage rate stabilized, and since 1972 it has been tending toward decline. In 1976 there were 2,133,000 marriages and 1,077,000 divorces, approximately one divorce for every two marriages, and an average of 1.08 children involved in each divorce (Bloom, Asher, & White, 1978, p. 867).

Thus, in 1976 alone, more than 2 million adults and 1 million children were personally involved in legal dissolution of their nuclear families. The numbers are impressive and underscore the social reality of divorce. By sheer statistical prevalence, a subgroup has evolved in our culture whose members have in common their deviation from the traditional two-parent nuclear family and its associated life-style.

The process by which individuals join the ranks of those with altered family structure is of concern to the mental-health profession. The stress of the emotional upheaval and disruption created by divorce is a familiar clinical phenomenon that has gained increasing attention in the professional literature and through the communications media with important implications for children as well as adults.* Yet the examination of parental divorce as a critical factor in child development has just begun.

By its very nature, divorce places both the separating couple and their children at risk. It is an announcement of the death of a marital relationship, and that announcement carries with it personal significance and consequences for each member of the family. Divorce necessitates a division of property, a change in economic functioning, a change in life-style, and changes in the relationships around, within, and throughout the family. It may be regarded as a crisis, for the changes set into motion by the decision are at once fundamental and far-reaching, and they are likely to create stress that cannot be handled by the family's customary coping patterns.

For the children, the family system as they have known it represents survival itself. The security provided by the wholeness of the family, the child's powerful attachments to both parents, and the comfort derived from the predictability of life in this familiar context far outweighs the painful and often disruptive atmosphere created by marital discord. Psychoanalyst James Anthony (1974, p. 467) has commented that "the final act of disruption, even in the worst marriages, can tax [the child's] coping capacities to their limit," for "however prepared, [the child] is never ready for and is rarely able to accept [the divorce]." This does not imply that divorce per se is destructive or pathogenic to the child involved. Intrinsic in the progression and resolution of such a crisis is the potential for growth and enhanced maturity as much as the potential for regression and dysfunctional adjustment. The growing number of children affected by parental divorce strongly suggests a need for careful evaluation of the risk factors involved. We do not know, for instance, which children seem most clearly to suffer regression and poor adjustment. We do not know what the long-term effects of the experience are, other than to note that statistics indicate that children of divorced parents are themselves likely to terminate marriages by divorce.

The picture is a complicated one. On the one hand, the increasing incidence of one-parent families tends to diminish the stigma with which these children have to live. On the other hand, the mere knowledge that this life circumstance is shared cannot be expected to compensate for the multidimensional losses imposed upon a child whose parents divorce. Further, there is a perplexing range of vulnerability to stress among individuals and throughout the life span. This, in interaction with the myriad variations in parenting styles,

---

*For example, an entire issue of the *Journal of Social Issues* was devoted to this subject. See *Journal of Social Issues*, Vol. 35, No. 4, fall 1979.

communication, expectations, values, and roles among families, makes it unproductive to think in terms of simplistic causal explanations.

A systematic investigation into the effects of parental divorce on children was initiated in 1971 by Wallerstein and Kelly in Marin County, California. Their ongoing work is of particular interest for several reasons: the subjects, judged by their parents to be developing normally, are derived from the normal population and have no history of contact with mental-health professionals. The study investigates 161 children ranging in age from 2½ to 18 years of age and is an in-depth look at both children and parents at two points in their family experience: soon after the parental separation, and 1 year later. The research seeks to sort out the responses of children to family restructuring at various age levels, to identify high-risk factors, and ultimately to develop clinical-intervention strategies specific to divorcing and post-divorce families (Kelly and Wallerstein, 1976).

In 1968 McDermott published a report of an observational study of the impact of parental divorce on preschool children, deriving his data from nursery school contact with 16 children, aged 3 to 5. While the studies by Wallerstein and Kelly and McDermott do not compare in depth or breadth, their findings are both harmonious and sobering. Clearly, the family disruption does evoke crisis responses in the children throughout the ages examined. Kelly and Wallerstein (1976, p. 32) have found the nature of the divorce process as opposed to the actual event of the divorce itself to be the critical factor influencing outcome. Most disquieting was their finding that approximately half the children they studied from early childhood to later latency demonstrated difficulties consequent to the divorce and/or significant psychologic deterioration by the time of the 1-year follow-up.

The implications for clinical practice are enormous. From the standpoint of primary prevention, we have before us a population with a core of common problems, responses, and needs that identifies them as a group at risk. These children are being confronted in their formative years with a situational crisis that may thwart their adjustment and progress to healthy and satisfying adulthood. Being mindful that the median duration of marriages ending in divorce is 6.5 years, the majority of children affected are under and within school age (National Center for Health Statistics, 1977; Bloom, Asher, & White, 1978, p. 868). This chapter seeks to examine the capacities and age-engendered vulnerabilities that come into play as the family system undergoes the process and aftermath of divorce. It will explore the affective, cognitive, and social dimensions of the child from preschool through the juvenile years in an attempt to bring into focus a developmental understanding, on the basis of which strategies can readily be formulated for intervention into the crisis and later adjustment. Practical considerations will be discussed for helping both the divorced parent(s) and child. There are indeed measures that can be taken to facilitate an improved resolution of the child's difficulties and to enhance the functioning of the altered family system. In so doing, not only is the child's current life experience likely to be enriched, but also an investment is made in the development of healthy parents for the future.

THE PRESCHOOL CHILD

The years from infancy to school age are dynamic and formative ones marked by rapid development from total dependency through active exploration and diligent efforts at gaining mastery over everyone and everything in the environment. Intellectually, the child operates by what Piaget has termed "egocentrism," meaning that everything is interpreted by the child in terms of his or her own experience and activity, and the child has not yet learned to differentiate him- or herself from others (Piaget & Inhelder, 1969, p. 13; Kessler, 1966, p. 31; Ginsberg & Opper, 1969, pp. 103–104). The child is unable to imagine the existence of places, property, things, or people not experienced and assumes that his or her notions, feelings, and experiences are simultaneously shared by everyone. Lacking self-perception, the child is unable to imagine or see anything from other than his and her own vantage point. It is clearly impossible for the preschooler to empathize or in any way put him- or herself in the place of another; it is simply beyond the child's cognitive capacities. His or her understanding of adult behavior, therefore, is richly laden with personal inferences. It does not occur to the child that his or her parents have needs or any mission in life separate from relating to and caring for their child. Thus, parental preoccupations, forgotten promises, or any unusual absences are interpreted as punitive or hostile. Prolonged absence, such as may occur following marital separation and even if resultant from hospitalization or death, is perceived as abandonment (Goldstein, Freud, & Solnit, 1973, p. 12). Any such disappointment perpetrated by adult behavior is unconsciously assumed by the child to be a deliberate response to the child's "badness." The greater the loss, the more intense the rebuke and the consequent need for defense against acknowledging it.

While much of the child's experience and environment defies his or her understanding, the child nonetheless attempts valiantly to assimilate the complexities of reality. The child's conscious processes are filled with non sequiturs, contradictions, and magic; explanations of how unfamiliar things work are adaptations of the child's limited understanding of the familiar, and the child's attention span is short.

Magic pervades the child's thinking, filling in the gaps of understanding and compensating for the child's smallness and realistic limitations. With it the child imbues him- or herself with wondrous power derived in part, no doubt, from the obvious impact of his or her needs, words, and actions on both parents and surroundings. Inherent in these processes is the belief that the child's thought or wish is tantamount to the deed. In the child's limited experience, this has frequently held true. The gradual yet dashing disappointment in learning that his or her wishes do not always come true brings with it reassurance, inasmuch as many of the child's feelings are ambivalent, some wishes are hostile, and most of them are everchanging.

The preschool child experiences time as protracted and slow-moving. From "now" until suppertime is a very long time to wait for Daddy to come home, for example, as every need felt is accompanied by a sense of immediacy (Goldstein, Freud, & Solnit, 1973, p. 40). Compounding the child's relative urgency for gratification is his or her inability to anticipate the future. Future time and circumstances not yet experienced are abstractions too complex for his comprehension. Assurances of gratification to come, therefore, are of little value to the child and can placate only insofar as the adult dealing with the child is trusted and conveys confident patience. Similarly, the preschooler is unable to anticipate loss. If the child is led, for example, to talk about the imminent departure of a parent, the talking will be done with enviable equanimity. Continued discussion, however, will reveal that the child has no idea that the departure will create changes in that person's availability and relationship to him or her. The child knows life only in terms of the present.

The foundation of the preschooler's security is his or her parents: their care, "omnipotence," and "omniscience." The child is certain that despite his or her own insecurities in the face of the unknown, there are no unknown or unmastered elements in the parents' lives. It is reasonable, for example, to ask of a parent in a crowded public place, "Who is that standing there?"— fully expecting to be given a name and brief biographical sketch. It seems reasonable to the child that since we make our rooms warm or cool and light or dark and have the ability to make radios, televisions, and other mysterious objects perform, we certainly ought to be able to stop the rain, turn on the sun, or take him or her to see Grandpa, who is 2000 miles away, right now. It is impossible for the child to imagine a problem that parents cannot resolve. The child's greatest and usually unnamed fear is that of being abandoned, for parents represent survival itself.

The Preschooler's Experience of Parental Separation

When marital discord erupts between the preschooler's parents, he or she is quite likely to assume responsibility for it since all things are assumed to be a consequence of the child's needs, thoughts, wishes, or deeds. As the child's identity is continuous with his or her parents', so the child's sense of well-being is dependent upon the parents' comfort and harmony. Parental anxiety and tension are readily perceived and threaten the child's sense of security in vague, inexpressible ways. Frightening and uncontrollable elements of life universally lurk in the recesses of the preschooler's mind and take on concretized form as monsters, lions, goblins, tigers, and carnivorous vacuum cleaners. Such fantasies are particularly stimulated when anxiety levels rise in the parents and subsequently in the child. For if the parents are upset, their omnipotence is called into question. If the parents are angry—and presumably the child's actions or thoughts caused it—if the parents are fighting—and his or her identity is not separate from theirs—the child is obviously in the thick of the fray, vulnerable, guilty, and a target for anger.

This is the preschooler's situation as his or her parents separate and divorce. The crisis in the family constitutes crisis for the child, whose world is virtually crumbling. If one parent has left the child, what then will prevent the other from leaving as well? The child's very survival is in question. His or her preexisting dependency is heightened as life (schedules, significant others, and relationships) becomes less predictable. Concurrently, his or her parents are involved in their own crisis and less able to perceive the child's needs while being quite unable to understand the child's involvement.

Defense mechanisms are mustered by all family members in response to the personal meanings of the strife and change. Additionally, the remaining parent's emotional state impacts upon and reflects itself in the child. Foremost in the child's experience is loss: seeming abandonment. The child is unable to understand or deal with the loss through other than denial and/or regressive behavior (McDermott, 1968, p. 1426; Wallerstein & Kelly, 1975, p. 602). It is not difficult, then, to understand the frequency with which mothers report that their preschooler has not asked questions about the father's absence or that the child appears to be acting the same as always.* The parent may assume this means that the child is unaware or undisturbed by the change. Usually the parents fail to inform the child's nursery school teachers of marital disruption, apparently not suspecting that tell-tale changes in the child have already emerged there (McDermott, 1968, p. 1430).

The child's loss, if not total, is at least qualitative. One of the parents is not home with the child as before and devotes considerably less time to the relationship than previously. One half of the child's foundation for security is physically removed from the home, and with it, the regularity and predictability of that contact is lost.

The stress of the separation experience is compounded by the emotional response of the removed parent. Most often this is characterized by anger, depression, and grief resulting from the extensive loss the divorce creates for him. Fathers frequently report the difficulty they have in pursuing relationships with their children inasmuch as this necessitates contact with the ex-

---

*As child custody is awarded to the mother in an overwhelming number of divorce cases, particularly when young children are involved, the noncustodial parent is referred to here, for convenience, as the father.

spouse, as well as working out a diluted, time-specific fraction of the former relationship with the child (Greif, 1979, pp. 316–317). This working-through process requires the adult to recognize and deal with both the attachment and the relative loss that has occurred. He will be confronted by variability in the child's responses to his visits as the ebb and flow of both parties' needs and defenses cloud their communications. Negotiating this post-separation relationship is a difficult task requiring emotional energy and strength from the parent at a time when his resources are most likely to be depleted.* Many fathers, for purposes of their own coping, defer or altogether neglect making the effort, thus confirming the child's sense of abandonment (Greif, 1979, p. 317).

Responses of preschool children to marital separation of their parents include shock, disbelief, and anger. As the shock gives way to acceptance, signs of depression become apparent. It is interesting to note that the responses of these children parallel those of the children who have lost their primary caretaking parent as described by Bowlby (1960; 1963), which would seem to indicate that the process is one of childhood mourning.

The observations of this writer, as well as those reported by McDermott, Wallerstein, and Kelly, indicate a variety of age-determined capacities and coping styles for managing this loss. The preschooler's shock and anger are manifested by heightened anxiety, irritability, and aggression. Specific forms include temper tantrums and aggressive or hostile play with peers, increased dependency on caretaking adults for physical contact and approval, and heightened separation anxieties. Play during this time appears to be unsatisfying, unpleasurable, and less imaginative, indicating feelings of great loss and emptiness with underlying themes of helplessness, aimlessness, and searching. Puppetry and doll play often act out the child's perceptions of the drama at home and demonstrate restitutive efforts or sheer denial of the reality of the loss.

Regressive behavior is not uncommon among the preschool group, particularly those under 3 years of age. Intense separation anxieties, fretting, whining, general fearfulness, sleep disturbances, regression in toilet training, and bewilderment over their own aggression or tears are all common to these youngsters as they live through the crisis in their families. The cognitive capacities of children under 3 are simply inadequate to grasp any meaning from the disorder they are experiencing, and general confusion and bewilderment are seen along with the aggressive and regressive behavior they demonstrate. If these children are supported by a consistent and loving caretaking adult, be it the parent or a substitute, they seem to adjust satisfactorily with time. The actual turbulence settles down in a matter of weeks (which to the child, it must be remembered, is a very long time). In the

---

*For further consideration of this subject, see Cassidy (1977, Chap. 5).

absence of consistent and loving care, long-term indications of the trauma experienced are continued neediness in relation to adult contact and approval and overcompliance in behavior and attitude (Wallerstein & Kelly, 1975, p. 615).

Parental divorce during the 3- to 5-year age span impacts on the child in accordance with his or her developmentally determined view of self in relation to others and his or her early superego development. The effect of the event has implications for the child's self-esteem and self-image secondary to his or her assumed responsibility for the parents' difficulties. Indeed, McDermott and Wallerstein and Kelly found the play of children in this age group to demonstrate self-blame and attempts to master threats to their survival as perpetrated by imagined natural disasters. Unlike the younger child who is unable to verbalize concerns, these children voice confusion over the loss of a parent and fear as to its consequences for their own survival. The concept of human ties and relationships concerns 3- to 5-year-olds, and these children are clearly shaken by the apparent uncertainty of their future in the face of ruptured parental ties. While regressive behavior is much less common in this age group than in the youngest preschoolers, they are clearly anxious and irritable and cry easily. Minor provocations, normally taken in stride, may set the 3- to 5-year-old experiencing family crisis off into tears and wails. These characteristic responses are evoked whether the precipitating factor is recent parental separation or revival of custody or visitation battles. One 5-year-old poignantly expressed her worry to me over the custody battle her mother had waged, asking, "Could you please talk to the judge and tell him I should stay here?" When I acknowledged her concern over the import of this for her relationships and future she sighed, "I really worry a lot these days." While her custodial father and stepmother were unaware of her worrying, they reported a sharp change in her flexibility over minor changes in daily activities and were amazed and concerned over the frequent tears and protests from their formerly aggreeable, affable daughter.

Children of 5 and 6 years of age are, in general, better able to absorb the experience of parental separation following their immediate reactions to the loss. They too react with shock, anger, confusion, and outbursts of aggression and sadness but are less troubled with regressive coping mechanisms and seem better able to express their questions and concerns than are their younger counterparts. Undoubtedly, the expanded ability to conceptualize, the greater sense of fledgling autonomy, and the age-connected increase in life outside the home and family contribute to their ability to cope.

Adjustment difficulties stemming from failure to negotiate such a family change healthfully during this era are often related to the "family romance." One parent is gone from the home scene and that has obvious oedipal ramifications for the child who remains there, whatever that child's gender. Boys hold the dubious victory over their rivals, ousted precisely at the time when their identity has begun shifting to the now disfavored role model. How is the boy to proceed in testing assertiveness, masculinity, and his desire to take his father's place? At what cost or with what encouragement from the mother will he evolve his role in the newly modified system?

Wallerstein and Kelly (1975, pp. 609–610) found that girls of this age who do not adjust well frequently respond to the father-loss associated with divorce with strong denial and prolonged efforts, through fantasy and visitation, to sustain the romantic yet frustrating relationship with their part-time fathers. Underlying the massive denial are consuming efforts to ward off the impact of the loss and the associated depression, the manifestations of which include poor peer relations, fear of failure, excessive day-dreaming, and clinging to teachers. Significantly, there is delay in moving on to school-age tasks.

Of utmost importance to the young child's ability to weather the storm of parental divorce is the emotional intactness and strength of the parents, particularly the parent rendering the major portion of the care of the child. A parent absorbed in his or her own grief, anger, humiliation or bitterness has considerably less energy or attention to devote to parenting. Beyond this, the remaining parent may have little inclination to empathize with the child's attachment and positive feelings for the departed parent.

The remaining parent often does have to deal with changes involving living arrangements, economic status, employment pursuits, and altered social and emotional supports. Solutions to matters such as these often evolve slowly and have fundamental impact on the quality of life and availability of emotional energy for parenting.

THE SCHOOL-AGE CHILD

The interaction of factors, including the emergence from the oedipal state, combined with state-mandated schooling and maturational forces, shift the focus of the child's learning away from the family and out of the home. The ensuing years, to age 11 or 12, see a dynamic process in which the child's subjective world becomes decentralized cognitively, socially, and morally (Piaget & Inhelder, 1969, p. 95). His or her position in the family is clearly established in terms of gender identity, birth order, and role, and affords the child security while demanding little of his or her energized attention.

While the social realm of the preschooler is quite simple and restricted to a small group of significant others, the juvenile years, in contrast, are marked by rapid expansion of his or her world's population and boundaries. Horizons are suddenly broadened to include not only knowledge of siblings and parents but of great numbers of peers and a variety of authority-carrying adults and older children. Given fortunate experience up to this time, the child's energy is free for diligent work at gaining a broader notion of who and what he or she is, and an understanding of how the larger world operates. The social expansion confronts the child with the new awareness of variations in authority, rules, custom, expectations of others, and the complexities of personal status in nonfamily groups. This plunge into socialization brings with it the first real opportunity to correct erroneous notions generated by the limited social learning obtained up to this time within the confines of the family. It fosters the juvenile's obtaining quite a different view of him- or herself. The child may, for example, have seen him- or herself as the least capable of the sibling reference group, coincidentally happening to be the youngest; alternatively, the child may have seen him- or herself as the most capable and powerful by virtue of being the oldest, or as the center of adult attention by virtue of being the only child. Becoming one of a large group of matched-aged children, all with family-derived expectations and feelings of significance and self-worth, of necessity alters the child's self-concept.

The school experience requires the child's exposure to nonparental authorities. To them, the child naturally transfers whatever levels of trust, respect, obedience and independence have been developed thus far in relation to parents. The assortment of authority figures encountered subsequently, with their inevitable differences and less personal ties to the child, gives rise to the child's ability to perceive authority as role-based behavior. By the conclusion of the juvenile years, the child will have achieved some grasp of the notion that authority figures, and even parents, are people (Sullivan, 1953, p. 230).

For all the human status they gradually achieve, the parents retain an unquestioned ethical authority from which the child derives the sense of right and wrong, good and bad. They are the role models and cultural models and thereby provide the predictable security and sense of permanence needed to buffer the exponential exposure to variations in ideas and life-styles with which the child is in growing contact.

Parents remain the juvenile's major source of identity and become a conversational topic with peers as comparison and competition introduce themselves into the child's modes of thinking and interacting. "My father's *stronger*"; "My dad knows *all* about that"; "My mom can do that too": These are common themes in exchanges between children of school age as they attempt to enhance their own worth by virtue of their parentage.

Mastery and self-esteem undergo rapid development during these years as the juvenile is increasingly exposed to opportunities to learn and perform, i.e., in the classroom, in the playground, in the neighborhood, in church groups, and in scout and family groups. Each arena provides a laboratory in communication, cognitive and physical skills, social accommodation, and emotional maturation. These are the dimensions that underlie social differentiation as it evolves at this age and that contribute to or diminish the juvenile's sense of worth and self-esteem. They are the criteria that distinguish individuals as being in the group or as outsiders; a social awareness that clearly emerges in the school-age years.

Conceptually, juveniles are still unable to see themselves as others do, and, lacking self-awareness, they are unable to identify or understand most of their feelings. Their inability to empathize undoubtedly underlies the striking insensitivity to the feelings of others characteristic of this age. It is a time of crudeness and cruelty in interpersonal relations, wherein anything that distinguishes a peer as different from the rest is likely to be loudly pointed out with mockery and taunting. Bases for such abuse cover the spectrum of handicaps, from physical disability and disfigurement to social factors, such as being the "new kid around" or having a parent with a stigmatizing feature. It is a painful experience for the child who is targeted, and, if prolonged, it has negative and enduring ramifications for the child's self-esteem and self-image (Sullivan, 1953, pp. 230, 241). This phenomenon is an unfortunate function of the interplay between cognitive limitations and the social need to compete inherent in this stage of development.

Intellectually, the 7- or 8-year-old is in the process of giving up and forgetting the egocentric understanding that brought him or her this far; it is no longer serviceable. The child is working toward a concrete operational understanding of events that can afford him or her the comfort of being able to deduce and predict (Piaget & Inhelder, 1969, p. 113). Development of concrete operations constitutes a great step forward cognitively because it allows greatly expanded understanding of the juvenile's daily reality. Later, adolescence will bring him or her to examining the roles, values, traditions, and mores taught by life in the family. For now, things seem to "make sense" to the juvenile, and what does not is selectively unattended (Sullivan, 1953, p. 223). The child's thinking, in other words, is categorical and rather discrete and absolute; those experiences that validate or fit his or her categories make sense, while those that do not are ignored. Things and people are seen as completely good or completely bad, obviously right or completely wrong, fair or totally unjust. In this cognitive framework, justice becomes a central notion by which the juvenile reviews the expectations and behavior of authority figures toward her- or himself; it is a notion readily applied to those around him or her, and most frequently to parents.

The School-Age Child's Experience
of Parental Separation

When the announcement of parental divorce is made to the school-age child, the inevitable shock and anger emanate from the personal injury it creates. The proposed changes totally exceed the juvenile's understanding. How these two who have created the child and cared for him or her this long, who have sat as the child's teachers and judges, can now tear asunder the unity that defines who and what the child is, is overwhelming and baffling. Long-standing tension, discord, or turbulence in the home prior to the divorce announcement does not prepare the juvenile for the parents' decision to separate. The child's inability to empathize results in his or her experiencing their decision as a personal affront. Understandably, the response to being told of the separation is shock and anger that is not reduced in the least by the child's having lived with the parents' obvious unhappiness. "Why did you wait till I was so old!" and "Why did you have us if you didn't love each other enough to stay married?": such outcries convey the child's perception of life and relationships. Investment in relationships that are changing despite the child's needs, brings pain so poignant as to leave the child feeling that the relationships should never have begun in the first place.

The parents' complete goodness and rightness is transformed in the child's eyes as he or she wonders whether they may be trusted to do right anywhere when they have made such a serious mistake. They suddenly appear shabbily unworthy of the esteem and power vested in them. The child's standard bearers of ethical and behavioral values are at least momentarily divested of their status and a sense of anomie develops. The child's ability to deduce and predict based on past experience is now obsolete, rendering him or her more dependent on the adults in charge when he or she feels least able to count on them. That sense of permanence and predictability that gave the child security to explore and grow in the larger world is gone as family and home are redefined, and the injustices of the current circumstances are enraging and frightening.

In the service of self-defense, the juvenile most often goes into a stance now familiar to clinicians and teachers as the "divorced child syndrome." Parental separation initiates withdrawn and sullen behavior from the child who also shows marked decline in participation at school and in peer activities. Relationships in general are highly suspect to the child now because he or she is fearful and confused about who (and whose) he or she is, what his or her future is, and whom he or she can trust. The child is socially blighted and vulnerable to peer sanctions, and sad and lonely at a level he or she is often unable to share with anyone. Often, academic achievement drops noticeably as the child's ability to concentrate is short-circuited by heightened anxiety. Some, however, find school work to be increasingly gratifying as a manageable focus for their attention at a time when they so desperately need to feel control and mastery. The juvenile's difficulty in making sense of anything that is happening during this period is reflected in a good deal of selective inattention. This, together with the child's withdrawal from relationships, creates a lot of solitary time that many choose to fill with the safe company of their favorite toys, hobbies, or books.

Wallerstein and Kelly (1976) found most of the 7- and 8-year-olds reacted to their parents' separation in a frantic, disorganized manner, while the older

344 / Understanding the Family

school-age children were better focused in their expressions of anger and pain. Undoubtedly, the added experience and cognitive maturity in the older group was of some assistance in the juvenile's ability to pinpoint the source of their pain.

Many juveniles respond with desperate attempts to pull their parents together, whether through obvious efforts at diplomacy or dictatorship or through camouflaged means, including illness and acting out. For example, normally well-behaved youngsters may suddenly begin to shoplift, create disciplinary problems at school, or get involved in petty property damage in the neighborhood. They are finding expression for the diffuse anger they feel while simultaneously crying out for parental cohesion, attention, and control. At this time it seems crucial to the survival of the child's identity during the crisis that he or she neutralize the opposing parents, using whatever means are available. The profoundly stressful situation both within and surrounding the child whose family is reorganizing greatly increases vulnerability to infection, allergies, or chronic illness. Development of sickness in the child may be effective in attracting attention and nurturing care from otherwise preoccupied parents. It can interrupt parental conflict and redirect and unify their energies when all else is lost as common ground. Meanwhile, the child has not willfully placed demands upon the already burdened parents, for the child truly does not wish to do anything but restore peace and acceptance within the family.

Typically, the child's own unidentified feelings of anger, fear and sadness are pushed aside in solicitous deference to parental unhappiness and myriad situational changes. Together, the upset of these two priorities rocks the child's foundations. Even when asked by a parent, the juvenile is usually unable or reluctant to express his or her feelings, responding with uncomfortable replies, e.g., "I don't know." The difficulty lies in the child's lack of insight, the need for parental stability, and sensitivity to their pain. When the inevitable anger is released, it is usually disguised, projected, or displaced in ways and scenarios baffling to the parent.

Few children manage their anxiety in such a way that no aspect of their functioning is disturbed. Eating patterns are commonly disrupted, shifting to either extreme in barometric response to the child's anxiety level. For some, food serves as an available and immediate gratification when all else seems bleak and unsatisfying. For others, food is dangerously symbolic of the relationships that are causing so much pain and is clearly unappealing during anxious times. Sleep is unwelcome for it necessitates giving up control. In the wake of so much uncertainty, any diminution in control carries with it vague and threatening dangers. Once the child is asleep, nightmares signal that anger, pain, and fear are brewing beneath the surface of his or her mind.

After separation is an undeniable reality, the child often resolves the sense of loss by splitting ambivalent identification with and attachment to both parents such that one comes to embody all that is bad, and the other all that is good. The parent who initiated the divorce process is readily seen by the child as the villain, responsible for everyone's loss and pain. On the other hand, the nature of the circumstances and relationships can be such that one parent is seen to have been so unbearable or cruel that the "good" parent had no choice but to seek divorce. While this "taking sides" may have negative consequences in the long run, it affords the child temporary relief from the sense of being "torn in two," or "split down the middle."

The child's overriding need is for the altered system to stabilize. In the service of this, many try to rescue their parents, taking on nurturing, protective, or companionship roles in an attempt to satisfy the needs of the parent. Others adopt role-linked behaviors of the departed parent, attempting to fill the void created by his absence. This often serves the dual purpose of allowing the child to vent inner chaotic and angry feelings—feelings that never would have been expressed in the child's former role. Still other children attempt to be as inconspicuous as possible, fearful of the unpredictable, and fearful that expression of their needs or wishes would only make matters worse.

Ambivalence and loyalty toward both parents compounds the child's difficulties during the adjustment phase following separation. If the juvenile has dichotomized the parents into the "good" and the "bad" one, anger can hardly be expressed straightforwardly toward the "good" one: The child fears being rejected as the "bad" parent was. If favorable feelings are expressed (e.g., a wish to be with or communicate with the other parent), the child risks losing ground with his or her allied parent. If the separated family has succeeded in avoiding adversarial alliances, the child is in less of a strategic quandary, yet there is no less reluctance to say or do anything that could hurt the already unhappy parents. Already having absorbed loss, the child feels vulnerable to dual parental rejection and abandonment. Nothing in his or her developmental armamentarium assures the juvenile that he or she is any more secure in his or her relationship with either parent than was the ex-spouse.

WHEN INTERVENTION IS SOUGHT

The divorced families referred to this writer have uniformly sought assistance for understanding and relieving adjustment problems exhibited by the child. Inasmuch as the child, as a part of the family system, is in mutual and simultaneous interaction with the other elements of the system, it is not surprising that many of these cases have also revealed, upon examination, a variety of familial problems. Those of the child have simply been easier to identify and have been a more acceptable focus for outside help.

While a child may certainly have a problem of adjustment or coping due to greater sensitivity and vulnerability than other family members, he or she may, on the other hand, be manifesting symptoms that serve to maintain the functioning and stability of the family system. When the latter is the case, assessment and intervention into the symptom behavior must address itself to the total family system in order to be effective; this subject is dealt with extensively in the clinical writing and work of family therapists. However, it exceeds the scope and intent of this chapter to deal with symptom-bearing children on this level. Rather, what follows will be focused on the divorced or divorcing family in which the child, by virtue of age, stage of development, role and experience, gives evidence to having difficulty in adjusting to the changes the parents' divorce has created in his or her life.

Approaching the Family

Intervention begins, of course, with a psychosocial data base obtained through interviewing the altered family, and particularly the parent who initiated contact with the mental-health professional. This writer's preference is to meet with the family in their own home because being on familiar territory increases the comfort of family members and makes the nature of the living situation and relationships more readily apparent. During this phase, while the primary intent is identification of problems the child may be having, there must also evolve a rapport between the parent(s), child(ren), and therapist, and the sense of trust prerequisite to allowing an outsider to enter the family system.

In the beginning, it is very helpful to elicit information regarding the evolution of the now split nuclear family: roles, relationships, goals, belief and value systems, the backgrounds of the parents, sources of pain that contributed to the divorce, as well as current problems. It is important to know the circumstances surrounding the advent of children in the marriage. Specifically, was the child planned, wanted, looked forward to, and did conception occur during a period of contentment in the marriage or in response to strife—perhaps for purposes of cementing the threatened relationship? This content may well reveal conflicts, implicit assumptions, or negative messages with which the child is struggling but of which the parent is unaware. Further, it affords a backdrop against which the current behavior, relationships, assets, and problems present a meaningful picture. An assessment of a child cannot be done in isolation from the family system of which he or she is a part. It must take into consideration the past as well as the present circumstances and direction of the family group and its members.

An immediate benefit from this initial phase of contact is the therapeutic experience of being carefully attended to, and being helped to organize and verbalize the family's history and current functioning. This provides a degree of clarification and perspective from which problem solving can proceed in the developing relationship between the therapist and family.

Working with the Parent*

Common parental concerns that readily emerge include bewilderment over the child's behavior and affective states, anger at the other parent for whatever his perceived participation has been, guilt with associated low self-esteem over the parent's own sense of failure, and often a sense of helplessness with regard to relieving the child's anger, sadness, or anxiety. Questions foremost in the parent's mind include "What have I done wrong?" and "What can I do to help this child?" (or "What can *you* do?"). Parental explanations attempt to convey awareness of the child's needs and their attempts to accommodate them, as well as presenting the realistic constraints and barriers to resolution by the parent.

Parental self-esteem and vulnerability become issues as assessment and intervention proceed. The very personal, emotionally loaded nature of sharing one's problems and assumed shortcomings with a mental-health professional, while focusing on the child who is bearing symptoms, underscores the parent's sense of failure. This undoubtedly underlies my finding that in the early stages of relationships with such parents at least some of the sought-after data are withheld, denied, or "purified." Acknowledgment and support of the parents' positive efforts, feelings, and intentions assist both the parent and the therapist to proceed in exploration of the family's problem or problems.

In working with parents, I have found their concerns and questions over a child's behavior to be best answered with information couched in terms of support and encouragement. Specifically, this takes the form of conveying understanding of the child's view of him- or herself and the world, as presented in the preceding sections. It is useful for the parent to understand the child's age-related limitations in cognitive understanding and communication. Most adults are unaware of childrens' sensitivity to loss or their need to mourn and work through associated feelings. Understandably, such a parent misinterprets the disguised age-appropriate expressions of the child's feelings and needs, expecting that reassurances that deny any problems will settle whatever prompted each round of tears or fears. Helping the parent to translate the child's expressions in terms of his or her recent loss, followed by concrete suggestions for how to deal with the child when these occur, are

---

*In my experience, the custodial parent is the one who seeks help for the child, and since custody is most often awarded to the mother, for expedience, the parent will be identified in this section as the mother.

most helpful. It is reassuring to the parent to learn that any time one incorrectly interprets the child's behavior to the child, it is like water off a duck's back, whereas to do so correctly may result in a wondrous breakthrough for the child. Information of this sort serves to reduce or eliminate the parent's sense of bafflement and helplessness over what had seemed incomprehensible child behavior and also tends to promote a greater regard for the child as a sentient person who does indeed "make sense" and can be understood and worked with.

It is not uncommon for a parent to have asked for help for her child when it is in fact the parent who is feeling tenuous in her ability to cope, and the child is the challenging variable, the activator, or the uncontrolled element that keeps equilibrium and a strong "foothold" just out of reach. Under these circumstances, assistance from an outside source might be expected to help stabilize the situation and benefit both child and parent. When this is the case, splitting the therapeutic visit to devote time individually to the child and then the parent is very useful in providing support for the parent, and concomitantly it defuses the child's demands for attention. It has been remarkable to me that once the child has been closely attended to, as will be described later, he or she is usually able to separate from the parent and other adults and go off to play, apparently contentedly, on his or her own. This allows the parent to have the balance of the time relatively free of interruptions, during which time her needs and concerns take priority. The therapist's acknowledgment of the parent's authority in the system has immediate ramifications for the well-being of the child. The emotional significance of the parent, together with her proximity, result in the child's being unavoidably affected by her stress, fatigue and pain. Additionally, as this is relieved, the parent has more free energy and interest in parenting the child.

The primary goal in working with parents is to assist them in relationships with their child(ren). Parenthood is a difficult and demanding life-role, harder still in the wake of disorganizing and reorganizing the family. Crisis and its aftermath bring heightened needs for security, comfort, direction, and support to family members, along with disrupting many of their patterns for communicating, relating, and getting needs met. The child's proximity and emotional closeness make him or her a ready yet inappropriate resource to the crisis-worn parent. Particularly if both feel abandoned by the departed spouse, such an alliance serves to blur the distinctions that are so vital for healthy problem resolution and the adjustment of both parent and child. Assisting the parent to clarify the distinction between her needs and the needs of the child is prerequisite to both parties' achieving healthy resolution to their problems. Clarifying the separateness of parent and child reveals a very real need for both to communicate clearly with each other in order for each to know what the other feels, wishes, or thinks. In an emotionally fused state, there is far greater reliance on nonverbal communication, unvalidated assumptions, and projections. It is highly beneficial to the growth of the parent-child relationship for regular periods of high-quality times to be set aside, perhaps no more than 10 or 15 minutes a day, in which the two share thoughts, feelings, concerns, activities of the day, or whatever. Simply to take care that the child receives this commitment of time and attention validates his or her significance and therein goes far to buffer unavoidable turbulence.

Working with the School-Age Child

Objectives of the therapeutic relationship center on facilitating the child's expression of those feelings that are causing trouble: anger, fear, and sadness. The child whose parents have separated has undergone loss and must acknowledge and mourn that loss in order to restore his or her wholeness and integrity in order to move on in growth and healthy personal development. Efforts to stabilize the system, together with loyalty to both parents, interfere with the child's willingness to grieve. This is compounded both by the child's fear of retaliation from the caretaking parent and by the child's role- and age-engendered limitations in expression. Even the best-intentioned and most empathetic parent may be unsuccessful in helping the child confront and mourn his or her loss. However skilled at opening communication, the parent cannot escape personal involvement and significance to the child in relation to that loss. The therapist has the distinct advantage of being personally uninvolved and can greatly assist the child with an approach that conveys permission, indeed expectation of painful, perhaps turbulent feelings. In the privacy of this relationship the child need not worry about the impact of his or her feelings on the adult listener. The therapist can reassure the child that grieving is not a permanent condition but a necessary process, that expression of sadness does not make it grow or proliferate, and that anger is natural and not lethal. Relaxing control over those feelings brings great relief, and ultimately amazement, to the youngster who never would have guessed that letting feelings out would in any way diminish their strength.

The therapeutic relationship presents a safe opportunity for the child to do this and work through painful feelings if the therapist demonstrates unwavering truthfulness and reliability. Only then can the child trust that he or she is not risking further loss. Confidentiality is a relevant issue to the extent that the child is aware and concerned about the therapist-parent relationship and what will be shared at that level. Clearly, the child's wish for privacy must be consensually validated and respected. It is not necessary for feelings to "go public" for the work to succeed, and reassurance of this to the child who is worried is an important step in development of a therapeutic relationship.

Children unfortunately assume that when things go badly they carry blame, and in their guilt they seek to cover, ignore, and move past the source of their pain. The natural outcome, of course, is the child's failure to initiate any questions or comments even remotely related to the area of his or her concern. This, together with immature cognitive processes and limited experience with relationships, makes for serious distortions, misguided assumptions, and fears that often can block the child's progress in achieving resolution. Management of these concerns constitutes the remaining therapeutic task. To accomplish this, it is necessary to unearth and define the child's worries and fears, because the child lacks facility in confronting them alone. Finding words to express fears, sharing them with another person, and bringing them out into the light of day does a lot to make them manageable. Unrealistic fears can be eliminated with information and validation, while those that are real become less painful when dealt with in a supportive therapeutic relationship.

As indicated in previous sections, the child's most potent fears emanate from his or her dependence on both parents. The child dreads losing them through abandonment, illness, death, or natural disaster. Some parents do, in fact, abandon their children, and some give no hint of caring about them. Adults do this for a variety of reasons and in an infinite variety of ways, consistent only in their failure to terminate clearly and fairly with the child. There is only one way to help the youngster over the pain of such blatant rejection and that is by sensitive, supportive communication that explores the needs and problems of the absent parent, accounting for but not excusing the rejecting behavior. This, in effect, clears the child of personal responsibility for the rejection. Realistic assessment of the absent parent, disappointing as he or she may be, can be tolerated more easily by the child than a web of fantasies involving personal unworth and an idealized parent who loves but is too busy to visit, call, or remember the child except (or *even*) on special occasions. Promises or reassurances that fail to materialize serve only to diminish the child's sense of his or her own worth.

In working with a school-age child, these issues can most often be dealt with in straightforward discussion. Many are delightfully forthcoming and candid as they approach the therapist, apparently recognizing this as an opportunity to unleash their feelings without fear of repercussion. Others have to be coaxed into talking about the problems they are having. Children have a propensity for assuming that they are absolutely unique and alone in their troubles and are stunned to find someone who understands them, and more so to find a person who can guess what they are feeling. Taciturn stoics are responsive to hearing concerned comments regarding what "most people your age think/feel/fear" when their parents divorce. For the same reasons, group therapy with these children can work very well to bridge the sense of desperate isolation, fostering mutual support as well as a safe forum for expression.

Working with the Preschooler

Developing a relationship with a preschooler proceeds most readily for this writer through actively meeting the child at his or her own level. The young child cannot find words to adequately express his or her questions or feelings. Neither can the child quickly trust or respond to a new adult whose medium of expression is predominantly verbal. Going with the child to his or her favorite play area and getting involved with the child's toy or game of choice achieves a wordless rapport from which multilevel communication can develop.

Doll play and puppetry are wonderful activities to progress to because they are readily available and foster or necessitate expression of ideas, feelings, and assumptions about others. In the early stages, when assessment is the primary task, it is best to follow the child's lead and avoid interjecting therapist-based ideas. What may seem neutral or realistic may in fact shape or direct the play of a child who is insecure and overcompliant. Reflective comments that simply restate what the child has said or done are more successful forms of nondirective confirmation and further cement the child's sense of his or her own acceptability. Drawing and painting are very useful activities, if the child likes to use them. The child's choice of subject, use of color, level of activity, concentration, and pleasure tell much about his or her life that could not be conveyed with language. Painting along with the child, taking turns creating a picture together, and building a story through a painting are all means by which the relationship grows and greater understanding is achieved. Verbalizing the mood conveyed by the child's painting and naming the details or activities seen in the picture are useful techniques that serve to recognize the child's communication, expand the exchange, and allow mutual validation to occur between adult and child.

In the context of such play-based interaction, intervention can flow easily through a variety of channels appropriate to the skill of the therapist and the responsiveness of the child. For example, developing a shared painting on the subject of family composition or mutual storytelling can convey plausible solutions or alternatives in symbolic form by way of the therapist's contributions. If the child is comfortable enough and has adequate language skill, straightforward comments that elicit and recognize feelings, fears, and concerns seem to work well, while attention can appear to be centered on play activities. I worked with one 4-year-old who demonstrated perpetual uncertainty over the existence and involvement of her noncustodial mother. She acted out in doll play symbolic resolution of the problem. In one scenario, her mother was dead. At another time, she was painted as a tiny background figure. At other times, the youngster omitted her mother entirely in her pictures of the family. In the midst of painting with her, I commented that she must wonder when she would see her mommy again. "Yes, I *do*," she said with some surprise as she went on painting. "Do you ever ask about your mommy?" I followed. "No," she explained patiently and, looking at me, added, "It's better not to ask." As we continued to paint and talk it became apparent that no one had ever offered any explanation to this 4-year-old sage for her change in living arrangements 10 months earlier, and that her future and residual ties to the past were mysterious, uncharted, and best left untouched. Opening communications, however, that explained both the past and plans for her future were soon followed by diminution and eventual disappearance of the nightmares and tears that had been interrupting her sleep.

CONCLUDING REMARKS

While divorce is a legal event, it is more accurately understood to be a process in which the lives of each family member are disorganized and rearranged. Research indicates that the process is a slow one, involving emotional, psychologic, social, and economic dimensions that settle into place at varying rates over a span of several years (Wallerstein & Kelly, 1977, p. 5). Further, it is the *nature* of the process that impacts significantly on the child. Favorable and speedy adjustment is determined by a host of variables, yet it is fostered most significantly by the emotional maturity and resilience of the parents. When present, this enables them to sustain consideration of the child and his or her needs through a time when their own personal needs require disruption and abandonment of the structure and setting that the child has grown to see as his or her main support.

It is, after all, the *parents'* divorce. At best, it will terminate daily living with discord and pain and allow the adults to change course—frequently, for everyone's eventual benefit. Divorce does not, however, sever the ties created by marriage. Invisible loyalties, connectedness, and emotional significance survive through the course of the lives of those who once shared nuclear-family identity. The event of divorce does little to end the dynamics between the dissonant spouses and allows improvement only insofar as it provides distance between them. Children live on as the one indivisible residual of the marriage, defining by their very existence a shared role for two adults who in all other ways have publicly renounced their commitment to each other. They are often the only reason for continuing contact between their parents and therein become the medium through which unresolved feelings are likely to be expressed. Their position renders them highly vulnerable to being used as ammunition or pawns in the ongoing battle that rages and wanes between the two who are their parents. When such is the case, outside help in the form of psychotherapeutic intervention can serve to shortcut the course and duration of destructive patterns and facilitate improved resolution for everyone involved. First of all, everyone who has taken part in the war must participate in the peace-making process. For the sake of the child whose pain has become apparent, divorced couples often can be brought together when they are otherwise unable to negotiate fairly. Opening communication between all family members, bringing into focus the positions, wishes, and needs of each, and protecting the rights of the powerless ones is the most promising route to each achieving, through compromise, what each needs.

Litigation, by contrast, seeks to resolve conflict by identifying adversaries, gathering ammunition, discouraging communication and conquering by shrewd wit. In this process the child is unavoidably reduced to highly prized property, becomes the focus of competition, and is silenced by the rules of the courtroom game. Responsible counseling is often successful at averting litigation by aiming to help the parties accept the realistic losses imposed by the divorce, while maximizing continuity or growth of those relationships not necessarily aborted by the event. Findings indicate that solutions to custody and visitation developed in the supportive atmosphere of counseling, work satisfactorily over time (Wallerstein & Kelly, 1977; Greif, 1979), whereas solutions obtained through litigation are rarely felt to be fair compromises by those involved. They are frequently contested and renewed in ongoing legal (power) struggles that can become a way of life.

Not every family needs professional help in order to negotiate successfully the profound changes inherent in divorce. We must keep sight of the fact that this legal process is intended to provide a social and emotional remedy while we attempt to measure its human cost in the lives of the children. Optimal progress for everyone involved is achieved through the adults getting the distance they need from each other while maintaining their chosen roles as parents. If neither adult wants to relinquish custody, joint custody can be worked out to everyone's benefit. Certainly, the child does not wish to relinquish such a caring parent, and he or she retains investment and loyalty to both parents and gains an opportunity for the relationship to grow (Greif, 1979).

That 1 million children per year join the ranks of those whose parents are divorced is a sobering fact. Moreover, the toll and consequence of divorce-related experiences on the long-term development of these youngsters has not been fully measured. Currently, they are voiceless in the legal processes that determine their future, and we have no established remedy with which to ensure their immediate or eventual well-being. They are, nevertheless, tomorrow's parents.

REFERENCES

Anthony, E.J. Children at risk from divorce: A review. In Anthony, E.J., & Koupernick, C. (eds.), *The Child in His Family*, Vol. 3. New York: Wiley, 1974.

Bloom, B., Asher, S., & White, S. Marital disruption as a stressor: A review and analysis. *Psychological Bulletin*, 1978, 85, 867–894.

Bowlby, J. Grief and mourning in infancy and early childhood. *Psychoanalytic Study of the Child*, 1960, 5, 9–52.

Bowlby, J. Pathological mourning and childhood mourning. *Journal of the American Psychoanalytic Association*, 1963, 11, 500–541.

Cassidy, R. *What Every Man Should Know about Divorce*. Washington, D.C.: New Republic Books, 1977.

Ginsberg, H., & Opper, S. *Piaget's Theory of Intellectual Development*. Englewood Cliffs, N.J.: Prentice-Hall, 1969.

Goldstein, J., Freud, A., & Solnit, A. *Beyond the Best Interests of the Child*. New York: The Free Press, 1973.

Greif, J.B. Fathers, children and joint custody. *American Journal of Orthopsychiatry*, 1979, 49, 311–319.

Kelly, J.B., & Wallerstein, J.S. The effects of parental divorce: Experiences of the child in early latency. *American Journal of Orthopsychiatry*, 1976, 46, 20–32.

Kessler, J.W. *Psychopathology of Childhood*. Englewood Cliffs, N.J.: Prentice-Hall, 1966.

McDermott, J.F., Jr. Parental divorce in early childhood. *American Journal of Psychiatry*, 1968, 124, 1424–1432.

National Center for Health Statistics. *Final Divorce Statistics, 1975* (Monthly Vital Statistics Report, 26, No. 2, Suppl. 2, May 19, 1977). Washington, D.C.: U.S. Government Printing Office, 1977.

Piaget, J., & Inhelder, B. *The Psychology of the Child*. New York: Basic, 1969.

Sullivan, H.S. *The Interpersonal Theory of Psychiatry*. New York: Norton, 1953.

Wallerstein, J.S., & Kelly, J.B. The effects of parental divorce: Experiences of the preschool child. *Journal of the American Academy of Child Psychiatry*, 1975, 14, 600–616.

Wallerstein, J.S., & Kelly, J.B. The effects of parental divorce: Experiences of the child in later latency. *American Journal of Orthopsychiatry*, 1976, 46, 256–269.

Wallerstein, J.S., & Kelly, J.B. Divorce counselling: A community service for families in the midst of divorce. *American Journal of Orthopsychiatry*, 1977, 47, 4–22.

ADDITIONAL READINGS

Bowlby, J., & Parkes, C.M. Separation and loss within the family. In Anthony, E.J., & Koupernik, C. (eds.), *The Child in His Family*, vol. 3. New York: Wiley, 1974.

Despert, J.L. *Children of Divorce*. Garden City, N.Y.: Doubleday, 1962.

Gardner, R.A. *The Boys and Girls Book about Divorce*. New York: Jason Aronson, 1970.

Gardner, R.A. *Psychotherapy with Children of Divorce*. New York: Jason Aronson, 1976.

Salk, L. *What Every Child Would Like Parents to Know about Divorce.* New York: Harper & Row, 1978.

Steinzor, B. *When Parents Divorce: A New Approach to New Relationships.* New York: Pantheon, 1969.

Stuart, I.R., & Abt, L.E. (eds.). *Children of Separation and Divorce.* New York: Grossman, 1972.

Victor, I., & Winkler, W.A. *Fathers and Custody.* New York: Hawthorn, 1977.

Wallerstein, J.S., & Kelley, J.B. The effects of parental divorce: The adolescent experience. In Anthony, E.J., & Koupernik, C. (eds.), *The Child in His Family.* Vol. 3. New York: Wiley, 1974, 479–505.

18

Genetic Diagnosis and Counseling

Gillian Ingall

Although screening for latent health problems is recognized as an essential component of health care, genetic screening is a comparatively new process that has given rise to many legal, ethical, and political questions. While such screening is considered inappropriate if the goals are political or eugenic in nature, some health professionals have attempted to come to terms with the issues by proposing that the legitimate aims of screening are scientific, that is, to provide information for those who are genetically threatened. Ingall describes those disorders that can now be detected by genetic screening and underlines some of the inherent dilemmas that confront affected families. Those living under such a threat are often desperately in need of information on which to base crucial life decisions, and it is here that genetic counseling is seen as providing a vital service through diagnosis and anticipatory guidance. Ingall emphasizes the importance of establishing a linkage between genetic services and others available in the community. Professionals in community agencies must be alert to potential genetic problems if they are to engage in appropriate client referral. Similarly, the genetic counselor must develop an awareness of the necessity of referral for skilled family counseling or other services in those situations in which more than diagnosis and help with decision making is required for successful resolution of client problems.

Medical genetics is a rapidly expanding area of medicine related to all clinical specialties. Today, genetic disorders account for an increasing proportion of morbidity and mortality because of the relative decline of infectious diseases and nutritional deficiencies. For example, until the 1930s, infectious diseases such as tuberculosis, pneumonia, and gastrointestinal infections had accounted for 75 percent of all deaths, whereas today they account for approximately 10 percent. In the 1930s, 4 percent of all infant deaths were attributed to congenital malformations, but now the figure is in the range of

20 percent (Porter, 1977). This is not, however, because of an absolute increase in genetic diseases but because genetic disorders are better recognized and diagnosed. For example, before the use of antibiotics, cystic fibrosis was indistinguishable from the vast number of infections. Today, it is the most common single-gene recessive disorder in white children, not because the incidence has increased but because it is now identified (Thompson & Thompson, 1980). It is estimated that about 1 out of 20 pediatric hospital admissions and 1 out of 10 childhood deaths are the result of disorders that are largely, or even entirely, genetic in causation (Emery, 1977). Tremendous advances in genetic knowledge and greater ability to diagnose, treat and prevent genetic diseases have resulted in an increasing demand for genetic diagnosis and counseling services. What do these services consist of and whom are they designed to help?

There are two relatively common situations in which genetic counseling may be sought. The first arises when a child is born with an inherited disease or a congenital anomaly, one that is present at birth. The parents want to know why it happened and whether it will happen again.

The second situation occurs when a couple is contemplating marriage, and one of them has a family history of an inherited defect. They come to find out what risk they run of producing a child with the same disorder. To provide this information, it is essential to have the correct diagnosis: to ascertain that the disorder is genetic and, if it is, the inheritance pattern it follows. This requires a very careful evaluation of the family history as well as physical examinations of certain family members, and it involves the collaboration of the genetic team.

A typical genetic consultation requires a complete family history, access to medical records, and the preparation of a pedigree chart. Chromosome studies, biochemical investigation and other laboratory work, x-rays, and hematologic analysis are often required in addition to the usual clinical examination. Some of these tests are time consuming, and definitive results may not be available to the referring physician for several weeks. Disorders that appear the same clinically and in which the medical treatment will be the same can vary genetically. That is, the disorder is inherited in a different pattern, and the recurrence risk for one is not the same as for the other. This of course is of extreme importance in answering the client's question, "Will it happen again?" Thus, when genetic counseling is discussed, correct genetic diagnosis is a crucial prerequisite and an integral part of the service.

Genetic counseling is given to the individual and his or her family after the diagnosis of a hereditary disorder is established. It is concerned with risks of recurrence and indirectly with the prevention of genetic disorders within the family. It is, however, not only a matter of quoting risk figures, but of interpreting these in a relevant fashion so that the individual and/or family understand and therefore make an informed decision.

TABLE 18.1
Characteristic Onset Ages of Some Genetic Diseases

TYPICAL ONSET AGE	CONDITION
Lethal during prenatal life	Some chromosome aberrations; some gross malformations
Prior to birth	Congenital malformations; chromosomal aberrations
Soon after birth	Phenylketonuria; galactosemia; cystic fibrosis
During the first year of life	Tay-Sachs disease; Duchenne muscular dystrophy
Variable onset age	Diabetes mellitus (0–80 yr); Huntington's chorea (15–65 yr)

Adapted from Thompson, J.S., & Thompson, M.W. *Genetics in Medicine*, 3rd ed. Philadelphia: Saunders, 1980.

BACKGROUND TO GENETIC DISORDERS

A disease is genetic if genes are clearly implicated in its etiology. The genes are the units of heredity (approximately 100,000 per cell) and are arranged in linear order on each chromosome. Chromosomes are arranged in pairs; in human beings there are 46 chromosomes in each cell, including a pair of sex chromosomes (XX for female and XY for male). Genes in the two corresponding loci of the chromosome pair may be identical (homozygous) or different (heterozygous). A child receives one of the pair from the mother and one from the father.

The term *congenital* means that the disorder is manifest at birth, but all genetic diseases are not congenital. The onset of genetic diseases varies during the life span. For example, Tay-Sachs disease does not become evident until the baby is 4 to 6 months old, Duchenne muscular dystrophy does not manifest itself until the child is at least 1 year of age, and Huntington's disease not usually until adulthood. This creates undesirable strains on families and will be commented upon later. Characteristic ages of onset are illustrated in Table 18.1.

MODES OF INHERITANCE

Genetic disorders can be divided into three main groups. First, there are the single-gene disorders. These are individually rare but collectively contribute a notable percentage of disorders at birth (1 to 2 percent). Second, there are the chromosome abnormalities, which account for at least 0.5 percent of liveborn infants; third, the multifactorial or polygenic disorders, which refer to genetic variations that are due to an interaction of several abnormal genes with environmental influences. Major congenital anomalies that are classified as multifactorial disorders occur in approximately 3 percent of live births (Lubs, 1977).

Single-Gene Disorders

Genetic diseases due to single abnormal genes have typical patterns of inheritance; first studied and confirmed by Gregor Mendel in 1866, they are referred to as Mendelian inheritance. Man and woman have 22 pairs of chromosomes (called autosomes) and one pair of sex chromosomes: XX for the female and XY for the male. The mutant gene responsible for the disorder in question can be on any of these chromosomes and, depending on which, can be classified autosomal dominant, autosomal recessive, or X-linked.

An autosomal dominant disorder is one in which those who possess the abnormal gene are clinically affected. When such a person marries a normal individual, half the children, irrespective of sex, can be expected to be clinically affected, while the rest will be normal. If the affected children reproduce, on average half of their offspring will also be affected, but their unaffected sibs will produce normal children. Autosomal dominant gene disorders often show considerable variation in their clinical manifestations. For example, if a child is diagnosed as having a disease that is genetically determined as an autosomal dominant, and the rest of the family, including the parents, appears normal, the disorder could be a new mutation, in which case neither the sibs nor the parents would be at an increased risk of producing another affected child. However, if on closer examination one of the parents has some of the features of the disorder, then the risks of producing another child with the same disorder will be 50 percent. Examples are Marfan syndrome, which includes elongated extremities, cardiovascular abnormalities, and dislocation of the lens of the eye, and Huntington's disease, which is characterized by choreic movements and progressive mental deterioration.

An autosomal recessive disease is one in which those affected carry the mutant gene on both members of a chromosome pair, meaning that they have inherited the disorder because they have received the affected gene from both parents, who are known as "carriers." The double dose has resulted in the disease expressing itself. The single dose present in each parent does not usually result in any manifestation of the disease. Examples of recessively inherited disorders are sickle cell disease, cystic fibrosis, and phenylketonuria.

Disorders with a sex-linked pattern of inheritance are due to genes on the X chromosome, one of the sex chromosomes. Males receive an X chromosome from their mother and a Y chromosome from their father; females receive an X from each parent. There are no known diseases in human beings that result from the presence of abnormal genes on the Y chromosome. Disorders with a sex-linked pattern of inheritance are generally due, therefore, to genes on the X chromosome, and the disease appears almost always in males whose mothers are unaffected but are in fact "carriers"; hence the term *sex-linked*. Hemophilia and Duchenne muscular dystrophy are X-linked inherited disorders.

Chromosome Abnormalities

In human beings, as already mentioned, there are 23 paired chromosomes, each pair being similar in appearance except for the sex chromosomes. Chromosomes are classified into seven groups according to size and other features, and the arrangement is called the karyotype. It is now possible to study the chromosome constitution of an individual in specific detail by culturing cells from blood, bone marrow, or skin. Each chromosome can be identified, and aberrations in the chromosome complement can be readily noted.

Chromosome abnormalities may arise from extra chromosome material, fragmentation of chromosome material, or rearrangement, resulting in various clinical disorders such as Down syndrome (mongolism), Turner syndrome, and Klinefelter syndrome. Chromosome aberrations are a significant cause of fetal loss, occurring in approximately one-third of spontaneous first-trimester abortions (McKeown, 1976).

Multifactorial or Polygenic Inheritance Disorders

Many of the disorders do not follow the "simple" pattern of inheritance of those described in the section on single-gene disorders because they are caused by a combination of genetic and environmental factors. These disorders include many of the common congenital malformations, such as cleft lip and palate, pyloric stenosis, congenital dislocation of the hip, spina bifida, and anencephaly. Neither the genetic factors nor the environmental ones have been clearly identified, but there is an increased incidence of these conditions in relatives of those affected. In order to calculate the probabilities of recurrence in a family, one must rely on empiric risk figures. These figures are determined by studying the recurrence of certain defects in relatives of affected individuals. Many family studies have been undertaken to establish such risk figures (Carter, 1976). A generally accepted recurrence figure for a multifactorially inherited disorder after the birth of one affected child is 5 percent.

GENETIC EVALUATION

In order to provide reliable genetic counsel, great emphasis must be placed on using the correct genetic diagnosis. Although this will not necessarily alter the medical treatment of the disorder, the inheritance pattern may be different, thus changing the recurrence risks and the genetic counseling. For example, in certain kinds of dwarfism that look similar clinically (achondroplasia and thanatophoric dwarfism), the pattern of inheritance varies from autosomal dominant, with a risk of recurrence of 50 percent, to autosomal recessive, with a recurrence risk of 25 percent (McKusick, 1978). The variability of expression of some genetic diseases can also make it difficult to establish the inheritance pattern. For instance, members of a family may be so mildly affected by a disorder that it is never diagnosed, never defined. Consequently, with no apparent family history, a solitary affected individual might be considered to have a new mutation with little risk of recurrence for the progeny of either his parents or his sibs. On closer scrutiny, however, one of his parents may prove to be affected, and this would indicate an autosomal-dominant inheritance pattern, carrying a 50 percent recurrence risk.

Diagnostic procedures include, among others, physical examination, cytogenetic and biochemical tests, x-rays, hematologic analysis, dermatoglyphics, and, of course, family history. The family history will help reveal the inheritance pattern of the disorder. When the diagnosis is confirmed the family history will also identify those in the family who are at risk and should be followed and counseled.

Gathering the family history can be time consuming and complicated. It involves creating a family tree or pedigree, showing dates of births, deaths, age at death, number of children, stillbirths, miscarriages, etc. In addition to collecting information about other family members, it is often necessary to contact and examine them. This means that one has to explain to the relatives, who have not sought advice in the first place and who are not requiring medical attention, why they should, for example, submit to a blood test or x-ray. Sometimes it is not possible to trace a key member of the pedigree, or the family does not want certain individuals to know of their medical problem. This may prevent a diagnosis being made, and although the decision to withhold permission to contact other family members must be respected, it does raise certain ethical, moral, and legal issues. Some of these problems arise when genetic screening for chromosome abnormalities is planned as part of a genetic evaluation. For example, in the case of a family where translocation Down syndrome has been diagnosed it is important to test other family members who are at risk for being carriers of the translocation, and to counsel them accordingly.

Individuals who have translocation Down syndrome are a small group, about 4 percent of the total Down syndrome population. Instead of having the extra separate chromosome 21, this group has the extra chromosomal material attached to another autosomal chromosome. In this kind of Down syndrome, one of the parents may be a carrier of the anomaly. He or she will be phenotypically normal but will only have 45 chromosomes, and the karyotype will reveal the missing chromosome attached to another. If the mother is found to be the carrier, theoretically, one-third of her live offspring will be normal; one-third will be phenotypically normal like their mother and show 45 chromosomes including the translocation; and one-third will inherit Down syndrome. Thus, the chances of this mother's having another child with Down syndrome is theoretically one-third, which is considerably greater than the 1 to 2 percent risk carried by the mother who has a child with the more usual extra chromosome, Trisomy 21 (Thompson & Thompson, 1980). If the father is found to be the carrier there appears to be less risk of recurrence.

Sometimes the distinction between the familial sporadic cases of Down syndrome and the more common Trisomy 21 is not made until later in life. This is because cytogenetic techniques were not routinely available to newborns some decades ago, and many older patients have therefore never undergone chromosomal analysis. The example that follows concerns a young woman who was classified as having Down syndrome but had never undergone cytogenetic studies. She was 35 at the time of testing, and her mother had been more than 40 years old when giving birth to her. Surprisingly, although she was the last born to an older mother, the chromosome studies revealed that she belonged to the rare group of translocation Down syndrome individuals, and her mother was a carrier. She was the youngest of a family of four, each of whom had children of child-bearing age. The question was whether or not any of her brothers and sisters were also carriers and therefore at risk of passing on the translocation to their children. In this particular instance most of the family consented to be tested, and various other carriers in the family were identified and counseled accordingly. However, there was one older brother who had consented reluctantly to be tested, along with his two teenage sons. When he learned that all three of them were carriers he wanted to know nothing more. He refused to tell his sons on the grounds that "what they don't know does them no harm." These boys were under age at the time, but in a few years they were contacted again by the genetic team who explained to them that they were all carriers and that there was a chance that they could produce a child like their affected aunt. They were told about prenatal diagnosis and that amniocentesis would detect this disorder in utero. Thus, although they found this news unwelcome, they were now alerted and fully informed of the options available to them.

Screening for Genetic Disorders

Screening for genetic disorders includes testing for carrier status of recessively inherited disorders such as sickle cell, Tay-Sachs disease, and thalassemia. During the past few years detection of genetic carriers has become an important field of research in medical genetics. In some conditions, carriers can be recognized with a high degree of certainty, for example, for Tay-Sachs disease and sickle cell anemia. Genetic counseling can then be accurately given, based on this information. A couple who are both carriers for such disorders have a one-in-four chance of having a child with the disease, and if prenatal testing of the fetus is possible, as is the case with Tay-Sachs disease, the affected fetus can be detected. There are, however, many recessively inherited disorders in which the carrier state is not yet detectable, the most common of these being cystic fibrosis.

Screening for genetic disease has raised many ethical, moral, and legal problems. Genetic counseling is now accepted as an essential prerequisite for any screening program; however, there is a wide variety of controversial issues relating to this area of practice, some of which will be discussed in the following section.*

Prenatal Diagnosis

During the past ten years, prenatal diagnosis followed by selective abortion has become an increasingly important option for those at risk of severe fetal abnormalities in future offspring. The possibility of diagnosing certain genetic disorders in utero in early pregnancy, so that termination of that particular pregnancy can be an option, has resulted in many and varied issues in genetic counseling. Such conditions fall into two main groups: (1) those conditions due to chromosomal abnormalities, such as Down syndrome or mongolism, occurring in approximately 1 in 600 births, and (2) gross malformations of the nervous system, as in anencephaly and spina bifida, affecting approximately 1 in 1000 in the United States. In addition, there are also more than 60 rare metabolic disorders detectable in early pregnancy, but the families at risk are not always identified until an affected child is born. However, once this has happened and the child's diagnosis has been established, amniocentesis can be offered if a prenatal test is available. Sex-linked abnormalities, such as Duchenne muscular dystrophy, are not directly detectable, and even the carrier status of the mother is not precisely reliable. However, the sex of the fetus can be obtained by amniocentesis, and couples

---

*For a full exposition of the issues, refer to National Academy of Sciences (1975).

at risk can elect an abortion of all males, thus avoiding the 50-percent chance of producing an affected son.

The procedure itself carries very little risk to either the mother or the fetus (NICHD, 1976). The sample of amniotic fluid is generally obtained trans-abdominally as an outpatient procedure. The timing of amniocentesis is critical and is best performed 14 to 16 weeks after conception. It usually takes 4 to 6 weeks to grow enough cells in tissue culture to make a satisfactory chromosome diagnosis, and it may take longer for some enzyme assays or other biochemical tests. If a termination of the pregnancy is contemplated, the diagnosis must be completed by 20 to 22 weeks in order to allow time for a legal abortion. This is an extremely anxious time for the couples, and if the pregnancy is to be interrupted, there is little time to spare once the analysis of the sample is complete.

The most important condition for which prenatal screening can be done at present is Down syndrome. It is a severe disorder resulting invariably in mental retardation, but it can be detected with extreme accuracy prenatally. The frequency is related to maternal age: The empiric risk of having a child with Down syndrome at age 35 is in the region of 1 in 300; at age 40 it is nearer 1 in 100; at age 25, however, it is about 1 in 1500 (Trimble & Baird, 1978). Thus, it is now an accepted obstetrical practice to inform all pregnant women of age 35 and older of the test and to recommend it to all over age 40 who are pregnant. This has meant that those older couples who may have been aware of an increased risk because of their age but were prepared to take the risk are now faced with options from which they have to make a choice. In the same way, other couples who have a close relative (for example, a sibling or previous child) with a neural tube defect, or where both are known to be carriers of a detectable recessively inherited disorder, such as Tay-Sachs disease, should be informed about prenatal diagnosis since they will have to make a decision about prenatal testing.

There are many and varied decisions that some of these couples have to face, and during this time they need support and understanding from someone in the health team. Too often a woman is referred for amniocentesis with little knowledge about the procedure or the reason for referral: "My doctor wants me to have the test as I am over 35, and that is all he told me." When it is explained that the procedure is a form of screening for certain birth defects and that the only "treatment" is an offer of termination of pregnancy, the test is sometimes refused. Others, however, want the test done for reassurance and in order to prepare for the worst, if necessary. Some couples make their position very clear from the start. They would under no circumstances consider abortion, but they would like amniocentesis performed in order to prepare themselves to cope with a child with a disorder. It is difficult to anticipate the idiosyncratic responses of prospective parents under these circumstances. For example, an older mother whose first child was expected when she was age 42, expressed her wish to have amniocentesis not because she would terminate an affected fetus but, surprisingly, because she intended to give a healthy child up for adoption. On the other hand, if the baby was found to have Down syndrome, for which she was at high risk, the mother said she would keep the baby and would look after it herself. She explained that she would need time to prepare herself for this event, and amniocentesis would allow her to do this.

Prenatal diagnosis has allowed some couples, whose family histories or advanced age might have prevented their contemplating pregnancy, to be assured that the defect is *not* present. However, it is well to point out that only certain disorders can be prenatally diagnosed at present. The number is steadily increasing, but there are still many other undetectable congenital anomalies and metabolic disorders causing mental retardation and birth defects. Every couple, regardless of family history or age of the mother, runs a 3- to 5-percent risk of having a baby with a serious congenital disorder despite prenatal diagnosis (Lubs, 1977). Prenatal diagnosis has also focused on the problem of deciding how serious a defect has to be to merit termination of pregnancy. "Should *any* defect, regardless of how minor, that causes consternation to the parents, be an acceptable indication for termination?" write Epstein and Golbus (1977, p. 710). How far might a parent want to go to avoid having a child with a genetic problem, and how serious does the defect have to be? To terminate a pregnancy when the fetus is found to have Down syndrome may be an easier decision to make than to terminate a male fetus who is calculated to have a 50-percent probability of having Duchenne muscular dystrophy. In the latter instance, the mother may already have had two brothers with this disorder and have seen them deteriorate over the years until death in early adulthood. This woman would be fully aware of the quality of life her unborn son might have to face. On the other hand, her son may not have inherited the gene and so be at no risk whatsoever of developing the disease. What is she to do? Until there are tests to detect Duchenne muscular dystrophy positively, these are harrowing choices to have to make.

Decisions to be taken when other, perhaps less severe, chromosome disorders are detected vary with family situations. For example, a mother who was undergoing amniocentesis because of her age and her higher risk of having a child with Down syndrome, was found to be carrying a male with Klinefelter syndrome, a chromosomal anomaly in which affected men are sterile, have very small testes, sometimes have breasts, and are often mentally retarded (Emery, 1968). She and her husband found it very hard to know what to do. They already had four healthy children, and by the time the diagnosis had been completed, gestational age was already 22 weeks. The disorder for which she was at high risk (Down syndrome) was not found, but this new development was something quite unexpected. The mother, however, felt that "the baby belongs to me now," and as the rest of the family were already in high school, she could cope with a boy who might be retarded. She therefore, did not elect to terminate the pregnancy. Fortunately for the marriage, her husband supported her in this decision.

Another difficult situation can arise in a family where one child already has the defect, such as a neural tube defect that results in confinement to a wheelchair and severe disability. The child may be of normal intelligence, however, and well aware that his mother, who is pregnant, has been recommended an amniocentesis to detect the very disorder from which he or she suffers. If the disorder is identified in the fetus, the likelihood is that his mother will terminate the pregnancy—or will she? How do the parents decide whether to accept or destroy another child with the same disorder, and how will the brother or sister feel about this decision?

Those who decide to terminate a pregnancy on the basis of the results of prenatal testing have made the decision after much thought and soul searching. However, no matter how well-adjusted they seem to be, they should be prepared, too, for the depression that is likely to follow. This is an area where professional follow-up is of the utmost importance (Blumberg, Golbus, & Hanson, 1975). Such follow-up is essential in order to assess the depth of the disturbance and the available family and environmental supports, and for referral for family or individual therapy if needed.

EXPANSION OF GENETIC SERVICES

It has been estimated that probably 98 percent of the people who need counseling are not seen by genetic counselors (Sly, 1973). This does not mean that they receive no counseling, but those with obvious diagnoses, such as hemophilia, muscular dystrophy, cystic fibrosis, and sickle cell disease, where the diagnosis is confirmed, do not get referred to genetic counseling as such. The need for this is not generally appreciated. However, families in which these disorders occur need access to current genetic information at different stages of their lives. Parents of affected newborns often need to find out, more than once, what the risks of recurrence are for future pregnancies. It is not enough to explain to the father and mother soon after the delivery of a baby with a severe meningomyelocele that prenatal diagnosis is an option they might like to consider when the wife next becomes pregnant. The parents are probably overwhelmed by the diagnosis at this initial meeting, and they are certainly not at this time considering future pregnancies. However, in some months or even years, when the situation has been resolved, those parents may be looking for up-to-date information and an opportunity to discuss the genetic prognosis. Other relatives of affected individuals, particularly brothers and sisters, need to know their risks of having similarly affected children, and the affected individuals themselves need counseling as they reach adulthood.

If counseling is to be made acceptable to those who need it, when they need it, more trained personnel will be required. Health professionals in touch with families at different stages are an obvious continuing source of information. The nurse or medical social worker is particularly well suited to this role as he or she already has experience and training in approaching families with medical problems, and is familiar with the working of the medical and scientific professions. However, it is extremely important that the elements of genetic diagnosis and counseling be taught and learned before responsibility for any genetic counseling is assumed. Contact with genetic centers and attendance at continuing-education programs should be encouraged. Courses in medical genetics should be included in the core curriculum of nursing schools and schools of social work, but so far not many have taken up the challenge. The passing of the National Genetic Disease Act (PL 94-278, 1976) has given recognition to the need for state-wide access to genetic counseling services. Genetic associates have been hired to implement this act, and they will be a liaison between the community health worker and the genetic center.

Genetic centers, where a varied medical and scientific staff are concentrated, exist in most large cities in the United States. These centers are usually closely connected to or part of a university medical school. There is consultation between centers, especially in the area of the more rare diseases, where one center may specialize in prenatal detection for a certain disorder and another will have the most experience with some other diagnostic test. The March of Dimes Birth Defects Foundation regularly publishes a directory of genetic centers throughout the world, and this is readily obtainable through their offices (Lynch, et al., 1980).

There is a need for genetic diagnosis and counseling services available in wider rural areas and in more isolated places. A recent development in the delivery of genetic services has been the outreach or satellite clinic that has been established in areas some distance from the genetic center but staffed by personnel from the center. The missing feature from this network of genetic services is often the link between the community and the center. This is where the public health nurse or school nurse, for example, has a most important role to play. In the same way, the social worker attached to agencies for handicapped children can also be an essential link. Genetic services are now available. A crucial remaining task is the promotion of their accessibility.

REFERENCES

Blumberg, B.D., Golbus, M.S., & Hanson, K.H. The psychological sequelae of abortion performed for a genetic indication. *American Journal of Obstetrics and Gynecology*, 1975, 122, 799–808.

Carter, C.O. Genetics of common single malformations. *British Medical Bulletin*, 1976, 32, 21–26.

Emery, A.E.H. Genetic counseling—its genetic and social implications. In Chester, R., & Peel, J. (eds.), *Equalities and Inequalities in Family Life*. London, N.Y., San Francisco: Academic Press, 1977, 71–80.

Emery, A.E.H. *Heredity, Disease and Man. Genetics in Medicine*. Berkeley: University of California Press, 1968, Chap. 3.

Epstein, C.J., & Golbus, M.S. Prenatal diagnosis of genetic diseases. *American Scientist*, 1977, 65, 703–711.

Lubs, H.A. Frequency of genetic disease. In Lubs, H.A., & de la Cruz, F. (eds.), *Genetic Counseling*. New York: Raven Press, 1977, 1–16.

Lynch, H., Fain, P., & Marrero, K. (eds.). *International Directory: Birth Defects—Genetic Services*. New York: March of Dimes Birth Defects Foundation, 1980.

McKeown, T. Human Malformations: Introduction. *British Medical Bulletin*, 1976, 32, 1–3.

McKusick, V.A. *Mendelian Inheritance in Man. Catalog of Autosomal Dominant, Autosomal Recessive and X-Linked Phenotypes*, 5th ed. Baltimore: Johns Hopkins University Press, 1978.

National Academy of Sciences, National Research Council, Committee for the Study of Inborn Errors of Metabolism. *Genetic Screening—Programs, Principles, and Research*. Washington, D.C.: The Academy, 1975.

The National Institute of Child Health and Human Development, National Registry for Amniocentesis Study Group. Mid-trimester amniocentesis for prenatal diagnosis—safety and accuracy. *Jounal of the American Medical Association*, 1976, 236, 1471–1477.

Porter, I. Evolution of genetic counseling in America. In Lubs, H.A., & de la Cruz, F. (eds.), *Genetic Counseling*. New York: Raven Press, 1977.

Sly, W.S. What is genetic counseling? In *Contemporary Genetic Counseling: Proceedings of a Symposium of the American Society of Human Genetics* (Philadelphia, October 1972). Birth Defects: Original Article Series, 1973, 9, 5–18.

Thompson, J.S., & Thompson, M.W. *Genetics in Medicine*, 3rd ed. Philadelphia: Saunders, 1980.

Trimble, B.K., & Baird, P.A. Maternal age and Down's Syndrome. *American Journal of Medical Genetics*, 1978, 2, 1–5.

ADDITIONAL READINGS

Apgar, V., & Beck, J. Is my baby all right? *A Guide to Birth Defects.* New York: Trident Press, 1972.

Hendin, D., & Marks, J. *The Genetic Connection.* New York: Morrow, 1978.

Kelly, P.T. *Dealing with Dilemma: A Manual for Genetic Counselors.* New York: Springer-Verlag, 1977.

Reisman, L.E., & Matheny, A.P. *Genetics and Counseling in Medical Practice.* St. Louis: Mosby, 1969.

Riccardi, V.M. *Genetic Approach to Human Disease.* New York: Oxford University Press, 1977.

19

The Hospice Concept:
An Alternative Approach to
Terminal Care

Irene Mahar

Medical hospitals have as their mission the preservation of life. Under these circumstances it is not surprising that the care given the terminally ill, however technically efficient, is often deficient in provision for the psychosocial needs of those who are not expected to recover and yet continue to linger. Further, these acute-care institutions are the domain of professionals whose task it is to carry out highly specialized treatment functions. As a result, family and friends tend to be excluded from participating, instead of being seen as essential contributors to the patient's welfare. In addition, their own lives having been disrupted, they are left to manage on their own. These deficiencies in hospital services have prompted a search for alternative approaches to the care of the dying. Mahar describes the hospice concept, a humanistic system of care that has evolved as a means of meeting the broad spectrum of needs of the dying person and his or her family.

Hospice, originally a medieval name for a way station for pilgrims and travelers, where they could be replenished, refreshed, and cared for, today refers to an organized program of care for patients going through life's last station (U.S. Congress, 1976). While authors frequently speak of the joys associated with the first station of life, until recently they had made relatively little reference to life's last phase. Certainly, a newborn can bring joy to many. The new life is nurtured and loved. The newborn's dependency and need for security is an acknowledged fact. Why then does society look so differently upon this same individual when he or she has been diagnosed as having a terminal illness?*

Proponents of the hospice concept believe that human dignity always should be respected and that quality of life should be maintained as long as one lives. Further, they believe that each individual, just as each situation, is unique and that care for a particular individual, whether given at home or in a special in-patient facility, must be comprehensive and provided by a select group of trained personnel available on a 24-hour, 7-day-a-week schedule. Just the knowledge that service is available can do much to change attitudes toward terminal or even long-term illness. In fact, by reflecting briefly on some considerations relative to long-term illness, we may better visualize some of the precipitating factors that led to the modern definition of hospice and the promise it holds for terminally ill people and their families.

LONG-TERM ILLNESS: ITS EFFECT ON SOCIETY

Each of us is a potential candidate for some type of long-term illness. Young persons of today, as products of a youth-oriented culture, give very little, if any, thought to this fact. Adults, on occasion, discuss the devastating effects that long-term illness could have on their lives. The aged often reflect on what long-term illness has done to their friends and families, openly expressing their hopes and prayers that such illness does not strike them. It is only when we or one close to us, young or old, have been stricken that we experience the true meaning of long-term illness and its myriad ramifications. The diseases and disorders responsible for long-term illness are various, each having its own natural history resulting from the interaction of host, agent, and environmental factors (Leavell & Clark, 1965).

Long-term illness is no respecter of age, social class, or economic status. When it occurs in any family, all members experience its rippling effect. Some of the general considerations that accompany the news that one has long-term illness include concerns about cost, availability of care, amount of suffering to be experienced, and uncertainty about the future. In addition, the ill individual may have to cope later with rejection and may experience a loss of identity. Is it any wonder, then, that patients and families alike faced with this crisis often experience anger, depression, frustration, and despair?

---

*In this discussion a terminally ill person is defined as one who no longer can benefit from medical treatment directed to control the disease and whose life expectancy is estimated at 3 to 5 months.

Throughout history, families have coped with long-term illness in many different ways. Individual differences have ranged from rejection to overprotection, but one common need surfaces. That commonality is the need for support, which may manifest itself in a biologic, psychologic, social, or spiritual form. In early times when long-term illness was managed primarily within the home, neighbors, family physician, religious leaders, and relatives were among those who met identified needs as those needs occurred and provided the patient and family with the support deemed appropriate. Later, as technology advanced, changes in our health care system also occurred. More and more frequently, patients were admitted to hospitals where health professionals and paraprofessionals provided the care. This move proved advantageous in terms of meeting the physical needs of the patient, but concurrently his or her total environment and role changed. No longer surrounded by family and friends in a familiar environment, the patient found him- or herself being cared for by strangers who were often skilled but impersonal in their interactions with him or her. Coupled with this, agency regulations limited the hours family and friends could visit, and loved ones were no longer allowed to participate in the care. The illness, rather than the person, seemed to have become the focal point of interest.

Observations of the care provided the terminally ill so gravely concerned a young woman in England during the middle of this century that she was stimulated to action. Cicely Saunders, a nurse and medical social worker, went back to school at age 33 to become a physician. Miss Saunders believed that health personnel should listen carefully to what patients say. Further, she maintained, in our preoccupation with patients for whom there is hope, we cut ourselves off from learning from *all* patients, particularly those with terminal illness (Saunders, 1969, p. 111).

After observing and caring for terminally ill patients for a number of years, Dr. Saunders opened St. Christopher's Hospice in London in 1967. This was made possible by donations from numerous patients and friends. At St. Christopher's, patients with terminal illness were kept alert but free from pain and other distressing symptoms, and patients and families were given the emotional and spiritual support so sorely needed during this period. Hospice care was provided either at home or in a facility made as homelike as possible. In this facility patients were allowed to bring some of their personal belongings (a favorite chair, a lamp, etc.), and families, including children and grandchildren, were permitted to visit as desired. On occasion a favorite pet was brought to see its owner. Kindness was the keynote in this institution. Comfort measures were provided by caring people, and those who were able to remain at home were given the same comprehensive care by a team of skilled persons dedicated to helping a fellow human being and his or her loved ones. The person, not the disease, was of major importance. Quality of life was the central theme. Dr. Saunders, the founder and still medical director of St. Christopher's Hospice, was selected to receive an honorary doctorate of medicine from the Archbishop of Canterbury in April 1977. She was the first person in nearly 100 years to receive such an honor (Mills, 1977).

SUPPORT SYSTEMS: HOSPICE CONCEPT

While the most important needs of a person going through the last phase of life have been identified as freedom from pain and discomfort, emotional and spiritual support and a pleasant environmental setting, the needs of significant others who help him attain and maintain quality of life must also be considered. Families, though experiencing some of the same needs as the patient during this crisis period, may indeed have additional concerns.* A third group, the care providers, also has needs that, although different, are equally significant. Support systems can be of tremendous assistance. Caplan (1974, p. 7) refers to a support system as "an enduring pattern of continuous or intermittent ties that play a significant part in maintaining the psychological and physical integrity of the individual over time." He further contends that support systems do not suggest weakness but rather augment a person's strengths to facilitate his mastery of his environment (Caplan, 1974, p. 69). The hospice concept, as it is developing in the United States, encompasses support systems that will meet the needs of each of the previously identified groups.

Person with Terminal Illness

Glaser and Strauss (1968, pp. 5–7) report that a person with terminal illness proceeds through a course of dying, or "dying trajectory." They describe common "critical junctures" in all trajectories; however, each one has special characteristics. Just as the course of dying is individualized, so too are the pain and other distressing symptoms experienced by the terminally ill.

If pain is present, this is usually the person's primary concern. However, contrary to common belief, not all experience pain. Saunders (1976, p. 13) states that "the few studies that have been carried out in this area suggest that of those who die of all forms of malignant disease some 50% are unlikely to experience pain at all." For those who do, effective control can often be accomplished by the use of oral medication, frequently a narcotic combined with a phenothiazine. The phenothiazine enhances the effect of the narcotic,

---

*In this regard Barbara Giacquinta (1977) introduces a model of the stages a family must confront when a member is dying of cancer.

serves as an antiemetic, and acts as a tranquilizer. It has been found that if medications are titrated carefully according to individual needs and given on a regular 4-hour basis (not "as needed" or when the person has to ask for it), often the dosage can be reduced for a period of time and increased as the condition worsens. Through the use of this method of pain control, the patient's fear or expectation of pain is diminished, and anxiety, so often associated with pain, is reduced.

Nausea, insomnia, itching, and bowel and bladder problems are a few of the whole gamut of possible symptoms. Each must be evaluated carefully by the hospice team of health professionals (physicians, nurses, and pharmacists) who, after careful assessment and collaboration, will prepare a therapeutic plan. This blending of the skills of a multidisciplinary team can produce maximum effectiveness in the provision of care. Physical-comfort measures (positioning, turning, and cleanliness) play a large part in the day-to-day care plan. Ambulation and nutrition, too, can be vital therapeutic agents. Since the hospice team of professional experts will be developing an individualized plan of care for each person in the program, specifics have been avoided here. We are dealing with human beings, not machines, and thus there is no single routine that is best suited to all.

The psychologic needs of terminally ill persons vary. Kübler-Ross (1969) finds five stages of dying: denial and isolation, anger, bargaining, depression, and acceptance. Elaborating on each stage, she cites information gleaned from dying patients in terms of coping mechanisms effective at the time of a terminal illness. Not all patients progress systematically through each of the stages of dying as described by Kübler-Ross; however, it is believed that the majority do. Certainly, anger, depression, and the fear of being rejected or isolated are not uncommon responses associated with terminal illness. Hospice personnel and family members must be cognizant of any emotional changes they perceive. Sometimes honest communication is obscured by evasion. However, by listening attentively, picking up cues, and closely observing actions, one can often respond in a most assuring way. Timing can make a significant difference in the effectiveness of communication. Indeed, the mere presence of a caring person is an indication that one is not being rejected or isolated.

Spiritual needs, often not acknowledged until the end of life approaches, can now assume considerable importance and be met by any of the care givers when the need is expressed. Ideally, it would be the spiritual advisor of the individual's choice who could function best in this capacity, but the person close at hand at the moment the patient wishes to pray or talk of his or her religious beliefs should encourage him or her to do so. To be joined in prayer by a caring person can provide much solace to one who is ill.

For many, the old saying, "There's no place like home," is particularly true when they realize life is coming to a close. To be in familiar surroundings with family and friends near, to be able to lead a life as normal as possible, and to know that one's identity can be maintained is as therapeutic as drugs in some instances. Home is usually the ideal place for terminally ill persons whose family members can provide care, while the hospice team members serve as their support system. Unfortunately, today a large segment of our population does not have this good fortune.

At some point it is possible that even the terminally ill person cared for at home will need to be admitted to an in-patient facility specifically designed to meet his or her needs. Reasons for this admission might be the worsening of the ill person's condition or the inability of the in-home care provider to continue necessary care. It is then that the home-like environment of a hospice—a home away from home—should be available. Pleasant, cheerful surroundings, competent, understanding personnel, and an "open-door" policy make transition and adjustment to such an in-patient facility less traumatic. The hospice may be housed as a special unit (frequently referred to as a palliative care unit, or PCU) within an acute or general hospital, or it may be a separate building (a free-standing facility) specifically designed for terminally ill patients and their families. When possible, individuals are encouraged to be up and about and to join hospice personnel at mealtime. Accompanied by a staff member, they might even enjoy a short outing to a local store or bar. The park-like setting in which a well-planned hospice is situated will provide natural beauty, serving as a spot where silence or conversation with family and friends can be appreciated. Though some private rooms are available, units large enough to accommodate two, four, or more beds are more common. One advantage of such an arrangement is that each patient and family can see, or at least be aware of, the concerted support provided by the staff when death nears. Identification in this situation enhances peace instead of fear.

If the home situation changes and his or her condition warrants it, a patient may return to his or her own environment, with all the hospice support services. Ideally, the same team members known to the patient and the family in the in-patient facility will continue to provide assistance in the home. Much can be done to comfort and support a fellow human being through this phase.

The Family

It may be that at no time in life do family members mean as much to one another as when one member is diagnosed as having a terminal illness. A closeness and understanding that only suffering can bring may become overt (Kübler-Ross, 1969, p. 143). Initially, concerns about finances, separation, and future plans are overshadowed by genuine concern to assist the individual who is stricken. Without doubt, it is the person or persons residing within the patient's home whose equilibrium and daily life may be most upset, but often they will be willing to make greater adjustments than anyone else. Once the emotional hurdles have been coped with, family forces are mobilized and the members are able to work closely with the hospice team. Secure in the knowledge that help is as near as their telephone and that assistance is available in the home 24 hours a day, family care givers can do a superb job. Frequently, personal care provided by a spouse, daughter, or son is more pleasing to a patient than that provided by a skilled professional. Favorite foods prepared by a family member may be more appealing than the most palatable meal prepared in another setting. Highly motivated family members often are excellent students and most conscientious about assuming responsibility for patient care. Thus, in addition to providing some direct care in the home, demonstration, teaching, and counseling are major functions of the hospice team.

Reactions to the illness may precipitate unprecedented family problems. In young family members school problems, bed wetting, even stealing may occur. Children may be receiving less attention than usual and thus be aware that something unpleasant has invaded their environment. Adults, unable to cope with their own feelings, may find themselves avoiding discussion of the illness and its outcome with anyone, including the patient. On the other hand, it may be the patient who purposely avoids the subject. Denial may be the basis for this avoidance. Resulting behaviors may in no way resemble the usual family interactions. It is at this point that a team member can provide the counseling essential to helping them identify problems and plan appropriate approaches.

The combined efforts of the total hospice team (professional, paraprofessional, family, and ill person) may make it possible for the terminally ill person to remain in his or her natural environment during most of the illness. Indeed, if family needs can be met and appropriate physical care be provided, many may remain at home throughout their illness; such is the choice of most patients, according to one study (Mikolaitis, 1978, p. 19). However, should admission to the hospice be necessary, consideration for the family is shown in a variety of ways. Children are allowed to visit and make use of a supervised play area, available at the facility for children of staff and patients. Family members are encouraged to continue participating in the care of the ill member and may receive counseling by staff members in areas ranging from feelings and attitudes to concerns regarding finances, children, and future plans. Here the family is not frightened by unfamiliar life-saving equipment so often seen in an acute-care facility since only those measures essential to patient comfort are employed.

By using every opportunity to support the family, the hospice staff can establish a trust relationship that is a source of strength during the illness and continues on throughout the mourning process. Sometimes the family member who has been the most stoic during the illness needs support for the longest period following the death. Conversely, that individual may provide untold support to other families who later must cope with similar circumstances. Throughout the mourning period, it may be the spiritual advisor who assumes the primary role in helping the family accept the loss of a loved one and make necessary adjustments.

Care Providers

People who elect to devote their time and expertise to helping others—especially the terminally ill—must possess certain qualities not easily identified. Dedicated, caring, religious, unselfish: these are all terms which have been used to describe such care providers. Indeed these terms sometimes sound "Pollyanna-ish," but the adjective "humanistic" seems to come closest to an adequate delineation of the necessary characteristics. It is often part of human nature to want to help others in distress. While kindness, compassion, and a desire to serve others are admirable qualities, personnel on a hospice team must have more. They must choose to work in this program because of a real commitment to the concept. Actually, many professionals would not elect this area of care where daily interfacing with terminal patients and their families is the mode, for, as stated by Carpenter and Wylie (1974, p. 403), "When death becomes inevitable, many health professionals withdraw from its bruising assault and redirect their efforts elsewhere." For this reason professional members of a hospice team, in addition to possessing expertise in their discipline, must also understand their own attitudes toward death. These attitudes can be reflected in their interactions with other team members as well as with care consumers. Empathizing, communicating, and acting appropriately under stress place great demands upon the team members. However, many highly motivated professionals feel comfortable in coping with such stressful situations and receive satisfaction in their roles as contributors to the common goals of the hospice team.

Recognizing that health professionals representing different disciplines are essential to delivery of the broad spectrum of caring services so sorely needed at this time, collaboration and cooperation are keystones to effective multidisciplinary team functioning. Each team member must divest him- or herself of vested interests and subscribe to the philosophy that a multidisciplinary effort is essential to the effective carrying out of the multiple tasks that may surface throughout and after the terminal illness. Planned or spontaneous conferences may be initiated at any time by any team member. Leadership and decision making at such conferences depend on the situation, and no two situations are identical. Flexibility, respect for colleagues, and willingness to place patient/family welfare above professional hierarchy are true signposts of the team approach so often referred to but seldom seen in an acute-care setting.

Paraprofessionals who comprise a large and vital component of the team can contribute in numerous ways to a hospice program. As clerical workers, friendly visitors, nurse's aides, transportation aides, readers, etc., they are essential cogs in the wheel of daily operations. Eager as they may be to assist in the program, their motives must be much deeper than those based on emotionalism. For this reason they, as well as professionals, should be carefully screened and required to take an attitudinal test before appointment so that team members can be selected as objectively as possible from applicants who express interest.

Everyone participates in an orientation program. The number of sessions may vary, although it is essential that all disciplines receive the same information regarding the hospice philosophy, goals, communication patterns, and interpersonal relations. This can best be done in joint meetings, with individual subgroups arranging additional programs to meet their own particular needs. Thorough orientation to the hospice philosophy and a commitment to a multidisciplinary approach to care can do much to develop the esprit de corps so vital to the success of the program. Open communication among hospice colleagues, families, and the terminally ill person will result in clarification of shared goals. On-going group sessions will assist the staff members to express their concerns and share problems. In addition, support from resource persons will be forthcoming during regularly scheduled staff meetings, since emotions can be strained, no matter how satisfying the working environment, when a person one has come to know and care about does not recover. To cry or otherwise share feelings with families or co-workers may provide the bond that identifies professionals as being human first and care givers second. It is essential that each care provider individually maintain physical and emotional strength. To do that, time must be taken outside of working hours for self-refreshment and restoration drawn from those sources that are relevant to the individual's needs and values.

DEVELOPMENT OF THE HOSPICE CONCEPT IN THE UNITED STATES

During the period when Dr. Saunders was seeking support for St. Christopher's, she traveled to the United States to share her hopes and dreams with interested people. Untiring in her efforts to share with others her philosophy of terminal care, Saunders lectured at Yale University during 1963. Out of the receptive audience who heard this courageous woman speak came the nucleus of a group who worked diligently to develop a hospice in New

Haven, Connecticut. Within a relatively short time, with the support of many interested citizens, plans became reality, and a home-care program for the terminally ill was opened in New Haven in 1974. This home-care program demonstrated the need for hospice care in the community and has been expanded to include an in-patient service modeled primarily on St. Christopher's, which continues to serve as the prototype for others. Hospice, Incorporated (New Haven), now named Connecticut Hospice, Incorporated, is recognized as a leader in developing the concept, which has spread throughout the United States.

As a leader in the hospice movement, Hospice New Haven hosted the First National Hospice Symposium in Branford, Connecticut, in the fall of 1975. At that time there were approximately 21 hospice groups in different stages of development, most on the East and West coasts. Patterns varied for delivery of care. Some offered home care only; others were developing an in-patient program within a hospital; still others were planning an in-patient program in a free-standing facility. The symposium evoked much enthusiasm, and those present returned home armed with much valuable information and an even stronger conviction that a new arm of the health-care delivery system was emerging.

In 1976 the term *hospice*, as recorded in the United States Library of Congress, was defined as a program that provides palliative and supportive care for terminally ill patients and their families either directly or on a consulting basis with the patient's physician or another community agency such as a visiting nurse association (U.S. Congress, 1976). Further recognition of the hospice concept by the federal government was signified in the fall of 1975 when a request for proposal was sent out by the National Cancer Institute through its Division of Cancer Control and Rehabilitation, making available grants for interested groups to set up experimental hospices for terminal cancer patients (Holden, 1976, p. 389). Soon after, federal- and state-supported demonstration projects began evaluating the hospice program as an alternative approach to the care of the terminally ill. Such willingness to support research in this area of care indicates concern for this facet of our present health-care delivery system.

The Second National Hospice Symposium was held in Boonton, New Jersey, in the spring of 1977. This time there was representation from 60 units in different stages of development in 21 states. The rapid increase, both in the number of participants and in the states represented, indicates that hospice care is now recognized nationally as an alternative approach to the care presently offered to terminally ill patients and their families. Formation of the National Hospice Organization took place at this symposium.

The National Hospice Organization (NHO) held its first annual meeting in Washington, D.C., during the fall of 1978. At the meeting, attended by more than 1000 participants, purposes and goals of the organization were identified (National Hospice Organization, 1978, pp. 7–8): The purposes were to:

1. Develop a clear understanding of the hospice concept among health care professionals, as well as the public.
2. Provide for a steady flow of information and communication among existing hospice groups and others that are evolving.
3. Develop and maintain standards of care in program planning and implementation.
4. Provide technical assistance to hospice organizations in their formative years and evaluation of their programs.
5. Make available basic training materials to assist new groups, their boards, members, and volunteers.
6. Monitor health-care legislation and regulation at all governmental levels relevant to the hospice movement.

Immediate goals outlined were to:

1. Define a common data-collection base to be used for the purpose of demonstrating definitive national trends in the care of the terminally ill and their families.
2. Design policy to be considered by legislators and governmental agencies for provision of care for the terminally ill and their families.
3. Develop standards and procedures for giving accreditations to hospice organizations.
4. Provide opportunities for training through workshops, seminars, and other similar programs.

Two issues of particular concern in terms of the future development of the hospice concept were finances and legislation. Both are being researched. Some communities provide third-party coverage for hospice care, but further studies must be made before there can be a comparison of the differential between actual hospital costs for terminal illness and hospice care. Legislation, supported by many United States political luminaries, advocates the hospice concept of death with dignity. Changes in federal and state laws to include hospice care have been made or are imminent.

SUMMARY

The hospice concept that originated in England more than 10 years ago is spreading rapidly throughout the United States. Leaders of government and the private sector in concert with the NHO have given momentum to the development of the hospice concept throughout the country. Truly a concept as opposed to an institution or mode of service delivery, it has as its core a commitment to helping the terminally ill person to maintain quality of life rather than the mere preservation of life itself. Further, it is concerned not only with the patient but also with supporting and otherwise assisting the family both throughout and following the terminal phases of the illness. In order to carry out the central tenets of the hospice concept, a multidisciplinary team provides the necessary services within the patient's home or in specially designed residential facilities.

There is still much to be learned, but caring persons committed to a common goal can help a fellow human being die in peace and dignity. In the words of Cicely Saunders (1976, p. 3):

> We have an armoury—not against death itself—but against pain, suffering, loneliness. As professionals we should master the weapons that are so readily at hand; psychology, pharmacology, and nursing expertise. . . . It is in the hospices that the weapons are forged and refined. Their use requires trained hands, trained minds, and educated hearts.

REFERENCES

Caplan, G. *Support Systems and Community Mental Health.* New York: Behavioral Publications, 1974.

Carpenter, J.O., & Wylie, C. On aging, dying and denying. *Public Health Reports,* September–October 1974, 89, 403–407.

Giacquinta, B. Helping families face the crisis of cancer. *American Journal of Nursing,* 1977, 77, 1585–1588.

Glaser, B., & Strauss, A. *Time for Dying,* Chicago: Aldine, 1968.

Holden, C. Hospices: For the dying, relief from pain and fear. *Science,* 1976, 193, 389–391.

Kübler-Ross, E. *On Death and Dying.* New York: Macmillan, 1969.

Leavell, H., & Clark, E.G. *Preventive Medicine for the Doctor in His Community.* New York: McGraw-Hill, 1965.

Mikolaitis, S. Choosing the circumstances of death. *Forum,* 1978, 2, 18–23.

Mills, N. London hospice helps steer calm voyage through Valley of Death. *New York Daily News,* February 25, 1977, p. C10.

Saunders, C. The hospice movement. *A Nursing Times Publication: Care of the dying,* London: Macmillan, 1976, 72, 3.

Saunders, C. The moment of truth: Care of the dying person. In Pearson, L. (ed.), *Death and Dying: Current Issues in the Treatment.* Cleveland: Case Western Reserve University Press, 1969.

Saunders, C. Control of pain in terminal cancer. *A Nursing Times Publication: Care of the Dying.* London: Macmillan, 1976, 13–15.

U.S. Congress, House Committee of Interstate and Foreign Commerce, Subcommittee on Health and the Environment. *A Discursive Dictionary of Health Care.* 94th Cong., 2nd Sess., February 1976.

Newsletters òf the National Hospice Organization, New Haven, Conn. 1978–79.
National Hospice Organization, *Hospice in America*, Brochure of the National Hospice Organization, New Haven, Conn. 1978.

ADDITIONAL READINGS

Abbott, J. Hospice—new way to help the dying. *United Church of Christ A.D. Magazine*, August 1978, 7, 19–23.

Brim, O.G., (ed.) *The Dying Patient.* New York: Russell Sage Foundation, 1970.

Chaney, P. (ed.) *Dealing with Death and Dying. A Nursing Skillbook.* Interned Communications, Jenkintown, Pa.: Eugene Jackson, 1977.

Craven, J., & Wald, F. Hospice care for dying patients. *American Journal of Nursing*, 1975, 75, 1816–1822.

Duff, R., & Hollingshead, A. *Sickness and Society.* New York: Harper & Row, 1968 1968.

Elder, R. Dying in the U.S.A. *International Journal of Nursing Studies*, 1973, 10, 171–184.

Epstein, C. *Nursing the Dying Patient.* Reston: Reston, 1975.

Goleman, D. We are breaking the silence about death. *Psychology Today*, September 1976, pp. 44–52.

Hackley, J.A. Full-service hospice offers home, day, and inpatient care. *Hospitals, Journal of the American Health Association*, 1977, 51, 84–87.

Halman, M., & Suttinger, J. Family-centered care for cancer patients. *Nursing '78*, March 1978, 8, 42–43.

Hauptfuhrer, F. Kids, and pets are welcome at Dr. Cicely Saunders' hospice for terminally ill people. *Medics*, December 22, 1975, pp. 40–41.

Ingles, T. St. Christopher's Hospice. *Nursing Outlook*, 1974, 22, 759–763.

Kassakian, M., Bailey, L., Rinker, M., Stewart, C., Yates, J. (eds.) The cost and quality of dying: A comparison of home and hospital. *Nurse Practitioner*, January–February 1979, 4, 18–23.

Krant, M.J. Sounding board—the hospice movement. *The New England Journal of Medicine*, 1978, 299, 541–549.

Kron, J. Designing a better place to die. *New York Magazine*, March 1, 1976, pp. 43–49.

Kübler-Ross, E. *To Live until We Say Good-Bye.* Englewood Cliffs, N.J.: Prentice-Hall, 1978.

Lack, S. Hospice helps patients "live until they die." *Hospital Administration Currents*, 1978, 22, 27–29.

Libman, J. Death's door: Hospices stress home care for the terminally ill. *Wall Street Journal*, March 27, 1978, 58, 1, and 22.

Markel, W., & Simon, V. The hospice concept. *CA—A Cancer Journal for Clinicians*, 1978, 28, 225–231.

Marino, L. Cancer patients: Your special role. *Nursing '76*, September 1976, 6, 26–29.

McCorkle, R. The advanced cancer patient: How he will live—and die. *Nursing '76*, October 1976, 6, 46–49.

Melzack, R., Ofiesh, J.G., & Mount, B.M. The Brompton mixture: Effects on pain in cancer patients. *Canadian Medical Association Journal*, 1976, 115, 125–128.

Neal, H.K. Why can't the dying have heroin? *New York Magazine*, October 2, 1978, 76–80.

Plant, J. Finding a home for hospice care in the United States. *Hospitals, Journal of the American Health Association*, 1977, 51, 53–62.

Stoddard, S. *The Hospice Movement*. Briarcliff Manor, N.Y.: Stein and Day, 1978.

Wald, F.S. Hospice movement must recognize human needs. *The American Nurse*, March 20, 1979, 11, 4–5.

Will, G.F. A good death. *Newsweek*, January 9, 1978, 72.

Williams, J.C. Understanding the feelings of the dying. *Nursing '76*, March 1976, 3, 52–56.

Williams, J.C. Assumptions and principles underlying standards for terminal care. *American Journal of Nursing*, February 1979.

section
IV
WORKING WITH
FAMILIES

Contemporary American families are called upon to function under increasingly difficult circumstances, at a time of diminishing economic and social resources. Because society's demands are highly complex, facile and narrow definitions of problems are unlikely to be useful in capturing the nature of the situations facing troubled families. As a result, it is necessary for professionals to exercise both creativity and flexibility in modifying services so as to be responsive to those who are in need of help. Total reliance on traditional models of service provision can no longer be considered satisfactory. This section, combined with selected material from earlier portions of the book, provides the reader with an opportunity to examine a variety of approaches to family intervention. The selective use of family therapy is the focus of some authors; others consider modes of treatment as divergent as behavior modification and psychic healing.

20

Issues Facing Beginning Family Therapists

Winnifred Humphreys

In the past two decades a family-system orientation has assumed increasing importance in guiding human-service practitioners in their work. This orientation has given impetus to the development of family-centered treatment approaches, spurring seasoned professional and novice alike to examine their practice and expand their skills. As students of family therapy become involved in clinical work, they are confronted at first hand with the infinite complexities of family systems, often finding that therapeutic strategies previously relied upon are not always productive. In this chapter Humphreys explores some of the hazards attendant on this change in practice and elucidates dilemmas that have particular urgency for beginners.

This chapter has been prompted by questions posed repeatedly by students in family therapy. Because they fall into a small number of basic categories, they can be addressed in a broad way in a single place. It is not my intention to deal specifically with the plethora of complex problems stemming from the personal "family baggage" brought by the individual student to the work of family therapy or with issues of methodologic "doctrine," although beginners in this form of therapy yearn for guaranteed guides to therapeutic success just as do those attempting to master other orientations. Such multifaceted matters fall beyond the scope of the present work. On the other hand, it would be erroneous to suggest that there are not clear and recurrent methodologic issues focusing around decision making and technique in the on-going work of family therapy.

My orientation toward understanding and working with the family is firmly rooted in an ecologic view of this unit as a social system dynamically interconnected with its environment. In addition, I align myself with those whose experience, knowledge, and preferences lead them to view *any* psychotherapeutic work as impinging on (and as being impinged upon by) a family. However, the work of family therapy places particular demands on practitioners both in terms of the special characteristics of the unit of therapeutic attention and in relation to expected outcomes. The demands generate particular problems for beginners (for students), and it is with these that we are concerned here. The first demands emerge *prior* to the first contact.

IDENTIFYING AND INVOLVING FAMILIES

Not unexpectedly, most descriptions of family therapy begin with the family already in hand and, by their presence, implying a degree of willingness to examine, if not to deal with, some version of their problems. This, in fact, happens at times, usually in a setting whose organizational title indicates that it is a "family agency" of one sort or another. That is, these agencies represent themselves publicly as being primarily interested in families. Yet even here, families do not *commonly* present themselves as units. Our culture, with its strong emphasis on individual responsibility, is not one that provides much acceptance and/or reinforcement of group responsibility and mutual concern.

This being the case, how are family problems to be identified? The question is clearly not so much a matter of whether the family initially presents as a unit, but rather what types of problem situations lend themselves to family therapy. The issue must be decided on the basis of which troubled situations coming to the attention of an agency (health, mental health, or social) appear (1) to involve intrafamilial relationships to such an extent that it is unlikely to yield to treatment that does not include most or all of the members; (2) to be so deeply embedded in the family members' way of dealing with each other and the world that it is unlikely that they can come to terms with it on their own; and (3) to involve a family whose concern about the problem is such that its members are, at the very least, prepared to make themselves accessible to an examination of the situation in conjunction with a family therapist.

Under what guises do "family problems" present themselves? Often the problem is depicted as specific to a particular family member—frequently a child—or in relation to a social institution (school, clinic, or community center) that may be viewed as magnifying or mishandling the situation. On other occasions, careful assessment of what at first blush appears to be a response to externally-induced stress—the loss of a job, a natural calamity, the necessity to secure new housing—may reveal long-term family patterns that have all along been problematic. Several examples come readily to mind though they do not, in any way, represent a full array.

Mrs. A. telephones a Child Guidance Center and reveals that her 9-year-old son is doing very poorly in school. He is of better-than-average intelligence but has never done well academically and, in fact, has always been reluctant to engage in new experiences or to play with other children in the neighborhood, in marked contrast to his bright and outgoing younger sister. The mother describes her son as a pleasant child who gives his parents "no trouble." In fact both she and her husband have been rather inclined to believe that he will "grow out of" the problem. They view him as "slow to mature." However, since the school has continued to take "an alarmist view," they (the parents) have decided to accept the referral.

Mr. B. telephones a mental-health clinic, saying that he feels that he needs help. He and his wife separated the previous week, and he has become increasingly depressed and anxious since he moved out of the home. He misses his children dreadfully and, despite the long-term nature of the problems in the relationship with his wife, he finds it impossible to get through a day without being in touch with her.

Mr. and Mrs. C. come to a social agency, both of them greatly distressed because they fear that their two-year marriage is on the verge of breaking up. This is the "second time around" for each of them, and both brought with them children from their previous marriages. While the blending of the families was not without its problems, things seemed to have begun to work out well until, 3 months previously, they agreed to take into their household Mr. C.'s eldest daughter, Karen. After electing to live with her mother at the time of the divorce, Karen became very unhappy and begged to join her father. Since the girl moved in, however, she has become increasingly upset about the limits placed on her behavior, maintaining that her stepmother is too restrictive and intrusive. She has told her younger siblings that they need not comply, that this is not their "real" mother, and that therefore she has no right to make demands on them. Both marital partners have been feeling increasingly trapped by their relationship. Mr. C. is troubled over his daughter's insistence that his wife is harsh with the children, yet at the same time he feels unsettled and irritated by his wife's pleas for support in dealing with the children and drained by her appeals for acknowledgment of her worthiness as a wife and mother. Mrs. C. is feeling overwhelmed by the situation, increasingly unsure of her capacity to function, and is both injured and angry over her husband's less than wholehearted support in her difficult situation. Separation has begun to seem the only viable solution because their every conversation seems to become an escalating, pitched battle.

Mrs. D. calls a clinic for children, pouring out her concern that her normally responsive 9-year-old daughter has closed herself off in her room for most of the past couple of days with the claim that she wants to be by herself and does not want to talk. At the same time, her 10-year-old son has been finding it almost impossible to eat anything. She is terribly distressed since she feels torn between the children who clearly need her badly and her husband who was hospitalized two days ago in critical condition. She wonders whether someone could help the children.

In each of the foregoing situations, as the problem is initially presented, the practitioner may not tune in immediately to the likelihood that the difficulty can best be understood and dealt with as a family problem. For example, Mrs. A. might well be asked to accompany her son to an agency where he would be "evaluated" by one or more professionals while she provided background information to another. However, even on the basis of the scanty information presented by Mrs. A., there is reason to believe that the boy's long-term problems may have some significance for the entire family. His "bright and outgoing" younger sister is apparently quite different from him, yet the mother speaks of her timid, academically handicapped son as being seen by his parents as "pleasant" and "no trouble" despite his serious difficulties in school and his social isolation. Why would parents exhibit this total unconcern in our achievement-oriented society? What are their expectations for him? How is it for him to have a little sister who does so well in the areas in which he is constricted, and how does the younger child feel about her fearful and unprepossessing older brother? Since it seems unlikely that these areas can be effectively addressed without in some way involving each family member, why not focus from the outset on the family unit?

Mr. B., a depressed and anxious man, might well need to be seen individually in view of the degree of his distress. However, he also gives clear evidence that although he is physically separated from his family, he still has strong ties, whatever their nature, to his wife as well as his children. Is his wife deeply distressed also? What are the children's reactions, and to what extent are these related to Mr. B.'s current upset? He still seems to look to his wife for some form of response, and she has apparently not refused to talk with him daily. Does *she* want to be involved in reexamining or otherwise dealing with their relationship? Although one cannot predict the outcome, is it not possible that all members of this family may, at the very least, wish to take advantage of an opportunity jointly to examine their current circumstances: their responses to it, as well as their plans for continuing their lives, together or apart?

Mr. and Mrs. C. have come to an agency for help in relation to their marriage, but, at least initially, both identify one child in their far-from-blended family as the central focus of dissonance in a marital situation that previously had been working well for both of them. Clearly, a volatile situation has developed in this triangular relationship among husband, daughter, and wife, and there are rumblings of trouble with at least some of the other children. Although, once again, outcomes cannot be predicted, it is possible that Mr. and Mrs. C. may be able to do much of the work with the children themselves if, with marital therapy, their relationship regains its equilibrium and is judged rewarding by both of them. However, it would seem important at least to *assess* this very complex situation with the entire family, in view of the apparently serious problems in relation to the taking on of family roles and in assigning responsibility and blame.

It appears that the D. children are suffering greatly at a time when their father's life may well be in question and their burdened mother, reaching for outside help, is feeling unable to meet the needs of her very ill husband and her troubled children at the same time. Her own probable desperation, while implied, is not explicit. Here again is a situation in which the practitioner has alternative routes available. The children might be viewed as the focus of attention or Mrs. D. might herself be seen by another professional, both in relation to the children's problems and her own distress. Once more, however, the family might be approached as a unit, though presumably without the father at this time. This would provide an opportunity for family members, alone with the therapist, to gain some understanding of whether and how they can respond to each other in this difficult time and for the therapist to move toward rapid intervention in a crisis in which all family members are finding their resources severely strained.

Often it is not easy for beginners in family therapy to move from a focus on the individual, "the identified client," to one in which the interactions of a social system constitute the unit of attention. It is crucial that a shift be made from viewing problems as residing in one person to an approach that recognizes and treats them as interactive in nature and their causation as circular rather than linear (Wachtel, 1979, p. 123). Wachtel suggests that the transition is less arduous for those whose approach to individual psychotherapy has involved a clear awareness of the systemic implications of the problems of the individual. Easy or not, the shift must be made.

In addition, eager to learn and anxious to meet an academic requirement that depends on their securing client families, students tend to experience particular stress with regard to involving family groups in work on their common problems. The difficulties here relate to the vulnerability of the beginner who almost inevitably views a family's unwillingness to participate or continue as a therapeutic failure in some form or degree. In turn, untoward pressures are sometimes exerted on the family, which is likely to respond in its own characteristic ways to the perceived external threat (whether of public exposure of guilt, inadequacy, blame, or dissolution): a response that is not likely to advance the therapeutic work. Unquestionably, the help of a preceptor or supervisor is essential under these circumstances if the interaction is not to spiral toward increasing destructiveness for all concerned.

Family therapy is not uncommonly undertaken with a subunit of the total group. While in some situations this may be an effective approach, it is one that is attended by certain risks for both family and student therapist. By agreeing to meet with some and not with others, the therapist may be playing into an already established pattern of scapegoating in which one or two "problem bearers" have been singled out as defective members of the household. Similarly, the inclusion of certain members means the exclusion of others, which may serve to reinforce a split within a family which is already struggling for survival as a unit. For example, beginning therapy with a mother and son may lend support to a family alliance in which the father is seen by both as punitive and destructive and therefore "to blame" for the behavior problems presented by the son. The mother may view herself as needing to protect the boy from her husband and, by placing herself in the intermediary position, effectively prevent father and son from relating directly to each other. This is not to say that such chances are never to be taken; it is critical, however, that the practitioner taking them does so consciously.

On the other hand, although a family assessment may be completed with all members present, at times much—even all—of the continuing work may be done with the parents. This is often characteristic of those situations in which the major difficulties emanate from their relationship. Certainly, those who need to work on sexual problems require an opportunity to do so without the presence of the children. Further, while the anxiety of the beginning therapist is most frequently focused on "the reluctant family," careful thought must be given to the possible centrality of the role of a member of the extended family in the problems brought to therapy. Inclusion of such persons on a regular or time-limited basis may be crucial to the remediation of the difficulties (Napier & Whitaker, 1973, p. 110).

Clearly, it is vital that the therapist achieve growing freedom to base therapeutic decisions on the characteristics and requirements of each *family's* situation. In Haley's terms (1972, p. 164), "The *problem* is the method."

ISSUES IN BEGINNING

Family therapy begins with the therapist's first contact with the family; this may be in a telephone call, a letter, or a brief face-to-face meeting with a "walk-in" applicant. Students are uneasy about these beginnings since they must undertake them with little or no knowledge of the situation in question and are therefore unable to secure specific prior consultation from a preceptor or supervisor. In any event, it is in this crucial encounter that the first ground rules can be set for working together. A family-systems approach is set forth as constituting the context of the therapy (Franklin & Prosky, 1973, p. 31). A "mapping" process is begun whereby the players in the family drama are identified, and initial moves are made toward setting the problem in an interactionist frame. This early reconnaissance provides an opportunity for the therapist to make essential preliminary decisions as to who will be seen during the evaluation period and to be explicit about the plans. Students are often intimidated by the recognition that this first contact has such vital implications for the ongoing work. Some of the discomfort may be mitigated by initially contracting with families for a minimum of two interviews for evaluation purposes. The continuing availability of consultation is usually of some help. However, as in all risk-laden learning situations, only the sense of mastery gained through repeated experience followed by careful critical analysis and planning can be expected to reduce the inevitable anxiety effectively.

Beginners frequently find it difficult to decide whether the initial meetings would be held best in the family's home or in the office. Practical considerations aside (for example, the physical confinement of a key family member or an irremediable transportation problem), the implied control and the freedom from interruption of an office setting recommends it as the more promising location when the therapist is new to family work. Later, home visits may well be planned, as dictated by the requirements of the ongoing work. In fact most family therapists would agree that home visits always reveal aspects of the family's life that would otherwise be much harder to come by.*

As already indicated, the familiarity and implied control of the office milieu provides a certain support for the student who, freed at least from environmental distractions, can focus on the business at hand. For example, the chairs can be arranged so as to permit some choice on the part of family members; the therapist can choose to be seated last if this promises to be useful in developing early clues to family interaction patterns, and members are more likely to include the therapist in any decision about removing themselves from the room (the therapeutic "territory"). It is also especially useful for the beginning therapist to have the security of having made arrangements for the supervision of very young children, should it be necessary for them to leave for part of the time; such a plan may provide for more effective work on the part of experienced clinicians as well.

Initial Interviews

Students are likely to be concerned and indecisive if family members do not arrive together for the interview, especially if some are markedly late. It is useful to consider this possibility prior to the first meeting since some patterns will be laid down here for all that follow. Usually it is very important to wait for the missing persons to arrive in order to reinforce in action what has

---

*See, for example, Bloch (1973).

been dealt with verbally in the initial contact. However, if it is clear that those who are absent will not attend at all, it will probably be necessary to meet with those present in order to assess the situation further and to re-negotiate further contacts. Careful exploration frequently reveals that at least some of those present have had a stake in the "defection" of the absent member or members. Under these circumstances the therapeutic enterprise is, at best, off to a rocky start and may well founder along the way.

In this first meeting the beginner is faced with the necessity for starting to grapple actively with issues hinging on family interaction patterns; si-multaneously, family members usually work hard to keep the focus on the person or persons they see as having the problem. There is sometimes an irresistible temptation for the neophyte therapist to join the family in this comparatively familiar territory, yet focusing on the "symptom bearer" en-tails the risk of reinforcing a pattern of scapegoating that keeps the family in a state of precarious equilibrium while leaving one member in a great deal of misery. On the other hand, to ignore or reject the symptoms is to imply an insensitivity to the plight of both individual and family. A laissez-faire approach is unlikely to be effective here. If the therapist is to be useful in helping to initiate needed changes in the situation, it is essential that she or he move steadily toward gaining a more comprehensive picture of how family members interact with each other, working with them to recognize how these patterns relate to the problems they have defined and to others, as such are revealed.

Beginners frequently feel that they must do this without revealing their intent; perhaps they are worried that "showing one's hand" will somehow alert the clients to tricks that belong only to practitioners of the trade. There are indeed times when, in the interest of increasing the likelihood of certain outcomes, the family therapist may consciously choose not to share the basis of her or his thinking, but this is not one of those times. If a family is to gain new perspectives on old problems, its members must be given the opportunity to begin making sense of their situations with the open and active involvement of the therapist who may begin with a straightforward approach such as: "One of the things we know about family members is that because they've lived close to each other for a long time, each member is likely to be affected, one way or another, by what happens to the others. I can see that X has been having a good deal of difficulty, but what I'm not clear about is where everyone else stands in all this."

The therapist here has been open about alignment with the "experts" in her or his business (often a comforting position for a student) implying (1) that she or he has a fairly clear idea of how one goes about family therapy; (2) that she or he, therefore, is assuming certain responsibility for structuring the current encounter; (3) that although "the problem" is pressing and may elsewhere appear to reside in a particular member, that individual is not to be viewed as blameworthy here; and (4) that it would be a rare person indeed who would not react to problems in another family member. The stage is then set for an examination of the family interaction, and the therapist can return to a reiteration of this stance as needed throughout the course of therapy.

Having made the position clear, the student is often dismayed when communication lines continue to flow from the individual family member to the therapist. This behavior is clearly tied to many of the issues already discussed and, depending on the content, has additional elements of testing the reactions of both therapist and (without direct interaction with them) other family members as well. It provides the communicator with the security of a higher degree of control over the communication since it is much less difficult to deal with the response of a single person at any one time. Each member feels vulnerable in one way or another, and each feels the need to manage the impression that she or he is making on the therapist. Issues related to blaming, responsibility, and guilt are clearly involved here, and concerns about privacy and confidentiality are usually closely interwoven. Some of the constriction in the interaction may be partially relieved by an open statement that these are always matters of concern and that certain rules will need to be developed and observed.

For the therapist whose experience has previously been confined to work with individuals, management of confidentiality takes on some new characteristics in family work. Clients can still be given the usual assurances that information will not be made available to anyone outside the agency or clinic. However, issues of privacy and confidentiality between the therapist and the family are more complex. The family must be made aware that while a member may be understandably uneasy about sharing certain information lest it expose them to attack from another member (or from the therapist), the work cannot be productive for the family if the therapy is hamstrung by "secrets" that mark forbidden territory on all sides. Similarly, the practitioner must be clear that she or he cannot be party to any "privileged communication" from one family member because that would render untenable the role of therapist for the entire family unit. It is important, that all concerned know from the beginning that contacts outside the family session will be considered "shareable" at the next meeting. This latter is especially important in situations that involve cotherapists, either one of whom may find that she or he is cast in the role of "protector of a family secret" by a family member who does not wish the other therapist to know. This position clearly cannot be taken on if the therapeutic team is to be productive and the therapy effective.

Questions regarding history taking frequently emerge from these early efforts at getting the enterprise afloat. Unquestionably, the implied structure of history taking has considerable appeal for neophytes who, looking for a means of "gathering data" on that seemingly ephemeral process, "family interaction," are often attracted by the more familiar notion of an orderly assemblage of data along a timeline. They are not alone in their view of history taking, which is a clearly specified part of the approach of many family therapists. Notable in this regard is Virginia Satir, who advocates setting aside the first two family interviews for the taking of a detailed "family life chronology" (Satir, 1967, p. 112). Others—Jay Haley, for example—take a different stance; with characteristic style he states his view:

> The beginner tends to see the family as a collection of individuals who have introjected their pasts. The more experienced family therapist learns to see the present situation as the major causal factor and the process which must be changed. He inquires about the past only when he cannot understand the present, and thinks the family can discuss the present more easily if it is framed as something from the past (Haley, 1972, p. 159).

There is little question that history taking in the hands of a skilled practitioner may be managed in such a way as to further the prime goals of family therapy, namely, to facilitate change in family functioning through examining and intervening in family interaction. However, this involves making the assembling of the chronology subsidiary to the central goals of dealing with the interaction, and it demands a flexibility and skill that beginners are not likely to possess. The result is that the history taking is likely to become an end in itself and often gets in the way of both student's and family's sense of here-and-now priorities. On the other hand, as Haley suggests, it is indeed often necessary to "dip into" the past briefly where it seems likely that this will be useful in further illuminating some aspect of the present. In general, beginners seem better able to adapt this approach to the requirements of the ongoing work since it is less likely that the family interactional focus will be derailed by lengthy historical excursions.

An additional cluster of issues concern students at the time of initial interviews. These center around the development of an explicit set of agreements or contract: in short, a plan of therapeutic action that is worked out with the family when the therapist has begun to develop some clarity about the situation. While the work of contracting frequently includes reaffirmation or renegotiation around such matters as confidentiality and deciding which family members will participate on a regular basis, students frequently experience dilemmas concerning other elements as well. The setting of limits on the length of the initial contract is often a source of uneasiness for students; they sometimes fear that what they view as their own ineptitude may hamper the family in achieving "enough" change before the time comes for evaluation and renegotiation.

Clearly, contracting calls for a spelling out of the therapist's initial formulations regarding the nature of the difficulties as well as those aspects of the family's functioning that seem comparatively free of trouble. Here, once more, the role is active. It is one that entails what the beginner often sees as the risk of being "wrong." The setting forth of initial treatment plans, including what the therapist has to offer, may also be viewed in a similar light. Students are especially concerned that the family, when given the choice, may reject them and what they have to offer. Clearly, if their clients are to have productive experiences in beginning (and continuing) family therapy, supervisory consultation adequate to the demands of the situation must be made available, and it must be accepted. Contracting has a crucial role in the active work of family therapy, and therapists are obliged to learn to participate in it actively and well.

ISSUES IN CONTINUATION

Having negotiated the troubled waters of the early interviews, it is a heady experience for the beginning therapist to see family members starting to interact more openly, including each other in communications and expressing their views and feelings with some degree of freedom. It is dismaying to find, however, that a prolonged indulgence in observing and commenting upon these processes is not, in and of itself, productive of the expected changes. Locating a golden mean between exclusive focus on process and active, direct intervention to promote change is a demanding therapeutic obligation—and one made more difficult by the fact that it must be discovered anew with each individual family. Moreover, judgment must be exercised by the family therapist insofar as encouragement of the venting of feelings is concerned. This is often a source of uncertainty for the learner who, doubtless, has seen clients in individual psychotherapy considerably relieved through the experience of emotional "ventilation." Nevertheless, it is important that students learn early that although the sharing of feelings may at times serve a very useful purpose in helping family members relate to each other, the identifying and expressing of feeling as an end in itself is not effective in family therapy. For example, where rage is involved, it must be carefully assessed for the degree to which its continued expression is helpful in the family's ongoing work together. This does not imply indifference to the upset of the individual member who may, in fact need to be given the opportunity for additional help elsewhere.

Apropos of the foregoing, students frequently raise the question whether an individual or subgroup within a family may appropriately be referred elsewhere for assistance of another type—and if so, when that can be done. Clearly, the basis for such decisions must include an assessment of the degree to which the problems are so idiosyncratic to the persons concerned that they are unlikely to be addressed adequately within the context of the family therapy. A serious and unyielding parental sexual problem might be a case in point. Under most circumstances, discussion of the difficulty would already have been moved out of the family context to one that included only the therapist and the troubled pair. However, for a variety of reasons, the practitioner may well reach the conclusion that the problems are beyond her or his knowledge and expertise and that the help of an outside expert is warranted. Whatever the difficulty, where the persons concerned are in great distress, a rapid referral must be attempted. Where the discomfort or disturbance is less serious and/or where it is seen as unlikely to impinge on the family therapy in a negative way, it may be possible to postpone the referral until a time more favorable to the work with the family as a whole.

It is important to note that scapegoating may once more be an issue here since, again, one person or a small segment of the family is singled out on the basis of a problem that may not be viewed favorably by the others. The therapist, whether novice or experienced, must be alert to this possibility and deal with it openly as the need arises.

As part of the continuing work with families, beginners may find it necessary to make decisions regarding the possible introduction of comparatively structured devices, such as parent education or family tasks. The latter may be designed to serve a variety of purposes and may either grow out of the mutual work of practitioner and family or be assigned by the therapist with the intention of enhancing some aspect of their functioning.* Students are often uncertain about the appropriateness of the design when tasks are contemplated, and also find it difficult to weigh alternatives in relation to timing. The usual considerations with regard to promoting family interaction and change apply here as elsewhere, but beginners require help in assessing the probable impact of "work assignments" at any given point in the clients' work with each other. It is especially important that these be tailored to a family's capacities. Otherwise the family will be put in the devastating position of repeatedly experiencing failure.

When it becomes evident that a lack of knowledge is hampering parents in dealing with each other and their children, some form of parent education is often contemplated. It is important that the therapist new to family therapy carefully assess and test out the *degree* to which the additional information (1) seems required by the parents and (2) seems likely to be accepted and used. Therapists are frequently surprised to discover a thoughtfully planned task or a well-phrased effort at education being managed by a family in such a way as to sabotage the goals: This may be an indication that it is more

---

*For a more comprehensive discussion of both the designing and uses of family tasks, see Chapter 23 of this volume.

important to the family to convey a message to the therapist than to achieve change. In addition, students, eager to "pass on" what they have been learning themselves, may believe that education must take a didactic form in order to be effective. In fact, their own behavior with the family may provide an ongoing model that is highly efficacious as an educational device with both parents and children alike.

On occasion, family therapists are dismayed to find themselves firmly caught up in a family struggle. Less experienced in rapid appraisal of interactional ploys, learners are especially susceptible to this frustrating and problematic circumstance. In summarizing the process Lynch (1974, p. 163) writes: "The family in treatment will work hard to maintain the homeostasis of its system and in doing so may draw the therapist into its field so that he becomes a part of that system, frequently losing himself in the process." The practitioner may, for example, align her- or himself quite unknowingly with one part of a family: perhaps with the child who is perceived as victimized by the parents or, conversely, with a father or mother who is viewed as oppressed by self-willed and difficult adolescents. The therapist, enmeshed in the family maelstrom, may begin to feel, uneasily, that she or he has to be far more active than usual, to "make up for" the apparent inertia in a family that is not "moving" or changing. At the same time the therapist usually has a sense of marking time or "running in place;" change is the family's responsibility, and no solo effort on the part of the practitioner can accomplish the goal.

Therapist entrapment in a family system may occur with bewildering rapidity, so beginners need help in early identification of situations that are likely to move in this direction (this is especially true of circumstances that stir up disturbing echoes of past personal experience). Where a cotherapist is a part of the family therapy, she or he can provide invaluable help in providing a "danger alert" when the problem is in its early stages. However, beginners are also much in need of the assistance of an experienced and skillful family-therapy supervisor if the difficulty is to be both understood and managed adequately.

A brief note concerning issues arising in relation to termination seems important before concluding this chapter. When family members have reached a point at which their ability to communicate and interact permit them to work effectively at problem solving on their own, they often begin to view family therapy as being somewhat superfluous. Termination under such circumstances is usually greeted with some comfort and gratification by student therapists, although it may be somewhat unsettling to them that, "having each other," family members are less distressed at the loss of the therapist than are individual clients. However, beginners are often in need of assistance in terminating productively with those families who, having achieved certain of their goals, are in need of the opportunity to end the therapy in order to test out their relationships and functioning. This is often worrying to students because, in the first place, "everything" has not been dealt with, and, in the second, there is always the possibility that, having once been "lost," the family will not return to therapy. But experienced therapists understand and students need the opportunity to learn that if this testing and consolidating period is not permitted, a family's continuing in therapy is likely to be unproductive and even destructive. At termination, then, the family therapist is acquiescing in—even fostering—the family's "reenmeshment" in the ecologic system of which it has all along been a part.

REFERENCES

Bloch, D.A. The clinical home visit. In Bloch, D.A. (ed.), *Techniques of Family Therapy*. New York: Grune & Stratton, 1973, 39–45.

Franklin, P., & Prosky, P. A standard initial interview. In Bloch, D.A. (ed.), *Techniques of Family Therapy*. New York: Grune & Stratton, 1973, 29–37.

Haley, J. Beginning and experienced family therapists. In Ferber, A., Mendelsohn, M., & Napier, A. (eds.), *The Book of Family Therapy*. New York: Science House, 1972, 155–167.

Lynch, C. On not getting caught up in the family system. *Family Therapy*, 1974, 1, 163–170.

Napier, A.Y., & Whitaker, C. Problems of the beginning family therapist. In Bloch, D.A. (ed.), *Techniques of Family Therapy*. New York: Grune & Stratton, 1973, 109–121.

Satir, V. *Conjoint Family Therapy*. Palo Alto, Calif.: Science and Behavior Books, 1967.

Wachtel, E.F. Learning family therapy: The dilemmas of an individual therapist. *Journal of Contemporary Psychotherapy*, 1979, 10, 122–135.

21

Considerations for Working with Single-Parent Families

Cathleen Getty

The rapidly growing number of families that include only one parent has generated considerable controversy as to how this variant structural form should be viewed. While it is often proposed that the family form itself is inherently dysfunctional, there is evidence that the problems believed to emanate from the single-parent status of such families are, in fact, related to one or several of a multiplicity of factors that are not unique to them. For example, financial insecurity frequently has a deleterious effect on a family's functioning, regardless of its structure. Like most urban nuclear families, the one-parent family is heavily burdened by a societal expectation that a small number of individuals will be capable of taking on all the role responsibilities previously shared throughout the extended-family network. In this chapter, Getty explores the pressures experienced by such families and offers some direction for the family therapist engaged in working with them as they attempt to manage their new circumstances.

There is a large and ever-increasing number of single adults who are living alone with their children as a result of various circumstances: the death of a spouse, marital separation or divorce, or the decision of an unmarried adult to keep the child born to her or him. More than one-sixth of the children in this country now live with only one parent, and it is estimated that nearly one out of every two of today's children will live in a one-parent family by age 18 (Glick & Norton, 1979, pp. 28–29). These changes are primarily due to the increasing divorce rate and the growing number of unmarried women who have children but do not give them up for adoption.* The chance of

---

*Most one-parent households result from divorce and separation (70 percent). The death of a spouse ranks next, accounting for 14 percent of these families (a relatively stable percentage); 10 percent of the single parents who head families have never been married (Weiss, 1979, p. iv).

an individual's becoming a single parent—having the unshared responsibility for the care of his or her children—approaches one in four; the likelihood of a woman's becoming a single parent (one in two) is far greater than that for a man (one in twenty) (Weiss, 1979, pp. x–xi).

The major challenge facing the family that includes only one adult is providing for the growth and development of the children, as well as meeting the needs of the adult (Satir, 1972; Weiss, 1979). In an era in which the effectiveness of the nuclear family has been severely criticized, Weiss (1979, p. xiii) underlines the concern of many regarding the capabilities of the one-parent family: "If two parents are too few, what about one?"

One adult becomes responsible for what two find difficult: securing an adequate financial income, maintaining a household, providing for the psychosocial as well as the physical needs of family members, and so forth. In addition, the one-parent family must do its job for a disapproving and rejecting society that expects it to fail, a society that views it as deviant, perhaps even un-American in its presumption that it can "go it alone," giving up the sanctioned and sanctified marital pairing. Little wonder then, if a single parent succumbs to the intense pressures generated by family and social situations and, feeling unable to continue, eventually finds need of an array of public services. Mental-health professionals attest to the fact that such families constitute a slowly increasing proportion of their "caseloads." This being the situation, what are some of the problems particular to the single-parent family, and, in turn, what considerations do they raise for the mental-health professional who undertakes work with such a family?

SINGLE-PARENT FAMILIES—SIMILAR YET DIFFERENT

Although all single-parent families face common problems deriving from their similar structural characteristics, they do, of course, differ remarkably. Much of their dissimilarity has to do with the route by which each became a one-parent family in the first place and the way in which each was able to adjust to the crucial changes precipitated by separation, death, or parenthood. A family's history in this regard greatly affects the self-image of each family member, the image the family has of itself as a unit, and the members' conceptions of their relationships to one another and to the missing parent. This past history also influences the family's ability to cope with its day-to-day functioning as well as its readiness to deal with future exigencies.

Emotional Impact of the Initial Disruption

It is useful, then, to conceive of all single-parent families as involved in processes precipitated by crucial events in their lives—processes that evolve over time. In this view, divorce, for example, would not be just an event, but "a process that occurs in a family over a period and that has far-reaching effects throughout the nuclear and extended family systems" (Beal, 1980, p. 241).

It has been proposed that divorce and separation require two separate but overlapping adjustments: first, the adjustment to the dissolution of the marriage and, second, the adjustment to the development of a new life-style (Spanier & Casto, 1979).* If one considers the adjustment that the widow and the never-married mother and their families must make to their changed circumstances, there is some rationale supporting the utility of this process model in conceptualizing the experience of widows and never-married mothers as well.†

Several tasks are involved in the initial adjustment. Both the single parent and family must cope with the emotional impact of the events that they themselves have brought about or that have befallen them. Willingly or unwillingly, they must deal with relatives and friends, alerting them to their circumstances. In addition, they must involve themselves in legal processes: working out property and child-custody settlements or other necessary arrangements (Spanier & Casto, 1979, p. 244).

All single-parent families resulting from divorce, separation, or death of a spouse have experienced loss; however, the response to loss in each case is unique. A spouse may be lost and a marriage ended through divorce, but the bonds between the pair remain remarkably strong, whatever the quality of the previous marriage, and they persist long after the dissolution of the marriage. Through an appreciation for the strength and persistence of the marital bond that has developed through time and shared experience, one can gain an understanding of both the anxiety and the ambivalent feelings experienced by the divorced and their often inconsistent behavior with their ex-spouses.‡ For example, although angry at and resentful about the mistreatment she has suffered during marriage and after, a divorced woman may still pine for her ex-husband and seek continued contact with him, even if renewed contact results in further conflict and disappointment. In contrast, one more readily understands and appreciates the loss and resultant grief

---

*The reader may wish to compare Spanier and Casto's work with an earlier crisis model developed by Hill (1965, pp. 45–48), who proposed that although each family's adjustment to unusual stress varies, common response patterns may be identified for the individual member, as well as for the family. His stages closely parallel those identified in the bereavement process and are labelled Crisis, Disorganization, Recovery, and Reorganization. The first response is "numbness": Members act as though nothing has happened. Then as they begin to acknowledge the impact of the precipitating events, disorganization occurs; the role behavior of family members is altered, and conflicts strain relationships. Later, members develop and put into effect new routines, establishing agreement regarding future organizational patterns.

†Although it is obvious that men can be divorced or widowed, and they can become fathers without marrying, since most single-parent families are headed by women, the single parent will be identified as female in most instances in this chapter.

‡For further exploration of the impact of divorce on marital bonding and attachment, the reader is referred to the excellent discussion in Weiss (1976).

experience of the person whose spouse has died: The finality of the loss and the "blameless" position of the widow or widower are potential factors shaping our perceptions in this regard.

The divorced and the widowed alike may experience similar emotions regarding their loss: sadness, loneliness, hurt, anger, and guilt are common and often intensely experienced feelings. However, while the anger and guilt of the widow or widower are soon muted and positive memories of the marriage remain (Weiss, 1979, p. 7), those negative feelings are likely to be kept alive for the divorced person by the necessity for continued contact with the ex-spouse. In addition, if the divorce was initiated by the action of only one partner, the other may be left struggling with feelings of failure, unworthiness, and self-doubt.

Obviously, the never-married parent faces a different set of circumstances: the addition rather than the loss of a family member. This is not to suggest that loss is not involved. The single mother, for example, is likely to find one or more important relationships disrupted, significantly changed, or ended as a consequence of becoming pregnant or of choosing parenthood while unmarried. If her relationship with the child's father is a tenuous one, it may not tolerate the strain imposed on it by this new event, and, as a result, it may be ended by a clear and mutual decision on the part of the couple or by the disengagement of one partner. Alternatively, the relationship may simply deteriorate as the couple experiences greater emotional estrangement. Similarly, relationships with parents, siblings, and relatives may also be adversely affected. The emotional impact of unmarried parenthood, then, will be greatly dependent on the response of the social network (a dimension elaborated on at a later point in this chapter). However, owing to the stigma attached to her status, the unmarried woman is likely to experience some degree of guilt, shame, and failure for not living up to her own expectations and/or those of others. She may also suffer hurt, pain, and sadness as relationships with significant others in her life are altered.

The addition of a new child will, of course, call forth a host of emotions; the unmarried parent's reactions are closely tied to the meaning that having a child and becoming a parent holds for her. While the unmarried parent may be somewhat relieved once she has made the decision to keep the child, she must thereafter deal with the realities accompanying that decision.

Therapeutic Considerations.   Single parents may seek help at any point in the adjustment process. Depending on the circumstances precipitating their need for services, they may single out themselves or one of the children as the client. It is somewhat unlikely, however, that the entire family is initially identified as needing assistance. From the first then, it is important that the therapist carefully consider whether it is most appropriate for the single parent to receive therapy individually, in a group with other clients who share similar concerns, or with his or her family. This issue must be read-dressed, too, at critical junctures throughout the treatment process. Whatever modality used by the therapist, a family-systems approach is indicated.* The overriding concern and ultimate therapeutic goal emanating from such an approach is the integrity and functionality of the reshaped unit: its ability to operate in a cohesive and organized manner, effectively managing tension, providing for the needs of its members, and relating to significant others in its social network.

In working with single-parent families, the therapist must be aware of the members' and family's position in the adjustment process and of what each phase requires of members, since this has implications for the therapeutic work (Salts, 1979). If the members are in the initial phase of adjustment, it behooves the practitioner to gain an appreciation for the impact the crucial event has had on them and the way in which they are coping with the accompanying stress and emotions. During this period, it is important for the members to express their feelings openly, whatever they may be, and to be heard and to hear one another—allowing for differing feelings and attitudes.

If it becomes evident that one or more members is having more than usual difficulty in coping, the therapist will then need to focus on the management of this intense stress. For example, the divorced woman who is having great difficulty detaching from her spouse will need support and understanding while she struggles with her ambivalence and perhaps acts in contradictory ways. She may need help in recognizing that although her teenage children do not share her resentment and anger for their father, they still care about her. (Their differing attitudes may be threatening to her; they may be taken to mean that the children are "siding" with their father.) It will be important that she be assisted in dealing more constructively with her negative, hostile feelings so that she will not act in ways that are ultimately destructive to herself, the children, and her ex-husband. If she can be assisted in doing so, the children are in a much better position to maintain their crucial relationship with their father. As the mother comes to terms with her own feelings and altered life situation, she is better able to invest productively in her new way of life.

Social Adjustment

The ability of the single-parent family to cope successfully with the traumatic events and the changes precipitated by them, and subsequently to establish a new life-style appropriate to the circumstances in which the family finds

---

*Humphreys elaborates on this issue in Chapter 20 of this volume.

itself, is intimately related to the members' readiness and ability to maintain old and develop new relationships with friends, relatives, and the community. While divorce, by virtue of its increased incidence, is no longer so negatively sanctioned as it was several decades ago, divorced persons may still find family and friends shocked and embarrassed by their marital upset and separation. They may even find others to be overtly hostile toward them. In such situations, divorced persons may find that the lack of support increases the overall difficulty in adjusting to the separation (Spanier & Casto, 1979, p. 246). Widows and widowers, on the other hand, are likely at least to receive initial support from their community, because in contrast to divorce, the rituals are clear, well established, and spell out the manner in which others are expected to participate with the grieving spouse and family members.*

An unmarried woman is in the least desirable social position as a single parent. Weiss (1979, p. 10) characterizes it in this way:

> Bereavement is clearly tragedy. Separation and divorce have their tragic elements, but they suggest something in addition: failure or at least bad judgment. Unmarried motherhood seems to elicit searches for explanation in the mother's personality. The mother who never married tends to be seen as unfortunate or thoughtless or easily misled, perhaps a disorganized member of a disorganzied family or a rebellious member of an organized one.

Despite the increasing divorce rate, marriage continues to be a highly valued social institution. Being married is especially valued by women, whose status is generally lower than that of men and whose opportunity to achieve status through other routes is more limited (Kitson et al., 1980, p. 291). Thus, when a woman becomes divorced or widowed, she is separated not only from a spouse but from the valued and central role of wife as well, and she is required to move into the formless status and "nonrole" of divorcée or widow (Nass, 1978, p. 470). The unmarried woman has not only cut herself off from access to the valued role of wife, she does not even have claim to past occupancy.

Such role changes require a redefinition not only of intrafamilial relationships but of those external to the family as well (Pais & White, 1979, p. 273). However, redefinition is a complex process. Our views of how others perceive us greatly affect the way in which we define ourselves (Stryker, 1972), and it is clear that the single parent is likely to be perceived as "different" both

---

*It is important to note, however, that many widows and widowers may find the responses extended them to be quite superficial and short-lived. Miles and Hays (1978, p. 213) report that widows often find others to be "gauche, insensitive and uncaring."

by others and by herself (Kitson et al., 1980, p. 292). These changed perceptions, then, contribute to the individual's feeling distanced by others or to her choosing to distance herself from others. In either situation, her social network is diminished, and increased isolation results.*

As single parents recover from the initial blow of their respective traumatic situations and attempt to reestablish old relationships, they may find themselves out of step with friends from the past. No longer united to old friends by similar life situations, they may indeed experience a period of social isolation before they are able to establish new friendships, most likely with persons with whom they have in common their new life circumstances and concerns.

Therapeutic Considerations. As previously noted, the nature of the therapeutic work either with the single parent individually or with the family as a unit will, of necessity, be integrally related to the stage of adjustment in which the family finds itself. This general principle also applies when the therapist is considering strategies concerned with fostering social interaction of the single-parent family. For example, with a family still in the process of adjusting to the dissolution of the parents' marriage, the therapist will need to assess the degree to which the family has been able to alert relatives and friends to its changed circumstances: Have they been able to make their private situation public? Fearing censure, the single-parent family may avoid disclosing information about its current circumstances. While this may be considered the family's prerogative, it does not provide for the open and public acknowledgment that is a crucial step by which the family begins to accept the reality of its new situation and to signal the family's social network that a response is in order. Not communicating with others may further shape members' perceptions of themselves and the family as deviant and delay the necessary work of redefinition.

Also of importance is the way in which family members communicate their distress, concerns, or needs to others. Can they do so in a manner likely to elicit supportive responses from their social network? Family members may have difficulty acknowledging that they have needs that they themselves cannot meet; they may fear further labeling of the family as inadequate and failing. Alternatively, they may be hesitant to solicit support openly, anticipating that it will be denied or that the significant relationships will be strained or unable to accommodate such requests.

Under such circumstances, family members may need an opportunity to

---

*In this regard, Kitson and associates (1980) found that divorcées felt more restricted in their relationships with others than did widows, and they believed these attitudes to be related to the status of the divorced women.

address their concerns openly, with the therapist functioning as an "agent of reality," assisting them in checking out the validity of their perceptions and testing the responsiveness of their network. In this way, the family may be less likely to distance itself from important figures in its network.

The therapist may begin work with a single-parent family that finds itself, although recovered from the initial traumatic impact, somewhat isolated and with its social network diminished. The practitioner may play an important role in this transitional period, for family members need support and encouragement as they seek out and attempt to establish new relationships. This is a difficult and crucial time inasmuch as members will be testing out their new identities while they are still feeling vulnerable because of their past history. This vulnerability is particularly felt by single mothers as they attempt to reinvolve themselves with men. Widows, for example, may tend to feel somewhat uncomfortable with the resurgence of sexual feelings (Miles & Hays, 1978, p. 214), while divorced women may feel discouraged and exploited because of the frequent sexual propositioning they experience (Kitson et al., 1980, p. 297).

As she tries out new relationships, the single parent is also likely to need help in evaluating this process: for example, how she goes about meeting and selecting the men whom she dates, how she finds herself participating in these relationships, whether she finds them gratifying, and so forth.

Once a single parent gains greater self-esteem, she is likely to feel that she has greater and more constructive options open to her. That is, she need not feel driven to find a new mate out of desperation because she feels unable to "make it" on her own, or she need not give up on finding a mate, feeling hopeless and unworthy. Instead, she is likely to feel more in control of her life, ready to invest in selected relationships while recognizing that they will not be the sole measure of her life's worth.

Life-Cycle Considerations

The family's response and adjustment to its changed circumstances are inexorably linked to chronologic factors: the age of members and the life tasks facing them individually and as a unit. For example, how old are the spouses at the time of divorce? Of what duration was their marriage? How old are their children? Statistics reveal that two-thirds of all women who divorce do so before the age of 30; consequently, most of the children involved are quite young: under the age of 7 at the time of the legal divorce (Beal, 1980, p. 243). The gravity of the situation is further suggested by data that indicate that children under 5 years of age appear to have greater difficulty in adjusting to divorce than do older children (Wallerstein & Kelly, 1974; 1975; 1976).

Children's age has also been identified as a factor related to the degree of trauma experienced by the mother: The younger the children at the time of divorce, the more likely that the mother's experience will be highly traumatic (Goode, 1956). Divorce, then, results in reshaped family households: units largely headed by young women who most often must seek or continue full-time employment while assuming sole responsibility for their young children. (Their still young husbands may remarry, thereby involving themselves in a new family unit, further distancing themselves from their ex-wives and the children of the first marriage.)

In such situations, one may well wonder how the single working mother manages the parenting of these children who are likely to have special need of her attention as they themselves cope with their new, bewildering, and painful circumstances.* Needing to perform well at work and at home, she may give one or the other short shrift or, more likely, feel impelled to "do everything" and, as a result, feel she has failed miserably in both important arenas. What energy is left to be expended in maintaining old social ties or in seeking and establishing new ones? No longer a wife but still a mother, how is she able to manage her new life circumstances so that she can experience and develop a clear sense of self?

Women generally become widowed somewhat after young adulthood, so their children, if there are any, are more likely to be adolescents or even young adults themselves. This situation is likely to entail a different set of problems. Her marriage now ended after many years, the widow may also be forced to seek employment, perhaps never having worked before. This added responsibility is likely to come at a time when she and her spouse had anticipated a lessening of familial burdens. Moreover, the prospect of parenting adolescents can be frightening, and she may feel ill prepared to tackle that task alone. With her dating experience far behind her and her relationship with her husband vivid in her memory, the widow may find it difficult to seek out new relationships with men.† Moreover, if she reengages in this behavior from an earlier period in her life, she may find herself in a situation remarkably similar to that of her teenage children. They may see this similarity of experiences as competition at a time when they may need to look to her for parental guidance.

For an unmarried woman, the age at which she becomes a parent in large measure determines alternatives open to her. If an adolescent, she may not

---

*For an in-depth discussion of the potential impact of divorce on children, see Chapter 17 in this volume.

†Pais and White (1979, p. 278) note that the age of the individual greatly influences his or her ability to find new reference groups, and that middle-aged persons may experience greater difficulties in this regard.

have sufficient financial resources or employment that will guarantee a steady income. Moreover, she may not feel prepared to assume full responsibility for the care of her child. Under these circumstances, some unmarried mothers choose to remain in their parents' home, thus attempting to take on a parental role while still dependent upon their own parents. The adolescent mother who chooses to live alone with her child, or of necessity must do so, takes on adult concerns and obligations while she really needs to be with her "unfettered" peers who, without the additional burdens, are likely to be better able to prepare themselves for the life tasks that face them.

In comparison, the unmarried woman who becomes a parent in her early or mid-adult years is in a much better position to accept the responsibilities attendant on parenthood. She has managed the separation from her own parents, and, sustained by her life and work experiences, she is likely to be more realistic and self-reliant.

Therapeutic Considerations. The therapist working with the single-parent family needs to be attuned to the therapeutic issues deriving from the unit's particular life circumstances and the time frame within which the family was confronted by them. In this regard, it is useful to identify the "usual" life-cycle tasks with which the family and its members were engaged at the time of the disruption. For example, was the under–30-year-old wife busy with rearing young children and investing in her husband's budding career at the time of the divorce? Was the couple middle–aged and in the process of "launching" late-adolescent children when the husband was killed in an industrial accident?

It is then necessary for the therapist to assess the degree to which this life work has been altered or affected by the disruption, to examine the way in which the restructured family unit and its individual members are able to take on the unfinished work and/or the new tasks required of them, as well as their capacity for meeting the age-specific needs of the members. Does the young divorced woman who has been left solely responsible for three children under the age of 6 find that, meeting the demands of a new full-time job, she is unable to care for the children as she did previously? Right on the heels of being separated from their father, are the children particularly threatened by the daily disappearance of their mother, fearful that she, too, may be lost to them? In yet another single-parent family, is the middle-aged mother who is still mourning the loss of her husband and the end of a 25-year marriage able to support her 19-year-old son's plans for college in a neighboring city? Or is she so anxious about additional separations that she thwarts her son's attempts to leave home despite the fact that two older, married children live within walking distance of her? Sensitized to such chronologic issues, the therapist can better appreciate the extreme complexity of the situation in which the single-parent family finds itself.

ESTABLISHMENT OF A NEW LIFE-STYLE

The second phase of adjustment involves the establishment of a new and functional life-style (Spanier & Casto, 1979, p. 244). Tasks belonging to this period may include finding a new residence, learning how to parent alone, arranging for financial income through employment or public assistance, and developing new friendships. It also includes the management of emotions evoked by these new and often difficult tasks—feelings of fear, frustration, inadequacy, and the like.

Redefinition of Parent-Child Relationships

By virtue of having experienced a special relationship, a couple may feel and pursue a connectedness even when they are no longer living together or legally defined as married. (This may be true for never-married as well as for divorced or separated couples.) On the other hand, estranged couples may no longer feel any sense of attachment, and were it not for their children, they would initiate no further contact with one another. Their former relationship as a couple, the nature of the disruption, and the way in which it was experienced and managed, will affect their readiness and ability to continue their parental partnership. The resolution of this problem, or lack of it, has important consequences not only for the parents but for the children and for the functioning of the new family unit as well.

If parents have intense and unresolved feelings toward their former partners and their post-separation relationships do not provide for satisfactory communication and absorption of tension, they are likely to involve their children in their distress, thus failing to differentiate their own and their children's relationships with their ex-spouses (Pais & White, 1979, p. 276). For example, they may attempt to punish the ex-spouse by interfering with visitation rights or by withholding child support, or one may attempt to pull the child into an alliance against the other spouse through denigration or by courting the child's favor. Such behavior has potentially grave consequences in that it prohibits a successful redefinition of the parents' roles vis-à-vis each other, leaving the single parent unable to expect or solicit coparental support from the ex-spouse, who may be further distanced from interaction with the children. It is also likely to have significant consequences for the children who are being given negative messages regarding the trustworthiness and capability of men and women, as well as the expectations one can hold for male-female relationships (Satir, 1972, pp. 170–172). In addition, children who are pressured into alliances may experience great tension and guilt as they attempt to please and remain loyal to each parent. If the parents' relationship is one of extreme conflict, the children's ties with the noncustodial parent may be ruptured, resulting in further loss for children and parents alike. It is unlikely, then, that children will emerge from such situations with good feelings about themselves and others as persons or as males and females (Satir, 1972, pp. 170–172).

On the other hand, if a good, working parental relationship is developed, they may negotiate for the noncustodial partner to assume some responsibility for care of the children. In addition, his or her consultation may be sought when decisions affecting the children are required.* Even brief and periodic respite from the inexorable demands of child care and a sharing of parental decision making may be important in preventing the emotional depletion of the single parent (Weiss, 1979, p. 284). And, importantly, the children will be better able to accept and adjust to the changed relationships with both parents if the partners have successfully dealt with the changes themselves.

Reallocation of Family Tasks

Because of the inordinate amount of responsible work required of it, the nuclear family is most often making full use of its resources in order to manage its everyday operations. Under such circumstances, there will be a certain amount of strain when one or the other parent is temporarily unable to fulfill his or her role obligations. However, nuclear families that have built flexibility into their role definitions and have internal resource reserves and/ or good access to the external resources of extended family and friends will be able to shift gears, modify their usual way of doing things, and "fill in" for the out-of-action parent. For example, if Mother is hospitalized, Father may absent himself from work and, with the help of a teenage daughter, say, take care of the 10- and 8-year-old children and run the household. Or he may not have to disrupt his work because Grandmother is able to substitute for Mother temporarily. But it is clear that these arrangements are sufficient only for a short period, since the family members and operations are greatly strained unless Mother is soon able to reassume her duties.

So when the family loses a spouse or parent, it loses not only an important individual but an important actor as well. His or her roles in family life are vacated, creating disruption and disorganization while the family attempts to reallocate the functions to other members. With its remaining members and limited resources taxed to the utmost by having to manage these additional demands, the single-parent family can readily find itself experiencing

---

*Consideration may need to be given here to the potential difficulty inherent in parents' being expected, after separation, to enact their parental roles in ways other than as previously defined. For example, a father who did not participate in nurturing ways with the children prior to divorce may find it difficult to take on such new role behavior successfully after divorce (Pais & White, 1979, p. 276).

several forms of overload. Weiss (1979, pp. 267–276) has found that three interrelated yet distinct forms of overload can result; he has defined these as responsibility, task, and emotional overload.

Responsibility Overload. While friends, relatives, and/or the ex-spouse may provide periodic or intermittent child care or financial assistance, it is the single parent who alone must bear the continuing responsibility for the maintenance of the household and the family's welfare. With such responsibility comes a never-ending series of worrisome decisions related to household financing, child-rearing practices, and so forth. Child care appears to be an especially difficult area; the single parent keenly feels the absence of a partner who might balance and diffuse his or her participation with the children (Weiss, 1979, pp. 270–271).

Task Overload. If finances are problematic, the single mother may need to get a job, perhaps for the first time in her life, or if she is already employed, she may need to increase her work hours. These new or increased responsibilities usually do not replace her other functions as homemaker and mother; rather, they are added to her normal load. This leaves her to juggle these demands herself, arrange for outside help, or enlist the children's aid.

Although the family may eventually find ways to get the work done (this often involves a redefinition of priorities and standards), there is little reserve capability for managing extra demands. Task overload may be "produced by the frustration of not being able to complete everything that must be done, and the feeling that failure is inescapable. It can occur when the single parent has been operating for some time at the limits of the parent's capability and has accumulated both fatigue and tasks not yet done" (Weiss, 1979, p. 273).

Emotional Overload. As the sole adult in the family, a single parent finds that she needs to be constantly on call, readily available, and responsive to the needs and demands of the children. Sensitive to the changes the family has undergone, and perhaps feeling responsible for the changed circumstances, she may be unable to define a period of time as her own. The parent's difficulty in defining priorities or delegating tasks may also figure in here. Whatever the causative factors, the result is the same: Without respite, the single parent becomes emotionally depleted, unable to continue giving.

Therapeutic Considerations. When the family has been unsuccessful in reallocating the absent parent's duties, the difficulties are readily apparent. There are likely to be signs of role strain and conflict: Members feel overburdened or unable to fulfill the obligations of their new roles or distressed over the behavior of others whose performance does not meet with their expectations. With family members (especially the mother) busily engaged in keeping the household running, the needs of an individual member may go unrecognized; perhaps if recognized, they are not perceived as meriting attention. Should this continue, the member may begin to exhibit symptoms and/or behavior changes that clearly indicate that it is not only the individual who is in trouble, but the family as well.*

Yet another set of difficulties may result from the family's attempts to manage its new situation. Children may be pulled into adult roles. This is not to be confused with situations in which the parent assigns age-appropriate tasks to the children or when they themselves take on tasks in which they are particularly interested or competent. Rather, it has to do with the parent's expecting and/or permitting the child to perform at levels for which he or she is sociopsychologically unprepared, and which may skew his or her child role with the parent and his or her sibling role with the other children (Satir, 1972, p. 171). For example, the single father may desperately feel the need for a confidante, someone with whom he can share adult concerns and experiences. As his wife is no longer meeting this need and his concerns are not ones he wishes to share with his work buddies, he may begin confiding in his 14-year-old daughter. Although alert to her father's distress and eager to be of help, she may be threatened by his confidences, the growing intimacy of their relationship, and the adult functioning it requires of her. The father's behavior is problematic for him as well: It keeps him from establishing new relationships with his peers or redefining old ones so that they might better meet his needs. The other children in the family may feel jealous and threatened. They are left out of this special relationship with Dad and may be ready to oppose their sister should the relationship result in her attempting to exert more power over them.

When it is evident to the family and/or therapist that reallocation of tasks and roles is problematic, the family needs an opportunity to examine the changes necessitated by the parent's departure, the means by which they have been managed, and the resultant impact on family operations. Although it appears to be a fairly straightforward proposition, this work is not so easily accomplished since it may give rise to hurt, anger, and fear—feelings that belong to their earlier experiences but have not yet been adequately resolved. In such circumstances, the therapist needs to assist them in refocusing on this unfinished business so that they can come to terms with and accept the reality of their current life situation.

Once the family members have accomplished the "sorting-out" process, they can be assisted in identifying and testing out alternatives. When at-

---

*Parad and Caplan's (1965) now classic study details a family's attempt to cope with the absence of the mother and illustrates how a young child's special needs prove problematic for the family, neither the father nor older sisters being able adequately to take on the nurturing functions previously performed by the mother.

tempting to arrive at new and functional solutions, the family members may need encouragement to draw on outside resources. They may find it useful and productive to "tap" friends, the ex-spouse, and/or community services for needed assistance. In this way, they may gain temporary respite, i.e., needed relief from onerous burdens, which may then provide additional time in which to plan and implement strategies for longer-term solutions. Or they may be able to develop long-term solutions that incorporate "outsiders" in productive ways. For example, a working single mother and her family may be assisted in working out a plan in which the children assume a greater share of the household tasks, thereby relieving the mother of certain responsibilities that may quite appropriately be taken on by the youngsters. In addition, the mother may be encouraged to rework her budget to allow for the part-time services of a neighborhood teenager. The mother, perhaps with input from the children, can then decide how best to use the teenager's services in order to free Mother to spend more unpressured time with the children and in activities for her own well-being.

As previously noted, families may need assistance in learning to assign tasks on the basis of interest and competence. A mother, for example, may need to learn to give clear messages to her teenage son (and to the other children as well) that she does not expect him to assume the role as her coleader (Satir, 1972, p. 172). However, she may very well ask him to take on some of the duties previously performed by his father, e.g., fixing the family car, because he may have both the interest and skills appropriate to the tasks.

Task assignments made on the basis of individual competence may have multiple beneficial consequences. Jobs are accomplished and contribute to the overall efficiency of family operations. In using the skills of its members, the family draws on its own resources to manage its day-to-day operations effectively. This sets in motion a process that Weiss (1979, p. 288) describes as "a kind of benign cycle . . . in which successful management of responsibility leads to enhanced self-confidence, which in turn makes easier further management of responsibility."*

CONCLUDING REMARKS

The single parents and their families who seek professional assistance are those who have had difficulty in coping with the critical events that set them on the road to single parenthood and/or in establishing a new and functional life-style. Disorganized and often demoralized by the events that have be-

---

*While Weiss' comments were directed to the development of self-reliance in the parent, they appear to have relevance for the family as a unit, as well.

fallen them, family members may question their ability to function effectively both as individuals and as a unit. Therapy, then, is likely to be a crucial experience for them, and the therapist has an important facilitative role in the process. However, the therapist will have difficulty in enacting this role if she or he views such families as inherently flawed, rather than as having potential capabilities and resourcefulness, or if she or he buys into the myth of family self-sufficiency, rather than recognizing and supporting the interdependence of families within communities.

REFERENCES

Beal, E. Separation, divorce and single-parent families. In Carter, E.A., & Mc-Goldrick, M. (eds.), *The Family Life-Cycle: A Framework for Family Therapy.* New York: Gardner Press, 1980, 241–264.

Glick, P.C., Norton, A.J. Marrying, divorcing and living together in the U.S. today. *Population Bulletin 32*, Population Reference Bureau, Inc., Washington, D.C., 1979.

Goode, W. *Women in Divorce.* New York: The Free Press, 1956.

Hill, R. Generic features of families under stress. In Parad, H.J. (ed.), *Crisis Intervention: Selected Readings.* New York: Family Service Association of America, 1965, 32–52.

Kitson, G., Lopata, H.Z., Holmes, W.M., & Meyerling, S.M. Divorcees and widows: Similarities and differences. *American Journal of Orthopsychiatry*, 1980, 50, 291–301.

Miles, H.S., & Hays, D.R. Widowhood. In Backer, B., Dubbert, P.M., & Eisenman, E.J. (eds.), *Psychiatric/Mental Health Nursing: Contemporary Readings.* New York: Van Nostrand, 1978, 211–215.

Nass, G. *Marriage and the Family.* Menlo Park, Calif.: Addison-Wesley, 1978.

Pais, J., & White, P. Family redefinition: A review of the literature toward a model of divorce adjustment. *Journal of Divorce*, 1979, 2, 271–281.

Parad, H.J., & Caplan, G. A framework for studying families in crisis. In Parad, H.J. (ed.), *Crisis Intervention: Selected Readings.* New York: Family Service Association of America, 1965, 53–72.

Salts, C.J. Divorce process: Integration of theory. *Journal of Divorce*, 1979, 2, 233–240.

Satir, V. Special families: One-parented and blended. *Peoplemaking.* Palo Alto, Calif.: Science and Behavior Books, 1972, 170–195.

Spanier, G.B., & Casto, R.F. Adjustment to separation and divorce: An analysis of 50 case studies. *Journal of Divorce*, 1979, 2, 241–253.

Stryker, S. Symbolic interaction theory: A review and some suggestions for comparative family research. *Journal of Comparative Family Studies*, 1972, 3, 17–32.

Weiss, R.S. *Going It Alone—The Family Life and Social Situation of the Single Parent.* New York: Basic, 1979.

Weiss, R.S. The emotional impact of marital separation. *Journal of Social Issues*, 1976, 32, 135–145.

Wallerstein, J.S., & Kelly, J.B. The effects of parental divorce: Experiences of the child in later latency. *American Journal of Orthopsychiatry*, 1976, 46, 256–269.

Wallerstein, J.S., & Kelly, J.B. The effects of parental divorce: Experiences of the preschool child. *Journal of the American Academy of Child Psychiatry*, 1975, 14, 600–616.

Wallerstein, J.S., & Kelly, J.B. The effects of parental divorce: The adolescent experience. In Anthony, E.J., & Koupernik, A. (eds.), *The Child in His Family, Vol. 3.* New York: Wiley, 1974, 479–505.

ADDITIONAL READINGS

Brandwein, R.A., Brown, C.A., & Fox, E.M. Women and children last: The social situation of divorced mothers and their families. *Journal of Marriage and the Family*, 1974, 36, 498–514.

Froiland, D.J., & Hozman, T.L. Counseling for constructive divorce. *Personnel and Guidance Journal*, 1977, 55, 525–529.

Hetherington, E.M., Cox, M., & Cox, R. The aftermath of divorce. In Stevens, J.H., & Matthews, M. (eds.), *Mother-Child, Father-Child Relations*. Washington, D.C.: National Association for the Education of Young Children, 1978.

Parkes, C.M. *Bereavement*. New York: International Universities Press, 1972.

Raschke, H.J., Social and psychological factors in voluntary postmarital dissolution adjustment. Unpublished Doctoral Dissertation, University of Minnesota, 1974.

Raschke, H.J., & Raschke, V.J. Family conflict and children's self-concepts: A comparison of intact and single-parent families. *Journal of Marriage and the Family*, 1979, 41, 367–374.

Speigel, J. The resolution of role conflict within the family. In Greenblatt, M. (ed.), *The Patient and the Mental Hospital*. Glencoe, Ill.: The Free Press, 1957, 545–564.

Wiseman, R. Crisis theory and the process of divorce. *Social Casework*, 1975, 56, 205–212.

22

Families in Crisis

Lee Ann Hoff

Situational and developmental crises are an inevitable part of family life. The degree to which individual families are successful in managing such exigencies varies. However, as indicated in earlier sections of this volume, there is growing concern as to the ability of the nuclear family to cope with the tasks assigned to it by our increasingly urbanized and technologic society. Many families can no longer count on the support formerly found in the extended family and in familiar community institutions. It has fallen to health and social agencies to act in place of these former resources. However, this must be viewed as an interim arrangement if families are to be supported in achieving autonomy again. Hoff offers an approach to these crisis situations that has the potential for helping families to buttress threatened interrelationships and to mobilize their capacities to function.

THE FAMILY AT RISK IN MODERN SOCIETY

Some type of domestic group exists in all societies, although the form and structure varies. In Western society the domestic group is generally synonymous with the nuclear or conjugal family, consisting of husband, wife, and child(ren), whereas in many non-Western societies the nuclear family structure is less common. However, as developing countries increasingly experience the impact of industrialization and urbanization, traditional extended-family forms tend to be replaced by the nuclear-family structure. While all families, regardless of form, experience crisis, it is in the nuclear-family structure that crises appear to be most acute. A most basic and perhaps obvious reason for this is that there are fewer interested and potentially helpful people in the immediate family setting to assist in cushioning the impact of various crisis-precipitating events, such as the death of a parent, divorce, illness, or a suicide attempt.* However, in spite of the fact that the nuclear family form with its lack of readily available support from extended kin is the predominant type in industrialized societies, family members nevertheless have certain basic needs that must be met if destructive outcomes of life crises are to be avoided.

In this chapter, people in families are considered in respect to their basic needs and in relation to human growth principles as these are manifested in a contemporary industrialized society. Crisis theory is applied to the family situation along with a case example illustrating how a family in modern society can be helped to weather the storms of life crises. The focus of the recommended helping process is on the establishment of social networks that can supplement or substitute for the kind of help that families in traditional societies could expect and most often received from extended kin.

We are conceived and born in a social system. We grow and develop among other people. We experience crises in relation to events in our social milieu. People around us—individuals, our families, the community—help or hinder us in the resolution of crises. And finally, death, even for those who die in isolation and abandonment, demands some response from the society left behind.

One's social network may consist of family, friends, neighbors, relatives, fellow workers, in fact, anyone with whom a person has regular social intercourse. However, for many in our culture, the family is the most natural source of support and understanding in time of trouble. At the same time, the family is also very commonly the sphere in which people experience their most acute distress. Whether a family is primarily helpful to its members or a source of distress, depends to a considerable extent on the resources available from the larger community. As previously noted, these community resources are particularly vital in modern society where routine support in the extended family is less common than in traditional societies.

Just as individuals are vitally entwined with their families for better or worse, so are families bound up with their communities or neighborhoods.† Individuals, families and whole communities can experience crisis. There is a network of interdependence between individuals, families, and communities; human needs cannot be met in isolation. Therefore, a person, family, or community in crisis can only be understood in terms of their systemic interdependence.

---

*This is not to imply that the nuclear family in modern society is not significantly involved with extended kin. It simply means that extended kin are physically less available than they are, say, in a joint family arrangement, and as a consequence the social and emotional supports of extended kin may also be less readily drawn upon in a crisis.

†For further consideration of this topic, see Hoff (1978, Chap. 4).

REQUIREMENTS FOR NEED FULFILLMENT

To lead a life free of excessive strain, an individual requires a balanced fulfillment of needs for privacy, intimacy, and community. With a suitable measure of privacy, intimate attachments, and a sense of belonging to a community, the person is in a good position to avoid the potentially destructive effects of the life crises she or he is bound to encounter. Central to the individual, family, and community interactional system is the individual with his or her unique personality, set of attributes and liabilities, view of self and the world, goals, ambitions, and set of values.

A self-accepting, self-actualized person not only has a need for privacy but a definite capacity for it. Such persons can retreat to their private world as a means of rejuvenating and coming to terms with self and the external world. In contrast, persons who experience privacy as isolation and loneliness or as rejection and abandonment by others are prone to crisis. They may adapt to their pain and distress when alone by engaging in self-destructive behavior. We all have differing needs and capacities for privacy. Life circumstances can interfere with fulfillment of this need in two crucial ways: A condition of consistent deprivation of normal privacy may develop, or the individual may be subjected to what may be experienced as an excess of privacy, that is, isolation. The child in a family with inadequate housing, or a marriage in which one or both partners are extremely clinging, exemplify conditions under which privacy deprivation may be expected to occur. The person "clung to" by an excessively dependent person is deprived of essential privacy need-fulfillment; he or she feels bombarded by the demand to relate continually to another person. The possibility of such intense dependency relationships is inherent in the modern nuclear-family structure, unless the couple makes deliberate efforts not to confine social relations and demands for emotional support to the conjugal unit.

In one sense an excess of privacy is the other side of the coin of lack of intimacy and community. A person can hardly have too much privacy so long as his or her social needs are also met. Individuals in charge of themselves and capable of living in their private worlds are in an advantageous position to reach out and establish mutually satisfying intimate attachments. Need fulfillment at this level of interaction may facilitate the establishment and enjoyment of additional relationships in the work world and the larger community or neighborhood. Such reaching out into the neighborhood or community meets the basic human need for involvement in significant groups in which one feels accepted and needed. The development and flow of the interactional system of privacy, intimacy, and community needs may be halted if, for example, an individual feels too insecure to establish intimate or communal attachments; a couple establishes an intimate attachment that is essentially closed and turned in on itself, thus limiting need fulfillment in the larger community; or a neighborhood or small communal group turns in on itself and fails to relate to society outside of its own narrow confines in such a way that newly arrived families experience serious problems in establishing themselves and in eliciting needed community support.

The capacity of individuals to live comfortably with themselves and move with ease in the world is influenced by families and communities. A child born into a chaotic, socially unstable family is off to a poor start in establishing him- or herself in the world. Such a child is more crisis prone at developmental turning points such as entering school, puberty, and adolescence. This child's family in turn is affected by the kind of community surrounding it. The crisis proneness of child and family are influenced by such factors as economic and employment opportunities, racial or ethnic prejudice, the quality of schools, availability of family or social services, and recreational opportunities for youth. When there is a sufficient number of individuals and families who are adversely affected by such factors, the whole community is more prone to crisis. It is within this framework of basic needs and human growth that family crisis will be considered in the following sections.

CRISIS THEORY APPLIED TO THE FAMILY

Having noted how the crisis experiences of individuals, families, and communities are mutually influencing, let us examine in detail the person or family in crisis. Stressful events and emergency situations are part of life and have the potential of becoming crises. However, a crisis does not necessarily follow a traumatic event. What is a crisis for one family may not be one for another. Crisis occurs when an individual's or family's *interpretation* of traumatic events leads to stress so severe that coping becomes impossible. A family in crisis cannot carry on its normal functions of mutual support and nurturance.

There are meaningful differences and relationships between stress, predicaments, emergency, and crisis (Hoff 1978, p. 6). Stress is not crisis; it is strain, tension, or pressure. Similarly, predicament is not crisis; it is embarrassment, unpleasantness, or potential danger. Emergency is not crisis; it is an unforeseen and potentially dangerous combination of circumstances that calls for immediate action. Webster's *International Unabridged Dictionary* defines crisis as "a serious or decisive state of things, a turning point." For example, when an adolescent makes a suicide attempt, the entire family may be in crisis. Such an individual and family crisis may be the "turning point" toward needed changes in the marital and family interactional system. Norris Hansell (1976, p. 14) describes crisis as any rapid change or encounter that is foreign to a person's usual experience.

Predicaments and emergencies lead to stresses that carry the potential to become crises. Whether such predicaments and emergencies become crises depends on individual and family ability to handle these stresses. For example, John, age 45, has a heart attack and is taken to a hospital by ambulance. This is clearly an emergency medical situation and a source of stress for John and his family. However, John's heart attack may also precipitate an emotional crisis for himself and his entire family. Whether that traumatic experience results in growth and enrichment for John and his family, or in a return to some lower level of functioning for all of them, depends largely on their previous problem-solving abilities and current level of support. If John or members of his family become extremely upset as a result of his heart attack and feel unable to handle the situation emotionally with their usual problem-solving devices, they are said to be in crisis and may need some help to resolve it. Crisis can be defined, then, as an acute emotional upset in which one's usual problem-solving ability fails.

Researchers (Hill, 1965; Parad & Caplan, 1965) consider family troubles according to their sources and effect upon family structure, the type of event affecting the family, and the effect of the type of family configuration. If the source of trouble is from within the family, the event is more distressing than are those related to external sources of trouble, such as racial prejudice or natural disasters. For example, if family members make suicide attempts or abuse alcohol, it is usually viewed as a reflection on the family's lack of basic harmony and internal adequacy. Eliot (1955) and Hill (1965, pp. 37–38) suggest that family configuration is affected by stress from dismemberment (loss of a family member), accession (addition of an unprepared for family member), demoralization (loss of morale and family unity), or a combination of all three. This classification of family stressors recasts in a family context the numerous traumatic life events that may lead to crises.

Caplan (1964, pp. 40–41) notes that crisis develops in identifiable phases and not instantaneously:

1. A traumatic event causes an initial rise in anxiety to which the person responds with familiar problem solving mechanisms.
2. The person's usual problem-solving ability fails to relieve the anxiety caused by the traumatic event while the source of tension continues.
3. Tension increases even further and spurs the person to use unusual means of problem solving.
4. Active crisis occurs as a result of failure in problem solving and unbearable anxiety.

The development of a family crisis can be illustrated by examining more closely the situation of Linda, a 15-year-old who attempted suicide.

CASE EXAMPLE: A FAMILY IN CRISIS

Linda's parents, Mary Jones, age 37, and Jack Jones, age 39, were married at 19 and 21, respectively. Mary had abandoned her college and career plans and quickly assumed the role of mother and caregiver at the birth of their son Robert, now age 17, while Jack worked his way up to the position of evening supervisor in a steel plant. The third child, Joan, now age 11, was born when Linda was 4 years old. She and Linda had frequent fights; Linda felt in general that Joan was "the spoiled child" of the family. Robert was clearly regarded as the "good boy" and had to do little or nothing to gain his father's attention and approval. Linda, on the other hand, could never do anything right. Mary and Jack had definite differences about child rearing, she tending to be more lenient and he more strict. The strongest difference, however, was in Jack's double standard of behavioral expectations for Robert and Linda. In Linda's view Robert could get away with murder while she felt the rules for her were unbearably restrictive. Linda was not so resentful of the special treatment Joan received, since she thought Joan was not old enough to be really responsible. Besides these discrepancies, Linda felt close to her mother, but no matter what she did she felt virtually ignored by her father.

The strain between Linda and her father was intensified by the fact that Jack worked the evening shift at the steel plant. Although Jack could have worked during the day, he preferred evenings, as he enjoyed more authority and status and a higher salary in that position than he would have had on the day shift. This situation also left Mary with the major task of nurturing and disciplining Robert, Linda, and Joan. Jack seemed to be either sleeping or working most of the time. Moreover, Mary and Jack felt increasingly isolated socially in their community, having practically abandoned even their occasional excursions with other couples to the movies and going out to dinner because of Jack's work schedule. Their chief outing was a bimonthly visit to Mary's parents' house—30 miles away in the country—for Sunday dinner, to which her sister's family was also invited. These visits were enjoyed by all, especially by Mary who was close to her mother, and by the children, since these were welcome occasions to be with their cousins. Jack's parents lived in another city hundreds of miles away, so visits with them occurred at most only once every year or two.

As tension rose, Mary and Jack fought more and more about "what to do with Linda"—when she did not obey, when she did not pick up her things, when she violated the evening curfew. Their fights escalated when they received a report from school that Linda's work was near failing and that teachers suspected she was taking drugs. Since Linda complained to her mother about her father's coldness, Mary tried to intervene with her husband to pay more attention to Linda, especially now with the new problems she was having. She also suggested that they talk with their pastor about their problem, but Jack refused.

Meanwhile, although Mary was very devoted to her children, she was becoming more and more dissatisfied with her marriage and her "wife-and-mother-only" role, feeling very pressured by the task of rearing the children alone. Moreover, as the stress of child tending and housework increased, she began to feel resentful about having given up her plans to go to college when she met and married Jack. She now had fantasies about how different her life might have been if she had gone to college instead of marrying so early and at the same time could not imagine herself functioning in any other role than that of wife and mother, even though at times the thought of divorce entered her head as a way out of her dilemma. She reasoned that since she was bringing up the children largely by herself anyway, she might be relieved in no longer expecting anything from Jack.

Tension in the Jones family reached a near-crisis point when Linda threatened to run away from home. Jack finally began to agree with Mary that they had a possibly serious family problem to cope with. He therefore agreed to take a couple of weeks off work and focus some time and attention on the problems at home. Everyone, especially Mary and Linda, seemed happy to have Jack around the house more. Things settled down for a few weeks. Linda in particular was less rebellious and appeared generally happier since Jack was more attentive to her than usual. Robert claimed, of course, that "things could always be this way if only Linda would shape up and act her age." Joan was just happy to see more of her father.

A few weeks after Jack returned to work the familiar tension and fighting were back in full force, along with new complaints from school about Linda. She again threatened to run away, this time to her grandmother's home, where she said she felt more wanted. Robert now blamed Linda more than ever for the problems he wished would go away. In addition, since Jack and Mary never communicated their real feelings about each other and their marriage, it was easy for them to believe that they would not be fighting if it were not for Linda's behavior problems.

One evening when Jack was off from work, he and Linda had a particularly harsh argument. She stormed off to her room. An hour later her mother heard her crying uncontrollably in the bathroom. She had cut her wrists and was sitting on the bathroom floor banging her head against the wall and sobbing, "Just go away and let me die . . . Nobody cares."

Stress and pain for Linda had reached the breaking point: She was in crisis. Her most natural support system, her family, either could not or would not give her the help she so desperately needed. From a family perspective, however, Linda was the identified symptom bearer, the "scapegoat," for a family in crisis. She functioned in this role to maintain the family balance, however disturbed that balance might be. For example, as long as the Jones family focus was on Linda's acting-out behavior, the mother and father could ignore their marital problems and Robert could assume that he and his privileged status in the family had nothing to do with Linda's problems. When Linda abandoned her scapegoat role and struck out in the form of self-destructive behavior, the family's shakily constructed balance gave way and the entire family was in crisis.

Duration and Outcomes of Crisis

A person or family in crisis cannot stay that way forever. The state of crisis and the anxiety that accompany it are too painful. The family must somehow bring itself back to a tolerable state of being within a few days or weeks (Caplan, 1964, p. 35). How do they accomplish this? The Jones' situation can be used to illustrate several conceivable alternatives:

1. After the initial shock from Linda's suicide attempt the family might return to its precrisis state. This would mean reinstating Linda in her scapegoat role to maintain the family balance. Nothing essential would change; there would be continuous stress, but at least the family system would not be in crisis.
2. After emergency medical treatment of Linda and a bit of initial sympathy, the entire family might take to "blaming" Linda for the family troubles even more, adding now the fact that she had disgraced them by her "childish and extreme way of looking for attention." Such an outcome would be destructive since it almost invariably would lead to another suicide attempt that might eventually culminate in death for Linda.
3. The shock and crisis of Linda's suicide attempt (demoralization) might serve as a "turning point" for the distressed Jones family. They might finally get the message implicit in Linda's "acting out" in her prescribed scapegoat role. This awareness might foster fundamental changes in the entire family system and in its individual members; for example, in the marital situation, the favoritism shown toward Robert and Joan, Jack's habitual absence from everyday family interaction, and Mary's personal frustration in her locked-in role.

The third and last outcome is, of course, the most desirable, because the crisis has provided the occasion for growth rather than stagnation, despair, or even death. Destructive outcomes of crisis occur only when an individual or family is unable to use other more constructive ways of solving life's problems and relieving intolerable anxiety.

ASSESSMENT OF A FAMILY IN CRISIS

Having considered how a family crisis develops and what its possible outcomes may be, let us examine in detail how to identify a family in crisis. One method of crisis assessment includes identification of the events leading to the family's acute stress. Golan (1969, pp. 390–393) differentiates between the hazardous event and the precipitating factor.

Hazardous Event

This is the initial shock or rise in tension within the family system that sets in order a series of reactions culminating in a crisis. In the Jones family the hazardous "event" or situation was the onset of Linda's adolescence and the subsequent conflict with her father. This led to her scapegoat role in the family. Her role as symptom bearer and her rebelliousness formed a vicious cycle leading ultimately to the despair she expressed in the suicide attempt. Hazardous events are, of course, a normal part of life. It is this fact that is the basis for viewing crises as normal, particularly those associated with transition states in the cycle of human development.

To the extent that developmental crises are anticipated, preparation can be made for them. Birth and death are, of course, universal transition states, and because of their great significance they are marked by a variety of social customs. These signify that an individual has either entered or departed from society, and they help the social community to deal with the addition or loss of a member. In traditional societies these two life events along with initiation into adulthood are marked by rites of passage. Modern Western societies do not have such formal social support mechanisms for the adolescent. Moreover, significantly, in light of the high incidence of divorce, while Western society has marriage rites, it lacks divorce rituals in the sense of public social support for the partners and their families who are undergoing that major role transition (Blumen, 1977). These societal facts place an even heavier responsibility on members of the social network on behalf of individuals and families at risk to prevent hazardous events from becoming full-blown crises.

Precipitating Factor

This is the proverbial "straw that breaks the camel's back." It is the final stressful event that pushes a person or family from a state of acute vulnerability into crisis. The constitution of the precipitating factor is intricately related to the person's or family's psychologic strength and social supports.

For Linda the precipitating factor leading to her breaking point, the suicide attempt, was the harsh argument with her father. If Linda's mother had not had so many problems of her own she might have been a preventive and supportive force for Linda following the argument. For the Jones family unit, the precipitating factor was Linda's suicide attempt. If the Jones family had availed themselves at an earlier point of counseling resources, such as the school guidance counselor or their pastor, Linda might not have attempted suicide.

Feelings, Thoughts, and Behavior during Crisis

Also important in assessing a family in crisis is the identification of the characteristics of the people in crisis, both individually and as a family unit. In crisis, usual ways of feeling, thinking, and acting are altered (Caplan, 1964; Hansell, 1976; Hill, 1965).

People in crisis experience a high degree of tension and anxiety. They may also feel fearful, angry, guilty, or embarrassed. Jack Jones' predominant feeling after Linda's suicide attempt was guilt about his harsh treatment of her earlier in the evening. He was also embarrassed about the "horrible thing" that was somehow tearing his family apart. Mary primarily felt anger toward her husband: "I *told* you to start treating her decently. She deserves at least as much as Robert does." She was also very fearful that Linda would really kill herself, and she was ashamed that she herself resented her confined wife and mother role. Robert, too, was acutely upset by the event. Suddenly, his favored position in the family seemed somehow like a burden he wanted to shed. He felt guilty about his special treatment and about his constantly blaming Linda for the family problems. Joan was afraid and confused. Linda felt guilt and remorse for once again disgracing the family. She also felt hopeless about herself and the future.

Feelings—especially high anxiety—have great impact on a person's perceptions and thinking process. Full attention is focused on the acute anguish being experienced and on a few selected aspects of the crisis event. People in crisis have a difficult time sorting things out, setting priorities, and achieving a perspective on their situations. Jack, Mary, and Robert Jones tended to blame themselves individually or each other for Linda's suicide attempt, and they could not relate the attempt to their total interaction as a family unit. The thought crossed Jack's mind that "maybe Linda is 'crazy'—why else would anyone do a thing like that?"* The family members' confusion

---

*For details regarding the understanding and assessment of suicidal danger, see Hoff (1978, Chaps. 5 and 6).

resulting from the high-anxiety state reduces their problem-solving ability. This results in the necessity for outside help if destructive outcomes are to be avoided.

Behavior usually follows from what people think and feel. A significant behavioral sign of a family in crisis is its inability to perform vocational functions in the usual manner. Jack could not concentrate at work, so he took "sick leave." Mary had all she could do to prepare meals and keep the house in some semblance of order. She also had weeping spells. Even Robert was so upset that he stayed home from school the day after Linda's suicide attempt. Joan tried to be more helpful than usual. The family as a whole was so embarrassed by the event that they avoided even their normally constricted social contacts for about 6 weeks.

A behavioral response of some people in crisis is the rejection of outside help. Fortunately, this was not the case with the Jones family. Although there were definite problems in the Jones marriage and family interaction, Jack and Mary were so stunned by Linda's suicide attempt that they were more than grateful to accept the emergency-room doctor's referral to a mental-health clinic. Both salvaged out of the event the hope that something might still be done to keep their marriage and family together. They knew that their family was in crisis and seemed ready to move from the dead-end spot that kept them in constant stress.

Another useful framework for assessment of people in crisis has been developed by Aguilera and Messick (1978). This assessment model is based on the concept that people in crisis are in a state of disequilibrium (imbalance). The authors propose that if equilibrium can be maintained or regained, crisis can be avoided. Equilibrium is affected by several balancing factors: realistic perception of the event, adequate situational support, and adequate coping mechanisms. When all of these are operational, the problem can be resolved.

The foregoing view of the elements involved in the reestablishment of homeostasis when people are in crisis was originally proposed by Menninger, Mayman, and Precyser (1963) and Caplan (1964). This stance has been criticized by Allport (1960), Taplin (1971) and Bartolucci and Drayer (1973). The problem with the homeostatic view is that, if applied too narrowly, it isolates crisis concepts from other important psychosocial concerns, such as learning, perception, emotion, and communication, and suggests that crises can be resolved by mechanistically reducing tension (Taplin, 1971). A closed system is implied; that is, the person is seen as a tension-managing social network. Such a view of the person in crisis is best avoided. For example, if equilibrium theory alone is applied to the Jones family, Linda or a substitute scapegoat would have to continue in the role of symptom bearer to maintain family equilibrium. It is important to identify and deal with the emotional, social, and communication factors that are intrinsic both to the Jones family problems and to Linda's scapegoat position. Extreme tension and anxiety associated with crisis may be regarded more productively as arising from interaction with others and at the same time affecting the individual's self-concept. People like the Joneses learn and grow by successfully resolving a crisis like that associated with Linda's suicide attempt by a systemic approach to the total family problem. In contrast, reassigning Linda to the scapegoat position merely reduces family tension in order to maintain an equilibrium that is at best tenuous. However, if understood in a broader psychosocial context, the concept of homeostasis can be helpful in ascertaining whether a person or family is in crisis.

HELPING A FAMILY IN CRISIS

What are the options open to the Jones family? How can this family develop more productive modes of functioning through an acute-crisis experience? From what has been observed it seems clear that they need help from someone outside their own family system. There are a number of prospective helping resources for families in crisis: a family doctor, crisis counselor, pastor, school guidance counselor, and family-service agency. The important considerations follow. Whoever attempts to help should:

- Understand the family as a social system since the lack of such understanding can result in perpetuation of the identified client's scape-goat role;
- Be compassionate and empathetic toward the special problems and needs of the family since a helper more interested in working with individuals may be unaware of the needs of the family group in crisis;
- Be knowledgeable about crisis and skilled in crisis-management tech-niques.

Planning with a Family in Crisis

Having determined that the Jones family needs and wants help, and assuming that helping resources are available, the next step is to develop with the clients a plan toward constructive resolution of the crisis. The good intentions of some would-be helpers may end in disaster or stop in dead center because of lack of planning. Sometimes helpers argue that the crisis situation is so acute that there is no time to plan: Something has to be done immediately, because lives might be at stake. This, rather than justifying the failure to plan, only underscores the urgent necessity for planning. A sound plan can be formulated immediately, if necessary, by a worker who knows the signs of crisis, is confident in his or her ability to help, and is able to secure additional assistance rapidly in the case of impasse or a life-and-death situation. The basic elements of planning for crisis resolution will be considered within the framework of the following definition:

> *Crisis intervention* is a short-term helping process for individuals or families in crisis which focuses on resolution of the immediate problem through use of personal, environmental and social resources (Hoff, 1978, p. 7).

A major feature of an effective crisis-management plan is that it is developed in collaboration with the people concerned. Successful crisis resolution is much more probable when things are done *with* people rather than *to* them. Whatever plan and crisis-management techniques are proposed should be formalized in a written service contract that makes explicit what the client and counselor can expect of one another and defines specifically how and when the counseling goals are to be achieved. The nature of the contract implies that family members are essentially in charge of their own lives and able to make decisions for themselves. It also implies that the crisis-counseling relationship is one between partners and that both parties to the contract have clearly stated rights and responsibilities.

When working with a family in crisis the contract is even more important than in individual situations because of the inevitable complexities of the family-communication network. For example, the Jones family service contract would need to contain a clear statement of what all family members would agree to do the next time, should Linda "act out." Presumably, this would be something more constructive than instantly blaming Linda for all the family problems. The contract should also include a specific discipline plan for all the children to replace the ineffective and vague response that "Linda never does anything right."

Other features of crisis planning include focus on the immediate problem, appropriateness to the functional level of family-member, concreteness and specificity as to time and action, flexibility, and provision for follow-up assessment (Aguilera & Messick, 1978; Caplan & Grunebaum, 1967). Each of these elements merits further consideration.

Problem Orientation. The immediate concrete problems that directly contribute to the total crisis situation constitute the focus of planning. In the case of the Jones family, Linda's suicide attempt and the feelings, behavior, and events surrounding it would provide such a focus and also avoid the delving into basic personality patterns or underlying psychologic problems that might contribute to the family's proneness to crisis. The latter concerns are more properly the aim of psychotherapy or ongoing counseling, which the family themselves may pursue after resolution of the immediate crisis.

Appropriateness to Functional Level.   While sound assessment is essential to any treatment strategy, it is crucial in crisis work, which, because of the inherent time factors, demands particular evaluative acuity. The functioning of family members in perceptual, emotional, and behavioral realms is central to such an assessment and basic to the planning of intervention.

Concreteness and Specificity.   People in crisis need to know that actions A, B, and C are planned to occur at points X, Y, and Z. This kind of structure is reassuring because it provides concrete evidence that something definite will happen to change the present state of acute discomfort. The seemingly endless confusion and chaos of the crisis experience can be handled in familiar terms, and the entire plan has a clearly anticipated end-point.

Flexibility.   Productive plans cannot be carved in marble. Full effectiveness requires that plans be alive, meaningful, and flexible. Therefore, a mechanism for dealing with changes must be included in order to anticipate those situations in which the original plan no longer fits the family's needs. The absence of such a mechanism can result in the family's perceiving certain outcomes as "failure" rather than as indications of a need for change in the plan. The assurance, "If this doesn't work, we'll examine why and try something else," may in itself be very supportive to persons who are feeling hopeless about their circumstances.

Provision for Follow-up.   An effective contract includes an agreement for follow-up after apparent resolution of the crisis. The management of future crises will be favorably affected not only by successful crisis management, but also by awareness of help before stress situations develop into acute crises. Provision of information regarding available resources should be included in any adequate follow-up contact (Langsley & Kaplan, 1968).

Working Through the Crisis

Helping a family through constructive crisis resolution involves carrying out the plan developed after identifying the problems and reactions associated with the crisis. Specific intervention techniques should flow from the cognitive, emotional, and behavioral manifestations of crisis in the people concerned. The aim should be to promote effective crisis coping in these three areas:

- *Cognitive.*   Help the family develop a realistic grasp of the situation and sort out any distorted perceptions they may have. For example, in working with the Jones family it would be important to emphasize that Linda did *not* make a suicide attempt because she was "crazy," that, in fact, the family troubles are not the fault of any particular person.

● *Emotional.* Help family members accept and express feelings appropriate to the situation and avoid denial of any strong feelings. Again, with the Jones family, it would be crucial for Mary to tell Jack *directly* how angry she is. Linda should be encouraged to express her hopelessness and despair verbally and not in the form of suicide attempts.

● *Behavioral.* Help the family to mobilize and use all the personal and social resources possible to resolve their crisis and avoid further destructive outcomes in the future.

Effective crisis coping is fostered by the use of several techniques (Hoff, 1978, pp. 60–65):

● *Active listening.* When people are listened to they feel important and deserving of help, and are better able to dispel feelings of shame they may have in the face of ineffective problem solving. The experience of being listened to also aids in the process of thoughtful reflection about the crisis and understanding of it. In the Jones family, for example, Linda apparently could not make herself heard except through a suicide attempt. Listening, therefore, to what each family member has to say can help the entire family to understand and accept the reality of their crisis.

● *Encouragement of feeling expression.* The open expression of negative or pent-up feelings is facilitated by effective listening and can represent the beginning of healthier coping with crisis in the future.

● *Exploring new ways of problem solving.* Since the very nature of the crisis experience involves failure in effective problem solving, this technique is fundamental to the successful resolution of a crisis, especially for those whose ineffective coping with crisis, e.g., through alcohol abuse or suicide attempts, has made them crisis-prone in the first place.

● *Linkage with other helping resources.* For example, Mary and Jack may be referred to a marriage counselor following resolution of the immediate crisis.

● *Decision counseling.* This helping process is cognitively oriented and allows people in distress an opportunity to put distorted thoughts, chaotic feelings, and disturbed behavior into some kind of order (Hansell, 1970). The counselor facilitates crisis resolution by helping the family identify problem areas, set priorities, and decide on appropriate problem-solving measures.

● *Reinforcement of newly learned coping devices.* It is crucial that the proposed problem solutions be tested in the family's daily interaction. Successful problem-solving mechanisms may then be reinforced by the counselor; unsuccessful solutions can be discarded and new ones sought.

These planning and crisis-management techniques might be applied in a variety of ways in working with the Jones family. For example, it would be extremely important to help all members to see the relationship between Linda's suicide attempt and the family's interactional and communication system. This would be facilitated through family members' learning to develop listening skills and to give and receive affection. Since it is apparent that the couple has difficulty in perceiving alternative solutions to problems, they will need support in working out an overall disciplinary stance that provides Linda with better controls and eliminates favoritism toward Robert. It will be crucial to assist Mary and Jack in managing their own relationship so that they can work cooperatively, resolving their differences in a manner that is not destructive to the family. Because the Jones family members have spent very little time together, they will have had little experience in planning and securing gratification from common pursuits. Active consideration of a variety of means of gaining such experiences may constitute an important part of the process, especially since this will provide opportunities to work on the compromises that will be inherent in each member's taking into account the interests and needs of the others.

In all likelihood the counselor's efforts will need to extend beyond the bounds of the family itself. Troubled families are frequently either lacking in external relationships or are for some reason unable to make use of those that are available. The latter is more clearly the case with the Jones family. Some success in work as a couple may make Mary and Jack more open to reaching out to and accepting support from the maternal grandparents, for example. This might be of particular help to Mary and the children. Another significant resource might lie in Linda's school guidance counselor with whom a joint conference might be especially productive. Other community agencies may well need to be called into the picture in a situation as serious as that of the Jones family. There is no question that Jack and Mary are deeply embroiled in serious marital problems and might well benefit from ongoing marital counseling in order to resolve some of the underlying conflicts contributing to their family's proneness to crisis.

Families, like individuals, can gain from the productive management of crisis situations. The challenge for the crisis worker is to help the family mobilize the resources necessary to move in the direction of growth rather than stagnation or further family disruption and the despair of its members.

REFERENCES

Allport, G.W. The open system in personality. *Journal of Abnormal and Social Psychology*, 1960, 61, 301–310.

Aguilera, D.C., & Messick, J.M. *Crisis Intervention*, 3rd ed. St. Louis: Mosby, 1978.

Bartolucci, G., & Drayer, C. An overview of crisis intervention in emergency rooms of general hospitals. *American Journal of Psychiatry*, 1973, 130, 953–60.

Blumen, J. Divorce as life crisis. In Chapman, J.R., & Gates, M. (eds.), *Women into Wives*. Beverly Hills: Sage, 1977.

Caplan, G. *Principles of Preventive Psychiatry*. New York: Basic, 1964.

Caplan, G., & Grunebaum, H. Perspectives on primary prevention: A review. *Archives of General Psychiatry*, 1967, 17, 331–46.

Eliot, T.D. Handling family strains and shocks. In Becker, H., & Hill, R. (eds.), *Family, Marriage and Parenthood*. Boston: Health, 1955.

Golan, N. When is a client in crisis? *Social Casework*, 1969, 50, 389–94.

Hansell, N. Decision counseling method. *Archives of General Psychiatry*, 1970, 22, 462–67.

Hansell, N. *The Person in Distress*. New York: Human Services Press, 1976.

Hill, R. Generic features of families under stress. In Parad, H.J. (ed.), *Crisis Intervention*. New York: Family Service Association of America, 1965, 32–52.

Hoff, L.A. *People in Crisis*. Menlo Park, Calif.: Addison-Wesley, 1978.

Langsley, D., & Kaplan, D. *The Treatment of Families in Crisis*. New York: Grune & Stratton, 1968.

Menninger, K., Mayman, M., & Precyser, P. *The Vital Balance*. New York: Viking, 1963.

Parad, H.J., & Caplan, G. A framework for studying families in crisis. In Parad, H.J. (ed.), *Crisis Intervention*. New York: Family Service Association of America, 1965, 53–72.

Taplin, J.R. Crisis Theory: Critique and reformulation. *Community Mental Health Journal*, 1971, 7, 13–23.

23

A Task-Based Approach to Family Treatment

Anthony N. Maluccio

The raison d'être of the practitioner is to act in such a way as to promote change. When action is the valued mode, it is essential to be wary lest the activity become an end in itself. The spirit of the times further promotes this propensity with the proliferation of "how-to-fix-it" prescriptions for all predicaments. On the other hand, pressing human problems cry out for solution, leaving the practitioner feeling that there is little opportunity for a more measured approach. In this chapter, Maluccio elucidates a framework for the thoughtful use of activity as a therapeutic means toward families' mastery of their own life circumstances. He views goal-directed tasks as central to this work.

Task is a key concept in the life-model perspective on family treatment discussed in Chapter 1 of this volume. Within this perspective, the focus of help is on identifying, supporting, and setting in motion natural adaptive processes of the family and its members. The main objective is to aid family members in promoting growth-producing environmental conditions and in mobilizing their own resources and coping patterns. There is emphasis on life experiences, family tasks and activities, and other opportunities for enhancing personal autonomy and competence.

In the context of the life model, the central thrust of family treatment is the carefully planned use of tasks or activities. Through purposive and systematic engagement in meaningful tasks, family members have experiences that are conducive to the fulfillment of their mutual needs as well as mutual meeting of needs. The family as a unit is thus helped in carrying out its integrative and adaptive functions.

This chapter further defines the concept of task, discusses its purposes and varieties as well as major practice principles, and illustrates its application through clinical examples from a range of practice settings.

DEFINITION OF TASK

Task is a term with multiple meanings. In Webster's *New Twentieth Century Dictionary of the English Language*, it is defined as "a piece of work assigned to or demanded of a person," "an undertaking involving labor or difficulty," and as being synonymous with such words as *labor, function, drudgery*, and *toil*. In the behavioral sciences, there is extensive discussion of the developmental, role, and situational tasks of individuals and families. In family treatment, there is reference to family adaptive tasks as well as to use of therapeutic tasks in the course of intervention. In social work, task describes "the demands made upon people by various life situations" (Bartlett, 1970, pp. 94–97).

As used in this chapter, *task* refers to explicit definition of *what is to be done by the family or its members in any specific situation so as to meet their needs or enable them to deal successfully with environmental challenges*. This view of task is derived from two central features of the life model: (1) the notion of people as engaged in ongoing, dynamic interaction with their environment; and (2) the conviction about the importance of the person's active and purposive participation in the helping process.

In this context, task is deliberately focused on the client system rather than on the therapist. It is assumed that the client has the major responsibility as "the primary worker in task accomplishment," while the therapist has a secondary responsibility "to provide the conditions necessary for the client's work on his task" (Studt, 1968, pp. 24, 42). Task is not, as some writers* indicate the same thing as the therapist giving a *directive* to the family, although on occasions directives are necessary. There is, on the contrary, mutuality between family and practitioner, as both participate actively in formulating and negotiating each task as a basic part of their interaction.

A brief, if somewhat oversimplified, case example illustrates this conceptualization of task and its relationship to family goals as well as to family and practitioner activities:

> This was the situation of a young couple referred to a marriage counselor by their minister. The husband had suddenly been laid off his semi-skilled job in the aerospace industry. A few months earlier, the wife had terminated employment as a secretary because they planned to start a family. The

---

*See, for example, Haley (1976, pp. 48–80).

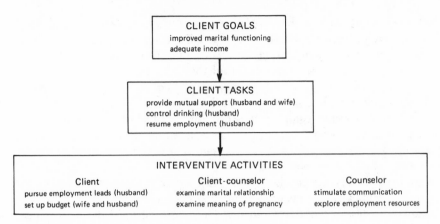

FIGURE 23-1. Goals, tasks, and interventive activities.

anxiety aroused by the husband's job loss, coupled with the wife's recent pregnancy, reactivated dormant marital difficulties. These were manifested primarily in her verbal attacks on him, his withdrawal from her, and his resumption of heavy drinking.

In the early sessions, the counselor engaged this couple in a careful analysis of their situation, leading to a formulation of an interrelated set of goals, tasks, and interventive plans, as shown in Figure 23-1.

The goals, tasks, and interventive activities in Figure 23-1 are intended as examples and are not presented in any order of importance or timing. The main purpose is to illustrate that client goals determine client tasks, out of which flow a number of interrelated actions to be carried out either jointly by the couple and the counselor or separately by client(s) or counselor. The interventive activities may be viewed as subtasks or specific actions that need to be completed by the participants in order to carry out successfully the agreed-upon tasks.

PRACTICE PRINCIPLES

A task-based approach to family treatment can maximize client opportunities for quick and active engagement in the helping process. Various principles guide the practitioner in making effective use of tasks. I will delineate at this point the major principles that are illustrated through case examples later in this chapter.

First of all, each task should be defined as explicitly and concretely as possible and in terms that are meaningful to all family members. Toward this end, family or individual problems, needs, and conflicts are redefined as adaptive challenges. There should be congruence in problem definition and goal formulation among the different family members.

In addition to explicit formulation of the task, there should be clear instructions to all family members regarding their responsibilities. Beyond clarity, there should be simplicity in task formulation. In instances in which a given task is rather complex, it is essential to break it down into smaller components or subtasks. Otherwise, there may be insufficient understanding, lack of agreement or mutuality among family members, or discouragement on the part of one or more of them.

Second, the task should be relevant to the family's life situation and the unique qualities and needs of its members. It should be consonant with the "growth processes, and developmental stage" of the family and its members (Maluccio, 1974, p. 34). As Haley (1976, p. 56) observes: "The therapist must fit the task to the people. As he interviews a family, he will observe what sort of people the members are and can fit the task to the family style." This means, in part, that to encourage their active involvement, a task should embody some potential benefit for each participant. Without the promise of gain for themselves, family members may not be properly motivated to engage in it. In addition, the techniques used by the practitioner to aid the family in implementing a task need to make sense to its members. For instance, the value of artificial tasks such as role playing may have to be explained before some clients can accept them.

Third, a task should be carried out as much as possible within the family's natural life context. Following whatever rehearsal may be necessary within the clinical setting, family members should be helped to practice desired skills or behaviors at home and in interaction with other significant persons in their environment.

Fourth, implementation of each task should be geared to the family's readiness. Proper timing is crucial, since family members may vary in their capacity. One or more of them may need additional explanation or encouragement. The family's readiness is also dependent upon such factors as the quality of its members' relationships with the therapist.

Above all, formulating and implementing each task must include the active participation of the family as a whole or any appropriate subsystem. In this process, the family is helped to draw as much as possible upon its own actual or potential resources and its customary adaptive strategies.

PURPOSES OF TASKS

There are several distinct therapeutic purposes of tasks, although these are in practice interrelated: (1) changing a family's structure or interaction, (2) enhancing the family's decision-making process, and (3) promoting the competence of family members. A discussion of the theoretical and pragmatic rationale underlying each of these purposes follows, as does illustration of their use in intervention with families.

Changing Family Structure and Interaction

In the life-model perspective on treatment, the practitioner makes active use of the family matrix in the "process of healing." People are helped to cope with life challenges or problems by modifying family structure and organization and by transforming dysfunctional patterns of interaction.

Internal processes and structures within the family exert a strong influence on the family's functioning and that of its members. Frequently, family members are not aware of these processes and therefore are unable to effect change. Tasks can help to confront the family with its problems, to stimulate possible ways of changing, and to offer new opportunities for restructuring. As noted by Minuchin (1974, p. 150):

> Tasks create a framework within which the family members must function. The therapist can use tasks to pinpoint and actualize an area of exploration that may not have developed naturally in the flow of family transactions. Or he can highlight an area in which the family needs to work.

Through selected tasks, family members may be helped to shift their interactional processes sufficiently to go on changing and growing on their own.

The following examples illustrate the use of tasks to achieve specific changes in family structure, communication, and interaction. In the first case, a family becomes aware of its dysfunctional patterns and gradually changes them.

THE BREWER FAMILY

Mrs. Brewer was a middle-aged widow who had been referred to a mental-health clinic by her physician because of her hypertension, obesity, and pervasive unhappiness and depression. She was desperate for help as a result of the physician's warning that her hypertension had been increasing steadily. Mrs. Brewer for years had been unsuccessfully trying to lose weight.

In a family session involving Mrs. Brewer's two teenage daughters, it became apparent that the family as a whole had considerable difficulty in expressing anger or dealing with anxiety. Whenever Mrs. Brewer got angry, upset, or discouraged, she withdrew to her room. The daughters were quite concerned about her behavior but avoided discussing it with her. Instead, they typically brought plates of rich food to Mrs. Brewer, who quickly devoured everything.

Choosing to deal directly with family dynamics, the therapist pointed out how the daughters were interfering with their mother's efforts to lose weight and how each family member found it difficult to express her feelings, particularly negative ones. Focusing on their mutual concerns, the therapist helped the family to formulate these goals: communicating their feelings more openly with each other, becoming engaged in more gratifying joint activities within as well as outside the home, and helping Mrs. Brewer to lose weight.

When it was clear that all family members concurred in these goals, the therapist helped them to define several pertinent tasks. First of all, they were to plan at least one pleasurable joint activity every other day, such as watching a favorite movie on television. Second, Mrs. Brewer and her daughters were to express their feelings of anger openly during several family sessions at the clinic. Third, the daughters were not to bring any food to their mother whenever she retreated into her room; instead, they were to reach out to her by making themselves available to talk. At the same time, Mrs. Brewer agreed to talk or do something constructive while one of the daughters was in her room.

As each of these tasks was defined, the therapist systematically elicited each family member's understanding of it as well as her feelings about it. In addition, she explained the rationale for each task. For example, she indicated that, by expressing their negative feelings within the therapeutic sessions, they would release natural pent-up feelings that were preventing them from achieving the kinds of relationships that they desired with each other.

As Mrs. Brewer and her daughters carried out these tasks, a number of significant changes began to take place within the family system. For instance, its members learned to convey feelings and concerns directly rather than through food. At the same time, as Mrs. Brewer received from her daughters some of the attention that she had been craving, she had less need to overeat.

As each family member had the experience of expressing her feelings within the therapeutic environment, the therapist faced them with another more complex task, namely, expressing their angry feelings toward each other at home. During each session, she reviewed with them how each task was proceeding and provided encouragement and positive feedback whenever appropriate. Slowly and with much difficulty, after several months Mrs. Brewer and her daughters were able to change their mutually destructive patterns of communication and interaction.

The example of the Brewer family demonstrates that even a small improvement in communication can enhance the relationships within a family and facilitate further gains. This is also seen in the following case, in which another family is forced to confront its negative transactional patterns in such a way that it is challenged to effect some change.

THE MARTIN FAMILY

Mr. and Mrs. Martin had been referred by the school to a family-service agency for help in coping with their three preadolescent children, who had been acting out increasingly in school, at home, and in the community. In the initial family session, the Martins presented themselves to the social worker as insecure, inadequate parents who felt more and more incompetent in dealing with their children. They seemed unable to set limits and dealt with the children through angry outbursts. The children, in turn, interacted with the parents and with each other through yelling and fighting.

In early counseling sessions, Mr. and Mrs. Martin seemed desperate for help. They indicated that their immediate goal was to get the children to be more cooperative at home and to respect their authority. The children wanted their parents to give them more freedom. All family members also expressed their wish for greater family happiness and harmony.

In response to these goals, the social worker proposed that the family develop and carry out a household-chores contract. He viewed the contract as a means of quickly focusing on the issues of parental authority and control that divide the family and also as a way to teach concrete ways to work together more efficiently and with greater mutual satisfaction as members of their family system. The worker explained that the contract would entail the making up of a chart in which all of the children's chores would be listed. In return for chores completed, the parents would agree to set aside specific times for activities with the children, e.g., going out for pizza, playing a Saturday afternoon poker game, etc.

The family readily agreed to three trial sessions to put such a plan together and to see how it would work out in practice. The next three treatment sessions therefore were focused on setting up the contract, going home to try it out, and reviewing with the worker how it worked out from week to week. During these sessions, the agenda was pretty much in the parents' hands; they emphasized getting the children to do their chores, showing little consideration of their own part in the bargain. The worker unsuccessfully tried to encourage the children's input. Communication between the parents and children was highly negative, with frequent accusations and counteraccusations. It was soon evident that the chore-contract system was falling apart and all therefore agreed to abandon the effort.

The worker then capitalized on the material that had emerged in these sessions, especially the evidence of intense resentment between the two subsystems of parents and children and among the children themselves. He engaged family members in formulating another task, namely, dealing with their angry feelings toward each other by expressing them in the treatment setting first, and eventually in their natural surroundings. In contrast to the rapid way in which he had influenced this family to establish the earlier task of a chore contract, the worker carefully delineated the methods and purposes of expressing their mutual feelings. Since it was evident that all family members understood this task, he encouraged each of them to bring out his or her feelings, attitudes, and concerns about it. By the time the task was actually implemented, a great deal had already begun to happen. Family members had the opportunity to express some of their feelings within a safe environment. They were required to listen attentively to each other as well as to the practitioner. And they experienced some sense of mastery and control, since they were asked by the worker to give their opinions about the task and to decide whether or not they wanted to participate in it.

The Martins then went on with the task of expressing their feelings in the office and at home and also reviewing their experiences during each family session. As they engaged in this task, various gains became evident. There was some recognition of the positive meaning that parents and children had for each other after they had ventilated some of their intensely negative feelings. There was a beginning awareness of the family's pattern of yelling and screaming and scapegoating. Family members could see that a better way might be to try listening and to take responsibility for one's own behavior. Above all, they realized more dramatically than ever that they could not go on in their usual way. There ensued some motivation to change and family members began to respond more positively to the worker's efforts to help them to modify their transactional patterns.

Among other points, the above example illustrates the importance of selecting a task that makes sense to the family and that is formulated through the active participation of each member. As often happens in practice, the early choice of a task, such as the chore contract with the Martins, resulted from the worker's enthusiasm rather than from the family's readiness. The family needed to deal with some of its underlying anger before it could tackle such a concrete task. In addition, there was very limited involvement of family members in formulating that task. As with many families who are desperate for help, the Martins readily agreed with the social worker's suggestion to develop a chore contract, but they had little conviction about it or understanding of it. Without adequate preparation, the task therefore fell through, although the worker managed to salvage enough out of the experience to go on with the Martins in a more successful fashion. As this example shows, the selection, formulation, and assignment of a task should be carefully considered, to insure that it is responsive to the family's needs and readiness and that it is based on their meaningful participation.

Enhancing Decision Making

In family intervention there are often opportunities for encouraging family members to exercise and enhance their skills in decision making. Tasks can be used effectively toward this purpose. Family members can be helped to choose among different courses of action, to select appropriate tasks, or to set priorities among various goals. Where there are discrepant goals among them, the practitioner can encourage family members to be responsive to one another and to find areas of common expectations (Gitterman & Germain, 1976, p. 605). In addition, by being involved in the process of defining and negotiating a task, family members are provided with natural opportunities to express their feelings and concerns and to become more sensitive to each other's needs and qualities. Moreover, in the process of negotiating a task, family members can acquire skills in organizing their energies toward common goals. In various ways, therefore, task assignment in and of itself can be therapeutic.

THE PAINTER FAMILY

Mr. and Mrs. Painter were in their late twenties. Mrs. Painter was referred to a mental-health clinic by a visiting nurse due to post-partum depression. The visiting nurse, who had known the family for more than a year, had become aware of the mother's acute unhappiness following the birth of her third child. The father, who had been unemployed for 5 months, spent most of his time at home sleeping or watching television and gave little attention or help to his wife in the care of their children.

During several sessions, Mr. and Mrs. Painter defined as their dual goals (1) being more responsive to each other's needs, and (2) becoming involved in constructive activities outside of the home. In response to the first goal, the therapist pointed out that they needed to engage in bringing out their personal aspirations and their expectations of each other. This need was then established as an explicit task, and the therapist urged them to carry it out in several ways: writing down their most compelling needs, aspirations, and expectations; reviewing these and discussing them in the office; practicing expression of their feelings and needs directly with each other, first in the therapeutic setting and later at home.

As the Painters became freer with each other, they brought out an overwhelming range of mutual expectations. Consequently, a key role of the therapist then was to help them to see that they could not accomplish everything at once and to decide what were their *most urgent* needs at this time. Gradually, Mr. Painter became more sensitive and responsive to his wife's increased need for affection at this point in her life. Mrs. Painter became more aware of her husband's sense of inadequacy as a result of his unemployment and his consequent need for support. The Painters thus became better prepared to meet one another's emotional needs. At the same time, Mrs. Painter was able to let her husband know firmly how and when she expected him to help out with the children. As her expectations in this area were made explicit and concrete, he began to assume increasing responsibility for child care.

In response to the second goal of becoming involved in constructive activities outside the home, the therapist also began by urging each partner to list the kinds of activities that would offer him or her satisfaction. This task was very complex for the Painters, who had been isolated for so long that they were unable to imagine what might be available or even what they might like to do. The therapist consequently took a more active role, bringing them information about possible community resources and offering suggestions as to what the Painters might do in the way of social, cultural, and other involvement outside of their home. As the Painters thus learned about various possibilities and resources, the therapist guided them in clarifying their own interests and in considering the advantages and disadvantages of each opportunity. Ultimately, the therapist confronted the Painters with the need to choose from various alternative courses of action those that might be attainable, and most responsive to their current needs and life situation.

As a result of this process, Mr. and Mrs. Painter decided that they wanted to resume some of their earlier separate social or recreational activities—for example, involvement in a bowling league in the case of both, and pursuing a long-dormant interest in writing lessons in Mrs. Painter's case. In addition, she decided that she wanted to find a part-time job that involved working with people, while he realized that he needed vocational training in order to have better job opportunities. To promote the Painters' efforts to work on their respective tasks, the therapist and the visiting nurse then collaborated to see that various resources were provided for this family: a homemaker who relieved the parents of child care for several afternoons or evenings each week; a part-time job as a hospital aide for the mother; and vocational training that might lead to skilled employment for the father.

As the Painter case illustrates, family members become better able to make critical decisions affecting their lives when their needs are formulated in terms of clear and specific tasks that help to make their problems less overwhelming and more understandable. In addition, as they carry out their tasks and their decisions, family members often need social supports and resources from their social networks and other helping systems outside the family unit. In many case situations, the use of external supports is in fact essential in a task-based approach to family treatment, since it facilitates and complements the family's own problem-solving efforts.*

In addition, frequently, a key role of the practitioner is to provide infor-

---

*For an excellent discussion of strategies for using social networks and informal helping systems in practice, see Collins and Pancoast (1976).

mation that stimulates the clients' cognitive functions and enables them to make decisions. Family treatment often involves an instructive process: the practitioner provides information, imparts knowledge, and stimulates new ideas and concepts. He or she consequently plays an educational role—a role that could be further exploited in practice. It is also important to offer family members regular feedback in relation to their situation, to encourage them to assess the potential risks and benefits inherent in alternative courses of action or in choosing different environments, and to help them to monitor and measure change.

The contract between client system and practitioner can be used as a dynamic tool for engaging family members in assessing their situation, selecting appropriate tasks, and implementing interventive plans.* Participation in contract negotiation can serve to stimulate the person's cognitive growth and mastery, broaden his or her knowledge of different alternatives and their consequences, and mobilize his or her decision-making function. In an increasingly mass-oriented society, human beings desperately need to be able to make important decisions affecting their lives on the basis of adequate knowledge. The practitioner has a responsibility to assist the person in seeking and processing the knowledge needed to reach decisions about complex matters. In a real sense, the availability of adequate information about—and understanding of—the environment is an essential condition for effective human adaptation.†

Promoting Competence

Successful participation in purposive life experiences and activities contributes to the person's self-esteem, autonomy, and competence.‡ Since tasks are generally action-oriented, they can serve as excellent means of promoting competence in family members.

Furthermore, through emphasis on tasks, life problems or events may be redefined to generate opportunities for enhancing the clients' coping efforts and facilitating their involvement in goal-directed action.

Tasks based on action can be especially useful in promoting family members' competence in interpersonal skills and in meeting each other's needs more effectively. Several brief examples from diverse practice settings illustrate this point.

---

*See Maluccio and Marlow (1974).
†For a penetrating discussion of this point, cf. Moos (1976).
‡See Maluccio (1974 and 1981).

THE FORT FAMILY

Mrs. Fort was a middle-aged woman who seemed incapable of functioning since her husband's death a year ago. She had become extremely dependent on her adolescent children, who were frightened and frustrated by her behavior. The children had been avoiding her, thus contributing to her loneliness and depression. Their physician referred the Forts to a psychologist.

After helping Mrs. Fort to work through some of her grief reaction, the psychologist involved her and the children in formulation of multiple tasks designed to promote her independent functioning as well as to change the family's interactional patterns. For example, instead of constantly avoiding their mother, the children agreed to go with her to visit relatives at least once weekly. Mrs. Fort agreed to let them go out on their own several evenings weekly, and not to feel that all of them should always keep her company. The children were instructed to sit down individually with their mother on occasion and to share with her their hopes for the future—they had done so routinely with their father. The mother was encouraged to make necessary decisions, for example, about housing repairs. She was also encouraged to pursue a variety of activities, including shopping for some badly needed clothes for herself and beginning to look for a job.

As they performed these varied tasks, Mrs. Fort and her children developed a new interactional equilibrium in their family system, which had been severely threatened by the loss of the husband and father. New role behaviors and communication patterns emerged, enabling them to offer each other some gratification as a changed family unit. In addition, as she gradually performed her individual tasks with the psychologist's and children's support, Mrs. Fort enhanced her sense of autonomy, gained some desperately needed feelings of competence, and improved her skills in dealing with the environment. All family members thus profited through engagement in their joint as well as individual tasks.

THE TURNER FAMILY

Mr. and Mrs. Turner went to a child guidance clinic for help with their 13-year-old son, Rick, the oldest of five children, following referral by the juvenile court. Rick had been involved in delinquent activities, including stealing from a store and beating up younger children. Psychiatric evaluation revealed that Rick had been increasingly neglected by his parents, who were preoccupied with their younger children. The father, in particular, had withdrawn from Rick, as he became more and more difficult to handle. Mr. Turner expressed concern as well as resentment toward Rick. The major underlying problems seemed to be his pervasive sense of inadequacy as the father.

In the course of treatment, Rick and his father agreed that, although they would like to have a better relationship, they did not know how to get along without getting upset or screaming. Learning how to get along with each other therefore became a major task focus for father and son. Among other approaches, the psychiatrist suggested that Mr. Turner ask Rick to visit him daily after school in his small grocery store, where Rick could perform minor chores. In each treatment session, Rick and his father were then encouraged to review their experiences together and to express their feelings toward each other. It became evident in this process that Rick's emerging adolescence had been arousing Mr. Turner's conflicts over his own turbulent adolescence. With considerable input from the psychiatrist, Mr. Turner learned that much of Rick's belligerent behavior as well as the turmoil that he himself experienced as a teenager was quite natural and was to be expected. Mr. Turner was then better able to relax with Rick, who at the same time provided him with positive reinforcement as they became more involved with each other.

After several weeks, Mr. Turner and Rick reported that they enjoyed the time they spent together and that they had become good friends. Mr. Turner conveyed a renewed sense of competence in his role as the father and a hopefulness about Rick that had been totally absent earlier.

THE MOSLEY FAMILY

Mrs. Mosley was a divorced woman who had been struggling to care for her children. Two of them were now teenagers who were experiencing much difficulty in school. Mrs. Mosley blamed the school for her son's problems and lately had been refusing to attend the parent-teacher conferences to which she was repeatedly invited. Eventually, the school nurse reached out to Mrs. Mosley. The nurse had gotten to know her as a result of a minor accident that one of her sons had had in the woodworking shop several months earlier. Following repeated calls and two home visits by the nurse, Mrs. Mosely agreed to attend a school conference, if the nurse would also be there.

The nurse reassured Mrs. Mosley that she would also participate. Together, they formulated a major, joint task in connection with the conference: improving the collaboration between school and parent on behalf of the children. The nurse agreed to support Mrs. Mosley in her concern for her children and their right to be treated fairly by school personnel. On her part, Mrs. Mosley agreed to listen to what the teachers had to say and to consider ways in which she could support the school's expectations from them.

In the conference, Mrs. Mosley spoke assertively about her children's rights and expressed her concern for them. She responded to a teacher's obvious hostility toward one of her sons by pointing out that the teacher was rejecting Bob, and that Bob, therefore, reacted negatively. She heard the interest and concern of the other teachers regarding her children. She offered suggestions as to how the boys might be handled in school and emphasized ways in which she could discipline them at home and expect more from them in relation to their school work.

In short, with support from the school nurse, Mrs. Mosley succeeded in expressing her feelings, confronting school personnel, and gaining their acceptance. School personnel responded more positively to her as they saw her in a different light, as a result of her performance during the conference. In dealing with her children's continuing school difficulties, she then began to move from angry outbursts against the school system toward making realistic expectations clear to the children. The school nurse maintained regular contacts with her and reinforced her greater competence as a parent through informal family sessions also involving her three sons.

VARIETIES OF TASKS

Case examples have been used to illustrate the different types of tasks that can be used for therapeutic purposes:

1. *Clinical tasks* that promote the therapeutic relationship or other aspects of the helping process, e.g., talking together for the purpose of developing a relationship between the therapist and the family or asking family members to list their problems and concerns for purposes of problem assessment (Haley, 1976, pp. 76–77).
2. *Natural life tasks* that are designed to achieve structural changes in the family system through active involvement in real-life experiences, e.g., having family members work at being more sensitive to each other's needs and at giving emotionally to each other.
3. *Artificial tasks*, such as role playing, that provide the opportunity for family members to practice desired behaviors or develop interpersonal skills.
4. *Homework assignments* that afford opportunities to learn or practice more effective behavioral patterns or interpersonal skills (Shelton & Ackerman, 1974).

Another use of tasks is in the *paradoxical task assignment*, in which the therapist directs the family to do something that he or she actually does not want them to do or to continue doing. In other words, the clients are instructed to engage in behavior that seems totally contrary to their goals and expectations. The family or one of its subunits is directed to engage, often in exaggerated form, in precisely the kinds of behavior that family members ostensibly wish to change, such as yelling at each other or arguing violently.

These instructions initially do not make sense to the family. They appear to be "paradoxical to family members because the therapist has told them he wants to help them change but at the same time he is asking them not to change" (Haley, 1976, p. 67). However, it has been demonstrated through clinical practice that, in response to such incongruous demands by the therapist, some families do begin to change. The assumption is that the paradoxical task places family members in the position of resisting or "rebelling" against the therapist, thus becoming motivated to assert their own will and to decrease or otherwise modify their unproductive behavior:

> . . . having the usual behavior occur under the therapist's guidance makes it a different behavior, and because of the confusion about how to resist, the usual patterns are altered, new perceptions occur, and change results (Hare-Mustin, 1976).

This technique seems to be especially effective with families that have reached an impasse in therapy or are locked into mutually hostile and destructive relationship patterns. A brief example follows.

MR. AND MRS. CORMIER

Mr. and Mrs. Cormier were a middle-aged couple who over the years had developed a pattern of getting into violent arguments that were never resolved. During an argument, Mr. Cormier usually left the house after calling his wife crazy. Mrs. Cormier was becoming increasingly dissatisfied with this pattern and her threat of divorce brought the couple to a marriage counselor.

In the early sessions with the counselor, both Mr. and Mrs. Cormier expressed their dissatisfaction with each other and their mutually hostile behavior, along with their wish to change. Their explicit goals were to improve their communication and to have more enjoyable sexual relations. However, they resisted the counselor's efforts to discuss their feelings and concerns further and persisted in unproductive behavior, such as blaming each other for their problems.

Among other approaches, the counselor chose to tell the Cormiers that they were not doing a very good job of "fighting" and directed them to engage in the fighting behavior even more intensely whenever they were at home.

Furthermore, the counselor instructed Mrs. Cormier to work harder to show her husband what a good fighter she was. Mr. Cormier, on the other hand, was directed to do a better job himself by not leaving the scene whenever there was an argument.

Although the Cormiers were puzzled by this task and indicated that it did not make sense to them, the counselor gave no other explanation and insisted that they carry it out. Following several interviews, the Cormiers reported that they had made only feeble attempts at fighting, emphasizing that the whole idea was "silly." Gradually, they realized that their long-standing pattern of fighting with each other was mutually destructive and laughingly noted that there "must be a better way of doing it." At the same time, the counselor recognized and helped them to express the negative feelings that had long been pent up within each of them, as well as their needs and expectations of each other. This process eventually led to their better communication, including renewed ability to express tender feelings toward one another and a more satisfying sexual relationship.

As this example suggests, paradoxical tasks constitute another effective tool in family intervention:

The use of paradoxical tasks is a powerful lever in producing change in the family by using the resistance in the family system. The selection of tasks of an absurd or confounding nature breaks up the family's usual ways of behaving and perceiving each other as it enables them to achieve some detachment from the disturbing behavior (Hare-Mustin, 1976, p. 130).

Paradoxical tasks may be effective for different reasons with different families. In some cases, as in the preceding example, by being confronted with the futile or destructive nature of their interaction, family members are helped to achieve a "breakthrough" of recognition that their behavior patterns are not productive. This awareness helps to free the members toward new directions: developing different attitudes toward each other, expressing their feelings more constructively, initiating new interactional patterns, and learning new behavior in their functioning as a system. In other situations, the experience of engaging with greater intensity in painful or anxiety-provoking behavior leads to a sense of mastery and control in members of the family unit.* Above all, paradoxical tasks seem to be an effective way of dealing with family resistance to change. The task apparently shocks the family into different behavioral patterns or mobilizes it toward "spontaneous" change, so as to show the therapist that it is as good as other families (Haley, 1976, p. 69).

---

*This explanation is suggested especially by Frankl (1960), who uses paradoxical tasks as an integral part of his logotherapy with individuals crippled by anticipatory anxiety.

Unlike other tasks in which the family is actively involved with the therapist in a reciprocal process of formulation and selection, paradoxical tasks require the therapist to take the initiative and give directives. As Haley observes, this calls for a complex set of skills and qualities. Therapists must be comfortable in giving directives; they should be able to think about problems and their solutions in a playful way; they must be ready to tolerate the potentially negative reactions of the family toward them, and they need to convey that the task is part of the framework of trying to change the family in relation to its own goals (Haley, 1976, pp. 70–76).*

Although we are concerned here primarily with the therapeutic purposes of tasks, it is also worthwhile to note how such methods may be of use in family assessment. Tasks such as the structured family interview, family sculpting, and drawings can be helpful in the diagnostic process. For example, the Bing Conjoint Family Drawing (Bing, 1970) can serve as an excellent tool in assessment of family functioning. In the course of an early session, the clients are asked to collaborate on drawing a picture of their family. In doing so, they reveal a great deal about the family's structure and interaction through the completed drawing, as well as their communication patterns while working on the task. The therapist can take advantage of this material not only in reaching diagnostic understanding of the family but also in increasing the members' awareness of their problems and interactional patterns. As with the Bing Conjoint Family Drawing, other action-oriented tasks, such as sculpting, can serve as effective and quick methods of bringing out underlying feelings and conflicts of family members and cutting through intellectualization, defensiveness, and projection.†

A SUMMARIZING CASE EXAMPLE

In this chapter I have developed the concept of task and its key principles, purposes, and varieties and have illustrated its application in intervention with families in a range of practice settings. Most of the examples, however, have been necessarily brief and fragmented and may not have conveyed the full impact and varied possibilities of a task-based approach to family treatment within any one case situation. For this reason, a more extensive case illustration follows in which a social worker deliberately follows the life model of practice and uses tasks as the major thrust of her intervention with a family at a community mental-health center.

---

*For further discussion of paradoxical tasks, see Watzlawick, Weakland, and Fisch (1974, pp. 110–157).

†See, for example, Duhl, Kantor, and Duhl (1973); Papp, Silverstein, and Carter (1973).

THE FOLEY FAMILY*

Mr. and Mrs. Foley, in their fifties, and their 15-year-old son David were referred to a mental-health clinic by the guidance counselor. David had a history of problems in school ever since first grade. He was of average intelligence but uninterested in school and was failing every subject in the ninth grade. In addition, he had been repeatedly suspended for "bullying" younger children and skipping school several times weekly.

In the evaluation sessions at the clinic, Mr. and Mrs. Foley came through as insecure and unhappy people who were very upset and overwhelmed by their son's behavior. The had been brought up in multiproblem families where they had experienced considerable emotional and economic deprivation. Mr. Foley was generally detached in his relationship with David and periodically blew up in angry outbursts. Mrs. Foley and David were constantly yelling and fighting with each other. The parents were uninvolved with one another but occasionally expressed a joint wish that their son get out of the house.

On the basis of a careful assessment, the social worker concluded that this family's identity and structure and the adaptive capacities of its members were seriously affected by their destructive interactional patterns and dysfunctional communication processes. Family homeostasis, which had been maintained by the family members' lack of relatedness, was now threatened by the son's adolescence. Mr. and Mrs. Foley seemed unable to fulfill their roles as parents or to provide the necessary environment in which David could grow and develop. Although they had sought outside help in the past to improve the family's functioning, they had been unable to use it productively, partly because they blamed their son for all problems. In the process, they had increasingly isolated themselves from him and his acting-out behavior and virtually retreated from their parental roles. The greatest source of friction apparently resided within the dyad of Mrs. Foley and David. Both mother and son had difficulty in effectively transacting with their respective environments, resulting in their taking out their frustrations on each other. In addition, Mrs. Foley lacked the autonomy necessary to motivate her to improve her situation or to view her life as having choices.

Following several joint sessions in which they expressed a wish to improve their family relationships, Mr. and Mrs. Foley and David formulated a variety of goals and tasks with the worker's help. Mr. and Mrs. Foley realized that they needed to reassume their roles as parents. In order to do so, they agreed to examine in joint sessions with the therapist their current patterns of functioning, their respective parent-child relationships, and the roots of their unhappiness and inability to interact effectively with their environments. Over the course of several sessions, the social worker carefully

---

*Adapted from a case summary by Barbara Loh, to whom I am deeply grateful.

explained what this kind of examination would involve for each of them and also tried to sound them out as to their readiness to undertake it. For instance, for Mr. Foley it specifically meant that he would need to explore his fear of intimacy and emotion with his son and with his wife and also his resultant pattern of withdrawal from them. For Mrs. Foley it meant considering the reasons for her unhappiness, her pattern of using her son as a scapegoat, and what she needed from her husband and her environment in order to become happier. For David, it involved exploration of his need to blame his parents and to use his mother as the focus of his negative feelings about himself and his inability to take responsibility for his own life.

While the tasks that were thus formulated were rather complex and threatening, Mr. and Mrs. Foley and David seemed to be quite motivated to work on them. In order to facilitate their performance of the tasks, they also agreed on a variety of related activities or subtasks. The worker was to be responsible for providing a supportive environment in which the Foleys could more successfully complete their tasks, acting as an advocate for David in getting his individual needs met from the school system, serving as educator and model for the Foleys in helping them to be better parents, and supporting Mrs. Foley in her attempts to achieve a better "fit" with the environment. David was to take responsibility for going to school, doing his chores so that he could receive his allowance, and for attending individual sessions every week and family sessions periodically. Together, Mr. and Mrs. Foley were to be responsible for attending sessions for the two of them and periodic family sessions, giving David an allowance for doing his chores, doing various homework assignments such as thinking about their own adolescence in order to understand David's better, and giving David more freedom as a teenager. Mrs. Foley agreed to be less negative and accusing in her dealings with David, to look into possible participation in activities outside of the family, and to take more responsibility for such things as calling a repairman and buying clothes for herself. Mr. Foley agreed to become more involved with his son through such means as working together on projects around the house. He also concurred that he should be more responsive to his wife's need for support by becoming more attentive to her.

In view of the multiplicity of tasks and activities that have been outlined above, it should be emphasized that they are not formulated quite as rapidly or simply as it appears. Rather, they emerge as the worker and the family go on working with each other toward solution of identified problems. In trying to achieve their agreed-upon goals, this family and the practitioner were in fact engaged in active work for 8 months. At the beginning, family sessions proved quite unproductive therapeutically but gave the worker a clear picture of the dysfunctional elements. Early sessions consisted primarily of ventilation. In addition, David's school trouble, only one month into the year, set off a crisis situation in the family and afforded the therapist the opportunity to assume the role of advocate for David and his parents in their transaction with the school. David was clearly not going to make it in the regular junior high school, and the worker facilitated his placement in an alternative program after meeting repeatedly with guidance counselors and school officials.

After this crisis had been resolved, the worker continued to play a supportive role with all family members, in addition to that of educator about adolescence and appropriate parenting. The parents remained skeptical, however, that anything worthwhile would be accomplished, in view of their frustrations with mental-health workers in the past and their seemingly unsupportive environment. In light of their understandable pessimism, the worker suggested that a step-by-step contract be negotiated, to help in coping with their overwhelming situation. By becoming involved in the process of breaking down their problems into smaller and more easily manageable components, Mr. and Mrs. Foley as well as David became less passive, more action-oriented, and more positive in their outlook. In addition, contract negotiation gave clients and therapist the opportunity to clarify and reaffirm treatment goals and methods and to confront discrepancies in their mutual expectations.

Family sessions then became focused on the family's lack of structure, their problems in interactional patterns, and each member's inability to tackle effectively his or her "problems in living." For instance, much energy went into attempts to negotiate an agreement on basic family tasks: chores, allowance, bedtime, etc. The worker played the role of negotiator or bargainer. She tried to get family members to bring out their expectations of each other in respect to these family tasks, to reach agreement regarding key expectations, and to try to fulfill them as a part of their daily functioning as a family unit. Although the Foleys reached a working agreement in these areas, it did not work out, reflecting how poorly the family was operating even in relation to concrete and essential activities.

At this point there followed a period of deterioration in the family's functioning as well as within the therapeutic context. David began cancelling his appointments at the last minute. Mrs. Foley was frequently ill with headaches and stomach pains. Mr. Foley felt that the situation was hopeless and complained to the worker that treatment was not helping in any way. The worker herself was quite discouraged, since she sensed this family's desperation and was also frustrated in trying to help them change their fixed dysfunctional patterns.

A major problem was that while David had been trying hard to change, his parents seemed to be rigidly fixed in their destructive relationship and unable to give to one another. Furthermore, they continued to project all problems onto David as the scapegoat. Consequently, the worker at this point decided to concentrate her interventive efforts for a while on Mr. and Mrs. Foley as a couple. For instance, she helped them to connect their past feelings, disappointments, and hopes to the present. They became less resistant and defensive as they were gradually able to explore the roots of their unhappiness and disappointments in life. Each interview with the Foleys became less and less of a gripe session about David and more and more focused on themselves as people. Slowly, the worker and parents were able to redefine the problem and no longer view the son as the cause of family difficulties.

As the client-therapist relationship became stronger, Mrs. Foley was able to share her depression in several individual sessions. In one of these, the worker concentrated on short- and long-term planning for her, with which Mrs. Foley hesitantly went along. She began to admit that she had been using her son as a focus for her unhappiness and that their fights helped her to escape her boredom and gave her life some "meaning." Mrs. Foley was then able to tackle various tasks designed to improve her skills in transacting with her environment and to enhance her sense of competence. These included compiling lists of her interests and possible activities out of the house, discussing her future, beginning to explore the possibility of a job, and successfully completing a clothes-shopping spree she had been wanting to do for nearly a year.

There were also separate individual sessions with Mr. Foley. These were focused on supporting him in his sense of success as an office manager, encouraging him to support his wife in her strivings toward greater autonomy and to engage in recreational activities with his son. The husband's increased attention to the wife, coupled with her greater insight into her feelings, lessened the hostility in the mother-son dyad and alleviated the son's role as the scapegoat.

Individual sessions with David were also resumed during this period. David at first was very uncomfortable with the worker, remaining detached from her and verbalizing only after constant questioning. However, he did continue with treatment contacts. Later, as his parents began to function more constructively and to be more positive in their interaction with him, David reported that things were better at home. He indicated, for example, that although disagreements between his mother and himself still occurred, they were now minor skirmishes rather than major crises. He also noted with satisfaction that he and his father were becoming a little closer and that they enjoyed doing things together.

Following this concentrated program of joint as well as individual sessions, Mr. and Mrs. Foley and David learned to cope more constructively with everyday problems and events that in the past would have totally disrupted the family system. They became more supportive of each other and better able to carry on with their life tasks. Mr. and Mrs. Foley gained some insight into their feelings and qualities. At the same time, the worker helped them to translate their growing awareness into *behavior* through such means as role playing and communication training. Plans were also made for David to return to his regular class at the high school the following September.

Considerable pathology was evident in the family in the preceding example, and it would have been easy to become pessimistic. The problems were long standing and the behavior patterns, well established. The parents had sought help in the past, to no avail. There was serious question as to whether they could change. The therapist was aware of the family's pathology but not excessively preoccupied with it.

Emphasizing the life model in general, and the use of tasks in particular, the worker concentrated on the family's strengths and adaptive capacities rather than its underlying weaknesses. Despite periodic setbacks, she persisted in her efforts to help family members in confronting their problems, considering alternative courses of action, selecting treatment goals and methods, and formulating and implementing multiple tasks designed to achieve their goals. As they were faced with the need to think and choose in this ongoing process of negotiation and renegotiation among themselves as well as with the worker, family members were stimulated to exercise and enhance their decision-making powers and to learn better ways of coping with family conflict.

Through the purposive use of selected tasks, the family was also helped to change its structure and transactions sufficiently to enable its members to communicate and interact more constructively with one another. Similarly, by carrying out a variety of individual tasks, each of them was helped to increase his or her competence and autonomy. For example, the parents became more secure and effective in their parenting roles. The father became more comfortable in his relationship with his wife, as well as with his son. The mother gained a better sense of herself as she successfully completed on her own, various significant tasks. The son strengthened his identity as an adolescent as he experienced his ability to control his situation.

In this family's case, as in others, the positive results did not happen easily. On the contrary, they demanded tremendous persistence on the part of the worker as well as the family. Perhaps most importantly, they required that the worker continue to have faith in the family's capacity to change in the face of numerous obstacles.

CONCLUSION

Through its orientation to action and experiential quality, the task-based approach to family treatment can be an effective means of mobilizing client and practitioner energies toward achievement of family and individual goals. To attain this purpose, much effort is required beyond the simple definition of tasks. Family members need to struggle and to receive consistent encouragement and support through the practitioner. This approach places the clients squarely in the heart of the helping process and affirms the preeminence of their participation in therapeutic intervention.

REFERENCES

Bartlett, H.M. *The Common Base of Social Work Practice.* New York: National Association of Social Workers, 1970.

Bing, E. The conjoint family drawing. *Family Process,* 1970, 9, 173–194.

Collins, A.H., & Pancoast, D.L. *Natural Helping Networks.* Washington, D.C.: National Association of Social Workers, 1976.

Duhl, F.J., Kantor, D. & Duhl, B.S. Learning, space, and action in family therapy. In Bloch, D.A. (ed.), *Techniques of Family Psychotherapy: A Primer.* New York: Grune & Stratton, 1973, 47–63.

Frankl, V.E. Paradoxical intention. *American Journal of Psychotherapy,* 1960, 14, 520–535.

Gitterman A., & Germain, C.B. Social work practice: A life model. *Social Service Review,* 1976, 50, 601–610.

Haley, J. *Problem-Solving Therapy.* San Francisco: Jossey-Bass, 1976.

Hare-Mustin, R.T. Paradoxical tasks in family therapy: Who can resist? *Psychotherapy: Theory, Research and Practice,* 1976, 13, 128–130.

Hare-Mustin, R.T. Treatment of temper tantrums by a paradoxical intervention. *Family Process,* 1975, 14, 481–485.

Maluccio, A.N. Action as a tool in casework practice. *Social Casework,* 1974, 55, 30–35.

Maluccio, A.N., & Marlow, W.D. The case for the contract. *Social Work,* 1974, 19, 28–36.

Maluccio, A.N. (ed.). *Promoting Competence in Clients—A New/Old Approach to Social Work Practice.* New York: The Free Press, 1981.

Minuchin, S. *Families and Family Therapy.* Cambridge, Mass.: Harvard University Press, 1974.

Moos, R.H. *The Human Context—Environmental Determinants of Behavior.* New York: Wiley, 1976.

Papp, P., Silverstein, O., & Carter, E. Family sculpting in preventive work with "well families." *Family Process,* 1973, 12, 197–212.

Shelton, J.L., & Ackerman, J.M. *Homework in Counseling and Psychotherapy.* Springfield, Ill.: Thomas, 1974.

Studt, E. Social work theory and implications for the practice of methods. *Social Work Education Reporter,* 1968, 16, 22 ff.

Watzlawick, P., Weakland, J., & Fisch, R. *Change—Principles of Problem Formation and Problem Resolution.* New York: Norton, 1974.

24

Families of the Developmentally Disabled: Helping Models

Sharon S. Kern

In the past it was customary to view the developmentally disabled as mentally deficient. The term mental deficiency *in itself implies an irremediable deficit, while inherent in the notion of developmental disability is recognition of capacity for change through learning. Similar biases have influenced service to this segment of the population, particularly among those professionals who have valued so-called insight therapies over supportive, reeducative, and action-oriented approaches. The helping models presented by Kern are rooted in the belief that the developmentally disabled not only have a right to assistance but that help must be firmly based on the conviction that these individuals have a right to become all that they potentially may. These models propose habilitative and interventive roles for the family, collaborating with professionals in enhancing the functioning of the individual in his or her life setting. Benefits accrue to the family as well since they learn new and more productive ways of coping and interacting.*

The recognition that the family is the most effective setting for enhancing the development of a handicapped child and the current shift from institutional care to community-based services have given rise to a number of family-oriented social treatment models for helping the developmentally disabled child. These models emphasize the importance of the family as both habilitative and interventive agent. They provide a framework in which parents and professionals can work as partners in developing and providing services for children with handicapping conditions in order to enable them more successfully to lead satisfying lives in the community.

INFORMATION AND OUTREACH

Work with families of mentally retarded and other handicapped children has traditionally focused on helping parents to cope with their disappointed expectations, feelings of guilt, shame, anger, and persistent grief and sadness.* These feelings do exist in varying degrees, depending on the parents' past experiences, personal resources, values, and life situation. They are never altogether resolved.† Insensitivity of relatives and the community, protracted dependency, the need for special or time-consuming procedures, recurrent medical crises, frequent clinic or agency visits, and frustration over lack of services exacerbate the hurt and anger. Many parents of older children today struggle with mixed feelings: gratitude for new services and regret that they were not available earlier.

When the stress of having or caring for a developmentally disabled child is so great that it produces a family or personal crisis, professional counseling or psychotherapy may be needed. For most families, cooperative efforts at reaching out that link professionals with other parents in offering immediate practical information and emotional support are sufficient to help them maintain equilibrium. New parents need to talk about their experiences, including their fears and misconceptions, and they need someone to listen to them. However, it is equally important that they know their child will grow and develop, and that there are programs as well as activities they can do during the child's first years of life that will help him or her stay closer to a normal rate of development.

Information Is Therapeutic

When parents first learn their child has a handicapping condition, it is natural for them to be disturbed. A major part of their disturbance is realistic fear and confusion compounded by a sense of isolation. They know little or nothing about the diagnostic label that has been applied to their child, and they probably have never known anyone else—at least not well—in the same situation. They have no conception of what the immediate or distant future holds for their child. Most do not completely understand medical, psychologic, or educational terminology. They may not be aware of what services are available to them or even that services exist.

Parents should be given as much information as they can comprehend.

---

*For a brief historical review of the theoretical models with which parental responses have been viewed, see Wolfensberger & Menolascino (1970).
†For a parent's own account, see Searl (1978).

Contrary to the opinion of some, information is reassuring rather than frightening if it is presented in a supportive manner. Parents should always receive information, especially the initial diagnosis, when they are together. They are each other's primary source of emotional support. Single parents should have the opportunity to be with a supportive friend or relative.

Explanations at the time of diagnosis should include realistic but tentative and positive descriptions of the child's potential development, rather than emphasis on limitations inherent in the condition. Beginning at the time of diagnosis, the parents should be taught basic principles of development. They need to know that all persons grow and develop in similar stages, and that their own child will, too, but probably at a slower or more uneven rate. It is helpful to give some concrete examples for development stages. Parents should be told that with appropriate stimulation activities, primarily involving movement and play, they can help their baby develop farther and faster than he or she might without special help. The child can progress at a rate that was once believed impossible. They should be told, too, that development continues throughout life (this is also a fairly new idea). Thus, provided with a stimulating environment, their child can go on learning through adulthood. This developmental approach, in contrast to the old static model, permits family members to begin with a positive attitude, one which helps to offset the "so sorry, how awful" responses they have received from their well-meaning but ill-informed friends and relatives.

Physicians are reluctant—sometimes understandably so—to use such a positive approach, for fear of raising false hopes. My experience suggests that it is better to err in the positive direction. Far greater harm is done to children who are constrained by limited expectations.

Written materials describing developmental sequences and play activities* given or loaned to parents right away serve an additional therapeutic function: Parents feel they can *do* something, even if at first they are only reading. They begin to feel some control over the situation. In the past parents described their situation as feeling helpless, "in the dark," and "at the mercy of the doctors" (or other professionals). Having positive information to share with grandparents and friends in the beginning has the additional benefit of helping the parents to strengthen their own support systems.

Explanations of professional terminology should be written down in language that avoids jargon, and the parents should be encouraged to maintain a file of records for their child. It is, after all, the parents who must shop for services, and the better they understand their child's situation, the less confusing will be the process. Giving parents copies of diagnostic and educational reports they can submit with program applications may cut weeks or even

---

*An excellent 1978 pamphlet, *Growing . . . A Guide for Parents* is available from the Canadian Association for the Mentally Retarded, 4700 Keele St., Downsview, Ontario.

months from the process of obtaining the desired service and add those weeks and months to the benefits derived by the child.

Professionals must be sensitive to the abilities of parents with whom they are working. Some may not like to admit they do not read. Others, who do read, may not learn well that way, and could benefit from tapes or a home teacher. At the other extreme is the highly educated parent who may need the information just as badly but will be offended if he or she feels the professional is talking down to him or her. Even the most intelligent parents need to have things repeated more than once. Stress affects both perception and memory. The parents may nod as if they understand, but pride, reserve, or deference to authority may prevent them from asking questions.

As soon as the parents learn what is "wrong" with the child, they should be told the kinds of services that are available. Most practitioners do not have a comprehensive directory of services. In fact, many physicians who are not knowledgeable about current practices in early intervention and parent training are still advising parents to institutionalize moderately retarded children. Admission criteria in most state facilities today are such that this is not a viable option. Some hospitals, with the help of private agencies, are attempting to educate pediatricians to greater awareness of developmental and educational needs of young children with handicapping conditions. Pediatric residents at Children's Hospital National Medical Center in Washington, D.C., spend 12 hours at an experimental preschool program in conjunction with curriculum activities and readings in developmental and behavioral pediatrics. Residents reported that they gained most in relation to their understanding of community resources available for handicapped children. They reported an increased understanding of behavioral characteristics and greater ability to communicate and plan with parents and teachers about the developmental and educational needs of children (Richardson, Guralnick, & Tucker, 1978).

Many specialized state and local agencies and parent groups operate information and referral services. The task of locating appropriate services and evaluating them is a difficult one for parents who have no experience in programming for the handicapped. Staff and parent members of a voluntary association for the developmentally disabled are familiar with the service-delivery system and therefore can negotiate with it. Development of linkages with representatives of such organizations saves precious time for families.

Many parents, at the first realization of their child's handicapping condition, become frightened in anticipation of a greater financial burden for special services. Information regarding Public Law 94-142, which mandates that their local school district must pay for and provide transportation to a suitable educational program for their handicapped child from 5 to 21 years of age is an immediate anxiety reliever. In most states publicly funded preschool and infant programs are available as well.

First-hand observation of older handicapped babies and children is a great help to parents in overcoming their fears and doubts. A family visit to an integrated early-intervention program where there are happy, personable youngsters with similar conditions will contribute as much as or more than the best counseling techniques to the family's sense of well-being. Likewise, for the family of a profoundly handicapped baby (even though he or she will remain at home), a carefully planned visit to an infant home can provide important reassurance that resources are available if the family cannot cope or has an emergency. The important thing for the helper to communicate is that the family *can* cope and that assistance will be there when needed.

Self-Help Groups

Parents who have a handicapped child, especially those who have recently given birth to such a child, often want to talk with other parents who "have been there," who have had similar experiences with doctors, neighbors, and grandparents—a need most professional counselors cannot fill. Sharing with another parent on a one-to-one basis, or in a group, reduces feelings of aloneness. A visit to another home where there is a developmentally disabled child has the potential for providing psychologic support for the entire family; it permits them to see a real family that has absorbed a handicapped child on a day-to-day basis as it would any other child.

Many informal networks exist, but a number of agencies have begun to formalize one-to-one parent-counseling programs. The agency usually provides back-up services such as training and consultation. The Parent Resource Program in Buffalo, New York, and the Parent Outreach Program in St. Louis, Missouri, both sponsored by local associations for retarded children, are examples. The St. Louis group has published a guidebook for developing a parent-to-parent program (Bassin & Kreeb, 1978).

Parent groups can provide more than emotional support. They can arm their members with information about the developmental, educational, and social needs of their children and about their own legal rights in order to become advocates for their children. They can monitor the quality of existing services and work in partnership with agencies and schools to develop new and better programs. They can operate their own information and referral services. The most effective parent-information and advocacy groups have access to and commitment from legal advocacy services. Professionals must accord parents full status as working partners to increase their self-esteem and, thus, their ability to improve services for their children.

Sibling groups have received attention in the professional literature.*

---

*See for example, Schruber & Feeley (1965).

Usually composed of adolescents, with guidance from a trained group leader, the groups have offered information and support about such topics as curious or hostile peer attitudes; feelings of anger, embarrassment or shame; anxiety about dating, marriage, and parenthood; guardianship; and disagreement with parents about behavior management. It has been observed that not only does the group experience relieve anxiety for the sibling by giving him or her information and an opportunity to deal with his or her feelings openly and constructively, but it frequently results in greater interest in and empathy for the handicapped brother or sister. Siblings, because of proximity in age, can contribute to the learning of social skills through play and by including the developmentally disabled child in a broader social group. Siblings with a realistic and accepting attitude can be a source of support for parents.

The dramatic experience of Craig and Jan Cole in the following case serves to illustrate the importance of providing immediate practical information and outreach to parents of newborns. Much anguish could have been avoided had it been offered to the Coles earlier. Fortunately, it was available in time to prevent a tragic ending to their story.

THE COLE FAMILY

Jan Cole gave birth to twins 2 months prematurely. Denise, who had the higher birth weight, progressed more rapidly than her brother, Danny, who was in trouble from the start. Denise was discharged from the hospital 6 weeks later, but Danny remained in the premature nursery for 4 months.

The Cole's marriage was shaky before the twins' birth, but things got worse afterward. The pregnancy had been unplanned. Craig blamed Jan, and she resented his lack of support. When there was only Denise to care for, Jan could manage, but after Danny came home and there were two infants who required more than the ordinary amount of attention, the stress became too great. She began to have hostile impulses toward Danny and specific fantasies of harming him.

One night Jan telephoned the countywide child-abuse hot-line, expressing fear that she would hurt Danny. The parent manning the hot-line that evening happened to have had experience with developmentally delayed children as a foster mother. She called the Association for Retarded Children. The following day an outreach social worker visited the Cole home.

After she had listened to Jan's story, watched her interact with the two infants, and made a cursory developmental assessment, the worker understood some aspects of the case very well. Seven months after birth, Denise was functioning developmentally in the 4- to 5-month range, as expected for 2 months' prematurity. Unfortunately, Jan did not know that. Denise was responsive to Jan's demonstrations of affection and a bond existed between mother and child. Danny, on the other hand, was passive and unresponsive, and his motor development was severely delayed, although his muscle tone was good. The worker speculated that when the second baby came home from the hospital, Jan who was giving her emotional energy to Denise and was already stressed, related only mechanically to the unresponsive Danny. With two strikes against him, Danny's developmental retardation was exaggerated. His unresponsiveness and lack of progress made Jan feel less and less competent and more and more frightened and angry. They were caught in a dangerous cycle.

The worker began at once to give both emotional reassurance and reassuring facts, teaching Jan basic behavioral-reinforcement concepts and a few specific stimulation activities for Danny. The worker fed lunch to Denise while Jan fed Danny. Later, the two women played with the babies together. As if by some good omen, Danny smiled responsively for the first time that afternoon, and Jan shed tears of relief and hope. Before the worker left, she called another parent who visited Jan the following day and continued to offer support. The Coles were linked with a marriage counselor and with a local child-development program, where Jan became involved in a mothers' group.

Because she had been carrying twins and had had a troublesome pregnancy, Jan had delivered at a university-affiliated children's hospital 30 miles from the town where she and her husband lived, rather than at the local general hospital. Coincidentally, one of the best early-intervention programs in that part of the state was located in their home town, but the Coles did not know they could get help for their infants there. How did it happen that in all the months the family had contact with the nearby pediatric hospital and their family physician, they could have been so uninformed?

At follow-up 1 year later, Jan reported that both children were involved daily in the preschool learning program. Denise's development was within the normal range, and although Danny was developing more slowly, she was pleased with his progress. Jan and Craig had worked out an amicable separation, in which he was actively involved with the children. Jan had opened her own interior decorating business and was able to afford a live-in nanny who was warmly attached to both children.

PARENT TRAINING

More and more programs for children with handicapping conditions are beginning to concentrate on the development of the infant and young child. The maturation process is very complex; the development of skills in one area affects the development of other areas. For example, the acquisition of motor skills influences the development of intellectual skills and social skills and, thus, total development. Atypical growth patterns can frequently be identified very early, and assisting a child in acquiring certain skills can enhance his or her overall functioning. A variety of stimulating activities geared to the child's developmental needs can lessen the impact of the handicapping condition.

Parents as Teachers: Infant Stimulation and Skill Building

Because parents are the natural teachers of their children and are with them more than are any other persons, especially in the early years, they have the greatest opportunity to influence their development. Since home is usually the most supportive environment for a baby, he or she may learn best there. Most agency programs are carried out in the home through visits from a home teacher or trainer. Sometimes home training is offered in conjunction with an agency preschool program in order to offer a total continuum of services. Additional support staff, such as physical therapists or speech and language specialists, can become involved, depending on the individual child's needs. Some agencies offer parents the option of parent-training groups, where they can socialize and compare notes with other parents.

In home training programs, the parents assume the role of teachers with their children, and the worker assumes the role of trainer and consultant to the parents. First the home trainer begins by teaching the parents about normal developmental sequences, using charts, pamphlets, and video tapes. Second, the trainer helps the parents assess their child's place in each area of development. Together they compile a list of the child's strengths and weaknesses based on the premise that babies and young children, like all people, learn best in a framework that builds on their strengths while working on their weaknesses. An example of this would be to incorporate an exercise, tedious by itself, into play activity the child enjoys. Such a framework also helps the parents focus on what the child can do rather than on what he or she cannot do.

The trainer encourages parents to expect their child to learn one or two behaviors or skills at a time. This focus limits the task to manageable proportions and defines specific goals to be achieved. Next, the trainer helps parents break down the targeted behavior or skill into small increments, or objectives. The trainer further assists the parents by demonstrating or modeling and by having the parents rehearse the particular activities suggested for accomplishing their objectives. Modeling effective interactive responses and praising parents' productive efforts reinforces their appropriate responses. Videotaping allows parents to observe themselves interacting with their child and to identify effective and noneffective responses. These methods are more instructive than simple didactic ones, and they increase the parents' confidence in their ability to teach as well. In most programs the trainer makes weekly or twice-monthly home visits with more frequent telephone follow-up to support and encourage continued progress. Parents can help children develop motor skills, focus attention, acquire language, and learn play behavior and self-help skills, such as feeding, toilet training, and dressing. Moreover, parents can feel successful and competent as they aid their child's development. There are several excellent home teaching guides.*

Parents as Interveners: Behavior Management

In recent years parents have learned to employ behavior-modification techniques in the home to eliminate problematic or maladaptive behaviors in their children and to teach adaptive behaviors or skills.† Behavior management based on operant techniques is particularly effective when parents have unwittingly become "stuck" in patterns of reinforcing a child's inappropriate or negative behavior with negative attention such as scolding, nagging, or inconsistent punishment. Temper tantrums; an inability or refusal to follow directions, sit at the table at mealtime, or stay in bed at bedtime; running away; and self-abusive behaviors are all amenable to behavior management.

Home training in behavior management has several advantages. It permits the trainer to observe the child with the family in ordinary daily activities and interactions in their mutual setting. The trainer can identify negative reinforcement patterns more readily and more accurately than in the office on the basis of parents' verbal descriptions. Because the family members' life-style and unique circumstances are known, the home trainer can better help them design a realistic management program that they are able to carry out.

Behavioral trainers may write their own teaching materials and charts for recording data, or they may use programmed texts designed to teach parents principles of behavior change.‡ It is important that parents chart the frequency of behaviors before they begin their efforts at change. Continuation of the charting allows them to see that they are making progress; this is especially important when the desired change takes place over a long period of time. The programmed texts are useful for group work with parents if their children have similar problems and learning abilities. Parent-training groups offer parents the advantage of learning and receiving support from one another. Parents may learn and become more confident from sharing the teaching role.

---

*See, for example, Baker, Brightman, Heifetz, & Murphy (1976).
†See, for example, Hawkins, Peterson, Schweid, & Bijou (1966).
‡See for example, Patterson & Gullion (1976); Baldwin & Fredericks (1973).

THE BRAMER FAMILY

Ed and Cathy Bramer referred themselves to the local Association for Retarded Children for help with their 3-month-old son, Carl, who had Down syndrome. Their first child, Lisa, aged 4, had been a typical infant. The Bramers' initial fears and misconceptions were heightened by the fact that Cathy had had a severely retarded sister who died during adolescence. They described Carl as being lethargic and limp when they brought him home from the hospital. This gloomy situation was reinforced by their physician who said Carl would "probably not do much." At 3 months, Carl showed some motor lag on the left side, and there was a question of hearing impairment because he had no startle reflex and did not respond to the sound of a bell by turning his head.

The home trainer who worked with the Bramers noted that Carl had excellent eye contact and was making many nonspecific sounds. She recommended a pediatric hearing evaluation and prescribed and taught Ed and Cathy specific activities to elicit auditory responses and encourage head control and equal movements; as well, she suggested general tactile and sensorimotor-stimulation activities.

The home trainer pointed out that Carl *was* responding to noises by blinking and changing the degree of his motion and breathing. The pediatrician subsequently confirmed this and supported the trainer's efforts. The infant-stimulation program proceeded, supplemented by reading materials and audio and video tapes. The Bramers were careful, too, to balance their family acitivities so that Lisa's needs were not overlooked.

At 7 months of age, Carl had no developmental delays. His once skeptical pediatrician had been converted to the idea of early intervention. Carl sat independently, finger fed, passed objects from hand to hand, stood briefly holding furniture, said "da-da" and "ma-ma" specifically and other sounds nonspecifically, vocalized to his toys and sibling, was shy with strangers, played "catch," and pulled off his socks and shoes.

Carl became a source of pride and joy to Ed and Cathy. Their ability to teach him was satisfying. They recognized that the time would come when his rate of development in some areas would be slower than the norm, but they were comfortable in the knowledge that they had the ability and available resources to help Carl make the most of his potential for growth and learning.

FAMILY SYSTEM INTERVENTION

A problem with a developmentally disabled family member may be the symptom of a dynamic family problem in the same way that the "problem child" in any family can be the symptom of family dysfunction. Watzlawick,

Weakland, and Fisch (1974) note that problems sometimes arise in families as the result of off-target attempts to change another problem in the family system. For example, a husband and wife in marital conflict may swing from extremes of verbal and even physical combat to withdrawal and isolation from one another. Problems with a disabled child offer such a couple an opportunity to relate to one another indirectly, avoiding both the conflict and the isolation. Hence, the child's problem becomes the solution to the marital problem, and the child's behavior is reinforced. The child becomes the focus or the scapegoat for the family.

It is not our intention here to discuss the family as a system or family-therapy techniques based on that model; the reader is directed elsewhere.* However, it is important that those who work with the developmentally disabled be familiar with family-systems theory and family-therapy strategies. When a behavioral intervention aimed at changing a developmentally disabled member is ineffective, it may be because the family needs to maintain his behavior as a "solution." Since the developmentally disabled individual has an identifiable disorder and might have unusual or inappropriate behaviors for other reasons, his or her behavior problem may not be readily recognized as the symptom of family dysfunction. Such oversight, coupled with a lack of experience and discomfort on the part of many professionals in dealing with retarded persons, leads many family-counseling and mental-health agencies to refer families with a retarded member to a specialized agency, with the statement that mental retardation is the primary problem, when this may not be the case.

THE WALTERS FAMILY

The Walters family consisted of Mrs. Walters, a widow for 7 years, and her son, Donald, a moderately retarded adult, who worked in a sheltered workshop. Mrs. Walters' mother and married brother and sister lived nearby, but there had been no contact for 7 years.

Mrs. Walters requested help in dealing with Donald's problems. In recent years, she felt she "had" to shave and dress him, although he was capable of self-help. He had frequent temper tantrums when he did not get what he demanded. Recently, he had decided to walk to work instead of riding in the car pool, even though his workshop was not within realistic walking distance.

A home trainer helped Mrs. Walters work out a behavior-management program for Donald with the use of his radio, television, and record player,

---

*See, for example, Ackerman (1973); Minuchin (1974).

his favorite possessions, as reinforcement contingencies. It was briefly successful, but Mrs. Walters was unable to use the reinforcers consistently. The home trainer called on her supervisor, who was experienced in family therapy, for help in understanding Mrs. Walters' problems in implementing the program.

Mrs. Walters had no social role to perform after her husband's death other than to mother Donald. She had no work skills, outside interests, or close friends. She had not arrived at a satisfactory adult relationship with her mother or her siblings. Donald's behavior was the reason given for her estrangement. Focusing on Donald allowed Mrs. Walters to avoid the difficult and frightening task of establishing new adult roles for herself. Once the workers understood how Donald's behavior was a solution to his mother's problems, they were able to help her, through the use of paradoxical instructions and other strategic tasks.* Within a matter of weeks, Donald was taking care of his own personal needs, and tantrum behavior was infrequent. Fairly quickly, Mrs. Walters was able to begin relating to her family of origin again, and she received help and support from them. Subsequently, she renewed some adult friendships and became involved in social activities. The workers then turned their attention to finding suitable social and recreational programs for Donald.

The preceding case illustrates a situation in which a developmentally disabled individual is symptom bearer for the family. In this instance, Donald's behavior is not the "real" problem; thus it is not directly amenable to behavior change. In addition, the family is not a typical family: that is, a two-parent, two-generation system. (Nonetheless, however, it *is* a family system.) Furthermore, the example demonstrates how strategic intervention with only one member, Mrs. Walters, changed the entire system.

PARENT MODELING

Certain families must have specialized and intensive help in parenting their developmentally disabled children. The inadequately socialized family requires that special attention be given to the parents in order for them to meet the needs of their children. The term *inadequately socialized* might be applied to multiproblem, low-income families in which parents lack employment and transportation, have marginal literacy and related social handicaps, and commonly were themselves deprived, neglected, or abused children. These parents, most often single mothers, frequently have difficulty disciplining their children because of problems in their own personalities and early socializa-

---

*For a discussion on paradoxical tasks, refer to Haley (1976, pp. 67–76). Elsewhere in this book, Maluccio elucidates a task-based approach to family therapy in Chapter 23.

tion. They may, for example, not trust others, have little self-respect, or be impulsive and childishly needy. As a result, they may relate to their children punitively and defensively as peers or rivals. Mothers with these characteristics require a great deal of gratification and feedback, explicit acceptance and nurturance.

A greater risk of neglect or abuse is likely to exist when these immature and needy parents interact with a developmentally disabled child. Not only may the child who progresses at a slower rate be less gratifying in his or her accomplishments, often that child has a longer period of dependency for feeding and toileting. He or she may have related medical problems necessitating frequent clinic visits, regular medication, or other special needs that place unusual demands on a mother whose tolerance is already low.

The goal in work with the poorly socialized family is not merely to teach behavioral skills in relation to the child's developmental needs but to enhance the parent's competence as a parent. It is necessary for the helper to engage the parent intensively over a long period of time to establish a trustful relationship, meeting the parent at her level of need so that she acquires a stake in the approval of the helper. Initially, it means letting the parent know the helper as a person, as well as the purpose of their contact. This includes exchanging experiences and offering concern and concrete assistance by participating in the daily life of the family.

The helper becomes a parent surrogate to the adult, filling the expressive parental role through a nurturing, accepting attitude, and the instrumental role by modeling and teaching skills and rewarding the parent for new and more mature behavior. The helper may also model related adult social roles by accompanying the parent to school conferences, clinic visits, and meetings with the landlord or welfare worker. Jehn (1962, p. 102) suggests that imitative learning occurs in the context of a warm, affectionate, nurturant relationship, and, at the same time, the client's perception of the helper as an expert or authority increases learning. The client might gain some of the helper's competence, prestige, or control of resources through imitation.

The gains achieved by Frances Jones and her children in the following case study demonstrate how an intensive, caring relation with her worker over a span of 2 years resulted in growth for the entire family.

THE JONES FAMILY

The Jones family consisted of Frances, her son James, who was 6 when the worker first met the family, and her niece, 11-year-old Ruth, who was mentally retarded. James was labeled hyperactive and learning disabled. Both children were in public school special-education classes, and the family received public assistance.

The social worker, representing a community agency committed to preventing the institutionalization of developmentally disabled children, initially became involved with the family when Ruth came to live with her
aunt as a foster child. The wisdom of the placement was questioned by the
agency worker, but Ruth had been shuffled from one family member to
another and was repeatedly rejected, most recently by her father and the
woman with whom he lived. Ruth was depressed and easily upset. She
cried at night for her father. She cried when she spoke of school and her
frustration at not being able to learn to read. Frances had taken Ruth in
periodically over the years and really cared for the girl. She identified with
Ruth's rejection. Frances had been an abused child of alcoholic parents, and
she had grown up in an institution. She expressed a sincere desire to help
Ruth, and Ruth loved her aunt.

Frances was moody and had many somatic complaints. She could be warm
and giving when she felt in control of her life situation, but if she perceived
any threat to her security and sense of competence, she became depressed
and volatile. If the children were not compliant, she hollered and cursed
and banished them to their rooms, whereupon James would have a tantrum.
His behavior would escalate until Frances threatened him physically.

When the worker's initial concern for Ruth's depression evoked a resentful
and rivalrous response from Frances, the worker realized that to secure this
home for Ruth and teach Frances to meet Ruth's needs, she would first have
to meet Frances' needs for nurturance. The worker spent several hours
weekly the first year, listening, sharing stories about her own children, and
warmly supporting Frances. Often she stayed for dinner. Frances was a
good cook and was gratified by the worker's appreciation. Gradually, as
Frances came to trust and respect her, the worker began to model positive
parenting behaviors toward the children. After a while, she and Frances
were able to discuss, in a didactic manner, particular issues: how to instruct
Ruth about menstruation and appropriate, related social behavior, for example. Evidence of Frances' growing confidence emerged when she asked
the worker to spend time with Ruth, who had been having frightening
dreams. Finally, the worker was able to engage Ruth in a therapeutic relationship. The worker subsequently taught Frances "how to help Ruth
with her problems" by using active listening skills. Along the way Frances,
with the worker's help, tackled concrete problems with various social agencies.

As the worker eased her way out of the family, the case was turned over
to a social-work student for continued supportive casework. Many problems
remained: inadequate resources, Frances' health problems, and crises created
by relatives coming and going. Much had changed, however. Ruth, now
13, was moving into satsifying peer relationships. She was outgoing and
well liked at school. She could deal with Aunt Frances' moods philosoph-
ically. She could talk about her painful feelings regarding adults letting her
down. She and Frances were able to communicate verbally in a mutually

helpful way, and Frances could set appropriate limits for James, who no longer had tantrums.

ECOLOGIC FAMILY APPROACH

An ecologic model of service delivery, one that views the family in relation to all of its environmental systems and facilitates the learning of adaptive behaviors and roles within each of these systems, is well suited to the needs of developmentally disabled families. This view is consistent with the focus on adaptive behavior in the current definition of mental retardation accepted by the American Association on Mental Deficiency (Grossman, 1973, p. 102).

Developmentally disabled families, even more than families termed "inadequately socialized," need intensive and extensive help if they are to maintain functioning as family units that can provide for the growth and development of children. In the developmentally disabled family, one or both of the parents is handicapped by mental retardation, and the children may be at risk because their parents lack knowledge and training, social skills and good judgment, and the ability to secure adequate resources independently.

Ecologic intervention with developmentally disabled families encompasses four major components. First, an ongoing, family-oriented, comprehensive evaluation of needs should assess the family's strengths and weaknesses in the areas of financial resources, occupational training, housing, maintenance of basic needs (food and clothing), medical care, child development, social skills and social supports, legal needs and transportation. Second, specific goals related to the family's needs in each area are developed, keeping in mind the overall goal of teaching the family adaptive behaviors and skills for independent living. Third, a flexible system of interdisciplinary services is designed to accomplish the stated goals by bringing together a cooperative network of governmental, educational, and social agencies. Fourth, a case manager coordinates and monitors the family service plan. Regular comprehensive planning and evaluation conferences include the family in addition to agency representatives involved with the family.

The case manager interfaces between the family and the various environmental and social systems and arranges the linkage of the systems. This is a difficult and complex role, requiring a high level of what Horejsi (1979) calls "boundary skills." The case manager must be flexible, patient and have a strong commitment to assisting retarded persons who choose to have families in becoming capable and responsible parents. The worker must be able to change roles regularly; he or she must be teacher, counselor, advocate, social broker, surrogate parent, and friend. Often, the family does not comprehend or appreciate this role. The worker must therefore rely on personal commitment, and on that of the agency, to continue offering the intensive, long-term service necessary to assist developmentally disabled families in rearing children. The vital importance of the case manager–coordinator to the success of ecologic casework cannot be overemphasized.

Developmentally disabled families present a challenge. They are the families most in need of early intervention. Pomerantz and his associates (1978) are engaged in an intensive educational-intervention program for developmentally disabled parents and families. It is believed to be the first organized program of its kind. These authors, in their preparatory search of the literature, found no published material dealing with services for this population. Their work underlines the need for professional literature that describes successful techniques for working with developmentally disabled families.

THE DUTCHER FAMILY

That Mary and Ronnie Dutcher were managing to make an adequate home for their 14-month-old daughter, Sandra, who was now developing normally, might be viewed as the outcome of the combined efforts of an extensive network of support services provided by a variety of public and private agencies as well as the inexhaustible dedication of the extraordinary social worker who had coordinated it all. Mary was diagnosed "moderately mentally retarded" and was a full-time homemaker. Ronnie, who was mildly retarded and stunted in physical growth, attended an occupational-training program. They received public assistance and Supplemental Security Income.

The worker had known Mary for several years, since she came with her relatives from the South to the urban area where they now live. Mary had been economically and sexually exploited. A son born in her early teenage years remained with relatives. When Mary again became pregnant, she refused to give up her baby and she and Ronnie decided they would make a home for it. The couple's determination, together with the fact that Mary's adaptive ability was believed to be higher than suggested by her I.Q. score, convinced the worker to help them. He felt that Mary, who suffered from malnutrition when she lived at home, might be a better homemaker than her alcoholic mother. The worker initially attempted to help Mary and Ronnie set up housekeeping in a flat in their old neighborhood where they would have support from family and friends. This proved to be a mistake, for they were constantly taken advantage of by neighbors and relatives. Their money, food, and furniture disappeared. As a result of this, the worker then set up a comprehensive treatment plan and helped Mary and Ronnie obtain public housing in another area.

TABLE 24-1
Dutcher Family Intervention Plan*

NEEDS	CLIENT GOALS	AGENCY GOALS	METHODS
Financial	Learn to budget money for food and clothes Learn to cash checks and avoid being cheated	Arrange for Mary and Ronnie to receive public assistance and SSI on their own Set up overall budgetary system	CETA worker from private agency facilitates applications and follow-up Social worker/case manager arranges voucher system so major bills, e.g., utilities, can be paid directly from Dept. of Social Services DDS home economist and CETA worker cooperatively teach these skills
Occupational	Regular attendance at occupational training center (Ronnie)	Assure that occupational training is continued for Ronnie	Public school officials cooperate in assuring Ronnie's continued participation Interested teachers cooperate with social worker/case manager in encouraging Ronnie's attendance
Housing	Learn to pay rent independently	Ensure certification for public-housing eligibility and annual recertification Secure furniture	Municipal Housing Department calls social worker/case manager, who accompanies Mary to recertification hearing County department of social services provides grant for furniture County home economist helps purchase furniture CETA worker trains Mary regarding paying rent

(continued)

Table 24-1 (continued)
Dutcher Family Intervention Plan*

NEEDS	CLIENT GOALS	AGENCY GOALS	METHODS
Maintenance	Learn to purchase food and clothing Learn simple cooking and nutrition Learn laundry and clothing repairs Learn house cleaning	Devise "curriculum plan" to teach Mary basic homemaking skills	Home economist and social worker share responsibilities for teaching Mary homemaking skills
Medical	Attend clinics independently and use Medicaid card Make decision regarding birth control Obtain birth control	Ensure prenatal, postnatal, and pediatric care Assist Mary in making decision and in obtaining birth control	CETA worker and reach-out workers from family agency accompany Mary to health department clinic and monitor attendance
Child development	Learn to care for Sandra, e.g., feeding, toilet use, recognizing illness, etc. Learn to stimulate Sandra's development	Monitor Sandra's development Provide teaching regarding child stimulation Ensure appropriate early childhood health intervention when needed	Public health nurse visits two to three times per week Periodic development evaluation by ARC Additional language stimulation provided by ARC Sandra eventually to attend ARC preschool program
Social	Attend to personal hygiene Learn to save money for social activities Learn to avoid being taken advantage of by neighbors	Eliminate sabotage by relatives who formerly profited from special income	Counseling and rapport from social worker/case manager Include extended family in care conferences and support their constructive interest
Transportation	Learn to walk or travel by bus to pay rent and visit clinics (Mary) Accompany Mary on complicated trips (Ronnie)		CETA worker "travel-trains" Mary and teaches bus routes to Ronnie as needed

*Daniel W. Barton, a developmental disabilities counselor with the Erie County Association for Retarded Children in Buffalo, New York, is responsible for this family-service plan.

He called together representatives of the agencies from whom services were needed, and together with Mary and Ronnie they established and agreed to a complex of goals and methods that would facilitate the Dutchers' ability to live independently. Goals for Mary and Ronnie were prioritized. The worker made two or three home visits per week in order to provide the continuous support and teaching necessary for their accomplishment. He had regular and continuous telephone contacts with the agencies involved to communicate progress and ensure ongoing support. Periodic intraagency conferences to update or revise the plan included not only the Dutchers but also significant members of the extended family who previously had sabotaged the worker's efforts. The total intervention plan is summarized in Table 24-1.

Mary and Ronnie required a great deal of attention, encouragement, and sometimes confrontation from the worker regarding their ability to help their child in order to follow through on their commitments. At follow-up, the worker reported that Mary had become warm and affectionate with Sandra. As she learned how to parent and felt more confident, she became more and more responsible. She kept clinic appointments and paid the rent independently, walking or traveling by bus. She could cook adequate meals and shopped with assistance. She and Ronnie remembered to keep their apartment locked. Mary decided she would not have more children and secured an intrauterine device.

Continued intensive involvement with this family would be necessary, especially in relation to Sandra, but the functional family unit that now existed, however limited, was an improvement over the extremely marginal lives these young people would have lived without intervention.

SUMMARY

A variety of family-oriented models of service delivery involve parents as partners with professional helpers in increasing the capabilities of developmentally disabled persons for community living. The most effective initial approach for the families with such children is a counseling model that incorporates knowledge about developmental needs of the child with a handicapping condition. This model calls for the active participation of parents. Using this framework, the worker lets parents know that they can help their child develop closer to a normal rate of growth, links them with support from other parents, and provides information and advocacy regarding available services. The parent-training model enables parents to become teachers of their own child as well as agents of behavior change. A family-therapy model is appropriate when presenting problems with a developmentally disabled child are not directly related to his or her disability but are symptoms of family dysfunction. Multiproblem, inadequately socialized families and developmentally disabled families need creative, long-term, intensive help in order to parent their children adequately. A body of knowledge regarding productive methodologies must be developed for this population.

ACKNOWLEDGMENTS

The author gratefully acknowledges Molly Averill Miller, Daniel W. Barton, Nancy M. Doyle, and Kathleen O'Mara, who have provided some of the case material in this article. Names and identifying data have been changed.

REFERENCES

Ackerman, N. *Treating the Troubled Family*. New York: Basic, 1973.

Baker, B.L., Brightman, A.J., Heifetz, L.J., & Murphy, D.M. *Steps to Independence: A Skills Training Series for Children with Special Needs*. Champaign, Ill.: Research Press, 1976. (Copies can be ordered from the publisher at 2612 North Matthis Avenue, Champaign, Illinois 61820.)

Baldwin, V.L., & Fredericks, H.D. (eds.) *Isn't It Time He Outgrew This? Or a Training Program for Parents of Retarded Children*. Springfield, Ill.: Thomas, 1973.

Bassin, J., & Kreeb, D.D. *Reaching Out to Parents of Newly Diagnosed Retarded Children*. St. Louis: St. Louis Association for Retarded Children, 1978.

Grossman, H.J. (ed.). *Manual on Terminology and Classification in Mental Retardation*. Washington, D.C.: American Association on Mental Deficiency, 1973.

Haley, J. *Problem-Solving Therapy*. San Francisco: Jossey-Bass, 1976.

Hawkins, R.P., Peterson, R.F., Schweid, E., & Bijou, S.W. Behavior therapy in the home: Amelioration of problem parent–child relations with the parent in a therapeutic role. *Journal of Experimental Child Psychology*, 1966, 4, 99–107.

Horejsi, C.R. Developmental disabilities: Opportunities for social workers. *Social Work*, 1979, 24, 40–43.

Jehn, D. *Learning Theory and Social Work*. London: Routledge and Kegan Paul, 1962.

Minuchin, S. *Families and Family Therapy*. Cambridge, Mass.: Harvard University Press, 1974.

Patterson, G., & Gullion, M.E. *Living with Children: An Introduction to Social Learning*. Champaign, Ill.: Research Press, 1976.

Pomerantz, D., Towne, R., & Pomerantz, P. *An Ecological Model for Intensive Home Education of Developmentally Disabled Parents and Families*. An unpublished pilot study at the Cantalician Center for Learning, Buffalo, New York, funded by P.L. 89-313, ESEA Title 1, through the New York State Education Department/ Division for Handicapped Children, 1978.

Richardson, H.B., Jr., Guralnick, M.J., & Tucker, D.H. Effective involvement with handicapped pre-school children and their families. *Mental Retardation*, 1978, 16, 3–7.

Schruber, M., & Feeley, M. Siblings of the retarded: A guided group experience. Children, 1965, 12, 221–225.

Searl, S.J., Jr. Stages of parent reaction. *The Exceptional Parent*, April 1978, 8, 27–29.

Watzlawick, P., Weakland, J., & Fisch, R. *Change—Principles of Problem Formation and Resolution*. New York: Norton, 1974.

Wolfensberger, W., & Menolascino, F.J. A theoretical framework for the management of parents of the mentally retarded. In Menolascino, F.J. (ed.), *Psychiatric Approaches to Mental Retardation*. New York: Basic, 1970, 475–492.

25

Scapegoating: A Survival Phenomenon

Ann McCreery

Scapegoating is often described as a phenomenon related to severe family pathology, as when a member, singled out to bear the burden of maintaining the system, becomes the focus of family interactional stress, begins to show symptoms and is subsequently labeled mentally ill. However, the same process may also be found operating in families that are not characterized by such blatant dysfunction. For example, parents may relive unresolved aspects of their own conflicts through the acting-out behavior of a child. This often functions to preserve a pseudoharmony in the marital relationship and ultimately to maintain the integrity of the family. This chapter is useful to clinicians in that McCreery elucidates the intricacies of this process and provides a close look at family scapegoating through a detailed case illustration. She points out that while the dysfunctional outcomes for the scapegoated individual may be striking, it is vital to consider the fact that the group's very survival as a family may depend on this mechanism. Therefore, any intervention in such a situation must be weighed against the inherent risks for both family and individuals.

In the ancient Hebrew religion, a rite was observed in which the high priest came out of the sanctuary and, taking a goat, intoned a public confession of all the sins of the people, commanding that the scapegoat be taken into the desert and hurled from a precipice. The death of the scapegoat freed the people of their collective guilt (Craveri, 1967, p. 290). The magical symbolism of this ritual is to be found in many other religions as well. The scapegoat, symbolically carrying the guilt for human error, has appeared throughout history in literature and in folklore. In more recent years, the term has been reconceptualized in social-psychologic theories to account for a similar process in small groups and families.

The primary purpose of a group is to perpetuate its existence. Multiple mechanisms occurring within the group enable it to continue. Scapegoating, based on mechanisms of projection and displacement, is a prevalent group and social survival phenomenon (Toker, 1972). However, it is only when it becomes a frequently recurring interactional pattern with reference to a specific target that it assumes the full proportions of the scapegoating process. The family is a special group with intense pressures toward survival. This chapter examines the purpose and process of scapegoating within the framework of family structure and function.

When a group, in this case the family, experiences stress and tension, its management of them depends on members' abilities to openly express and acknowledge their reactions. Paul and Bloom (1970, p. 37) view the "healthy" family unit as one in which "strong and jarring emotions can be borne because they can be discussed freely and without fear of retribution or annihilation from other family members." On the other hand, an inability to deal with the effect leaves the family with severe unresolved conflicts. At times of crisis the unresolved tensions become unbearable. In order for the family to survive, relief is achieved through the use of a selected family member.

There are many sources of tension for a family. They may stem from relationships with the larger community or with families of orientation. Poverty can be a prime operating factor (Cornwall, 1967). In addition, negative feelings inevitably build up between members of a family. Vogel and Bell (1967) contend that scapegoating is produced by the existence of tensions between parents that have not been satisfactorily resolved in other ways.

A scapegoat is selected from within the family because projection of internal tensions would entail the risk of conflict with the larger society. Frequently a child is chosen since a child is dependent and is unable to leave the family or to counter the parents' power (Vogel & Bell, 1967). Selection focuses on the particular child who best symbolizes the conflict. For example, birth order, sex, level of intelligence, resemblance to a parent, or other physical characteristics may contribute to the process of symbolization. Although members of a family may share many similarities, there are, of course, differences among them, and a particular difference may be perceived to be threatening to others in the family. Ackerman (1971) has written of this prejudicial selection process in which several or all of the family members who share this sense of threat combine to attack the source.

However, the foregoing portrays only one side of what is actually a complex interactive process. Although the scapegoat is a victim of projection, he or she concomitantly works to maintain his or her position (Rollins, 1973). Berkowitz and Green (1972) stress that the scapegoat has certain qualities that stimulate scapegoating. The scapegoat is not an innocent bystander and in fact interacts in many ways that serve to perpetuate his or her status. In addition to the rewards accruing to the child for accepting this role assignment from the family, the performance of this group-perpetuating function is literally essential to his or her own survival.

The necessary interactive process having been established, one further condition must be satisfied in order for it to be maintained. Parents are often made to feel guilty by internal and external criticism regarding their behavior with the scapegoated child. The parental response typically takes the form of rationalization that defines *them* as the victims of the child's behavior, rather than the reverse (Vogel & Bell, 1967, p. 435).

In sum, for scapegoating to occur, there is first a source of unresolved tension. In the face of the family's need to survive, the tension is relieved by the choice of a family member to carry the guilt.* The family member most symbolic of the conflict is chosen, accepts, and contributes to maintaining this crucial role in the maintenance of family homeostasis. The family members then rationalize their hostile behavior by defining themselves rather than the child as victim.

The following family study provides an opportunity for further examination of the process.

THE RANDALL FAMILY

The Randall family was seen by cotherapists in seven family-therapy sessions. Craig, 16, the oldest child in a family of four siblings, had become the identified patient. The goal of therapy was to assess the family situation, and to focus on the interaction patterns in the family as a possible source of difficulty and/or support for Craig. He was the child of his father's first marriage; his three siblings were offspring of his father and stepmother. Craig was first identified as a problem to the family at the age of 5, when he entered public school for the first time. His behavior was described as disruptive in class and at home, disobedient, and uncontrollable. His parents felt that he did not exhibit feelings of affection toward them or toward his siblings. He did not obey household rules, such as telling the family when and where he was going, staying in with the family on some evenings, or eating meals with the family. This behavior increased in frequency and intensity as he grew older. Added to this in more recent years, was behavior such as stealing from family and friends. Craig was also diagnosed as having diabetes mellitus at the age of 12. His behavioral response to the knowledge of his disease was to deny its importance, continuing to eat as he had formerly done, and refusing to test his urine, etc.

---

*Beavers (1976, p. 63) describes a scapegoating process in certain families he labels as "centrifugal" that varies inasmuch as the focus of the incessant blame and attack shift from one family member to another.

Mr. Randall, at the age of 16, had left his parents' home and married. Craig was born; Mr. Randall had gotten divorced and returned to his family of origin with custody of Craig who was then cared for by his grandmother. When Craig was 15 months old Mr. Randall was remarried to his current wife, Craig's stepmother.

During the earliest sessions with the Randalls the parents seemed to share similar concerns. During later sessions it became apparent that there was an unspoken source of tension between them. Although a reason for the tension was never identified by Mr. and Mrs. Randall, the nature of the struggle appeared to center on power and control issues within the family. Mr. Randall was an outspoken man who directly demanded to be the head of the family: to control what happened. Mrs. Randall, on the other hand, was a more passive person who outwardly deferred to the wishes of her husband. However, she undermined Mr. Randall and his decisions in a passive-aggressive manner when she disagreed.

Also, in later sessions it became apparent that Craig was an unspoken source of tension between the parents. As the son of a woman about whom the spouses harbored negative feelings, as the only son in the family until the birth of his 7-year-old brother, as the child with a disease requiring special dietary treatment, and as the first child to move into new situations, e.g., school, Craig was seen to be "different" and to behave in ways unfamiliar to, and sometimes unprescribed by, the family. The Randalls presented to the community the picture of a hard-working, "respectable" middle-class family. Their scapegoat was within the family; their tensions were reposited in Craig.

Mr. and Mrs. Randall appeared unable to discuss sources of tension between them. Mr. Randall was easily angered, especially when his word or orders and rules were questioned. It was apparent in the course of therapy that neither the mother nor the other siblings were able to approach Mr. Randall directly without fear of his volatile temper. Craig served as a drain for this tension. As long as he was present the family could depend upon him to divert his father's anger to himself. This was further demonstrated in the silence of the siblings when Craig called upon them for support in the course of therapy.

There were several reasons for the choice of this boy to be the family scapegoat. As the choice of scapegoat is intimately related to the sources of tension (Vogel & Bell, 1967), it may be assumed that Mr. Randall's unfinished business with his first wife and family was a source of tension. Craig represented the first family and was never allowed to fit into the new one. This was demonstrated in a session in which Mrs. Randall attempted to bring up a statement made to her by her husband in which he claimed Craig as his responsibility and referred to the other children as "your children." Mr. Randall denied that the statement had been made, or that it had importance, and his wife was forced to drop the subject. Immediately after this interchange, he again expressed anger toward Craig.

The function that Craig fulfilled in the family at the age of 5 was negligible; for this additional reason, he was an appropriate scapegoat. He was powerless and dependent, in contrast to Mr. Randall who was needed to support the family. Craig was the first child to go to school and to interact with the community. School became a vehicle for acting out that caused shame for the family in light of their desire to maintain "respectability" in their community. He was the oldest child and the first one available for scapegoating. He was assigned the role, and once assigned, he continued in it. In Laing's terms, "We indicate to them how it is: they take up their positions in the space we define" (1972, p. 79). Although the scapegoat cannot permanently relieve the pain experienced by the family, he or she believes and is allowed to believe, that this is possible so continues in the role, partly by his or her own choice (Satir, 1967).

When parents criticize the scapegoated child, they present him with mixed messages that in some way implicitly support the persistence of the explicitly condemned behavior (Vogel & Bell, 1967). This was an important dynamic in Craig's continuing as the scapegoat for the family. Mr. Randall consistently failed to follow through on threats and he delayed punishments. In addition, all of the family showed considerable interest in and therefore reinforcement of Craig's behavior, especially in relation to his diabetes. The parents were at all times inconsistent in their treatment of Craig, resulting in his being caught in the conflict. Mrs. Randall was alternately warm, accepting, and understanding and cold, aloof, and rejecting. Mr. Randall became angry and threatening but then backed down, offered "another chance" to his son, at the same time contending that offering another chance to Craig was useless since he knew he could not live up to expectations.

Craig had to deal with inconsistencies between his parents, inconsistencies within each of their behaviors, and also with the changes they exhibited over time. These are all examples of the means of inducting Craig into the scapegoat role. As he became older and was labeled "disturbed" by courts, doctors, and institutions, his role as family scapegoat was set; this thesis is supported by Vogel and Bell (1967), who maintain that the scapegoated child's disturbed behavior adds stability to the role system.

As treatment continued, it became increasingly apparent that Craig could not easily give up the role he had maintained in the family for many years. The family members had indicated that they were happy and at peace while he was away. His role as scapegoat confirmed his sense of importance, since he received a great deal of attention from everyone in the family. They could not easily "forget" him. As a result, the boy maintained his role in order to remain an integral part of the family.

Craig was unable to accept emotionally and therefore to care for his diabetes. There were occasional incidents in which his self-neglect produced serious medical consequences. He had, for example, experienced a diabetic crisis at school and had later been found by his family unconscious in the garage. This quite literal need to survive actually contributed to the maintenance of Craig in the role of scapegoat, since his labile physiologic balance necessitated constant attention from the family, often to "save" him.

The related literature stresses the essential function of the scapegoat in keeping a group together, i.e., staving off disintegration (Toker, 1972). In the family that scapegoats a child, part of the maintenance of equilibrium involves rationalization of the process by the parents. In rationalizing their treatment of Craig, Mr. and Mrs. Randall were able to deny giving sanction for his behavior, since their permission was implicit. The Randalls could also shift the blame onto Craig alone, since their other children had "turned out so well." Another means of rationalization is to define the parent rather than the child as the "victim" (Vogel & Bell, 1967). Mr. Randall repeatedly did this. He pointed out to Craig that although *he* had had it much harder as a boy in *his* father's home than Craig ever had, Craig was not appropriately grateful. In one instance, Mr. Randall brought forth a bill from the correctional facility in which Craig had been detained as proof that it was he who had to pay for Craig's misbehavior, rather than Craig himself. These successful rationalizations of the scapegoating allowed the process to continue and the family to remain a unit.

It is important to mention the mechanism of denial in relation to the Randall family, since it played an important part in the family dynamics. Denial may be defined as "the ability to deny the existence of something disturbing" (Lidz, 1968, p. 258). Both Mr. and Mrs. Randall used this mechanism frequently in their interactions with each other and with the other family members. Craig employed it as well. This was seen especially in relation to his diabetes mellitus. In spite of increasingly frequent reminders by his parents that he should eat properly and test his urine, Craig continued to ignore symptoms and to refuse even to discuss his disease. The inconsistencies described earlier helped to contribute to Craig's denial. In spite of many threats by his father to extrude him from the family, Craig refused to admit that this could happen to him. This denial later played an important part when his extrusion became a reality.

According to Ackerman (1971, p. 629), disturbed families tend to break up into warring factions with each faction attaching a specific meaning to individual difference and organizing around the device of scapegoating. A leader emerges in each subgroup; a particular member of the family is chosen as a victim of prejudicial attack; a defensive counterattack is mobilized.

In the Randall family two factions existed. The first was headed by the father, who wanted Craig, as his son, to remain in the family. The second was led by the mother, who preferred to extrude Craig. The balance was maintained by the inconsistencies in their approach to the boy, as when the mother allowed Craig to stay and the father expressed a desire for him to leave on many occasions. Yalom (1970, p. 239) refers to a group's "sacrificing" the selected member unless the therapist intervenes, and Ackerman (1971, p. 631) refers to this interventive role in work with families as that of the "family healer" who may or may not be the therapist. It is necessary for someone to provide an emotional antidote to the destructive effects of the "prejudicial assault." Craig's father served in this role by reaccepting Craig into the family. However, when the mechanism of scapegoating no longer serves to help the family to survive or when it becomes divisive, they must make a change in their patterns of interaction. When the scapegoating process in the Randall family became dysfunctional, when it was more of a problem to them than a solution to their problem, they sought therapy.

When a child becomes emotionally disturbed, secondary complications are generated (Vogel & Bell, 1967). This creates extra tasks for the family, such as providing constant surveillance for the child (for example, Craig could not be trusted to be in the family home alone) and the expending of time and money for treatment. In addition, the child may develop behavior involving fighting back and punishing his parents for the way they treat him. Craig did this very effectively with his father. Mr. Randall would frequently drive Craig beyond a point that he could tolerate in an attempt to "get him to stand up to him like a man." Craig would merely walk out of the house instead of demonstrating the behavior his father would have liked to produce. He used other means of counteraggression, such as fighting with his siblings, stealing, and bringing unacceptable friends into the house. Craig's mother was home most of the day, accounting partly for her desire to get treatment for him and for her wish to have him out of the family. These secondary complications contributed to making the scapegoating process less functional for the Randalls. Their survival as a unit was also threatened when, although Craig was still performing the necessary role in the family, it came into conflict with his role as representative of the family in the community.

The Randalls brought Craig in for therapy, saying, "We think this boy has a serious emotional problem and that he needs help." The entire family became involved in treatment at the therapist's suggestion "only because it might help Craig." Although Craig was able to make several behavioral changes in the course of therapy, the family was unable to recognize them. He was kept in the role of scapegoat. However, as the focus of treatment made the entire family aware of their individual roles in the process, they became burdened with additional guilt and anxiety (Raymond, Slaby, & Lieb, 1975). Since they perceived the situation as hopeless, the only course that promised relief was to extrude Craig from the family. The situation became intolerable for the boy; he ran away from home and eventually attempted to rob a gasoline station. He was imprisoned; the family refused to bail him out or to accept him at home again.

In the last session with the Randall family, Craig was not present since he had left home 2 weeks before. At this time, Mr. and Mrs. Randall gave voice to some previously unexpressed hostility toward each other. Mr. Randall was obviously angry, sitting with his back toward his wife for the entire session. He made a statement concerning the behavior of the other children, naming especially his younger son, to the effect that if they were to behave as Craig had, they would be "handled differently." This statement was made within hearing of all of the other children, seemingly to prepare the way for one or all of them to become the family scapegoat. Extrusion of Craig had not solved those underlying conflicts in the family that his presence had served to ameliorate.

The scapegoating process can be stabilized for a long time within a family. As is frequently the case, the role took its toll upon Craig's personality development. Although he had been given several opportunities to be part of the larger community through school and other organizations, he failed to function effectively in any of them, continuing to cast himself in the scapegoat role. His inability to cope productively with life stress was also clearly evident in his denial. Along with his refusal to acknowledge his diabetic condition, he consistently denied that he had problems at home, at school, or in his relationships with friends and community. While the scapegoating mechanism was functional for the family as a group, it was clearly dysfunctional for the emotional health of the child and for his adjustment outside the family of orientation. When last seen, Craig expressed a belief that he would be let off lightly by the judge, that he could return to his home, and resume his place in the family.

SUMMARY

Family group behavior is determined to a great extent by a need for group survival. Role allocations, among them that of scapegoat, are frequently made on this basis. The role is maintained with the chosen member's active participation. Extrusion of the scapegoat also occurs as a result of the family's need to survive. The Randall family has been presented as a clinical example of these phenomena.

REFERENCES

Ackerman, N.W. Prejudicial scapegoating and neutralizing forces in the family group, with special reference to the role of "Family healer." In Howells, J.G. (ed.), *Theory and Practice of Family Psychiatry*, New York: Brunner/Mazel, 1971, 626–634.

Beavers, W.R. A theoretical basis for family evaluation. In Lewis, J.M., Beavers, W.R., & Phillips, V.A. (eds.), *No Single Thread—Psychological Health in Family Systems*. New York: Brunner/Mazel, 1976, 46–82.

Berkowitz, I., & Green, J.A. The stimulus qualities of the scapegoat. *Abnormal and Social Psychiatry*, 1972, 72, 203–301.

Cornwall, F. Scapegoating: A study in family dynamics. *American Journal of Nursing*, 1967, 67, 1862–1867.

Craveri, M. *The Life of Jesus*. New York: Grove Press, 1967.

Laing, R.D. *The Politics of the Family and Other Essays*. New York: Random House, 1972.

Lidz, T. *The Person*. New York: Basic Books, 1968.

Paul, N.L., & Bloom, J.D. Multiple family therapy: Secrets and scapegoating in family crisis. *International Journal of Group Psychotherapy*, 1970, 20, 37–47.

Raymond, M.E., Slaby, A.E., & Lieb, J. Familial responses to mental illness. *Social Casework*, 1975, 56, 492–498.

Rollins, N., Lord, J.P., Walsh, E., & Weil, G.R., Some roles children play in their families. *Journal of the American Academy of Child Psychiatry*, 1973, 12, 511–533.

Satir, V. *Conjoint Family Therapy*. Palo Alto: Science and Behavior, 1967.

Toker, E. The scapegoat as an essential group phenomenon. *International Journal of Group Psychotherapy* 1972, 72, 320–332.

Vogel, E.F. & Bell, N.W. The emotionally disturbed child as the family scapegoat. In Handel, G. (ed.), *The Psychosocial Interior of the Family*. Chicago: Aldine, 1967, 424–442.

Yalom, I.D. *The Theory and Practice of Group Psychotherapy*. New York: Basic, 1970.

26

The Family That Gives Up

Sr. Joan Thérèse Anderson

Human beings have a remarkable capacity for mastering their environment. However, there are times when previously reliable coping devices are no longer effective, leaving the individual feeling hopeless and helpless to deal with the exigencies of life. This phenomenon has been termed giving up *and has been found to be a not uncommon response to stress. Anderson finds the* giving up *concept useful in attempting to understand the behavior both of families and of individuals. In this chapter she presents the case study of a family for whom giving up became a central dynamic, shaping their interactions with one another and their environment. She identifies issues crucial to work with such families and introduces the reader to essential elements in the process of engaging them in therapy. The chapter also explores the means through which members were helped to gain a renewed sense of control and mastery over their lives.*

The family may be viewed as an ongoing system. It tends to maintain a dynamic balance that is established as the family structure evolves. Families tend to develop certain repetitive and enduring techniques for interaction—patterns that hold whether the stress is internal or external, acute or chronic, trivial or gross (Speer, 1970 p. 262). These techniques are then characteristic for a given family. The currents of feeling that move between components in the family system differ in kind and in intensity. The emotional tone prevalent in the relationships among any individuals in the system has a development peculiarly its own, but this development is continuously influenced by the emotional climate that characterizes the whole family (Charny, 1969, p. 19). It is within this context that I have selected Engel's delineation of the giving-up–given-up complex as a frame for examining the functioning of families demonstrating particular patterns of interaction.

THE GIVING-UP–GIVEN-UP COMPLEX

Engel describes the giving-up–given-up complex as a significant dynamic in his work with depressed individuals.* However, it is one that I have seen as an enduring pattern of interaction operating in a family for the maintenance of its equilibrium when confronted by stress. This presentation first examines the individual dynamic as conceptualized by Engel and then discusses the same phenomenon as it operates in a particular family.

The giving-up–given-up complex includes five psychologic characteristics.

1. Feelings of helplessness and hopelessness are often reported by persons exhibiting this complex. They may describe feelings of being at the end of the rope, of being at a loss, or of uncertainty and may verbalize these feelings in such phrases as, "It's too much," "It's no use," "I give up," and the like. These feelings may be experienced as helplessness when the failures and deficiencies are attributed to the environment and as hopelessness when attributed to the individual's failures or inadequacies (Schmale & Engel, 1967, p. 135). The experience of helplessness arises from feelings of being incapable of changing or altering the situation since the potential for help or relief is seen as residing only in the environment. Despite the perceptions of these people that their environment has failed or frustrated them, they still look to it to resolve their dilemma. By contrast, the experience of hopelessness arises when the persons hold themselves responsible for their "failure" or inability to cope. They do not believe that any relief from the environment is possible because each sees everything as being his or her "fault." They feel responsible for their fate and assume that help, if offered, will be of no avail (Engel, 1968, p. 297).

2. A depreciated image of self that is commonly found among those who exhibit the giving-up–given-up complex is frequently related to loss. Loss of a loved one, home, status, or a valued possession have often contributed to making these individuals feel incomplete or damaged, as if a part of them has been destroyed. They may perceive themselves as less whole, less competent, less in control, and less capable of functioning than in the past, although they may make efforts at coping (Schmale & Engel, 1967, p. 135).

3. A sense of loss of gratification from relationships or life roles pervades all aspects of the life of those who demonstrate this complex. They feel a lack of support, and rebuffs, humiliations, and loss of status in the family may contribute to the feeling that even simple gratifications are denied them.

---

*The concept has also been found useful in planning nursing intervention with individual patients hospitalized for medical-surgical conditions. See Schneider (1980).

Relationships with other people and/or crucial roles in life are felt to be less secure (Schmale & Engel, 1967, p. 136).

4. A feeling of disruption of the sense of continuity between past, present and future as well as a lessened ability to project into the future with hope and confidence may be experienced as the present is viewed as diverging widely from the successes of the past (Engel, 1968, p. 297).

5. Memories of earlier periods of giving up are commonly reactivated. Past failures tend to be relived while past successes do not seem to matter and therefore cannot serve a supportive function. Thus, the old feelings associated with the previous loss surface again and strengthen the current hopeless/helpless syndrome. Each successive loss, no matter how trivial, may be experienced as symbolic of the original loss, and given-up feelings may be reactivated (Engel, 1968, p. 297).

Giving-up and given-up experiences differ. The giving-up phase opens with the failure of the defenses and coping mechanisms that had previously assured gratification and is marked by an awareness that the troubled person is unable to reachieve gratification. The given-up stage which may or may not follow, is marked by the apparent finality of the loss of gratification that for a time must be endured since no alternative source of gratification is perceived as being available (Schmale & Engel, 1967, p. 136).

The giving-up–given-up complex is rarely found to exist as an uninterrupted condition for any length of time. It appears to wax and wane as the person gives in and struggles with the situation alternately. The ultimate consequences of the complex fall into three major categories: (1) The person may succeed in achieving new and more effective coping behaviors or, if the external environment changes, may regain his or her former level of adjustment; (2) the person may become physically ill, which may lessen or intensify the complex; or (3) he or she may use psychopathologic or sociopathologic methods to attain relief, in which case he or she may be perceived as mentally ill or socially deviant (Schmale & Engel, 1967, p. 136).

THE JOHNSON FAMILY

The Johnson family exhibited this individual dynamic as a family pattern. The family consisted of the father, Bart, age 49, who had been divorced for 8 years and had custody of his 15-year-old son, Greg; his wife, Rita, age 47, who also had been divorced and had received custody of Neil, age 17; and the couple's own son, Jimmy, who was 6. In addition, Mrs. Johnson had two daughters who were married and living outside the home. Although the parents had initially requested help in relation to Jimmy, the family was seen in family therapy because of the complexity of its structure and the obvious differences of opinion between the marital partners regarding how to parent their youngest son.

Bart appeared to be a dominant, hard-working perfectionist. He had a tremendous need to be heard yet was afraid to assert his authority for fear he would not be liked. He won most arguments with the family by continuous verbal overload, which caused the family to give up trying to be heard, saying in their frustration "What's the use!" He never clearly used his authority since he did not really believe he had any. In addition, he felt almost totally responsible for what his children would become and therefore seemed to avoid acting openly for fear of his impact.

Rita appeared to be quiet and passively aggressive. She did the typical household chores but had an underlying desire to go back to work, which was threatening to Bart's image of himself as breadwinner. She attempted to intervene with Bart on behalf of the boys. She had great difficulty with interference from Bart's former wife in the rearing of Greg. Bart sided with his former wife in most arguments to avoid an unpleasant scene, leaving Rita unsupported, silently hurt and angry.

Neil was a fairly active teenager who quit school to get a job and buy a car and then went back to high school to finish his senior year. He was independent but frequently displayed a great desire to be an active member of the family although he did not feel like one.

Greg was a quiet, pale, unhappy-looking, and frequently withdrawn boy. He acted very depressed during several family meetings. He was constantly put down by his father, and he frequently degraded himself. He felt he did little or nothing right and appeared to be quite inactive. Most activities, for example, bowling, swimming, and baseball, had been "spoiled" for him since his father did them better and demanded perfection from Greg, with little or no expressed praise or affection.

Jimmy was an intelligent, talkative, playful child who knew his ability to control his parents by acting out and crying and frequently used that behavior effectively to gain his own way.

The therapist's first impression was one of heaviness in the family setting. There was very little interaction between the members. Feelings were not expressed or, if they slipped out, were made light of or excused. Each member of the family expressed needs, but members did not respond to them.

Satir (1972), who does not see the "blending" process as inevitably deterring the family from achieving a rewarding family life, does identify characteristic "potential handicaps."* Many of these were present and operative in the Johnson family although not all were currently problematic. Pain and disappointment from a previous marriage and a sense of failure increase the need to succeed in a second marriage. Both Rita and Bart had great expectations of their second marriage and therefore "a harder row to hoe" to satisfy each other's uncommunicated and frequently unconscious expectations.

The degree and nature of the authority exercised by their ex-spouses in relation to the children was not recognized or dealt with, although it was a continuing issue and frequently problematic. To compound the problem, Bart frequently saw his former wife's behavior in Greg's and responded to simple actions with anger and hurt reactions belonging to his unfinished relationship with his first wife. A frequent remark in derogatory tones was "You're just like your mother."

The parents had lived many years with their own children before the present marriage. There had been time to develop rituals, traditions, even private jokes, which made the new mate and children feel outside or excluded. Despite an opportunity to develop present family traditions, the old ones continued to exert their influence (Satir, 1972, p. 177). This presented a particular problem for the Johnsons, since they were trying to start anew and deny a past that was, however, continually operative. Previous friends, belongings, and contacts also impinged on the present, along with a quadruple set of in-laws, grandparents, and other relatives. Room was not being made for integration of these important others into the present family.

For Bart and Rita the danger of treating their own children as private property was continuously present. The common problem of parents each giving conflicting directions to children was magnified by feelings ("He is my son," "I am in charge"). The need for clearly defined roles and communication between spouses over child discipline was heightened by the need to come to terms with "his," "mine," and "our" children. This added a great burden to the already poor communications between husband and wife. For *their* part, while the children of the blended family are pressured to give their love and allegiance to their biologic parents, they are also expected to transfer their love and acceptance to the new spouse and siblings. This, in fact, is seen by Satir (1972, p. 179) as being the most serious single problem faced by these children. A frequent source of such tension in the Johnson family stemmed from Neil's love for his father and Rita's concomitant expectation that he would be loyal to her even to the extent of siding with her in an argument with his father.

The Johnsons, not equipped to deal with these problems openly, denied their presence. It was difficult for the couple to admit to any problem in their

---

*The tasks facing the blended family are explored in depth in Chapter 5 in this volume.

relationship since this fed into previous feelings of failure. This dysfunctional communication pattern had an impact on the family as a whole and on each individual member. Their needs were not being heard, let alone met. There was a tremendous amount of daily hurting of one another. The family demonstrated a tremendous desire for closeness, but they were constricted in their expression of feelings, particularly those involving positive sentiments. They were all extremely vulnerable and, to defend themselves, had constructed the myth of a happy family despite their despair over ever achieving the reality.

The Experience of Helplessness and Hopelessness

In one therapy session each family member expressed feelings of helplessness and hopelessness. Bart was giving up on his job. He was exhausted. He was overworked because of staffing problems in the job situation and it had become his responsibility to have the work of the department finished at the end of the day: "There is nothing you can do. That's the way it is, and so much for that." Neil was disgusted with looking for a new job and getting nowhere. He was also concerned about the discontinuation of the school's evening program in which he was enrolled, since this endangered his credits; he responded to this disappointment, "So, what's the use?" Greg had lost out in school dramatic tryouts and had also decided to give up trying out for sports since he "probably wouldn't make it anyway." Rita and Jimmy threw their despair into the pot as well. It was almost as if each was trying to top the others' expressions of woe. As long as a story implied a negative outcome, there was silent listening or agreement about the hopelessness of the situation. All members of the family appeared to have acquired a dynamic of giving up as soon as resistance was met from other family members or from outside forces. A feeling of helplessness and hopelessness permeated the family.

Depreciated Self-Image

Mr. Johnson and Greg exhibited a sense of hopelessness at their own personal inadequacies. The father's inability to get his children to do outdoor chores was perceived as a personal shortcoming since he was unable to evoke in them the "proper" filial response; instead, it seemed to him "Everything has my name on it." "I might as well do it," he would say; "If I ask them they will be mad at me, and I won't be a good father." Greg felt hopeless about his athletic ability. He had failed at football, swimming, and track and at getting a part in the school play. He felt nothing could be done about it: "I must have weak blood; no use trying anymore." He expected and programmed himself for failure.

Mrs. Johnson and Neil exhibited more of the quality of helplessness, not so much in response to personal failures and inadequacies, as to failures in the environment. Neil had lost his job, and the school was not going to give him credit for his night course. He responded, "What's the use? You can't fight it; just do something else; no use fighting." The mother felt she could not do anything with the children regarding tidiness and picked up after them since "there is no use telling them." If she refused to wash Greg's clothes as punishment, he would simply take them to his own mother to be washed. Rita feared that his mother would think she did not take care of him, but she felt "you can't stop him." She saw no other alternative and believed the children were in control.

The feelings of hopelessness and helplessness were evident in every family member in every session. The energy in the system was bound up in expressions of defeat: "What's the use?"; "It won't work anyway"; "Everything I do is wrong." Their self-images were poor since they got little support or help from each other except for giving up and so they rarely succeeded individually or in a family endeavor. This family did not believe in giving compliments. The father stated, "So you get a pat on the head one minute and then turn around and get a kick in the seat of the pants the next. So, what's the use?" The sense of an increasing loss in control and a decrease in gratification, key experiences in the stages of giving up and of having given up, appeared to be daily phenomena.

Sense of Loss of Gratification

The family had experienced many losses. The father had lost out in a career in music because of the war, had given up a job with computers that he had highly valued because his first wife needed money and he could not take time for the course, and his first marriage had failed. He felt he had suffered much more in his divorce than had his first wife since she had retained the family home that Bart prized. His present wife stated that she had had a happy first marriage until her husband had started to drink after the birth of their third child. She had left him and had gone to work to support the children. She had enjoyed working and found it difficult to settle down as a housewife in her second marriage after Jimmy was born. She felt the loss of freedom and frequently spoke of the happy earlier days of her first marriage, thus increasing Bart's sense of failure as a husband. Her son, Neil, missed his father and spoke of him often. Greg had tried very hard to keep his father and mother together, and he had been sent to live with his paternal grand-mother after their divorce. He was happy there and found it very difficult to leave his grandmother and his friends to move to his new home with his father and stepmother. He had been going clear across town to see his grandmother and play with his friends for nearly a year after the marriage, when he had been only 8 years old.

Jimmy was losing his opportunity to become independent because his parents were overprotective. He was not allowed to play with other children and was afraid of them. When he did play, he was overdemanding and expected to get his own way as he did at home. He was not free to play as a child but was expected by his father to do everything perfectly. For ex-ample, he was to stand just right and hold the ball precisely when using his toy bowling set. He had never played in a park or used a slide or swing since he might get hurt. He appeared to be losing his opportunity to be a child. Jimmy's problem of relating with other children fed back to the father's sense of failure: "You try to give him everything, protect him, and now that's wrong. There's no use trying. I give up."

Little time was really spent on developing relationships within the Johnson family. The family communication network did not allow for exchange of information or feelings. The family as a whole found it very difficult to communicate with each other in family sessions and rarely talked together as a family in their daily ongoing interactions. Feelings were rarely expressed and when a person did express a feeling or relate an incident that was very important, he or she was responded to out of the needs of the other person. Each person's need to be heard appeared so intense that there was no one to listen and respond. Gratification, however, did appear to come from the message that others were in the same boat, that nothing could be done, with resultant reinforcement of the giving up.

Roles within the family were traditionally defined. Inside the house was the mother's territory, and outside was the father's. Children were expected to listen, obey, and do well in school and in sports. Both parents felt they could not make the children obey, and the children felt that the parents did not listen. The rigidity of role patterns in the family lessened the opportunity for gratification. Greg failed at sports but liked to cook. However, this was the mother's job. Similarly, Rita wished to go back to work, but this con-flicted with Bart's defined role as husband.

When the children made requests, the father laid down the law and the children gave up. Greg went to his room and Neil took off in his car because there was "no sense in arguing with father. He's always right." According to Ackerman (1958, p. 117), parents' preoccupation with their own needs limits their capacity to make room for their children's needs. The absence of confidence and natural pleasure in parenthood is expressed in attitudes of rejection, overindulgence, anxious overprotection, and inconsistent and inappropriate discipline. Mr. Johnson's inability to get his needs met was very evident. He tended to dominate and overload family sessions and was very difficult to bring back to the here-and-now. He focused on his job, his younger days, his family, the cost of living, what other people did and thought, quoted from books, philosophized, and sermonized. His wife rarely challenged him openly but frequently failed to support him. She often escalated the conflict by engaging in parallel behavior, saying, for example, "If you don't, I won't either." The boys made small attempts at communicating their feelings about their father's critical behavior but were inhibited by Bart's ongoing verbal gymnastics.

The family was unable to show aggression verbally and handled it by denial. The father actually retained little respect and prestige in the home because of his behavior and his wife's covert disagreement with him. When he strove to dominate he forced the family to conspire to circumvent him. Communication was greatly impeded by mutual withdrawal and masking of motives. The parents experienced shame and anguish in their defaulting as parents. In Ackerman's terms: "Precisely because control patterns are weak, erratic, and undependable, there is exaggerated concern with issues of control and discipline" (Ackerman, 1958, p. 118). When control did not work, Mr. and Mrs. Johnson were reinforced in their feelings of helplessness.

Disruptive Sense of Continuity

The Johnson family exhibited some feelings of disruption of the sense of continuity between past, present, and future. There was also a lessened ability to project into the future with hope and confidence. Both parents and older children had a sense that their early years had been happy and rewarding but that the past few years (the present) and the future were hopeless. Rita's first husband had been an alcoholic and was seldom at home so she had developed her own methods of discipline and had been able to work to support herself and her children. She currently missed this freedom. Bart also looked to the "good old days" of his first marriage. The past with all its problems was somehow idealized, while the present seemed bleak. The family's difficulty in projecting into the future is exemplified in Neil's attitude; he wanted another job, but if he could not find one, he said it was "Okay," because "you can't let it upset you." Greg talked of leaving home as he would not be able to do anything if he stayed home, but no one offered him either opposition or support. Bart said he was going to start taking it easy when he was 50, the following year, and Rita responded with, "Okay, I'll just give up too."

REACTIVATION OF MEMORIES OF PREVIOUS LOSS

The family members frequently referred to past losses and failures that were present in their minds. The "last straw" phenomenon (Engel, 1968, p. 297), in which a minor event can reactivate old sensitivities, was fairly common, especially since the children interacted with their absent parents, and Mr. and Mrs. Johnson used past events to manipulate present behavior. The parents were placing a high priority on making this marriage work and kept reminding each other of past failures to be avoided. This opened old wounds.

The family had experienced great losses and was still experiencing feelings of emptiness, anger toward others and themselves, self-pity, and feelings of worthlessness. They used a good deal of denial; and the lid was kept tightly on all strong feelings. One sensed the underlying hostility, but overt signs of anger were so well hidden that even arguments were conducted in well-modulated voices.

Grief appeared unresolved and there were signs that depression had evolved as a family dynamic. The parents were also facing loss of roles and cherished hopes for their children and themselves. These may have been reviving unresolved feelings of loss leading to renewed feelings of helplessness and hopelessness that contributed to the process of giving up. This sense of hopelessness and helplessness became the constant internal environment of this family system. The literature is replete with examples of people who, confronted with a hopeless situation, simply give up. Some may actually die from helplessness; alternatively, if they discover the situation is not hopeless, they may continue to struggle (Seligman, 1974, p. 83). The Johnson family believed that they were helpless in dealing with most of their day-to-day situations. They believed that they could do nothing about these situations either as a family or as individuals. They became passive and depressed and gave up.

INTERVENTION

The change sought in family therapy must be preceded by modification of dysfunctional transactions among family members. This can only come about after disruption of the usual patterns (Smith & Mills, 1969, p. 115). The Johnson family was entrenched in its pattern of giving up. It was necessary for the therapist to join in family-interactive processes in order to assist them to face problems realistically and to provide corrective, positive experiences. The major issues in this family, identified by the therapist to be those of control, power, and aggression, contrast sharply with the giving-up dynamic. The family also needed to be assisted, individually and collectively, to complete their grieving process so that they could be free to enter into new relationships within the present family system.

Control

The family's belief in the futility of members' efforts to bring about change in their environment and the strong acceptance by members of their own helplessness parallels the findings of Seligman (1974) in describing "learned helplessness." A person's beliefs about his or her control over life events and environment are very significant in determining how that person acts: "Learned helplessness is the assumption of no control—the belief that nothing one does makes a difference" (Hooker, 1976, p. 194). The individual's experience with life events shapes his or her belief in his or her own ability to influence outcomes. If an individual consistently attempts to exert control over uncontrollable events, where nothing can be done that will affect the outcome, he or she may come to the conclusion that his or her responses are of no avail. By the same token, an individual may repeatedly use ineffective strategies to modify potentially controllable situations, with equally negative results. This may well lead to the belief that the individual is unable to control the outcome of any event. The person, failing to see his or her actions as making any difference, becomes less motivated to try: He or she experiences helplessness and fails to take action even when the situation is potentially controllable (Hooker, 1976, p. 195).

Intervention in the Johnson family requires prompt, effective action to help members to have an impact on their environment. It requires assisting them to assess the situation accurately and review the alternatives for action and the probable consequences of the action (Hooker, 1976, p. 197). They need to experience the relationship of positive action to outcome continually, until they can begin to believe that what they do makes a difference. This family needs to experience control over its destiny. Members need to see that their actions are not futile, that they have a measure of control over their lives. Therapeutic tasks should, therefore, be planned with an eye to providing the family with a much-needed taste of success.*

Power

In the Johnson family, the power issue is most noticeable with the parents who undermine their own authority in verbal and nonverbal ways. They also abdicate their power in relation to the children. The parents need to be assisted to explore their understanding and use of authority. The entire

---

*For an elucidation of the use of family tasks, see Chapter 23 in this volume.

family requires education as to their rights as individuals and help in acting assertively.

Role conflict also undermines power within this family. The parents' roles are traditionally defined. However, the partners are not meeting each others' (felt but not articulated) expectations. According to Spiegel (1957), when complementarity fails, the role systems tend to move toward disequilibrium as the partners fail to measure up to each others' expectations. The partners become aware of the failure of complementarity as tension, anxiety or hostility and self-consciousness occur (Spiegel, 1957, p. 548). Restoration of equilibrium when complementarity is threatened is a complicated process. Spiegel suggests role modification (the setting up of new roles through insight and communication) or role induction, in which one partner agrees, submits, or is persuaded to assume a role that will restore equilibrium (Spiegel, 1957, p. 555).

Areas of parental role conflict within the Johnson family are those emanating from the sharp distinction between breadwinning and housekeeping tasks and discipline based on the territorial jurisdictions implied in this sexual division of labor. Therefore, the therapist needs to collect family data on these roles. This would include listing or describing the roles, exploration of the assignment and adoption of particular family roles, securing of consensus among family members as to their mutual roles, eliciting the role bearer's views and feelings about the role, determining how role bearers would like to see the roles changed, and negotiating ways to bring about changes in roles. Through this process, rigidity and dissatisfaction with current definitions of the roles of housekeeper and breadwinner could be explored and modified. This would have the potential for increasing gratification in the role as well as for ensuring family support for it. The family would also be learning a process for future modification of roles.

The role of disciplinarian in the family might best be handled by role induction, since there is a great deal of undermining of discipline by both parents because of mutual dissatisfaction with this role. Bart refuses to set limits with the boys or to back up limits set by Rita. The only thing he takes responsibility for is allowing the boys time away from home and setting times for them to be in the house. He needs to work through fears of assuming and exercising his authority and to become aware of how he undermines his own authority. He may then be helped to assume his share of the disciplinarian's role, thus earning a more central place in the family's life.

Grieving

The Johnsons have experienced a great number of losses and both unresolved grief and repressed anger are evident. An "operational mourning" experience, in order to attempt resolution or closure of past grief experiences, may be beneficial. Such an experience consists of a grief response induced by the therapist's inquiring about reactions to losses sustained by specific family members (Paul & Grosser, 1965, p. 339). Through repeated review of remembered details surrounding the losses, the therapist first invites expression of the feelings of those members directly involved. Other family members may then be asked to share any feelings stimulated by witnessing this grief reaction. The losses of each person in such an experience tend to be similar or intertwined. Therefore, if members are helped by the therapist to stay with the painful experience, they may be able to identify quickly with one another, thereby increasing their understanding and capacity to help each other give vent to bottled-up emotions. Since experiencing and expressing the wide range of painful feelings associated with loss is essential to the healing of the grief wound, it is crucial that the therapist intervene to assist the family members in expressing the range of guilt, anger, resentment, remorse, and ambivalence surrounding the losses—experiences that have been too painful for them to face alone. If they can learn new patterns of response, they may be able to "let go" of the lost person or object and release the energy to reinvest in new relationships or goals.

The process, in its provision for the resolution of unresolved grief, may serve as a powerful empathetic experience that injects new life into the family system. Because of the overwhelming nature of the helplessness and hopelessness in families like the Johnsons, and the fact that the "operational mourning" experience would tend to intensify this dynamic at first, it would be wise to have more than one therapist available to support them throughout this process.

Aggression

The Johnsons need assistance in handling aggression. They tend to sweep disagreements under the rug and deny the existence of problems. There is a fairly high level of tension, dissension, anger, and conflict between the spouses. Bart and Rita need to learn that they can survive the experience of openly expressed anger. They need to learn to fight fairly and openly. It may be necessary for the therapist to participate in initiating open expression of differences and to intervene frequently to keep the process going until resolution is reached, in order to give family members "fight experience" (Bach & Wyden, 1970).

The energy generated by fights may be a force missing in this family. Interplay of complementary qualities and the clash of opposites have the potential of producing energy, life, and power than can be drawn on by all family members (Charny, 1969, p. 19). The atmosphere of the Johnsons' home is so "heavy" that a "good fight" monitored by the therapist might well have the effect of helping the family learn to unleash and channel energy.

Notes to the Therapist

The therapist can readily succumb to the feelings of helplessness and hopelessness prevalent in a family such as the Johnsons. In the face of such strong feelings it is tempting to give up on helping the members to complete the small, "bite-size" tasks requisite to their experiencing a sense of control of their environment. It is easy for the worker to believe that his or her actions with the family will not influence the outcome. The therapist begins to question his or her own adequacy and to hold negative expectations. Therefore, it is important to identify areas over which the therapist can exert control and make a difference—in precisely the same way as the family needs to be helped. It is easy to feel helpless when all the energy one introduces into the system tends to be rechanneled into bringing up more evidence that everything is hopeless.

Another pitfall in working with such a family lies in viewing the members as helpless and therefore moving to assume control that only increases their experience of their own helplessness. Such a move would encourage the family to become dependent upon the therapist for action and decrease further their feelings of control over their own lives.

In working with the Johnsons, the therapist was frequently aware of being drawn into the family pattern. It was easy to focus on the content and miss the process. This was initially problematic because it was necessary for family members to become aware of the process as governing their interactions and to experiment with new methods of exerting control. In order to assist family members to express their feelings and respond to each other in different ways, it was necessary to model and role play in order for them to gain experience in demonstrating expressions of anger, affection, and assertiveness. It was also important to examine new experiences and explore with the family members what it was like for them to respond and be responded to in a new way. Productive experiences could then be reinforced and others explored further.

REFERENCES

Ackerman, N. *The Psychodynamics of Family Life*. New York: Basic, 1958.
Bach, G. R., & Wyden, P. *The Intimate Enemy—How to Fight Fair in Love and Marriage*. New York: Avon, 1970.
Charny, I. Marital love and hate. *Family Process*, 1969, 8, 1–24.

Engel, G. A life setting conducive to illness—the giving-up–given-up complex. *Annals of Internal Medicine*, 1968, 69, 293–300.

Hooker, C. E. Learned helplessness. *Social Work*, 1976, 21, 194–198.

Paul, N., & Grosser, G. Operational mourning and its role in conjoint family therapy. *Community Mental Health Journal*, 1965, 1, 339–345.

Satir, V. *Peoplemaking*. Palo Alto: Science and Behavior, 1972, 173–195.

Schmale, A., & Engel, G. The giving up–given up complex. *Archives of General Psychiatry*, 1967, 17, 134–145.

Schneider, J. Hopelessness and helplessness. *Journal of Psychiatric Nursing and Mental Health Services*, 1980, 18, 12–21.

Seligman, M. Giving up on life. *Psychology Today*, May 1974, 80–85.

Smith, L., & Mills, B. Intervention techniques and unhealthy family patterns. *Perspectives in Psychiatric Care*, 1969, 7, 112–199.

Speer, D. Family systems: Morphostasis and morphogenesis, or Is homeostasis enough? *Family Process*, 1970, 9, 259–278.

Spiegel, J. P. The resolution of role conflict within the family. In Greenblatt, M., Levison, D., & Williams, R. (eds.), *The Patient and the Mental Hospital*. Glencoe, Ill.: The Free Press, 1957, 545–564.

27

Perspectives on Psychic Healing

Joan Evans Rawson

Western medicine, with its rational base in the scientific model, has long dominated our health-care delivery system. Parallel technologic advances, despite their contributions to patient well-being, have tended to emphasize mechanistic aspects of care at the expense of more humanistic concerns. Consumers, unwilling to settle for the limitations in this conception of service provision, have sought alternatives and are joined in this movement by growing numbers of professionals. Content related to alternative forms of healing appears with greater frequency in the professional literature and in medical and nursing school curricula. In this chapter Rawson focuses on family experiences with psychic healing, a therapeutic mode that currently has increasing appeal for consumers and professionals alike. She describes three different traditions in psychic healing and provides examples of the healing experiences of several families. These intriguing accounts should prove useful for professionals seeking to augment their knowledge about this therapeutic form and its potential for meeting the needs of selected families.

Our daughter, Lisa, is one of the joys of our lives! Three years ago we were experiencing a crisis that centered around her. We had been presented with the recommendation of several eminent cardiologists that Lisa, then 5 years old, undergo open-heart surgery. It was not an unexpected recommendation. Although we were aware of the phenomenal technologic advances in the field of cardiac surgery, and although we had no question about the level of expertise of Lisa's cardiologists, we were experiencing unanticipated levels of procrastination and indecision. We were plagued by the life-threatening potential of the surgical procedure if we chose one course and by the low life-expectancy predictions if we chose the other. We felt that through our decision we held Lisa's life in our hands. The burden seemed overwhelming.

Psychic healing as an alternative for Lisa occurred in what I can best describe as an instantaneous flash. Since the flash we have learned and experienced many things about psychic healing, about ourselves, and about the nature of "reality." Since that time we have witnessed a healing not only of Lisa but of the whole family.

In this chapter, I will discuss the definition of psychic healing, forms of psychic healing, and psychic healing as it relates to current health-care models in America. I will look at psychic healing from an experiential perspective, from an historical perspective, and from a scientific perspective. I will relate psychic healing to the concept of the family where this is relevant.

TOWARD A DEFINITION OF PSYCHIC HEALING

The derivation of the word *"psychic"* is from the Greek word meaning "soul" or "spirit." *Healing* derives from the old English *haelan* meaning "to make whole."

A striking lack of uniformity exists in the use of the term *psychic healing* both in the literature on healing and in general usage. *Psychic healing* may be used interchangeably by some with "faith healing," "spiritual healing," "mental healing," and "magnetic healing"; others make precise differentiations of these terms. At times the term may be used in a general, all-encompassing sense to include almost any form of healing outside the methods used within the Western medical model; at other times *psychic healing* is used in a restrictive sense to refer perhaps to one method of healing, for example, the laying on of hands. The particular usage seems to depend at least in part upon the user's frame of reference and world view or upon the source to which the individual attributes the healing power, be it God, the Great Spirit, magnetic power, or cosmic energy.

For the purposes of this chapter I will use the following definition of the term *psychic healing.* Psychic healing is a "paranormal" phenomenon, that is, a healing event "not within the range of normal experience or scientifically explainable phenomena" *(The American Heritage Dictionary).* Psychic healing is a process in which a healer performs certain mental activities and perhaps physical activities and the one undergoing healing responds with positive physical, psychologic, spiritual, or social changes when there appears to be no adequate medical, physiologic, or psychologic explanation for the change.

FORMS OF PSYCHIC HEALING

Psychic healing is practiced by a number of disciplines and traditions that have evolved a variety of techniques, behavior, and explanations for the healing power. Reverend Harold Plume, Rolling Thunder, and Dolores Kreiger are three healers in America who represent different traditions and different forms of psychic healing.

A Spiritual Healer

The Very Reverend Harold Plume, the healer to whom we took our daughter 3 years ago, had been ordained through the Ancient Catholic Church in England several years before. He performed healings in small chapels known as St. John's First Chapel of Healing, located in two California cities.*

Reverend Plume believed that his power to heal was a God-given gift, and that he was merely a channel for God's healing power. He believed that he was also a channel for physician guides from the spirit realm: Hoo-Fang, a Chinese doctor who had died some 2500 years ago, and several medical specialists skilled in the treatment of humans or animals.

Reverend Plume had highly developed psychic abilities, including clairvoyance, with which he was able to "see" auras† and spirits and "see into" physical bodies, and psychokinesis, through which he was able, with Hoo-Fang's assistance, to dematerialize his fingers so that they entered the body of the person undergoing healing, there dematerializing diseased tissue. There was no pain, no blood, and no scar. After Rev. Plume had withdrawn his fingers from Lisa's chest during her first healing, she lifted her blouse, scrutinized her body and exclaimed, "There's no blood! And there's no hole!" This psychokinetic ability was a unique characteristic of Rev. Plume's healing and one he tended to deemphasize. To the witness, whether skeptical of or open to the impossible, the experience was awesome. David St. Clair (1974, p. 90) has reported that this phenomenon of Rev. Plume's hand disappearing into a patient's body "has been seen by hundreds, photographed by skeptics,

---

*Many healers believe that death is a transitional phase in a cycle that moves from existence within a physical body to a spiritual existence without a physical body. In July 1976 Rev. Plume "went into transition." His healing mission is being continued by his wife, Bertha, who has been his able partner and assistant throughout the years, and by four or five other healers, most of whom had previously assisted Rev. Plume. I am told that the "miracles" continue. Bertha Plume attributes these healing miracles to her husband, who now works "from spirit," and to the continued guidance of God, Hoo-Fang, and the other spirit entities who worked through Rev. Plume.

†An aura was described by Rev. Plume as an electric field of energy with colors that pulsate and constantly change, depending on one's physical and mental state at the moment.

and even filmed by a CBS television studio crew that was so shocked by what they captured they refused to show the film." Rev. Plume's mental activity in relation to healing is exemplified by his words:

> I don't dwell upon defects. People will come in wheel chairs and tell me they can't walk. Well I can see that! But I *know* that with God *nothing* is impossible. That's how I work. I *see* that person walking. I don't see the defect when I work on them. I only see it when they come in. As soon as they are sitting in the chair (in the healing room) I see them as completely cured. . . . I see them immediately cured. They are, as far as I'm concerned in my soul's eye, perfect. Perfect as God made them (St. Clair, 1974, p. 108).

An American Indian Medicine Man

Rolling Thunder, medicine man for the West Shoshone nation, has evolved his method of healing within the traditions of the Native American medicine man. He regards most physical disease as the reflection of a spiritual malaise. He emphasizes the need to understand the connectedness of man and the earth, and the need to treat all things, including one's own body and the earth, with understanding and respect:

> Too many people don't know that when they harm the earth they harm themselves, nor do they realize that when they harm themselves they harm the earth. . . . Understanding is not knowing the kind of facts that your books and teachers talk about. I can tell you that understanding begins with love and respect. It begins with respect for the Great Spirit, and the Great Spirit is the life that is in all things—all the creatures and the plants and even the rocks and the minerals. All things—and I mean *all* things—have their own will and their own way and their own purpose; this is what is to be respected (Boyd, 1974, pp. 51–52).

Rolling Thunder believes that there is a reason for all sickness, that everything has a cause that is at the same time the cause of something else. He takes this into account when he is making a decision about whether to treat someone—a decision that may take up to 3 days. According to Rolling Thunder: "If we take away an illness or a pain when we are not supposed to, the price the person pays in the future might be even greater. The sick person's spirit knows this even if, on the surface, the person is not aware of it" (Krippner & Villoldo, 1976, p. 61). During healing ceremonies Rolling Thunder uses many ancient symbols and rituals that include "all the natural things about us": herbs, eagle claws, feathers, waters, gestures, and incantations to the Great Spirit. During healings, the medicine man has perfect mental control, for he knows the power of thought. As did the medicine men of the past, he has the ability to leave the physical plane to visit the spirit world when this is necessary. Rolling Thunder claims that he does not do the healing: It is the Great Spirit working through him.

Therapeutic Touch

Dolores Kreiger, a professor of nursing at New York University, conducts workshops throughout the country in the philosophy and techniques of "therapeutic touch," a practice of healing derived from the ancient tradition of the laying on of hands.* Kreiger relates this healing process to the yogic concept of *prana*, the closest English equivalent of which is the vigor or vitality that underlies the life process. According to Kreiger the healthy person has an abundance of *prana*, while the ill person suffers from a deficit. Indeed, the illness is the deficit. During therapeutic touch there is a channeling of *prana* to the person undergoing healing and a balancing of this person's energy by the healer; in addition, a mobilization of the person's own self-healing processes seems to occur.

The behavior that Kreiger teaches for healing by therapeutic touch is basically as follows. The mental activity of "centering" is the essential first step. During centering, the healer quiets the mind, and reaches a state of harmony within the self. Next the healer makes an assessment of the "energetics" of the person undergoing healing by moving the hands around the individual's physical body, and determining, through differences in sensation experienced in the hands, the areas of deficit, imbalance, or blockage in the person's energy field. The information gained from the assessment determines the specific behavior of the third step, which is the healing itself. During therapeutic touch, the hands of the healer are placed on or near the body of the person to be healed for approximately 10 to 15 minutes. During this time a repatterning of the energy fields of both persons occurs.

According to Kreiger, healing by therapeutic touch is a natural human potential that can be actualized, given three prerequisites. The potential healer must be reasonably healthy, thereby possessing an overflow of *prana*; he or she must have a strong intent to help or to heal; and the healer must be educable, that is, capable of change. A healer may be taught the techniques of healing in a few hours, says Kreiger, but the art of healing comes from the self and may take a lifetime to develop.

There are numerous other forms of psychic healing: distant healing by individuals or by groups, self-healing through meditation and visualization techniques, psychic surgery as practiced by healers in the Philippines, healing

---

*The information in this section was presented by Kreiger during workshops attended by the author in April 1976 and June 1977.

by the use of color or of sound, healing through a blend of Western and alternative methods, and so forth. Many psychic healers view their healing methods as adjuncts rather than as alternatives to the techniques used within the Western medical model.

WESTERN SOCIETY, HEALTH-CARE MODELS, AND PSYCHIC HEALING

A revolution in consciousness is taking place in Western society. Increasing numbers of people are questioning their basic beliefs and values, the adequacy of their materialistic, mechanistic, rational, Western world view. More people are permitting themselves to explore beyond the physical dimension; psychic and spiritual realms are being rediscovered. The cultural taboo on intro-spection—on dreams, fantasies, and meditation—is weakening and even breaking down. A reevaluation and a redefinition of our world view is taking place. For many the results are renewing, expanding, and liberating.

Reverberations from the consciousness revolution are being experienced in the health-care field. The holistic health model has recently reemerged and is gaining attention and support. It represents an alternative in practice and in viewpoint to the Western medical model that has ruled supreme in this society's health-illness arena for the past 40 to 50 years. Psychic healing is one of the practices within the holistic model of health care.

The Western Medical Model

At present some of the basic assumptions and practices of the Western medical model of health care are being questioned. For example, are practices that are particulate and tend to blur the image of the holistic human being the most effective? Is knowledge that is scientific, quantifiable, and objective the only valid and relevant knowledge? Should invasive interventions such as chemicals and surgery so frequently be the treatments of choice? Is it rea-sonable for the populace to relegate to the physician total responsibility for the restoration and maintenance of its health (and to present him or her with a malpractice suit if he or she is unable to comply)? Within the medical model highly significant advances have been made, particularly in the areas of combatting acute infections and increasing longevity. Are the assumptions and practices of this model effective, however, in dealing with the problems we face today—for example, the chronic and degenerative stress-related dis-eases (cardiovascular disease, arthritis, respiratory disease, and cancer), which are so prevalent in this society?

The Holistic Health Model

Within this model of health care the individual is regarded as a physical, mental, spiritual, and social whole: inseparable and harmonious. Any malfunction or imbalance in one part is invariably reflected as a disequilibrium in the whole. Thus, illness is seen as a disorder of the total person. The acceptable sources of information are broader: Subjective and intuitive as well as objective and scientific knowledge are considered valid. The focus within this model is on the dynamics of health rather than on disease. Holistic health practices are frequently techniques for turning consciousness inward and for healing the self, as in meditation, biofeedback, autogenic training, visualization, and fantasies. The model incorporates other cultural healing practices into the Western technologic system, for example, acupuncture, meditation, and psychic healing. The holistic health model raises the issue of responsibility. The client becomes the expert in his or her own well-being; health care practitioners are used as collaborators and consultants, and health becomes the responsibility of the individual. In addition to representing an expansion in treatment modalities, this health model represents an expansion or a change in viewpoint regarding the *cause* of disease and the *purpose* of disease.

A Paradigm Shift

At the present time, medical treatment in accordance with the tenets of the Western medical model is what most of the populace demands. It is the treatment Western physicians have been trained to supply. Consequently, resistance to the expansion of health care practices is a potent force. These facts notwithstanding, there is evidence of the incipient stages of a paradigm shift: a shift from the beliefs and practices of the Western medical model to the beliefs and practices of the holistic health model.

- In June, 1976, a conference entitled "The Bicentennial Medicine Show: The State of Medicine 1976" was presented by the University of California Extension at Santa Cruz. During this conference the podium was shared by proponents of such seemingly diverse philosophies and disciplines as Max H. Parrott, immediate past president of the American Medical Association, 1975–1976; Rolling Thunder, a Native American medicine man; Olga Worrell, a renowned psychic and spiritual healer; and Elisabeth Kübler-Ross, a psychiatrist well-known for her work with death and dying.

- During 1977, Johns Hopkins University in Baltimore, Maryland, one of the most highly respected medical institutions in the country, presented a lecture series in alternative health techniques that included demonstrations and talks by practitioners in psychic healing, laying on of hands, yoga, meditation, and nutritional therapy.
- The First Congress of Nurse Healers, held in San Francisco in June 1977, addressed itself to the renaissance of humanistic nursing care and to the transformation of the nurse, in the words of Dolores Kreiger, "a new type of nurse for a new type of age—the nurse healer." Papers and workshops were presented in such practices as acupressure, biofeedback, therapeutic touch, creative dreaming, holistic massage, hatha yoga, and movement-dance therapy.
- Malcolm Todd, president of the International College of Surgeons and former president of the American Medical Association, told a medical audience at a conference entitled, "New Dimensions in Health Care," held in Houston, Texas, in July 1977: "It is proper and timely that medicine should become informed and involved in some alternative programs of health care. . . . We need to learn and evaluate skills derived from ancient cultural traditions, to integrate them with new technological discoveries." Todd pointed out that more than 2300 years ago Hippocrates had said that the physician must consider the whole person in order to diagnose and treat health-care problems properly. Referring to holistic medicine Todd said, "The spectrum of components might range from biofeedback, biorhythms and the psychology of consciousness to paranormal phenomena and psychic healing." (Ferguson, 1977, pp. 1–2.)

PSYCHIC HEALING FROM
AN EXPERIENTIAL PERSPECTIVE

The essence of experience is difficult to convey within the framework of our language, which has been designed to communicate primarily about objects. Experience, the living through or participation in an event or series of events, is inherently subjective and unique; the experience of no two individuals is the same. For this reason the experiences within my family vis-à-vis psychic healing will be discussed primarily from my own personal point of view. Examples of the experiences of individuals in other families in which one or more members have sought the services of a psychic healer will be described as they were related to me. The data presented will be anecdotal and subjective in nature; no claim is made to scientific objectivity or scientific validity.

My Family and Psychic Healing

Shortly after the instantaneous flash of which I wrote at the beginning of this chapter, during which psychic healing as an alternative to open-heart surgery for our daughter Lisa occurred to me, there began a sequence of events that seemed coincidental at the time. My husband and I learned of Rev. Plume, and took Lisa to him for healing. In his healing room we experienced the wonder and the mystery of coming face to face with forces that we had discounted as magical or religious—forces that were totally outside the "reality" we had accepted. And we came face to face with the fact that these invisible forces were producing "miracles." We discovered that a "psychic institute" was offering healing and meditation classes in a community center located on the very block on which we lived. There we were introduced to the philosophy that we are all healers. We began to take an active role in Lisa's healing. We began to experience a lightening of the burden. Classes led to healing conferences, to the experience of others whose lives included "the miraculous," and to an expansion of our knowledge relating to alternative methods of healing.

Significant changes seemed to be taking place in members of my family. Lisa appeared to be thriving. My husband was experiencing changes related to a reordering of priorities, to his development on psychic and spiritual levels, and to an expansion in the methods of treatment used in his practice of psychiatry. Our son Brian, who had developed indications of a probable need for surgery to correct a hernia, having received psychic healing, had no further symptoms. Even our German shepherd, who had become severely incapacitated due to paralysis related to a ruptured disc, had received a healing and was showing signs of recovery.

I was personally experiencing a sense of expansion and renewal, reassessing and revising beliefs relating to the nature of reality, to the universe and the self, to life and death, and to illness and healing. I felt less bound by unrelenting, self-imposed boundaries and beliefs. I was more open to other points of view, to other dimensions.* Let me elaborate with brief examples.

I once viewed the self as a skin-encased ego, mortal and finite. This has been supplanted by a point of view in which the self is regarded as a closely interrelated body-mind-spirit trinity that is continuous and harmonious with

---

*I wish to acknowledge the following for providing opportunities for expansion: est (Erhard Seminars Training) and its founder Werner Erhard; Harold and Bertha Plume of St. John's First Chapel of Healing; Richard Hanuman and Robbins of the Church of Hanuman; Lenard Orr of Theta Seminars; and the many psychics, healers, and healed persons with whom I have had contact.

the forces of the universe. In a sense, we are one. The experience of the oneness, or unity, of the universe can have far-reaching effects, relating, for example, to the significance of life and death for one, and to the nature of one's relationships. It has led me to expand my definition and experience of the concept of "family," to include not only our membership in a nuclear family and an extended family but also our membership in a superextended family: the family of mankind.

In discussing the sense of unity that exists in the state of consciousness he called the clairvoyant reality, LeShan (1974, p. 52) has written the following:

> If I *know* that in a real and profound sense you and I are one and are both integral parts of the total One, I treat you in the same way I treat myself. In addition, I treat myself with love and respect because I am part of the total harmony of the universe (or "a part of God" or "contain the indwelling light" or "an expression of Brahma"). If I regard you and me as separate, and do not accept that we are part of one another, I tend to treat you differently than I treat myself. Further, because of my cut-off-from-the-universe state, I may treat either or both of us badly. The Clairvoyant Reality contains within it the answer to the question of Cain: we *are* each our brothers' keepers and we are each our brothers.

I formerly held illness to be an admixture of hereditary predispositions and various noxious agents in the environment, including invading organisms and invading stress. All illness was considered a burden, a condition to be endured. I have begun to view illness from other perspectives: as a blockage in the free flow of cosmic energy, as a spiritual malaise, or as a product of our own thought-forms.* I have come to view illness as a possible vehicle to expedite growth rather than as a burden. This view is consistent with Kübler-Ross' statement that "all happenings are gifts to learn from." In this sense Lisa's heart anomaly has served both my husband and me, probably Lisa herself, and possibly other members of the family.

In September 1976, when we learned through definitive cardiac studies that Lisa's heart was "functionally normal" and that surgery was no longer recommended, our response was one of ineffable joy, relief, and thanksgiving. We had sought a physical healing of Lisa's heart, and this she had received. Healing on the physical level, however, seemed but one dimension of the healing. Our experience of the family being healed was the other. Were our experiences unique? What accounts would be given by others who had received psychic healing? Would there be instances in which reverberations

---

*It has been suggested that the world is crystallized thought. By that it is meant that one's mental image of empirical reality may possibly be creating that reality.

from psychic healing would be experienced by other family members or others in significant relationship to the person undergoing healing?

Experiences of the Healee

Individuals who receive psychic healing report variable experiences, possibly including momentary sensations of temperature change, tingling sensations, deep relaxation, peace, incredulity. Beyond these momentary effects, changes of a more protracted nature may be experienced in relation to psychic healing. These changes may be on a physical, psychologic, spiritual, or social-relationship level. Frequently, the divisions are not clearly demarcated; I will discuss them separately, however, for the sake of clarity and comprehension. In presenting examples of individuals who have experienced healing at various levels, I will include descriptions of some reverberating effects to significant family members or friends.

Physical Level.   The literature abounds with examples of physical changes or cures related to psychic healing in all periods of history, some instantaneous, some requiring the passage of time. Healings at the physical level are the most readily observable, categorizable, and verifiable. They are the cures most frequently sought; however, the terms *physical cure* and *healing* are by no means synonymous. Healings are frequently manifest on levels other than the physical. They are also frequently manifest on levels other than that requested by the person undergoing healing. "All men know what they want," said Pythagoras, "but only the Gods know what they need."

The Patterson family exemplifies one in which members requested and received healing at a physical level. In addition there appear to be radiating effects to significant others. I will describe this family's experiences in some detail.

Ten years ago Barbara Patterson was severely incapacitated. She had had a mastectomy for cancer and had subsequently developed metastatic cysts in her hips. She was unable to walk without using either a cane or crutches. Three physician specialists were of the opinion that this condition was inoperable, that hip-joint replacement was infeasible, that there was nothing they could do. Barbara stated that the physicians advised her to stay on her crutches as long as she could, then to go to a wheelchair. Through a "chance" meeting Barbara learned of the healer, Rev. Plume. She attended his clinic that day, and received her first psychic healing.

Barbara had this to say of the period immediately following the healing: "I went home with my cane, and I got in the house and one of my cats started to cry because it was hungry. I hadn't been able to bend over for all these years. My son, in fact, had to put my shoes and socks on. Well, without thinking I took the bowl and just squatted down and I couldn't believe it when I realized what I'd done. I could bend over!" Barbara took off her shoes and socks herself that night, an extraordinary feat for her.

After 2 weeks and three healings, Rev. Plume told Barbara, "You don't need that cane anymore!" Barbara walked out of the chapel, and locked the cane in the trunk of her car, where it remains to this day. At present Barbara is an active woman who enjoys a full range of activities, including remodeling her house and hiking in the hills. And Barbara herself has become a healer, working with Bertha Plume and others at St. John's First Chapel. "It changed my life," claims Barbara of her healing experience. "Now I'm trying to do for others."

Radiating effects from Barbara's healing experiences appear to have touched others, notably her son, her parents, and a friend. A few months after Barbara's healing, her 17-year-old son, George, sustained a major injury during basic training in the army. He had fallen from a height of 20 feet, landed on his wrist, and in addition to injuring muscles he had broken a bone in his hand. George was keenly aware of the recent changes in his mother's physical condition; he asked to be taken to Rev. Plume for healing. Rev. Plume did one healing on George, using characteristic clairvoyant and psychokinetic abilities. He then declared, "All right son, you can take that cast off in 3 days. It will be healed." Being sufficiently astute to recognize that if the army says to remove a cast in 2 months you do not take it off in 3 days, George decided to go to a nearby base for x-rays. From the evidence of x-rays taken 3 days after the healing session, the army physician assured George that there was nothing wrong with his wrist, that it had completely healed.

George's healing, in turn, profoundly affected his mother. Though she herself had experienced a physical healing, she had been somewhat skeptical of the basis for it and consequently of its probable duration. "Was this the power of suggestion?" she asked herself. "Was it my mind that made me free? Or is this for real, did my hip really regenerate?" Following her son's healing, with its documentation of x-rays before and after healing, Barbara was convinced that it "was not just in my head." She was able to accept the healing, and to proceed with her life.

Barbara's parents appear to have been influenced by reverberations from her healing experiences. Barbara described her father before her healing as a "typical businessman," neither aware of nor interested in "new-age things," such as psychic healing. Her parents' response, in particular her father's, to her remarkably increased physical capacity was skeptical and pessimistic. He was of the opinion that the effects of the healing would not last, that "it was all in Barbara's head." Changes in her parents have been noted over the past 5 years. Gradually, their world views have expanded to include an interest in and an acceptance of psychic healing and related phenomena. Both parents have attended Rev. Plume's clinic, the mother for a healing herself. They have encouraged friends to consider using the services of healers. Said Barbara of her father, "It has opened his eyes."

Barbara's experiences led her to an interest in the phenomena of distant healing. When she received a letter from an old friend stating that her physician had diagnosed an inoperable malignant brain tumor and that she had been given a limited time to live, Barbara responded by putting her friend's name on the Plumes' absent healing list as well as by "sending out" healing energy herself to her friend. A short time later Barbara heard from her friend; she had been back to her physician who could find no evidence of a brain tumor. "And this has affected her life," said Barbara, "because now she's trying to do for others. Her biggest reason for living now is so that she can help someone else."

Psychologic Level. Some individuals who have received psychic healing report experiencing healings of a psychologic nature manifest as change in emotions, mood, attitudes, or resultant behavior. Ann and Mark are individuals who have experienced change in the psychologic dimension.

A friend related to Ann some of the changes she had observed since Ann began receiving psychic healing: "It's an attitude change. It's a more relaxed attitude. And I think it helps your sense of humor. You seem happier. Maybe you were always happy inside, but you're more happy outside now. You seemed more depressed at one time. It seems to have lifted." Ann acknowledged that in addition her problem with difficult breathing and the associated feelings of fear and panic have subsided.

A year ago Ann took her daughter for healing for the treatment of allergies. These symptoms have been alleviated and there has been no recurrence. Ann was of the opinion that there had been no other reverberations from healing to members of her family or friends.

Mark is a young man who 4 years ago was involved in a car accident in which he sustained a spinal-cord injury that left him quadriplegic. During the past 4 years he has made marked progress. Two years ago Mark began attending workshops related to psychic healing and other psychic phenomena. One year ago he began attending Rev. Plume's healing clinic. Though he still uses a wheelchair, he is able to function totally independently, driving his own van, attending school, and so forth. Mark says that although physically he cannot claim anything has happened since psychic healing began, mentally and spiritually he has definitely grown. He attends St. John's First Chapel of Healing on a regular basis in order to "maintain my energy and level of health, and to be in contact with positive people." A most striking quality about Mark is his positive attitude toward his situation. "I see my paralysis as a temporary thing that's going to help me grow; well, it has helped me grow quite a bit, and it's preparing me for something else. It's just part of a cycle that I'm going through."

Spiritual Level. Many individuals have become aware of changes on a spiritual level associated with the experience of psychic healing. The changes have been manifest in several ways: the experience of spiritual uplift and renewal, an awareness of expansion beyond one's physical boundaries, the development of interest in the metaphysical, an increase in the desire to love and serve others, and a sense of being in touch with the "higher self," "the inner truth," "a higher consciousness," "love," or "God."

> Mark has experienced healing on the spiritual level. According to him, spirituality has become a much more integral part of his personality. He refers to establishing a personal contact with God and to getting in touch with his "higher self" or the "power within," which, he believes, has been responsible for the progress he has experienced since his accident: "The more I concentrated on the power that was in me, and that if I relied on that power it could never be taken away from me, and it would always help me through things, the more I was able to accomplish. And everything changed! I became very positive. And as I concentrated on the power within, I was able to project it." Mark believes that his being in touch with the power within has hastened his recovery; for example, his discharge from a rehabilitation hospital in 3 months rather than in the predicted minimum of 6, was, he feels, directly attributable to this fact.*

By the same token, some people experience growth on the psychic level. Ruth, following psychic healing 10 years ago, began to see colors or "auras" coming from people. A short time before receiving a telephone call from her close friend, Ann, for example, she will "see" the pinkish-red color she associates with her.

The Healing Shrine of Lourdes, France, provides numerous illustrations of spiritual renewal experienced both by the recipients of psychic healing and by the relatives and friends who accompany them. More than 2 million pilgrims visit Lourdes every year, including more than 30,000 sick. The reported frequency of cures of organic disease varies widely depending on the criteria used. For example, in the century of the shrine's existence, fewer than a hundred healings—62 to be precise—have passed the stringent test required by the Roman Catholic Church before they can be declared miraculous. Yet the piles of crutches at Lourdes are evidence of numerous additional cases of at least improved functioning. An old pilgrim reported: "Of

---

*I am reminded of the statement, "Any event in life can have the function of putting us in touch with higher consciousness," made during a presentation by Naomi Remen, during the Prescription for Health symposium, June 17, 1977, in Los Altos, California.

the uncured none despair. All go away filled with hope and a new feeling of strength. The trip to Lourdes is never made in vain." (Frank, 1974, p.69.)

The experiences of relatives and friends who accompany the sick to Lourdes is noteworthy. They go for the spiritual uplift and renewal of life that, it is said, they unfailingly receive. Bonnell (1968, p. 32) tells of a conversation with a young Irishman who was for the seventh year spending his 3-week vacation at Lourdes working as a *brancardier*, one of the sturdy helpers who carry the sick on stretchers. Said the young man:

> I am only one of scores of men and women who do the same thing. I get such a spiritual lift in this place—where everybody seems to be busy trying to help someone else—and the whole place is throbbing with enthusiasm and good will. I wouldn't miss it for the world.

One of the doctors who was actively engaged on the International Medical Committee of Lourdes said the following:

> It is unfortunate that so much of the publicity about Lourdes is concerned with the expectation of sensational healing miracles. Actually these healings when they occur are little more than fringe benefits. If Lourdes were a secular medical clinic and had produced only sixty-two authenticated healings in more than a century we should go out of business in a few months. The chief product of Lourdes is spiritual uplift and renewal (Bonnell, 1968, p. 33).

Social-Relationship Level. Another level at which individuals may experience psychic healing is that of relationships. A change at this level may be due to primary change on the part of the healed person; it may be due to the secondary effects experienced by that person's family or significant others. The source is frequently difficult to determine. In either case, the healing is manifest as a change in the dynamics of the relationships.

> Johanna, a 10-year-old girl whose mother was receiving psychic healing for a physical disorder, described succinctly the changes in her family's relationships: "The family has changed. We have gone more together. We help each other more. And we are closer to God." Mark, whom I have discussed above, is of the opinion that the changes he experiences in his relationship to members of his family are due primarily to a change in *his* role in the family. He decided to take a more active role; he is more willing to take the initiative and is more willing to share the responsibility for problems. This has been evident in his attitude toward his father's recent depression. Mark says that he is trying to help his mother, realizing that his father's illness is not her problem alone, that she should not have to bear the whole thing by herself.

Dolores Kreiger, the nurse-healer whom I discussed earlier, has found that healing related to therapeutic touch is not necessarily manifest as physical change. It may be a transformation of personality; it may be a healing of family relationships. During healing workshops Kreiger has taught members of families the techniques of therapeutic touch for the purpose of healing an ill member. She has reported that this is an excellent vehicle for nonverbal communication that has resulted in changes in the dynamics of the families concerned.

Impact on Families

My experience with psychic healing both in my own family and in other families with whom I have communicated has led me to conclude that reverberations are frequently experienced by members of the family besides the identified person or persons undergoing healing. In the majority of cases these reverberations are experienced as positive, and change is oriented in the direction of health, growth, and harmony. One could speculate that the change might be attributable to a response on the part of family members to change in the person undergoing healing or to a disequilibrium created in the family group by change in that person. It might be a response to the ambience of love and caring frequently experienced during the receiving, witnessing, or participation in healing sessions; it might be related to the realization that one is more than a skin-encased ego; it might be a combination of factors.

In a few families, members assessed the impact on the family as being negligible or absent altogether. One young woman saw the response of significant others as negative. According to her, following her remarkable healing on physical and spiritual levels, those close to her responded at first by avoiding her and finally by completely excluding her.

The qualitative response of significant others did not appear to be determined solely by the impact of the experience itself on the person who had undergone healing. For example, 22 years ago Mrs. Williams' 2½-year-old daughter was suffering from acute leukemia and was hospitalized. Against medical advice, the mother removed her from the hospital to take her to a healer. She did this with great reluctance for at the time she believed neither in doctors nor in other healers. Three-and-a-half weeks later the child died.* However, Mrs. Williams reported that since this healing experience she has become open to anything that is helpful in relation to healing. In recent years both her teenage daughters have received psychic healing treatments, one for

---

*Mrs. Williams reported that the hospital physicians at the time of discharge were of the opinion that the child would not live for 24 hours without blood transfusions. That she lived for 3½ weeks without a blood transfusion was described as a miracle by the same physicians.

a large growth that was removed by psychic surgery, the other for an emotional disturbance. Mrs. Williams' situation exemplifies a remarkable change in attitude despite what may appear to have been a failure of psychic healing in the case of her 2½-year-old child. She is in fact, now of the opinion that if one truly believes in healing, it is 100 percent effective.

A Complete Healing

It is believed by many that for a healing to be lasting or permanent it must have been a complete healing, that is, all dimensions of the individual must have been involved. Physical cures, it is thought, will be only temporary unless the healed person experiences growth on other levels, such as the psychologic and the spiritual.

Rolling Thunder, for example, believes that for the person undergoing healing to get the most value out of a healing experience, he or she must have a "proper attitude." "The people who are being 'doctored' must have cleared up their thinking so that they can accept the Great Spirit's work," he has said (Krippner & Villoldo, 1976, p. 57).

In discussing those who have experienced healing at the shrine at Lourdes, Frank (1974, p. 70) has written the following:

> . . . cures at Lourdes involve the person's total personality, not merely his body. The healed, whatever they were like before their recovery, all are said to be possessed of a remarkable serenity and a desire to be of service to others.

Yogi Ramacharaka, who wrote extensively during the early part of this century about the philosophies and spiritual practices of India, stressed the importance of observing certain natural laws of the body relating to proper nutrition, proper elimination, and proper breathing in order to attain and to maintain psychic healing:

> And no matter if the patient were cured instantaneously by the most powerful form of psychic healing, still, if he were to continue to neglect the primary physical laws of his being he would sooner or later get back to his old diseased condition (1919, p. 188).

PSYCHIC HEALING FROM
AN HISTORICAL PERSPECTIVE

My experiences with psychic healing stimulated my interest in tracing the origins of these healing practices. I have found that although there has been an increasing awareness of psychic healing in recent years, psychic healing is far from new. Its origins date back to prehistory. Of the two great traditions involved in the history of healing—the "religiomagical" and the "scientific-rationalistic"—the roots of psychic healing can be found in the former. It is interesting to note that psychic healing and Western psychotherapy have many origins in common.

In early civilizations, such as those of Babylonia, China, and Greece, all disease was believed to be of supernatural origin. It was the responsibility of the healers and the magicians to ward off the offending evil spirits. Illness was regarded as a misfortune involving the entire person, including the person's relationships with the spirit world and with members of the terrestrial group. These beliefs were evident in the practices of Aesclepius and Hippocrates in ancient Greece and in the early healing methods of the Chinese, the Hunas of Hawaii, and the North American Natives.

Touch in Healing

That touch has been an important aspect of healing from earliest times is attested to in the cuneiform of Sumeria from the fourth millenium B.C. The early rock carvings of Egypt and Chaldea, the ancient traditions of India and Tibet, and the Old and New Testaments indicate the predominant role of touch in healing rituals. Certain historic figures such as Pyrrhus, King of Epirus (319–272 B.C.) and the Roman emperor, Vespasian (A.D. 9–79) were able to cure through touch. Pyrrhus is said to have healed colics and other illnesses by passing his toes over the bodies of patients brought before him. Vespasian is believed to have cured blindness and lameness by touching patients with his saliva (Ehrenwald, 1976, p. 38).

The early Christian period provides many accounts of miraculous healing by the laying on of hands. Christ's cleansing of the leper is one example:

> While he was in one of the cities, there came a man full of leprosy, and when he saw Jesus, he fell on his face and besought him, "Lord, if you will, you can make me clean." And he stretched out his hand, and touched him, saying, "I will; be clean." And immediately the leprosy left him (Luke 5:12–13).

In medieval times kings of France and England were known to effect cures by what became known as the "Royal Touch." The following is the account of a young woman suffering from scrofula, who was cured by the Royal Touch of Edward the Confessor (1042–1066):

> A young woman . . . got into an ill state of health by an overflowing of humors in her neck which broke out in great nobbs. She was commanded in a dream to apply to the King to wash it. So to Court she goes and the

king being at his devotions all alone, dipped his fingers in water and dabbled the woman's neck and he had no sooner taken away his hand than she found herself better. The loathsome scabb dissolved but the lips of the ulcers remaining wide and open. She remained at Court till she was well which was in less than a week's time; the ulcers being so well closed, the skin so fair, that nothing of her former disease could be discovered (Ehrenwald, 1976, p. 38).

Invisible Energies

Records of early civilizations from around the world make reference to "invisible energies." The ancient Egyptians called it *ka*; the Chinese, *ch'i*; the Yogis, *prana*; the Hawaiians, *mana*. The invisible energy was thought to be linked to a healing power that could be channeled through a healer—shaman, witch doctor, or medicine man—to a person suffering from disease. It is noteworthy that in China the concept of invisible energy, *ch'i*, was encoded into a medical model: Acupuncture has been a primary traditional Chinese medical treatment for several thousand years.

The theories and techniques of the eighteenth-century physician, Franz Anton Mesmer, appear to be related to "invisible energy." Mesmer postulated an invisible "magnetic fluid," disturbances of which resulted in manifestations of illness. Mesmer, discoverer of "animal magnetism," found that by means of "magnetic passes" made by the hands over the body of a patient he was able to induce trance-like conditions, and to cure apparently organic disorders, such as blindness, convulsions, and paralyses. Mesmer's theories and practices were met with disapproval and censure by the medical community of the day. His discoveries, however, appear to be precursory to seemingly diametric lines of endeavor: on the one hand, scientific hypnotism, hypnoanalysis, and psychoanalysis; on the other hand, Spiritualism, the Theosophical Society, and Christian Science (Wyckoff, 1975, pp. 131–142).

The Era of Witch-hunting

An historic phenomenon that had a profound effect on the course of psychic healing, and on the course of all nonmedical healing as well, was the persecution of practitioners of witchcraft. The early Christian Church was intolerant of any metaphysical healing outside the Christian faith, regarding it as the work of the devil. The medieval men of medical science viewed with suspicion the "widow women" who served the needs of the lowly and the poor, that is, the vast majority of the population, by practicing unorthodox magical medicine. Some of these widow women gained considerable renown for their remedies and were consulted by persons of consequence. With the resultant indignation of men of science, the intolerance of the Christian Church, and the devil fixation of the times, the era of witch-hunting was begun. Persons possessing psychic gifts were singled out as special victims; such gifts were held as proof of their possessors' being in league with the devil. The mass mania of medieval witch-hunting brought misery to millions, horrible death to hundreds of thousands, and a complete weakening of the spiritual point of view (Hall, 1971, pp. 125–154).

The Age of Science

Since the Renaissance we have entered a developing Age of Science in Western civilization. During the Reformation of the sixteenth century, Protestant reformers chose not to perpetuate the Christian ministry of healing. The Roman Catholic Church alone continued to recognize miraculous healings. (The shrines at Lourdes in France, of Fatima in Portugal, and of Sainte Anne de Beaupré in Canada are examples of Catholic shrines to which multitudes of pilgrims travel yearly in search of miracles). Paranormal healing outside the church was in disrepute following the persecution of witches. It was left to the secular branch of medicine to tackle, almost single-handedly, disease-related problems. As a result the spirit of the Age of Science was felt in medicine.

What impact has science had on healing? During the scientific era *materia medica* became completely divorced from areas of magical practices and life forces that could not be particularized and demonstrated. The mechanistic interpretation of nature totally negated the role of "higher consciousness" in cause-and-effect relationships; most Western scientists became skeptical of anything that seemed to involve the notion of higher consciousness or the paranormal. There were no longer any spiritual or psychic considerations in matters of health and illness. Physicians became the sole authentic healers.

We in the twentieth century are profoundly aware of the powerful medical technologies that have been developed during the scientific epoch. Has the secularizing of medicine, purportedly initiated by the Greek priest-physician, Hippocrates (fifth century B.C.), had a salutary effect on the healing arts, however? Most modern materialists would respond in the affirmative. Manly P. Hall, founder of the Philosophical Research Society, represents another viewpoint. Hall (1971, pp. 95–123) is of the opinion that the division has led not to progress but to confusion. Spiritual values were left behind by physicians in their search for physical knowledge; the human being lost his identity as the child of God and became a case history; medicine severed its connection with religion and became a business, and medical commercialism began.

The Present Era

There are recent indications, as discussed earlier in this chapter, that the pendulum has begun to reverse its direction. The present era offers an opportunity for the acceptance of "all means physical and magical that contribute to the recovery of the patient."* The present era offers an opportunity for the synthesis of the forces of ancient wisdom and the forces of modern science in the quest for health.

PSYCHIC HEALING FROM
A SCIENTIFIC PERSPECTIVE

A diversity of opinion exists regarding the appropriateness of scientific methodology and verification in paranormal phenomena like psychic healing. Many Westerners, operating from a scientific world view, consider invalid anything that cannot be verified scientifically. The psychic, the spiritual, and the metaphysical, being largely subjective, do not lend themselves easily to exploration based upon scientific methodology. They are given little credence by many for this reason.

The recent interest in Eastern philosophies and practices is having an influence on the point of view of some Westerners. Traditionally in the East, there is little concern with explanation; cause-and-effect relationships are considered irrelevant and unimportant. Of greater concern is the direct experiencing of the oneness of the universe. Referring to the Eastern mystics, Fritjof Capra, a physicist, has written the following:

> Being well aware of the unity and interconnectedness of the universe, they realize that to explain something means, ultimately, to show how it is connected to everything else. As this is impossible, the Eastern mystics insist that no single phenomenon can be explained. They are generally not interested in explaining things, but rather in obtaining a direct non-intellectual experience of the unity of all things (Capra, 1977, p. 52).

In spite of the difficulties in subjecting phenomena such as psychic healing to the scientific method, some Western scientists believe that method to be the best vehicle for securing reliable explanations of reality. Krippner and Villoldo, humanistic psychologists and researchers of paranormal phenomena, give this explanation for their advocacy of scientific methodology in investigating healing:

---

*A great metaphysical physician and pioneer of medicine, Paracelsus of Hohenheim (1493–1541), stated that the true end of medicine is the recovery of the patient. All means, physical and magical, are justified, he said, if they contribute to this end (Hall, 1971, p. 148).

In surveying the realms of "healing," the authors have searched for one quality above all else—truth. The authors have emphasized the scientific method because, for all its faults, science is the best procedure that human beings have invented for discovering truth and obtaining agreement about their knowledge of the universe. Its aim is to surmount the foibles of superstition and wishful thinking by a method aimed at discovering facts and relationships that can be known, communicated, and verified by others (Krippner & Villoldo, 1976, p. 314).

It is only in recent years, since the 1960s, that significant scientific studies have been conducted in the area of psychic healing. These studies indicate that there are forces involved in the complex process of such healing that go beyond the psychologic forces of suggestion, placebo effect, relaxation, and change of attitude. A number of scientific studies of psychic healing are described below.

Experiments in the Laying on of Hands

Bernard Grad, a Canadian biochemist, did a series of experiments with Oskar Estebany, a Hungarian healer renowned for his ability to heal people and animals by the laying on of hands. Double-blind studies were conducted with mice and also with barley seeds. In the former study Grad et al. used 300 laboratory mice (Grad, Cadoret, & Paul, 1961). The mice were surgically wounded and then divided into three groups: one experimental group and two control groups. In the experimental group each mouse was treated daily by Estebany. The mouse was placed in a paper bag; then the paper bag and the mouse were held in his hands for a specified period of time. In one control group the mice received equivalent daily treatment from medical students who claimed not to have unusual healing ability. In the second control group the mice were allowed to heal without outside intervention. Meticulous measurements of the rate of healing demonstrated that by the end of 2 weeks significantly faster healing had occurred in the mice that had been treated by Estebany.

In another series of experiments, Grad (1964) used barley seeds that were "wounded" by being soaked in a saline solution. The seeds were then divided into three groups, as in the experiment with mice. The seeds in the experimental group were watered from flasks that had been held by Estebany; those in one control group, from flasks that had been held by persons who did not claim to have healing powers; those in the second control group, with tap water. At the conclusion of the experiment it was found that the seeds that had been watered from the flasks held by Estebany sprouted more quickly, grew taller, and had more chlorophyll than the seeds in the control groups.

In a related series of experiments Sr. Justa M. Smith (1972), a biochemist, and enzymologist, studied the effects of the laying on of hands on various enzymes of the body. Her previous research had shown that the reactivity of enzymes was increased when they were treated by a strong magnetic field. In a double-blind study using the enzyme trypsin and the ministrations of the healer Estebany, Smith found that the effect of Estebany's treatment on the sample of trypsin was similar to that of the enzyme when it was exposed to a high magnetic field. Testing with a magnetometer revealed that there was no unusual magnetic field around Estebany's hands. Another finding of the Smith studies was that the healer's ability did not affect all enzymes the same way; in fact, some were not affected at all. Within the context of what enzymes do in the human body, all the substantive effects seemed to contribute to improving or maintaining health.

In the early 1970s Dolores Kreiger (1975a) designed experiments to further study the effects of the laying on of hands, which she called "therapeutic touch." The effects of laying on of hands on the level of hemoglobin, the oxygen-carrying component of red blood cells, was studied in human subjects. In a series of controlled studies in which experimental group subjects were treated with a laying on of hands by Estebany, Kreiger found significantly increased hemoglobin levels in the experimental group.

In a further study Kreiger (1975b) investigated the hypothesis that therapeutic touch was a natural human potential that could be actualized by those who had three prerequisite conditions: a fairly healthy body, a strong intent to help or heal ill persons, and educability. With registered nurses as healers under her direction, using therapeutic touch in a study designed similarly to the one above, it was found that the hemoglobin levels of those in the experimental group were again significantly increased. This study has important implications for the theory that we are all healers.

Experiments in Distant Healing

Robert N. Miller, a chemical engineer, conducted a number of laboratory experiments with Olga Worrall and the late Ambrose Worrall, healers well known for their ability to heal at a distance. In one experiment, the growth rate of a rye plant in Atlanta was measured while the Worralls sent healing energy to it from Baltimore, a distance of more than 500 miles. Using a sensitive device, Miller (1972, p. 25) was able to measure the growth rate of plants to an accuracy of a thousandth of an inch per hour. Before the experiment began, the growth rate of a new blade of rye grass had been stabilized, under controlled conditions of lighting, temperature, and watering frequency, at 0.00625 inches per hour. On a prearranged evening at their usual healing-meditation time (9 P.M.) the Worralls "prayed" for the plant by visualizing it as growing vigorously in a white light. At exactly 9 P.M. the trace began to deviate upward, and by 8 A.M. the next morning the grass was growing 0.0525 inches per hour, a growth-rate increase of 840 percent.

Commenting on Miller's experiments, Mishlove (1975, p. 146) wrote:

> His experiments imply that the interactions found in psychic healing can easily traverse great distances of space guided simply by the mental intentions of the healer. The mere notion of energy radiating from the hands of the healer is insufficient to account for the known phenomena. It may simply be that the hands form a psychological tool for the focusing of concentration.

The work of Lawrence LeShan is particularly useful in elucidating the experience of psychic healing from the perspective of the healer. LeShan is an experimental psychologist who has done extensive research in the paranormal. In his investigations of psychic healing he studied the behavior and writings of many serious psychic healers such as Olga and Ambrose Worrall, Harry Edwards, Edgar Jackson, the Christian Science group, Paramahansa Yogananda, and Katherine Kuhlmann. He then extracted the "commonality behaviors," a set of behaviors engaged in by all the healers when they were trying to heal someone. From the healers' experiences LeShan (1974, pp. 153–154) was able to delineate an altered state of consciousness, a way of "perceiving and reacting to the universe as if it were run on a different set of laws and principles than those which we 'normally' believe to be operating." He called this state of consciousness the "Clairvoyant Reality." Our usual way of being in the world LeShan referred to as the "Sensory Reality."*

Within the experience of the Clairvoyant Reality LeShan differentiated two types of healing. In Type-1 healing, after going into an altered state of consciousness, the healer views him- or herself and the person undergoing healing as one entity; that is, the healer seems to merge with the healee. There is no active attempt to heal; the aim is simply to meet, to be one with, to unite with the person undergoing healing. In Type-1 healing it is not necessary for healer and healee to be in close proximity, in fact, they can be separated by great distances. In Type-2 healing, the healer experiences a flow of energy between the palms of his or her hands when they are "turned on." The healer then tries to heal by placing the hands on each side of the pathologic area of the person undergoing healing. This is healing by the

---

*LeShan later differentiated two additional states of consciousness or modes of being in which human beings are capable of functioning. He called them the "Transpsychic Reality" and the "Mythic Reality."

laying on of hands. In both types of healing the healer must care deeply and intensely, at least for the moment.

After developing this theory of the process of psychic healing, LeShan was able to train himself to go into an altered state of consciousness and to do psychic healing, that is, to effect positive biologic changes in the body of the healed. In a further step, he has been able to train others to heal.

Joyce Goodrich conducted an investigation of LeShan's Type-1 healing in an attempt to determine whether healing at a distance actually worked. In the study healers were assigned to persons with whom they did a face-to-face healing. Later at various intervals the healers attempted to merge with the healees from a distance of several miles. The healees kept a journal in which they carefully assessed their experiences. The results of this study were found to be statistically significant. By examining the journals kept by the healed persons, independent judges were able to identify correctly the times that the healers were at work (Krippner & Villoldo, 1976, p. 36).

Discussion of the Experiments

The above experiments illustrate that effects from psychic healing can be demonstrated through scientific methodology. In the studies cited the effects were manifest and measured at various levels such as that of healing and growth rates, and the physiologic level of enzyme and hemoglobin counts. It is noteworthy that the studies pertain to *physical* manifestations in relation to psychic healing. More difficult areas to investigate scientifically are changes at the spiritual level, the psychologic level, and the social relationship level—aspects that would be of particular interest in the study of family life. Because of the subjective nature of these areas, it is considerably more difficult to design studies to demonstrate and instruments to measure them.

The studies in distant healing indicate that for the "unseen force" or the "invisible energy" to heal, proximity of healer and healee is not a requirement. From the studies it appears that the "invisible force" is capable of being directed by the mind as well as by the hands; one might postulate that its direction may be determined solely by the mind. It may be useful to consider electrical energy as an analogue for the healing force. We can experience the manifestations of both, but we can see the actual force of neither.

The studies of Kreiger and LeShan support the hypothesis that the ability to heal is a human potential available to everyone rather than the gift of a select few. This finding does not deny the existence throughout the ages of a small number of highly developed individuals who have evidenced an extraordinary gift of healing.

The words of Francis Bacon provide a valuable guideline for attempts to understand and verify psychic healing:

For the world is not to be narrowed till it will go into the understanding (which has been done hitherto), but the understanding is to be expanded and opened till it can take in the image of the world (cited in Wyckoff, 1975, p. 19).

SUMMARY AND CONCLUSIONS

In this chapter psychic healing has been discussed from several perspectives: from that of the healer and the healed, from that of the individual and the family, from times present and times past. It has been presented as a method of healing that exists in many forms, three of which were elaborated: that of spiritual healer, that of Native American medicine man, and that known as "therapeutic touch." Psychic healing has been explored as a healing method whose effects can be experienced on different levels: the physical, the psychologic, the spiritual, and the social relationship level. Using data from my own family and from other families, I have explored the premise that reverberations from psychic healing may be experienced not only by the identified person undergoing healing but also by significant others in his or her environment. Psychic healing has been presented as an ancient method of healing that is presently gaining some recognition and acceptability in Western societies, at least in part because of the emergence of the consciousness revolution and the holistic model of health care. Recent scientific studies relevant to the area of psychic healing have been described and discussed.

Many unanswered questions remain. What, for example, are the *essential* ingredients, the sine qua non, of psychic healing? Is it the mental state or mental activity of the healer? Is it the intention, the faith, or the experience of the healer? On the part of the healed person, how essential is openness or receptivity, faith, intention, or world view?* How does one account for the healing of children and animals or the healing of skeptics? Questions continue about the psychic healing process itself. Is an actual transfer of energy involved? What part do the healed person's self-healing mechanisms play? Much that pertains to psychic healing remains paradoxical. If the ability to heal is a natural human potential, and if the capacity to be healed is dependent primarily upon such qualities as one's degree of openness, can psychic healing be described as "paranormal"? And can it be considered "miraculous"?

In recent times LeShan (1976, p. 125) suggested, "There is no such thing as a paranormal event. There are only events that do not fit into your current

---

*A recent Rosicrucian study (Holloway & Buletza, 1977, p. 18) indicated that a lack of receptivity to cosmic harmony on the part of the person undergoing healing was the greatest cause for failure in psychic healing.

system of organizing reality." St. Augustine, before him, believed that there was no such thing as a miracle that violated natural laws; there were only events that violated our limited knowledge of natural laws. I have concluded that the labels, epithets, and descriptions we use to describe psychic healing frequently reveal more about ourselves (our beliefs, world views, and realities) than about the phenomenon of psychic healing.

It is my opinion that much that could be called "psychic healing" occurs outside the healing rooms and chapels. The loving touch of a parent comforting a hurt child, the gentle care of a health worker for a patient, the focused concern of an environmentalist toward our planet: all provide a powerful, harmonizing force—a force that heals. It is my belief that what is required in the health-care arena is not a shift from one healing modality to another, but an expansion in the concept of healing to include anything that works to alleviate suffering. The combination of ancient wisdom and modern technology could be a potent healing influence.

Finally, I have concluded that psychic healing may be a step toward achieving wholeness, toward unlocking the spirit, freeing the psyche, experiencing love, or reaching inner truth. If it is approached with a degree of openness, receptivity, perhaps even adventure, it has the potential to transform individual and family life.

REFERENCES

Bonnell, J.S. *Do You Want to Be Healed?* New York: Harper & Row, 1968.

Boyd, D. *Rolling Thunder*. New York: Dell, 1974.

Capra, F. Ancient Buddhism in modern physics. *New Realities*, 1977, 1, 48–54.

Ehrenwald, J. (ed.) *The History of Psychotherapy*. New York: Jason Aronson, 1976.

Ferguson, H., Todd Urges Medical Profession to Integrate Old, New. *Brain Mind Bulletin*, July 1977, 1–2.

Frank, J.D. *Persuasion and Healing*. New York: Schocken, 1974.

Grad, B. A telekinetic effect on plant growth. *International Journal of Parapsychology*, 1964, 6, 473–498.

Grad, B., Cadoret, R.J., & Paul, G.I. The influence of an unorthodox method of treatment on wound healing of mice. *International Journal of Parapsychology*, 1961, 3, 5–24.

Hall, M.P. *Healing: The Divine Art*. Los Angeles: Philosophical Research Society, 1971.

Holloway, A., & Buletza, G.F., Jr. Metaphysical healing: A scientific demonstration. *Rosicrucian Digest*, August 1977, LV 17–20.

Kreiger, D. Therapeutic touch: The imprimatur of nursing. *American Journal of Nursing*, May 1975(a), 75, 784–787.

Kreiger, D. Therapeutic touch: A mode of primary healing based on a holistic concern for man. Presentation at the Physician of the Future Conference, International Cooperation Council, San Diego, California, June 21, 1975(b).

Krippner, S., & Villoldo, A. *The Realms of Healing*. Millbrae, Calif.: Celestial Arts, 1976.

LeShan, L. *Alternate Realities*. New York: Evans, 1976.
LeShan, L. *The Medium, the Mystic, and the Physicist*. New York: Viking, 1974.
Miller, R.N. The positive effect of prayer on plants. *Psychic Magazine*, April 1972, 3, 24–25.
Mishlove, J. *Roots of Consciousness*. Random House, New York, 1975.
Ramacharaka, Yogi. *The Science of Psychic Healing*. Chicago: Yogi Publication Society, 1919.
Smith, Sr. M.J. Paranormal effects on enzyme activity. *Human Dimensions*, 1972, 1, 15–19.
St. Clair, D. *Psychic Healers*. Garden City, N.Y.: Doubleday, 1974.
Wyckoff, J. *Franz Anton Mesmer*. Englewood Cliffs, N.J.: Prentice-Hall, 1975.

ADDITIONAL READINGS

Buletza, G., Jr. Your personal healing power. *Rosicrucian Digest*, September 1977, 17–20.
Edwards, H. *The Healing Intelligence*. New York: Hawthorn, 1971.
Flammonde, P. *The Mystic Healers*. New York: Stein and Day, 1974.
Fodor, N. *Encyclopedia of Psychic Science*. Secaucus, N.J.: Citadel, 1974.
Hammond, S. *We Are All Healers*. New York: Harper & Row, 1973.
Holzer, H. *Beyond Medicine*. New York: Ballantine Books, 1973.
Leek, S. *The Story of Faith Healing*. New York: Macmillan, 1973.
Maple, E. *The Ancient Art of Occult Healing*. New York: Samuel Weiser, 1974.
Oyle, I. *The Healing Mind*. Millbrae, Calif.: Celestial Arts, 1975.
Palos, S. *The Chinese Art of Healing*. New York: Herder and Herder, 1971.
Shealy, C.N. *Occult Medicine Can Save Your Life*. New York: Dial Press, 1975.
St. Clair, D. *The Psychic World of California*. Garden City, New York: Doubleday, 1972.
Worrall, A.A. & Worrall, O.N. *The Gift of Healing*. New York: Harper & Row, 1965.

Index

Value system
  in black female-headed families,
    163–164, 168–170, 175–176, 182
  definition of, 160
Ventilation, emotional, 397
Verbal abuse, 257, 259, 294
Vasquez, E., 196
Villoldo, A., 506, 519, 523, 524, 527
Violence. *See also* Child abuse; Family
    violence; Wife abuse
  abusive, 257
  against women, 83, 88
  normal, 257
  problem of, 255–257
  resource theory of, 313
  television, 273–274, 314
  in U.S. society, 261, 273–274, 314
Vogel, E. F., 62, 133, 480, 481, 482,
    483, 484, 485

Wachtel, E. F., 391
Wake, M., 201
Walker, K. N., 126
Wallace, A., 28
Wallerstein, J. S., 334, 337, 338, 339,
    340, 343, 352, 353, 408
Wand, D. H., 235
Wang, L. C., 236
Ward, R., 206
Warrior, B., 275, 283
Wasserman, S., 315
Watanabe, B., 201
Watanabe, C., 238
Watts, J. C., 31
Watzlawick, P., 241, 243, 451, 467
Wax, M., 137, 138, 140
Wax, R. H., 138
Weakland, J., 451, 468
Weiss, R. S., 401, 402, 403, 406, 412,
    413, 415
Western Interstate Conference for
    Higher Education in Nursing, 132
Whitaker, C., 392
White, B. L., 31
White, P., 406, 409, 411, 412
White, R. W., 5, 14
White, S., 332, 334

Whitehurst, R. N., 274
Whitenack, J., 201
Widowed families. *See* Blended
    families; Single-parent families
Widows
  impact of death of spouse on, 403–404
  and life cycle, 409
  social adjustment of, 406, 408
Wife, subordinate status of, 112
Wife abuse, 254, 259, 268, 270,
    272–295. *See also* Family violence
  and case finding, 290–291
  and characteristics of woman,
    277–279, 285
  and community, 275–277
  and definitions, 290, 294
  incidence of, 273
  and needs of the victim, 279–280
  and personal values and professional
    ethics, 292–293
  research on, 288, 293–294
  and role adaptation for
    professionals, 291–292
  as social problem, 274–275
  and social service agencies,
    deficiencies in, 280–281
  and stigma, 276–277
  and trends in services, 282–289
  and view of provider, 277–279
Wilson, E., 281
Winnicott, D. W., 37, 38
Wolfe, D. M., 58
Wolfensberger, W., 459
Women
  and employment discrimination, 96,
    97, 98, 111
  fear of change among, 88–89
  gains for, in marriage, 84
  as head of household, 83, 90, 99,
    102–103. *See also* Female-headed
    household
  losses of, in marriage, 84–85
  oppression of, 78, 79, 89, 91
  organizing, 91–92
  and power relations in marriage,
    77–93, 114
  role of, in Chicano family, 195–196
  and role strain, 111–112, 114–116